"Unabashed and undeterred, Peter McLaren offers a new ma
lean-to room' of the American hall-and parlor house that is . .
Pedagogy of Insurrection is yet another example of Peter's unflinching critique of our
contemporary moment of neoliberal capitalism and its contribution to our crisis of
democracy. Beautifully written, creative, and broad and ambitious in its conceptual scope,
Pedagogy of Insurrection offers a radical vision of human possibility and social transformation; a
reclaiming of critical pedagogy's connection to a political struggle—a philosophy of praxis. As
Peter has argued for nearly four decades, nothing less than a global revolution can be our
collective aim and, once again, with *Pedagogy of Insurrection*, McLaren has leapt into the
breach, challenging, no, demanding that we follow him."

> *Ernest Morrell, Macy Professor of Education; Director, Institute for Urban and*
> *Minority Education; President, National Council of Teachers of English;*
> *Teachers College, Columbia University*

"In this dark night of the soul of global political economy, *Pedagogy of Insurrection* comes like
a wild prophetic yell through the streets that would teach us of the radically democratic
demand for revolutionary intolerance that must sound across the planet as never before. Here
McLaren's unparalleled pedagogical poetics rises up with new moral urgency to speak true
words for and with humanity—an enflamed series of critical communiqués from the heart,
these almost incantatory and expressionistic critical visions courageously unveil the global
imaginary of violent corruption and terror and inveigh against the transnationally
institutionalized denigration of the educational hope that we the people may still yet learn
that the beloved community can be here now as soon as we demand it. Then, like non-GMO
seeds scattered everywhere, this book salutes the diverse movements for the total liberation of
life on earth that move us toward the eschatalogical omega point that will be the abolition of
the masters of war and their historical domination of nature. ¡Hasta siempre, Comandante!"

> *Richard Kahn, Core Faculty in Education, Antioch University Los Angeles*

"The modernist separation of church and state has functioned well to silence both radical
discourses of spirituality and public life, even when they might point us toward formidable
theological, pedagogical, and communal practices of resistance, insurrection, and
transformation. In this unique and courageous revolutionary volume, Peter McLaren
cultivates exciting new ground for rethinking a pedagogy and politics of global liberation,
including formidable re-readings of historical figures and reasserting their place in the long
recalcitrant struggle for human emancipation. At the very heart of this passionate manifesto
lies a deep yearning for an ethical world that can propel us beyond the mania of racialized
capitalism and its advancing destruction of the planet."

> *Antonia Darder, Leavey Endowed Chair in Ethics and Moral Leadership,*
> *Loyola Marymount University, Author of* A Dissident Voice:
> Essays on Culture, Pedagogy, and Power

"With *Pedagogy of Insurrection*, McLaren again makes it clear that he simply has no equal
today in writing revolution as critical pedagogy. In this book, he brings a photorealist poetics
to a searing political vision; he applies a street-savvy Marxism and a salvaged Jesus to
contemporary social movements. His is a rage against the machine with the facts lined up,

with history present, with teeth and heart bared. If this be McLaren's manifesto for a new humanity, it is also, without missing a beat, his Ginsbergian *Howl*."

John Willinsky, Stanford University

"With this latest volume, one can almost hear McLaren's pen raging away on the page. Evoking Jesus, one of our first documented critical pedagogues, McLaren shouts back at policy wonks and corporate babblers that feed the frenzy of failure dominating twenty-first century mainstream discourse in education. Theorists and critical practitioners will find themselves challenged again by McLaren's clarion call for us to do better in service of the world's most vulnerable youth."

Jeff Duncan-Andrade, Associate Professor, Raza Studies & Education,
San Francisco State University

"*Pedagogy of Insurrection* is both a call to arms and a call to reflection, from the foremost critical educator working today. McLaren's unparalleled exegeses invite us out of the dead ends offered by neoliberal capitalism and toward a horizon of revolutionary love and solidarity. Simultaneously challenging the value-form of capital, the violent legacies of colonialism, and the conservative monopoly on theology, McLaren shows brilliantly how teaching must be tied to the project of transforming the fundamental conditions of life. For the contemporary malaise produced by both corporate education 'reform' and postmodern abstentionism, this book offers the cure. There is simply no text that should be more urgently read by those committed to social justice."

Noah De Lissovoy, Associate Professor of Cultural Studies in Education,
University of Texas at Austin

"With his encyclopedic mind and laser-like vision, his agile wit and acrobatic imagination, Peter McLaren once again draws his flaming red-hot pen as a sword against the banksters and their hedge-fund homies, the marketeers and their brother barbarians in the political class. McLaren illustrates in compelling cadences that imperialism is in decline and capitalism exhausted—its brief parenthesis in history is at an end. Another world is coming, but the outcome is far from certain: chaos or community, brutality or solidarity, barbarism or socialism. Here is a clarion call to love one another or die."

William Ayers, Author of Fugitive Days, Public Enemy, and Teaching the Taboo

"In *Pedagogy of Insurrection*, Peter McLaren passionately embraces life, while forcefully denouncing the violently predatory capitalist system that sucks life out of humanity as well as those who masquerade as revolutionaries. In this brilliantly provocative series of essays, McLaren has the courage to call out neoliberalism's king for wearing no clothes, and to reclaim the revolutionary power of critical pedagogy."

Christine Sleeter, Professor Emerita, School of Professional Studies,
California State University, Monterey Bay

"*Pedagogy of Insurrection* is without question McLaren's boldest book to date. Inspired by a deep Fanonian rage, he unleashes a cogent critique of neoliberal capitalism and its assault on the mind, body, and spirit of its global subjects. Summoning the best of his own catholic-schooling, McLaren engages in a clever inversion of the Right's appropriation of religion to serve the un-godly aims of capital. McLaren offers what he terms a 'new aperture' through which to examine the modern human predicament. In so doing he aims to suture critical pedagogy back to a revisioned liberation theology, one that reclaims Christ as a postulate for humanity and radical love. This is the exact right book for the exact right time."

Sandy Grande, Associate Professor, Connecticut College; Author of Red Pedagogy

"With passion and provocation comes this newest book by Peter McLaren that dissects the now of U.S. capitalism, neoliberalism, and imperialism with a historical juxtaposition of liberation theology that is nothing short of startling. Read this book, share in the rage that catapults to collective action, and bring to life the promises of a *Pedagogy of Insurrection.*"

Kevin Kumashiro, Author of The Seduction of Common Sense

"Peter McLaren has done it again. For several decades, McLaren has given us different treatises on Marxist revolutionary education. In his newest intervention, he takes us through the paradoxes of a materialist spirituality. At once lyrical and disturbing, apocalyptic as well as humanizing, McLaren's new direction is bold. Like a particle collider, he fuses two seemingly incommensurable perspectives. What results is an explosive argument imbued with beauty, symmetry, and a new physics of liberation."

Zeus Leonardo, Professor of Education and Faculty of the Critical Theory Designated Emphasis, University of California, Berkeley

"Professor McLaren has been a forceful and influential voice in the arena of critical pedagogy for four decades. In *Pedagogy of Insurrection* he has not only reached his strongest and most creative phase but also begun to carve out a new theoretical terrain with his pulsating style of writing."

Juha Suoranta, Professor of Adult Education, University of Tampere, Finland

"This book will make the feathers fly and the blood boil. Always dangerous, always incisive, always poetically *puissant*, McLaren hauls in, among others, Comrade Jesus and [the] biblical roots of communism in his permanent war for economic, social, and educational justice. This is like McLaren pouring out a part-surrealist, part Marxist manifesto in a spoken word salon where everyone has imbibed a pint of absinthe and a quart of anger."

Dave Hill, Professor, Anglia Ruskin University, England

"In this wide-ranging work, renowned critical educator Peter McLaren lays bare the human condition under neo-liberal capitalism and delivers us, in his own words, a revolutionary critical pedagogy for a new humanity. Drawing on his broad experiences in the United States, Latin America, and elsewhere around the world, he puts forth a devastating critique of the misery and exploitation generated by the capitalist system, the bankruptcy of neo-liberal education, an alienating consumer culture, and the banality of post-modern academics who substitute a politics of representation for a politics of revolution. McLaren proposes in place of the current transnational capitalist dystopia a transformative project that would draw vision and inspiration from a fusion of a Marxist humanism emphasizing transcendence with the spiritual and Christian communist teachings of Jesus. At this time of severe global crisis, when the fate of humanity rests in the balance, McLaren's critical pedagogy could not be more urgent. This book should be studied by all those who seek inspiration in the struggle for survival and the construction of a more just and humane future."

William I. Robinson, Professor of Sociology and Global Studies, University of California at Santa Barbara; Author of Global Capitalism and the Crisis of Humanity

"In *Pedagogy of Insurrection* McLaren reconnects us to the essence of *true words*, and its ability to elevate and guide the human spirit in its efforts to promote critical transformation, build hope, and to impart love. As critical educators, McLaren encourages us to stand strong and remain true to conviction as we battle the anti-humanistic projects that attempt to dilute our spirit and corrupt our consciousness. *Pedagogy of Insurrection* reaffirms our souls as critical educators, and deepens our commitment to our *true words*."

Augustine F. Romero, Co-Founder, The Social Justice Education Project

"As the crisis of global capitalism deepens, and as the neoliberal straightjacket on public education tightens its belt, plagued with the new corporate consumer managerialism, Peter McLaren's latest offering, *Pedagogy of Insurrection*, invites educators to challenge the dominant political, economic, cultural, and ideological arrangements that mask contradictions rooted in capitalist social relations of production. This managerialism, whose hallmarks are characterized by accountability, efficiency, performance-based outcomes through Common Core Standards, Pearson's sponsored Teacher Performance Assessment (EdTPA), and high-stakes summative assessments, has permeated public education today. In spite of the fact that some have criticized McLaren for a challenging and, perhaps, inaccessible writing style, his work has enduring value in its efforts to push conceptual boundaries to further critique existing structures of power and domination. *Pedagogy of Insurrection* is a must-read for teacher activists and education policymakers."

Ramin Farahmandpur, Professor, Department of Educational Leadership and Policy,
Graduate School of Education, Portland State University

"Apocalyptic, poetic, messianic, and revolutionary. Following in the footsteps of don Lorenzo Milani, liberation theology, Oscar Romero, Gustavo Gutiérrez Merino, Ignacio Ellacuría, Paulo Evaristo Arns, Enrique Dussel, Frei Betto, and many others, Peter McLaren sees radical Christianity as a source of social transformation for greater social justice. Echoing Paulo Freire, he finds kindred spirits in Karl Marx and Jesus Christ. This book treads new ground in the idea of critical pedagogy as ongoing struggle, with hegemony recognized as having a series of pedagogical relationships at its core. A new world governed by a strong sense of spirituality and justice is in the making but it must be forged in the revolutionary efforts of movements exercising radical democracy from below, with revolutionary emancipatory learning a crucial and indispensable feature."

Peter Mayo, University of Malta; Author of
Hegemony and Education under Neoliberalism, *and* Politics of Indignation;
Co-author of Lorenzo Milani, the School of Barbiana and the Struggle for Social Justice

"This is McLaren's masterpiece with new angles, innovations in theory, and original contributions to what is becoming to be known as Decolonial Pedagogy, a new field of scholarship and activism. While keeping alive his previous contributions, he brings them to another level. This is his major work."

Ramón Grosfoguel, University of California, Berkeley

pedagogy
of insurrection

Peter McLaren

pedagogy
of insurrection

FROM RESURRECTION TO REVOLUTION

Foreword by E. San Juan, Jr.

PETER LANG
CLASSICS
Lausanne • Berlin • Bruxelles • Chennai • New York • Oxford

Bibliographic information published by **the Deutsche Nationalbibliothek.**
The German National Library lists this publication in the German National Bibliography; detailed bibliographic data is available on the Internet at
http://dnb.d-nb.de.

Library of Congress Control Number: 2023906441

Cover art:
Gemma Galgani: Patron Saint of Students by Erin Currier
Mixed media collage and acrylic paint on panel 36"x24"

Back cover photo by Challenge

ISBN 978-1-63667-440-7 (Print)
ISBN 978-1-63667-441-4 (ePDF)
ISBN 978-1-63667-447-6 (ePub)

© 2023 Peter Lang Group AG, Lausanne
Published by Peter Lang Publishing Inc., New York, USA
info@peterlang.com - www.peterlang.com

First published in 2015 by the same author in the series *Education and
Struggle* (Vol 6, ISBN 9781433128967).

Never having met an angel face-to-face, I was skeptical that they existed until I met you, Wang Yan (Angie). When I am surrounded by jackals, you protect me; when I despair, you give me hope; when the world around me erupts into chaos, you take me to a place of peace. Dearest Angie, you are a miracle in my life.

TABLE OF CONTENTS

ACKNOWLEDGEMENTS

This book was conceived several years ago, during a dark time in which it was difficult for me to maintain much faith in humanity. What existed around me seemed little more than a vortex of deep-seated repression, envy, political scapegoating and entrapment, self-interest and subterfuge. Solidarity, love, compassion and understanding seemed absent in the world. The survival and well-being of the oppressed seemed everywhere secondary to the petty needs of the non-oppressed. Coming to Chapman has taught me that spaces of solidarity, trust, friendship and a commitment to truth and dignity for every human being can survive within the walls of the academy. My deepest gratitude goes to Suzi Soohoo, Lilia Monzó, Tom Wilson, Don Cardinal and Anaida Colón-Muñiz for revealing a loving and compassionate side of the world of education and displaying such integrity and faith in our collective humanity as educators. And my most heartfelt thanks go to two women in my life. Jenny Jones I met and married in 1975; Wang Yan (Angie) I married in 2012. Without these two miracles in my life I could not continue to do the work to which I have committed my life. I am also indebted to Father Alan Roberts of Holy Cross Seminary in Auckland, New Zealand, who picked me up from the streets of despair and clothed and fed me spiritually until I was on my feet again.

Bernardo Gallegos was a continent away yet proved that real brotherhood knows no distance. Peter O'Connor became a bright light in a very dark universe. His companionship and blue suede shoes are forever engraved in my memory. Thanks to Sergio Quiroz Miranda, who housed and fed me for months in Mexico until my ill-fated return to Babylon. Thank you Sergio for enabling me to learn once again what it means to be a revolutionary. Trapped once more in the belly of the Anti-Kingdom, words of encouragement from Noam Chomsky and Cornel West were greatly welcomed. I wish to acknowledge especially the support of my six brothers, Carl Boggs, Henry Giroux, Bernardo Gallegos, Richard Kahn, Juha Suoranta and Donaldo Macedo, and of my four Sisters of Mercy, Karen Richardson, Sheila Macrine, Karen Anijar and Antonia Darder. And I would also like to express my gratitude to Sam Fassbinder for his editing assistance. A warm thanks goes to Bernadette Shade for her perceptiveness and her patience. Bernie and Phyllis Korper went beyond the call of duty to include last minute adjustments to the book, and without their capacity to endure my obsessive email requests, this book would not have seen the light of day. Chris Myers was able to put my eccentricities into perspective and with a deep breath give me the support that I needed to finish the book. For all these reasons, and more, Peter Lang remains my publisher of choice. Of course, the very idea of creating this book would have been impossible without Wang Yan, who left her world in the northeast of China to stand in loving solidarity with me at each moment of every day.

The author wishes to thank the following publications for permission to reprint from the following sources:

Introduction

McLaren, Peter. (2013). A Critical Patriotism for Urban Schooling: A Call for a Pedagogy Against Fear and Denial and For Democracy. *Texas Education Review*, volume 1, pp. 234–253. As retrieved from: http://txedrev.org/wp-content/uploads/2013/11/McLaren_A-Critical-Patriotism-for-Urban-Schooling_TxEdRev.pdf

Jose María Barroso Tristán and Peter McLaren. (2013). Critical Pedagogy Against Capitalist Schooling: Towards a Socialist Alternative. An Interview with Peter McLaren. *Global Education Magazine*. As retrieved from: http://www.globaleducationmagazine.com/--

McLaren, Peter and Farahmandpur, Ramin. (2005). *Teaching Against Global Capitalism and the New Imperialism: A Critical Pedagogy*. Lanham, Maryland: Rowman & Littlefield Publishers, Inc.

McLaren, Peter. (2000). *Che Guevara, Paulo Freire, and the Pedagogy of Revolution*. Lanham, Maryland: Rowman & Littlefield, Inc.

McLaren, Peter. (2010). Afterword: Matters Change: And Why Change Matters. In sj Miller and David E. Kirkland (eds.) *Change Matters: Critical Essays on Moving Social Justice Research from Theory to Policy*. (pp. 219–240) New York: Peter Lang Publishers.

Peter McLaren, (2005). *Capitalists and Conquerors: A Critical Pedagogy Against Empire*. Lanham, Maryland: Rowman & Littlefield Publishers, Ltd.

McLaren, Peter. (2011). Preface: Towards a Decolonizing Epistemology. Erik Malewski and Nathalia Jaramillo, (eds). (2011). *Epistemologies of Ignorance in Education*. (pp. vii–xxviii) Charlotte, North Carolina: Information Age Publishers.

McLaren, Peter. (2010). Revolutionary Critical Pedagogy. Interactions. *UCLA Journal of Education and Information Studies*, 6(2). As retrieved from: https://escholarship.org/uc/item/7qj2b570#page-2

Chapter 1

Peter McLaren. (2014). Education agonistes: An epistle to the transnational capitalist class. *Policy Futures in Education*, *12*(4), 583–610.

Peter McLaren. (2014). Comrade Jesus: An epistolic manifesto. *Knowledge Cultures*, 2(6), 55–114.

Peter McLaren. (2015). On dialectics and human decency: Education in the dock. *Open Review of Educational Research*, 2(1), 1–25. DOI: 10.1080/23265507.2014.986187

Chapter 2

Peter McLaren. (2014). Reflections on love and revolution. *International Journal of Critical Pedagogy*, 5(1), 1–10.

Peter McLaren. (2015). Reflections on Paulo Freire, critical pedagogy, and the current crisis of capitalism. In Michael Peters and Tina Besley (Eds.), *Paulo Freire: The global legacy* (pp. 17–38). New York, NY: Peter Lang.

Chapter 3

Peter McLaren. (2013, March 7). The man in the red beret. *Truthout*. Retrieved from http://truth-out.org/speakout/item/14997-the-man-in-the-red-beret

Peter McLaren. (2013). Farewell to the man in the red beret, enter the man in the white silk mitre: 'There is a crack in everything, that's how the light gets in.' *Policy Futures in Education*, *11*(4), 477–480.

Peter McLaren & Mike Cole. (2014, June 11). Austerity/Immiseration capitalism. What can we learn from Venezuelan socialism? *Truthout*. Retrieved from http://truth-out.org/news/item/24264-austerity-immiseration-capitalism-what-can-we-learn-from-venezuelan-socialism. Also reprinted in *Venezuelanalysis*, June 14, 2014. Also reprinted in *Iberamericano Social*, 2014. Retrieved from http://iberoamericasocial.com/austerity-immiseration-capitalism-can-learn-venezuelan-socialism/

Chapter 4

Peter McLaren. (2009). Guided by a red star: The Cuban literacy campaign and the challenge of history. *Journal of Critical Education Policy Studies*, 7(2), 52–65. Retrieved from http://www.jceps.com/?pageID=article&articleID=161

Peter McLaren. (2009). Foreword: A possible praxis. In Mark Abendroth (Ed.), *Rebel literacy: Cuba's national literacy campaign and critical global scholarship* (pp. vii–xix). Duluth, MN: Litwin Books.

Chapter 5

Peter McLaren. (2007). Foreword: The future of the past. In Michael Löwy, *The Marxism of Che Guevara* (pp. vii–xxiv). Lanham, MD: Rowman & Littlefield.

Peter McLaren. (2008). The Marxism of Che Guevara: Searching for 'Che' in capitalism's nightmare. *Indigo*. 'Shared Visions,' 3, 102–117. Retrieved from http://pages.gseis.ucla.edu/faculty/mclaren/Images/INDIGO_Info.pdf

Chapter 6

Revolutionary critical pedagogy: The struggle against the oppression of neoliberalism—A conversation with Peter McLaren. This was an interview by Sebastjan Leban for the Slovenian journal, *Reartikulacija*. The interview was reprinted in the following texts: In Peter E. Jones (Ed.). (2011). *Marxism and education: Reviewing the dialogue, pedagogy, and culture* (pp. 216–234). New York, NY: Palgrave Macmillan; and in Sheila Macrine, Dave Hill, & Peter McLaren (Eds.). (2010). *Revolutionizing pedagogy: Education for social justice within and beyond global neoliberalism* (pp. 87–116). New York, NY: Palgrave Macmillan.

Chapter 7

Petar Jandrić & Peter McLaren. (2014). Revolutionary critical pedagogy is made by walking—In a world where many worlds coexist. *Policy Futures in Education*, 12(6), 805–831.

Chapter 8

Peter McLaren. (2013). Seeds of resistance: Towards a revolutionary critical ecopedagogy. *Socialist Studies/Études socialistes*, 9(1), 84–108.

Peter McLaren. (2012). Objection sustained: Revolutionary pedagogical praxis as an occupying force. *Policy Futures in Education*, 10(4), 487–495.

Chapter 9

Peter McLaren. (2011). Radical negativity: Music education for social justice. *Action, Criticism & Theory for Music Education, 10*(1), 131–147.

Chapter 10

Lilia D. Monzó, Peter McLaren, & Arturo Rodriguez. (forthcoming). Deploying guns to expendable communities: Bloodshed in Mexico, US imperialism and transnational capital—A call for revolutionary critical pedagogy. *Cultural Studies/Critical Methodologies*.

Lilia D. Monzó, Peter McLaren, & Arturo Rodriguez. (2014). Distribución de armas a comunidades prescindibles. Baño de sangre en México, imperialismo estadounidense y capital transnacional: Por una pedagogía crítica revolucionaria. In *Tiempos violentos: Barbarie y decadencia civilizatoria*. Buenos Aires, Argentina: Ediciones Herramientas.

Chapter 11

Peter McLaren. (2011, September 25). Education as class warfare: Interview with scholar/author Peter McLaren. *The Socialist*.

Chapter 12

Peter McLaren. (2014). Education agonistes: An epistle to the transnational capitalist class. *Policy Futures in Education, 12*(4), 583–610.

Peter McLaren. (2014). Comrade Jesus: An epistolic manifesto. *Knowledge Cultures, 2*(6), 55–114.

Peter McLaren. (2015). On dialectics and human decency: Education in the dock. *Open Review of Educational Research, 2*(1), 1–25. DOI: 10.1080/23265507.2014.986187

FOREWORD

E. San Juan, Jr.

Professorial Lecturer, Polytechnic University of the Philippines, Manila, Philippines; former Fellow, W. E. B. Du Bois Institute, Harvard University; Harry Ransom Center, University of Texas, Austin

For citizens of the informed public sphere everywhere, Peter McLaren needs no introduction. He is one of the world's most distinguished educators, the key architect of "revolutionary critical pedagogy," to quote his colleague Paula Allman. His substantial academic record of over 45 books and hundreds of scholarly articles, beginning from his pathbreaking *Life in Schools* to his epoch-making *Che Guevara, Paulo Freire and the Pedagogy of Revolution*, is widely known. It unfolds a chronicle of passionate engagement with radical social movements and popular-democratic forces of change spanning over 30 years. It serves as a testimony to an examined life in the service of humanity, in particular "les damnés de la terre."

"Wretched of the earth," Frantz Fanon's rubric for the colonized peoples of the global South, signals what is crucial in McLaren's new endeavor. It is a point of departure for the finessing of the weapons of critical pedagogy in the age of the wars of terror, planetary surveillance, legal torture, genocidal drone assassinations, in this mystifying regime of disaster capitalism. As a leading public intellectual, McLaren seeks a rearming of the collective spirit to explore possibilities for resistance and transformation of social life.

Here we witness a novel turn in McLaren's career. But it is a dialectical move, negating but also preserving elements of the old in a new configuration.

McLaren began as a school teacher in Canada. After involvement in youth activism and the international anti-Indochina wars protest movement, McLaren earned his doctorate from the Ontario Institute for Studies in Education, University of Toronto. His early, rich experience in frontline teaching (1974–1979) is intimately documented in *Life in Schools*. It was followed by his scholarly dissertation on *Schooling as a Ritual Performance: Towards a Political Economy of Educational Symbols and Gestures* (1986).

In his early teaching and research, McLaren's expertise in critical literacy, ethnography, and curriculum studies reflected his Weberian interest in the politics of consumption and lifestyle identity nuanced with Frankfurt Critical Theory. With the outbreak of global capitalism's crisis after the end of the Vietnam War, and the attempt of the neoconservative bloc (Reagan and Thatcher's reactionary attacks on unions and the social-welfare consensus) to roll back revolutions in Central and South America, as well as in Africa and Asia (support of dictatorships in Chile, the Philippines, apartheid rule in South Africa, etc.) until the explosion in 2008, McLaren's thinking underwent delicate recalibration, if not a subtle retooling of the critical-pedagogy paradigm.

In the trajectory of McLaren's development, 1994 is marked as the pivotal year of change. His encounter with the ideas and example of Paulo Freire, the great Brazilian thinker, functioned as a heuristic and catalyzing influence. Freire negated the neoliberal hubris of possessive individualism and replaced it with the secular ideal of a community of learners-teachers. Freire's vision of education as freedom for action was simultaneously realistic, utopian, and self-critical. Meanwhile, McLaren was fully engaged in teaching at Miami University, Ohio (circa 1985) and the University of California, Los Angeles (from 1993). But his focus was less on classroom methodology than on the critique of political economy, cultural contacts, and racialized identity. In my view, this period signaled the more self-reflective process of actualizing the principle of Marxist-humanist praxis, the combination of theory and practice, in and outside the schoolroom. It is a project of inscribing the work of teaching and learning in the concrete totality of the prevailing social relations of production, in the complex dynamics of everyday life. In Freire's *Pedagogy of the Oppressed*, the cardinal lesson is that genuine education is not possible without the self-reflective change in the learner in the process of a transformative, emancipatory praxis. The production of ethical-critical consciousness, a historical commitment by the community of the oppressed to their own liberation, is called by Freire "conscientization."

McLaren's "conscientization" has its roots in his early involvement with youth and communitarian movements in which he acquired a mode of resistance-postmodernist outlook. This rebellious stance metamorphosed with his involvement in the struggles for social justice around the world, particularly in Latin America. He participated in the landless workers' movement in Brazil, with the Zapatistas in Mexico, with the Bolivarian Revolution in Venezuela, and the insurgent partisans in Colombia and South Africa. Grasping what he deemed "the differentiated totalities of contemporary society," McLaren sharpened his critique of the epistemological and axiological dimensions of democracy with his knowledge of actual struggles of peasants, workers, women, youth, and other marginalized peoples in the "peripheries" once dominated by the colonial and imperial metropolis. In the critique of "the coloniality of power," he encountered the work of José Porfirio Miranda and other theologians of liberation who argue that "option for the poor" is not preferential but an obligation for all conscientized humans.

McLaren's "conscientization" has its roots in his early involvement with youth and communitarian movements in which he acquired a mode of resistance-postmodernist outlook. This rebellious stance metamorphosed with his involvement in the struggles for social justice around the world, particularly in Latin America. He participated in the landless workers' movement in Brazil, with the Zapatistas in Mexico, with the Bolivarian revolution in Venezuela, and the insurgent partisans in Colombia and South Africa. Grasping what he deemed "the differentiated totalities of contemporary society," McLaren sharpened his critique of the epistemological and axiological dimensions of democracy with his knowledge of actual struggles of peasants, workers, women, youth, and other marginalized peoples in the "peripheries" once dominated by the colonial and imperial metropolis. In the critique of "the coloniality of power," he encountered the work of Jose Porfirio Miranda and other theologians of liberation who argue that "option for the poor" is not preferential but an obligation for all conscienticized humans.

This encounter harbored germinal insights for McLaren's future work. The re-discovery of Jesus of the Gospels as a foundational communist, the origin of the narrative of Christian communism, has given his Marxist humanism a new line of approach in the "war of position" against predatory capitalism. McLaren now wrestles with questions prompted by his synthesis of critical pedagogy as a praxis of class struggle and a neo-Gramscian approach to constructing the counter-hegemony of the "wretched of the earth." He asks: "How can we reclaim Jesus as a fellow communist? ... After all, it was not

Marx who established the final criterion for judging the authenticity of one's life as a concern for all peoples in need. It was comrade Jesus. How do we move beyond a new left narrative of redistribution and defence of public services? How do we get up and run an antagonistic social and political paradigm to neoliberalism? How can forms of popular power from below be transferred into a new historical bloc?" These are urgent questions not to be postponed for a future agenda of organic intellectuals.

The application of historical-materialist methodology leads us to "Comrade Jesus." As Enrique Dussel (in *The Ethics of Liberation*) has pointed out, we find the ethical criteria of those subjugated by the Empire in the primacy of "corporeal carnality," the community and its carnal needs, summed up in Matthew 25:35–36: "For I was hungry and you gave me food, I was thirsty and you gave me drink, I was a stranger and you welcomed me, I was naked and you clothed me, I was sick and you visited me" (for a feminist angle, see Elisabeth Fiorenza, *Bread Not Stone*, 1995). In this context, McLaren affirms that Jesus's "intransigent condemnation of the rich" and the vision/prophecy of a classless society that emerges from the abolition of private property and alienated labor, is a message "grounded in the establishment of justice and life now, at this very moment."

This detour to the Gospels actually brings us back to the real world of contradictions, to the historicity of lived experience. We rediscover the world of sensuous practice which resolves the classic duality of immanence and transcendence, idealism and materialism, and the historic disjunction of manual and mental labor. Social agency reveals itself in the metabolism of human needs and nature, of cognition and material conditions. We grasp anew the "community of life" where bodies with their potential and actual powers interact with the natural life-world—Marx's fundamental insights expressed in the *1844 Manuscripts* and *Grundrisse*. A similar experience occurred in the Philippines during the nightmarish U.S.-Marcos dictatorship (1972–1986), when partisans of the movement against U.S. imperialism invented a theology of struggle and organized the Christians for National Liberation. Both lay persons and church workers joined hands with national-democratic movement guerillas in the fight for social justice and genuine sovereignty. "People's war" waged by the Communist Party of the Philippines since the 1960s articulated a program of structural transformation partly inspired by the Latin American theology of liberation initiated by Gustavo Gutierrez, Leonardo Boff, and others.

In the essay on "Comrade Jesus," McLaren revitalizes the principles of materialist dialectics with his account of his visit to San Juan Chamula where the indigenous farmers of Mayan lineage now struggle with the Zapatistas. He also celebrates the people's mobilizations in Detroit and in Cochabamba, Bolivia, for basic rights to water and other vital resources, against corporate greed and cynical bourgeois reforms. They serve as examples of self-management and decolonizing collective praxis. These enduring struggles for food, health care, housing, education, and other basic human rights on an international scale (including the phenomenal Occupy Wall Street insurrection) have now expanded and enriched the revolutionary critical pedagogy that McLaren initiated in the last decades of the last century.

Operating on the terrain of ideological struggle, McLaren's militant cultural politics evolves in resonance with the times. It continues to confront state apparatuses of reification, media commodity-fetishism, and networks of power that construct identity/performative subjects. It strives to expose the limits of nihilistic deconstruction, anarchist pragmatism, and the biopolitics of the multitude. His interventions into the embattled sites of popular culture, of common-sensical *habitus* in the urban life-world colonized by racist-sexist politics of white supremacy, seek to analyze institutional relations of power and their reproduction. McLaren's vocation has always been to discover opportunities in classroom and community life susceptible to mediation, resistance, and transformation. His commitment to advance the project of producing subjects or agencies of liberation empowered with sensuous rationality and reflexive structures of feeling is vibrantly demonstrated in this new work.

As Paulo Freire noted in his preface to McLaren's *Critical Pedagogy and Predatory Culture*, we are fortunate to become "intellectual cousins" of McLaren by sharing (through his discourse and his example) the knowledge and skills needed for conscientized participation in changing our world by sharing with, and cooperating in, the struggle of the "wretched of the earth" for our all-encompassing liberation from the barbarism of global capitalism and for the survival of the planet.

PREFACE

Peter McLaren's Emancipatory Humanism

Michael A. Peters

Critical pedagogy locates the production of critical knowledges leading to praxis in its social, spatial and geopolitical contexts, and reveals the workings of the production process and how it operates intertextually alongside and upon other discourses, but it does so with a particular political project in mind—an anti-capitalist, anti-imperialist, anti-racist, anti-sexist and pro-democratic and emancipatory struggle.

—Peter McLaren

Peter McLaren is one of the few who from the beginning of his career as a teacher clearly knew where his sympathies lay—with teachers, with students, with ordinary people struggling against injustice and with other critical scholars and researchers who are committed to the principles of fairness, equality and social justice in public education. He has been one of a small group of scholars and activists based in the US who, in solidarity with the Brazilian educator, Paulo Freire, initiated the U.S. project of critical pedagogy. This is a movement barely fifty years old that has established itself as a powerful philosophy of education that grows out of and extends the humanist paradigm based on praxis, agency and emancipation.

Peter McLaren has gone through various theoretical phases to embrace a form of revolutionary Marxism. His latest work, *Pedagogy of Insurrection*, is a stunning culmination of thought and action, reflecting many years of engagement around the world. Distinctively, his work weaves together two powerful strands of thought that help to shape and define the Western tradition of critical humanism and radical philosophy: Karl Marx and Jesus Christ. A revolutionary critical pedagogy based on Marx and Jesus immediately expresses McLaren's sense of community with Freire and with much of Latin America and other parts of the world that see revolutionary praxis as an expression of love, community and social justice against the neoliberal ravages of the age. This strategy of combining Marx and Christ in one recuperative gesture conditions Marxist revolutionary praxis and resituates Christian socialism and liberation theology. I say "recuperative" because he makes a form of humanism the anchor that holds revolutionary Marxism and Christian socialism together in a new brutal age when the forces of neoliberal capitalism have created a new global class of financiers, bankers and insurers—alongside broader "financialized" global cybernetic capitalism and traditional industrial oil and gas—that exploits world resources to the edge of environmental doom and increases global inequalities, creating the global precariat (Peters & Besley, 2015). Increasingly, many of the world's inhabitants live in conditions of existence that leave them without any form of security and exposed to the risks and whims of global finance capitalism.[1]

Above all the term "precariat" refers to a restructuring of labor that has strengthened the power of management and weakened the power of workers and unions, rendering them increasingly as temporary and casual labor. Neoliberal labor reforms call this the creation of a market-sensitive, flexible workforce based on the shift from manufacturing to services in a postindustrial economy. It has the effect of systematically dismantling the legacy of the welfare state and any commitment to full employment. In the age of austerity, this means that youth populations around the world have no future. The covenant between education and work has been ruptured. Education is no longer a guarantee of employment.

Through his intelligence, his work and his talks and seminars in various parts of the world, Peter is aware of the forces that increasingly use education as a source of profit and a disciplining technology, rather than one designed to open horizons and to encourage a sense of community, solidarity and belonging in short, rather than as a humanizing force. The twin pillars of Marxism and Christian socialism provide McLaren with the deep resources of a revolutionary humanism that at once assert a humanity, a transformative agency, and an uncompromising commitment to the plight of the oppressed.

The embrace of a Christian anarchism that pictures Jesus as a revolution-ary thinker should come as no surprise. I remember talking with Peter recently about the "desert fathers and mothers" and their role in the development of the Western monastic system—the very beginnings of secluded spiritual communities and communal living based on self-renunciation and the vows of poverty, chastity and obedience. He knew immediately what I was talking about. He had been there before me and was not only aware but also well informed and shaped by the Western humanist tradition.

Sometimes the logic of place that unfolds while traveling embodies a set of associated thoughts that provides its own justification or rationale. On a recent trip to Burgundy, where we stayed for a week, we visited the various monasteries and abbeys, including the magnificent L'Abbaye de Fontenay that is one of the oldest Cistercian monasteries in France. It was founded by St. Bernard in 1118 and flourished over three centuries.[2] Reflecting on the origin of monasticism in the West, I became aware of the origins of West-ern asceticism and of the significance of doctrines of self-repudiation, self-denial and self-control that have pervaded Western Christianity and Western education for many years. The elevation of the mind and the renunciation of the body in rituals and exercises of self-discipline, self-denial, restriction and surrender—along with fasting, sexual abstinence, poverty, withdrawal, and sometimes with physical and mental pain—characterize Western ascetic humanism disciplining the body. But these privations did not originate in the hatred of the body, but rather illuminated the future glory of the body on the day of Resurrection. It is a curious fact that the Church can be a source of innovative humanizing theology working for liberation on the one hand and the seat of conservative moral values, on the other.

Both Freire and Illich began their revolutionary struggles with the Chris-tian idea and insight of liberation. Liberation theology began its life within the Catholic Church in Latin America during the 1950s as a reaction against the extreme poverty of the *Latifundia* system imposed by Spanish and Portu-guese colonizers who recruited and exploited local peasant labor. Later the term was widely adopted by Black and feminist thinkers. The Vatican admon-ished the Peruvian theologian, Gustavo Gutiérrez[3] (credited with coining the term), and other proponents for using "Marxist concepts." This is the appropriate context within which to situate Peter McLaren, in the forge of Western humanism, that brings together the sources of Western humanism as a revolutionary force for social justice. Thus he stands in the tradition inaugu-rated by Freire and Illich, and he seeks deliberately to develop the theoretical resources that are not always made explicit and to connect the skein of praxis, as he says, to comrade Fidel, comrade Che and comrade Chávez.

The chapters that comprise this book of essays are vintage McLaren— perhaps McLaren at his very best—with his inimical, whimsical and iconic style, his hope, his community, his revolutionary love, and his transformative critical pedagogy. Considered as a global movement, McLaren is certainly one of the founding intellectuals. He has gone on to fashion his own radical theory of revolutionary humanism in a highly distinctive manner, placing him in the pantheon of critical educators and critical thinkers. While of his age, he also transcends it, joining a small group whose message of justice to global humanity seeks the equality and betterment of all human beings.

Michael A. Peters
University of Waikato, NZ
University of Illinois, Urbana-Champaign, USA

Notes

1. The term "precariat" is neologized from the words "precarious" and "proletariat," and was first coined by Léonce Crenier, a Catholic monk who used it as a theological and political concept to describe the conditions of austerity within the monastery to pay off huge accumulated debt. In contemporary discourse the term is used to describe "contingent labor" that characterizes a flexible exploitation of casualized labor in the service sector—mostly women, youth and immigrants—who can be hired and fired at will. Precarity here refers to an existential positioning of those who are at high risk of social exclusion from job insecurity. In contemporary discourse the term has become synonymous with global justice movements, especially in Europe. It is a theological concept that emerges from Catholic social teaching and anarchism that is deeply humanist, referring, as it does, to the existential condition of the proletariat.
2. See http://www.abbayedefontenay.com/en/
3. See Gustavo Gutiérrez, A Theology of Liberation: History, Politics, and Salvation, 15th anniversary ed., trans. Caridad Inda and John Eagleson (Maryknoll, NY: Orbis, 1988; 1st ed., Maryknoll, NY: Orbis, 1973). Originally published as Teología de la liberación: Perspectivas (Lima, Peru: CEP, 1971).

OUT OF THE RUBBLE,
STAKING A CLAIM

An Introduction

Critical pedagogy currently exists today as precariously as a shabby lean-to room added to a typical American hall-and-parlor house. I'm referring to the type of house that formed the basic English prototype for the classic American building we see everywhere in New England and on the East Coast. If the hall-and-parlor house represents education in the main, then we critical educators are as rare as hen's teeth, shunted to the rear of the house, squatters huddled under a slanted roof, wearing fingerless gloves, clutching our tin cups of broth and spearing biscuits and dreaming of the day when we will become an official part of the architecture of democracy.

Those of us who practice revolutionary critical pedagogy, who comprise the night shift of critical pedagogy, are more marginalized still. Our push for democracy in U.S. schools is drowned out by the clamour of the parlors and chambers being enlarged above to make room for more policies such as No Child Left Behind, Race to the Top or even the current Common Core. Charter schools, while making up only a fraction of the overall schools in the country, are more accepted into the floor plan than are public schools in communities struggling with unemployment and urban infrastructure damage.

And what happens when students exit those floor plans and enter into the university system? Here students enter a more ominous structure because they are given the appearance of having some autonomy over the process of their learning, of having some control of the production of knowledge and the formation of their own political subjectivity. Yet here, alas, wisps of consumer whimsy disguised as truth trickle out of the smokestacks of knowledge production; intellectual chloroform wafts from corporate furnaces towering over the entire system, anesthetizing young brains and putting dreams into deep sleep in the digital furnace of the knowledge economy.

Life since Year Zero of the Capitalocene to the advent of technoecosystems and their toxic and eutrophicating chemicals has not been a pleasant ride. Soon we will be fracking the noosphere of human thought in our lecture halls, making Freire's critique of banking education seem utterly tame. Teachers' work will be routinized and rationalized to that of stoop laborers (as Henry Giroux would put it) weeding celery fields. As far as job satisfaction goes, a Walmart cashier or a Radio Shack clerk would feel more fulfilled.

As any awake teacher is aware, we live at a time of intensified race and class warfare in U.S. society. The crisis is epidemic and readily visible in our schools. As each generation tries to move forward on the path to liberation, we remain ensepulchered in the vault of hubris, like insects frozen in amber.

I intend to reflect upon the tragic irony of the current crisis of education that leads Stan Karp (2011) to characterize it as follows: "If you support testing, charters, merit pay, the elimination of tenure and seniority, and control of school policy by corporate managers you're a 'reformer.' If you support increased school funding, collective bargaining, and control of school policy by educators you're a 'defender of the status quo.'" Largely as a result of huge marketing campaigns in the corporate media, it is the ideological right wing that now claims the mantle of reformer and progressive teachers and defenders of public schooling have been placed on the defensive. Critically minded educators are not so easily fooled.

Decades ago I sounded a little-heeded alarm that urban education in the U.S. increasingly was susceptible to the intentions of neoliberal capitalism and a jaundiced corporate-infused perspective. Today, in a world where capitalism has monopolized our collective imagination as never before, befouled our bodies through a frenzied pursuit of narcotizing consumption and turned education itself into a subsector of the economy, such a remark would be read by most critical educators as a gross understatement. Because today, more than at any other time in human history, the perils of capitalism have been exposed. It is no longer controversial among many of us in the teaching profession to acknowledge that "governments seek to extend power and domination and to benefit their primary domestic constituencies—in the U.S., primarily the corporate sector" (Chomsky, 2013).

Over recent years educators who work within the critical tradition have been especially vociferous in their criticisms of education—urban education in particular—in relation to issues of social justice and what they perceive as persistent racism, the exploitation of urban working families, white supremacy, the containment of students with disabilities, homophobia, the attack on teacher education and the war on youth (Duncan-Andrade & Morrell, 2008; Sleeter 2011, 2012; Leonardo, 2009; Ayers, 2004, 2004a; Giroux 2013, 2013a; Gabel and Miskovic, 2014; Kumashiro, 2009, 2010; Ladson-Billings, 2005). Yet solutions to these problems appear persistently out of reach.

U.S. democracy once lit up the sky of the American dream like a glitter helix launched from a girandola. With the advent of neoliberal capitalism and the success of groups such as Citizens United and the American Legislative Exchange Council, the seams of democracy have been ripped asunder. The contradictions that for so long have been held in check by the violent equilibrium of market regulation have unchained themselves and as a consequence the mythic unity of capitalism and democracy has been exposed as a trussed-up fraud.

The shards of a dashed hope have been sent spinning like whistling bottle rockets into a firmament of sputtering stroboscopic dreams and titanium salutes, under a red glare and bombs bursting in air. The pursuit of democracy has given way to the waging of war, and there certainly is unanimous agreement worldwide that the U.S. "does war" better than any country in history.

Yet in the academy few have chosen to speak about the crisis of democracy and instead are self-admiringly recapitulating all the articles they wrote before getting tenure, that is, before they decided to overhaul what is left of the pursuit of knowledge so that it fits better into the corporate brand of their institution. They even might be working on university–Pentagon joint partnerships on crowd control or cyber warfare. The good professors don't bother to offer up any excuses for not jumping into the public fray other than maintaining that they are still collecting "data" and aren't ready to make any judgment calls about politics.

As I have written elsewhere about some of the etherized minds I have met in the academy over the past twenty years:

> Many of my academic colleagues, looking for some final vantage point from which to interpret social life, remain politically paralyzed, their studied inaction resulting from a stubborn belief that if they wait long enough, they surely will be able to apprise themselves of a major, messianic, supra-historical discourse that will resolve everything. Presumably this *ne plus ultra* discourse will arrive on the exhausted wings of the Angel of History! There seems to be some naïve belief that a contemporary codex

will eventually be announced (no doubt by a panjandrum at an Ivy League university) which will explain the quixotic mysteries and political arcana of everyday life. At this moment intellectuals will have the Rosetta Stone of contemporary politics in their possession, enabling them to know how to act decisively under any and all circumstances. Establishment academics under the thrall of technocratic rationality act as if the future might one day produce a model capitalist utopia in the form of an orrery of brass and oiled mahogany whose inset spheres and gear wheels, humming and whirring like some ancient clavichord melody, will reveal without a hint of dissimulation the concepts and practices necessary to keep the world of politics synchronized in an irenic harmony. All that would be necessary would be to keep the wheelworks in motion. (McLaren, 2008, pp. 474–475)

Clearly, there are spaces devoid of intellectual and moral putrefaction in the academy and I am fortunate finally to have found such a space with Freirean educators at Chapman. Such spaces are crucial at a time in which the tendrils of capitalism's poisonous vine are spreading into all the spaces and virtual spaces of potential capital accumulation. We desperately need cadres of teachers to speak out and to create spaces where their students can assume roles as razor-tongued public instigators for the social good. Globalized finance capitalism is the most widespread authoritarian structure in the history of civilization, giving the rich even greater riches and forcing the dispossessed to set up markets on moonlit streets to augment their exiguous incomes. We might be living in what is now called the "age of greed" but we should not be fooled that the current crisis of capital is linked mainly to the greed of corporate capitalists captured by Hollywood figures such as Gordon Gekko, since we believe that it is endemic to the system of capitalism itself.

Our shadow grows large beside the flames of capital's vast furnace, a grotesquery out of Dante's *Inferno*. We appear specter-like, Nosferatu the Vampyre with fingers extended across the wall of our flickering cave that we call civilization, all the better to grasp profits wherever our bloodlust for capital finds them, and to palpate the farthest rim of the earth if necessary, even to squeeze out from the vacant eyes of the poor their last tears of sorrow, if they could fetch a handy price in the market. All human and non-human animals inhabiting the planet have been stuffed stone-eyed into the vaults of capitalist social relations, a mausoleum of tortured beings writhing in the toxic vomit of the earth. We weep with all sentient beings, even as we shift from our anthropocentric cosmovision to a biocentric one.

According to Noam Chomsky (2014),

This is the first time in human history that we have the capacity to destroy the conditions for decent survival. It is already happening. Look at species destruction. It is estimated to be at about the level of 65 million years ago when an asteroid hit the earth, ended the period of the dinosaurs and wiped out a huge number of species. It is the same level today. And we are the asteroid. If anyone could see us from outer space they would be astonished. There are sectors of the global population trying to impede the global catastrophe. There are other sectors trying to accelerate it. Take a look at whom they are. (Cited in Hedges, 2014).

This behemoth we call capital is not some creature encountered in the medieval surrealism of Hieronymus Bosch or a *Bestiarum vocabulum* of the Middle Ages or in a sideshow banner in a county fair midway where you might be expected to find, in the abhorrent language of the carnival, Melvin Burkhart the Anatomical Wonder; Zippy the Pinhead; Chang and Eng, the original Siamese twins; Johnny Eck, the King of the Freaks; or Koo Koo the Birdgirl. The beast of the apocalypse, which I could name Exploitagus, is here among us, among both the living and the dead. Besmirched with a feral lunacy, and driven by a lust for the spoils of labor power, it towers over our world and all of our imaginings of what other worlds could, or should, be like. Its pallid countenance, lolling tongue and bloodless skin disguises its gluttonous and perverse appetite for profit, an appetite so ravenous that it would swim across an ocean of excrement, even risking the trident of Britannia, in order to ingurgitate a half farthing wrung from the aching arms of a bootblack. Its indelicate stride is not an evolutionary gallop as we are much too worldly wise to label it progress. Quite the contrary, it's a devolutionary sprint, a conquest of the globe that has laid waste to the land and has made civilization into a mausoleum, a place of dry bones in what once was a thriving metropolis of pulsating, fibrillating and undulating flesh; it's now a place of hollow sockets and empty brainpans that once held the vitreous and the electrical charges that fashioned for humanity the gift of sight and foresight.

Even a premonitory lunge from capital's febrile hand can cause havoc to cascade from its fingers of fire. And when it goes on a rampage, squatting on its precious platinum haunches and depositing its larvae as it has this past decade into the gin and tonics of our political leaders, nothing can stand in its path and survive, least of all the impecunious bystanders who seek out whatever diversions they can to avoid staring directly into the darkness of their own souls. Inside the darkness, they can see the junkyard world of the future. Finding relief in the light, they become blind to any and all alternatives to capital's value form.

The free-market economy is championed as the protector of democracy, like the fierce Chinese guardians or warrior attendants in a Tang dynasty temple. They protect us from any competing alternative, such as the dreaded socialism. The new citizens of this tilt-a-whirl domain of American politics remain functionally unaware, studiously refusing to see capitalism as a means of the exploitation of the labor-power of the worker and even less as accumulation by dispossession. As David Harvey (2010) puts it, accumulation by dispossession "is about plundering, robbing other people of their rights ... capitalism is very much about taking away the right people have over their natural resources" (Harvey, 2010, p. 99). Accumulation by dispossession is interrelated with neoliberalization or institutional reforms that are premarket and pro-privatization and against state interventions into the marketplace and so on.

The champions of neoliberalism—the antinomians, the pre-millenialists and post-millenialists—see those who would oppose their master—the socialists, liberals and communists—as in league with the anti-Christ. Some of these "warrior Christians" (as they like to see themselves) send their children to "Jesus camps," while others join the Christian militias, like Hutaree, and plot to kill government law enforcement agents and train to wage war against the anti-Christ (a recent poll indicated that one-quarter of Republicans believe that Barack Obama could be the anti-Christ, the Beast of the Apocalypse in the Book of Revelation). Of course, the Jesus of these militant evangelical extremists bears little resemblance to the Jesus of the Bible, even though their serpent-handling pastors and fellow sign-followers like to brag in their tent crusade revival meetings (once the copperheads and water moccasins are carefully secured in their baskets) that their values and politics derive from a 'literal' interpretation of holy Christian scriptures. Theirs is the Jesus of the prosperity preachers, a Jesus who wears a revolving Krispy Kreme donut as a halo, complete with sprinkle candy.

Those who do not want to talk critically about capitalism should keep quiet about the barbarism we are witnessing all around us. Be my guest and keep complaining about violence in schools, and how poorly teachers teach, and how immigrants are spoiling the country, but we don't need your advice. For those Anglos who feel a secret glee when Donald Trump, the capitalist id, calls undocumented Mexicans murderers and rapists, we ask: Can't you hear the earth shuddering in agony beneath your spit-and-polished jackboots? People aren't falling on the streets like spent bullets. Violence is more than a metaphor. People are falling in the street because they have been shot with bullets! And these are disproportionately people of color. Is it so difficult to connect this destruction systematically to capitalist relations of production rather than simply foisting it off as the result of greedy capitalists (we are tired of psychologizing what is clearly a structural crisis built into the dynamics of value production under capitalism)?

Present attempts at resisting the hydra-headed beast of capital are frozen like dried blood on history's stale proscenium where we dream our dreams and are dreamt by dream machines in an overcrowded theater of destruction. In this country of strangers, the scourge of capitalism is too infrequently accompanied by a momentous uprising by the oppressed but instead is met by isolated individuals enshrouded in a cynical resignation and a calcified hope, resulting in a paralyzing quietism awaiting its own dispersion. We will not be bequeathed another Che Guevara or Paulo Freire who will lead the fated triumph of the hardscrabble workers over the succulent and savvy bourgeoisie, will transubstantiate the graveyards of political defeat into a victory march of the Left, and will bring us into a world of unbearable beauty and harmony, a land of Cockaigne devoid of Breughel's slothful peasants. Those days are gone. But we do have Julian Assange, Chelsea Manning and Edward Snowden, and we should acquaint ourselves of their gifts of courage.

In our world of hand sanitizers, willfully disenfranchised youth, high-gloss reality shows, television commentaries on world events that have as much analytical depth as sparkle dust sprayed from a vintage-style perfume bottle, and benign varieties of televised adolescent rebellion with fast-food marketing tie-ins, we try in vain to find a way out. But that proves as difficult as asking your eyeball to stare back at itself. Or Benjamin's Angel of History to turn her head and face the future. Yet even against logo-swathed backdrops and image-based commentaries of daunting corporate grandeur, we keep ransacking Marx's tomb, especially when an economic crisis hits that demands some kind of explanation not afforded by the pundits of the *Wall Street Journal*.

Everywhere it seems—perhaps especially in education—you find Marxism being derided with a leering flippancy or galvanized indifference. You can't escape it, even in coffee shops for the urban literati, as a recent visit to a popular Los Angeles establishment taught me. There, among the hard-nosed espresso drinkers, a stranger approached me waving heavy hands. Bobbing over a thin nose and pair of succulent lips were a pair of tarsier eyes, looking as if they had been clumsily plopped onto plump, fleshy stumps that sprung out ominously from deep within his sockets. Escaping his overly caffeinated oral cavity was a stage-whispered admonition delivered with requisite theatrical intensity: "Oh, you're McLaren, the one that writes that Marxist shit." I responded with a simple retort, as quickly as if I had rehearsed it in advance: "I assume you're already so full of capitalist shit that I wonder how you noticed mine."

Today's capitalism is spawned in a petri dish of virtual Faustian space, as dank and suffocating as the inside of a hot air balloon. Capitalism dresses itself up in corset-like vocabularies of common sense. It can adapt to and absorb any language—even the language of the Left. It works its discourse in the service of its self-expansion, having no master to serve but itself. Its favorite language is the language of mystification, of progress, of democracy. By fashioning itself out of the contradictory logic of progressivism and traditionalism, it can confuse and obfuscate unobstructed.

In these times the tears of the poor do not help nourish the seeds of revolution; before they can fall to the ground they are swept up into the tornado of fast capitalism that passes them like minuscule batons around and around from crisis to crisis in an arena of corruption where the race is never finished, only suspended like an image in a frozen computer screen until the next corporate bailout. Resistance cannot take hold. Freedom is slipping away.

Arguably it is the case today that corporate greed constitutes the epochal spirit of our times. But to my thinking it is not the central antagonism at this current juncture in world history that is witnessing the ongoing trauma of capitalist formation within national security states such as the U.S. The problem is not entrenched corporate interests. This is merely the symptom that we mistake for the disease. The main problem—dare we say it?—is not that corporations and the banking industry (what used to be called the "Big Mules") are mulcting the public (which they are). The problem is global or transnational capitalism itself.

Capitalism is the very Eye of Sauron, the Hammer of Havoc, a heinous blight upon the planet that sees all, consumes all and destroys all in its path. We, the people, are lodged fast in the fetid bowels of the capitalist state, buried deep inside a monological regime of untruth, ensepulchered within the monumentalism and U.S. exceptionalism of the dominant culture—spread-eagled in the vortex of conflict that Bakhtin (in his work on dialogism, polyphony, heteroglossia and open interpretation) calls the authoritative discourse of the state and the internally persuasive discourse of our own making that expresses our values and our aspirations. The discourse of the state—that positions the "other" as irredeemably evil, as a monolithic alien species that is so barbaric as not to merit the rule of law—along with the functional existence of the state as an instrument of exploitation and repression, clearly need to be overcome.

How can this be possible? Cold War ideology prevails and U.S. citizens in the main bear the ideological marks of their times. The term "American empire" is being championed by the Right out of a sense of noblesse oblige—to be part of an empire is a duty and a responsibility that comes with being the leader and protector of the "free" world. With their paternalistic toy trumpets, and their willingness to jettison their critical faculties in favor of embracing an iron certainty and ineffable faith that the United States has a providential mission in the world, the far right boasts that free-market democracy has to be delivered to the far corners of the earth (by bombing runs, if necessary) if civilization is to prevail on the planet.

We learn this in our Steven Spielberg suburbs waiting for E.T. to return, in our double-mortgaged farmhouses, in our Appalachian towns ravaged by crystal meth, in our urban barrios where children with shipwrecked eyes and remastered smiles dream of Marvel Comics lives. We learn this from *Lamp Unto My Feet*, from *Our Gang*, from *Leave It to Beaver*, from *Happy Days*, from *The Fresh Prince of Bel Air*, from *Soupy and Pookie*, from *Tom Terrific*, from *What's My Line?*, from *Winky Dink and You*, from *Ding Dong School*, from Jack Bailey on *Queen for the Day*, from *Twin Peaks*, from *Jeopardy*, from *Teletubbies*, from carnival barkers, from television commercial scripts, from rodeo announcers and commentator hosts from the Superbowl to the Final Four. We are all infected.

The corbelled vault of our imagination from which memories cry out and dreams are born has been constructed out of the windswept debris of dead cities, destroyed civilizations, nations brought to servitude by the mailed fist of the world eaters, those whose imperial eyes sweep over the clearings when the dust of destruction has settled and seek to plunder the resources of entire nations, caring nothing of the aftermath, nothing of the blood that soaks into the earth or pools in the sewers of the heart, nothing of the blight brought to humankind.

Is it too late to re-enchant the world, to remold the planet in mytho-poetic terms, to create a past dreamtime, a mystical milieu in the present, to give ourselves over to dream divinities, to live in the eternal moment, to mold sacred totems from the damp clay of the riverbed? And while we ponder this possibility, the armies of the night march on, sneering at the pious surrender of the oppressed.

Because through the medium of experience the ego-driven individual is mistaken as the source of social practices, this process of misidentification has become a capitalist arche-strategy that marginalizes collectivity and protects the individual as the foundation of entrepreneurial capitalism. As a consequence, the well-being of the collectivity is replaced by the "politics of consumption" that celebrates the singularities of individuals by valorizing the desire to obtain and consume objects of pleasure. Experience in this view becomes non-theoretical and beyond the realities of history.

This is why we need to locate all human experience in a world-historical frame, that is, within specific social relations of production. Revolutionary critical pedagogy, as we have been trying to develop it, attempts to create the conditions of pedagogical possibility that enable students to see how, through the exercise of power, the dominant structures of class rule protect the practices of the powerful from being publicly scrutinized as they appropriate resources to serve the interests of the few at the expense of the many (Ebert & Zavarzadeh, 2008).

While we do not seek to live life with caprice or with an insouciant smirk, our project is anti-normative as long as schools seek to normalize students to an unjust world of stultifying toil for the laboring classes. We challenge this natural attitude of capitalist schooling and its moralizing machinery by climbing out of our spiritually dehydrated skin and re-birthing ourselves into relations of solidarity and *comunalidad*. We are assigned roles in the transnational workplace by our neoliberal overlords, and Heidegger's phrase, *das nicht-zuhause-sein* (not-being-at-home), is apposite in reminding us that we are not at home in the capitalist schoolhouse. Our place, our assignment in the world must be interrogated. As Tanya Loughead (in press) writes, "Radical education undoes the assignment of place. It unassigns and rebirths, not just once, but sets up that re-volting to occur throughout one's life."

Since we remain engulfed by a malefic capitalist bureaucracy radiating outwards from the center of the earth like a shockwave from hell, in a world that demands ever more hecatombs and suffering, I argue that today we need an intervention through a pedagogy of commitment and obligation. What does this mean, exactly? I emphasize the words "commitment" and "obligation" because no necessary logical connection exists between our interpretation of reality and our ability to transform such reality; that is, there is no strict rational move from premises in the indicative ("this is") to conclusions in the imperative ("therefore you must") mode. There is no formal logical link between judgments of fact and value-choices, between "is" and "ought" or "explanation" and "valorization" (Löwy, 2005). We need to mediate dialectically interpretation (subjectivist) and explanation (objectivist) by fusing hermeneutic (subjectivist) and structural (objectivist) approaches. In this way, it is possible for ideas to be critically appropriated following the historical-materialist stance of E. San Juan (2007). San Juan's brilliant work is characterized both by a multidetermined specificity and counterhegemonic imperatives framed by an internationalist worldview and grounded in concrete universals. In other words, specifics and universals are deftly combined strategically and tactically depending upon the context in which we, as agents, are called to act. Here, race and ethnicity are sometimes conceived as determinants for the totality of social relations that serves as the backdrop San Juan's decidedly Marxist theory of revolutionary praxis. And success is often conditioned by the skill employed and consistency achieved by the bricoleur so that the results do not remain a mere eclectic collage. We must not let our refuge only be in our dreams, for we are always bumping up against reality and must account for it. There is more to this universe than interpretations and metaphors and I am not simply talking about the corporeal body and the law of gravity.

I also believe that it is not only possible but imperative that academics and researchers make a "commitment" to a specific action or consider as an "obligation" their actions regarding the relationship between a specific premise and their concluding interpretations and explanations. That, of course, depends upon whether or not they agree to consider both creatively and dialectically the idea that our interpretation of the world is inseparable from our transformation of the world—both are linked socially and ethically. As such, a dialectical and critical self-consciousness of the relationship between being and doing (or being and becoming) becomes a part of the very reality one is attempting to understand and requires an ethical rather than an epistemological move, which is why ethics always precedes epistemology in the field of critical pedagogy. Only ethics of compassion, commitment and respect can guide us out of the neoliberal impasse that we face. Such critical self-consciousness steeled by a commitment to the oppressed becomes revolutionary if, for instance, your analysis is placed within the class perspective of the oppressed, that is, within the class perspective of the proletariat, cognitariat, precariat, etc. Logic and reason must be anchored by values and virtues that are grounded in an obligation to help the most powerless and those who suffer most under the bloody and bloodying heel plates of the capitalist behemoth and the devil's cartels. Che Guevara, whose reputation as a revolutionary basks in durable acclaim worldwide, was born into a middle-class household in Argentina. Yet Che was able to transcend his bourgeois roots and identify with the oppressed and fashion a storied life right out of a Homeric epic of great deeds. Unlike Che, Charles Dickens did not voluntarily commit class suicide. His father was committed to Marshalsea Debtor's Prison while young Charles worked for six shillings a week in a boot-blacking factory. Paulo Freire was born into a middle-class household yet the crisis of the world economy in the 1930s forced the young Freire into a world of hunger and poverty. Living among Brazil's rural poor while developing his pedagogical work, Freire

was able to understand their lives and identify with their struggle. His identification with the poor and powerless was forged during his youth when his own
bifurcated class position needed to be reconciled with real-life situations facing both his own family as well as the *campesinos* with whom he chose to work
and to whom he became committed. All of these figures held a commitment
to the poor and dispossessed accompanied by a vision of a socialist alternative
to capitalism.

But the vision for socialism in this book is not of ordinary stock. It is
grounded in the notion that a philosophy of praxis is not simply a stance one
takes toward the world, but a commitment to changing the world through
the "onto-creative" process of becoming fully human. It is grounded in the
notion that we discover reality in the process of discovering our humanity
within the continuity and fullness of history. While capitalism abstracts from
our subjectivity and turns us into objects and instruments of exploitation, our
personhood can never be reduced to this set of abstract social relations since
we are both the subject and object of history and play a part in pushing back
against the economic system that produces us. While we reflect the ensemble of social relations that inform our humanness we also have the ability
of transforming those social relations by assigning meaning to them. Those
meanings, of course, vary in time and place. The set of meanings that inform
this book attempt to animate what the gospels refer to as the Kingdom of God,
the Kingdom announced by Jesus. I am not here concerned with whether the
Kingdom is constructed before, during, or after eschatological judgment. My
goal is not to use a Western historical-critical approach to create a secular
messianism or transhumanism but, echoing the motto of the Italian Marxist Antonio Gramsci, through a militant optimism of the will and pessimism
of the intellect to build a pedagogical case for a truly Christian socialism,
drawing upon the inner fire of our apocalyptic call to usher into oblivion
the last epoch in human prehistory we call 'capitalism'. My approach—in
which Christian hope, Marx's historical materialism, and our obligatory call
to help all those who suffer needlessly are intertwined—underscores the need
to address the fraught issues of race, class, gender, disability, homophobia, spe-
ciesism and other forms of oppression not only in terms of what they might
mean for the agents themselves but in terms of how they function institution-
ally and in terms of the interests and purposes that they serve. The goal is not
to found some "pre-Q" tradition of Christian communist societies or uncover
an esoteric wisdom tradition—some pre-Templaristic ecology of symbols—
in accordance with an ancient Middle Eastern agrarian society. Nor are we

contemporary members of the Dolcino brotherhood who wish to resurrect the legacy of Fra Dolcino as the apostle of the socialist Jesus, although we do acknowledge the value of his ideals upon which his commune of impoverished penitents was founded. Our goal is, rather, to uncover Jesus' message of love and justice in the context of creating a society absent of differentiating wealth and to integrate this message into the field of revolutionary critical pedagogy as both apocalyptic warning and cause for joy in the possibility of redeeming the earth from ecocide and bringing about an alternative to value production, and in so doing, participating in our own redemption.

Critical pedagogy has done much to inspire dissidents to engage culture in the agonistic terrain of the cultural imaginary so as to break with dominant relationships of power and privilege through forms of pedagogical subversion. While some dimensions of subversion have led to interventions and new communal relationships of solidarity and struggle, others have been dominated by forms of postmodern self-absorption and self-fashioning where the embattled agent engages in acts of symbolic inversion within the contradictions of consumptionist capitalism. What interests me are the ethical imperatives driving such acts of subversion. Is the protagonist subject not codetermined by discourses of resistance and possibility, as Henry Giroux might put it? If this is the case, then I would argue that within the field of critical pedagogy today, there is a disproportionate focus on the critique of identity formation at the expense of examining and finding alternatives to existing spheres of social determination that include institutions, social relations of production, ideologies, practices and the cultural imaginary—all of which are harnessed to value production.

Manos Sucias (Dirty Hands): The Sins of the State

I am staunchly opposed to the violence of the state. This is a complicated issue and I draw here upon the work of liberation theologians and especially from Michael Rivage-Seul (2008). Frantz Fanon (2004) wrote about how the European elite undertook the creation of a native elite and in doing so legitimated and monumentalized the idea of non-violence and attempted to mystify the working classes, the toilers of the world, into thinking that they have the same interests as the oppressed, the exploited, the dominated. Of course, the ruling class does not have the same interests. It often uses state violence to achieve its ends, yet officially preaches non-violence except in instances where it enforces its judicial code, which, of course, privileges the interests of the wealthy and mainly white property owners.

The first-level violence, or the violence of the state, is a violence whose idol is "empire," and whose patron is "capitalism"; a violence that justifies itself in fighting terrorism; a violence which, here in the U.S., puts African Americans and Latinos in the prison system in vastly disproportionate rates compared to whites. And when they are not incarcerating them at breakneck speed, the security forces of the state are slaughtering them on the streets for not acting white. Now second-level violence is what we could call revolutionary violence, a violence directed against the state, against the first-level violence of the state, its legal system, its police forces, its economic system. And then there is third-level violence, which is reactionary violence, a violence enacted by the state, a violence directed by the state against revolutionary violence.

It bears mentioning that all violence is divinized, it is a form of worship, a form of the sacred based on the feature of scapegoats and stereotypes and gives justification for our actions. However, it doesn't take much insight to see that the armies of the U.S. empire and its client states that undertake state violence are far less vulnerable than those who undertake revolutionary violence. Just look at the 200,000 slaughtered in Guatemala, the 80,000 slaughtered in El Salvador, the 70,000 slaughtered in Nicaragua and the perhaps 2 million slaughtered in Iraq—all by the U.S. military or forces receiving support from the U.S. empire. How much has really changed in those countries? People are still being used as cheap labor for multinational corporations.

So you can see how even revolutionary violence—the violence most justified—can feed into the military-industrial complex, inflating it even further, giving it more reason to produce weapons of mass destruction which are incomprehensible in their ability to kill and maim and are sold to both sides of the conflict. This point has been made, as noted earlier, by Michael Rivage-Seul (2008) and other liberation theologians. We know that the violence of the state is not called violence, is not called terrorism. We know, of course, that this is not the case. But if any act of violence is at least partly justified by "just war" standards (the U.S. cites its own "patriots" in the Revolutionary War against England), it is revolutionary violence. We cannot condemn those who practice revolutionary violence as long as we participate in state violence. That is my point. But revolutionary violence must be proportional, must be a last resort, must have the right intention and reasonable prospects for success.

We also need as Leftists to recognize that we have as much intrinsic capacity for abuse as those on the Right. We need to avoid both moral absolutism and political dogmatism and not be part of a righteous vanguard. The idea is not to defeat "evil," because good and evil are inextricably connected, and human depravity is ubiquitous and persistent, but to figure out how to create a society in which we can establish the conditions of possibility to transcend the antimony of good and evil.

Hence, we cannot condemn others who engage in revolutionary violence—or second-level violence—when we who choose not to engage in such violence sit back and allow our tax dollars to fuel corporate interests and the military-industrial complex without taking action. It is important to develop forms of non-cooperation with injustice and to reform judicial systems, to create sustainable and just economic systems through the struggle for freedom. On an international level, we need to take away the moral authority of those who, in the name of the interests of state security, exercise violence. We need to have confidence that in many instances, non-violent direct action can stop structural violence if the world community can put pressure on the perpetrators.

In a political arena where the Grand Ole Opry meets slick Beltway hustlers, grim patriots with sandpaper smiles under faded NASCAR peaked caps are ready to believe almost any explanation of why their faith in America has collapsed. They lurch lockstep in drumbeat resignation that it must be the bankers who are to blame for their ills, or it's Obamacare, liberals, socialists, multiculturalists, gays and lesbians or immigrants who have stolen their dreams. The focus is rarely on the real structural problems of living in a capitalist economy that is prone to crisis.

Capitalism clearly is structurally incapable of permitting democracy to live up to its own definition even minimally, as it can no longer tolerate, let alone absorb, the principle of economic justice and equality. Yet even in the face of this disquieting fact, there are few aspects of our teacher education programs or our graduate schools of education that focus on the perils of education reform in the context of examining the perils and pitfalls of contemporary capitalist society.

Any hope we have for a future that does not resemble the sets of *Blade Runner* (Deely & Scott, 1982) is increasingly land-filled. We are heirs to a time when voices calling for reason and sanity are the new unreason and victims of corporate media blackout. The warnings of Marxists, ecologists, environmental scientists—and even Pope Francis—about the impending crisis of the planet sound to many as irrational as the sports bar ravings of a besotted town crazy and find an echo only in the conscience of those already considered part of the lunatic fringe.

Potential conscripts for fighting those who are waging war on the working class, the phalanxes of spindle-shanked inner-city youth who are consigned to big-box retail stores like Target and Walmart where they are paid salaries well below the official poverty rate, are as dependent upon The Man as corporations are dependent upon fossil fuels, and return home too exhausted from work to mount much of a political opposition, although those that manage to pull themselves into the streets and picket lines to protest are surely to be congratulated. Computers displace clerical workers and many middle-class jobs and college degrees, if the right kind, might give a tiny edge to recent college graduates resigned to a grim enslavement to the corporate wage as non-union workers. Unions have been eviscerated, except in some instances at the local level, but most are enfeebled by laws constraining labor relations and workers' rights that prohibit the right to organize and act collectively. Union strikes in the U.S. are few and far between.

The structural unconscious of "America" has an enormous capacity to assist the citizenry in escaping the reek and corruption of everyday life. It sends us skittering away desperately into hinterlands of social amnesia, far enough away from facing the harsh reality of our potential destiny as planet slum and entraining us in the short-term gratification of media culture. Revenge scenarios in television shows, the proliferation of television sports and the collective mockery of "losers" on reality shows are able to siphon away our energies that elsewhere could be committed to creating sites of collective dialogue and political organization.

We are, as the cultural critics tell us, libidinally invested in the delights of popular culture. It has replaced in our structural unconscious what was once the call of a loon or the howl of a wolf in some mythic woodland in the darkness of an eclipsed moon. Instead, we get images of Miley Cyrus's atomic wedgies and tinsel pasties flopping around in our minds as we awake gravel-headed from our media-enforced stupor (when we should be praising her support of the GLBTQ community and for raising money and awareness for marginalized and homeless youths, including those from LGBTQ communities).

Irretrievably entangled with our mission to bring social justice to the world are the thousand-armed Bodhisattvas who appear to us in our frivolous and restless minds today not as Buddha or Krishna or Christ but as Gomer Pyle, Pee Wee Herman, Ipana Toothpaste's Bucky Beaver, 20 Mule Team Borax, Soupy Sales, Lassie, Monty Python's Flying Circus, Jimmy Durante, The Monkees, Jack Benny, *The Prisoner*, Rawhide, Red Skelton, Liberace, Mother Mabel Carter, Mr. Magoo, Perry Como, *Hee Haw*, *Catweasle*, *The Twilight*

Zone, Marvin the Martian, Roy Rogers, Dale Evans, Trigger, Ricky Nelson, Robert Tilton, a.k.a. the Farting Preacher or Pastor Gas, *Hopalong Cassidy*, Kookie and his comb, Robbie the Robot, Miley Cyrus's disco ball nipple pasties, Ryan O'Neal's sheepskin jacket, Sacha Baron Cohen's Bruno thong, *The Glenn Campbell Goodtime Hour*, Mr. Spock, Vanna White, Geraldo, Jiminy Cricket, *Buffy the Vampire Slayer*, *Breaking Bad* and *Game of Thrones*.

Less well known perhaps—but no less tantalizingly seductive—than the history of American charter schools is that of performance contracting in the education sector, specifically Supplemental Educational Services (SES), facilitated through Title I of the No Child Left Behind Act (NCLB) and mandated in Obama's Race to the Top neoliberal platform. Schools that fail to meet adequate yearly progress (AYP) benchmarks for 3 consecutive years are legally required to pay for the use of SES for their students. SES is designed to divert Title I funds to private (and faith-based) tutorial companies that are not compelled by law to follow civil rights statutes yet who claim the language of equality and human rights in their efforts to improve students' high stakes standardized test scores. Originally hatched in the 1970s by infamous Iraq war profiteers Donald Rumsfeld and Dick Cheney during their eerie tenure in Nixon's Office of Economic Opportunity, SES is part of yet another neoliberal scam. In the 1970s, Rumsfeld and Cheney tried to shift billions of tax dollars earmarked for public schools into the greased palms of for-profit venture capitalists and speculators who would be able to remain legally unaccountable to the public trust (Rosa and Rosa, 2015). Such a scam failed miserably in the 1970s but eventually came to fruition in the Bush Jr. White House under NCLB when Cheney and Rumsfeld finally unlocked the nuclear codes to their neoliberal unconscious and launched a warp drive surplus-value offensive. SES betrays a scandalous affinity to Cheney and Rumsfeld's storied re-allotment of taxpayer dollars from the military budget to accountability-adverse private contractors such as Halliburton and Blackwater (Rosa and Rosa, 2015).

It was not long ago that we heard that 93 of 206 charter schools in Texas were in hot water for bilking the state out of millions of dollars by over-counting their enrollment. Approximately $9 million of the $23 million owed to the taxpayers was from shuttered "academies of learning" that the Business Roundtable intended to be funneled into the for-profit, or non-profit corporate tax credits (Schools Matter, 2008).

It is not enough to complain about the egoism of economic life with moral-advocative denunciations, although that is certainly a good beginning. What drives the logic of capital relentlessly forward at such a tremendous pace is not egoism alone, but the structural contradictions of the labor/capital relationship within advanced capitalist societies—the alienation of humanity's labor and products from humankind through the commodification of everyday life.

Greg Palast (2013) exposed what he called the "End Game Memo," which signaled part of the plan created by the top U.S. Treasury officials to conspire "with a small cabal of banker big shots to rip apart financial regulation across the planet." In the late 1990s, the U.S. Treasury Secretary Robert Rubin and Deputy Treasury Secretary Larry Summers pushed hard to de-regulate banks, and they joined forces with some of the most powerful CEOs on the planet to make sure that happened. The "end game" was tricky and seemed indomitable because it required the repeal of the Glass-Steagall Act (1933) to dismantle the barrier between commercial banks and investment banks.

It should come as no coincidence that the Glass-Steagall legislation was passed the year that marked the end of the Banana Wars. The Banana Wars (1898–1934) marked a sordid time of U.S. military interventions and occupations in Latin America and the Caribbean. Countries that were targeted by the U.S. included Cuba, Puerto Rico, Nicaragua, Mexico, Honduras, Haiti and the Dominican Republic, where the U.S. was intent on protecting its commercial interests (largely via fruit companies such as The United Fruit Company) and extending its sphere of political influence through military means in countries that were unable to pay their international debts.

The Glass-Steagall Act was designed to help regulate Wall Street and strengthen the regulatory power of the Federal Reserve. Palast called the repeal of the Glass-Steagall Act "replacing bank vaults with roulette wheels." The banks wanted to venture into the high-risk game of "derivatives trading," which allowed banks to carry trillions of dollars of pseudo-securities on their books as "assets." However, the transformation of U.S. banks into "derivatives casinos" would be hampered if money fled U.S. shores to nations with safer banking laws. So this small cabal of banksters decided to—and successfully did—eliminate controls on banks in every nation on the planet in one single move by using the Financial Services Agreement (FSA).

The FSA was an addendum to the international trade agreements policed by the World Trade Organization that banksters utilized to force countries to deal with trade in "toxic" assets such as financial derivatives. Every nation was thus pushed to open their markets to Citibank, JP Morgan and their derivatives' "products." All 156 nations in the World Trade Organization were pressured to remove their own Glass-Steagall divisions between commercial savings banks and the investment banks that gamble with derivatives. All nations were bribed or forced in other ways to comply, and only Brazil refused to play the game.

Of course, as Palast (2013) noted, the game destroyed countries such as Greece, Ecuador and Argentina, to name a few, and contributed catastrophically to the global financial crisis of 2008. Of course, by then the model of the American imperialist war was no longer modeled on the small-scale Banana Wars, but the Iraq War, which privatized the Iraqi oil industry and allowed it to be dominated by foreign companies.

Solving the Problem of Inequality: The Market Is Not a Sustainable or Liveable Community

Schools in the main reflect the inequality found in the structure of capitalist society. We need to face this grim reality of what has now become a truism in our society. New standards and high-stakes testing will not solve the problem of inequality; in fact they could even intensify the problem. High-stakes testing for the promotion of cognitive ability is more likely to create inequity than it is to eradicate it. The issue is not simply how the tests are used, but the very act of testing itself, which ignores non-cognitive factors which contribute to human (endogenous) development.

Schooling in the U.S. (and in most Western democracies) is successful to the extent that it betrays an uncritical acceptance of the doctrine of meritocracy and refuses to examine itself outside of the hive of capitalist ideology and its cloistered elitism—its precepts, concepts, its epistemicides and its various literacies of power through which ideas become slurred over time and actions on their behalf are guaranteed to remain as inactive as a drunken fisherman lost at sea in a leaking boat. In their belief that the industrious and ambitious are justly rewarded, they unwittingly and unsparingly legitimize the existing structures of inequality. They resign themselves to the fact that answers to the questions of social justice and equality will remain predesigned before questions can even be formulated.

This vision of democracy is inevitably preformed and must be engraved on the minds of its citizens through ideological state apparatuses such as schools. As long as the ideas of the ruling class rule us—and they can certainly rule us with the help of the partnership between the state and corporate media—we will remain apprentices to the anguish of the oppressed. Ideas for eradicating poverty and injustice will be guaranteed to remain vacant, hidden in a thicket of "feel-good" bourgeois aesthetics whose complicity with inequality bulks as large as its opposition to it, making it an appropriate ideological form for late capitalist society. Such ideas will be guaranteed not to transgress the "comfort zone" of those who tenaciously cling to the belief that with hard work and a steeled will, they will reap the rewards of the American Dream—regardless of race, class, gender or geographical location.

If we want to participate in educational reform, then it becomes necessary to challenge the proponents of the competitive market whose corporate outlawry is driving the reform initiatives of education today. We barely can distinguish what augments and entrenches corporate power today from the brutal logic that powers the narco-cartels that wreak havoc throughout Mexico. Today we not only are besieged by a world-historical crisis of capitalism, we also face a crisis of human decency. The future proffers an ominous stillness, an illusion already sucked dry by gluttonous speculators and the new transnational robber barons.

We in the field of education should be gravely disquieted by the power of this claim. We see the wake of capitalism's devastation in the privatization of public schooling following Hurricane Katrina in the Gulf Coast to myriad ways that No Child Left Behind and Race to the Top transform public schooling into investment opportunities—not to mention corporate efforts to turn New Orleans into a city of white yuppies. We see it in the retooling of colleges in order to serve better financial and military-industrial interests, in overuse and exploitation of contingent faculty, in the growth of for-profit degree-granting institutions and in rising tuition and student debt (student debt in the U.S. now exceeds that of credit cards, totaling over $1 trillion; see Cauchon, 2011), not to mention the assault on critical citizenship in favor of consumer citizenship.

The crisis of the "free" enterprise system today, the naked money-grabbing practices that might accurately be described as gangster capitalism, or drive-by capitalism, lacks any sincere connection with human dignity and is reconstructed as a mere "greed-is-good" formalism and proffered to the American people as self-protection: a harsh and unavoidable reality of the times. This legally unrestrained self-initiative that enables all barriers to the market to be dismantled in the interests of profit making by the few is built upon a negative definition of freedom—the freedom from having to enter into the necessary conversations with humanity that permit the full development of human capacities for fairness and social justice.

Not only is this an acceptance of the current distribution of wealth and the transvaluation of social into individual needs, it is also the freedom to enjoy your wealth and success without having to accept any moral obligation for the suffering of others. Expenditures of any kind must be made from the principle of self-interest and individual advantage, and in proportion to that advantage—and all such brutal vindictiveness of the capitalist class towards the 99 percent is egregiously justified under the term "human nature." People come to be judged solely in terms of human capital: for their economic contribution is measured by the market. There is no motive of social amelioration. Further, in times of crisis, it is the bankers and huge corporations that can "socialize" their risk by transferring it to the taxpayers who are used by the government to bail them out.

But the market is not a community. It is only possible to realize your humanity if you are educated in an authentic community. And how do we achieve true community? Only by analyzing and understanding the distinction between how the social system understands itself, and how it exists in objectivity, that is in reality—in other words, only by working through false consciousness towards critical consciousness, towards a more dialectical understanding of how capitalism affects the very way we approach social problems, including educational problems. At present there is a huge disconnect between the two; that is, there is a tremendous gap between how U.S. society comprehends itself and how it is structured to be co-extensive with inequality. In a community, social wealth is distributed by means of the principle of equality in response to need. For me, education is about creating community in a society that has forgotten the meaning of the term.

Critical pedagogy is strongly assertive of its epistemologies and premises, its obligations and its practices, as well as its normative prescriptions and prohibitions with respect to engaging with others in the world. Even though critical pedagogy has been on the scene for decades, it is still argued by many in the educational establishment that the problem with working-class families has to do with the culture of poverty, in which it is assumed that there is an egregious deficit in working-class culture when read against the values and cultural capital of bourgeois culture.

But for critical educators, this is taking what is fundamentally a structural problem—capitalist-produced inequality—and turning it into a cultural problem: the problems of values, attitudes and the lack of high culture and preponderance of low or middlebrow culture within working-class families, which suggests erroneously that class privilege has something to do with merit. It reflects a paternalistic presumption implicit in contemporary school reform approaches, namely, that the poor lack the proper attitudes and values to help them succeed in consumer capitalist society.

Of course there is a racial dimension to all of these measurable inequities when examining the statistical facts of gaps between the outcomes of students disaggregated by race and affluence and comparing them with the statistical facts of disproportionate numbers of teachers among races. Moreover, when you compare these to the realities of the school-to-prison pipeline, and the resegregation of schools, we see a national trend. Consider the following statement from Dr. Martin Luther King (2009):

> We have come a long way in our understanding of human motivation and of the blind operation of our economic system. Now we realize that dislocations in the market operation of our economy and the prevalence of discrimination thrust people into idleness and bind them in constant or frequent unemployment against their will. The poor are less often dismissed from our conscience today by being branded as inferior and incompetent. We also know that no matter how dynamically the economy develops and expands it does not eliminate all poverty.

Relatos Salvajes (Wild Tales): The Illogicality of the Market

The fact that the logic of the market is a regulatory principle of life within capitalist societies is now commonplace. Over time, this regulatory principle has led the state to react harshly to fomenting opposition, especially from the current generation whose futures seem, in the words of Henry Giroux, disposable. This has led to various incarnations of "soft fascism" that we saw increase exponentially throughout the U.S., especially after September 11, 2001, and the global slump of 2008. We have witnessed the militarization of the police, the often fatal assaults on black men by the police, harsh sentences for whistleblowers, etc. and the push to privatize public spaces such as schools and universities where dissent can be more effectively controlled by private owners and conservative and well-heeled boards of trustees. Clearly, the corporatocracy is worried about political dissent. Capitalism is in the process of reconstituting itself transnationally. And those who are hit hardest are learning from alternative sites in the social media to see through the veil of deception and lies of the corporatocracy. They know that the state is recalibrating its plans for reacting to hostile opposition from the poor, from students saddled with debt, and from those who are committed to the process of democratization in all spheres of public and private life. They have been aided by critical educators who are intent on helping their students read both the word and the world dialectically, recognizing power as a constitutive dimension of both pedagogy and politics.

Revolutionary critical pedagogy has attempted to give substance to the lie that the U.S. is fighting evil empires around the globe in order to protect its vital interests, interests that must be met for it to continue as the prime defender of the 'free' world. Critical educators assume the position that equality is both a precondition and outcome for establishing community, and a community is a precondition for deep democracy. This demands that students question the various roles played by the U.S. on the stage of history and nurture a radical imagination where they can consider other forms of organizing society and collectively providing for themselves and others their economic, social, cultural and spiritual needs.

The U.S. ceased to become a democracy long before John Foster Dulles, who served as U.S. Secretary of State infamously under Republican President Dwight D. Eisenhower from 1953 to 1959, helped to overthrow the democratically elected Iranian government through the efforts of the CIA. A significant figure in the early Cold War era who advocated an aggressive stance against communism throughout the world, Dulles sought to duplicate the CIA's overthrow of Prime Minister Mohammad Mossadegh in Iran in the same manner in the Congo, Guatemala, Indonesia and Egypt, which later was used as a model in Vietnam, Guatemala, Cuba, Afghanistan and Nicaragua. All of this can be verified in countless sources, the most vivid by the ex-CIA agent who was directly involved, Kermit Roosevelt.

The U.S. has accepted "low intensity warfare" as its normal foreign policy. For instance, a vitally important and thoroughly documented report on the impact of Obama's drone campaign was just released by researchers at Stanford University Law School and NYU (see International Human Rights). The Stanford–NYU report details the effects of Obama's drone assaults in Pakistan, which not only targeted individuals, but also targeted those attempting to assist and rescue those who had been injured, including those attending the funerals of those who had been recently assassinated.

Can you imagine structuring a lesson plan around this in Texas or anywhere in the U.S. public school system? Students are surprised to learn that the World Court in the 1980s issued a judgment in favor of Nicaragua, condemning the U.S. for what it called "unlawful use of force," and ordered the U.S. to desist training and funding assassination squads and pay substantial reparations for what was tantamount to terrorism (Cleaver & Tran, 1986). We are referring here, of course, to President Reagan's support for the Nicaraguan Contras, whose sole purpose was to terrorize and kill men, women and children (and especially schoolteachers) in the countryside.

How many students today know that the U.S. rejected a Security Council resolution calling on all nation states to observe international law? Not engaging and understanding the history of imperialism and the instrumental role played by the U.S. can have devastating consequences in that we will continue to repeat that history.

As I write this, the U.S. again publicly condemns countries that have been accused of using chemical weapons. While the use of chemical weapons should be outlawed, the U.S. government fails to consider that what it defines as conventional weapons—cluster bombs, napalm, depleted uranium shells and white phosphorus (that melts the flesh from bones)—are condemned by countries worldwide for being tantamount to weapons of mass destruction. Why hasn't the U.S. joined the Convention on Cluster Munitions to this date? Didn't the U.S. military finally admit to using napalm during its invasion of Iraq? Is not depleted uranium, which the U.S. military used during its 1991 and 2003 invasions of Iraq to penetrate walls and pierce armor, a type of genotoxic chemical weapon that vaporizes upon contact and can be inhaled with devastating genetic consequences? Did it not cause Iraqis who lived in the areas where shelling with depleted uranium was prevalent to suffer astronomical rates of genetic damage? Is it not the case that in cities such as Basra and Fallujah, where U.S. and British forces used depleted uranium shells at the start of the war, it is estimated that over half of all babies conceived after the start of the war were born with heart defects?

Should such questions form our ongoing debates in our classrooms? Or do we continue to claim that classrooms must be "neutral" spaces devoid of political debates and discussions and leave such questions to the "experts" (likely certified by the Pentagon)? Do we pander to those who claim that such discussions are anti-American? Do we hide behind the lie that the U.S. military does not commit war crimes, or do we hold our government accountable for what are by any sane standards incontrovertible facts?

If you truly are a patriot and wish your country to be a force of real democracy and peace in this world, it would seem reasonable to assume that a first step you would want to take would be to acknowledge the atrocities your country has committed in the name of democracy. To refuse to take such a step is to fall into an opaque attempt at offering a rational defense of those atrocities and to provide a way of distancing ourselves from reality. It is a form of self-deception that indirectly "naturalizes" all behavior on the part of the U.S. as a force for good.

But when we are working with students in our elementary schools, trying to help them understand their behavior towards others, do we not ask them to own up to their misbehavior as a first step in transforming themselves into more productive and considerate citizens? Regrettably, when we try to apply this principle to U.S. foreign policy, we are met with a fierce defensiveness and often warned to back off from our criticisms for fear of being labeled anti-American or providing sympathy and solace to America's enemies.

It is a regrettable characteristic of any plutocracy, but especially ours, that the wealthier you are, the greater influence you have in impacting public opinion. It is a tragic truism that only a fraction of a percentage of the U.S. population determines the policy for the rest of us. So when we discuss U.S. democracy with our students, do we provide them with the opportunity to explore the current crisis of democracy that haunts all of us today?

This is not a charge that I have simply stumbled upon adventitiously. This has been pointed out since the 1960s and to the present day by Noam Chomsky (2013) and other intellectuals who are marginalized by the mainstream media. Where do we engage this ugly reality in critical dialogues in our schools?

While a large percentage of the public and approximately half of the wealthy believe that the minimum wage ought to be indexed to the cost of living and high enough to prevent falling below the poverty line, why is the minimum wage far below this standard? Our health system has twice the per capita costs of other OECD countries and less-than-desirable outcomes, yet opinion polls show that the public wants a national healthcare system (Toner & Elder, 2007). But that is unlikely to happen. Large majorities of the public believe that corporations and the wealthy should pay higher taxes. Yet, taxes on those groups actually have declined.

So how is it that the U.S. as a democracy actually moves in the opposite direction from what the public wants? Part of it has to do with the opinion of the sentinels of the capitalist class that the American people are not considered intelligent enough to be the best judges of their own interest. A fundamental role of the bankers and the intellectual elites is to keep the American people from actually acting on their beliefs. The elites accomplish this through the machinations of the public relations industry (Chomsky, 2013).

Democracy is not a condition that the U.S. elites want to see obtained in this country. Far from it. They perceive democracy as too deeply dangerous to their own financial interests. So the corporate elites and their government handmaidens want to keep the public in a state of terminal confusion.

Chomsky (2013) noted that the American Legislative Exchange Council (ALEC) is instituting a new program "to try to overcome the excessive rationality of the public," stating succinctly that:

> It's a program of instruction targeted for K-12 (kindergarten to 12th grade in schools). Its publicity says that the idea is to improve critical faculties—I'd certainly be in favor of that—by balanced teaching. "Balanced teaching" means that if a sixth grade class learned something about what's happening to the climate, they have to be presented with material on climate change denial so that they have balanced teaching and can develop their critical faculties. Maybe that'll help overcome the failure of massive corporate propaganda campaigns to make the population ignorant and irrational enough to safeguard short-term profit for the rich. It's pointedly the goal and several states have already accepted it.

To the extent that liberating one's own words becomes a basis for liberating one's deeds, understanding the role that inequality plays in urban education reform is urgently needed for understanding both the perils and the promises affecting human life at a time of capitalist retrenchment and reconstitution. It also is a mechanism for working towards an alternative to the capitalist organization of human affairs. When a vocabulary of liberation takes root and a vision of common ownership becomes our herald, a path to action is created and a doorway is opened by the union of critique and possibility.

It is time for progressive educators worldwide to enter into serious dialogue with critical patriotism in order to advance the necessary re-ordering and reconstruction of the economy, society and polity built on the imperatives of economic equality and social justice for all. Occupy Wall Street as well as popular social movements worldwide has put the concept of social and economic justice back into the public vocabulary. Let's not permit it to disappear, but rather begin to build upon it. Democracy will surely be a contested terrain during this global crisis of capitalism. Yet a democracy built upon critical patriotism has a potential to thrive and grow, whereas a democracy distended by the rancid bile of social amnesia and denial will ossify and wither.

Ethical deficiency and logical contradiction are connected insofar as capitalism has dehumanized humanity and treated human beings as inert matter that can be swept under the toxic ruins of the world's industrial wasteland. It becomes therefore necessary to find an alternative to capital's value form— which is another way of saying that we need to consider an alternative to capitalism as a way of achieving democracy.

This alternative need not follow the historical path of European or North American struggles but can be illuminated by the many current efforts of indigenous peoples worldwide to protect the natural environment and build sustainable communities constructed on the principle of reciprocity and co-operation. By all means, let's celebrate the positive features of U.S. democracy, but at the same time we must be willing to consider the fact that democracy's sweetheart deal with capitalism has become a liability for the vast majority of the wretched of the earth and continues to drown our hopes for a better world in the tears of the poor.

Only when we can recognize the discrepancy between truth and false-hood will we be able to cease believing that slavery is freedom; only when we can create a renaissance of belief in humanity can we create that necessary and unflagging optimism of the will and stimulate the necessary emancipatory impulses among the insurgent masses of workers, youth, women, indigenous activists and environmentally conscious groups that can bring about a better future. We must refuse to surrender our independence and integrity and will-ingly take up the struggle.

I retain here the concept of democracy as synonymous with communism but not in the same sense as Hardt and Negri and other autonomous Marx-ists. I use the term "communism" as a horizon that "impresses upon us the necessity to abolish capitalism and to create global practices and institutions of egalitarian cooperation" (Dean, 2012, p. 6). My notion of democracy as communism pushes all political actions for and of the people into solidarity with the actually existing transnational workers' struggle in order to create a fundamental antagonism against the ruling class that can be met with strate-gies and tactics of class struggle. But it is not only a matter of participation by and of the people that is lacking in bringing about a communist alternative to capitalism, but the fostering of a vision of what a world absent of value production might and could look like. I believe that such a vision can initially be seeded within the discourse of socialist democracy as the first stage of har-vesting a communist future.

Critical Pedagogy

Critical pedagogy locates the production of critical knowledges leading to praxis in its social, spatial and geopolitical contexts, and reveals the work-ings of the production process and how it operates intertextually alongside and upon other discourses, but it does so with a particular political project in mind—an anti-capitalist, anti-imperialist, anti-racist, anti-sexist and pro-democratic and emancipatory struggle. It works against what Anibal

Quijano and Michael Ennis (2000) call the "coloniality of power." Here a critical pedagogy serves to make the familiar strange and the strange familiar (i.e., refiguring how we see the relationship between the self and the social so that we can see both as manufactured, as the social construction of multiple dimensions and, at times, as the observers of each other, and the suppressed underside of each other); in addition, it attempts to bring out the pedagogical dimensions of the political and the political dimensions of the pedagogical and to convert these activities to a larger, more sustained and focused project of building alternative and oppositional forms of sustainable environments, of learning environments, of revolutionary political environments.

The *differentia specifica* of critical pedagogy is located within a wider optic than classroom teaching, or popular education that takes place in community settings. It is defined as the working out of a systematic dialectic of pedagogy that is organized around a philosophy of praxis. Here, the dialectic involves a process of mutual understanding and recognition, a movement between an outlook on reality and a method of analysis. In the words of Anna Stetsenko, the dialectic involves "an emphasis on and attention to the constant movement and dynamism, change and transition, fluidity and historicity, totality and interdependence" (2008).

This praxis begins with an immanent critique of conventional pedagogies in order to see if their assumptions and claims are adequate to the type of praxis needed both to understand and challenge and eventually overcome capitalism's expansionistic dynamic. So we need both a philosophy of praxis that is coherent and forms of organization—horizontal and democratic and sometimes possibly vertical—that best reflect our praxis.

Now it is a praxis of being and becoming, of mental and manual labor, of thinking and doing, of reading and writing the word and the world (in the Freirean sense); in short, it is a practice of the self, a form of self-fashioning but not simply in the Foucauldian sense or in the Nietzschean "will to power" sense.

Theory and practice are contradictions in a unity where they interpenetrate, define and presuppose each other while co-evolving in the process of development (Stetsenko, 2008). Theory and practice do not exist separately from each other. Theory and practice are intrinsically linked in a dialectical unity (Stetsenko, 2008). With respect to critical pedagogy, we can thus pose the questions: What are the theories that guide the production of critical knowledge? What are the actions that need to be undertaken to help inform our theories of knowledge in the production of social transformation? How can the development of critical consciousness inform a theory of knowledge, or a theory of social transformation? How can a theory of knowledge production aid in the development of critical consciousness that leads to acts of social transformation?

As Anna Stetsenko (2009) notes, in the classical worldview, knowledge is defined as the inner depiction of an outer mind-independent reality and phenomena, but this has little to do with practical actions in and on the world. The focus, then, in a revolutionary critical pedagogy is to bring together knowing and doing, words and deeds. In this way, the production and product of critical knowledge cannot ever be thought of as separate realms.

A revolutionary critical pedagogy, then, is both a reading practice where we read the word in the context of the world, and a practical activity where we write ourselves as subjective forces into the text of history—but this does not mean that making history is only an effect of discourse, a form of metonomy, the performative dimension of language, a rhetorical operation, a tropological system. No, reality is more than textual self-difference. Praxis is directed at engaging the word and the world dialectically as an effect of class contradictions. A critical pedagogy is a way of challenging the popular imaginary (which has no "outside" to the text) that normalizes the core cultural foundations of capitalism and the normative force of the state. In other words, the ruling capitalist ideology tells us in numerous ways that there is no alternative to capitalist social relations.

Critical pedagogy is a reading and an acting upon the social totality by turning abstract "things" into a material force for liberation, by helping abstract thought lead to praxis, to revolutionary praxis, to the bringing about of a social universe that is not based on the value form of labor and financial gain but based on human need.

Yes, ideas and reason have an important role to play in any meaningful account of life. We need to understand our place in the rational unfolding of the world, but more important, we need to play an active—and indeed, protagonistic—role in the unfolding of history. As critical educators, we can't move history through ideas alone, we need to transcend the capitalist law of value and the social relations that constrain us. We transcend the alienation of this world by transforming the material world. Critical pedagogy is illuminated by an insight made foundational in the work of Paulo Freire: that politics and pedagogy are not an exclusive function of having the right knowledge via some kind of "ah-ha" awakening of the revolutionary soul. Critical consciousness is not the root of commitment to revolutionary struggle but rather the product of such a commitment. An individual does not have to be critically self-conscious and well-versed in the theories of the Frankfurt School or the writings of liberation theologians in order to feel the obligation to help the poor and the dispossessed. In fact, it is in the very act of struggling alongside the oppressed that individuals become critically conscious and aware and motivated to help others. Praxis begins with practice. This is the bedrock of revolutionary critical pedagogy's politics of solidarity and commitment.

While radical scholarship and theoretical ideas are important—extremely important—people do not become politically aware and then take part in radical activity. Rather, participating in contentious acts of revolutionary struggle creates new protagonistic political identities that become refined through theoretical engagement. Critically informed political identities do not motivate revolutionary action but rather develop as a logical consequence of such action. And the action summoned by revolutionary critical educators is always heterogeneous, multifaceted, protagonistic, democratic and participatory—yet always focalized—anti-capitalist struggle.

For some, making a commitment to help humanity liberate itself from its capitalist chains provokes an almost obsessive desire to understand everything that that commitment entails. For instance, a commitment to the oppressed is frequently postponed because of a fear that such a commitment might turn out to be all encompassing. This can be accompanied by an almost obsessive desire to know the full implications of serving the oppressed (i.e., how much time will it require; to what extent could it interfere with my other commitments; what kind of sacrifices will it require?). But as Luigi Giussani (1995) presciently remarks, "Making a commitment only after understanding it completely would mean never making a commitment" (p. 72). And it is through exercising our commitment (which is always undertaken in the realm of spirit) that critical consciousness begins to develop through action and doing, that is, through praxis.

The preceding pages have been occupied with various reflections on dialectics and praxis, so it would seem prudent at this time to summarize what we mean by praxis in the context of education, specifically transformative praxis. Imagine it as learning from our actions and acting from our learning. Theory and practice, knowing and doing, they are mutually constituting, and which comes first depends on historical and situational contexts. But it is invariably an intervention. As I have written previously:

> Teaching critically is always a leap across a dialectical divide that is necessary for any act of knowing to occur. Knowing is a type of dance, a movement, but a self-conscious one. Criticality is not a line stretching into eternity, but rather it is a circle. In other

words, knowing can be the object of our knowing, it can be self-reflective, and it is something in which we can make an intervention. In which we *must* make an intervention. (McLaren, 2008, p. 476)

This brings us then to the distinction between *abstract utopian praxis* and *concrete utopian praxis*. Abstract utopian praxis remains at the metaphysical level, locked into the beatific hinterlands of the imagination, disconnected from the asymmetrical relations of race, the power-sensitive relations of privilege, and dependent hierarchies of class that plague everyday life in capitalist societies. By contrast, a concrete utopianism (see the writings of Ruth Levitas [1990] on the important theories of Ernst Bloch as well as Bloch's magisterial three volumes, *The Principle of Hope* [1986] that offers a redemptive and revelatory synthesis of apocalypse and Marx that is at once sublime and heretical) is grounded in the creative potential of human beings living in the messy web of capitalist social relations—in the here and now—to overcome and transform their conditions of unfreedom. Here we are in agreement with what Santos (2009) means when he talks about *acto in proximis* and *acto in distans*. Knowledge production as a liberatory act must include an *acto in proximis*, meaning that the epistemology in question must have a practical effect in the world. This echoes Walter Benjamin's argument that if we merely contemplate the world we will only arrive at a knowledge of evil (see McNally, 2001). Knowledge of the good is knowledge of a practice designed to change reality; it derives from action, from contemplation. We judge the truth of our actions in their effects on the lives of the oppressed.

But an epistemology of everyday praxis is not enough, because such acts or forms of praxis need a larger rudder, something to give the emancipatory act not only ballast but also direction. That is, it must also be implicated in an *acto in distans*, or the utopian aspect of knowledge production, which, in our case, is part of our struggle to diminish exploitation and suffering and promote justice. An *acto in proximis* is very much like a form of concrete emancipatory praxis, whereas the *acto in distans* is the larger movement within which these forms of praxis move in their perilous journey towards a long-standing utopia built upon the principles of equality and participatory democracy. It is precisely the double valence, or mixture of the two acts, that prevents the utopia from becoming abstract and metaphysical and prevents everyday acts of emancipatory praxis from becoming free floating and directionless, detached from the larger project of global emancipation. It directs the praxis towards a concrete utopia, grounded in everyday struggle.

The repressed part of critical pedagogy returns, but it returns from the future. And, it is this delay, this deferral of action that allows us the space for dialogue, a dialogue that can serve as the conditions of possibility for a new beginning. Revolutionary critical pedagogy is a trauma that can be acted out hysterically or with a sufficient distance. We can create a liminal classroom where all identities are levelled and we confront each other in an existential void as equals, or we can create the necessary distance for critical self-reflexivity, or we can engage in a dialectical dance involving both. Of course, there are those critics who say that we cannot have critical distance today since the society of the spectacle necessarily subsumes criticality under distraction, given the nature of the new technologies and the media, where separations are concealed by an imaginary unity (Foster, 1996).

A critical pedagogy is about the hard work of building community alliances, of challenging school policy, of providing teachers with alternative and oppositional teaching materials. It has little to do with awakening the "revolutionary soul" of students—this is merely a re-fetishization of the individual and the singular under the banner of the collective and serves only to bolster the untruth fostered by capitalist social relations and postpone the answer to the question: Is revolution possible today? It falls into the same kind of condition that critical pedagogy had been originally formulated to combat. It diverts us from the following challenge: Can we organize our social, cultural and economic life differently so as to transcend the exploitation that capital affords us?

It is difficult for many to love others in this age of madness, in these dark times of capitalist horror. How can we love someone whom the times and circumstances have driven mad, especially when we have become mad ourselves? John Berger (2001, p. 176) has described such contemporary madness as being confronted with "the inadequacy of all given explanations to explain the everyday pain being suffered." He further describes it as being haunted by a phantom and confronting "the terrible space existing between spoken words and what they are meant to mean" (2001, p. 176). It is this suffocating existential vacuum that is the pain, "where madness rushes in and fills the space and there is no longer any distinction between state and world" (2001, p. 176). This all-absorbing vortex of interiority, this empty space of desolation exists "between the experience of living a normal life at this moment on the planet and the public narratives being offered to give a sense to that life, the empty space" (2001, p. 176).

Berger writes that this opens us up to listen to racist demagogues, such as France's Le Pen, because the evil story that he tells "seems closer to what is happening in the streets" (2001, p. 176). I would add that this is one of the reasons that oppressed people often listen to Limbaugh, to Hannity, to O'Reilly, to Ingraham, to Malkin. We are desperately trying to collapse the vacuum of our lives, to close the gap. Any fatuous, pompous, blustering gasbag will suffice. Berger takes us even further:

> this is also why people dream of 'virtual reality'. Anything—from demagogy to manufactured onanistic dreams—anything, anything, to close the gap! In such gaps people get lost, and in such gaps people go mad. (2001, p. 176)

Simone Weil wrote: "Love for our neighbor, being made of creative attention, is analogous to genius" (cited in Berger, 2001, p. 175). She went on to offer the following reflection:

> The love of our neighbor in all its fullness simply means being able to say to him: 'What are you going through?' It is a recognition that the sufferer exists, not only as a unit in a collection, or a specimen from the social category labeled 'unfortunate', but as a man, exactly like we are, who was one day stamped with a special mark of affliction. For this reason it is enough, but it is indispensable to know how to look at him in a certain way. (cited in Berger, 2001, p. 175)

Do we today possess the genius of which Weil speaks? Are we able to pull ourselves and others out of the gap of contemporary madness? Can we return the characters we are playing to the actors playing them? And can we assist the actors in distinguishing the everyday roles they are forced to play from their spiritual essence and their ontological vocation as agents of social justice? Can we prepare a space for Oneness, for the essence of the divine to flow through our veins as sap flows through ripe Canadian maple trees or Chinese elms? Can we once again live in the world of exteriority, affirming our history, values, practices and spaces of liberty, without them being rooted in narcissistic, pretentious and totalizing systems of intelligibility that would legislate uncritically for us all manner of thought and activity?

We have taken the position over the years that transcendence must always remain within the immanence of human possibilities. But first you need to have some idea of where you want to go. If you don't know where you want to go, it is pretty clear that no path will take you there (Lebowitz, 2010). What we need in critical pedagogy are strategic and tactical approaches in creating a world free from value production and a vision of the future that is gleaned from understanding how we are made by society and the educational system to be unfree, chained inside the prison house of capitalist social relations. This is the direction that we, as critical agents, wish to travel.

Marx's vision of a society was one that would permit the full development of human beings as a result of the protagonistic activity of human beings in revolutionary praxis—the simultaneous changing of circumstances and human activity or self-change. This key link in Marx's lapidary articulation was the concept of human development and practice. In other words, as Marx makes clear, there are always two products as the result of our activity, the change in circumstances and the change in people themselves. Socialist human beings produce themselves only through their own activity (Lebowitz, 2010).

So the question that I am obligated to ask at this early juncture in this book becomes: How do we transcend the conflicts today that lead to over-identi-fication and dis-identification with class struggle? Marxist humanists believe that transcendence means not only abolishing the dehumanizing conditions of human life under capitalism but also going beyond the given to create the conditions of possibility for individuals to shape their own destiny, read anew the past, de-mythify and generate meaning from the multiple contexts people inhabit. It is a process, one in which we have in mind the betterment of our social condition. Of course, it is impossible to create a classroom free of the totality of social relations that make up the social universe of capital such that students or teachers can take charge of the rudder of history. Pedagogical struggle will always be contingent, and provisional, and relational as well as disciplined and most certainly at times mutinous.

We struggle to negate social structures and social relations that negate us as human beings. This includes aspects of classroom life: of authoritarianism but not authority; of apathy and a heightened sense of individualism; of fear of speaking about difficult topics; of a resistance to move outside disciplinary boundaries and of questioning the interrelationship of ideas and practices. If we could depict our own unity, what would we create? But such a vision and struggle will not be absolute, a once-and-for-all moment—or even a series of moments. It is a protracted struggle waged every day in the schools, the facto-ries, the boardrooms and the churches and community centers.

The self-transcending formation of the meanings and values that illumi-nate our lives isn't restricted to the realm of ideas. It is an exigency and a demand. Our future has to be fought for through our projects, in the various realms of class struggle itself, in the productive dimension of history, within history's process of humanization as we become more and more conscious of ourselves as social beings—that is, within all dimensions of human creativity.

The ideas of critical pedagogy—as well as its practices—are never inde-pendent of the social conditions of the actions and processes that produced them. The concept of a revolutionary critical pedagogy implies some form of relation between knowledge of a domain formally constituted as "the social setting" in which learning takes place (such as classrooms) and another domain formally constituted as "the pedagogical" or where "teaching" occurs in the most general sense (and this includes venues other than classrooms).

Revolutionary critical pedagogy analyzes pedagogical practices with protocols that are specific to the humanities and social sciences in general and Marxist and critical theory in particular, including contributions from liberation theologians. Depending on the level of detail at which analysis takes place, the object of critical pedagogy may take the gross form of a totality (capitalist society in general), or it may exist in nuanced forms: specific classroom practices or sites of knowledge production such as the media, community centers, conferences, church basements, coffee houses, etc., or some subset of pedagogy as such (i.e., definitions or generalizations about teaching and learning found in encyclopedias, education journals or handbooks of education).

But critical educators recognize that pedagogical acts of knowing and engagement can neither be given in advance nor arbitrarily constructed by an analytic choice, but are, rather, necessarily implicated in and derived from particular interpretations that are grounded in our social life, that is, in our everyday experiences. They have an experiential existence, a social existence, before they have an analytic existence. Experiences are never transparent, and they require critical languages that can interpret them and actions that can transform them. Otherwise, we are all guided by our quick-tempered opinions, our raw emotions, our unconditioned reflexes. And where is the morality in this?

Indeed, critical pedagogy seeks to challenge the core cultural foundations of capitalism that normalize the idea that there exists no alternative to capitalist social relations, no way of challenging the status quo, and no way of defeating inequality, injustice and suffering among human and non-human animals that populate this vast planet of ours. Revolutionary critical educators question capitalist concepts—such as wage labor and value production—alongside their students in order to consider alternative ways of subsisting and learning in the world so as to continually transform it along the arc of social and economic justice. They seek new democratic visions of organizing our schools and our communities through a conscious praxis that self-reflexively examines the historical context of our ideas, social relations, institutions and human relationships while opening space for the possibilities of the popular imaginary. As such, critical pedagogy calls for a movement that is anti-capitalist, anti-imperialist, anti-racist, anti-sexist, anti-heterosexist and pro-democratic.

This movement I see myself as heralding—to challenge capitalism at its roots while at the same time using the figure of Jesus as a spiritual guidepost and groundswell of faith—requires that we question normative ways of thinking about the world that corporate advertising and consumer-based culture continuously push upon us both blatantly and deviously. We must look beyond Western, Euro/U.S.-centric ways of knowing the world that are based in capitalist wastefulness and a lack of regard for the planet, in order to consider alternative and oppositional ways of thinking about and acting towards/against the imperialism of free-market, neoliberal, global capitalism.

Rather than fall into the epistemologies of empire that designate certain knowledges as normative and non-dominant knowledges as "other," revolutionary critical pedagogy must find creative purpose and protagonistic agency in embracing all epistemologies by acknowledging how peoples everywhere engage in a reciprocal relationship with the world from their own sociohistorical contexts. It is through such a process of denying epistemologies of empire and recognizing the entirety of diverse human lifeways and thought that a new social order can be envisioned.

Indeed, this new social order should not be limited to Western/European responses to liberalism and capitalism alone, but rather should include the views of those who continue to suffer under the expansion of Western civilization while recognizing that their perspectives in response to colonization may not fully overlap with communist/Marxist responses to capitalism.

Developing another artisanship of pedagogical practices also means interrogating Eurocentered epistemologies as well as producing decolonizing and decolonial knowledges through understanding our subjectivities as historical and biographical loci of enunciation. In other words, we need to engage in a geopolitics of knowing that will produce a geopolitics of knowledge that follows from a process of political and epistemic delinking from what is destructive about the grand Western episteme and cosmology.

Communication is born out of the experience of opposites, out of antagonisms structured in relation to the central conflict between capital and labor. There is a "withness" to knowing precisely because the experience of consciousness is always meaningful within the presence of another. In other words, consciousness emerges out of conflict between the ego experienced as a subject versus the ego experienced as an object; between the ego experienced as worthy of respect and praise and the ego experienced as bad, degenerate and less than human; between the ego experienced as an active agent of history and experienced as a passive victim of oppression, betrayal, domination or exploitation. We strive to become active beings who can affect the world around us, but capital has, instead, embalmed us (through processes such as alienation and reification) so that we experience ourselves as constantly empty, as never being able to heal the jagged tear inside of our hemorrhaging self, never being able to stem the loss of our own agency as citizens from capitalism's saber slash across the cheekbone of history. We are placeless subjects having not been satiated by the determinations of bourgeois life. Critical pedagogy makes this conflict an object of knowledge.

It is the power of critical reflection that separates the knowing subject from the object of knowledge so that the anguish and misery of everyday life can be examined; but critical pedagogy also enables the knowing subject to experience being the object of knowledge, as the "other" then becomes the knowing subject. Thus critical pedagogy enables the knowing subject and the known subject to co-exist within the hydra-headed Medusan horror of capitalist exploitation. Critical pedagogy therefore functions as Athena's mirror shield that enabled Perseus to view Medusa through a reflection rather than directly; it protects the knowing subject through an acto in distans from being consumed by the alienation of capitalism and the coloniality of being by means of a dialogical approach to reading the word and the world.

Our identity is over time given continuity and coherence when we engage others not simply linguistically, as a set of linguistic relations, but as body-selves. The process of individuation—*Auseinandersetzung*—has as its most characteristic feature the encounter of oppositions (which in the capitalist world are really often distinctions within structural hierarchies that are metaphysically classified by the mind as oppositions) often experienced as antagonisms. This engagement—this dyadic relationship between self and other—gives form and substance to our sense of self. We don't just "language forth" our social universe, we "body forth" our social universe. Human consciousness is not the mere "reflection" of material processes and relations—as this would be a pre-dialectical stance—rather, consciousness and language are modes of our embodied being with others. Physical objects have culturo-technological meaning because they are embedded, as McNally (2001) notes, in networks of human meanings. Commodities have meaning according to the social relations and contexts that situate the individuals who interact with them. Every context is intercontextual, referring to other contexts of meaning. They interact, creating what is called a linguistic sphere. The body is integral to history and language. Consciousness, language and culture are all vital aspects of our bodies.

We are "seeing bodies"—bodies that are the experiential sites of spatiality and temporality rather than the transcendental category of mind (McNally, 2001, p. 124). Rather than teachers viewing students as disembodied minds, apart from teachers and other students and the outside world, we can only overcome the fragmentary character of our experience of our fermenting subjectivity and the world through our interactions with others. We need to instate the corporeal individual into our educational theorizing in and through the dyadic relationship between teacher and student, between the word and the world.

The dominant culture tries to drive socialist arguments underground but even in the homogenizing experiences of official culture, signs can never be rendered uniaccentual, we all struggle to accent signs differently. If the dia-lectic is about self-mediation, then theory and practice are already unified in the immanence of their self-unfolding (McNally, 2001). But many of the new avant-garde cadre of art house poststructuralists who wield with such aplomb the project of deconstruction disavow the dialectic. They foist on all of us the sceptical notion that a knowledge of truth is impossible, not admitting that they are contradicting themselves. As Miranda notes,

> The fundamental problem is that anyone who maintains that the human mind can-not know reality is by the same act affirming that his own mind knows that reality called the human mind, and knows it so well that he can say what it is capable of and what it isn't; he claims that his own mind knows the way things are and, therefore, tells us; hence he is contradicting himself. (2007, p. 77)

McNally makes the case that poststructuralist linguistics erases the laboring body, reproducing capital's myth of self-birth, the notion that capital can create itself without the mediation of labor (2001, p. 230). Poststructuralists often suggest that language can create itself outside of bodies and material practices.

A Pedagogy of Critique Against a Pedagogy of Desire

Clearly, critical pedagogy as it stands is no panacea for change. Before we recreate it, we need a vision of what it could be. I describe such a refurbishing as follows:

> Critical pedagogy needs to be renewed. It can no longer remain as a bundle of classroom methodologies removed from a larger politics of socialist struggle nor a

compendium of gnomic maxims that have a roborant effect on hardscrabble youth, such as "become an active agent of history rather than its casualty." It needs to be rhetorical, but not merely rhetorical. This time around it has to be concerned with the problem of reasserting human action, what we call praxis. The depredations of the postmodern pedagogues often subordinated praxis to the realm of ideas, theory, and the regime of the episteme. But critical pedagogy needs not only to disambiguate the otiose claims of the postmodernists and reject their cult of fashionable apostasy but begin with public political action, what has been called "public pedagogy." (McLaren, 2008, pp. 475–476)

The vision of what critical pedagogy could be, while certainly indebted to advances in postmodernism, in my view needs to embrace a Marxist problematic.

A critique of the scourge of poverty and oppression inflicted on masses of people throughout Latin America and other parts of the world and the dead and starving in our own streets must be the focal point of any revolutionary critical pedagogy. As Sobrino (1993, p. 32) warns: "The current European debate about modernity and post-modernity becomes at this point absolutely unintelligible and scandalous: we can opt out of many things, but we cannot opt out of the deaths of the poor."

In my opinion, the radical aesthetics of postmodern theorists represent what could be called a pedagogy of desire which fails to address the basic material needs of humanity. To this I wish to counterpose a Marxist pedagogy of critique grounded in historical materialist analysis. I believe such a model need not remain trapped in the negative dialectics of Adorno or (the later) Marcuse, trapped between the sublime and the despotic, with no way out. The vision that I embrace enables students' forward movement out of the never-ending oscillation of these two poles.

My work here is based very much on some of the work developed by Teresa Ebert and Mas'ud Zavarzadeh (2008). Paraphrasing Ebert and Zavarzadeh, the pedagogy of desire is about the thrill of corporeal pleasure; it mirrors the conditions of alienated capitalism, because, in reality, the pedagogy of desire is about teaching adjustment to existing social relations. It is about the transference of a teacher's desire to smash the norms of everyday life, about the emotional thrill of going against the grain of the social order, and not about a commitment to build a more just society. A pedagogy of desire is isolated from the social contradictions and historical contradictions that determine their relations.

Within a pedagogy of desire, arguments, modes of inquiry and concepts are irrelevant. What matters most is how the teachers and students feel— not what they think or do, but how they feel. A pedagogy of desire considers itself a "post" class pedagogy based on lifestyle, and irony, in which the rul-ing class avoids confronting the reality of others whose misery is the condi-tion of their prosperity. A pedagogy of desire does not emancipate students from economic oppression but is designed to free teachers and students from emotional distress. The purpose of pedagogies of desire is not understanding, but seduction and emotional investment in teaching as an affirmation of power.

Further paraphrasing from Ebert and Zavarzadeh (2008), pedagogies of desire are those developed by teachers whose fundamental needs have already been met. It is the pedagogy of an isolated, alienated, bourgeois subject. It is a pedagogy of free expression. It enforces anti-intellectual and trans-social individualism.

A pedagogy of desire sees oppression as a question of identity—the expe-rience of being black, gay, Latino, white—but oppression cannot be explained by experience. We need an analysis of experience, of experience effects, an analysis that, in other words, goes beyond experience. You only learn from experiences that you learn from, as Myles Horton once put it, and this requires a language to interpret experience, a language of dialectics that can help us unpack the material conditions of experiences. A pedagogy of desire takes the position that one can only learn what one already knows. This needs to be contrasted with a pedagogy of critique.

A pedagogy of critique is aimed at freedom from necessity. Teresa Ebert (2009) writes that a pedagogy of critique is a materialist critique whose purpose is not simply to perform an immanent examination of the cognitive validity of categories and forms of knowledge (by locating contradictions in the rules and systems necessary to the production of those forms) but to relate these categories to the outside, material conditions of their possibility. The role of materialist critique is to begin with an immanent investigation of a system or a practice on its own terms but to relate these inside terms to their outside historical and social conditions. Materialism consists of the objective, produc-tive activities of humans that involve them in social relations under definite historical conditions that are independent of their will and are shaped by struggle between contesting classes over the surplus produced by social labor. The more important question is not one of norm, truth or totalization—part of all discourses and practices—but how they further or resist the interest of a particular class. On which side of history do you struggle? Marx maintains that the question of whether objective truth can be attributed to human thinking is not a question of theory but a practical question—hence, we must prove the truth of our own thinking in practice, that is, in our revolutionary praxis as critical educators.

Further paraphrasing Ebert (2009), a pedagogy of critique is a mode of social knowing that inquires into what is not said, into the silences and the suppressed or the missing, in order to un-conceal operations of economic and political power underlying the concrete details and representations of our lives. It reveals how the abstract logic of the exploitation of the division of labor informs all the practices of culture and society. Materialist critique disrupts that which represents itself as natural, and thus as inevitable, and explains how it is materially produced. Critique, in other words, enables us to explain how social differences—gender, race, sexuality and class—have been systematically produced and continue to operate within regimes of exploitation (namely, within the international division of labor in global capitalism), so that we can fight to change them.

Thus, a pedagogy of critique is about the production of transformative knowledges. It is not about liberty as the freedom of desire, because this liberty, this freedom of desire, is acquired at the expense of the poverty of others.

A pedagogy of critique, as Teresa Ebert (2009) points out, does not situate itself in the space of the self, or in the space of desire, or in the space of liberation, but in the site of collectivity, need and emancipation. A pedagogy of critique is grounded not in desire, but in revolutionary love, that is, recognizing that love can only exist between free and equal people who have the same ideals and commitment to serving the poor and the oppressed and it is this moral affinity that constitutes the conditions of the possibility of love. In all sites of everyday life under capitalist social relations we have institutional power relations which are not free spaces that foster equality—quite the contrary. Revolutionary love can only thrive in the struggle for transforming these social relations. As Monzó and McLaren (2014) write:

> Under capitalism, love has become a term that people are almost afraid or embarrassed to utter. It is seen as a weakness, something that as human beings we cannot control, something that allows us to become vulnerable to the injustices of those who are presumed to love us. Its ultimate proclamation is an economic contract that secures each individual's interests (in capital terms) in the event of divorce. Under capitalism, everything is a commodity to be had, owned and controlled. Within the family, women and children are often seen as property and treated as subordinates. The family is, thus, a microcosm of the larger society's social relations of production and an important context for understanding relations of domination and subordination, the values necessary for maintaining capitalist production, such as individualism, a strong work ethic, meritocracy, and the belief in competition and ownership.

In the working class family, women, through childbirth and rearing, produce what Karl Marx termed the special commodity—labor power or the capacity to labor which determines value. Thus, women, their bodies and the ways they relate to the world, must be controlled through a patriarchal structure that becomes complicit with the interests of capital. A family structure that creates the conditions of possibility for true love—a love between an intimate couple and their children or other family members that is based upon mutual respect, equality, creative labor and social responsibility for each other within the family, sows a seed for a love that seeks to know the Other, that cannot conceive of violating an Other, that recognizes their own development as a function of the Other and that validates the others' differences. This type of love cannot be found within capitalism. Rather it can only spawn from a socialist alternative, a society free of capitalist social relations such that notions of equality, freedom, and love are the foundation of how family members interact. Within this socialist family, racism and other forms of domination and exploitation have no place, cannot be bred.

Critical pedagogy has a role to play both locally, regionally, nationally and transnationally. I have previously described this path as follows:

> The struggle for a critical pedagogy is perhaps best animated by the poetry of Antonio Machado (1962): *Caminante no hay camino, se hace el camino al andar* [*Traveler, there is no road. The road is made as one walks*]. There is no predetermined path, but we can look to the past, the future and to the present to see possible directions that our struggle can take. We don't struggle in some absolute elsewhere, lamenting having missed our rendezvous with truth. Our struggle is warm-blooded and it will end where its gestation began: in the fertile soil of class struggle. We know where we are going, because it is the only destination where we can divest our human condition of its many disguises and even then, we need to realize that we can only contest the ideological production of the capitalist class and not abolish it unless the social relations of production generating it cease to exist.

> The path to socialism, while continually created anew, is not a solitary one. Others before us have kicked up a lot of dust along the trail. Some of that dust is mixed with blood, and we need to tread carefully, yet not lose the determination in our step. And while workers may drop to the ground like spent cartridges in their conditioned effort to overthrow the regime of capital, their struggles exit the chambers of necessity with such an explosive force that history lurches out of its slumber in abstract, monumental time into the liminal present where the past is no longer and the future is not yet. Such a journey demands a critical pedagogy for the twenty-first century. (McLaren, 2008, p. 475)

A critical pedagogy for the twenty-first century demands that we address the reality of the spiritual dimension of our struggle to build a better world for ourselves and for generations to follow. Our spiritual selves have often been neglected in critical pedagogy and, as the saying goes, "to deny one facet of what is human is to contradict the totality of what is" (cited in Giussani, 1995, p. 76).

Italian mystic Maria Gemma Umberta Pia Galgani, known since 1940 as Saint Gemma Galgani, the "Daughter of Passion" and the "Gem of Christ," who bore in her flesh the wounds of Christ, is the patron saint of various and sundry collections of peoples but especially perhaps of students (see the cover of this book). She received the stigmata on June 8, 1899, during the Vigil of the Solemnity of the Sacred Heart of Jesus and shared the mighty suffering of His passion. She was effusively and fervently devoted to assisting those who were insensible to the presence of the divine. Her detractors thought her to be insane. While in no way saints (after all, they have committed the sin of critical thinking for social transformation!), revolutionary critical educators likewise are targeted in fierce attacks from the proprietors of the educational establishment in their attempts to weave together the threads of the spiritual and the material in the fabric of active, liberating knowledge, knowledge designed to break the chains of oppression.

The subtle alchemy of critical pedagogy rarely admits—let alone seeks—the irreplaceable divine assistance attributed to saints and mystics, and while I modestly attempt to redirect the current of critical pedagogy into the waters of religious salvation, I do so not out of a wish to convert readers to mystical Catholicism but to acknowledge the hunger that people of all faiths (as well as agnostics and atheists) have for a spiritual connection to that which speaks to us outside of ourselves, to that which is larger than ourselves yet encompasses and accompanies us along a path of personal and social transformation that would eliminate needless suffering.

I am well aware that forces of moral turpitude sanctioned by the highest powers in the land regularly conscript biblical references into the service of destruction. And that the mainstream media serve as instruments to sell the vileness and wrongdoing of their corporate masters and the political administrations that are beholden to the corporations. McLaren and Jaramillo (2008) highlight the masterful way that the Bush Jr. administration used biblical references to frame and to sanctify their criminal invasion of Iraq:

> Not only has Bush acted like an emperor who has received the laurel wreath (when he should be wearing a wreath of myrtle, signaling in ancient Roman times a hollow victory over an unlawful enemy or one that constituted an inferior force), he has also skillfully used the corporate media to present his foreign policy measures in light of Biblical history. When, on the freshly mopped deck of the carrier, USS Abraham

Lincoln, the U.S. warrior president emerged in a snug fitting flight suit from an S-3B Viking aircraft, helmet under his arm (a brazen move considering his military records reveal that he stopped flying during his final 18 months of National Guard duty in 1972 and 1973 and was not observed by his commanders at his Texas unit for a year), his swagger and grin were greeted by wild cheers from throngs of assembled officers and sailors. Appearing topside before a bold banner that announced "Mission Accomplished" he declared the "battle of Iraq" a "victory" in the ongoing "war on terror." This event was carefully choreographed by Bush's team of seasoned image-makers that included a former ABC producer, a former Fox News producer and a former NBC cameraman paid for out of an annual budget of 3.7 million that Bush allots for his media co-ordinators. We do not believe that it's coincidental that a comparison clearly can be drawn between this example of rightwing showmanship and Leni Riefenstahl's infamous propaganda film about the 1934 Nazi Parteitag in Nuremberg, *Triumph des Willens* (Triumph of the Will) that displayed Adolf Hitler as the world savior. In the German version, Hitler emerges from a Junker 52 aircraft that had been filmed landing at Nuremberg airport to the lofty strains of Wagner. Thousands of Nazi onlookers chant, Sieg heil! as the musical score builds to a crescendo. And while the scene was carefully crafted to suggest that Hitler was a modern manifestation of the ancient Aryan deity Odin (see *The Internationalist*, May 2003), the event on the USS Abraham Lincoln was pitching George Bush as a major player in the decidedly Christian drama known as the Second Coming. Bush's speech on the carrier paraphrased Chapter 61 of Isaiah, the very book that Jesus used when proclaiming that Isaiah's prophecies of the Messiah had come true, suggesting perhaps that Bush believes the Second Coming has begun (Pitt 2003) and that his war on terror is playing an important role in this Biblical prophecy.

Only communities of trust, solidarity and cooperation striving for moral rectitude can combat such injustice. And universities have the potential to provide such communities.

But what is missing in most classrooms in public schools, in university seminar rooms and perhaps especially in universities, is the establishment of true communities. Of course, those of us who are part of the academy always talk about creating "communities of learners" and the like, and all too frequently it turns out that these communities end up as little more than groups organized in particular ways, perhaps around a certain subject matter or interest in a particular topic or theme.

Sometimes a faculty will advertise itself as a "family," and while that is often done out of affection or loyalty, such a union remains too superficial to constitute a real community. In the past, I have been part of such aerosolized and deodorized communities and found them to be little more than associations of some kind or another, gatherings of frustrated faculty members prone to gossip, dominated by careerists, and who will remain colleagues in name only until you face some hardship or trouble of some sort and then these fair-weather colleagues will have no hesitation in throwing you under the bus if it will advantage them in some way. Fortunately, I have managed recently to find a home in the academy in which real communities do exist, but I believe these communities are not the norm in academia.

But the question still remains: What is a true community? Here we can turn to the sage reflections of Luigi Giussani (1995, p. 74), who describes a community as "a deep union born from a life shared together, which arises from the recognition of a common structure." Giussani (1995, p. 74) is worried here about teachers who "lack the energy to wage war against a pervasive negativity, choosing traditional, formalistic positions instead of renewing the eternal redeeming Word in the fact of the new struggle." Students seeking a total (as opposed to a partial) meaning of reality should not, in other words, be left alone in a world of abstractions while attempting to develop critical reflectivity, but should know and appreciate what it means to partake of community, since the communal dimension of learning enables intersubjective dialogue along with participating in "a way of conceiving life, a way of facing the problem of being, a way of studying history, and a way of living love" (Giussani, 1995, p. 75). In order for communities to exist in our capitalist society, it is necessary to move beyond the hyper-individualism, narcissism, extreme competitiveness and technocratic rationality that capitalism promotes and upon which it feeds.

What Giussani (1995, pp. 77–78) describes as Christian consciousness could easily apply to critical consciousness when he laments that consciousness requires that certain fundamental needs be met. He notes that students lack commitment when

> the method of calling lacks the capacity to "touch" the essential structures of consciousness with "motives" that, as the word says, are capable of "moving." Or maybe the mode of calling does not correspond to the "dimensions" of the spirit, to those structural needs which, once touched, could mobilize all of a person's energy.

Critical pedagogy manages to gather unto itself—sometimes through the theft of memory or its purposeful demise—what doesn't officially exist. And that includes writings by Marxists such as Walter Benjamin, Karil Kosik, Margaret Randall, E. San Juan and others. Here approaches to education open up to the immediacy and fullness of what Benjamin called messianic time, a shattering of the homogeneous empty time of capitalist schooling and making manifest through profane illumination the realm of possibility that does not fall along the linear continuum of history. Such a messianic time enables us to pull the brake-stop to this history and actively inaugurate a new beginning that is radically exterior to the history of progress.

This radical exterior is the already manifest but not-yet fully revealed—what I call in this book The Kingdom of God, a kingdom towards which we are called to make our home. This is not an exodus from the messy world of excremental culture to the good old days of German romanticism but away from such superannuated ideas to the very life force of Marx's work. Here, we can only lament the demise of Benjamin and wonder: Is he gazing from his cloth-lined coffin across the shimmering bay into the Mediterranean or is he pointed towards the stone wall of his cemetery niche in the graveyard of Port Brou, nestled in the wings of his Angel of History where he is busy unionizing the dead?

It should be clear from reading the introduction thus far that this book is not your typical critical pedagogy volume. I care little that some escapist theologians may abominate it as scholarly knavery or outlawry because of its association with Christian communism since their understanding of what Marx wrote about communism is more flimsy and insubstantial than many critics who profess to be Marxists. The reprobation by some Christian evangelicals—especially prosperity preachers—that I have misinterpreted biblical scriptures must be read against the coherent and unequivocal biblical reprobation of differentiating wealth and the condemnation by Jesus of wealth acquired by any form of profit in an economic system, specifically by expropriating the produce of a worker's labor. What distinguishes this work is its attempt to bring together various strands of critical pedagogy—with special attention to what I have been developing over the years as "revolutionary critical pedagogy"—and inviting that work into conversation with critical spirituality and various incarnations of liberation theology.

Michael Dantley (2010) writes that spirituality is an ethereal dimension of our being that makes challenging ontological and teleological inquiries that can assist us in achieving ontological and ethical clarity. Spirituality, as described by Dantley, serves as an instrument that enables us to build community and connectivity with others and provides us with vectors of possibility that allow us to chart our lives in such a way that we can more effectively contribute to the struggle for a better world. In this way, spirituality becomes a major source of compassion, a sense of equity, understanding and passion towards others as well as the life's work to which one has been "called" (2010, p. 215). A critical spirituality juxtaposes "the truth of social, cultural, and political realities with a hope of dismantling and constructing a different reality grounded in equity and social justice" (2010, p. 216).

This book is an act of mobilization as much as an act of refusal; it announces the possibilities of a new world through developing critical pedagogy as a philosophy of praxis. Please understand that this is what I believe makes up the foundation of all critical pedagogy—a philosophy of praxis, the arc of which extends beyond that which any materialism can afford us. Just as I believe that all social sciences should be approached philosophically, I believe that pedagogy should be approached the same way—through philosophical reflection on our actions and on the discourses that are constitutive of such reflection. What makes critical pedagogy different from other philosophical/praxiological approaches is that it acts upon the world as much as it reflects upon the world.

It enables us to reflect upon why we acquiesce to the root-and-branch deceptions of our political and religious leaders and to abuses of power by the government and its corporate courtiers, and it emboldens us to take action in order to gain our emancipation from the fear instilled deep within our structural unconscious by the masters of officialdom who possess all the latest technologies for manufacturing our loyalty to them and the capitalist class which they serve.

Reflection here is always active and our actions in and on the world are always self-reflective, the sword arm of revolution that for the past 30 years I have referred to as critical reflexivity.

This book is not trying to immanentize the eschaton by creating some kind of secular messianism ruled by a secret cabal of gnostics or dark-arts priestcraft organizations sworn to defend us from the geoplutocratic elite or global corporatocracy. On the contrary, *Pedagogy of Insurrection* presupposes that the eschaton has been with us for two millennia and that in order to bring about the Kingdom of God, we are obligated to live justice in our lives (both in our hearts and inside the messy web of material social relations in which we are objectively located) and that justice and love are mutually constitutive and confirming acts that critically mediate—through critical pedagogy and a philosophy of praxis—the idealism of what ought to be and the materialism of what is. The eviscerated amalgamation of culturally imposed religious positions, the uniquely American religion of deregulated capitalism and right-wing politics that passes for Christianity in the United States has little in common with the Jesus of the New Testament and his way of life. *Pedagogy of Insurrection* not only attempts to develop further critical pedagogy as the submission of the structural consequences of capitalist schooling to the revealed norm of the gospel but to establish some foundations for Christian socialist teaching and a critical spiritual pedagogy.

This volume is not meant to be a treatise in postsecularism, or a reassertion of spiritual ecology so much as an attempt to provide a new aperture—perhaps a "pinhole" along the lines of a camera obscura is more accurate—through which to examine the modern human predicament as it pertains to education; that is, through which to inherit a new educational topos where we can project Christ as a postulate for liberation, one that ruptures the anamnesis of mainstream education with its closed ontology, and affirms the project of revolutionary critical pedagogy against the prevailing current of our dystopia-soaked world. If it attempts to add anything to christology, soteriology or post-conciliar theology, it would be to bring these domains into deeper conversation with critical pedagogy in order to revalue hope as a central criterion for liberating education from its shackles so that we and our students can live as risen beings in history (Sobrino, 2001).

Bibliography

Ayers, W. (2004). *Teaching the personal and the political: Essays on hope and justice*. New York: Teachers College Press.

Ayers, W. (2004a). *Teaching toward freedom: moral commitment and ethical action in the classroom*. New York: Beacon Press.

Berger, J. (2001). *The shape of a pocket*. New York, NY: Vintage Books.

Bloch, Ernst. (1986). *The Principle of Hope*. Three volumes. Translated by Neville Plaice, Stephen Plaice and Paul Knight. London: Blackwell.

Brecht, B. (1959). *Selected poems of Bertolt Brecht*, Translation and introduction by H. R. Hays, London: Evergreen Books.

Cauchon, D. (2011, October 11). Student loans outstanding will exceed $1 trillion this year. *USA Today*. Retrieved from http://usatoday30.usatoday.com/money/perfi/college/story/2011-10-19/student-loan-debt/50818676/1

Chomsky, N. (2002). *Understanding power: The indispensable Chomsky*. P. R. Mitchell & J. Schoeffel (Eds.). New York, NY: The New Press.

Chomsky, N. (2013, August 17). A roadmap to a just world [Web log comment]. *Reader Supported News*. Retrieved from http://readersupportednews.org/opinion2/277-75/18946-focus-a-roadmap-to-a-just-world

Cleaver, M., & Tran, M. (1986, June 28). U.S. dismisses World Court ruling on Contras. *The Guardian*. Retrieved from http://www.theguardian.com/world/1986/jun/28/usa.marktran

Dantley, M. E. (2010). Successful leadership in urban schools: Principals and critical spirituality, a new approach to reform. *Journal of Negro Education, 79*(3), 214–219.

Dean, J. (2012). *The communist horizon*. London, England: Verso.

Deely, M. (Producer), & Scott, R. (Director). (1982). *Blade runner* [Motion picture]. United States: Warner Bros.

Duncan-Andrade, J. & Morrell, E. (2008). *The art of critical pedagogies: possibilities for moving from theory to practice in urban schools.* New York: Peter Lang.

Ebert, T. (2009). *The task of cultural critique.* Urbana, IL: University of Illinois Press.

Ebert, T., & Zavarzadeh, M. (2008). *Class in culture.* Boulder, CO: Paradigm Press.

Fanon, F. (2004). *Black skin, white masks.* R. Philcox (Trans.). New York, NY: Grove Press.

Foster, H. (1996). *The return of the real: The avant-garde at the end of the century.* Cambridge, MA: MIT Press.

Friedman, M. (2002). *Capitalism and freedom.* Chicago, IL: University of Chicago Press.

Gabel, S. L., & Miskovic, M. (2014). Discourse and the containment of disability in postsecondary education. *Disability and Society* 29, pp. 1145–1158.

Giroux, H. (2013). *America's education deficit and the war on youth.* New York: Monthly Review Press.

Giroux, H. (2013a). *Youth in revolt: reclaiming a democratic future.* Boulder, CO: Paradigm Publishers.

Giussani, L. (1995). *The risk of education: Discovering our ultimate destiny.* New York, NY: Crossroad.

Harvey, D. (2010). An interview with David Harvey. In A. L. Buzby (Ed.), *Communicative action: The logos interviews* (pp. 99–105). Lanham, Maryland: Lexington Books.

Hedges, C. (2014, June 17). Chomsky: American Socrates. *Truthdig.* Retrieved from http://www.truthdig.com/report/item/american_socrates_20140615

Hudis, P. (2005, November). *Marx's critical appropriation and transcendence of Hegel's theory of alienation.* Paper presented at the Brecht Forum, New York, NY.

Hudis, P. (2012). *Marx's concept of the alternative to capitalism.* Chicago, IL: Haymarket Books. Retrieved from http://dx.doi.org/10.1163/9789004229860

Hudis, P. (2014, November). *Frantz Fanon's contribution to Hegelian-Marxism.* Paper presented at the Historical Materialism conference, London, England.

International Human Rights and Conflict Resolution Clinic at Stanford Law School and Global Justice Clinic at NYU. (2012). Living under drones: Death, injury, and trauma to civilians from U.S. drone practices in Pakistan. Retrieved from http://www.livingunderdrones.org/download-report/

Karp, S. (2011, October 25). Challenging corporate school reform and 10 hopeful signs of resistance. *Rethinking Schools.* Retrieved from https://www.commondreams.org/view/2011/10/25-1?print

King, M. L. (2009, May 3). Martin Luther King on guaranteed income social dividend. *The Progress Report.* Retrieved from http://www.progress.org/2009/05/03/martin-lutherking-on-guaranteed-income-social-dividend/

Kumashiro, K. (2009). *Against common sense.* New York and London: Routledge.

Kumashiro, K. (2010). "Seeing the bigger picture: Troubling movements to end teacher education." *Journal of Teacher Education, 61*(1/2), pp. 56–65.

Ladson-Billings, Gloria J. (2005). *Beyond the Big House: African American Educators on Teacher Education.* New York, NY: Teachers College Press.

Lebowitz, M. (2010). Socialism: The goal, the paths and the compass. *The Bullet.* Socialist Project. *E-Bulletin, 20*(315). Retrieved from http://www.socialistproject.ca/bullet/315.pdf

Lebowitz, M. (2015). The book is a weapon. *MRZine*. July 11. As retrieved from: http://mrzine. monthlyreview.org/2015/lebowitz110715.html

Leonardo, Z. (2009). *Race, whiteness, and education*. New York: Routledge.

Levitas, R. (1990). Educated hope: Ernst Bloch on abstract and concrete utopia. *Utopian Studies*, *1*(2), 13–26.

Löwy, M. (2005). *The theory of revolution in the young Marx*. Chicago, IL: Haymarket Books.

McLaren, P. (2008). This fist called my heart: Public pedagogy in the belly of the beast. *Antipode*, *40*(3), 472–481.

McLaren, P., & Jaramillo, N. (2008). Alternative globalizations: Toward a critical globalization studies. *Rizoma freireano • Rhizome freirean*, 1–2. Retrieved from http://www.rizoma-freire-ano.org/index.php/global-studies

McNally, D. (2001). *Bodies of meaning: Studies on language, labor, and liberation*. Albany, NY: State University of New York Press.

Miranda, J. P. (2007). *Rationality and democracy*. Mexico City, Mexico: Universidad Autonoma Metropolitana.

Monzó, L., & McLaren, P. (2014, December 18). Red love: Towards racial, economic and social justice. *Truthout*. Retrieved from http://www.truth-out.org/opinion/item/28072-red-love-toward-racial-economic-and-social-justice

O'Neill, A. (2015, January 3). On patrol with skid row's 'angel cop.' *CNN*. Retrieved from http://www.cnn.com/2015/01/02/us/skid-row-cop/

Palast, G. (2013, August 24). Confidential memo at the heart of the global financial crisis [Web log comment]. *Vice Magazine*. Retrieved from http://readersupportednews.org/opinion2/279-82/19053-confidential-memo-at-the-heart-of-the-global-financialcrisis

Quijano, A., & Ennis, M. (2000). Coloniality of power, Eurocentrism, and Latin America. *Nepantla: Views From South*, *1*(3), 533–580.

Rand, A. (1994). *The fountainhead*. New York, NY: Plume.

Rivage-Seul, M. (2008). *The emperor's god. Imperial misunderstandings of Christianity*. Kuala Lumpur, Malaysia: The Institute of Economic Democracy.

Rosa, Ricardo & Rosa, Joao. (2015). *Capitalism's educational catastrophe and the advancing endgame revolt!* New York: Peter Lang.

San Juan, E. (2007). *In the Wake of Terror: Class, Race, Nation, Ethnicity in the Postmodern World*. Lanham, MD: Lexington Books.

Santos, B. S. (2009). A non-Occidentalist West? Learned ignorance and ecology of knowledge. *Theory, Culture & Society*, *26*(7–8), 103–125.

Schools Matter. (2008, April 7). Charter schools: Mismanagement, fraud, enormous debt [Web log comment]. Retrieved from http://www.schoolsmatter.info/2008/04/charter-schools-mismanagement-fraud.html

Sleeter, C. E. (2011). "Becoming white: Reinterpreting a family story by putting race back into the picture," *Race Ethnicity & Education*, *14*(3), 421–433.

Sleeter, C. E. (2012). "Confronting the marginalization of culturally responsive pedagogy," *Urban Education*, *47*(3), 562–584.

Sobrino, J. (1993). *Jesus the liberator: A historical-theological view*. Maryknoll, NY. Orbis Books.

Sobrino, Jon. (2001). *Christ the liberator*. Maryknoll, NY. Orbis Books.

Stetsenko, A. (2002). Vygotsky's cultural-historical activity theory: Collaborative practice and knowledge construction process. In D. Robbins & A. Stetsenko (Eds.), *Vygotsky's psychology: Voices from the past and present*. New York, NY: Nova Science Press.

Stetsenko, A. (2008). Collaboration and cogenerativity: On bridging the gaps separating theory-practice and cognition-emotion. *Cultural Studies of Science Education*, 3(2), 521–533.

Stetsenko, A. (2009). Vygotsky and the conceptual revolution in developmental sciences: Towards a unified (non-additive) account of human development. In M. Fleer, M. Hedegaard, J. Tudge, & A. Prout (Eds.), *Constructing childhood: Global-local policies and practices* (pp. 125–142; World Year Book of Education series). London, England: Routledge.

Toner, R., & Elder, J. (2007, March 1). Poll shows majority back health care for all. *The New York Times*. Retrieved from http://www.nytimes.com/2007/03/01/washington/01cnd-poll.html?_r=0

· 1 ·

COMRADE JESUS

s critical educators we take pride in our search for meaning, and our metamorphosis of consciousness has taken us along many different paths, to different places, if not in a quest for truth, then at least to purchase more perspicuous conditions of possibility from which to inaugurate a radical reconstruction of society through educational, political and spiritual transformation. The different pathways I have trodden in my intellectual as well as my activist work has taken me to the rare book collections of libraries throughout the world, to radical bookshops selling cheap plaster busts of Marx, to coffee shops where stacks of second hand anarchist works were free for the taking, to streets convulsed in tear gas and chants demanding freedom, to the favelas and barrios of grassroots activists, to meeting places in communities where the land had been seized by the campesinos, to South African classrooms in shack dweller communities, to alternative community centers in Roma neighborhoods, to education conferences in Muslim and Hindu countries, to schools where martyred teachers adorn the murals on the walls, to universities occupied by radical students and to the mahogany and brass offices of university administrators. Our journey has also taken us along different spiritual pathways no less important to us. It has taken me from Buddhist temples in Thailand, to Taoist temples in China, to Shinto temples in Japan, to Christian churches throughout Europe, to the Vatican, to Maori *whare whakairo* in New

Zealand, to Santeria ceremonies in Havana, to Umbande and Candomblé *terreiros* in Bahia, Brazil, to Hare Krishna temples, to an abbey in Ireland, to the Self-Realization Fellowship temple of Paramahansa Yogananda and to evangelical churches in the U.S. where the Lord is praised in whoops and hollers. This sojourner thirsting for salvation and social justice has taken off his thirsty boots in decrepit hostels in Mexico, rested his feet on the mini-bars of luxury hotels in Spain and boarded for the night in rooming houses in Caracas while supporting the Bolivarian revolution. Over the years I have joined groups of religious pilgrims on a spiritual path. This has been as important to me as my scholarship and political activism. To me, they go hand-in-hand. Together, we have tried to break through all the barriers that constrain us from realizing the Kingdom of God, not realizing that it is already upon us. We have tried to make our own consciousness the object of our thought. We have tried to bolster our potential to think about thought itself. We have tried to blast open the continuum of history in order to arrive at Benjamin's messianic "now-time," at Leary's "white light," at Suzuki's satori, seeking our "profane illumination" as we smashed our fists through the prison doors of homogeneous, empty time, searching for that flashpoint moment where the temporal-ontological distance between the past, present and future vanishes and we are engulfed by an orgasm of history. We have been crazy fools and holy fools both. Some of us have found in revolutionary critical pedagogy an opportunity to bring together our spiritual and political struggles. Forces busy at work disabling our quest are neither apparent nor easily discerned and critical educators have managed to appropriate many different languages with which to navigate the terrain of current educational reform. This chapter adopts the language of Marxist humanism, revolutionary critical pedagogy and Christian socialism. What this chapter recriminates in official education is not only its puerile understanding of the meaning and purpose of public knowledge but also its hypocrisy in advocating critical thinking—as in the case of the recent educational panacea known as "Common Core"—while at the same time publicly suturing the goals of education to the imperatives of the capitalist marketplace. The idea of the new global consumer citizen—cobbled together from a production line of critically minded consumers who have been educated to make good purchasing choices—is a squalid concept lost in the quagmire of bad infinity and will only advance the notion that growth through the expansion of neoliberal capitalism automatically means progress for humanity. Critical pedagogy offers an alternative vision and set of goals for the education of humanity. Critical pedagogy is the lucubration of a whole philosophy of praxis that predates Marx and can be found in biblical texts. If we wish to break from alienated labor, then we must break completely with the logic of capitalist accumulation and profit, and this is something to which Marx and Jesus would agree. Consequently, we covenant our participation in the life history of the world through an endless struggle that constitutes the permanent revolution ahead.

It is no exaggeration to say that public education is under threat of extinction. The uneven but inexorable progress of neoliberal economic policies clearly provided the incubus for transferring the magisterium of education in its entirety from the womb of Minerva to the cradle of the business community. The world-producing power of the corporate media has not only helped to castrate Hermes and sterilize the Muses but has created a privatized, discount store version of democracy that is allied with the arrogance and greed of the ruling class. And it has also turned the public against itself in its support of privatizing schools. The chiliasm of gloom surrounding public schooling that has been fostered by the corporate attack on teachers, teachers' unions and those who see the privatization of education as a consolatory fantasy designed to line the pockets of corporate investors by selling hope to aggrieved communities is not likely to abate anytime soon.

Erudite expositors on the "what," "how" and "why" of effective teaching understand that it cannot be adequately demonstrated by sets of algorithms spawned in the ideological laboratories of scientific management at the behest of billionaire investors in instrumentalist approaches to test-based accountability. At a time in which exercises in "test prep" have now supplanted the Pledge of Allegiance as the most generic form of patriotism in our nation's schools, critical pedagogy serves as a sword of Damocles, hanging over the head of the nation's educational tribunals and their adsentatores, ingratiators and sycophants in the business community.

In an age of "advocacy philanthropy," in which the business elite and other financial opportunists sit comfortably at the helm of educational policy making, in which advocates for programs supported by funds from the student loan business to increase access to college for students who must borrow heavily to attend are not judged to be enemies of democracy but rather held up as examples of good citizenship, and in which the overall agenda of educational reform is to establish alternatives to public education at public expense, we shudder at just how retrograde public education has become in their hands.

If we could play education like a fiddler, more specifically like a fiddler from the Appalachian highlands of Virginia, who uses the technique of double stopping (in which two strings are played by the bow at the same time with one string serving as the drone string), then genuine education would represent this drone string that is never noted but always heard. The fiddler plays melodies on the other strings but the drone never changes. Mainstream reformers bedazzle the public with all kinds of melodies that do nothing to affect the aging drone strings, while revolutionaries want to replace the drone strings which are sagging and have grown drastically out of tune and which no longer complement the melodies.

We are not interested in arcana but in salvation. We don't waste our time debating whether Giordano Bruno was a martyr to science or a throwback to Hermetism but are more intrigued by his thoughts on the dialectical structure of the mind. We are simply searchers of the truth.

All of us indignantly reject social inequality as a major impediment to our goals of reforming the state through education, but many of us have chosen to follow a path that takes the struggle against inequality further than simply denouncing the peremptory mandates of austerity capitalism. My own goal is to use education to support critically minded citizens willing and able to consider alternatives to capitalist value production. One of the major obstacles has been imputing to socialism false maxims that we socialists "hate America" and attributing to us irreformably demonic characteristics—contemporary spin-offs that we are all dirty "reds" hiding under America's "beds." One of the key problems here, of course, is the confusion of capitalism with market anarchy and socialism with planned production by a centralized state. The bulk of social wealth is consumed not by people but by capital itself. The answer is not to be found in exchange relations in the market but rather in preventing the domination of dead over living labor. The inability of capitalism to reproduce its only value-creating substance—labor power—means that capitalism can be defeated should the working-class decide to withhold their labor power and refuse to feed the furnaces of capital. We need a philosophically grounded alternative to capitalism (Hudis, 2012).

The inexorable reprobation to which socialists have been subjected and their execration by the public-at-large has less to do with a willful ignorance than with a terrifyingly motivated historical forgetfulness created through the decades by the corporate media, a learned ignorance that Chomsky famously coined as "manufacturing consent." This has led over time to an instinctive repugnance towards socialism and a knee-jerk anti-Marxism. The culpable absence of the public in looking beyond capitalism can be ascribed to many factors, but in particular to a willful amnesia about the history of class struggle in the U.S., to an unscrupulous crusade against welfare and social programs carried out by both Republicans and Democrats and to a celebratory adherence to official doctrinal propaganda that claims that capitalism might be flawed but it is the only viable alternative for economic prosperity and democracy. The idea of a socialist alternative to capitalism is not an idea that needs to be immediately amenable to scientific investigation. Suffice that for the purposes of this chapter, I view it as moral exhortation—a categorical imperative, if you will—that some other sustainable form of organization has to be adopted in order for the planet to survive and human and non-human life along with it.

Clearly, this is a pivotal moment for humanity, when the meanings, values and norms of everyday life are arching towards oblivion, following in the debris-strewn wake of Benjamin's Angel of History; when human beings are being distributed unevenly across the planet as little more than property relations, as "surplus populations"; when a culture of slave labor is increasingly defining the workaday world of American cities; when capital's structurally instantiated ability to supervise our labor, control our investments and purchase our labor power merits new levels of opprobrium; when those who are habitually relegated to subordinate positions within capital's structured hierarchies live in constant fear of joblessness and hunger; and when the masses of humanity are in peril of being crushed by the hobnailed boots of Stormtrooper Capitalism.

The winds of critical consciousness, generated by outrage at the profligate use of lies and deceptions by the capitalist class—a class that gorgonizes the public through a winner-takes-all market fundamentalism and corporate-driven media spectacles—are stirring up the toxic debris from our austerity-gripped and broken humanity. Wearing the nationalist armor of settler-colonial societies, capitalism subordinates human beings to things, splitting human beings off from themselves, slicing them into pieces of the American Dream with the nonchalant dexterity of the Iron Chef wielding an eight-inch Honbazuke-processed knife.

Capitalism turns living and breathing bodies into things, ensepulchering humanity in a vault of silence, engulfing it in darkness and transforming it into the living dead through the occult process of commodity production. Capitalism is little more than an alchemic compendium of valorized abstractions, a world-producing monster adept at misplacing the abstract for the concrete, at reducing relational being to the form of appearance of socially average labor time, and destroying the concrete relationality of nature by misplacing the concreteness of all processive being (Pomeroy, 2004a). Capitalism therefore entails a loss of subjective and inter-subjective meaning

(Hudis, 2014a). Correlative to a capitalist economy is an unconscious schema of rational calculation governing an erotically exuberant pursuit of knowledge, which involves a possessive mastery over commodities, a squandering of human nature, abstracting from the wholeness of human beings and thus turning them into fragments of each other, creating the impersonal, quantifying and utilitarian rationality and alienated consciousness of *homo economicus*.

We confront ourselves as people who have ownership of the means to purchase wealth (the ideologists and apologists of the bourgeoisie) against those who must sell their labor-power to those who do not possess such ownership (the working class). We are trapped in the economic bowels of neoliberal capitalism whose closed and putrefied futures are visible in the pockmarked cultural skin of our consumer culture. Thousands of Miley Cyrus addicts whose lives turn on her accidentally-on-purpose wardrobe malfunctions and her high-cut leotards can still view themselves as cultural subversives after being declared redundant in their local Costco job and lining up for lunch in their neighborhood soup kitchen where they can share Miley's psychedelic Instagrams.

Amidst the turmoil and conflagration of the current historical moment, capitalism keeps a steady hand with the flippant arrogance of the most famous smirking apologist of U.S. imperialism, William F. Buckley, his Yale-educated tongue wagging jauntily from the pillow-feathered clouds of his heavenly perch as he adroitly deploys his clipboard-prop gently upon his succulent lap, otherwise reserved for his King Charles spaniels. There seems to be nothing standing in the way of capitalism's continuation, save a few irritants in the alternative media that are flippantly swatted away from time to time, like flies on the arse of a barnyard goat. Today's unrelenting urgency of redeeming life from the belligerent forces of social reproduction—the internally differentiated expanding whole of value production, inside of which is coiled the incubus of misplaced concreteness—marks a watershed in the history of this planet.

The paradigmatic innovation of anti-colonial analysis in North America has been significantly impacted by what has been taking place since capital began responding to the crisis of the 1970s of Fordist-Keynesian capitalism—which William Robinson (1996, 2000, 2004, 2008, 2011a, 2011b) has characterized as capital's ferocious quest to break free of nation-state constraints to accumulation and twentieth-century regulated capital (labor relations based on some [at least a few] reciprocal commitments and rights)—a move which has seen the development of a new transnational model of accumulation in which transnational fractions of capital have become dominant. New mechanisms of accumulation, as Robinson notes, include a cheapening of labor and the growth of flexible, deregulated and de-unionized labor, where women always experience super-exploitation in relation to men; the dramatic expansion of capital itself; the creation of a global and regulatory structure to facilitate the emerging global circuits of accumulation; and, finally, neoliberal structural adjustment programs which seek to create the conditions for unfettered operations of emerging transnational capital across borders and between countries.

In my work with teachers, education scholars, political activists and revolutionaries worldwide, I've repeatedly visited mean and lonely streets that span numerous counties, countries and continents. Whether I've been visiting the Roma district of Budapest, the barrios on the outskirts of Medellin, the cartel-controlled neighborhoods of Morelia or Juárez, the favelas of Rio or São Paulo, the markets of St. Petersburg, the crowded alleys of Delhi, the alleyways of Harbin (not very far from the Siberian border) or the streets of South Central Los Angeles, I've encountered pain and despair among the many as a result of the exploitation by the few.

Whether I've been speaking to hitchhikers caught in a snowstorm, Vietnam vets in overflowing homeless shelters, elderly workers in emergency warming centers whose food stamps had just been cut by Republican legislation, jobless men and women resting on pillows of sewer steam wafting through the cast-iron grates of litter-strewn streets, a group of teenagers hanging out in strip malls festooned with faded, pockmarked signs offering discount malt liquor or day laborers crowded around hole-in-the-walls offering cheap pizza, I hear the same voices of desperation and resignation.

Even in such concrete situations that reek of economic catastrophism, I would like to stress the importance of philosophy—that is, class struggle as cultivating a philosophy of praxis. Without such a struggle we will remain blank-faced and sullen, immobilized for all eternity like the death's-heads carved on gravestones by Ebenezer Soule of Plympton, Massachusetts, in the 1750s.

On a recent visit to the Universidad Autónoma de Chiapas and the Escuela Normal Rural Mactumactzá in Tuxla, Chiapas, I passed through San Juan Chamula and Zinacantán and stopped for several days at San Cristóbal de las Casas to meet some environmental educators from the government. On a lonely street of San Cristóbal, an old man with fire opal eyes, a straw hat and a Zapatista bandana passed me, and our shoulders almost touched. His eyes were fixed for a moment on the wall across the street. Emblazoned on the wall were the words "nos falta 43" (we lack 43), in reference to the 43 escuela *normalistas* from La Escuela Normal Rural Raúl Isidro Burgos (the Raúl Isidro Burgos Rural Teachers College) of Ayotzinapa in Iguala, Guerrero, Mexico, who were captured, tortured and executed and whose bodies have yet to be fully recovered at the time of this writing. The old man's face was world-weary and I watched him walk haltingly into the distance while I paused for a few minutes to contemplate the words that had been hastily sprayed on the wall. How many people in the U.S., even well-intentioned and caring people, would acknowledge in the face of hard evidence, that their comfortable lifestyle is, in part, at the expense of the exploitation not only of Mexico but also all of America Latina?

While authors such as Thomas Piketty—especially his far-famed book, *Capital in the Twenty-First Century*—have brought international attention to the exponential and inglorious growth of inequality associated with global capitalism today, we need to be careful about making too much of the very popular and trenchant metaphor of the 1 percent (the elite capitalist class and its comprador affiliates) versus the 99 percent of the rest of us (the exploited class). For Piketty (2014), today's "patrimonial capitalism," dominated by rentier wealth and a financial and political oligarchy of CEOs and financiers, has ushered in a new Gilded Age whose upward concentration of wealth poses a grave threat to democracy (Krugman, 2014).

While I agree with him on this, it is important to emphasize that Piketty understands capital more from the perspective of the conceits of bourgeois or neoclassical economics than from Marxist economics, that is, from the perspective of ownership and exchange such as assets tied to market prices that capture a return on output such as real estate, rents, profits, dividends (Andrews, 2014). His focus is on the capital/income ratio and the valuation placed on financial assets, and the distribution of financial resources in rich countries. Piketty admitted that he has never read Marx's *Capital* and he conflates material or personal wealth with capital. He therefore can't answer the question concerning where the additional money comes from that makes it possible to accumulate capital in Marx's general formula of capital as self-expanding value articulated by Marx as M-C-M.

As Hudis (2014a) points out, Marx argued that "money increases in value only if it is invested in commodities whose production entails the employment of labor power whose value is greater than the amount of value that goes to the worker." Money accrues in value only because of the exploitation of labor. In Hudis's (2014a) words, Marx is able to understand the "distorted and alienated character of human relations at the innermost recesses of society, at the point of production."

Thus, it is no surprise that Piketty ignores Marx's labor theory of value where commodities function as capital. Labor (concrete and abstract) and surplus value are not examined as obtaining in relations of exploitation and accumulation (Andrews, 2014; see Harvey, 2014). He ignores the findings of Marxist economics (the impossibility of full employment, incessant class struggle, recurring crises or slumps, the inevitability of impoverishment and precarious employment as the victories following class-based political activism and government-provided benefits won through social struggles are inevitably rolled back) built on the authority given to the capitalists to extract surplus value from the worker (see Andrews, 2014; Despain, 2014; Tengely-Evans, 2014).

While Piketty importantly emphasizes economic reforms associated with the social state such as an increase in the minimum wage, reducing the age requirement for Medicare, greater taxes on the rich and support for unions, he clearly believes that democracy must be paired with capitalism, as do most social democrats. That poses a problem for those of us who are searching for a democratic alternative to capitalism.

Piketty's book is important in drawing attention to the inexorable economic polarization occurring in countries worldwide and for its call for narrowing income differentials in countries such as the U.S., where the moneyed disproportionately live (the U.S. has become more unequal than many emerging countries such as China and India). But my worry is that an overweening concern over inequality can distract us from the misery experienced by masses of people at this particular historical juncture who, as the victims of structural forms of capitalist genocide, cannot find work or feed their families. We need to fight against rising inequality, but we also need first and foremost to understand the causes of capitalist exploitation and immiseration.

The notion of the 99 percent can be misleading too, since an unmarried person with an income of $366,622 in 2011 was part of the 99 percent (Kliman, 2013). There are great disparities in that group. And furthermore, the causes of the crisis of capitalism are more complicated than simply having to do with the upward redistribution of income. In fact, a downward redistribution of income that takes away the profit from capitalists will also help to destabilize the system (Kliman, 2013).

Most critics of capitalism that manage to get into the mainstream debates refrain from an unqualified condemnation of free markets themselves and instead denounce the unmourned cupidity associated with a robber baron mentality that they believe has been resurrected by finance capitalism, winner-take-all markets, family dynasties and super-salaries and that lies at the core of our present and persistent problems with economic inequality and disparity. I have no problem with emphasizing the social responsibility of governments and organizations that have become increasingly aggressive and ethically indolent in today's digital economy, but I want to underscore the structural violence of capitalist inequality and the necessity of creating a socialist alternative to capitalism's impending form of outlawry in our increasingly disjointed and dissolute world.

If we arrive at a socialist alternative, it will be the result of class struggle. And I want to make the argument, made by others in the international Marxist-humanist initiative, that class struggle needs to be incorporated into a philosophy of praxis, that is, a concretization of philosophy that confronts, rather than excludes, the dialectic. Dialectical philosophy can help us undress capitalist ideology; that is, it can help us unpack our uncritical acceptance of social forms that bind us to the social relations of capitalist exploitation in our anticipation of a liberated future. The founder of Marxist humanism, Raya Dunayevskaya, maintained that the task of Marxists is not to "abolish" philosophy, but rather "to abolish the conditions preventing 'realization' of Marx's philosophy, i.e., the reunification of mental and manual abilities in the individual himself, the 'all-rounded' individual who is the body and soul of Marx's humanism" (1965, p. 76).

The ideological imperatives unleashed by organizations such as the Council on Foreign Relations, the Bilderberg Group, the Trilateral Commission, the National Program Office, the Central Intelligence Agency, the Federal Bureau of Investigation and the National Security Organization, and their Faustian counterparts in the banking industry, help to establish the framework in which citizenship and patriotism are alloyed; these Stygian imperatives epitomize imperial power and the quest for world cultural domination, and are designed to root out apologists for socialism.

Nearly three decades ago, Robert Higgs (1987) cautioned that the U.S. was becoming a participatory fascist state. Today, Nafeez Ahmed (2013) ominously warns that the Pentagon is currently preparing for massive social unrest over climate change and energy shocks; Ahmed (2014) reports disturbing instances in which U.S. military agencies are supervising and funding investigations by universities into "tipping points for large-scale civil unrest across the world" in order to supply these agencies with "warfighter-relevant insights."

As one example, the U.S. Department of Defense through its Minerva Research Initiative has partnered with Cornell University to study "social movement mobilizations and contagions." In this research scenario, non-violent activists are considered national security threats, equated with supporters of political violence and described as "social contagions." Social science is being militarized in the service of war, and social scientists are being con-scripted into their patriotic duty of counteracting grassroots protest move-ments in the interest of the national security state.

There is now a proliferation of domestic surveillance operations against political activists, particularly those linked to environmental and social justice protest groups, such as Greenpeace and anti-fracking activists, as strategic part-nerships have been created between the FBI, the Department of Homeland Security, the private sector and the academy to create a "corporate security community" protecting the interests of Wall Street and corporate America.

So what about activists among the professoriate? A fresh new breed of post-modern rebels festooned with brand-name-theory knock-offs and thrift-shop identity politics now exercise their fashionable apostasy in the new techno-mediated social factories known as universities. They are very much present in our graduate education programs through their postmodern theorizing of identity, which hinges on the linkage of identity-formation and the creation of a discount store version of democracy as a mixture of meritocracy and the American Dream.

Rather than challenging the marriage of the university and the capitalist class or fighting for the emancipation of the oppressed worldwide through pedagogies of liberation that have a transnational reach, class antagonisms are universally normalized through the performative pettifoggery, the aero-sol spray sophistry, the pseudo-profundities, the convulsions and casuistries of political disengagement and the vertigo-inducing terminology that has distinguished these disquieting hellions of the lecture hall over the past few decades—not to mention their dismissal of class struggle in favor of questions of ethnicity, race, gender and sexuality.

Furthermore, these knavish coffeehouse philosophers and suave prodigies of subversive criticality and analytic subterfuge equipped with air-conditioned imperatives to discredit all enlightenment meta-narratives such as Marxism and to demarcate critical introspection as a prison house of language games fail to identify as self-deception their own participation in language games. This domestication of the economic and divine activation of the cultural has led to the exfoliation of some of the most verdant contributions of socialist pedagogy during these decades.

From this vantage point, postmodernism appears to be an ideology of the prosperous, "which itself is a product of the type of capitalism that arose in the imperialist core of contemporary capitalism during the 'Golden Age of Capitalism' between 1945 and 1973" (Ahmad, 2011, p. 16). If, even during these years of prosperity, creating a democracy embracive of economic equality in the U.S. was about as realistic as Astroland's Burger Man seizing the controls on the rocket ship that sat atop Gregory & Paul's Hamburgers on Coney Island, and orbiting it around the Statue of Liberty, then economic equality through education today is about as realistic as the National Rifle Association calling for a ban on assault weapons, or McDonald's eliminating the Big Mac.

Much of the self-styled brigandage exercised by these postmodern outlaws involves turning away from the cultural and claiming to be materialists. But this so-called productive materialism grounded in immanence equates the material with the "thing-ness" of signs, symbols, discourses, values—part of the cultural "real"—rather than with how the mode of production of material life and social being determines consciousness. Teresa Ebert (2009) sees this move as a return to eighteenth-century materialism that stipulates experience as the limit of what can be known.

Never part of the cloth-cap crowd of workers, these ex-radicals, keen on the latest theoretical divertissement, are adept at giving encouragement to their students and peers for "dissent" through terse but pregnant commentaries about the corporate assault on higher education, but such impious outlawry on the part of the opposition is more bluster and bloviation than substance. Aware of the ever-darkening menace consisting of industrial-scale torture and brutality that have arrived on the doorsteps of the nation, these radicals stop short of examining how capitalism is implicated in such brutality, preferring instead to offer courses on images of costermongers, high steel workers or Rembrandt's spectacle-pedlar.

We have always had liberal centrists and conservatives who believe that education should be politically neutral. We also have liberals and left-liberals who have given up on class struggle as an engine for social transformation. Motivated by a fear that their left-leaning views might scuttle their careers should they go on to upset or challenge the propriety of the academy or the beneficed academic clergy or sacerdotal aristocracy who run the universities, many scholars and researchers in the academy choose to moot their personal opinions with the utmost discretion and circumspection while still trying to appear radical-chic. Hence, they are extremely cautious not to offend inadvertently those whose religious or political views have lain fallow and unchallenged for generations but who hold positions of power within the university establishment.

Erstwhile radicals once sympathetic to Marx but who became disillusioned and disgusted by revelations about the Gulag and traumatized by the failure of "really existing socialism" worried that they would be condemned as dusty dilettantes still clinging to the paltry spirit of socialism (or worse, traduced as Stalinists). They decided instead to ride the new wave of postmodern social theory that embraced a linguistic turn and managed in turn to find comfortable abodes in literature and cultural studies departments. Positioning themselves thus enabled them both to smite the gross profligacy of the capitalist class and its command structure comprised of greedy corporatists and bankers with self-aggrandizing tirades and at the same time put paid to their academic critics by adopting a more digestible "deconstruction." This was a deft academic move that allowed them to assume a political agenda through a stringent labyrinth of explanations, yet without dragging research and scholarship away from the compromise of incremental reformism. Here, the institutional framework informed by neoliberal assumptions is already prejudged as the only rational framework for a society bent on justice, and unwittingly supported by a postmodern embrace of playfulness and the un-decidability of the sign.

Reveling in the sagacity of cultural criticism and eager to keep their gladiatorial attitude intact without suffering an unsettling cost for their radicalism, these prodigies of cosmopolitan learning embraced an unutterably reactionary "anti-foundationalism" that condemns all "master narratives" of progress. Marx would occasionally find a polemical way into some of the debates but was mostly banished from serious consideration. And while the work of Marx is a bit more fashionable these days, with the current crisis of neoliberal capitalism, the postmodernists have to a large extent fallen into tacit agreement with their modernist adversaries and pushed themselves into self-limiting alliances with liberals. By leaving the challenge to capitalism untouched, their politics eventually and unwittingly colludes with that of those whom they despise.

In the arena of educational reform, these defanged revolutionaries abrade the cause of their more militant colleagues, often with self-serving maunderings and sententious commentary about educational reform that are mere coinages of the general currency used in mainstream educational debates, never challenging the primacy of capital. Here we need to recall the storied comment by Benjamin (1936) that those who call for a purely cultural or spiritual revolution without changing asymmetrical relations of power and privilege linked to class antagonisms can only be served by the logic of fascism and authoritarian political movements. But the worst of the lot are the self-styled liberals who try to retaliate against radical professors for their outspoken activism and who deploy haughty moralistic pronouncements to condemn those whom they feel transgress their ideal of the good university citizen—all which reveals in standard Schmittian fashion that there are mainly two existential positions taken among liberal university professors: friend or enemy.

And then there are the Marxists who attempt to descry the positivity ensepulchered within the negativity of Hegel's absolutes but who are shunned for their embrace of a dialectics of transcendence (transcendence could lead to the Gulag again; it is much safer to remain in a politics of immanence). This Marxist-humanist position that emphasizes transcendence holds that we are the flesh-and-blood idea of capital, waxed fat from our complicity in advancing class society, and in doing so enabling millions to be exiled into Marx's reserve army of workers (the unemployed). Thus we need to break out of the social universe of value production by creating a democratic alternative.

My agnostic relationship to liberal modernity with its emphasis on the apolitical drama of personal development while crucifying class struggle on the altar of culture such that the politics of "representation" is substituted for a politics of "revolution," does not mean that I rely on some ghostly psycho-pomp for advice; rather, I subscribe to the concept of praxis (an ordered chaos or irrational regularity) without retreating into the hinterlands of metaphysics and in doing so express critical pedagogy in germinal form as a philosophy of praxis, steering a path between the Scylla of an intractable rationalism and the Charybdis of metaphysical ravings. Yet at the same time I do not abjure either a yearning or a search for a dialectics of transcendence that involves both history and spirit.

The aggrieved, the oppressed and the immiserated, who have subordinated themselves to existing social systems practicing a developmental terrorism, are awakening fitfully from their social amnesia and reminding those who choose to delay their hypnopompic state that, in standing idle, they risk being suffocated by their own past. The window of opportunity is growing smaller for protecting the world against the ghastly panorama of increasing mega-droughts, global warming, ozone depletion, marine and tropical forest habitat destruction, the ongoing and methodological destruction of the biosphere, pandemics, mass extinctions (including the possibility of human extinction) and a possible 1000-year period of unchecked warming, which has been referred to as the "Venus effect," where all possibilities for life on earth will be utterly destroyed. Thus, the clarion call of First Nations peoples worldwide: "Idle No More!"

The annihilation of humanity that capitalism prosecutes with such an illustrious savagery is not some ramped-up bit of catastrophism, but the foundation of civilization's unfinished obelisk, against which we can only smash our heads in horror and disbelief. The chilling realization is that eco-apocalypse is not just some fodder for science-fiction movie fans who revel in dystopian plots, but the future anterior of world history that is upon us. Under the guise of responsible job-producing growth ("jobs for the jobless"), we have an infestation of eco-fascisms, whose distracting sheen belies the horrors lurking beneath the surface. Preoccupied with the beautiful, translucent hues of a soap bubble catching the noonday sun as it floats aimlessly down a seaside boardwalk, courtesy of a bulbous-nosed local clown, we fail to notice the fish floating upside down amidst the rank and stink of the nearby ocean sewage. As our biosphere goes, so goes the public sphere, including public schooling, with its mania for high-stakes testing, accountability, total quality management and a blind passion for privatization (which usually begins with private–public partnerships), effectively dismantling a public education system that it took 200 years to build.

The enthronement of the bourgeois political order has seen the transnational capitalist class power elite become fully ensconced in what Gramsci called the "integral state" (see Mayo, 1999, 2005; Thomas, 2009). While functionally entombed in their propertarian and liberal democratic values, the bourgeoisie are becoming historically deformed. Samir Amin (2010) warns us about changes in the structures of the governing classes (bourgeoisie), political practice, ideology and political culture. He argues that the "historical bourgeoisie is disappearing from the scene and is now being replaced by the plutocracy of the 'bosses' of oligopolies" (Amin, 2010).

Capitalism is more than the sheet anchor of institutionalized avarice and greed, more than excrement splattered on the coattails of perfumed bankers and well-heeled speculators—it is a "world-eater" with an insatiable appetite. Capital has strapped us to the slaughter bench of history, from which we must pry ourselves free to continue our work of class and cultural struggle, creating working-class solidarity, an integral value system and internal class logic capable of countering the hegemony of the bourgeoisie, while at the same time increasing class consensus and popular support. Inherent in capitalist societies marked by perpetual class warfare and the capitalist mode of production is structural violence of a scale so staggering that it can only be conceived as structural genocide. Garry Leech (2012) has argued convincingly and with a savage aplomb that capitalist-induced violence is structural in nature and, indeed, constitutes genocide.

Some critics dismissively opine that liberal capitalist regimes such as the U.S. cannot become truly fascist. I disagree. Economics is now the dominant science of human behavior and is providing the rationale for merging together sections of government, the military-industrial complex and corporations, creating zealots whose main prerogative is to bolster unrestricted and unilateral authority for the U.S. on the world stage and to command obedience and loyalty to the U.S. imperium. We have arrived benightedly at the twilight of democracy, the end of freedom's long and slippery road. Yet our leaders instruct our balaclava-clad protesters to decamp from the streets and make their case for economic reform with appeals to politicians and policy makers in the spirit of reason and good faith. However, appealing to the humanity of transnational corporate oligarchs will be about as successful in ending the crisis of inequality faced by the majority of human beings on the planet as trying to put out all the fires in hell with a bucket of lustral water from the aspersorium of the local Catholic church.

In my adoptive homeland today, we have the greatest amount of consumer debt in the world, staggeringly high rates of both child and adult poverty, skyrocketing unemployment and, with the exception of North Korea, more people in prison than anywhere in the world in proportion to our population size, and have all but sacrificed our civic sovereignty. The chief executive officer of our Walmart stores, Michael Duke, makes US$16,826.92 an hour whereas new employees making $8.75 an hour gross $13,650 a year (Gomstyn, 2010). Our infrastructure is crumbling and we continue to fight undeclared wars. Wages for workers in the U.S. are at their lowest level since the 1930s. Even so, massive cuts are being implemented at every level of government, justified by the claim that "there is no money" for healthcare, education or other basic social needs.

The wealth of the ruling class at this crisis-ridden historical juncture is almost entirely divorced from productive activity in the real economy through a process of financialization, in which the productive forces of the economy are steadily undermined. As I wrote several years ago:

> We know now that the financial crisis created the great recession, which then resulted in the fiscal crisis. Massive layoffs and unemployment followed the financial crisis .... [A]s inflated profits on fictitious capital dry up after the implosion of a speculative bubble, capitalism must reduce the amount of variable capital relative to constant capital to restore profitability. Costs associated with providing public services go up as workers get laid off and tax revenues decline. The government uses taxpayer dollars to bail out those financial institutions that helped to create the financial crisis while those workers suffering most from the crisis are told that they are consuming too much and must be punished even further through austerity programs. The relative amount of value that goes to workers must be cut so that the succulent capitalist class can once again retool its digestive tract for devouring the profits of speculative capital. Voters are told that debt levels threaten their economic well-being, so out of fear they agree to cutbacks in

government spending and this is how capital manages to redistribute value from labor to capital—forcing the poor to pay for the rising debt levels afflicting global capital.

Demanding that the rich or the financial institutions pay for the crisis is not the real answer, either, because, as [Peter] Hudis (2010) notes, the relative proportion of value going to capital as against labor must be increased to guarantee that capital accumulation is sustained, and this is true even though 80% of the economic growth in the United States over the past 20 years has ended up in the hands of the wealthiest 5% of the population. Hudis (2010) warns us not to be misled by conceiving of social wealth as reducible to the revenue paid out to workers on one hand and capitalists on the other. This is because most of the value produced in capitalism is not consumed by the capitalists or the workers, but by capital itself. When the left demands that wealth be distributed to the poor, this only intensifies the crisis of capital, so long as the capitalist law of value is not challenged .... We need to uproot the very law of value itself. But to do that, we must create a viable conception of social organization that can replace capitalist value production. The left has failed to do this and it is up to us now to take up the challenge. (McLaren, 2011, pp. 373–374)

The hyperbolic rhetoric of the fascist imaginary spawned by the 2008 recession is likely to be especially acute in the churches and communities affiliated with conservative groups who want a return to the economic practices that were responsible for the very crisis they are now railing against, but who are now, of course, blaming it on bank bailouts, immigration and the deficit. Fascist ideology is not something that burrows its way deep inside the structural unconscious of the U.S. from the outside, past the gatekeepers of our everyday psyche; it is a constitutive outgrowth of the logic of capital in crisis that can be symptomatically read through a neoliberal individualism enabled by a normative, value-free absolutism and a neo-feudal/authoritarian pattern of social interaction.

The U.S. has managed to conjure for itself—mainly through its military might and the broad spectacle of human slaughter made possible by powerful media apparatuses whose stock-in-trade includes portraying the U.S. as a democracy under siege by evil forces that are "jealous" of its freedoms—a way to justify and sanctify its frustrations and hatreds, and reconstitute American exceptionalism amidst the rampant violence, prolonged social instability, drug abuse and breakdown of the U.S. family. Of course, all of this works in concert with the thunderous call of Christian evangelicals to repent and heed God's prophets, and to welcome the fact that the U.S. has been anointed as the apotheosis of specific forms of divine violence (i.e., whatever forms of violence the U.S. deems to be part of God's divine plan for the world). Plain-spoken declarations abound, dripping with apocalyptic grandiosity, for dismantling the barriers of church and state, and creating a global Christian empire. This should not sound unusual for a country in which rule by violence was the inaugurating law of the nation, and which has, through its history, marked its citizenry indelibly in their interactions with others.

The conditions of inequality—stubbornly rationalized by the ruling class through the ideological state apparatus of schooling, religion and the media—beguile the people with everyday distractions and falsehoods, mystifying them with respect to their aspirations, loyalties and purposes. As new forms of development of the productive forces arise, existing economic relationships become a burden to the new economic system of production and, as a result of capital's internal conflict, society reorganizes itself to accommodate these new relationships as the ruling class increases its legal and political demands (McLaren, 2005; Pozo, 2003). These central commissars of knowledge production, these sentinels of common sense, cannot abjure the powers of the working class to resist their immiseration by simply wishing them away (Hill, 2012). They need to control ideological production through discourses that obtain canonical value by assigning high rank to capitalist intellectuals and through constant repetition by means of mind-numbing cultural productions designed to distract the people from their woes and to disqualify the claims of the oppressed as unreasonable, impractical and unpatriotic (Best, Kahn, Nocella, & McLaren, 2011).

John Bellamy Foster (2013a) argues that we are living in an "epochal crisis"—a term borrowed from Jason Moore—a tremulous period in which dire economic and ecological crises emerge inextricably entangled in each other. He cites systems ecologist Howard Odum's revelation that Latin Americans, in particular, are being systematically robbed of their environmental resources through an unequal exchange in trade and production, in which "embodied energy" is being withdrawn from the global South to the benefit of the global North—a situation which García Linera refers to as "extra-territorial surplus value" (cited in Foster, 2013b).

We are facing what Foster (2013a) describes as the unlimited expansion of a capitalist system geared to a process of abstract wealth creation. We are witnessing the displacement of natural-material use value by specifically capitalist use value, which does little more than enhance exchange value for the capitalist, so that the production of use value ceases and money creates money without producing any natural-material use value (Foster, 2013a).

The "real economy" is being hijacked by the irrational logic of monopoly-finance capitalism organized around financial-asset appreciation, which is dependent on an endless series of financial bubbles. Big corporations and wealthy investors, according to Foster (2013a), have "increasingly poured their surplus capital into the financial sphere in order to secure high speculative returns." The response to this additional demand for their products by financial institutions is to supply "an endless array of new, exotic speculative opportunities (junk bonds, derivatives, options, hedge funds, etc.)" (Foster, 2013a), which invariably leads to massive credit/debt. And all of this is occurring in the midst of human suffering, the magnitude of which is scarcely imaginable. According to Foster:

> Behind the worldwide veil of capitalist value relations, hundreds of millions, even billions, of people are poor and destitute, often lacking the most basic prerequisites of material existence—adequate food, water, clothing, housing, employment, healthcare, and a non-toxic environment—due to the failures and contradictions of accumulation. Meanwhile, what ecologists call 'real wealth,' i.e., the product of nature itself, is being extracted from the environment on an ever-increasing scale devoid of any concern for either the rationality of production or the sustainability of natural systems, thereby robbing both present and future generations. Since unequal exchange relations with respect to both nature and labor prevail within the international economy this robbery falls disproportionately on poorer nations, a portion of whose natural use values (and economic surplus) is systematically siphoned off to enrich nations at the apex of the global imperialist pyramid. (Foster, 2013a)

Samir Amin (2010) captures the general trends in the important evolution of capitalism by describing them in terms of generalized and financialized oligopolies run by plutocrats. According to Amin, since

> [c]apitalism has reached a stage of centralization and concentration of capital out of all comparison with the situation only 50 years ago, [it is best described] as one of generalized oligopolies. 'Monopolies' (or, better, oligopolies) are in no way new inventions in modern history. What is new, however, is the limited number of registered oligopolies ('groups') which stands at about 500, if only the colossal ones are counted, and 3,000 to 5,000 in an almost comprehensive list. They now determine, through their decisions, the whole of economic life on the planet, and more besides. This capitalism of generalized oligopolies is thus a qualitative leap forward in the general evolution of capitalism. (Amin, 2010)

Paraphrasing Amin (2010), all types of production of goods and services—small, medium and large—are now subordinated to the oligopolies, which determine the conditions of their survival.

The real reason for this is the search for maximum profits, which benefits the powerful groups who have priority access to capital markets. Such concentration—which has historically been the response of capital to the long, deep crises that have marked its history—is at the origin of the "financialization" of the system. Amin remarks that "this is how the oligopolies siphon off the global surplus value produced by the production system, a 'rent monopoly' that enables oligopolistic groups to increase their rate of profit considerably. This levy is made possible because of "the oligopolies' exclusive access to the monetary and financial markets which thus become the dominant markets."

Amin tells us not to confuse financialization with "a regrettable drift linked to the 'deregulation' of financial markets, even less of 'accidents' (like subprimes) on which vulgar economics and its accompanying political discourse concentrate people's attention." On the contrary, financialization "is a necessary requirement for the reproduction of the system of generalized oligopolies."

The capitalism of generalized and financialized oligopolies is also globalized, producing a growing gulf between the "developed" centers of the system and its dominated peripheries and is associated with the emergence of the "collective imperialism of the Triad" (the U.S. and its external provinces of Canada and Australia, western and central Europe, and Japan). According to Amin:

> The new globalization is itself inseparable from the exclusive control of access to the natural resources of the planet exercised by collective imperialism. Hence the center-peripheries contradiction—the North-South conflict in current parlance—is central to any possible transformation of the actually existing capitalism of our time. And more markedly than in the past, this, in turn, requires the 'military control of the planet' on the part of the collective imperialist center.

> The different 'systemic crises' that have been studied and analyzed—the energy-guzzling nature of production systems, the agricultural and food crisis, and so on—are inseparable from the exigencies of the reproduction of the capitalism of generalized, financialized, and globalized oligopolies. If the status of these oligopolies is not brought into question, any policies to solve these 'systemic crises'—'sustainable development' formulae—will just remain idle chit-chat. (Amin, 2010)

The grave threat of a capitalism of generalized, financialized and globalized oligopolies is enhanced as a result of its private status, since its continuation is bound to result in the destruction of the societies on the peripheries—those in the so-called "emerging" countries as well as in "marginalized" countries—and could very well mean the destruction of the entire planet. According to Amin:

> Not only do the oligopolies dominate the economic life of the countries of the Triad. They monopolize political power for their own advantage, the electoral political parties (right and left) having become their debtors. This situation will be, for the foreseeable future, accepted as 'legitimate,' in spite of the degradation of democracy that it entails. It will not be threatened until, sometime in the future perhaps, 'anti-plutocratic fronts' are able to include on their agenda the abolition of the private

management of oligopolies and their socialization, in complex and open-endedly evolving forms. (Amin, 2010)

Yet things are not going so well in some parts of the Triad. In Los Angeles County, in the most dominant country of Amin's Triad, close to where I am composing this chapter, an estimated 254,000 men, women and children experience homelessness during some part of the year. On any given night, approximately 82,000 people are homeless, and between 4,800 and 10,000 of them are young people. One-third of the homeless population in South and Metro Los Angeles holds a bachelor's degree or higher, compared to 25 percent of the population as a whole (Wells, 2013). A fifth of the homeless are veterans and another fifth are disabled, while a quarter are mentally ill and half are African American (Wells, 2013). Throughout the U.S., 80 percent of the population faces poverty or near poverty (Yen & Naziri, 2013).

Gun violence is astronomical in the U.S. According to Sean McElwee:

> The U.S. leads the developed world in firearm-related murders, and the difference isn't a slight gap—more like a chasm. According to United Nations data, the U.S. has 20 times more murders than the developed world average. Our murder rate also dwarfs many developing nations, like Iraq, which has a murder rate less than half ours. More than half of the most deadly mass shootings documented in the past 50 years around the world occurred in the United States, and 73 percent of the killers in the U.S. obtained their weapons legally. Another study finds that the U.S. has one of the highest proportion of suicides committed with a gun. Gun violence varies across the U.S., but some cities like New Orleans and Detroit rival the most violent Latin American countries, where gun violence is highest in the world. (McElwee, 2014)

Striking and largely unremarked-upon characteristics of the U.S. are that, in many American counties, and in the Deep South especially, "life expectancy is lower than in Algeria, Nicaragua or Bangladesh," and that the U.S. "is the only developed country that does not guarantee health care to its citizens" (McElwee, 2014). This remains the case even after the Affordable Care Act. McElwee notes that:

> America is unique among developed countries in that tens of thousands of poor Americans die because they lack health insurance, even while we spend more than twice as much of our GDP [gross domestic product] on healthcare than the average for the Organization for Economic Co-operation and Development (OECD), a collection of rich world countries. (McElwee, 2014)

The U.S. has a frightening infant mortality rate, "as well as the highest teen-age-pregnancy rate in the developed world, largely because of the politically-motivated unavailability of contraception in many areas" (McElwee, 2014).

As far as raising children goes, McElwee (2014) notes that the U.S. "is among only three nations in the world that does not guarantee paid maternal leave (the other two are Papua New Guinea and Swaziland)." Poor American mothers must face the choice between raising their children and keeping their jobs.

McElwee offers the following sweeping condemnation of the U.S. education system:

> The U.S. education system is plagued with structural racial biases, like the fact that schools are funded at the local, rather than national level. That means that schools attended by poor black people get far less funding than the schools attended by wealthier students. The Department of Education has confirmed that schools with high concentrations of poor students have lower levels of funding. It's no wonder America has one of the highest achievement gaps between high income and low income students, as measured by the OECD. Schools today are actually more racially segregated than they were in the 1970s. Our higher education system is unique among developed nations in that [it] is funded almost entirely privately, by debt. Students in the average OECD country can expect about 70 percent of their college tuition to be publicly funded; in the United States, only about 40 percent of the cost of education is publicly funded. That's one reason the U.S. has the highest tuition costs of any OECD country. (McElwee, 2014)

Of course, there is a racial dimension to inequities within the U.S. public school system. This is especially the case when examining the statistical facts of gaps between the outcomes of students disaggregated by race and affluence and comparing them with the statistical facts of disproportionate numbers of teachers among races. And, of course, when you compare these to the realities of the school-to-prison pipeline, and the re-segregation of schools, we can see a national trend.

We know that in nearly every indicator, the U.S. has the largest income inequality in the OECD countries. Its infrastructure is crumbling and, in places such as South Dakota, Alaska and Pennsylvania, century-old wooden pipes are used to transport water (McElwee, 2014). Sewer lines and wastewater capacity date back to the mid-nineteenth century in large portions of the U.S. One in nine bridges is considered to be structurally deficient.

In the midst of the current epochal crisis, the U.S. Department of Education and its spokespersons in the corporate media are diverting us away from the central issues of the crisis of capitalism and the ecological crisis by turning our attention to the failure of public schools (McLaren, 2006, 2012). They propose, as a solution, to smash public schools and the commons by unleashing the hurricane of privatization (the term "hurricane" is metaphorically appropriate here in a double sense, since New Orleans went from a public school system to a charter school city after Hurricane Katrina [see *Democracy Now*, 2007]), causing unionized teachers to drop from 4700 to 500. Of course, this is not symptomatic only of the U.S. We are facing the imperatives of the transnational capitalist class and so the challenge to public education is occurring on a transnational scale.

Yet violence is not simply linked to financial indexes, as frightening as those have been of late. Violence is more than a series of contingencies unleashed by the labor/capital antagonism that drives the engines of capitalism. It is more than a series of historical accidents transformed into a necessity. In fact, it is the very founding act of U.S. civilization.

While violence can be traced to worldwide social polarization linked to the phenomenon of capitalist over-accumulation and attempts by the transnational capitalist class to sustain profit making by means of militarized accumulation, financial speculation and the plundering of public finance (Robinson, 2008), it can also be traced historically to epistemologies of violence and linked to the genocides brought about by the invasion and colonization of the Americas (Grosfoguel, 2013). Here, violence can be viewed as foundational to the Cartesian logic of Western epistemology, as the universal truth upon which all our understandings of the world must rely. Such violence can be seen across a host of institutional structures, including education, and in particular through "banking" approaches to teaching that preclude dialogue and thus privilege Western epistemology, omitting and systematically erasing other worldviews. Indeed, Paulo Freire would maintain that dialogue necessarily brings forth the epistemologies grounded in particular social positions. Not surprisingly, the historical conditions that have brought us to a place of Western domination are linked to "undialogic" social relations (Grosfoguel, 2013).

Ramón Grosfoguel, Enrique Dussel, Anibal Quijano and other decolonial thinkers have argued convincingly that the *ego cogito* (I think, therefore I am), which underwrites Descartes' concept of modernity, replaced the prior Christian-dominant perspective with a secular, but God-like, unsituated and monolithic politics of knowledge, attributed mainly to white European men. The presumed separation and superiorization of mind over body of the *ego cogito* establishe a knowledge system dissociated from the body's positioning in time and space, and achieve a certitude of knowledge—as if inhabiting a solipsistic universe—by means of an internal monologue, isolated from social relations with other human beings (Grosfoguel, 2013). This *ego cogito* did not suddenly drop from the sky; it arose out of the historical and epistemic conditions of possibility developed through the *ego conquiro* (I conquer, therefore

I am), and the link between the two is the *ego extermino* (I exterminate you, therefore I am).

Grosfoguel and Dussel maintain that the *ego conquiro* is the foundation of the "Imperial Being," which began with European colonial expansion in 1492, when white men began to think of themselves as the center of the world because they had conquered the world. The *ego extermino* is the logic of genocide/epistemicide that mediates the "I conquer" with the epistemic racism/sexism of the "I think" as the new foundation of knowledge in the modern/colonial world. More specifically, the *ego extermino* can be situated in the four genocides/epistemicides of the sixteenth century, which were carried out

> 1) against Muslims and Jews in the conquest of Al-Andalus in the name of 'purity of blood'; 2) against indigenous peoples first in the Americas and then in Asia; 3) against African people with the captive trade and their enslavement in the Americas; 4) against women who practiced and transmitted Indo-European knowledge in Europe burned alive accused of being witches. (Grosfoguel, 2013, p. 77)

According to Grosfoguel (2013), these four genocides are interlinked and "constitutive of the modern/colonial world's epistemic structures" and Western male epistemic privilege, and we can certainly see these genocides reflected in the founding of the U.S., in particular the massacre of indigenous peoples, the transatlantic slave trade and the Salem witch trials.

This genocidal history has been repressed in the structural unconscious of the nation (the term "structural unconscious" is taken from Lichtman, 1982). The assertion here is that the contradiction between the claims of ideology and the actual structure of social power, and the need to defend oneself against socially constructed antagonisms, is the primary challenge that faces the ego.

The function of the structural unconscious is therefore to reconcile reality and ideology at the level of the nation-state, and this requires conceptual structures to help citizens adjust to its genocidal history (McLaren, 1999; Monzó & McLaren, 2014). These structures comprise the foundations for coping strategies and are provided by the myths of democracy, rugged individualism and white supremacy that lie at the heart of U.S. capitalist society. Racialized violence is the domestic expression of the American structural unconscious, whose function is to provide psychic power to the myth of America's providential history.

The untrammeled devotion to this god of violence can be seen in the near worship of U.S. troops by the general population and in those who support imperial wars of aggression and in the self-aggrandizing ordinances enacted by politicians, always in war mode, and of course in the ways that U.S. society degrades its children by teaching them through the capitalist catechism of the media that the quickest and most efficient way to solve problems is through violence and aggression. Ideologies such as religious exceptionalism that are especially hospitable to fundamentalist/Dominion Christianity have clearly overpopulated the military leadership, and we are not just referring to the distribution of videos from the *Left Behind* rapture series, Christian rock concerts, Jesus Rifles (Trijicon riflescopes inscribed with specific New Testament Bible references engraved into the metal casings on nearly a million high-powered rifle sights) or the mandatory "Jesus Loves Nukes" courses used to train USAF nuclear missile launch officers at Vandenberg Air Force Base in California (Weinstein, 2015). Clearly, the U.S. military is on a world-historical crusader mission from God to preserve capitalism and the American way of life.

Today, we see this totalizing effect on America's structural unconscious as we live out our lives through the whims of the market, seeking happiness in an ever-increasing consumption of things we feel we need and justifying our superficial existence as the "successful" outcome of our "hard work." We have stopped questioning, and perhaps even caring as a society, why some people are more deserving than others of the basic necessities of life—food, health and dignity—and simply accepted the myth that some people do not work hard enough to get ahead, and that individual social ascendance based on presumed merits and motivation is just and right—that our existence alone is not sufficient to deserve basic human needs and that these must be "earned."

Likewise, we have stopped questioning who benefits from the chaos that exists in particular communities and have accepted that the natural world has been antiseptically cleaved and cordoned off into binary oppositions—wealthy/poor, white/of color—and that it is the providential role of the U.S. to "democratize" by means of our mighty arsenal of weapons those populations who threaten our economic interests and geopolitical advantage. We operate, of course, by the divine mandate that mere mortals must simply accept—that accepting our role as the global policeman is "God's will" and is as "good" for us as it is for the rest of the world.

Anyone who spends time traveling throughout the U.S. would be hard-pressed to disagree that our cities and our countryside lie in ruins. Riven by greed, ignorance and a belief in the imperishability of the market, our civilization is collapsing as we tunnel underneath it with the hope of escaping the worst of its hubris. Transnational capitalism, which remains unhindered and sufficiently versatile despite its intemperate balance between retroactive and anticipatory forces, has shown itself to be a self-sustaining edifice chillingly untouched by the cataclysm which it has provoked. Wary of resorting to protectionism, statism, nationalism, militarism and possibly war, the elites of the world are pleased that the U.S. is maintaining its role as the world's policeman, keeping social order on a world scale in order to create the most fecund conditions for capital accumulation and to destroy any popular challenges to the existing structures of class relations.

The wrecking ball of capitalism has torn through the very earth itself, as if it were affixed to the highest rung of Jacob's ladder by an angel gone astray, perhaps the result of a drinking spree in one of those taverns hidden away in the catacombs running beneath the Tower of Babel. Despite the deeply pitted sense of fear and existential terror that has accompanied immiseration capitalism since the crisis of 2008, this all-pervading and all-propelling unholy scourge appears to be indefinitely self-replenishing.

I feel obligated at this time to make a few comments about critical pedagogy as a lodestone through which we can consider how to organize the social division of labor and the realm of necessity, so as to enable humans to satisfy their social and individual needs. This is a daunting challenge, given that public education today fails to acknowledge its full entanglement in the messy web of consumer capitalism. The solutions about what to do with public education are selectively adduced by blue-chip brokers in the flora-stuffed, starched-linen breakfast rooms of expensive hotels to remind the public in opulently elusive ways that the importance of education today revolves around increasing the range of educational choices—as in a supermarket or shopping mall—available to communities by privatizing education.

Higher education pundits propound the notion that university education creates democratic citizens who are ready to take the hefty helm of government and steer it to glory. Yet the hysterical nucleus of capitalism—in which systems of higher education are inextricably embedded—is one in which the labor of the working class is alienated and in which the surplus value created by workers in the normal functioning of the economic process is appropriated by the capitalist. The workers are paid wages that are less than the price of the force of labor expended in their work. This value beyond the price of labor is surplus labor and is made possible only because the workers themselves do not possess the means of production.

All the good works made possible by higher education are calamitously wasted in the pursuit of profit. While cautiously adjusting its role to the fluctuating needs of capital, and vigorously safeguarding its connections to corporate power, higher education has become unknowingly imprinted with an astonishing variety of reactionary social practices as it unsuccessfully tries to hide that it is in cahoots with the repressive state apparatuses and the military-industrial complex, and works to create the hive known as the national security state. Impecunious students are taught to be dedicated to the hive (as indentured servants as a result of soaring tuition fees), which is conditioned by the pathogenic pressures of profit making. Within the hive, the capitalist unconscious turns murderously upon what is left of the Enlightenment as the irresolutely corporate conditions under which knowledge is produced reduce the products of the intellect to inert commodities. Higher education offers mainly on-the-cheap analyses of how capitalism impacts the production of knowledge and fails, in the main, to survey ways of creating an alternative social universe unburdened by value formation, and, in the end, offers us little more than a vision of a discount-store democracy. In making capitalism aprioristic to civilized societies, corporate education has replaced stakeholders with shareholders and has become the unthinkable extremity towards which education is propelled under the auspices of the cash nexus—propelled by a hunger for profit as unfillable as a black hole that would extinguish use value if allowed to run its course.

Under earlier dispensations, education had many names—it was paidea, it was critical citizenship, it was counter-hegemonic, it was transformational, it was a lot of things. Over time, its descriptions changed as its objects changed, and now it is distinguished by a special nomenclature most often drawn from the world of management and business. While critical educators have striven to formulate their work clearly and have defended their arguments with formidable weapons of dialectical reasoning, there is a new call by some Marxists and eco-pedagogues to expand the struggle as anti-capitalist agitation. This is to be welcomed, of course, but education as a revolutionary process will likely not seem time-honored enough for most readers to take seriously, with the exception perhaps of the work of Paulo Freire, whose storied corpus of texts exerts a continuous subterranean pressure on the critical tradition, and amply and brilliantly demonstrates its best features.

Some, however, would argue that Freire's work is as much about what education should be like after the revolution as it is about forging the revolution through a pedagogy of praxis. But if one considers revolutionaries such as Amílcar Cabral, Frantz Fanon, Che Guevara and Hugo Chávez, Subcomandante Marcos, Martin Luther King and Malcolm X as educators, then socialist education will have some gold-standard forebears and will be less likely to be banished into the outer darkness. If we consider the above list of educators as ancestors, we can begin to see ourselves as part of a distinguished tradition of warriors fighting for the conditions of possibility for a socially and economically just society. A further long-term task awaits the critical educator who combines competence as a political historian with skills in dialectical theory, with an eye to sustainability studies. But creating a subalternist historiography of critical education and developing educational initiatives that foreground democratic national rights and the collective welfare of all peoples, assumes that the planet will survive the unipolar world of U.S. hegemony.

The U.S. enacts its "civilizing" mission in a hail of macabre counterterrorism methods employed by President Obama. There are those who are protesting in the universities and the workplace, but they pay a price. Inhumanity and exploitation are rife, and many natural and unnatural antiauthoritarians are now psychopathologized and medicated—or thrown out of the institutions of higher learning—before they achieve political consciousness of society's most oppressive strategies and tactics. Those who do achieve political consciousness and try to redress the injustices that are so acutely widespread throughout the U.S. might find themselves on a National Security Agency surveillance list.

One person with the vision and fortitude to consider a liberatory alternative to Obama's foreign and domestic policies is Cornel West. In the beginning of the Obama presidency, it was easy to see how Cornel West, who participated in 65 campaign events for Obama, was drawn to Obama's progressive-sounding politics, since Obama clearly displayed at that time some very impressive populist attributes, even though Obama had been mentored by the vulpine milquetoast and political quisling par excellence, Joe Lieberman. But early on, with the assembling of Obama's economic team, it became clearer to West that Obama had a Machiavellian side and was pandering to the Wall Street oligarchs. In time, his centrist neoliberal position became unwavering. West laments the lack of backbone in Obama, especially at this particular historical juncture that West, cited in Hedges (2011) describes as

> maybe America's last chance to fight back against the greed of the Wall Street oligarchs and corporate plutocrats, to generate some serious discussion about public interest and common good that sustains any democratic experiment ... we are squeezing out all of the democratic juices that we have. The escalation of the class war against the poor and the working class is intense. More and more working people are beaten down. They are world-weary. They are into self-medication. They are turning on each other. They are scapegoating the most vulnerable rather than confronting

the most powerful. It is a profoundly human response to panic and catastrophe.
I thought Barack Obama could have provided some way out. But he lacks backbone.
(West, cited in Hedges, 2011)

In April 2009, during a meeting of the 5th Summit of the Americas in
Trinidad and Tobago, President Hugo Chávez of Venezuela, one of the great
world leaders and courageous defender of the poor and powerless, gifted
President Obama with a copy of *The Open Veins of Latin America*, a brilliant
book by Eduardo Galeano of Uruguay, who happens to be one of my favorite
writers. The book, which was banned during periods of military dictatorship in
Chile, Uruguay and Argentina, documents the plundering of Latin America
by Europe and the U.S.

The book given to Obama was in Spanish but an English translation has
been available from Monthly Review Press since 1971. Somebody needs to send
Obama the English translation. But even if he did decide to flip through it one
night, would his imagination be able to focus enough so that his eyes could see?

In *Cypherpunks: Freedom and the Future of the Internet*, Julian Assange
puts forward an unambiguous—and I dare say poetic—indictment of government and corporate surveillance, anti-file-sharing legislation and the social
media phenomenon that has seen users willingly collaborate with sites such as
Google, Facebook and Twitter, which aim to collect their personal data.
Assange famously describes the Internet as similar to "having a tank in your
bedroom," and writes that a mobile phone serves merely as a "tracking device
that also makes calls" (Assange et al., 2012, pp. 33, 49). Assange continues
with the ominous prediction that "the universality of the internet will merge
global humanity into one giant grid of mass surveillance and mass control"
(Assange et al., 2012, p. 6). Resistance must therefore include encrypting your
online activity, so that it will be possible to create an information network
which the state will not be able to decipher.

We are moving very quickly towards a transnational dystopia—in particular, a postmodern surveillance dystopia. Assange is clear about the violence
brewing just below the surface of the state. He notes:

> Most of the time we are not even aware of how close to violence we are, because we
> all grant concessions to avoid it. Like sailors smelling the breeze, we rarely contem-
> plate how our surface world is propped up from below by darkness. (Assange et al.,
> 2012, p. 3)

Assange juxtaposes the Platonic realm of the Internet with the fascist designs
of the state—designs given force by the seizure of the physical infrastructure

that makes the global Internet culture possible—fiber-optic cables, satellites and their ground stations, computer servers. We are no longer safe within Plato's cave. Everything produced inside the cave has been hijacked, stored in secret warehouses the size of small cities, creating a frightening imbalance of power between computer users and those who have the power to sort through and control the information generated in the networld. The only force that Assange sees capable of saving democracy is the creation of a "crypto-graphic veil" to hide the location of our cybernetic Platonic caves and to continue to use our knowledge to redefine the state.

You do not have to inhabit the dank bowels of a cybernetic Platonic cave to recognize the egregious war crimes committed by the U.S. government. When it was Bush ordering the invasion of Iraq, or Cheney profiting from the spoils of war through his company Halliburton (one of the biggest oil services companies in the world), it was easy to feel chilled as much by Bush's fraternity prankster face and Cheney's permasneer as by one of John Wayne Gacy's grinning clowns. When we think of war criminals, we think of people such as Vasili Blokhin, Cheka member and Stalin's favorite executioner, who once personally dispatched 250 captured Poles each night over 28 consecutive nights (for which he holds the Guinness World Record of "most prolific executioner"). We can only imagine how execution-style chic Blokhin looked, all decked out in his leather butcher's apron, his jaunty leather cap and shoulder-length leather gloves, which he wore during his "irreproachable service" for Stalin during the Yezhovshchina purge, even blowing out the base of Nikolai Yezhov's skull (Stalin's infamous apparatchik, for whom the terror was named) in the very execution chamber designed by Yezhov, with a sloping cement floor, drain and hose, and a log-lined wall. But the fact that there are more heinous killers in the rogue's gallery of political leaders than those leading us into 'humanitarian wars' should not cause us to downplay the seriousness of their crimes.

But what about Obama? Obama's soaring rhetoric is now his downfall, as his policies, both foreign and domestic, seem harvested from a manufacturing plant miles away from his own brainpan and light years away from his heart. A president who publicly laments gun violence but deifies "the troops" and relishes the lethal effectiveness of drone strikes offers us a contradiction so stark as to leave us speechless. Obama's words and convictions are about as far apart as the poles of a refrigerator magnet you purchased on your last visit to Martha's Vineyard, and the latest General Electric French Door Refrigerator your neighbor splurged on to make you envious.

Obama's defenders are correct to remind us of Obama's offering of Pell grants and stimulus money that made it possible for hundreds of thousands of black state and local workers to keep their jobs; they remind us, too, about Obama's role in the Fair Sentencing Act of 2010, which reduced the disparity of sentences for powdered and crack cocaine. They also point out the extension of the Earned Income Tax Credit, which kept poverty at bay for millions of working poor blacks, and the extension of unemployment insurance and food stamps, which helped keep millions of blacks from starving on the streets. Yes, Obama must be applauded for this. Yet even with these accomplishments, Obama can hardly be considered a leftist when it comes to public policy.

Critics of Cornel West, such as Michael Eric Dyson, who claim that Obama has a progressive or left position on public policy, are disingenuous. As Giroux (2015) points out:

> Tell that to the parents of the children killed by drones, to the whistle blowers put in prison, to people harassed by the surveillance state put in place under Obama, or to the endless number of immigrants exported and jailed under his administration. Maybe we should also include his tolerance for the crimes of bankers and torturers and his intolerance for the children and others who live close to or below the poverty line.

According to West:

> Obama used [Martin Luther] King's Bible during his inauguration, but under the National Defense Authorization Act King would be detained without due process. He would be under surveillance every day because of his association with Nelson Mandela, who was the head of a "terrorist" organization, the African National Congress. We see the richest prophetic tradition in America desecrated in the name of a neoliberal worldview, a worldview King would be in direct opposition to. Martin would be against Obama because of his neglect of the poor and the working class and because of the [aerial] drones, because he is a war president, because he draws up kill lists. And Martin King would have nothing to do with that. (Hedges, 2013)

Despite self-aggrandizing attacks on West by Michael Eric Dyson and others, I find myself in general agreement with West's assessment, partly because my own formation—*Bildung*—as an educator was through the African American prophetic tradition, which deeply impacted the civil rights movement, as well as through the Marxist-humanist movement pioneered by Raya Dunayevskaya.

Will there ever be any justice in this regard for all of those responsible for launching wars and attacks in the service of U.S. empire that have killed millions of people and contributed to ongoing geopolitical instability and violence that continue to this day? And by justice I do not mean being forced to watch endless reruns of Kira and the Muses performing on roller skates at Xanadu, but to be held to account for their crimes in an international court of justice. To be fair, I must applaud Obama's remarks when he says, "we are not at war with Islam. We are at war with people who have perverted Islam," and I support his criticism of those who attempt to link extremism to the Muslim faith. Obama showed similar courage and foresight to veto a bill recently that would have approved the Keystone XL pipeline. But what about the U.S. airstrikes in Afghanistan, Libya and Yemen? Are we supposed to forget those? Many Americans, including myself, wondered why Obama took so long to speak up after the events in Ferguson and the increasing police violence targeting African American communities.

If we can put aside for a moment the sentimental inducements that accompany discussions of 9/11 in the public square, there is another 9/11 that we also need to take into consideration: September 11, 1973, when Richard Nixon and Henry Kissinger helped to orchestrate a coup of Salvador Allende's government in Chile. Mark Weisbrot quotes Richard Nixon on why he wanted the Allende socialist government to be overthrown:

> President Richard Nixon was clear, at least in private conversations, about why he wanted the coup that destroyed one [of] the hemisphere's longest-running democracies, from his point of view: 'The main concern in Chile is that [President Salvador Allende] can consolidate himself, and the picture projected to the world will be his success .... If we let the potential leaders in South America think they can move like Chile and have it both ways, we will be in trouble.' (Weisbrot, 2013)

Nixon and Kissinger led the way in Chile for a rule of terror by coup leader Augusto Pinochet, to whom they gave the green light to assassinate Allende and strategic assistance from the U.S. military:

> The U.S. government was one of the main organisers and perpetrators of the September 11, 1973 military coup in Chile, and these perpetrators also changed the world—of course much for the worse. The coup snuffed out an experiment in Latin American social democracy, established a military dictatorship that killed, tortured, and disappeared tens of thousands of people, and for a quarter-century mostly prevented Latin Americans from improving their living standards and leadership through the ballot box. (Weisbrot, 2013)

The rule of terror in Chile, courtesy of the U.S. government, is nothing new. The Vietnam War is closer to home for most Americans. Listening to the transcripts of White House tape recordings between President Nixon and his advisors on April 25, 1972, and in May 1972, leads us to believe that the outcome could have been much worse for the North Vietnamese:

White House tape recordings, April 25, 1972:

President Nixon:	How many did we kill in Laos?
National Security Henry Kissinger:	In the Laotian thing, we killed about ten, fifteen [thousand] …
Nixon:	See, the attack in the North [Vietnam] that we have in mind … power plants, whatever's left – POL [petroleum], the docks … And, I still think we ought to take the dikes out now. Will that drown people?
Kissinger:	About two hundred thousand people.
Nixon:	No, no, no … I'd rather use the nuclear bomb. Have you got that, Henry?
Kissinger:	That, I think, would just be too much.
Nixon:	The nuclear bomb, does that bother you? … I just want you to think big, Henry, for Christsakes.

May 2, 1972:

Nixon:	America is not defeated. We must not lose in Vietnam. … The surgical operation theory is all right, but I want that place bombed to *smithereens*. If we draw the sword, we're gonna bomb those bastards all over the place. Let it fly, *let it fly*. (Blum 2014b)

Dr. Arnold A. Hutschnecker, Nixon's secret psychiatrist, thought Nixon was neurotic. Such sentiments betrayed by Nixon appear to exceed neurotic symptoms, revealing a terrifying glimpse of Nixon's apocalyptic unconscious, or perhaps we should say his "Apocalypse Now" unconscious.

Over many years in the field of education, I have advocated for a critical patriotism (McLaren, 2013) in my work in critical pedagogy, a pedagogy that would identify and condemn crimes against humanity perpetrated by the U.S., (as well as other countries) as a way of avoiding future tragedies. And as a means of countering the attitude of government advisors such as Michael Ledeen, former Defense Department consultant and holder of the Freedom Chair at the American Enterprise Institute, who opines sardonically: "Every ten years or so, the United States needs to pick up some small crappy little country and throw it against the wall, just to show the world we mean business" (Blum, 2014a).

In high school history classes, we do not hear much about the U.S. atrocities during the Philippine-American War (1899–1902), the coup in Chile or about Pinochet's feared Caribellos; or the assassinations of Catholic priests organizing cooperatives in the Guatemalan towns of Quetzaltenango,

Huehuetenango, San Marcos and Sololá; or the failed coup against the Venezuelan government of Hugo Chávez in 2002; or the role of the CIA in destabilizing Latin American and Middle Eastern regimes throughout the years; or the
history of the U.S. as the supreme master of focused and unidirectional aggression, whose intransigent martial will has made it the most feared country in
history. Nor do we learn about the Zapatista uprising which occurred as a result
of government oppression in the towns of the Selva, Altos, Norte and Costa
regions of Chiapas, and took place in San Cristóbal de las Casas, Las Mar-
garitas, Altamirano, Oxchuc, Huixtán, Chanal and Ocosingo, and involved
Tzotzils, Tzeltals, Tojolabals, Chols, Mams and Zoques.

What is of most concern in teacher-education programs is not the impact
that neoliberal capitalism has had on the way that the U.S. deals with questions of public and foreign policy, and the implications of this for developing a critical approach to citizenship. What occupies the curricula in teacher
education is the question of race and gender and sexual identity formations.
And while, in itself, this is an important emphasis, identity formation is rarely
problematized against the backdrop of social class and poverty, and the history of U.S. imperialism. I do not want to downplay the importance of the
struggles over race and class or gender or sexuality, and the history of the civil
rights struggle. But I believe that it is necessary to see such antagonisms both
in relationship to a geopolitics of knowledge and in terms of the ways in which
capitalism has reconstituted itself over the years.

When I introduce the topic of finance capitalism to my classes and stress
the importance of class struggle in my work with teachers, students prefer to
use the term "classism" or "socio-economic status," as if these terms were equivalent to racism and sexism and heterosexism, for instance. They see no reason
to examine the centrality of class in what they refer to as their "intersectional-
ity" grid. I have found a quotation by Joel Kovel that I hope will help readers
understand why class is a very special category. I will use this quotation in full:

> This discussion may help clarify a vexing issue on the left, namely, as to the priority
> of different categories of what might be called 'dominative splitting'—chiefly, those
> of gender, class, race, ethnic and national exclusion, and, with the ecological crisis,
> species. Here we must ask, priority in relation to what? If we intend, prior in time,
> then gender holds the laurel—and, considering how history always adds to the past
> rather than replacing it, would appear as at least a trace in all further dominations. If
> we intend prior in *existential* significance, then that would apply to whichever of the
> categories was put forward by immediate historical forces as these are lived by masses
> of people: thus to a Jew living in Germany in the 1930s, anti-semitism would have
> been searingly prior, just as anti-Arab racism would be to a Palestinian living under

Israeli domination today, or a ruthless, aggravated sexism would be to women living in, say, Afghanistan. As to which is *politically* prior, in the sense of being that which whose transformation is practically more urgent, that depends upon the preceding, but also upon the deployment of all the forces active in a concrete situation ....

If, however, we ask the question of efficacy, that is, which split sets the others into motion, then priority would have to be given to class, for the plain reason that class relations entail the state as an instrument of enforcement and control, and it is the state that shapes and organizes the splits that appear in human ecosystems. Thus class is both logically and historically distinct from other forms of exclusion (hence we should not talk of 'classism' to go along with 'sexism' and 'racism,' and 'species-ism'). This is, first of all, because class is an essentially man-made category, without root in even a mystified biology. We cannot, in other words, imagine a human world without gender distinctions—although we can imagine a world without domination by gender. But a world without class is eminently imaginable—indeed, such was the human world for the great majority of our species' time on earth, during all of which considerable fuss was made over gender. Historically, the difference arises because 'class' signifies one side of a larger figure that includes a state apparatus whose conquests and regulations create races and shape gender relations. Thus there will be no true resolution of racism so long as class society stands, inasmuch as a racially oppressed society implies the activities of a class-defending state. Nor can gender inequality be legislated away so long as class society, with its state, demands the super-exploitation of woman's labor.

Class society continually generates gender, racial, ethnic oppressions, and the like, which take on a life of their own, as well as profoundly affecting the concrete relations of class itself. It follows that class politics must be fought out in terms of all the active forms of social splitting. It is the management of these divisions that keeps state society functional. Thus though each person in a class society is reduced from what s/he can become, the varied reductions can be combined into the great stratified regimes of history—this one becoming a fierce warrior, that one a routine-loving clerk, another a submissive seamstress, and so on, until we reach today's personifications of capital and captains of industry. Yet no matter how functional a class society, the profundity of its ecological violence ensures a basic antagonism which drives history onward. History *is* the history of class society—because no matter how modified, so powerful a schism is bound to work itself through to the surface, provoke resistance (i.e. 'class struggle'), and lead to the succession of powers. (Kovel, 2002, pp. 123–124)

While class retains a strategic priority, we need to understand that race cannot be reduced to class. But just as postmodern theory has ignored the strategic centrality of race in its discussions of racism, too often Marxists have ignored the intersection of race and class, relegating race as a minor trope within the larger framework of capitalist exploitation (Hudis, 2014b).

Since we are working within the Hegelian-Marxist tradition, attempting to re-create the revolutionary dialectic by engaging the realities and social antagonisms of the present, we feel it is necessary here to emphasize the important work of Frantz Fanon. In doing so, we recognize that it is important to stretch Marx when it comes to addressing the issues of race and colonialism within the larger social relations of transnational capitalism. We believe that Fanon's work can help to inform a Marxist analysis of race by recognizing it as a profound moment of dialectical philosophy. Here we summarize some recent insights of Peter Hudis (2014b), who comments on the importance of building a viable Hegelian-Marxism for the twenty-first century by building upon Fanon's insights on racial domination, internalized oppression and the impact of racial and ethnic pride in achieving disalienation.

I don't have space here to rehearse Hegel's famous master/slave dialectic except to paraphrase Hudis's perceptive reading of it. For Hegel, it was about how consciousness first posits the object as absolute, followed by a phase of self-consciousness when the subject posits itself as absolute wherein objects now become objects for oneself, having lost their claim to independence. In trying to overcome the otherness of the external world, self-consciousness desires unity, and this otherness of the external world is seen as an obstacle that can only be overcome by positing self-consciousness itself as absolute.

Desire aims to conquer the otherness of the external world—or the "other"—but as soon as one object is negated, it is followed by another that needs to be negated and so on. When desire learns that it cannot consume the other and thus satisfy itself, it therefore seeks to satisfy itself in another self-consciousness. Thus, it seeks recognition from the other, at first a one-sided recognition *from* the other without a recognition *of* the other. This goes well beyond a liberal plea to be acknowledged as a living being. Hudis (2014b) puts it thusly: "Hegel makes it clear that what each desires from the other is recognition of the *dignity and worth* of its being." In other words, both self and other want to be recognized as absolute. The other cannot be killed in this situation since there will be no one to recognize the self as absolute. So the other is made a slave. Hudis writes:

> The master demands recognition from the slave, but since the master sees the slave as a non-essential being he feels no need to recognize him. The master is dominant, active and independent while the slave is submissive, passive and dependent. However, fear makes us aware of ourselves as sentient beings; by fearing the master the slave gets to know himself as an independent, essential being. Moreover, in his work the slave becomes truly conscious of his essentiality, since the master can't survive without him. The master tries to prove his *independence* by consuming products made by the slave, yet this only confirms his *dependence* upon him. The slave thereby discovers his being for self, in that he develops an independent consciousness—*a mind*

of his own—whereas the master turns out to be a dependent and miserable entity, lacking any such self-certainty. (Hudis, 2014)

Hudis (2014) wants us to recognize two main points in the master/slave dialectic found in Hegel's *Phenomenology*:

> 1) Each phase immanently posits the absolute, even though each phase ultimately turns out to be defective. If the subject did not posit itself as absolute it could not endure the battle for recognition. 2) While the slave achieves a "mind of his own" in the battle for recognition, the effort to achieve recognition turns out to be unsuccessful. The master is not overthrown at the end of the master/slave dialectic, nor does the master fully recognize the mind attained by the slave. *The struggle for recognition is still unresolved.* Reciprocal recognition is not reached until much later in the *Phenomenology*—in the chapter on Morality, which discusses the Christian conception of confession and forgiveness.

When Fanon (2004) discusses the dialectic of Self-Consciousness in *Black Skin, White Masks* (in the five-page section on "The Black Man and Hegel"), Fanon recognizes that when this master/slave dialectic is viewed in terms of race, it becomes impossible to accept Hegel's argument. Fanon recognizes "that the historic context of Hegel's master/slave dialectic—more correctly translated as 'lordship and bondage'—is the ancient and medieval world, in which slavery was *not* based on race" (Hudis, 2014b).

Hegel cannot help us to comprehend the lived experience of black people because when you add the context of race to the master/slave relation, Fanon reveals that the master is not interested in receiving recognition from the slave. In fact, the master denies the very humanity of the slave. Fanon argues that the master wants not recognition from the slave but labor. But since no amount of labor can confirm the essentiality of the slave's being for the master, the black slave remains less independent than the Hegelian slave. Fanon concludes that the black slave is less likely to attain the independent consciousness of the Hegelian slave and thus seeks to mimic the master by trying to become white. This is what Fanon means by the term "white masks." Fanon argues that the black slave interiorizes oppression and seeks acceptance by trying to become like the master. It is important to note, according to Hudis, that the Hegelian slave did not actually achieve an independent mind of his own since he becomes aware of the gap between his subjectivity and the objective world, and this mutual recognition requires, according to Hegel, reaching Absolute knowledge itself. Both Hegel and Fanon recognize that the struggle for recognition is not resolved from the provisional slave of the master/slave dialectic. So how does the black subject manage to overcome an independent mind and discover the road to self-certainty?

Since racism so debases the human personality as to render mutual recognition between white people and black people impossible, the black subject, according to Fanon, can only inhabit "a zone of non-being," an unbearable insularity. Since blackness is a construction of white racism,

> there is no pre-existing essence for the black to marshal on its behalf in resisting the racist gaze of the other. *Nothingness therefore resists in the very heart of its being.* This is the basis of the inferiority complex and the effort by the victim of racism to affirm itself by desperately trying to appear to be like the other. (Hudis, 2014b)

Fanon's answer was to make himself known, by shouting forth his blackness. Yet even potential allies such as Sartre considered black consciousness and pride as a minor term. Hudis notes that race is the particular and class (in particular, proletarian class struggle) is the universal for Sartre. Sartre here is closer to Hegel than to Fanon. Fanon was sharply critical of Sartre's position, recognizing that "this born Hegelian, had forgotten that consciousness needs to get lost in the night of the absolute, the only condition for attaining self-consciousness" (Fanon, 2004, p. 112). Sartre had forgotten that the absolute is immanent in each phase of the battle for recognition and that the subject must posit its own subjectivity as an absolute. Otherwise, what you are left with, according to Hudis, is an abstract revolutionism—an empty, disembodied absolute.

Fanon was well aware of this. The black subject can only lose himself in the particular—in shouting forth her blackness—on the long road to the universal. Fanon notes that "this negativity [of the black subject] draws its value from a virtually substantial absoluity" (cited in Hudis, 2014b, p. 113).

You cannot skip over the particular in reaching the absolute and, as Hudis rightly notes, only a struggle that leads to a new humanism is one that can help us disalienate ourselves from the ever-growing tendrils of capitalism. This requires absolute negativity, an open-ended dialectic that rejects a closed ontology, and that can be put in the service of emancipatory ends, in this case, the struggle against racism, sexism, patriarchy, colonialism and capitalist exploitation. Absolute negativity rejects the old and can become the basis of a new positivity, a new movement forward towards human freedom by continually negating the conditions of unfreedom.

We need to develop a coherent philosophy of praxis based on a dialectics of transformation. Such a dialectics is grounded in absolute negation in the Marxist-Hegelian tradition of Marxist-humanism developed by Raya Dunayevskaya, Kevin Anderson, and Peter Hudis. Readers who might object to Marx's critical appropriation of Hegel's double negation as yet another example of western logic hostile to non-European societies, might want to read 10th century Islamic philosopher Abu Ya'qub al–Sijistani, a major scholar within Isma'ili Islam, who participated in the development of negative, dialectical thinking, which synthesized Neo-Platonism with Isma'ili Shiite theology (see Hudis, 2004).

While revolutionary critical pedagogy has made unwanted inroads into some tributaries of mainstream educational studies, it largely remains underappreciated, not so much for the pamphleteering exuberance that marks its tone, but for the fact that it has not been able to make successful inroads into public education. Yet such a failure is not due to the fact that critical pedagogy has chosen to remain in the stance of the "outsider," as an outlaw outlier who refuses to collaborate with those adjacent conceptual and pedagogical systems that are its most eligible neighbors in the social sciences and humanities, but rather because it cannot exist *in situ* within the public education system and still remain true to its principles. This is because it is fundamentally a pedagogy of class struggle, carried out through multiple modalities—anti-racism, anti-sexism, anti-homophobic education, critical disability studies. And the fact that each instantiation of critical pedagogy is traversed by the personal predilections of its exponents has given it an eclectic rather than a systematic feel. In its current phase of theoretical gestation, there is a lack of univocal, reliable terminology. For now, it remains a pedagogy of hope, which does not mean that it must remain at a fierce remove from the everyday struggle for school reform. Critical pedagogy is still in its early birth pangs. As it grows stronger, the more its deficiencies are named. This only demonstrates that it is destined for longevity, and that such longevity is not fated to dissipate its native strength.

We do more than embrace the *geist* of solidarity; we work in the spirit of comunalidad for a world-historical attainment in the pursuit of truth and justice. A commitment to truth is never unproductive because no transformative act can be accomplished without commitment. No true act of commitment is an exit from the truth, but tramps down a path along which truth is won (Fischman & McLaren, 2005). I do not want to use my political imagination to create something new out of the debris of the old, because that leads us to adapt our revolutionary work to that which already exists. My concern is to struggle to change the conditions of what already exists so as to provide human agents with conditions of possibility for deepening their critical reflexivity in order to create what was thought to be impossible.

Acknowledging fully the asymmetrical relations of power encapsulated in the uneven and combined development pervading the global South in relationship to the global North—a relation of extreme violence so necessary for us, as Western consumers, to enjoy our relatively middle-class lifestyles—we nevertheless struggle for something that is akin to Agamben's "non-state" or humanity, through a Gramscian attempt at a war of position, a Freirean praxis of conscientization or the permanent revolution found in Raya Dunayevskaya's philosophy of praxis grounded in "absolute negativity," and through an ecological general strike of which the environmental caucus of the Industrial Workers of the World now speaks.

We look at the potential of the communal councils of the Bolivarian Revolution, which serve as public pedagogical sites for socialism and endogenous development and to what Michael Lebowitz (2013) describes as "a vehicle for changing both circumstances and the protagonists themselves," and deepening the struggle for socialism for the twenty-first century. Such a struggle is founded on revolutionary practice, famously described by Lebowitz (2013) as "the simultaneous changing of circumstances and self-change." The new socialist society stresses that the control of production is vested in the producing individuals themselves. Productive relations are social as a result of conscious choice and not after the fact. They are social because, as Lebowitz (2013) perceptively notes, as a people we deliberately choose to produce for people who need what we can produce.

I do not want to diabolize reformists in the name of revolutionary socialism or any other ultra leftist position or give oxygen to any crude sectarianism, for that would be akin to echoing the sentiments of Martin Luther, who argued that, for the man who does not believe in Christ, not only are all sins mortal, but even his good works are sins.

A New Epistemological Alternative

To look mainly to the European social tradition for guidance in the belief that the struggle for a socialist alternative to capitalism is the monopoly of the West would be to succumb to the most crude provinciality and a truncated ethnocentrism. Thomas Fatheuer (2011) has examined recent innovative aspects in the constitutions of Ecuador and Bolivia. In Ecuador, for instance, the right to a "good life"—*buen vivir*—becomes a central objective, a bread-and-butter concern that cannot be relinquished. One of the subsections of the constitution deals with the rights to nutrition, health, education and water, for example. The concept of the good life here is more than economic, social and cultural rights. It is a basic principle that "forms the foundation of a new development model (*régimen de desarrollo*)" (Fatheuer, 2011, p. 16). Article 275 states: "*Buen Vivir* requires that individuals, communities, peoples and nations are in actual possession of their rights and exercise their responsibilities in the context of interculturalism, respect for diversity and of harmonious coexistence with nature" (cited in Fatheuer, 2011, p. 16). Fatheuer distinguishes the concept of *buen vivir* from the Western idea of prosperity as follows:

> *Buen Vivir* is not geared toward 'having more' and does not see accumulation and growth, but rather a state of equilibrium as its goal. Its reference to the indigenous world view is also central: its starting point is not progress or growth as a linear model of thinking, but the attainment and reproduction of the equilibrium state of *Sumak Kausay*. (Fatheuer, 2011, p. 16)

Both Bolivia and Ecuador have utilized their constitutions to re-establish their states in a post colonial context and are committed to the concept of plurinationalism and the preservation of nature. Here, the state promotes the ethical and moral principles of pluralistic society:

> *amaqhilla, ama llulla, ama suwa* (do not be lazy, do not lie, do not steal), *suma qamaña* (*vive bien*), *ñandereko* (*vida armoniosa*—harmonious life), *teko kavi* (*vida buena*), *ivi maraei* (*tierra sin mal*—Earth without evil, also translated as 'intact environment'), and *qhapaj ñan* (*Camino o vida noble*—the path of wisdom). (Fatheuer, 2011, pp. 17–18)

The concept of *Pachamama* (Mother Earth) and the rights of nature play a special role, designed to put human beings and nature on a foundation of originality, mutuality and dialogue, and the Defensoría de la Madre Tierra statute is designed to "monitor the validity, promotion, dissemination and implementation of the rights of *Madre Tierra*," and forbid the marketing of Mother Earth (Fatheuer, 2011, p. 18). Here it is stipulated that the earth has a right to regenerate itself. It is important to point out that *buen vivir* is not a return to ancestral, traditional thinking, but is a type of *ch'ixi*, or a concept in which something can exist and not exist at the same time—in other words, a third state in which modernity is not conceived as homogeneous, but as *cuidadania*, or "difference": a biocentric world view that permits the simultaneous existence of contradictory states without the need for resolution towards a given pole, and that conceives of life in a way which is not informed by the opposition of nature and humans (Fatheuer, 2011).

New indigenous discourses in Bolivia and those articulated by the Con-federation of Indigenous Nationalities of Ecuador advocate for an integral philosophy and a new plurinational, communitarian, collective, egalitarian, multilingual, intercultural and bio-socialist vision of sustainable develop-ment. They fight against a capitalism that militates against harmony inside and between society and nature (Altmann, 2013). Interculturality is seen as a relational and a structural transformation and an instrument of decolonization. It is something that must be created and it refers not only to groups but also to structures based on respect, cultural heterogeneity, participative self-represen-tation, communitarian forms of authority, mutual legitimacy, equity, symmetry and equality; furthermore, it is applicable to monoethnic and multiethnic ter-ritories. Here, interculturality in combination with plurinationality is linked to a postcolonial re-foundation of the modern state (Altmann, 2012). This is something that present-day critical multiculturalists would do well to ponder.

John P. Clark (2013), in his magnificent work, *The Impossible Commu-nity*, has offered an array of possible approaches to take from the perspective of communitarian anarchism. These include a revised version of the liber-tarian municipalism of the late Murray Bookchin, the Gandhian Sarvodaya movement in India, and the related movement in Sri Lanka called Sarvodaya Shramadana—the Gandhian approach to self-rule and voluntary redistri-bution of land as collective property to be managed by means of the *gram sabha* (village assembly) and the *panchayat* (village committee). Sarvodaya Shramadana offers four basic virtues: *upekkha* (mental balance), *metta* (good-will towards all beings), *karma* (compassion for all beings who suffer) and *mundita* (sympathetic joy for all those liberated from suffering). Clark's work focuses on the tragedies and contradictions of development and his discus-sion of India is particularly insightful (see especially pp. 217–245 and the elo-quently informative review of Clark's book by Sethness, 2013). More familiar to teachers are perhaps the examples of the Zapatistas and the Landless Peasants' Movement in Brazil. Clark mentions, as well, the indigenous Adi-vasi struggles and those by Dalits, fighting the paramilitaries of the transna-tional mining communities in India.

Instead of reducing citizens and non-citizens alike to their racialized and gendered labor productivity, as is the case with the neoliberal state apparatus, we wish to introduce the term *buen vivir* as an opposing logic to the way we approach our formation as citizen-subjects. We would advise the guardians of the neoliberal state—especially those who are now in the "business" of education—to look towards *Las Américas* for new conceptions of democratic life that could serve as a means of breaking free from the disabling logic of neoliberalism that now engulfs the planet—a new epistemology of living that has so far not been a casualty of the epistemicide of the conquistadores, past and present.

We still adhere to the proposition that the human mind lives in a largely self-created world of illusion and error, a defective system of false reality from whence we can be rescued only by the development of a critical self-reflexive subjectivity and protagonistic agency. But we would add that such self-creation occurs under conditions not of our own making. Many of those conditions have been created by social relations of production and the way in which neoliberal capitalism has produced nature/human relations as a total world ecology linked to a racialized social division of labor and hyper-nationalism.

Critical consciousness here becomes the inverse equivalent of the ignorance of our false consciousness under capitalist social relations of exploitation and alienation. Hence, we seek a social universe outside of the commodification of human labor, a universe deepened by direct and participatory democracy and a quest for *buen vivir*.

Samir Amin pitches the challenges thusly:

> Whatever you like to call it, historical capitalism is anything but sustainable. It is only a brief parenthesis in history. Challenging it fundamentally—which our contemporary thinkers cannot imagine is 'possible' or even 'desirable'—is however the essential condition for the emancipation of dominated workers and peoples (those of the periphery, 80 percent of humanity). And the two dimensions of the challenge are indissoluble. It is not possible to put an end to capitalism unless and until these two dimensions of the same challenge are taken up together. It is not 'certain' that this will happen, in which case capitalism will be 'overtaken' by the destruction of civilization (beyond the discontents of civilization, to use Freud's phrase) and perhaps of all life on this earth. The scenario of a possible 'remake' of the 20th century thus remains but falls far short of the need of humanity embarking on the long transition towards world socialism. The liberal disaster makes it necessary to renew a radical critique of capitalism. The challenge is how to construct, or reconstruct, the internationalism of workers and peoples confronted by the cosmopolitism of oligarchic capital. (Amin, 2010)

Clearly, while we need a new epistemology of *buen vivir* and of Sarvodaya Shramadana to help stave off the epistemicide of indigenous knowledges by means of violent Eurocentric practices, we also need a class struggle of transnational reach.

The learning curve of our politicized youth appears mercifully short, a condition created by necessity more than choice. Few of them doubt the seriousness of the situation that we are facing as inhabitants of our planet.

They know too much already, and the question remains as to whether they will use their knowledge to join the fight for socialism, in which they risk life and limb, or decide to give in to the distractions of our electronically wired world of infotainment. As I have written elsewhere:

> Global warming and nature–society relations, imperialism, racism, speciesism, sexism, homophobia, genocide and epistemicide are not independent of the capitalist accumulation process, but mutually inform one another. The youth of today comprehend these myths for what they are—diversions designed to enfeeble the struggle for social justice—and they will never have the same force that they once had. During an unprecedented time when capital permeates lines of demarcation and casts its oppressive force through institutions such as the World Bank, the International Monetary Fund, the World Trade Organisation and the U.S. empire, the young activists of today recognise that they cannot pluck wholeness out of the atomised continent of capitalist culture. They must start anew. The genie of transnational contestation and revolt is now out of the lamp, has identified as an ecological proletariat, and has the potential to alter the course of human history—a history that begins with the overthrow of capitalist regimes of accumulation. Although there is no guarantee that from the conflagration that is capital today socialism will find its redeeming application, there is a fervent willingness among our youth to explore new terrains of contestation and struggle. In the midst of increased surveillance, heightened policing, stop-and-frisk policies on the streets, overbroad gang injunctions, and spiraling rates of juvenile incarceration we see determined efforts by youth who are participating in the US Civil Rights Movement, the transnational lesbian, gay, bisexual, transgender and queer (LGBTQ) movement, in various incarnations of feminist struggle, environmentalism and environmental justice movements, and in the labor, antiwar and immigrant rights movements; we also see these determined efforts in struggles among youth movements worldwide, who are bearing witness to and participating in the production of various countersummits, Zapatista Encuentros; social practices that produce use values beyond economic calculation and the competitive relation with the other, and are inspired by practices of social and mutual solidarity, by horizontally-linked clusters outside vertical networks in which the market is protected and enforced; by social cooperation through grassroots democracy, consensus, dialogue and the recognition of the other; by authority and social cooperation developed in fluid relations and self-constituted through interaction; and by a new engagement with the other that transcends locality, job, social condition, gender, age, race, culture, sexual orientation, language, religion and beliefs. In short, they support a global comunalidad. (McLaren, 2014, p. 159)

The current generation faces a formidable and intimidating challenge of civic and social responsibility, and we cannot expect the young men and women who have inherited the chains forged by the centuries-old dogma of the capitalist class to struggle alone. We need to stand with them, on the picket lines, in the classrooms, the shopping malls, the pubs, the churches—wherever they gather to discuss their future and to struggle to liberate themselves from all that capitalism produces to negate their possible futures. If we offer today's youth hope at the expense of truth then we enter the bad infinity of political hubris and the swindle of prosperity. If the planet dies, who will be left to look for jobs? Optimism can be fatal if it is not accompanied by hope. And hope cannot follow the same well-worn pathways to nowhere, since human agency is always borne out in dwelling places of possibility despite the grim reality that the odds are not in our favor, and perhaps never will be.

As we recognize consciousness and external reality as mutually constitutive, and assert that there must be an ethical dimension which gives priority to the oppressed, we become midwives to the dialectics of reform and revolution. They no longer become an "either-or" relationship but instead a "both-and" relationship. Dialectics does not juxtapose reform and revolution, but mediates them.

Given the post-humanities attack on dialectics by Antonio Negri and others, it might seem antiquated to look to dialectics as a means of creating what Fischman and McLaren (2005) have called the "committed intellectual" as part of the larger development of a philosophy of praxis. However, critics such as Antonio Negri have abandoned dialectics in favor of substituting singular, unresolvable and non-dialectical "antagonisms" for dialectical "contradictions." Asserting that dialectics imposes internal balances in capitalist society, serving as a mechanism for both establishing and maintaining equilibrium, such critics reject the primacy of the forces of production and the shaping of the social relations of production in accordance to its needs (i.e., the correspondence between the forces and relations of production).

As Teresa Ebert (2009) and Ebert and Mas'ud Zavarzadeh (2007) have illustrated, Negri believes that the trans-historical power of the subjectivity of the living labor of the multitude gives labor autonomy from capital through acts of self-valorization and affirmation of singularities. He therefore replaces the proletariat as the agent of class struggle with the multitude, while insisting that capital is merely reactive to the self-valorization of the workers, that labor is in effect a subjective power, and that value is not about economic relations but about power relations. It is easy to see how, under Negri's unfocused eye, class struggle evaporates into a series of unresolvable paradoxes in a world reduced to unknowable, and basically unreadable, linguistic self-referentiality.

The problem with Negri and the other anti-dialecticians is that they reject all forms of transcendence in favor of remaining on the plane of immanence, taking the given social reality as a point of departure (Anderson, 2010). How-ever, Anderson rightly notes that we do not have to choose between imma-nence and transcendence:

> But we do not have to choose between such one-sided alternatives. Consider Hegel's standpoint, as summed up by Theodor Adorno of the Frankfurt School: 'To insist on the choice between immanence and transcendence is to revert to the traditional logic criticized in Hegel's polemic against Kant' (Adorno, Prisms, p. 31). In fact, Hardt and Negri regularly attack Hegel and the Enlightenment philosophers as conservative and authoritarian, while extolling pre-Enlightenment republican traditions rooted in Machiavelli and Spinoza. What they thereby cut themselves off from is the dialectical notion that a liberated future can emerge from within the present, if the various forces and tendencies that oppose the system can link up in turn with an [sic] theory of liber-ation that sketches out philosophically that emancipatory future for which they yearn.
>
> Marx certainly overcame the pre-Hegelian split between immanence and transcen-dence. The working class did not exist before capitalism and was a product of the new capitalist order, and was therefore immanent or internal to capitalism. At the same time, however, the alienated and exploited working class fought against capital, not only for a bigger piece of the pie, but also engaged in a struggle to overcome capital-ism itself, and was in this sense a force for transcendence (the future in the present). (Anderson, 2010)

Even the illustrious Marcuse in his Great Refusal (his analysis of the preda-tory capitalist system and neoconservatism or what he referred to as "counter-revolution") displaces the dialectical quality of classical Hegelian and Marxist philosophy, betraying an incapacity to overcome contradiction in his lurch-ing towards a metaphysical or antinomial (neo-Kantian) posture in which he vacillates between two poles of a contradiction, poles of which he regards as antiseptically independent rather than interpenetrating; at times he seemed tragically resigned to the perennial permanence of contradiction and paradox (Reitz, 2000).

Here we can benefit from Marx's focus on Hegel's concept of self-move-ment through second negativity, which leads him to posit a vision of a new society that involves the transcendence of value production as determined by socially necessary labor time. Unlike the popular misconception about Marx's critique of Hegel—that Hegel's idealism was opposed to Marx's materialism—Marx did not criticize Hegel for his failure to deal with material reality. When Marx noted that Hegel knows only abstractly spiritual labor, he was referring to the structure of Hegel's *Phenomenology* and philosophy as a whole, which was based on a dialectic of self-consciousness, in which thought returns to itself by knowing itself (Hudis, 2012). Marx's concept of transcendence, on the contrary, was grounded in human sensuousness, in the self-transcendence of the totality of human powers. Dialectics deals with the transformative contradictions that power the material historicity of capitalist life.

Hegel presented the entire movement of history in terms of the unfolding of the disembodied idea; in other words, he presented human actuality as a product of thought instead of presenting thought as the product of human actuality. Marx, therefore, inverts the relations of Hegel's subject and predicate. Marx criticized Hegel for failing to distinguish between labor as a trans-historical, creative expression of humanity's "species being" and labor as the reduction of such activity to value production. We need to understand the dialectic, the description of the means by which reality unfolds, the nature of self-activity, self-development and self-transcendence, and the way that human activity subjectively and temporally mediates the objective world.

The presence of the idea—as negation—in human consciousness has the power to alter the natural world. Marx was not interested in the returning of thought to itself in Hegel's philosophy, but the return of humanity to itself by overcoming the alienation of the objective world brought about by capitalist social relations. In other words, the human being is the agent of the Idea; the Idea is not its own agent. The human being is the medium of the Idea's self-movement. Self-movement is made possible through the act of negation by negating the barriers to self-development.

But negation, as Peter Hudis (2012, pp. 72–73) tells us, is always dependent on the object of its critique. Whatever you negate still bears the stamp of what has been negated—that is, it still bears the imprint of the object of negation. We have seen, for instance, in the past, that oppressive forms which one has attempted to negate still impact the ideas we have of liberation. That is why Hegel argued that we need a self-referential negation—a negation of the negation. By means of a negation of the negation, negation establishes a relation with itself, freeing itself from the external object it is attempting to negate. Because it exists without a relationship to another outside of itself, it is considered to be absolute—it is freed from dependency on the other. It negates its dependency through a self-referential act of negation.

For example, the abolition of private property and its replacement with collective property does not ensure liberation; it is only an abstract negation which must be negated in order to reach liberation. It is still infected with its opposite, which focuses exclusively on property. It simply replaces private property with collective property and is still impacted by the idea of owner-ship or having (Hudis, 2012, pp. 71–73). Hudis writes:

> [Marx] appropriates the concept of the 'negation of the negation' to explain the path to a new society. Communism, the abolition of private property, is the negation of capitalism. But this negation, Marx tells us, is dependent on the object of its critique insofar as it replaces private property with collective property. Communism is not free from the alienated notion that ownership or *having* is the most important part of being human; it simply affirms it on a different level. Of course, Marx thinks that it is nec-essary to negate private property. But this negation, he insists, must itself be negated. Only then can the *truly positive*—a totally new society—emerge. As Dunayevskaya writes in *P&R* [Philosophy and Revolution], 'The overcoming of this 'transcendence,' called absolute negativity by Hegel, is what Marx considered the only way to create a truly human world, '*positive* Humanism, beginning from itself.' (Hudis, 2005)

However, in order to abolish capital, the negation of private property must itself be negated, which would be the achievement of a positivity—a posi-tive humanism—beginning with itself. While it is necessary to negate private property, that negation must itself be negated. If you stop before this second negation then you are presupposing that having is more important than being (Hudis, 2012).

Saying "no" to capital, for instance, constitutes a first negation (Pomeroy, 2004b). When the subject becomes self-conscious regarding this negation—that is, when the subject understanding the meaning of this negation recognizes the positive content of this negation—then she has arrived at the negation of the negation (Pomeroy, 2004b). In other words, when a subject comes to rec-ognize that she is the source of the negative, this becomes a second negation, a reaching of class consciousness. When a subject recognizes the positivity of the act of negation itself as negativity, then she knows herself as a source of the movement of the real (Pomeroy, 2004b). This occurs when human beings, as agents of self-determination, hear themselves speak, and are able both to denounce oppression and the evils of the world and to announce, in Freire's terms, a liberating alternative.

I fully agree with Reitz (2000, p. 263) that critical knowledge "is knowl-edge that enables the social negation of the social negation of human life's core activities, the most central of which are neither being-toward-death [as Heidegger would maintain], nor subservience [as Kant would argue], but cre-ative labor." When subjects create critical knowledge, they then are able to appropriate freedom itself for the sake of the liberation of humanity (Pomeroy, 2004b).

Searching for an alternative to capitalism means mining the dynamic potentiality that is latent, but unrealized, in everyday life and, in this regard, it is redolent of a spiritual quest in the manner suggested by Robert M. Torrance (1994). It requires a deliberate and urgent effort by teachers and teacher educators to transcend, through self-transformation, the limits of everyday reality and the human condition under capitalism, and a willingness to marshal this unbounded potentiality in the direction of social justice. It means realizing the enlarging and transformative potential of the given through a pursuit of the liberation of our collective humanity, a humanity that transcends the individual self not by seeking refuge in an immutable past or inertial present, but by advancing from subjective knowledge to the independently and objectively real that is always oriented to the determinable, living future—a knowledge that is the product of the human mind yet transcends the mind; a knowledge gleaned from the particular through its relationship to the universal; a knowledge that can never be fully apprehended; a knowledge engendered by the seeker yet at the same time transcending the seeker.

We must open our lexicon of critique and transformation to a changing world. As Marx pointed out, any viable exercise of protagonistic agency among the oppressed requires the dialectical self-negation of the working class as a class in itself into a class for itself, a class in which it is imperative to become self-conscious of how its membership is embedded in relations of exploitation and how they have become alienated from their own "species being," or their own life activity. Of course, the overall purpose of this critical transformation is to become emancipated from labor's value form.

We cannot know what the alternative to capitalist value production will look like until the struggle moves forward and we are able to claim some decisive victories. Only then can we know how we will proceed in forging a new alternative to capitalist commodity production. What is clear is that we must dissemble the self-referential closure of the capitalist trance state in which we find ourselves hopelessly enthralled. Through our passive exposure to electronic media, we willfully submit ourselves to the rituals of everyday capitalist commodity production, to their formulaic and habituated repetitiveness and invariance, to their inert sufferance and wearisome recurrence of stasis—all of which ineluctably and fatally disciplines us to assent uncritically to our own acedia and torpor. The only way out of this impasse is to seek an alternative social universe to that of value production.

This involves an unrelenting pursuit of justice, despite the fact that the goal can never be fully foreknown or finally attained. Workers who toil away at the loom of history are weaving a red tablecloth from all the strands of liberation struggles for the victory banquet of socialism. There is room for all at the table of restoration, a creative site of possibility, where we can contemplate our existence in the present and the not yet, where we can set freedom in motion but not fully realize it, where we can move towards redemption but not quite achieve resolution, where art can bring forth subconscious truth, where we can reconcile ourselves with others and where we can embrace our brother and sister trade unionists, civil libertarians, anarchists, small peasant proprietors, revolutionary intellectuals, cognitariats, precariats, agricultural workers, students, anti-war activists, Marxists, black and Latino activists, teachers, eco-socialists, fast-food workers, factory workers and animal rights activists and all the while try to love our enemies. We seek to replace instrumental reason with critical rationality, fostering popular dissent and creating workers' and communal councils and community decision-making structures.

We continue to struggle in our educational projects to eliminate rent-seeking and for-profit financial industries; we seek to distribute incomes without reference to individual productivity, but rather according to need; and we seek to substantially reduce hours of labor and make possible, through socialist general education, a well-rounded and scientific and intercultural development of the young (Reitz, 2013). This involves a larger epistemological fight against neoliberal and imperial common sense, and a grounding of our critical pedagogy in a concrete universal that can welcome diverse and particular social formations (San Juan, 2007) joined in class struggle. It is a struggle that has come down to us not from the distant past, but from thoughts that have ricocheted back to us from the future.

As I mentioned recently in an interview with a Canadian sociology journal, life does not unfold as some old sheet strewn across a brass bed in the dusky attic of history; our destinies as children, parents and teachers do not flow unilaterally towards a single vertigo-inducing epiphany, some pyrotechnic explosion of iridescent and refulgent splendor where afterwards we lay becalmed, rocking on a silent sea of pure bliss, or where we are held speechless in some wind-washed grove of cedars, happily in the thrall of an unbridled, unsullied and undiluted love of incandescent intensity.

Our lives are not overseen by a handsome God who blithely sits atop a terracotta pedestal and with guileless simplicity, quiet paternalism and unsmiling earnestness rules over his eager and fumbling brood, every so often rumpling the curly heads of the rosy-cheeked cherubim and engaging the saints in bliss-ful conversation about quantum theory. Were there such a God, wrapped in the mantle of an other-worldly Platonism and possessing neither moral obliq-uity nor guilt, who brings forth the world through supernatural volition alone, the world would be nothing but a teleported echo of the divine mind. Hunger could be ended by merely thinking of a full belly and sickness eliminated by a picture of perfect health.

Most of us, however, sling ourselves nervously back and forth across the great Manichean divide of the drab of everyday existence, where, in our ele-mental contact with the world, our human desires, for better or for worse, tug at us like some glow-in-the-dark hustler in a carnival midway. We go hungry, we suffer and we live in torment and witness most of the world's population crumpled up in pain. We don't have to witness a final miracle of eschatologi-cal significance to reclaim the world. What we do have to accomplish at this very moment is organizing our world to meet the basic needs of humanity.

Christian Communism Reborn?

But the same message of meeting the needs of humanity was prevalent in the Bible, and occupied the message of Jesus. I do not suddenly mention this out of some otherworldly penchant, but for a concern for the here and the now. The majority of American citizens are Christians of some denomination or other, and it is important to point out as an incontrovertible fact that the message of Jesus in the Gospels is focused on the liberation of the poor from captivity and oppression, thus in Luke 4:18–19: "The Spirit of the Lord is upon me, because he has anointed me to preach good news to the poor. He has sent me to proclaim release to the captives and recovering of sight to the blind, to set at liberty those who are oppressed, to proclaim the acceptable year of the Lord."

Jesus was very much opposed to oppression and bondage, and it was no secret that he excluded the wealthy from the kingdom of God, noted in this very clear passage from Matthew 19:16–24 (this authentic logion of Jesus is also described in Mark 10:17–25 and Luke 18:18–25):

> And, behold, one came and said unto him, Good Master, what good thing shall I do, that I may have eternal life? And he said unto him, Why do you ask me about what is good? There is none good but one, that is, God: but if thou wilt enter into life, keep the commandments. He saith unto him, Which? Jesus said, Thou shalt do no murder, Thou shalt not commit adultery, Thou shalt not steal, Thou shalt not bear false witness,

Honor thy father and thy mother: and, Thou shalt love thy neighbor as thyself. The
young man saith unto him, All these things have I kept from my youth up: what lack I
yet? Jesus said unto him, If thou wilt be perfect, go and sell that thou hast, and give to
the poor, and thou shalt have treasure in heaven: and come and follow me. But when
the young man heard that saying, he went away sorrowful: for he had great possessions.
Then said Jesus unto his disciples, Verily I say unto you, That a rich man shall hardly
enter into the kingdom of heaven. And again I say unto you, It is easier for a camel to
go through the eye of a needle, than for a rich man to enter into the kingdom of God.

When this rich young man asked Jesus what he must do to achieve eternal
life, Jesus advises the man to obey the commandments. But since this young
man already observes the commandments, he asks Jesus what else he must do.
Jesus tells him that to be perfect he must sell his possessions and give them to
the poor and he will then have treasure in heaven. Then he told the man that
he should follow him. But when the young man heard this he went away with
much sorrow, since he owned much property. Let us not walk away from this
news with sadness in our hearts, but know that through our struggle for social
justice we will achieve a world beyond value production, where differential
wealth will not corrupt us and finance capital will not possess our souls.

Many of us—either openly or secretly—harbor a religious faith that often
remains hidden between the lines of our manifestos and treatises. When I
made a profession of faith in 1975, "I believe and profess all that the holy
Catholic Church believes, teaches, and proclaims to be revealed by God,"
I was well aware of the problems with the history of the Roman Catholic
Church and other organized religions. My faith was in the crucified Jesus and
risen Christ, not an organization. My father was raised Presbyterian and my
mother was Roman Catholic, but I was raised within the Anglican Church. I
have often maintained the position that the official church of Jesus has been
implicated in the indefensible falsification of the Gospel in order to protect the
hierarchies of the church. Of course, this is not a new position by any means.
But here I wish to amplify this idea by briefly summarizing the important work
of the late Mexican Jesuit theologian, José Porfirio Miranda, whose work is as
prophetic as it is profound. He may well be our new John the Baptist.

Miranda's work skillfully corroborates his own analysis of the Bible with
those of ecclesiastically sanctioned studies by recognized and prominent Catholic exegetes. According to Miranda (1977, p. 203), Christian faith is supposed
to "transform humankind and the world." Miranda (1980, 2004) claims the
persecution of Christians for the first three centuries constrained Christians
to present a version of Christianity that would no longer provoke repression.

After the fourth century, the church acquired a dominant status in class society, and this was what then motivated the continuing falsification of the Gospel.

Clearly, the message of Jesus is to create the Kingdom of God on earth, as it has been created in heaven. Jesus is the prototypical rebel, someone whom suburban U.S. parents would continuously warn their children to avoid, and certainly not to befriend. As Terry Eagleton (2009, p. 10) notes, "Jesus, unlike most respectable American citizens, appears to do no work, and is accused of being a glutton and a drunkard. He is presented as homeless, propertyless, celibate, peripatetic, socially marginal, disdainful of kinsfolk, without a trade, a friend of outcasts and pariahs, averse to material possessions, without fear for his own safety, careless about purity regulations, critical of traditional authority, a thorn in the side of the Establishment, and a scourge of the rich and powerful" (cited in Maeshiri, 2014).

The official teachings of the church falsify the Gospels since it is clear from reading the texts of the Bible that Jesus maintains an intransigent condemnation of the rich.

Jesus does not condemn wealth in the absolute sense, as when the wealth of the whole people is praised in Deuteronomy 28: 1–14. But when Jesus says "Happy are the poor" and "Woe to you the rich," he is attacking the fact that some people are poor and others are rich. As Miranda (2004) emphasizes, "rich" and "poor" are correlative terms. Jesus's "inexorable reprobation" to which he subjects wealth refers not to absolute wealth but to differentiating wealth, that is, to relative wealth, and Jesus does so "implacably," "intransigently" and "unexceptionably." (Miranda, 2004, pp. 21–22). Miranda rightfully warns that "Exegesis cannot bear this message" (2004, p. 23). How is it possible to follow the message of Christ when his dire warnings about economic inequality are ignored? If you accept Christ as your personal savior and support a system that creates inequality and injustice, then what does this say? This goes beyond whether you vote for a Democrat or a Republican. It is at the heart of the struggle to be human. It does not mean that a socialist country is more Christian than a capitalist country if that socialist country exercises a totalitarian grip on its population. While justice is more than economic, it remains the case that economic justice is fundamental to the Kingdom of God here on earth. Yes, we can pray for the eternal salvation of our soul, and those of our brethren, but we cannot ignore the fact that the Kingdom of God is at hand, and that only love and justice in the here and the now will usher in this Kingdom, made possible by the grace of God. The notion that differentiating wealth is an undisputed fact of life is, of course, false. It is a lie that we are fed every day in the media and through the ideological state apparatuses in ways that we have come to regard as common sense. Much of contemporary Christianity begins with this false premise. Differentiating wealth as it is produced today by the machinations of finance capitalism is not a given. It is an historical contingency that can be overcome though the struggle for a socialist alternative.

Even liberation theology gets this wrong when it asserts that there should be a "preferential option for the poor"—it is not an option, but, as Miranda notes, it is an *obligation*. We cannot shirk from this obligation without imputation of culpability and still remain Christians. There is no abstention from this struggle. The condition of the poor obliges a restitution since such a struggle is injustice writ large (Miranda, 1974).

Jesus died for participating in political transgression aimed at liberating Judea from the Romans. According to Miranda, Jesus clearly was a communist, and this can convincingly be seen throughout the New Testament but particularly in passages such as John 12:6, 13:29 and Luke 8:1–3. Jesus went so far as to make the renunciation of property a condition for entering the kingdom of God. When Luke says, "Happy the poor, for yours is the Kingdom of God" (Luke 6:20) and adds, "Woe to you the rich, because you have received your comfort" (Luke 6:24), Luke is repeating Mark 10:25 when Jesus warns that the rich cannot enter the kingdom.

The Bible makes clear through Jesus's own sayings that the kingdom is not the state of being after death; rather, the kingdom is now, here on earth. Essentially, Jesus is saying that "in the kingdom there cannot be social differences—that the kingdom, whether or not it pleases the conservatives, is a classless society" (Miranda, 2004, p. 20). Consider what Luke says in Acts:

> All the believers together had everything in common; they sold their possessions and their goods, and distributed among all in accordance with each one's need. [Acts 2:44–45]

> The heart of the multitude of believers was one and their soul was one, and not a single one said anything of what he had was his, but all things were in common. ... There was no poor person among them, since whoever possessed fields or houses sold them, bore the proceeds of the sale and placed them at the feet of the apostles; and a distribution was made to each in accordance with his need. [Acts 4:32, 34–35]

Benjamin Corey (2014, p. 44) describes the early Christians as forming strong communal bonds:

> These early Christians had a strong sense of community, often meeting in small, house churches—a practice that facilitated deeper intimacy as they wrestled with this

new faith, together. In addition to exploring their faith in a relational way, they also put undiluted community into practice by rejecting the concept of individual ownership in lieu of an "according to need, according to ability" redistribution of wealth system—a practice that enabled them to eradicate poverty in their community.

"From each according to his ability, to each according to his needs!" was a famous phrase used by Marx in a letter he wrote in 1875 to the Social Democratic Workers' Party of Germany which came to be part of his Critique of the Gotha Program. If you refer to Acts 4:34–35, you will see that Marx simply paraphrased what is written in the New Testament. Does that mean that the early Christians were communists? Perhaps it is better to say that communism proper is a Christian principle (that was perverted and distorted in the totalitarian communist regimes of the former Soviet Union and Eastern Bloc countries). The first part of the principle—from each according to their ability—can be understood to mean that all members of society will have the right to use their creative abilities to produce that which benefits the entire society. The second part of the principle—to each according to their needs—explains that citizens will receive from society a fair return for their labor, that is, what is necessary to fulfill their needs. Needs here does not simply refer to material needs, although material needs must be met in order for other needs to be satisfied.

On this point, Corey (2014, p. 45) is clear:

> The early Christians didn't have megachurches where people watched a pastor with a $250,000 salary preach via a Jumbotron from a satellite campus; they didn't "worship" beside people they'd seen several times before but never actually met, and they didn't preach a hyper-capitalistic, American version of Christianity. The first Christians lived in the context of community and wrestled with an emerging theology among a tight-knit group of friends—friends who shared every aspect of their lives together, including their wealth.

It is often thought that Jesus taught that poverty is something that can never be eradicated, and that the poor will always be a natural part of social life. But Jesus did not say that the poor will always be with us; he said that the poor are with us all the time. Miranda (2004, pp. 58–60) cites numerous translation sources attesting that this statement should be translated as, "The poor you have with you at all moments [or continuously]. And you can do them good when you wish; on the other hand, you do not have me at all moments [Mark 14:7]" (2004, p. 59). According to Miranda (2004, p. 65), Jesus didn't say, "My kingdom is not of this world," he said, "My kingdom does not come forth from this world" or "My kingdom is not from this world" since we can retain the original meaning only if we consider the preposition *ek* in the original Greek as meaning "from," signifying place of origin or provenance.

But didn't Jesus advocate paying taxes? Rendering unto Cesar what is due Cesar? Jesus's remark about giving Cesar what is due Cesar is decidedly ironic, and not a capitulation to Roman authority (Miranda, 2004, pp. 61–65). Consider the following quotation cited by Miranda (2004, p. 53) concerning economic transactions found in the Bible:

> For the sake of profit, many have sinned; the one who tries to grow rich, turns away his gaze. Stuck tight between two stones, between sale and purchase, sin is wedged. [Ecclus. 27:1–2]

Miranda (2004, p. 54) notes that biblical scripture condemns the term "interest" (the Hebrew word is "neshet") numerous times: Exodus 22:24; Leviticus 25:36, 37; Deuteronomy 23:19 (three times); Ezekiel 18:8, 13, 17, 22:12; Psalms 15:5; Proverbs 28:8. And numerous times profit making through commerce, loans at interest and productive activity itself (the process of production) are condemned (production likely here referring to agriculture). Does not James condemn the acquisition of wealth by agricultural entrepreneurs (see James 5:1–6)? And does he not, in fact, attack all the rich (James 1:10–11)? In James 2:6, does he not say: "Is it not the rich who oppress you and who hail you before the tribunals?" Does he not also say: "See, what you have whittled away from the pay of the workers who reap your fields cries out, and the anguish of the harvesters has come to the ears of the Lord of Armies" (James 5:4)?

Does it now surprise us that Jesus would call money, "money of iniquity" (Luke 16:9, 11)? On this issue Miranda (2004, p. 55) writes:

> What this verse is doing is explaining the origin of wealth. Its intention is not to refer to *some* particularly perverse rich people who have committed knaveries which other rich people do not commit. The letter's attack is against *all* the rich.

This is the biblical reprobation of differentiating wealth as Luke vituperates those who have defrauded workers and impugns all the rich. According to Miranda (2004, p. 53), profit "is considered to be the source of (differentiating) wealth." Miranda continues:

> For James, differentiating wealth can be acquired only by means of expropriation of the produce of the workers' labor. Therefore, following Jesus Christ and the Old Testament, James condemns differentiating wealth without vacillation or compromise. Profit made in the very process of production is thus specifically imprecated. (2004, p. 55)

Miranda (2004, p. 73) explains further what this implies: "Where there is no differentiating wealth, where economic activity is directly for the purpose of the satisfaction of needs and not for trade or the operations of buying and selling for profit, government becomes unnecessary." The Bible attacks not only acquired wealth but the means by which such wealth is accumulated, which is the taking of profit or what could be considered a form of systemic or legalized exploitation or robbery. Even the prophets such as Micha and Amos understood that "no differentiating wealth can be acquired without spoliation and fraud" (Miranda, 2004, p. 40).

Miranda notes: "If we want to know 'Why communism?' the response is unequivocal: because any other system consists of the exploitation of some persons over others" (2004, p. 55). Miranda sees Jesus as the true God grounded in himself, meaning grounded in the establishment of justice and life now, at this very moment, since "the hour is coming and it is now." Miranda is uncompromising when he notes:

> A god who intervenes in history to elicit religious adoration of himself and not to undo the hell of cruelty and death that human history has become is an immoral god in the deepest sense of the word. A god who is reconciled or merely indifferent to the pain of human beings is a merciless god, a monster, not the ethical God whom the Bible knows. We would be morally obliged to rebel against such a god, even if our defeat were inevitable. Equally immoral is the god for whom the end of injustice and innocent suffering is a secondary or subordinate imperative. (1977, p. 187)

The key point in Miranda's theological argument is that the eschaton has already arrived, the eschaton of justice and life for all, in the example of Jesus Christ. If Christians don't believe that the eschaton has already come, then they are likely to relegate Jesus to a non-temporal and eternal or Platonic realm. But the eschaton cannot be indefinitely held captive in some mythic future; the historical moment of salvation is not repeatable since Jesus is the divine singularity—the definitive "now" of history. If this were not the case, "then the imperative of love of neighbor becomes an intro-self concept. It does not speak as a real otherness, because anodyne time, even if it is present, truly has no reason to command me more than any other time" (Miranda, 1977, p. 192).

Christians, argues Miranda, can't postpone the commandment to love their neighbor in the fathomless future, because this would make of God an unassimilable otherness, a perpetual language game in which postmodernists would love to participate without a commitment to any political imperative except narcissistic self-cultivation. And thus we could never be contemporaneous with God. Eternal life is not life after death but the defeat of death, that is, the defeat of suffering and injustice in the here and now. Of course, what should be condemned are the totalitarian police states that *claimed* to be communist (such as the Soviet Union) but which were, in the final instance, formations of state capitalism (see Dunayevskaya, 1992).

We need to be reminded that the first writing by Marx in his Gesamtausgabe was composed in 1835 (when Marx was a 17-year-old student at the Trier Gymnasium) and was a devotional essay on the fifteenth chapter of St. John's gospel called "The Union of the Faithful in Christ." And the last 500 pages of *The German Ideology* certainly illustrate that Marx had a clear understanding and detailed knowledge of the New Testament. While Marx did not identify as a Christian during his life, it is clear that he was influenced by the message of the New Testament regarding differentiating wealth and the necessity for the struggle against it.

What is clear from a reading of the Gospel accounts of Jesus is that the world is in the thrall of the monetary god, and that the true Kingdom of God requires a commitment to social justice. Did not the very person who baptized Jesus and who was a major figure inaugurating the Kingdom of God—John the Baptist—proclaim: "The man who has two tunics is to share with him who has none; and he who has food is to do likewise" (Luke 3:11)? Did not Jesus Himself declare, "No one can serve two masters, for either he will hate the one and love the other, or he will be devoted to the one and despise the other. You cannot serve both God and money" (Matthew 6:24)? What does this say about capitalism, the greatest colonizing force in history, sweeping across the parched plains of the planet like a dust storm from hell and arriving as temples of usury called banks and investment firms?

Of course, to point out that Jesus did not support politico-ethical neutrality in the face of injustice is not a popular message, especially for those who use God-talk as a politically pacifying force. James Cone's words are apposite when he writes in his magisterial work, A *Black Theology of Liberation*:

> Oppressed and oppressors cannot possibly mean the same thing when they speak of God. The God of the oppressed is a God of revolution who breaks the chains of slavery. The oppressor's God is a god of slavery and must be destroyed along with the oppressors. (1990, p. 58)

I am in agreement with Cone when he writes that "God-talk is not Christian-talk unless it is directly related to the liberation of the oppressed. Any other talk is at best an intellectual hobby, and at worst blasphemy" (1990, p. 60). To be a Christian who follows the words and actions of Jesus of the gospels is to denounce injustice as much as it is to announce that the Kingdom of God is at hand. This automatically positions Christians against the sentinels of the corporate state and the guardians of the structures of authority (both religious and secular) that give legitimacy to those structures. As Cone proclaims:

> To speak of God and God's participation in the liberation of the oppressed of the land is a risky venture in any society. But if the society is racist and also uses God-language as an instrument to further the cause of human humiliation, then the task of authentic theological speech is even more dangerous and difficult. It is dangerous because the true prophet of the gospel of God must become both "anti-Christian" and "unpatriotic." It is impossible to confront a racist society, with the meaning of human existence grounded in a commitment to the divine, without at the same time challenging the very existence of the national structure and all its institutions, especially the established churches. (1990, p. 55)

What we are confronting today is an investigatory and punishing state structure depopulated of collective memory, a built environment that produces and rules by fear that can best be captured by the words of George Orwell:

> Do not imagine that you will save yourself, Winston, however completely you surrender to us. No one who has once gone astray is ever spared. And even if we chose to let you live out the natural term of your life, still you would never escape from us. What happens to you here is for ever. Understand that in advance. We shall crush you down to the point from which there is no coming back. Things will happen to you from which you could not recover, if you lived a thousand years. Never again will you be capable of ordinary human feeling. Everything will be dead inside you. Never again will you be capable of love, or friendship, or joy of living, or laughter, or curiosity, or courage, or integrity. You will be hollow. We shall squeeze you empty, and then we shall fill you with ourselves. (1950, p. 195)

Here, the redemptive mode of memory as a lived discourse that attempts to enter into a dialogue with the past, is leeched out of our capacity to be human (that is, our capacity to dream) so that individuals are remade and remastered as suppilcatory beings placatory towards dominative capitalist regimes. This, of course, is the task of the ideological state apparatuses that include schools, churches and the corporate media.

The greatest potential for the exercise of totalitarianism can be found in capitalist societies, as was the case with the former Soviet Union, what Raya Dunayevskaya (1941) termed a state capitalist regime in which the ownership of the means of production by the state in no way resembled the Marxist concept of a workers' state or even a bureaucratic socialist state. In some ways the United States exceeds the former Soviet Union in its potential for exercising ruthless totalitarian power through hegemonic apparatuses so sophisticated that former Eastern Bloc police states seem Pollyannaish by comparison. If you disagree that our corporate media apparatuses in the United States serve as tools for state propaganda and the manufacturing of consent (to repeat Noam Chomsky's famous phrase), then you have already made my point.

At least several times per semester, students and colleagues approach me with a version of the following question: Wouldn't socialism turn people into lazy ragamuffins because the element of competition is eliminated? My first response is generally to say, "I'm not sure how a famous socialist such as Albert Einstein would answer that, but I can tell you that in my reading of the scriptures, Jesus much preferred a world of leisure to one of work. And leisure here does not refer to 'doing nothing' but fighting for the conditions of possibility for leisure—i.e., not having to work in slave conditions in factories to improve the standard of living for the factory owner and his bosses—that is, for exercising one's creative capacities and talents in the service of building the Kingdom of God. Didn't God, after all, create the weekend"?

And don't we at present possess the technological capability to free humanity from the travails of brutal, backbreaking labor but we choose instead to burn our surplus crops and allow people to starve? The fruits of our labor should be the creation of the Kingdom of God, and not the Trump Towers!

Was Jesus not concerned with the salvation of the hungry, the immiserated, and the oppressed, including prostitutes and lepers, and those who were the political victims of the imperial Roman Empire? Did Jesus not compare the Kingdom of God to the man who says, 'Take your pay and go. I want to give the one who was hired last the same as I gave you. Don't I have the right to do what I want with my own money? Or are you envious because I am generous?' "So the last will be first, and the first will be last" (Matthew 20:14–16).

We are so paralyzed by the dark cosmovision of capitalism—the money nexus, individualism, ruthlessness, lack of compassion—that we fear being roundly chastised for having the temerity to denounce the incontrovertible presence of social sin, or structural sin or the sin of state capitalism. We are chastened and rebuked to restrict our concern to our own sins and our personal atonement and repentance and to eschew condemning structural entities such as the state or our economic system. After all, are we not all sinners? Who are we to attack capitalism at its roots since we ourselves have transgressed the word of God? Yes, of course we are sinners, but that knowledge should not paralyze us so that we submit to the sins of the state. We should not remain silent while watching the furnaces of capital being stoked. If corporations now have the same rights as individuals (since 1819, the U.S. Supreme Court has recognized corporations as having the same rights as natural persons to contract and to enforce contracts), then I should be free to criticize any capitalist structure I wish for not enforcing the social contract between the state and its members.

Doesn't the Book of Acts (2:44–45) state: "All the believers together had everything in common; they sold their possessions and their goods, and distributed among all in accordance with each one's need"? And did Jesus not write: "The kingdom of heaven is like a grain of mustard seed that a man took and sowed in his field. It is the smallest of all seeds, but when it has grown it is larger than all the garden plants and becomes a tree, so that the birds of the air come and make nests in its branches" (Matthew 13:31–32)?

William Herzog's various attempts at developing a historical-critical approach to investigate adequately the historical Jesus began with examining the eschatological-existential and theological-ethical meanings of the parables of Jesus. Herzog considered these approaches insufficient, and it finally led him to reject such approaches in favor of a Freirean "problem-posing" approach that involved a dialectical understanding of the parables of Jesus, i.e., reading them as micro-scenes within the macro-scenario in which they were told. Finally, Herzog (1994) attempted to understand these parables in relation to the social and economic world of agrarian societies and the political world of aristocratic empires. The major findings of Herzog's experiment revealed that the parables of Jesus were created to problematize systems of oppression and that the center of Jesus's spirituality was the call to social justice. Such a call to justice reminded me of the struggle of Mexico's indigenous populations.

Social justice is one of the most fundamental messages of Jesus. Does Jesus not echo the prophet Micah (6:6–8) who tells us that the Lord requires us to act justly and to love mercy? We read in Amos (5:21–24) that God demands that we bring forth a mighty flood of justice instead of religious festivals and pretentious assemblies:

> I hate, I despise your festivals, and I take no delight in your solemn assemblies. Even though you offer me your burnt offerings and grain offerings, I will not accept them; and the offerings of well-being of your fatted animals I will not look upon. Take away from me the noise of your songs; I will not listen to the melody of your harps. But let justice roll down like waters, and righteousness like an ever-flowing stream.

In Luke (3:10–11) we are told that John the Baptist warns sinners to do the following as an act of repentance:

> The crowds asked, "What should we do?" John replied, "If you have two shirts, give one to the poor. If you have food, share it with those who are hungry."

And in Matthew (25:31–46) Jesus makes clear that the Kingdom of God is reserved for those who do justice:

> When the Son of Man comes in his glory, and all the angels with him, then he will sit on his glorious throne. Before him will be gathered all the nations, and he will separate people one from another as a shepherd separates the sheep from the goats. And he will place the sheep on his right, but the goats on the left. Then the King will say to those on his right, 'Come, you who are blessed by my Father, inherit the kingdom prepared for you from the foundation of the world. For I was hungry and you gave me food, I was thirsty and you gave me drink, I was a stranger and you welcomed me, I was naked and you clothed me, I was sick and you visited me, I was in prison and you came to me.' Then the righteous will answer him, saying, 'Lord, when did we see you hungry and feed you, or thirsty and give you drink? And when did we see you a stranger and welcome you, or naked and clothe you? And when did we see you sick or in prison and visit you?' And the King will answer them, 'Truly, I say to you, as you did it to one of the least of these my brothers, you did it to me.'

> Then he will say to those on his left, 'Depart from me, you cursed, into the eternal fire prepared for the devil and his angels. For I was hungry and you gave me no food, I was thirsty and you gave me no drink, I was a stranger and you did not welcome me, naked and you did not clothe me, sick and in prison and you did not visit me.' Then they also will answer, saying, 'Lord, when did we see you hungry or thirsty or a stranger or naked or sick or in prison, and did not minister to you?' Then he will answer them, saying, 'Truly, I say to you, as you did not do it to one of the least of these, you did not do it to me.' And these will go away into eternal punishment, but the righteous into eternal life.

Justice, therefore, constitutes, in part, a refusal to surrender to the norms of society and the authority of the inherited institutions. After all, the depreciatory denomination of insurgent is perfectly applicable to Jesus. Was he not crucified for sedition in between two other insurgents (translated as "thieves" or "robbers" in the scriptures)? Crucifixion was, after all, reserved for political rebels. Was Jesus not the ultimate insurgent in that he went beyond nationalism to proclaim the kingdom of God to all men and women worldwide? Was Christ not the thunderous irruption into human history of the divine? Was he not more threatening to the Romans than the zealots themselves? Were not the Jewish leaders fearful of Jesus, as well, as they worried that Jesus might inspire the wrath of the Romans for inciting the people against Rome? Were they not afraid of the revolutionary character of Jesus's spiritual proclamations as well? As Gregory Baum (1975) writes:

> Jesus initiated his followers to conflict with the existing institutions including the family. "I have come to cause divisions: for henceforth in one house there will be divided father against son and son against father, mother against daughter and

daughter against mother, mother-in-law against daughter-in-law and daughter-in-law against mother-in-law (Lk. 12:52–53). The preaching of Jesus, in a trend amplified by his followers, accused "the world"—that is, the dominant structures and the received norms—as the principle of evil.

The gospels teach us that the world is under the power of darkness, in which the locus of sin can be seen not only as personal and privatized but also as structural, as, for instance, an ideology sanctioning individualism and leading to the atomization of the social order; as dehumanizing trends built into social, political, educational and religious institutions; as false consciousness that leads to destructive collective action, to collective decisions based on the distortions built into institutions and social practices (see Baum, 1975). Is this not the coming of darkness of which we have been warned (see John, 12:31; 14:30; 16:11)? We read, "Do not love the world or the things in the world. For if anyone loves the world, the love of the Father is not in him" (John, 2:15).

The great Brazilian Dominican friar, Frei Betto, close friend of and co-author with Paulo Freire, maintained that we in the ivory tower tend to view the Bible as a window whereas peasant or base communities see it as a mirror. According to Robert McAfee Brown:

> We tend to use the Bible as a *window*, enabling us to see what is happening somewhere else—"Bible times," for example, when God was fairly available—and we hope to be transformed to be what we see out there. Members of the base communities, by contrast, use the Bible as a *mirror*, in which they see their own reality reflected and hope to learn about themselves in the process. (1993, p. 81)

Ernst Bloch's ontology of not-yet-being (that exists in a tension between a meta-ontic full being and an ontic being-in-process) provides a new eschatology of religion (eschatological communism) grounded in the concept of concrete utopia, which opens the path to a new type of "praxis." Following from Wayne Hudson's critical exegesis on the theology of Bloch, from his magisterial study, *The Marxist Philosophy of Ernst Bloch*, "Jesus ... claimed equality with Yahweh, usurped his place, and then outbid him by promising immortality and showing that he was morally superior to the Creator God who allowed him to be crucified" (1982, p. 188). Here, "the 'ideal of man' takes on the form of an ensemble of utopian relationships adequate to what has been projected as the God postulate, with the result that the making of future man acquires a centrality and a utopian meaning in Marxism which it has not hitherto possessed" (1982, p. 185).

While this view might seem offensive to many Christians, it is important to appreciate Bloch's understanding of the true meaning of religion—"an explosion of absolute hope" (1982, p. 188). The orthopraxis of Bloch offers us a new way to comprehend Jesus in the context of the Bedouin communism of his time and place and the social egalitarianism of the Nazarites that was continued by the prophets "with their radical stress on social justice, their reinterpretation of Yahweh as a *futurum* who brings a moral-social apocalypse, and their teaching that men could determine the outcome of history by their actions" (1982, p. 188).

Here Bloch views Jesus "as a revolutionary who preached a communism of the poor against the rich and promised to bring 'not peace, but a sword'" (Hudson, 1982, p. 189). Jesus preached the beginning of a new aeon, the Kingdom of God, wherein the parousia of Jesus (the soul as extra-territorial to death, human beings can enter heaven, hominization of the world) became the futurum (Hudson, 1982, pp. 189–190). Jesus becomes the Jesus of the eschaton, of the messianic, post-theistic, meta-cosmic Kingdom of God, where futurism becomes the model for faith. Towards the end of Bloch's *Heritage of Our Times* he describes Jesus as

> the preacher of an unknown human glory, too bright for the human body still to be able to equilibrate it, let alone the now existing world. He is the conquest of the human glory even behind the smallest and most unexpected window, and precisely there, precisely in the already appeared ruling, and satiated into which the Church has falsified and diffused him. (1991, p. 331)

Jesus's words convey, according to Bloch (2000, p. 216), "the promise of the deepest logological contents." He argues that "only in us do the fruitful, historical hours advance; in the deepest soul itself the primrose must bloom" (2000, p. 216). Jesus becomes the concealed verbum mirificim of absolute knowledge. Jesus "proclaimed a wanting-to-create, a wanting-to-know or wanting-to-be-like God formerly called 'original sin,' as the highest postulate" (2000, p. 275).

Infinitude is nothing different from spirituality. We stand tall as spiritual agents in the vastness and expansiveness of God's reach. We breathe, we are breath and we are breathed into existence by God. We are like a child's sigh within the interstellar pulsations of God's lungs. We cannot be reduced to lumps of flesh to be probed, poked and reduced to algorithms on a chart clipped to the end of our beds. If we are spiritual beings then we cannot be reduced to data. We are not spiritual because we are naturally good. We are not naturally good. We are good insofar as we can remove ourselves from nature and exist in the realm of spirit and God's loving grace. It is an inveterate self-deceit to describe human beings as empirical data. According to Miranda (2011, p. 331), capitalism has benefited from the prevalent theological position that natural egoism—or seeking to benefit oneself—is not sinful. The notion that we are already God is pantheism and it is the traditional denial of original sin (at least according to Hegel). Man's animal nature is natural, but man is man only insofar as he is free from nature. Unlike the philosopher Rousseau, Miranda does not believe that natural man is good. The moral imperative emerges from the infinite dignity of the neighbor, and this criterion evaluates whether or not an action treats the neighbor as a subject or as an object. You can't found morality on nature, on natural tendencies towards irresponsibility, aggression, sloth, infidelity, etc. (Miranda, 2011, p. 332). Human beings are not empirical data; they are spiritual. When we say to treat men and women as a subject and not as an object, as a means and not as an end, we are essentially saying that we must treat human beings as possessing infinite dignity and spiritual infinitude.

While it is true that Marx was a great dialectician, he was not, according to Miranda, great enough to address the problem of death and resurrection. According to Miranda, "When Marx avoids the problem of death and therefore does not even glimpse the possibility of resurrection, it is not precisely his lack of faith in God but rather insufficient dialectics for which we must reproach him" (1974, p. 279). God's intervention sets in motion "the immanent and horizontal causality of human history itself" (Miranda, 1974, p. 278), and we need to remember that the dialectic is inherent in history. The resurrection of Jesus "unleashed the dialectics that results in the definitive realization of justice and the abolition of death" (Miranda, 1974, p. 279).

Now while it is true that Marx does not believe in the reality of the spirit, "the spiritual, profoundly spiritual character of the whole man and of the social relationships which are the axis and engine of history is affirmed by Marx explicitly or implicitly on every page of his writings" (Miranda, 1974, p. 274). For Bloch, "the martyr's name has an altar in the heart of the working class" (cited in Miranda, 1974, p. 284). But the martyr must move humanity towards a socialist future, and for that to happen the "authentically dialectical Marxist" must take pains not to renounce the resurrection of the dead, that is, renounce divine justice (Miranda, 1974, pp. 284–285).

Michael Rivage-Seul confirms that Jesus, while sympathetic to the zealots, was likely not a zealot since he did not approve of violence. His violent actions removing the moneylenders in the temple could hardly be considered an endorsement of violence.

As explained by Rivage-Seul (2008, pp. 169–170), religious figures such as Dom Helda Camera and Óscar Romero spoke of a "bloody trinity" of three levels of violence: (1) structural violence, first-level violence, or violence of the "father" (social, economic, political, and military systems and arrangements, codified in law and custom that are responsible for tens of thousands of innocent deaths throughout the world each day); (2) revolutionary violence, second-level violence, or violence of the "son" (responses to first-level or structural violence); and (3) reactionary violence, third-level violence, or violence of the "evil spirit" (the reply by the state to acts of rebellion against structural or first-level violence). While clearly structural violence prevails in today's imperial regimes and their client states, revolutionary violence is the only violence officially condemned by such states (Rivage-Seul, 2008, p. 171). However, revolutionary violence is the only violence that can at least be theoretically justified as, in Rivage-Seul's words, "peasants and workers [seek] to defend their families from aggressions of the rich represented in the first and third levels" (2008, p. 171).

Even the figure of Jesus reveals some sympathy for the goals of second-level violence since he was very likely sympathetic to the insurgency against the Roman occupation. While almost certainly an anti-imperialist, Jesus "distanced himself from second-level violence, as well as from the first as represented by the Roman Empire" (Rivage-Seul, 2008, p. 172). According to Rivage-Seul, Jesus understood that second-level (revolutionary) violence would necessarily provoke a reactionary third-level violence and nothing would be changed (as his parable about the absentee landlord and his tenants illustrated). Ultimately, Jesus rebuked the worship of a divinized violence.

Structural violence in the U.S. is very rarely addressed by the state, but revolutionary violence, especially post-9/11, is "rejected out of hand." On this issue, Rivage-Seul's comments are apposite: "the reality is, however, that violence at this level is the most understandable and even the most justifiable, at least from the viewpoint of American history, Just War theory, and perhaps even in the light of Jesus's own sympathies" (2008, p. 175). While Rivage-Seul agrees that the example of Jesus "challenges Christians to implement the practice of non-violent resistance, both as a matter of practicality and spiritual conviction" (2008, p. 175), it nonetheless,

> seems inappropriate for First World Christians to insist that Third World resisters adopt strategies and tactics of non-violent resistance in situations where they must actually defend the "least of the brethren" in contexts shaped by extremely violent structures financed by U.S. tax dollars. In any case, Christians living comfortably in the U.S.A. must overcome the impulse to condemn second-level violence while

excusing systematic aggression in service to U.S. corporate interests. Perhaps Philip Berryman says it best, "I would assert that people who have not actively opposed the violence of the powerful against the poor, at some cost to themselves, have no moral authority to question the violence used by the poor." (Rivage-Seul, 2008, p. 175)

As systems of domination breed forms of resistance, understanding revolutionaries such as Jesus is crucial if one wants to take the next step for humankind, which is building social harmony and lasting peace through the dialectical praxis of love through justice and justice through love.

Here I want to explore structural violence in a bit more detail. David Graeber famously captured the "boring, humdrum, yet omnipresent forms of structural violence that define the very condition of our existence" (2012, p. 105). These fundamentally bureaucratic structures shape and are shaped by the minutiae of everyday life and refer to spaces or environments defined by the ultimate threat of actual physical force. Such a constant threat permits social relations characterized by racism, sexism and poverty to reproduce themselves largely uncontested.

Structures are not abstract, free-floating entities. They are, according to Graeber, "material *processes*, in which violence, and the threat of violence, plays a crucial constitutive role" (2012, p. 113). Structural violence occurs as part of the humdrum of everyday life primarily because government bureaucracies inspire fear and enter into "relations of command" in which dominant groups attempt to render subordinate groups (i.e., the poor, people of color, gays and lesbians) extensions of their will in conditions that comprise a structural inequality of power and that rely on a fear of physical force.

Violence here is the possibility of a threat or the potential for a threat. In other words, violence is embedded in the norms sanctioned by the threat of physical harm. It is uncannily the case that people not inclined to interpret power relations or who do not wish to understand situations from another person's point of view are apt to resort to violence by "applying preexisting templates to complex and often ambiguous situations" (Graeber, 2012, p. 119). Violence here obviates the need for what Graeber calls "interpretive labor" and is most effective when conditions of inequality are deeply internalized.

Ironically, victims of structural violence are likely to care more about those who benefit from such violence than the victimizers care about them. Graeber argues that "structures of inequality produce lopsided structures of the imagination" as bureaucratic violence consists "first and foremost of attacks on those who insist on alternative schemas or interpretations" of existing institutional, social and economic arrangements (2012, p. 121). Consequently, we labor within "dead zones that riddle our lives, areas so devoid of any possibility of interpretive depth that they seem to repel any attempt to give them value or meaning" (2012, p. 123).

Graeber importantly avoids ascribing to violence an ontological status that masks violence from critical scrutiny. More important is the need to examine violence dialectically from a historical materialist perspective in order to ascertain just where direct violence and structural violence intersect or overlap.

Tyner and Inwood critique the inherited ontology of violence, reminding us that there is no pre-given, discursive reality since our understanding of everyday life is always inflected politically, because politics is a precondition of reality (2014, p. 773). Thus, the reality of violence is the outcome of the political. Violence is not unproblematic and needs to be studied as a dialectical process. According to Tyner and Inwood, violence is neither transhistorical nor transgeographical. Rather, violence "comes into being through political practice" (2014, p. 774). Violence must also be understood as embedded subjectivities and sociopolitical relations invariably linked to a specific mode of production. Tyner and Inwood propose a dialectical approach to understanding violence grounded in a historical materialist analysis. Understanding violence through measuring dependent and independent variables is insufficient since these disarticulated variables in reality are internally related and form part of the hidden totality of violence related to the dominant mode of production in a given society. Rather than conflating real concrete acts with specific abstractions, a far more sustained and comprehensive analysis would examine violence in terms of its social and spatial relations by investigating acts of violence as "historically and geographically contingent and dialectically related to the society from which they emerge" (2014, p. 776).

We need, in other words, to be attentive to the sociospatial dialectics of violence that perpetrate inequality and facilitate the valorization of capitalism. For instance, concrete forms of structural violence can be seen in the lack of public housing or inadequate healthcare or decrepit school facilities. These are not unfortunate by-products of capitalism but are constitutive of the social relations of capitalist production, circulation and exchange. They are the direct result of class antagonisms.

Here, direct violence and structural violence can be understood as dialectically related rather than discrete instances of occurence. As Tyner and Inwood (2014) note, each mode of production will structure the abstraction of violence in particular concrete forms, that is, according to particular class relations. And in capitalist societies, workers are anything but free since they are separated from the means of production and are dependent upon selling their labor power for a wage. I consider these structural conditions affecting workers as criminal, but the notion of criminality is in itself historically and morally determined (Tyner & Inwood, 2014), and this is another question that needs to be examined if we are to consider more deeply the problem of state-sponsored structural violence.

On a recent visit to Chiapas, some Marxist comrades and I drove from San Cristóbal de las Casas, to the town of San Juan Chamula. As we approached the town, we passed rambling fields of corn separated by clusters of mud-and-straw and cinderblock houses and found a place to park our van across the street from a building that hosted several large Coca-Cola advertisements. As we exited the van we could see in the distance the seventeenth-century structure of the town's church that may have extended as far back as 1562. Founded by the Dominicans and named after John the Baptist, this religious meeting place was storied among anthropologists as a unique syncretic mixture of Mesoamerican beliefs and Spanish Catholicism.

We entered the church, transfixed by the candlelight mixed with giant shafts of sunlight descending from the side windows like laser beams. We walked gingerly across an emerald carpet made of dazzling pine boughs strewn across the entire stone floor of the church. Amidst the giant cloth hangings, the crosses dressed in colorful fabric, the burning copal resin engulfing our lungs still adjusting to the altitude, the statues of saints covered in mirrors and pineapple ornaments and the Tzotzil chants of the worshippers interspersed with regular volleys from homemade firecrackers exploding outside the walls, we tried to make sense of what we were experiencing. Hundreds, possibly thousands, of glowing candles balanced precariously on the floor. Worshippers prayed fervently and drank Posh, an artisanal sugar-cane-based liquor. They also sipped Coca-Cola, to help them release malevolent spirits by belching them out, sometimes spraying the Coca-Cola in a fine mist over the candles.

Whether the green Maya crosses outside the church represented to the Maya the crucified Jesus or resurrected Christ was not our concern; we were not interested in whether the crosses were representations of the prickly Ceiba tree or the Mayan Tree of Life whose roots reached into the underworld. Or whether Jesus was worshiped as a sun god. Or whether the four points of the cross represented the sun, moon, earth and human beings.

We were there not for ethnohistorical references, but to respect a people whose ancestors survived the brutal conquest of Bernal Diaz del Castillo (an officer who served under Hernán Cortés), who received an encomiendo for Chamula that gave him unlimited power to demand free labor from the indigenous peoples in return for "Christianizing" them. Today, the people of Chamula support the Zapatistas who, since 1994, have continued to fight life-and-death policies and practices of neoliberalism, the privatization of land and other natural resources and to create autonomous systems of governance, independent schools and gender equality. What interested us most was not an academic exercise in comparative symbology but building a domain of social justice; for where justice lives, love can flourish through many portals of spirituality, cosmovisions and ecosystems of the mind.

However, just as there remain battles over land and freedom, fierce battles of the Gods continue. As Rivage-Seul writes:

> Yes, there's a battle of Gods. Yes, there's a battle of Christs. Yes, there is a battle of the virgins. And the God that has proven victorious in all of this (over Jesus and Yahweh) is Violence itself. Violence has filled the "hollow concept" of God—just as we have seen it being filled at various points in the Bible by the Gods of Eve, Cain, Abraham, David, the prophets and Jesus. From there it is the God of Cain's original sin that has triumphed worldwide. And he has subjected the world to the terrible arithmetic of Lemech, multiplied again by the United States. Not one death for one death, not seven for one, not five hundred for one, but one thousand (and more) for one. Walter Wink said it clearly: Violence itself is America's God. Our creed is that violence saves. (2008, p. 169)

Violence may be America's God, but for Jesus violence was not meant for conquest, for the creation of economic inequality, for the reproduction of the coloniality of power.

Jesus was likely no quietist who publicly repudiated his messianic role, avoided political involvement and rejected the idea of leading a nationalist movement against the Romans. What is clear is that he was executed for sedition at the hands of the Romans and if he was not a Zealot, then it is likely he was sympathetic to many of their principles (Brandon, 1967). For those Christians—especially the prosperity evangelicals who are so popular in the U.S.—who promote capitalism and equate faith with wealth, it would serve them well to reconsider their interpretation of the Gospels and to consider the fact that communism predated Karl Marx through the teaching of the Bible (Miranda, 1974, 2004).

Speaking of the here and now, at the time of this writing residents of Detroit who have not paid their water bills have had their water supply shut off by the city, affecting more than 40 percent of the customers of the Detroit Water and Sewage Department, and posing a serious health hazard for 200 to

300 thousand residents. Detroit is not Cochabamba, Bolivia, in 2000, when protests broke out after a new firm, Aguas del Tunari (involving the Bechtel corporation), invested in the construction of a dam and tried to pay for this by dramatically raising water rates of the local people. A community coalition, Coordinadora in Defense of Water and Life, organized a massive protest movement, which finally reversed the privatization. Protests by the people of Detroit have not yet forced the city to keep the water flowing to those who cannot afford their water bills.

Is this so surprising? The U.S. has a history of ignoring the basic needs of its population. William Blum (2014a) writes:

On December 14, 1981 a resolution was proposed in the United Nations General Assembly which declared that 'education, work, health care, proper nourishment, national development are human rights.' Notice the 'proper nourishment.' The resolution was approved by a vote of 135–1. The United States cast the only 'No' vote.

A year later, December 18, 1982, an identical resolution was proposed in the General Assembly. It was approved by a vote of 131–1. The United States cast the only 'No' vote.

The following year, December 16, 1983, the resolution was again put forth, a common practice at the United Nations. This time it was approved by a vote of 132–1. There's no need to tell you who cast the sole 'No' vote.

These votes took place under the Reagan administration. Under the Clinton administration, in 1996, a United Nations-sponsored World Food Summit affirmed the 'right of everyone to have access to safe and nutritious food.' The United States took issue with this, insisting that it does not recognize a 'right to food.' Washington instead championed free trade as the key to ending the poverty at the root of hunger, and expressed fears that recognition of a 'right to food' could lead to lawsuits from poor nations seeking aid and special trade provisions.

The situation of course did not improve under the administration of George W. Bush. In 2002, in Rome, world leaders at another UN-sponsored World Food Summit again approved a declaration that everyone had the right to 'safe and nutritious food.' The United States continued to oppose the clause, again fearing it would leave them open to future legal claims by famine-stricken countries.

I'm waiting for a UN resolution affirming the right to oxygen.

No matter how strained we may become in fathoming the calamity of capitalist globalization and its attending antagonisms, we cannot banish these harrowing realities or thrust them out of mind by taking refuge in our books, our theories, our seminar rooms or in the salons of our organizing committees. We do not possess everything necessary to be truly human by understanding ourselves as part of nature. We are, after all, also spirit.

To be fully human, we need to be attentive to moral criteria and the moral imperatives we set for ourselves as human beings, categorical as opposed to conditioned imperatives, that is, moral imperatives which do not make the precept's obliging force depend on any need of the person obliged (Miranda, 2007). Our imperatives are not conditioned by our own self-interest. They follow from our obligation to treat others as ends and not means (Miranda, 2007).

Our moral imperatives oblige us to duty, to action! We are obliged to treat people of the future as having infinite dignity, and we appeal to rationality to negate the distinction between what is just and what is supererogatory. Here we are not guided by procedural ethics imposed by democracy but by our judgmental criteria and content when we affirm that all people are to be treated with infinite dignity, which entails some degree of reciprocal respect and which, according to Miranda (2007), is the real meaning of Rousseau's general will. We have, after all, a new era to proclaim. Here educators committed to social transformation through incremental means can take heed from the words of Miranda:

> The true revolutionary abjures reformist palliatives, because these divert the efforts of the people most capable of fomenting rebellion against the bourgeois system into rejuvenating and refurbishing it; such palliatives thus constitute the system's best defense. By the same token, the revolutionary must find any change in the socio-economic system to be a priori inadequate, if that change does not involve a radical revolution in people's attitudes towards each other. If exchange-value (that 'imaginary entity') and the desire for personal gain continue to exist, they will inevitably create other oppressive and exploitative economic systems. (1977, pp. 21–22)

The revolution is now, it's the dialectic regained, it's the people unchained, it's the eschaton made immanent. The teachings of Jesus enfold the world in a new community of justice-seeking revolutionaries. While some might dismiss Jesus as an amalgam of myths spawned in the depths of the Mediterranean imagination, the teachings of Jesus inspire us to turn towards the world and create a society of freely associated producers related in profound mutuality and overflowing love. We find our praxis of universal solidarity in suffering and hope and in our collective recognition that we are not alone but exist in the world with others. We recognize the presence of Jesus in the poor and the oppressed, and our response to the call of the other is not an option but an obligation. Early followers of Jesus lived communally, shared their resources, held all property in common, engaged in a communist lifestyle and held on to communist ideals where goods were distributed "from each according to ability to each according to need" (Rivage-Seul, 2014).

Knowing and appreciating the communist ideals of the early Christians can help us wed the sacred sphere of the Messianic Age to the classless society of Marx's proletarian revolution, as a means of entering into a restorative—even redemptive—relationship with both the past and the future by plunging into the past and dragging it back to the present through an alchemical prism that points to a concrete utopia, not unlike Walter Benjamin's (1969, 1979) restitutionist approach. Benjamin sought to interrupt the history of progress via an amalgam of revolution and messianism—a Messianic-redemptive alchemy that blends the archaic and the not-yet, the collective memories of a lost paradise and the future as a subjunctive mode of what could be. Perhaps in this way can we avoid the catastrophe of progress that today has taken us to a national security capitalism and the jackboots of a militarized psuedo-democracy.

Miranda is correct when he writes that truth and imperative are identical; that to abide in the truth means to fight for justice and equality by making the eschaton immanent. In this way, we judge the authenticity of our lives by the criterion of meeting the needs of others, in the historical (and not simply existential) imperative of loving our neighbor. Our task is to understand how to organize ourselves the day after we rid ourselves of the birthmarks of capitalism, of a world in which every social gain must be sacrificed at the altar of profit. Will we be able to project a viable alternative to the dominance of capital? How can we avoid the horrors of existing capitalist society in our attempt to replace it with a socialist alternative? How can we avoid the terror of societies that existed in places such as the former Soviet Union that destroyed the soviets (workers' councils) and replaced them with a totalitarian dictatorship that suppressed communism and replaced it with state capitalism? How can we prevent ourselves from descending into a narrow nationalism?

How can we fully reclaim the biblical roots of communism that can be found in the Acts of the Apostles? How can we reclaim Jesus as a fellow communist? After all, it was not Marx who established the final criterion for judging the authenticity of one's life as a concern for all peoples in need. It was comrade Jesus.

How do we move beyond a new Left narrative of redistribution and defense of public services? How do we get up and running an antagonistic social and political paradigm to neoliberalism? How can forms of popular power from below be transferred into a new historical bloc? How do we re-compose ourselves into an anti-capitalist united front?

We need a leadership from below that can help us build political programs, articulate new non-commodified collective practices, including new forms of self-management and new forms of public ownership and networks of redistribution—in short, a credible alternative to capitalism that begins with an engagement in the struggles of and for our times. These are the questions that need to be exercised by critical educators everywhere. For these are the questions asked of us by the future of history, after which time, as Matthew tells us, "the Son of Man will send his angels, who will remove from his kingdom all scandals and all workers of iniquity"(13:41), a time when "the just will shine like the sun in the kingdom of their father" (13:43).

We are the mustard seeds of the new Kingdom which Jesus of Nazareth proclaimed—a society free from economic exploitation and inequality (a socialist society envisioned long before it was hatched in the brainpan of Karl Marx) and where individuals are treated as ends in themselves and not as a means for something else. And when the capitalist class tries to bury us deep in the ground with their cold dead hands, we take root again, and push our message of revolutionary love up through the soil of our struggle and into the sunlight. To echo Pablo Neruda, they can cut our flowers but they can't stop the spring.

Bibliography

Ahmad, A. (2011, January–March). On post modernism. *The Marxist, 28,* 4–38.

Ahmed, N. (2013, June 14), Pentagon bracing for public dissent over climate and energy shocks. *The Guardian.* Retrieved from http://www.theguardian.com/environment/earth-insight/2013/jun/14/climate-change-energy-shocks-nsa-prism

Ahmed, N. (2014, June 12). Pentagon preparing for mass civil breakdown. *The Guardian.* Retrieved from http://www.theguardian.com/environment/earth-insight/2014/jun/12/pentagon-mass-civil-breakdown

Altmann, P. (2012). *The concept of interculturality in Ecuador—Development and importance for its agents* (Center for Area Studies Working Paper Series No. 1). Berlin, Germany: Center for Area Studies, Freie Universitat.

Altmann, P. (2013). Good life as a social movement proposal for natural resource use: The Indigenous Movement in Ecuador. *Consilience: The Journal of Sustainable Development, 10*(1), 59–71.

Amin, S. (2010, February). The battlefields chosen by contemporary imperialism: Conditions for an effective response from the South. *MRZine, 7.* Retrieved from http://mrzine.monthlyreview.org/2010/amin070210.html

Anderson, K. (2010, August 18). Overcoming some current challenges to dialectical thought. *International Marxist-Humanist*. Retrieved from http://www.internationalmarxisthumanist. org/articles/overcoming-some-current-challenges-to-dialectical-thought

Andrews, C. (2014, March 22). Thomas Piketty's *Capital in the twenty-first century*: Its uses and limits. *MRZine*. Retrieved from http://mrzine.monthlyreview.org/2014/andrews220314. html

Assange, J., with Appelbaum, J., Müller-Maguhn, A., & Zimmermann, J. (2012). *Cypherpunks: Freedom and the future of the Internet*. New York, NY: OR Books.

Baum, G. (1975). *Religion and alienation: A theological reading of sociology*. New York, NY: Paulist Press.

Benjamin, W. (1936). The work of art in the age of mechanical reproduction. Retrieved from http://www.marxists.org/reference/subject/philosophy/works/ge/benjamin.htm

Benjamin, W. (1969). *Illuminations: Essays and reflections*. H. Arendt (Ed.); (H. Zohn, Trans.). New York, NY: Schocken Books.

Benjamin, W. (1979). *One-way street*. (E. Jephcott & K. Shorter, Trans.). London, England: New Left Books.

Best, S., Kahn, R., Nocella, A., & McLaren, P. (2011). *The global industrial complex: Systems of domination*. Lanham, MD: Lexington Books.

Bloch, E. (1991). *Heritage of our times*. (N. & S. Plaice, Trans.). Berkeley, CA: University of California Press.

Bloch, E. (2000). *The spirit of utopia*. (A. A. Nassar, Trans.). Stanford, CA.: Stanford University Press.

Blum, W. (2014a, August 11). Cold War Two. *The anti-empire report 131*. Retrieved from http:// williamblum.org/aer/read/131

Blum, W. (2014b). Edward Snowden. *The anti-empire report 129*. Retrieved from http://william-blum.org/aer/read/129

Brandon, S. G. F. (1967). *Jesus and the zealots*. New York, NY: Charles Scribner's Sons.

Brown, R. M. (1993). *Liberation theology: An introductory guide*. Louisville, KY: Westminster/John Knox Press.

Clark, J. P. (2013). The common good: Sarvodaya and the Gandhian legacy. In J. P. Clark, *The impossible community: Realizing communitarian anarchism* (pp. 217–245). New York, NY: Bloomsbury.

Cone, J. (1990). *A black theology of liberation*. Maryknoll, NY: Orbis Books.

Corey, Benjamin (2014). *Undiluted: Rediscovernits The Radical Message of Jesus*. Shippensburg, PA.: Destiny Image.

Democracy Now. (2007, August 30). The privatization of education: How New Orleans went from a public school system to a charter school city. Retrieved from http://www.democra-cynow.org/2007/8/30/the_privatization_of_education_how_new

Despain, H. G. (2014, May 8). Piketty: A Marxist review. *Shiraz Socialist*. Retrieved from https://shirazsocialist.wordpress.com/2014/05/08/piketty-a-marxist-review/

Dunayevskaya, R. (a.k.a. Freddie James). (1941, March). Internal discussion *Bulletin* of the Workers Party. Retrieved from https://www.marxists.org/archive/dunayevskaya/works/ 1941/ussr-capitalist.htm

Dunayevskaya, R. (1965). Marx's humanism today. In E. Fromm (Ed.), *Socialist humanism* (pp. 63–76). New York, NY: Doubleday. Also retrieved from: https://www.marxists.org/archive/dunayevskaya/works/1965/marx-humanism.htm

Dunayevskaya, R. (1992). *The Marxist-humanist theory of state capitalism*. Chicago, IL: The News & Letters Committee.

Eagleton, T. (2009). *Reason, faith, and revolution*. New Haven, CT: Yale University Press.

Ebert, T. (2009). *The task of cultural critique*. Urbana, IL: University of Illinois Press.

Ebert, T., & Zavarzadeh, M. (2007). *Class in culture*. Boulder, CO: Paradigm.

Fanon, F. (2004). *Black skin, white masks*. (R. Philcox, Trans.). New York, NY: Grove Press.

Fatheuer, T. (2011). *Buen vivir: A brief introduction to Latin America's new concepts for the good life and the rights of nature* (Vol. 17). Berlin, Germany: Heinrich Böll Foundation Publication Series on Ecology.

Fischman, G. E., & McLaren, P. (2005). Rethinking critical pedagogy and the Gramscian and Freirean legacies: From organic to committed intellectuals or critical pedagogy, commitment, and praxis. *Cultural Studies ↔ Critical Methodologies*, 5(4), 425–446. Retrieved from https://amadlandawonye.wikispaces.com/2005,+McLaren+and+Fischman,+Gramsci,+Freire,+Organic+Intellectuals

Foster, J. B. (2013a). The epochal crisis. *Monthly Review*, 65(5). Retrieved from http://monthlyreview.org/2013/10/01/epochal-crisis

Foster, J. B. (2013b, November 14). The epochal crisis, unequal ecological exchange, and exit strategies. *MRZine*. Retrieved from http://mrzine.monthlyreview.org/2013/foster141113.html

Giroux, H. A. (2015, April 27). The perils of being a public intellectual. *CounterPunch*. Retrieved from http://www.counterpunch.org/2015/04/27/the-perils-of-being-a-public-intellectual/

Gomstyn, A. (2010, July 2). Walmart CEO pay: More in an hour than workers get all year? *ABC News*. Retrieved from http://abcnews.go.com/Business/walmart-ceo-pay-hour-workers-year/story?id=11067470#.T1TpP4cgcsd

Graeber, D. (2012). Dead zones of the imagination: On violence, bureaucracy, and interpretive labor. The 2006 Malinowski Memorial Lecture. *Journal of Ethnographic Theory*, 2(2), 105–128.

Grosfoguel, R. (2013). The structure of knowledge in Westernized universities: Epistemic racism/sexism and the four genocides/epistemicides of the long 16th century. *Human Architecture*, 11(1), 73–90.

Harvey, D. (2014, May 20). Taking on 'Capital' without Marx: What Thomas Piketty misses in his critique of capitalism. *In These Times*. Retrieved from http://inthesetimes.com/article/16722/taking_on_capital_without_marx

Hedges, C. (2011, May 16). The Obama deception: Why Cornel West went ballistic. *Truthdig*. Retrieved from http://www.truthdig.com/report/item/the_obama_deception_why_cornel_west_went_ballistic_20110516

Hedges, C. (2013, September 9). Cornel West and the fight to save the black prophetic tradition. *Truthdig*. Retrieved from http://www.truthdig.com/report/item/cornel_west_and_the_fight_to_save_the_black_prophetic_tradition_20130909/

Herzog, W. R. (1994). *Parables as subversive speech: Jesus as pedagogue of the oppressed*. Louisville, KY: Westminster/John Knox Press.

Higgs, R. (1987). *Crisis and Leviathan: Critical episodes in the growth of American government.* Oxford, England: Oxford University Press.

Hill, D. (2012). Immiseration capitalism, activism and education: Resistance, revolt and revenge. *Journal for Critical Education Policy Studies, 10*(2). Retrieved from http://www.jceps.com/?pageID=article&articleID=259

Hudis, P. (2005, November). *Marx's critical appropriation and transcendence of Hegel's theory of alienation.* Paper presented to the Brecht Forum, New York, NY.

Hudis, P. (2012). *Marx's concept of the alternative to capitalism.* Chicago, IL: Haymarket Books. Retrieved from http://dx.doi.org/10.1163/9789004229860

Hudis, P. (2004). Marx among the Muslims. *Capitalism, Nature, Socialism, 15*(4): 51–67.

Hudis, P. (2014a, September). From philosophy to organization and back: Marxist-humanist tasks and perspectives. Retrieved from http://www.internationalmarxisthumanist.org/articles/philosophy-organization-back-marxist-humanist-tasks-perspectives-peter-hudis

Hudis, P. (2014b, November). *Frantz Fanon's contribution to Hegelian-Marxism.* Paper presented at the Historical Materialism conference, London, England.

Hudson, W. (1982). *The Marxist philosophy of Ernst Bloch.* New York, NY: St. Martin's Press.

Kliman, A. (2013, February 13). 'The 99%' and 'the 1%' ... of what? *With Sober Senses.* Retrieved from http://www.marxisthumanistinitiative.org/?s=The+99%25%E2%80%9D+and+%E2%80%9Cthe+1%25%E2%80%9D

Kovel, J. (2002). *The enemy of nature: The end of capitalism or the end of the world?* London, England: Zed Books.

Krugman, P. (2014, May 8). Why we're in a new Gilded Age. *New York Review of Books.* Retrieved from http://www.nybooks.com/articles/archives/2014/may/08/thomas-piketty-new-gilded-age/

Lebowitz, M. (2013, January 9). Socialism for the 21st century: Re-inventing and renewing the struggle. *Links.* Retrieved from http://links.org.au/node/3178

Leech, G. (2012). *Capitalism: A structural genocide.* London, England: Zed Books.

Lichtman, R. (1982). *The production of desire: The integration of psychoanalysis into Marxist theory.* New York, NY: Free Press.

Maeshiri, K. (2014, April 19). The kingdom of God, or, what shall Christians do? *The Harvard Ichthus.* Retrieved from http://www.harvardichthus.org//2014/04/the-kingdom-of-god-or-what-shall-christians-do/

Mayo, P. (1999). *Gramsci, Freire and adult education: Possibilities for transformative education.* London, England: Zed Books.

Mayo, P. (2005). In and against the state: Gramsci, war of position and adult education. *Journal of Critical Education Policy Studies, 3*(2). Retrieved from http://www.jceps.com/wp-content/uploads/PDFs/03-2-03.pdf

McElwee, S. (2014, March 8). Six ways America is like a Third-World country. *Reader Supported News.* Retrieved from http://readersupportednews.org/opinion2/277-75/22453-six-ways-america-is-like-a-third-world-country

McLaren, P. (1999). *Schooling as a ritual performance: Toward a political economy of educational symbols and gestures.* Lanham, MD: Rowman & Littlefield.

McLaren, P. (2005). Critical pedagogy and class struggle in the age of neoliberal globalization: Notes from history's underside. *International Journal of Inclusive Democracy*, 2(1). Retrieved from http://www.inclusivedemocracy.org/journal/pdf%20files/pdf%20vol2/Critical%20Pedagogy%20and%20Class%20Struggle.pdf

McLaren, P. (2006). *Rage and hope: Interviews with Peter McLaren on war, imperialism, and critical pedagogy*. New York, NY: Peter Lang.

McLaren, P. (2011). The death rattle of the American mind: A call for pedagogical outlawry. *Cultural Studies ↔ Critical Methodologies*, 11(4), 373–385. Retrieved from http://www.academia.edu/958870/Death_Rattle_of_the_American_Mind

McLaren, P. (2012). Objection sustained: Revolutionary pedagogical praxis as an occupying force. *Policy Futures in Education*, 10(4), 487–495. Retrieved from http://dx.doi.org/10.2304/pfie.2012.10.4.487

McLaren, P. (2013). A critical patriotism for urban schooling: A call for a pedagogy against fear and denial and for democracy. *Texas Education Review*, 1, 234–253. Retrieved from http://txedrev.org/wp-content/uploads/2013/11/McLaren_A-Critical-Patriotism-for-Urban-Schooling_TxEdRev.pdf

McLaren, P. (2014). Contemporary youth resistance culture and the class struggle. *Critical Arts*, 28(1), 152–160. Retrieved from http://dx.doi.org/10.1080/02560046.2014.883701

Miranda, J. P. (1974). *Marx and the Bible: A critique of the philosophy of oppression*. (J. Eagleson, Trans.). Maryknoll, NY: Orbis Books

Miranda, J. P. (1977). *Being and the Messiah: The message of St. John*. Maryknoll, NY: Orbis Books.

Miranda, J. P. (1980). *Marx against the Marxists: The Christian humanism of Karl Marx*. London, England: SCM Press.

Miranda, J. P. (2004). *Communism in the Bible*. (R. R. Barr, Trans.). Eugene, OR: Wipf & Stock.

Miranda, J. P. (2007). *Rationality and democracy*. Mexico City, Mexico: Universidad Autónoma Metropolitana.

Miranda, J. P. (2011). *Hegel was right: The myth of the empirical sciences*. (E. Charpenel Elorduy, Trans.). Frankfurt, Germany: Peter Lang.

Monzó, L. D., & McLaren, P. (2014). Critical pedagogy and the decolonial option: Challenges to the inevitability of capitalism. *Policy Futures in Education*, 12(4), 513–525. Retrieved from http://dx.doi.org/10.2304/pfie.2014.12.4.513

Orwell, G. (1950). *1984*. New York, NY: Signet Books (The New American Library).

Piketty, T. (2014). *Capital in the twenty-first century*. Cambridge, MA: Harvard University Press.

Pomeroy, A. F. (2004a). *Marx and Whitehead: Process, dialectics, and the critique of capitalism*. Albany, NY: State University of New York Press.

Pomeroy, A. F. (2004b). Why Marx, why now? A recollection of Dunayevskaya's *Power of negativity. Cultural Logic*, 7. Retrieved from http://clogic.eserver.org/2004/pomeroy.html

Pozo, M. (2003). Toward a revolutionary critical pedagogy: An interview with Peter McLaren. *St. John's University Humanities Review*, 2(1). Retrieved from http://facpub.stjohns.edu/~ganterg/sjureview/vol2-1/mclaren.html

Reitz, C. (2000). *Art, alienation and the humanities: A critical engagement with Herbert Marcuse.* Albany, NY: State University of New York Press.

Reitz, C. (2013). Conclusion: The commonwealth counter-offensive. In C. Reitz (Ed.), *Crisis and commonwealth: Marcuse, Marx, McLaren* (pp. 269–286). Lanham, MD: Lexington Books.

Rivage-Seul, M. (2008). *The emperor's god: Imperial misunderstandings of Christianity.* Radford, VA: Institute for Economic Democracy Press.

Rivage-Seul, M. (2014, April 26). (Sunday Homily) Christianity is Communism! Jesus was a Communist! *OpEdNews.* Retrieved from http://www.opednews.com/articles/Sunday-Homily-Christiani-by-Mike-Rivage-Seul-Christianity_Communism_Economic_Jesus-140426-205.html

Robinson, W. I. (1996). *Promoting polyarchy: Globalization, US intervention, and hegemony.* Cambridge, England: Cambridge University Press. Retrieved from http://dx.doi.org/10.1017/CBO9780511559129

Robinson, W. I. (2000). Social theory and globalization: The rise of a transnational state. *Theory and Society, 30*(2), 157–200. Retrieved from http://dx.doi.org/10.1023/A:1011077330455

Robinson, W. I. (2004). *A theory of global capitalism: Production, class, and state in a transnational world.* Baltimore, MD: Johns Hopkins University Press.

Robinson, W. I. (2008). *Latin America and global capitalism.* Baltimore, MD: Johns Hopkins University Press.

Robinson, W. I. (2011a, May 8). Global capitalism and 21st century fascism. *Aljazeera.* Retrieved from http://www.aljazeera.com/indepth/opinion/2011/04/201142612714539672.html

Robinson, W. I. (2011b, December 4). Global rebellion: The coming chaos? *Aljazeera.* Retrieved from http://www.aljazeera.com/indepth/opinion/2011/11/20111130121556567265.html

San Juan, E. (2007). *In the wake of terror: Class, race, nation, ethnicity in the postmodern world.* Lanham, MD: Lexington Books.

Sethness, J. (2013, June 16). The structural genocide that is capitalism. *Truthout.* Retrieved from http://www.truth-out.org/opinion/item/16887-the-structural-genocide-that-is-capitalism

Tengely-Evans, T. (2014, June 14). Piketty and Marx. *International Socialism, 143.* Retrieved from http://www.isj.org.uk/index.php4?id=991&issue=143

Thomas, P. D. (2009). *The Gramscian moment: Philosophy, hegemony and Marxism.* Amsterdam, the Netherlands: Brill. Retrieved from http://dx.doi.org/10.1163/ej.9789004167711.i-478

Torrance, R. M. (1994). *The spiritual quest: Transcendence in myth, religion, and science.* Berkeley, CA: University of California Press.

Tyner, J., & Inwood, J. (2014). Violence as fetish: Geography, Marxism, and dialectics. *Progress in Human Geography. 38*(6), 771–784.

Weinstein, M. (2015). Stop! Read! Look at shocking photo! U.S. Army officially recruits for 'Mission for God.' Retrieved from http://www.dailykos.com/story/2015/01/15/1358006/-STOP-READ-LOOK-AT-SHOCKING-PHOTO-U-S-Army-Official-Recruitment-for-Mission-for-God?detail=email

Weisbrot, M. (2013, September 14). Forty years on, much of Allende's dream has come true: The United States no longer has the same hegemonic stranglehold over countries within Latin America. *Aljazeera.* Retrieved from http://www.aljazeera.com/indepth/opinion/2013/09/2013913174222513256.html

Wells, M. (2013, November 30). Los Angeles moves toward restricting food distributions in public places. *World Socialist Web Site*. Retrieved from http://www.wsws.org/en/articles/2013/11/30/losa-n30.html

Yen, H., & Naziri, M. (2013, July 28). Shocking study: 4 out of 5 in USA face near-poverty and unemployment. *Political Blind Spot*. Retrieved from http://politicalblindspot.com/shocking-study-4-out-of-5-in-usa-face-near-poverty-and-unemployment/

· 2 ·

COMRADE FREIRE

I t surely is the case that the age which we inhabit so precariously demands manifestos, not desiderata or credos. Unless, of course, those creeds can become manifest as a rallying cry, a canticle for the undead slaves toiling in capitalism's grim hostelry, forceful enough to be heard beyond the sepulchers and catacombs where schooling, as a proprietary field entombed by its own unforgiving success, has been consigned for all eternity for desecrating the very heart of what it means to live and to learn. It is my wager that words can howl, and on this brittle quiver of hope I set mine into print.

I am in solidarity with today's youth, the heirs of Spartacus, the Paris Commune, the Levellers, the Diggers, the Ranters, the Zapatistas and the sans-culottes, the orgasms of history whose howls of indignation clash with the ear-shattering silence of the mainstream pedagogical tradition—a tradition that compelled me as a youngster, in baggy denim overalls stained with grease and oil and sporting a jaunty oversized newsboy cap, to keep my eyes squarely focused ahead and my hands folded together on top of my desk as neat as a crisply starched handkerchief and not to trust teachers. All I recall are charts, tables and formulae; wall diagrams and lists—dead letters for the living dead. I had little sympathy in 1959 for teachers. That came much later, in 1965. The countercultural zeitgeist had inspired me, and I felt alive for the first time inside the walls of the academic prison house, beginning with readings of *Beowulf*, Chaucer and Shakespeare, in that historical order.

After years of being victimized by the bloviating gasbags of the corporate media, those venal, unscrupulous and dilettantish charlatans who serve as little more than capitalist cheerleaders for a conveyor belt democracy, I realized that my fate as a student in the academy was in less peril than that of others who took the brunt of capitalism's brutal neoliberal assault—reserve armies of low-wage earners and the unemployed. For those communities that have harrowed the hell of this world-eater, some explanation is necessary, especially since many of these communities are searching for a role that education can play to free them and their children from the death grip of this seemingly unstoppable and imperishable Leviathan. Capitalism is so wretchedly powerful it possesses the ability to commodify our souls (by commodify I here refer to something created expressly for market exchange).

When we talk of the working class, it is easy to fall into the trap of seeing class solely or mainly in terms of culture, i.e., working-class culture. But I want to emphasize that it is the social relations of labor that determine a person's class location, not the opportunities for engorging your powers of acquisition through deregulated consumptive practices. With gold-filled pockets as large as the pouched cheeks of Dizzy Gillespie playing his trumpet, the rich and famous have set the standard for success as measured by human greed and an unquenchable thirst for power. But for those who sell their labor power to earn a living (i.e., those who produce the profit for the capitalist), life is tantamount to being enslaved to those who purchase human labor (the capitalist class) and who stash away all the profits for themselves in order to invest in new labor-saving technologies rather than help advance the quality of life for the workers themselves.

While, for instance, the stock market may seem to produce wealth, it is really just redistributing the wealth produced by the labor of the workers. Profit does not come from market relations (buying low and selling high), but from human labor power. In this, I follow Marx's focus on the development of human productive forces—a very complex process that is historically related to the material conditions of production and the class struggle. The profound incompatibility between the forces and relations of production produces tremendous social conflict.

In the field of education, I want to draw attention to an irresoluble tension that exists between the possibilities of education and economic efficiency, threatening the professional autonomy and working conditions of educators and the very purpose of education itself. Marxism's protean focus on proletarian self-activity and the self-organization of the popular majorities are anathema to much of the work that falls under the dubious classification of social-justice education. Although well-meaning progressive educators might be willing to criticize the manner in which humans are turned into dead objects (i.e., what Marxists refer to as fetishized commodities), they are often loathe to consider the fact that within capitalist society, all value originates in the sphere of production and a main role of schools is to serve as agents or functionaries of capital and its masters—the military-industrial complex, the surveillance state and the transnational capitalist class. Furthermore, these educators fail to understand that education is more reproductive of an exploitative social order than a constitutive challenge to it precisely because it rests on the foundations of capitalist exchange value.

Taxpayer bailouts of the financial sector in 2009 have made billionaires of hedge fund managers, further widening the gap between the rich and poor, making the U.S. one of the most unequal countries in the so-called developed world. Faced with gargantuan cuts to school aid and an evisceration of programs designed to serve working-class communities, assaults on teachers and teacher unions and a push for the privatization of schooling and test-based accountability, public schools are under siege, fighting for their very existence against the onslaught of the new Daddy Warbucks in postmodern corporate clothing—the Bill & Melinda Gates Foundation, the Eli & Edythe Broad Foundation, the Walton Family Foundation, the Laura and John Arnold Foundation, the Michael & Susan Dell Foundation, the Bradley Foundation, the Robertson Foundation, the Fisher Foundation and the Anschutz Foundation. And, as Diane Ravitch (2014) has pointed out, organizations support privately run school organizations with progressive-sounding names such as "the American Federation for Children, the American Legislative Exchange Council (ALEC), Better Education for Kids (B$K), Black Alliance for Educational Options, the education program at the Brookings Institution, the Centre for Education Reforms, Chiefs for Change, ConnCAN (and its spin-off, 50CAN, as well as state-specific groups like MinnCAN, NYCAN, RI-CAN), Democrats for Education Reform, the Education Equality Project, Education Reform Now, Educators 4 Excellence, EdVoice, the Foundation for Excellence in Education, the National Council on Teacher Quality, New Leaders for New Schools, NewSchools Venture Fund, Parent Revolution, Stand for Children, Students for Education Reform, StudentsFirst, Teach For America, Teach Plus" and others.

Under the rallying cry of accountability through test-based evaluations of teachers, wealthy entrepreneurs and hedge fund speculators who have never attended public schools or taught in a classroom have partnered with billionaires to advance a corporate reform agenda in our nation's schools. These new "reformers" span the ideological spectrum from Bill Gates to the Koch brothers. In fact, among some of the very persons responsible for championing the neoliberal economic policies that led to the current recession are those who are now anointing themselves as leading educational reformers.

Savvy members of the business community fresh from power lunches with insider Beltway lobbyists and underwritten by private education management firms cravenly cement their agendas to the desperate cries for help from aggrieved communities, despoiling education by turning sites of learning into deregulated enterprise zones such that the rhetoric of democracy and education has now become oxymoronic. This is not to say that all attempts to create community and business partnerships for the improvement of education are merely cynical attempts to use market-driven reforms to manufacture an unstable and de-unionized teaching force. But it is no coincidence that the push to privatize education has in many instances had the tragic effect of intensifying inequality through reproducing a government-subsidized class-tiered system of education, leaving many schools in working-class communities with inadequate resources and languishing in despair.

To overcome this juggernaut of capitalist cruelty that would profit from the tears of the poor if it knew how to market them effectively, revolutionary critical pedagogy flouts the frontier between scholarship and activism in order to outflank consensus and, in this way, works to create a counter-public sphere. We are askew to traditional academia and are not enmortgaged to its status and do not represent the ivory tower. In fact, we are often marginalized in and excoriated by various and sundry academic organizations.

We want to mediate human needs and social relations in publicly discussable form to create a transnational social movement of aggressively oppositional power. However, critical pedagogy is not yet in a position to play a substantial role in the struggle for a socialist future. A more productive role for critical pedagogy needs to be discovered so that educators can become more effective agents of revolutionary transformation.

The ferocity of today's immiseration capitalism leaves little semblance of the unsundered world of the 1950s suburbia, as it haunts the world like a fallen Tharmas, the bellowing beast with sea jelly eyes and filament-riven skin that haunts Blake's Apocalypse.

Gone are the days of *The Adventures of Ozzie and Harriet, Leave It to Beaver, Dobie Gillis, Father Knows Best, My Three Sons*—shows that I grew up with watching U.S. television from my native Toronto. An only child, I longed to have a brother like Wally or Ricky who would defend me from extortion by the "hard rocks" at my school whose Brylcreemed ducktails and leather jackets were forbidden me by my parents. But what were those days like for the poor and the powerless, those who slaved on the assembly lines and in the factories, those who lived in Queens or the Bronx in the 1950s, or in West Side Manhattan's Hell's Kitchen long before its gentrification in the 1990s?

We fight to make available those vernaculars that have been deemed oppositional and counter-hegemonic/contestatory/revolutionary. With a critical lexicon, born in blood-soaked struggles by those who have over centuries fought against the forces of domination and exploitation through poetry, art, philosophy, literature, politics, science, technology and a search for justice and equality, we can envision and create a new world. And finally, we can see those things which interdict a learner's ability to read the word and the world critically.

Zygmunt Bauman (2010) and others have argued that vulnerability and uncertainty are the foundation of all political power. The state no longer mitigates the degree to which citizens are at the mercy of the vulnerability and uncertainty of the market. In fact, the state deliberately intensifies our vulnerability and uncertainty through the social construction of fear resulting from a belligerent indifference and constant threat of violence. We can trace this historically to the Thatcher and Reagan administrations and the brutal dismantling of the welfare state as restraints on market forces were lifted. The market was seen as self-regulating. The promise of the self-regulating market resembles the promise of artificial intelligence in the film, *Ex Machina*. We believe we can subject the market to some kind of Turing test to confirm it has an emotional intelligence and would never let humanity suffer at the hands of the hedge funds and banks. And we are led to believe that somehow it will pass the test. In this view, the market has the potential to transcend the human and assume God-like attributes because it is the perfect autodidact. Already we submit ourselves to the Market God, giving over our faith to those with the power to control it. Doing so is tantamount to thanking them for giving us the opportunity to be exploited. Could it even be likened to kissing the "*horribile flagellum*" after a lashing at the stock (stock market)?

Reagan launched a war against the poor, especially poor African Americans who were out of work. This assuaged the bloodlust of unemployed and underemployed white constituencies who, after all, needed somebody to blame for their growing economic vulnerability. According to the logic of the market, unless poor people of color submit themselves with requisite deference to the God-speak of the market and allow themselves to become exploited in low level jobs without security or medical insurance, they must be held responsible for their own immiseration. And they can then be criminalized by the state for the sake of order-building and for boosting the prison economy.

The market then becomes our protector, the ultimate criterion of political legitimacy for its ability to create security through a surveillance state so formidable, no terrorists could survive. This is further facilitated by the construction of a national identity via the corporate media that is a toxic admixture of statecraft and garage sale apocalyptic mysticism: America must carry the torch of free market democracy to the far corners of the globe as our God-given duty, a providential version of manifest destiny, even if it means preemptive military strikes and, as George W. Bush famously put it, "kicking some ass." And this requires a homeland safe and secure from any type of threat of market regulation.

The current crisis of neoliberal globalization is re-patterning not only the objective world, but the subjective world as well, constantly breaking down cultures of oppositional political solidarity by trying to create a post-ideological universe of human experiences and selfhood consisting of commodified subjects whose affinity for any type of political solidarity has been replaced by participation in orgies of capitalist consumption and the creation of self-gratifying designer identities. A new imperialist vision of manifest destiny (Harvey, 2003) has shaped the foreign policy of the U.S., giving a grotesque new meaning to the phrase "military-industrial complex." That we live in a democracy is largely an ideological fabrication or illusion that lends legitimacy to the reproduction of this complex. In the language of the transnational capitalist class, this might be called a "beneficial untruth."

In the present theatre of class warfare there remains a profound confusion as to how to wage our fight against the global contagion unleashed by the Great Recession. The seriousness of this crisis extends beyond developing isolated tactics for deployment in the struggle against state repression, imperialist wars, climate change, geopolitical insecurity and forms of abstract labor that are crippling workers and their families with a cruel malignity. Some of our best-intentioned fighters who are putting themselves most at risk in the struggle for social justice are operating under ideological assumptions that are squarely encapsulated to serve the needs of capital, thereby recuperating the very conditions they are struggling against. What's missing is a well-defined *strategic* sense of how capital as a monstrous entity can neither be placated nor reformed—but must be utterly destroyed. When we plead with the behemoth for compassion, it curls its hands, pulls back its rictus to reveal a wickedly jeering skull beneath its corporate skin and retreats across a field of dried bones, only to return again with an even larger club with which to pound us laughingly into dust.

Any state devoted to abolishing terror must itself inspire terror and in fact become more terrifying than the terrorists it purports to be fighting. However, the current crisis of democracy has been able to demonstrate to many that egalitarian justice cannot be achieved within the framework of a capitalist market economy that relies on wars, the arms industry and ecocide to slake its endless thirst.

One of the foundational social relations that interdicts a student's access to resources necessary to see the world critically is, I believe, class exploitation—an exploitation that despoils communities and dispossesses workers of their humanity. Education opposes schooling. Education is that which intrudes upon our instincts and instruments of mind and augments them; it pushes us along the arcs of the stars where our thoughts can give rise to new vistas of being and becoming and to new solidarities with our fellow humans and non-humans alike. Our responsibilities for creating critical citizens should be proportional to our privilege. Today a good education is no longer seen as a social responsibility but as picking carefully from an array of consumer choices provided by a number of new gluttonous companies and corporations.

In the main, I would say that we need to strive for cooperative, freely associated labor that is not value producing. We need to look to the new social movements and uprisings throughout the world for new organizational forms, including those of non-Western peoples. Socialism is not an inevitability, despite what teleologically driven Marxists might tell you. Right now capitalism is reorganizing itself and attempting to reconstitute the working class by criminalizing it and disaggregating its revolutionary potential through new information technologies. Can democracy survive this historical self-immolation? I would say no, not without the rise of social fascism. And then what kind of democracy would that be? A democracy in name only—which is not far from what we already have in the U.S. at the moment.

As we fall prey to the all-pervasive influence of corporations and their attempts to re-create us as desiring-machines (desiring what the corporations

have to sell us), we have become a less mindful, less vigilant citizenry, watching passively as civil life becomes swallowed up by the logic of capital, consumption and corporatism. Many young and talented individuals no longer
want to become actors—they want to become celebrities. Our rhizomatous
culture has become corralled by capital, so that it appears as if we are autonomous and in a constant state of self-actualization but in reality we are making
ourselves more vulnerable to the crippling control of Big Brother. But of course
it is easy to sink into a dystopian malaise and to be so fearful of the future that
we end up in the thrall of paralysis.

In our pedagogies, in our public pedagogies more specifically (this term
was developed first by Henry Giroux), I follow the tradition of popular education, liberation theology and Freirean-based education. Freire's standing
within the lineage of critical pedagogy is that of a global advocate for praxis.
Freire's work demonstrates the possibility of what I would call a transformative volition, or protagonistic intent, that is, a movement of the human spirit
(that resides in the flesh of our bodies and of our dreams) in and on the world
designed to transform the material and social conditions that shape us and are
shaped by us so that our creative and productive capacities are enhanced and
our humanity enlarged.

Here I would draw attention to the enfleshment of Freire's concept of
praxis in which he weaves the human body into his materialist dialectics of
consciousness and praxis. For Freire, reality was a concrete totality, a reality
that is already a structured, self-forming dialectical whole in the process of coming into existence. Freire believes we as subjects can break out of the prison
house of discourse and its attendant subjectivism by changing the material conditions that shape us in our practical activity. Through a method of analysis
and a conception of the world that involves a dialectical undressing of reality
and a dialectical unity with the oppressed, Freire is able to avoid solipsism and
idealism.

In other words, Freire was concerned with interrogating the causal relationships that inform our material consciousness and subjective volition and
intentionality. In the process of understanding the world, we deepen our consciousness precisely through our actions in and on the world that enable us not
only to grasp our positionality in the world but also to transform the totality
of social relations that constitute the contradictory character of our existence.

Freire was committed to freeing ourselves and others from the relations
bound up in the dialectical contradictions of everyday life. His work was thus
connected to Marx's negative conception of ideology—to actions and symbols

that are really only partial and fragmented and therefore distorted. Here Freire admonishes us not to free people from their chains but to prepare them to free themselves through a dialogic praxis linked to a materialist dialectics of consciousness (see Au, 2007). Freire understood that the form of action people take is a function of how they perceive themselves in the world. The critical action for freedom that Freire advocates stems fundamentally from our dialogic relations with other human beings and leads to a critical consciousness embedded relationally in the word and the world as a form of praxis, an act of knowing through problem-posing/coding/decoding and reconstruction (see also Freire & Macedo (1987)).

Critical pedagogy invites students to understand everyday life from the perspective of those who are the most powerless in our society so that society can be transformed in the interests of a more humane and just existence for all. Understanding social life from the perspective of the oppressed goes beyond mere empathy. Here I would draw upon the insights of Augusto Boal (1979), in particular his important concept of metaxis as a pedagogical process. Boal, like Bertolt Brecht (1964) before him, was suspicious of the use of empathy and catharsis in theater, since empathy and catharsis can destroy the audience's capacity for critique. Brecht developed the concept of *Verfremdung*, or "alienation-effect," which helped to create a distance between the audience and the character, and the actor and the person portrayed. Boal's notion of metaxis replaced the Aristotelian mimetic relationship between the theater and reality, so that both "the real and the fictional could be experienced simultaneously" (O'Connor, 2013, p. 11), a process that Vygotsky described as a "dual effect" "whereby the person is directly engaged with what is happening in the drama, and at the same time is distanced from it, as he or she watches his or her own engagement with the drama" (as cited in O'Connor, 2013, p. 13). Gavin Bolton sees this dual effect as "the tension which exists between the concrete world and the "as if" world, sometimes leading to contradictory emotions" (as cited in O'Connor, 2013, p. 11).

This process is reflected in Freirean critical consciousness as participants remain distanced from problems that others are facing in the contexts of everyday life yet at the same time are open to an empathetic response to those facing problems. Critical consciousness demands acting "as if" you were experiencing a problem situation experienced by others and yet remaining at a critical distance as a percipient of your own actions. Here empathy towards the other is not uncritical or removed from the type of critical reflection necessary to transform the conditions responsible for the problems.

A critical approach to education needs to expand the issue of pedagogy beyond questions of management and governance to that of reclaiming the world for humanity. Technological revolution and the market will not be enough to solve the growing environmental challenge and alleviate the problem of ecological decline and overcome necessity. Educational inquiry, as well as pedagogy as a social practice, must be rethought from the standpoint of those who exist at the bottom of the global capitalist hierarchy if we are to prevail in the continuing wars over scarce resources. Whether we support models of eco-communalism, eco-socialism or new sustainability paradigms, it is clear that critical educational studies underwritten by a social justice agenda will require more than lifestyle change; it will require a concerted critique and transformation of the unbridled barbarism of capitalist social relations.

In order that our social amnesia remain resolutely unacknowledged, we hide behind an almost puritanical fear of any pedagogy that insists on opening the door to doubt, to recognizing our entanglement in the larger conflictual arena of political and social relations and how such an entanglement is itself deeply ensconced in merging religiosity into political ends. If we wonder how it is that here in the twenty-first century we are witnessing the steady erosion of human rights and civil liberties, we only have to examine the extent of our political denial and its implication for mis-educating our citizenry.

At this moment in history, the work of Paulo Freire threatens to explode the culture of silence that informs our everyday life as educators in the world's greatest capitalist democracy, one overarching saga of which has been the successful dismantling of public schooling by the juggernaut of neoliberal privatization and the corporatization of the public sphere.

I met Paulo for the first time at an AERA conference in Chicago in 1985. In 1986, his beloved wife Elza died. Shortly after Elza's death, Paulo wrote me a letter expressing the great sadness that had enveloped him completely. I was surprised to receive a letter from Paulo, and especially such a personal letter, having at the time met him only once. Years later, I came across the letter in my office at UCLA, and I remember thinking to myself that I wish the letter would be lost, as I feared giving into the temptation of showing this letter of considerable intimacy too hastily to friends or to colleagues—or even worse, publishing it. Within days of finding the letter, to my great relief I lost it, and have never been able to recover it.

I also remember the unmitigated joy Paulo felt when he married Maria Araújo Freire, and became a devoted husband to "Nita" who blessed his life with a reciprocal devotion, a fierce intelligence and a relentless dedication to social justice. Nita became an inspiration for Paulo; their mutual love saturated both their lives and their work. One might be tempted to compare Paulo and Nita with Sartre and de Beauvoir, Luxemburg and Kautsky or Karl and Jenny Marx, but that would be romanticizing a relationship that needs no comparison with other historical couples. They were simply Nita and Paulo, lovers and intellectuals who combined both dimensions in their protagonistic actions in the service of the people and their needs. And in so doing, they created a moral affinity that constituted the conditions for the possibility of love. This is the true meaning of revolutionary love, recognizing that love can only exist between free and equal people who share similar ideals and a commitment to serving the poor and the oppressed. The revolutionary love of Nita and Paulo thrived in such conditions.

I remember meeting Nita in an airplane in Rio, quite accidently, and asking her what she thought of my idea about writing a book about Paulo and Ernesto "Che" Guevara. Nita replied that she thought Paulo would approve of such an idea, and Nita's enthusiastic support helped to give me the confidence I needed to complete the book. Eventually, Nita wrote the preface to *Che Guevara, Paulo Freire and the Pedagogy of Revolution* in an emotionally riveting style that set a beautiful tone for the work that followed.

During the decade that I came to know Paulo professionally and as a friend, I was particularly impacted by Freire's discussion of university professors, since at the time I was frustrated with finding a place for myself in the academy. Freire, I noted, directed some harsh criticism towards university professors who maintained a willful ignorance about the dialectical relationship between pedagogy and politics:

> I feel so sad concerning the future of these people who teach at universities and think that they are just professors. They don't put their hands into politics because they think that it is dirty. It's precisely in escaping from politics that you have to know that you are a politician, and that your tactics are not merely pedagogical ones. But we cannot escape from this fact that politics and education are interwoven. You must develop your tactics there in response to the situation you confront in the field, not here, in the university, unless you wish to stop the project. In that case you don't need tactics. You could just come back home and leave the project. (Freire, 1985, p. 19)

Freire was especially disdainful of those professors who chose to remain isolated from the social contradictions of the day and who ignored the historical conditions that helped to exacerbate those contradictions. To such professors, modes of inquiry and concepts are generally irrelevant to the pedagogical process. What matters most is the "feeling state" occupied by the students and teachers—not what they think conceptually or do protagonistically—but whether or not they are emotionally enjoying what they do. Consequently and tragically, such professors exercise a "post" class pedagogy based on life-style, and irony, in which it is difficult—if not impossible—for students to confront the reality of others whose misery is the condition of their prosperity. At the very most, these professors muster their energy in order to free teachers and students from emotional distress rather than teach them about the social totality and its fatal entanglement in capitalist social relations. Such a peda-gogy of domestication enforces anti-intellectual and trans-social individual-ism based on sharing one's lived experiences.

Many of these types of Janus-faced professors—often in the course of seek-ing or maintaining administrative roles—are the first to turn on critical schol-ars whose work exposes their hypocrisy. Of course, you do find some professors who exhibit courage in challenging the liberal paralysis embedded in many schools of education and when you do find them, you certainly feel blessed.

Both Paulo and Nita recognized that a critical pedagogy needs to accom-plish more than facilitate the sharing of lived experiences with one another. What is needed is a concrete and critical analysis of experience, of experi-ence effects, an analysis that, in fact, goes beyond experience, that teaches us something that we don't already know. This requires a language or languages to interpret experience, languages that can help us unpack the material con-ditions of experiences. Our lived experiences and the knowledge gleaned from them cannot simply be read on their own terms; rather, critical educators must help students relate these experiences to their outside historical and social conditions. But also, we need to take into account the loss of experience, including inner experience, as Walter Benjamin has distinguished this.

Modernity has helped to replace remembering with memory, that is, collec-tive memory (a magic disclosure of the world often accompanied by synaesthetic experience and self-forgetfulness) with memory in the service of the intellect (a purely instrumental form of lived experience expressed in corporeally estab-lished habits and mechanical and purposive rationality). Like Benjamin, Paulo understood the need for political and moral redemption as a step in restructur-ing our modes of experiencing a world that has been shattered by modernity.

It was this lesson that stood out early in my university work and my task, as I saw it, was to provide students with the most powerful theoretical tools to use to help understand their own self and social formation in relation to larger social relations of capitalist production, relations created within a bru-tal and systematic extraction of surplus value from proletarianized regions of the world (usually festering in a climate of bourgeois-comprador nationalism) culminating in a condition of substantive inequality and an egregiously unequal division of labor. In my early work I would deploy contrapuntally critical pedagogy, neo-Marxist critique and cultural analysis, and in my later work I utilize a revolutionary Marxist-humanist perspective with a focus on the role of finance capitalism and the social relations of production and their ecocidal effects on the biosphere and planetary sustainability.

Paulo graciously wrote a preface for my 1995 book, *Critical Pedagogy and Predatory Culture*. In his preface he reflected on our "intellectual kinship" and our relationship as intellectual "cousins" while at the same time he lamented the preoccupation of so many academics and politicians with fighting among themselves when they should be uniting against their antagonists:

> If someone should ask if intellectual kinship is a sine qua non to our ability to influence or be influenced, to work together, to exchange points of view, build each other's knowledge, I say no. When such a kinship develops we need to cultivate within ourselves the virtue of tolerance, which "teaches" us to live with that which is different; it is imperative that we learn from and that we teach our "intellectual relative," so that in the end we can unite in our fight against antagonistic forces. Unfortunately, as a group, we academics and politicians alike expend much of our energy on unjustifiable "fights" among ourselves, provoked by adjectival or, even worse, by purely adverbial differences. While we wear ourselves thin in petty "harangues," in which personal vanities are displayed and egos are scratched and bruised, we weaken ourselves for the real battle: the struggle against our antagonists. (Freire, 1995, p. x)

Freire was able to break free from such "petty harangues" and the contemporary postmodern discourses that domesticate both the heart and mind, so that he could remain focused on his efforts to help students unlearn those myths produced by the dominant ideology that deform humanity. Nita Freire would later contribute a chapter in a book about my work, edited by Marc Pruyn and Luis Huerta-Charles. I especially appreciated Nita's chapter since at that time I was being subjected to criticisms not so much with respect to the substantive aspects of my work but more to the mysterious reasons behind my tattoos and eyeglasses. (So much for serious educational criticism.) Nita was able to put the tattoos into perspective and to focus on the deeper meanings of the critical pedagogy I was attempting to develop. She has contributed mightily to the development of critical pedagogy herself, and her legacy remains of great importance for critical educators worldwide.

It is surely striking the extent to which Freire's eviscerating pedagogical commentary, by planting the seed of catharsis and thereby placing in our hands the responsibility to overcome the political amnesia that has become the hallmark of teaching, cannot be welcomed into the classrooms of our nation by the guardians of the state. They have witnessed the unnerving intimacy and camaraderie he was able to forge among his admirers worldwide and were taken aback by the disseminating force of his liberatory language of hope and possibility. And while they have not been able to root him out of the philosophy of teaching, they have managed to domesticate his presence. They have done this by transforming the political revolutionary with Marxist ideas into a friendly old man who advocates a love of dialogue, separating this notion from that of a dialogue of love—hence, the importance of reclaiming Paulo Freire for these times.

What Freire teaches us is that truth is never about unmediated reflections of a real object—something resolutely immutable and transparent. Rather, it is always dialogic, always about the self/other. Instead of heeding a Freirean call for a multi-vocal public and international dialogue on our responsibility as the world's sole superpower, one that acknowledges that we as a nation are also changed by our relationship to the way we treat others, we in the U.S. have let a fanatical cabal of politicians convince us that dialogue is weakness, is an obstacle to peace.

Freire's dialectics of the concrete (to borrow a phrase from Karel Kosik) is very unlike that of the postmodernists who, in their artful counterposing of the familiar and the strange in order to deconstruct the unified subject of bourgeois humanism, mock the pieties of monologic authoritarianism with sportive saber slashes across the horizon of familiarity and consensus. Whereas postmodern "resistance" results in a playful hemorrhaging of certainty, a spilling forth of fixed meanings into the submerged grammars of bourgeois society, remixed in the sewers of the social as "resistance" and rematerialized in the art house jargon of fashionable apostasy, Freire's work retains an unshakable modernist faith in human agency consequent upon language's ineradicable sociality and dialogic embedment. What Freire has in common with the postmodernists is a desire to break free of contemporary discourses that domesticate both the heart and mind, but he is not content to remain in the nocturnal world of the subconscious; rather, he is compelled to take his critical pedagogy to the streets of the real.

Paulo Freire's legacy in the field of popular education and critical pedagogy is one characterized by an ontological commitment to deploying literacy and learning as a matrix of critical mediation, of humanization. The corpus of works left by Freire resembles the rings of a tree—a veritable tree of knowledge; they cover every aspect of pedagogy, reflecting the history of meaning-making in both historical and mythical time (see Freeman, 1998).

Freire was one of the first educational philosophers to underscore repeatedly the concept of "knowing" as a political act. One way of examining knowledge that is highly indebted to the ideas of Freire is to see educators as working within the intersection of temporality and narrative as a dialectical event. Here, experience, temporality, reflection and social action come together in what is commonly referred to in Freirean discourse as "praxis."

In the field of anthropology, the profane or historical time of contemporary social groups (involving the concreteness, linearity and irreversibility of time) is often juxtaposed with the mythical time of so-called archaic societies (time that repeats paradigmatic or archetypal gestures that are filled with deep meaning for the participants who use such recurrent mythical forms as a prism for personhood). Freire's notion of praxis, however, brings both conceptions of time into the narrative fabric of the emergent self.

The act of knowing is grounded in a type of mythopoetic desire (a desire to raise our own existence to a level of greater meaningfulness; see Freeman, 1998) linked to community, to a new level of sacred authenticity, to organizing life in imaginatively new ways that refuse to reproduce the alienation and objectification necessarily found in the world of abstract labor. Here, revolutionary praxis folds historical and mythical time into an act of negating what is, in anticipation of what could be. Schematically put, the line (the perpetual reappearance of the present in historical time) is folded into the circle (the primordial horizon of the irredeemably configured past).

One of Freire's goals is becoming conscious of and transcending the limits in which we can make ourselves. We achieve this through externalizing, historicizing and objectifying our vision of liberation, in treating theory as a form of practice and practice as a form of theory as we contest the psychopathology of everyday life incarnate in capitalism's social division of labor. We do this with the intention of never separating the production of knowledge from praxis, from reading the word and the world dialectically (Stetsenko, 2002, 2008, 2009). In so doing we maintain that practice serves as the ultimate ground for advancing and verifying theories as well as for providing warrants for knowledge claims. These warrants are not connected to some fixed principles that exist outside of the knowledge claims themselves but are derived by identifying and laying bare the ideological and ethical potentialities of a given theory as a form of practice (Stetsenko, 2002). Critical educators seek to uncover what at first blush may appear as the ordinary, transparent relations and practices that make up our quotidian existence—what we might even call mundane social realities. We take these relationships and practices and try to examine their contractions when seen in relation to the totality of social relations in which those particular relations and practices unfold. Such an examination takes place against a transdisciplinary backdrop that reads the word and the world historically.

Important Freirean-inspired revolutionary critical educators such as Antonia Darder and Peter Mayo do not use literacy to impose a matrix of reality upon the educand as some abstract desideratum to be followed but to interrupt the continuity of everyday life and seize opportunities at the intersection of historical and mythical time so that life can be grasped and lived within the horizon of the configured past and the anticipated future. The educand learns to live in the historical moment as a subject of history, but history is simultaneously re-animated and re-narrativized such that it is linked to the struggles of oppressed groups in various geopolitical contexts throughout the course of history and into the future.

Freire was one of the first educators to affirm that the process of understanding cannot be reduced to the formal properties of language alone but has to take into account its relationship to extra-linguistic forms of knowing, other forms of corporeal and praxiological meanings that are all bound up with the production of ideology. Meaningful knowledge is not solely nor mainly the property of the formal properties of language but is enfleshed. It is neither ultra-cognitivist nor traditionally intellectualist. It cannot be abstracted "from all the concrete, particular, embodied, erotic, and expressive features of language in order to invest emancipatory possibilities from its formal properties" (McNally, 2001, p. 109). Knowledge, in other words, is embodied in the way we read the world and the word simultaneously in our actions with, against and alongside other human beings. Of course, as Freire's Marxist followers have made clear, only the pre-Hegelian philosophers could think of transforming history in the head alone.

Freire writes that it is "impossible to think of transformation without thinking of getting power to transform" (1987, p. 226). He goes on to say that "education means a kind of action which on the one hand is explained by the power which constitutes it, on the other hand it works in the direction of preserving the power which constituted it or works against the power which constituted it" (Freire, 1987, p. 226). But Freire did not wish simply to organize political power in order to transform the world; he wished to reinvent power. Political power, of course, is based on economic power. Freire believed that resources for a dignified survival should be socially available and not individually owned.

According to Freire, there are distinct ways of thinking practiced by the rich or the "non-poor" that lead to ways of defending the interests and privilege of the ruling class and preserving and immortalizing their history (Freire, 1987, p. 221). It is a fatalistic way of thinking about the poor that rationalizes poverty as a constituent condition of living in a class-divided society. Such a fatalism also leads to political immobilization as teachers focus on "techniques, on psychological, behavioral explanations, instead of trying or acting, of doing something, of understanding the situation globally, of thinking dialectically, dynamically" (1987, p. 223). Freire asserts that the non-poor are often very liberal and progressive in their politics, yet when it comes time for them to confront the possibility of the poor becoming better off economically, they become reactionary. In addition to a failure to grasp critically the significance of class struggle, what the non-poor lack is an understanding of the role of dialogue in the process of knowing, which admits a social, historical and cultural relationship to knowledge production.

For Freire, dialectical inquiry should be at the heart of "the act of knowing" which is fundamentally an act of transformation that goes well beyond the epistemological domain. As Freire writes:

> The act of knowing, which education implies, must be understood in connection with organization for changing, for transforming. The transformation, for example, about which we talk, constantly, has to go beyond the understanding that we have sometimes of transformation as something which happens inside of us. We have the tendency to stop the understanding of transformation at the level of some change in our way of thinking, in our way of speaking, for example, and it is not enough. The individual dimension of transformation has to be completed by the objective transformation, or the transformation of the objectivity, of reality, and it is a question again of politics. (1987, p. 223)

But in order to understand the process of knowing as a political act and to complete the transformation of objective reality, we need to see this process in terms of the creation of historical, cultural and material spaces where the dialogic nature of knowing is acknowledged and respected. As we begin to grasp its internal movement, it becomes clear that it can never be neutral. Part of Freire's task of dialogic education is to provide opportunities for students to recognize the unspoken ideological dimension of their everyday understanding and to encourage themselves to become part of the political process of transformation of structures of oppression to pathways to emancipation.

Recognizing that we live in a pluricentric world, Freire's approach to critical pedagogy is undertaken with a certain directiveness, not manipulation, with authority, not authoritarianism. While speaking with authority, it is important always to understand the place from which you speak, and from which you are being heard or ignored. On this note, Freire specifically urged U.S. educators to understand the role of their own country, especially in the context of the suffering masses of Latin America and other parts of the world. He warned:

> You must discover that you cannot stop history. You have to know that your country (the US) is one of the greatest problems for the world. You have to discover that you have all these things because of the rest of the world. You must think of these things. (1985, p. 22)

For Freire, an important task for critical educators is to grasp, comprehend and generalize forms of resistance to oppression on the part of the oppressed (that is, resistance on the plane of immanence) and give some direction in challenging capitalism at its very roots with the purpose of offering an alternative social universe outside of capitalism's value form (that is, creating a concrete utopia). Critical educators should not take a passive role when it comes to spontaneous struggles; instead, they should elicit from the workers an understanding of the meaning of their own everyday struggles.

Peter Hudis (2010) notes that this follows Marx's concept of the task of the revolutionary: "… not to imbue or impart consciousness to the masses but rather to generalize and develop the social consciousness that is generated from their actual struggles." This requires that critical educators not regard their constituents as blank slates that need to be filled with revolutionary knowledge and strongly endorses Freire's critique of banking education.

Some critical educators—who to a certain extent could be accused of unconsciously endorsing a banking concept of education—believe that socialist consciousness cannot arise spontaneously from the masses; in fact, they vehemently oppose the (Platonic) notion that the critical educator is the "midwife" of knowledge (Hudis, 2010) and claim that the masses should be given the "correct" knowledge by an elite cadre of intellectuals. I share Freire's position that workers who are struggling against the alienation wrought by capitalism (at the attendant antagonisms of racism, sexism, ableism, homophobia, anthropocentrism), have themselves already acquired a sense of what kind of new society they want and that critical educators should not bring this knowledge to them from the outside. Rather, the idea of this new society is already implicit in the dialectic of negativity that characterizes the struggle of workers from practice to theory, and from theory back to practice. In other words, such knowledge is immanent in the workers' drive for total freedom (Hudis, 2010).

Freire believed that it wasn't a prerequisite to acquire a critical consciousness in order to struggle for social justice. Quite the contrary. Critical consciousness was the outcome—not the precondition—of struggle. It is in the act of struggling that educands become critically conscious.

Indeed, if Freire is right on this issue, and I believe that he is, what then is the role of the critical educator in the struggle to transform the world? Critical educators need in my view to make what is implicit in the educands' experiences explicit by linking their spontaneous development of a critical or socialist consciousness to a larger, more comprehensive theory and philosophy of revolution (Hudis, 2010). In other words, critical educators can hasten the outcome of mass struggle. This, in my view, is the real meaning of critical pedagogy.

One of the greatest panegyrists of praxis—Paulo Freire—understood that humans reflecting upon themselves and undertaking various historical determinations is not an act that can be reduced to a set of empirical facts. It can only come about when the spirit calls us to take up the moral imperative to treat others as ends and not as a means for something else, and it is this irremissible responsibility that generates self-awareness. It is our binding obligation to engage the other in a way that we would wish to be engaged.

I would like to share a description that I made of Paulo for a book edited by Tom Wilson, Peter Park and Anaida Colón-Muñiz called *Memories of Paulo*:

> He was a picaresque pedagogical wanderer, a timeless vagabond linked symbolically to Coal Yard Alley, to Rio's City of God, to the projects of Detroit and any and every neighborhood where working men and women have toiled throughout the centuries, a flaneur of the boulevards littered with fruiterers and fish vendors and tobacco and candy stalls, the hardscrabble causeways packed with migrant workers and the steampunk always of dystopian dreams. This man of the people was as much at home in the favelas as he was in the mango groves, a maestro who would cobble together the word and the world from the debris of everyday life, from its fury of dislocation, from the hoary senselessness of its cruelty, from its beautiful and frozen emptiness and the wrathfulness of its violence. And in the midst of all of this he was able to fashion revolutionary hope from the tatters of humanity's fallen grace. This was Paulo Freire. (McLaren, 2010, p. 177)

It is impossible for me to think of Paulo in a strictly prosaic way. This is because Paulo is very much a poetic figure. This is not tantamount to saying that Paulo is larger than life, that he strides the world like some unmatchable pedagogical colossus, or that he is immune to critique. It simply means that I carry Paulo in my heart, and memories of Paulo are stored by me in the language of poetry, not only to be emotionally caressed but to be unpacked, interrogated, analyzed and understood with whatever theoretical tools I have available and under the historical conditions in which I am working. I learned to understand Freire differently while working in Venezuela than I did while working in Colombia, differently while working in Mexico than while working in Argentina, differently while working in Brazil than while working in Turkey, differently while working in Canada than while working in Greece. And I have learned much about his work from bell hooks, Henry Giroux, Donaldo Macedo and Antonia Darder.

If there is a spark of light in these very dark times, it can be found in the practices of resistance of which Paulo and Nita Freire spoke, a resistance that I maintain is tethered to the fusty iron chassis of socialism. I use this metaphor with some irony since too often the term "socialism" evokes an image of spindle-shanked gangrels working the shop floor and agitating for better wages and improved working conditions, watched over in the panopticon-like factory by grim-faced men in dark frockcoats who report any infractions to the factory owners in quill penned messages (sprayed afterwards using a pounce pot of powdered cuttlefish bone to dry the ink). Socialism can be found today in many forms, just as brutal working conditions can be found everywhere in capitalist society. Today, not far from where I live, we have an example of the "electronic whip"—giant flat screen monitors that hang in the laundry rooms in the basements of the Disneyland hotels in Anaheim that serve to keep track of the fastest and slowest workers.

But socialism is not something that can only or mainly be found in the European tradition. It is alive and well in indigenous communities throughout *las Américas*. I believe that a socialism for the twenty-first century will need to look to indigenous communities for ways to fight what Anibal Quijano (2000) calls "the coloniality of power" and to secure an ecologically sustainable socialist alternative to the barbarism of capitalism.

For those who believe that it is human nature for some groups to dominate and control others, the goal of liberation is to make both the despot and despotic regime more benign. For Freire, such a solution is tantamount to cutting off our legs in the hope that one day we shall grow wings. If we make the road to emancipation by walking, then we need to know at some point whether we are on the right path in freeing ourselves from the many antagonisms that beset us. For Freire, being on the right path is to have a coherent and consistent vision towards which progress is directed and which can serve as a template for living fearlessly, knowing that moving forward implies overcoming many obstacles. It is to be guided by a vision that ultimately and irrevocably can bring justice to a world in perilous imbalance.

Grave changes are warranted in our political civilization—not only the abolition of the commercial helotry of the factories and sweatshops but also unclenching the fists we call our hearts, freeing us to reclaim our stolen humanity. Freire's struggle incorporated many dimensions: To be humble enough to wonder yet courageous enough to defy, to be sufficiently self-assured to rebel yet possess enough self-doubt to keep from backsliding, to have the audacity to be creative yet remain unburdened by socio-cultural dogma, to be vigilant against the new faces of tyranny yet ever conscious of the flaws and insufficiencies of our own struggles.

Freire worked with the generic potential to posit a world that does not make capitulation and defeat inevitable. Those liberals and conservatives alike who preach the virtues of democracy without recognizing that their vision remains beyond the recuperative powers of the prevailing capitalist system are laying the foundation for plutocracy, and in so doing sawing from the tree the branch upon which they are perched: wizened old vultures masquerading as feathery companions of Minerva.

For Freire, understanding the alienation of human labor is the skeleton key that unlocks the boneyard of capitalism and makes it vulnerable for transformation into its opposite—a world of economic, social, cultural, racial, sexual and gender equality. Freire's pedagogy is connected to the utopian impulse, freed from utopia's instrumental and petrified systematizing and idealist, totalizing form. It is a pedagogy committed to the historical, material and situationally specific needs of humanity. It is a pedagogy of and for our times.

The theogony of Freire's works is not derived from biblical scholarship and the hamartia of Adam nor does he reject this root and branch; rather, it can be linked at least implicitly to the pantheon of indigenous saints that stretches thousands of years into the past and that refuses to be whitened, refuses to capitulate to the avaricious ideology inherited from the capitalist world-eaters. This could be seen as anathema to those ensepulchered within the dogma of capitalist modernity, for whom politics and spirituality are two fundamentally separable spheres, each of which somehow loses its integrity insofar as it loses autonomy to the other. However, Freire sees no contradiction in a pedagogy informed by both practical consciousness and spiritual conviction (see Rivage-Seul, 2006).

Freire's work should be seen in the light of other great critical educators such as Italy's storied Lorenzo Milani, sometimes referred to as the Italian Freire, whose collective writing practices with his young students produced a humanizing pedagogy oriented towards social justice that can indeed inspire educators today (see Batini, Mayo and Surian, 2014).

It was my privilege to have witnessed Freire walking among us, laughing and light-footed, his tiny shoulders heaving like twin turbines beneath his crisp, freshly starched shirt, his slender legs gliding with a carefree, insouciant lilt, as if he were being helped along by a puckish breeze that served as a counterpoint to his steady, almost relentless gaze. To me, it seemed as though he was always peering into the present somewhere from the future, in some future anterior where dreams are on a collision course with what is occurring in the laboratories of everyday life we call reality, where light breaks through dark chambers that cannot be illuminated without love. To understand that collision is to understand the essence of Freire's work. Without a careful reading of Freire's intellectual roots, one can only witness the collision without understanding the systems of intelligibility that make such a collision inevitable and without understanding the possibilities of sublating such a collision in order to bring about alternative futures linked to the sustainability of the planet and humanity as a whole. This is the grand mysterium of Freire's work.

The field of educational reform has been overgrazed, emerging as a multitude of conflicting opinions, varying according to the disposition of the reformer and the facts he or she has selected. The topsoil has worn thin as the sun withers and scorches seeds without roots. It is time to enrich the soil of our education reform if we are to once again grow roots. Until now, the socialist imaginary has lain buried deep within our pedagogical unconscious awaiting this historic moment to be revealed once again. We can begin by affirming our commitment to a communal self, one that implies a continuum between mind and spirit. We must fight for free expression of our productive capacities and free association with other workers in productive works. We need to learn how we can use our labor capacity outside and beyond capitalist production relations. This is what critical pedagogy is all about.

My goal is to develop transnational interactions from below—from the exploited and the excluded—and this may be called a counter-hegemonic globalization process, if you want. These are local struggles that need to be globalized—and we know what they are. Boaventura de Sousa Santos (see Dale & Robertson, 2004; see also Santos 2005, 2009) has listed some of these as transnational solidarity networks, new labor internationalism, international networks of alternative legal aid, transnational human rights organizations, feminist movements, indigenous movements, ecological movements, alternative development movements and associations, literary, artistic and scientific movements on the periphery of the world system in search of non-imperialist, anti-hegemonic cultural and educational values.

Critical pedagogy needs to become activated through new social movements. The movements that I have witnessed of late—the Occupy movements, the uprising in Greece, protests of university students in Mexico, the Indignados—are making more than minor demands; they are struggling for an entirely different kind of future and the originality and creativity of their protests speak to that future. They are not just about negating the present but also about reclaiming space—parks, public squares, university buildings and other spaces where they can enact a new, more horizontal form of governance and decision making. They are moving beyond narrow sectarian interests and seeking to put participatory democracy into practice as an alternative to vertical forms of organization favored by liberal, representative democracy. And, of course, they are fighting state authoritarianism and a growing transnational fascism. They are seeking to challenge consumer citizens to become critical citizens again, as many citizens strove to become before the era of asset capitalism, or neoliberal capitalism.

But the movement goes beyond nostalgia for the past, since most of the youth have known only neoliberal capitalism all of their lives. The youth have also figured out that parliamentary forms of representation can no longer suffice in creating democracy in a social universe of asset or finance capitalism which requires a neo-fascist reorganization of the state in order to preserve massive profits for the transnational capitalist class.

Youth protesters today are struggling for participatory forms of association using new social media and new convergent media production as digital tools, as technological literacies to educate themselves and their comrades to link their experiences of struggle to goal-directed actions. They are struggling for different forms of social life. Here the digital media do not become ends in themselves but augment or supplement real-world experiences of struggle for popular sovereignty—and in the case of the Zapatistas in Chiapas or the Purépecha nation in Cherán, Mexico, an autonomous community within the state. As a result of these struggles, these tools become more integrated as part of an effort to create a collective intelligence with multiple visions of a socially just, fairer world.

The educational Left needs to be more proactive in helping to transform such movements from spontaneous uprisings to historical blocs in the Gramscian sense. That said, I do believe there is an ongoing danger of communitarian popular fronts. Popular-frontism could become reified as the "lost generation" versus the bankers and hedge fund profiteers. We have to be wary of the struggle becoming reduced to the "good capitalists" who are against monopolies, etc., versus the unproductive parasites in the finance sector who accumulate their fortunes on the sloping shoulders of others who are forced to sell their labor power for a wage. We must begin to advance a struggle for an alternative to capitalism based on the creation of real wealth rather than the value form of labor.

Following Freire's pedagogically impassioned argument that freedom and education should never be separated, we cannot simply ride the crest of some cosmogenetic wave, merely going along for the ride, the winding sheet of humanity serving as our topsail. We cannot retreat into some reynage or folklore kingdom, no matter how powerful the animal totem is that presides. Tambourines, stilts, drums and pantomime are good for the marches but not for the battle. We need gasmasks and a relentless drive that ends only in victory. We cannot afford to rest our hope on the appearance of some galactic supernova of the soul, some parabolic flow into and out of historical time, as if merely a spectator in some arcane sideshow.

We must liberate ourselves from the liberal indecisiveness that prevents us from escaping a sullied world. We must forge our vision on the anvil of class struggle, of revolutionary transformation, through a self-giving, inter-abiding collectivity of self-community grounded in an ethics of solidarity, love and *comunalidad*. We, as historical agents, are inseparable from the motion of praxis, entrusted to Marx and passed along to Freire, but pluriversal in scope.

Life is filled with an incandescent beauty. Who can deny the heart-clutching radiance of childrens' velvety smiles or the sounds of Gregorian chants sung by monks in the dusky abbeys of Ireland, sounds that cling to the heart like the flesh of an under-ripe peach clinging to its stone? I have seen such smiles on the faces of children playing in the *Plaza de la Constitución, Ciudad de México* (similar to what I would have expected to have seen were I to have been able to observe, centuries earlier, the mighty streets of México-Tenochtitlan). I have seen similar smiles on the children playing in the *Oaxaca de Juárez*, and in other *zócalos* throughout Mexico; on children in the markets of Karachi, in the kebab stands of Ramallah, in the violin shops of Budapest's Roma district, in the Market Square of Wroclaw; on the beaches of Tel Aviv and along the noisy, winding and politicized streets of Caracas. I have seen crystal sugar smiles on the faces of students who have found the strength to help themselves in order to help others. I have seen the same smiles on their teachers. I have seen shooting stars over the Pacific ocean, have been serenaded by whales under my boat in the *Golfo de México*, have trembled through electric storms from a lonely cabin in the Sonora desert surrounded by friendly mesquite trees, ironwood, *palo verde* and *huisache*, the only companions with the exception of the lizards that would never let me down. I have floated in the warm currents of the Aegean, under the Temple of Poseidan at Sounion, whose bleached-white columns stood brazenly in the sun, like the giant vertebrae of long-vanquished titans still proud to be brought to life from time to time by Warner Brothers and available in 3D and on IMAX; I have heard the voice of The Master humming in the heart of the wind as I turned south on the Tariq Bab al-Ghawanima, near the northwest gate of the Temple Mount, tremulously inching my way down the Via Dolorosa in Jerusalem, the route taken by Jesus between his scourging and his crucifixion and resurrection. But I warn you, all followers of Freire. There are those who would snatch away such beauty from the present and who would destroy the future. They will deride you as a political and pedagogical relic of the past, as a nostalgic old fool or, certainly not in my case, a young fool. You will be chastised and deplored, ridiculed and spat upon. But if we have anything to say about it, your descendants will raise a glass to your memory as they are still able to breath the air outside of an oxygen tent and live creatively and productively in a society where their needs and those of their families can be met outside of the slavery of the market.

The battle is one that must be multipronged and coordinated with numerous interconnected struggles. One such struggle, while never independent from the struggle against capital, is the struggle over the production of knowledge and the meaning and purpose of teaching—in other words, the struggle over education. Popular education is a tree that throughout history has found a way to burst through the blood-soaked pitch of the battlefield, its roots firmly planted in the restitution of our planetary soul, its leaves finding shafts of sunlight slashing their way through the carnage.

Bibliography

Au, W. (2007). Epistemology of the oppressed: The dialectics of Paulo Freire's theory of knowledge. *Journal for Critical Education Policy Studies*, 5(2). Retrieved from http://www.jceps.com/wp-content/uploads/PDFs/05-2-06.pdf

Batini, F., Mayo, P. and Surian, A. (2014). *Lorenzo Milani, The school of Barbiana and the struggle for social justice*. New York and Oxford: Peter Lang.

Bauman, Z. (2010). *Living on borrowed time: Conversations with Citlali Rovirsoa-Madrazo*. Cambridge, England: Polity Press.

Boal, A. (1979). *Theater of the oppressed*. New York, NY: Urizen Books.

Brecht, B. (1964). *Brecht on theater: The development of an aesthetic* (J. Willett, Trans.). London, England: Methuen Drama.

Dale, R., & Robertson, S. (2004). Interview with Boaventura de Sousa Santos. Retrieved from http://www.ces.uc.pt/bss/documentos/boainterview1.pdf

Freeman, M. (1998). Mythical time, historical time, and the narrative fabric of the self. *Narrative Inquiry*, 8(1), 27–50.

Freire, P. (1985). *Dialogue is not a chaste event. Comments by Paulo Freire on issues in participatory research*. Compiled by Paul Jurmo. Amherst, MA: The Center for International Education, School of Education. Hills House South. University of Massachusetts, Amherst.

Freire, P. (1987). Conversations with Paulo Freire on *Pedagogies for the non-poor*. In A. Frazer Evans, R. A. Evans, & W. B. Kennedy (Eds.), *Pedagogies for the non-poor* (pp. 219–231). Maryknoll, NY: Orbis Books.

Freire, P. (1995). Preface. In P. McLaren (Ed.), *Critical pedagogy and predatory culture: Oppositional politics in a postmodern era* (pp. ix–xi). New York, NY: Routledge.

Freire, P., & Macedo, D. (1987). *Literacy: Reading the word and the world*. Hove, England: Psychology Press.

Harvey, D. (2003). *The new imperialism*. Oxford, England: Oxford University Press.

Hudis, P. (2010, December). *The critical pedagogy of Rosa Luxemburg*. Paper presented at the Encuentro Internacional del Pensamiento Critico: Marxismo y Educacion Popular, Morelia, Michoacan, Mexico.

McLaren, P. (2010). Afterword. In T. Wilson, P. Park, & A. Colón-Muñiz (Eds.), *Memories of Paulo* (pp. 73–178). Rotterdam, the Netherlands: Sense.

McNally, D. (2001). *Bodies of meaning: Studies on language, labor, and liberation*. Albany, NY: State University of New York Press.

O'Connor, P. (2013). *Terrorists under the bridge: Applied theatre and empathy*. Unpublished manuscript.

Quijano, A. (2000). Coloniality of power, Eurocentrism, and Latin America. *Nepantla: Views From South*, 1(3), 533–580.

Ravitch, D. (2014, March 28). Public education: Who are the corporate reformers? Retrieved from http://billmoyers.com/2014/03/28/public-education-who-are-the-corporate-reformers/

Rivage-Seul, D. (2006). *The emperor's god: Misunderstandings of christianity*. Berea, KY: Berea College Press.

Santos, B. S. (2005). General introduction: Reinventing social emancipation: Toward new manifestos. In B. S. Santos (Ed.), *Democratizing democracy. Beyond the liberal democratic canon* (pp. xvii–xxxiii). London, England: Verso.

Santos, B. S. (2009). A non-Occidentalist West? Learned ignorance and ecology of knowledge. *Theory, Culture & Society*, 26(7–8), 103–125.

Stetsenko, A. (2002). Vygotsky's cultural-historical activity theory: Collaborative practice and knowledge construction process. In D. Robbins & A. Stetsenko (Eds.), *Vygotsky's psychology: Voices from the past and present*. New York, NY: Nova Science Press.

Stetsenko, A. (2008). Collaboration and cogenerativity: On bridging the gaps separating theory-practice and cognition-emotion. *Cultural Studies of Science Education, 3*(2), 521–533.

Stetsenko, A. (2009). Vygotsky and the conceptual revolution in developmental sciences: Towards a unified (non-additive) account of human development. In M. Fleer, M. Hedegaard, J. Tudge, & A. Prout (Eds.), *Constructing childhood: Global-local policies and practices* (pp. 125–142; World Year Book of Education series). London, England: Routledge.

· 3 ·

COMRADE CHÁVEZ

Peter McLaren and Mike Cole

... the act of reading and studying is a liberating act, education is liberating, let's go then, go ahead with education, towards the liberation of our people ...
—President Hugo Rafael Chávez Frías, cited in Muhr & Verger, 2006

The tectonic plates of history are shifting. Rumbling through the fathomless fissures of time and exploding to the surface are humanity's raw-boned cries—Ya Basta! After generations of abuse as nature's "free gift" to capital, Mother Earth is dying, her plangent death throes reverberating across the seas. Shining through their own effulgence, her pyroclastic tears light up the evening sky, spewed from rotting smokestacks in what were once pristine fields yielding bumper crops under a harvest moon. The world's slums no longer pockmark the planet but define its central features. Everything, including the tears of the poor, are up for sale.

If at any time a militant pedagogy of empowered citizenry is needed, it is now. To create a pedagogy that is up to the task of challenging the neoliberal behemoth that now bestrides the world, urinating its wastewater sewage over crumbling metropolises like a fracking colossus in overalls and a miner's hat who has had too much beer, conditions of possibility for an alternative to neoliberal capitalism must first be created.

We call this alternative, after the Bolivarian revolutionaries of Venezuela, a socialism for the twenty-first century. But the word "socialism," let alone the revolutionary-style socialism given birth by the Movement of the Fifth Republic (MVR), Movimiento de la Quinta República (Movement of the Fifth Republic), established to support the presidential candidacy of Hugo Chávez in 1998, has taken a defensive posture in an age in which social democracy is on the decline in the European Union and where, in the U.S., socialism is defined in the corporate media as if it were synonymous with the ex-Soviet Union or the Eastern Bloc police states.

The Decline of European Social Democracy and the Onslaught of Neoliberal Capitalism

As Dave Stockton (2013) points out, whereas ten years ago the social democrats were in office in fifteen European Union countries, almost every country in western Europe is now ruled by a conservative government. As of March 2013, only in France, Denmark, Norway and Slovenia are there still governments headed by social democrats. Moreover, as Stockton explains, "social democrats" no longer even dream of a return of the long boom of the 1950s and 1960s when the rising tide of capitalist production and wide profit margins allowed the skilled and stable workforces of northern Europe to force concessions: the "European social model."

Renewed crises in capitalism meant that by the 1970s, all this began to be eroded. Thus, in the UK, for example, the election of Margaret Thatcher in 1979 and the onset of a ruthless neoliberalism paved the way for New Labor, Tony Blair and the social democratic sell-out. In the late 1970s/early 1980s, Thatcher had successfully but falsely equated the Stalinist Soviet Union with Marxism, with socialism, with the British Labor Party, with militant trade unionism, and had urged their collective confinement to the dustbin of history (Cole, 2011, pp. 30–31). Stockton (2013) describes what the so-called Third Way ideology adopted by Blair in the UK and the Neue Mitte of Gerhard Schröder in Germany in the mid-1990s meant in practice:

> For Blair this meant sustaining education, health and social services not by taxes on the corporations or the rich, but a huge expansion of credit. "Reforms" now meant "freeing up the labor market," i.e. cutting workers' rights, marketisation and privatisation of public services and utilities, tax reductions for business and the deregulation of finance. In Europe this also meant accepting the neoliberal orthodoxies of the

Maastricht Treaty, and the "strong" euro policy imposed by the Bundesbank on the European Central Bank (ECB).

In Germany in 2003 under Schröder, the SPD, in coalition with the Greens, inaugurated Agenda 2010. This entailed tax cuts, the lowering of pension entitlement and unemployment benefits and the freeing up of the labor market. When Schröder entered office, there were 4 million unemployed; when he left in 2005, there were 5 million. At the same time real wages stagnated (Stockton, 2013).

The Dawn of Austerity/Immiseration Capitalism

Under austerity/immiseration capitalism, Europe is witnessing its deepest economic and social crisis since World War II. In 2012, more people lost their jobs than in any other year in the past two decades. The situation is particularly severe in southern and eastern European countries. For example, in Greece and Spain one person in four is officially unemployed, with over half of young people without work (Schwarz, 2013). As Peter Schwarz (2013) puts it:

> Despite the social catastrophe they have provoked with their austerity policies, European governments are intent on tightening the fiscal screws. They are no longer limiting themselves to the periphery of the euro zone, but are ever more ferociously attacking the working class in the core countries.

Thus new draconian plans are afoot for Italy, France and Germany, while in the UK, with almost a quarter living in poverty, the ConDem government (ConDem here refers to the previous UK Conservative/Liberal Democrat Alliance that 'condemned' the workers to austerity/immiseration capitalism) is systematically attempting to undermine the welfare state, to destroy the National Health Service, social welfare and state education (Schwarz, 2013). As Prime Minister David Cameron said of education: "In welfare reform we've been radical, in education almost revolutionary—busting open the state monopoly of education and allowing new Free Schools to start up, and crucially to compete in this global race" ("Minister David Cameron's Speech," 2013).

Echoing Margaret Thatcher's famous speech in which she defended neoliberalism by insisting that there is no alternative (TINA), Cameron recently declared, "There is no alternative" (to the continuance of ConDem economic policy). This statement needs to be seen in the light of what Jean Shaoul (2012) describes as a social counter-revolution, the aims of which are the drastic diminution of workers' rights and living standards, the latter having been pushed back thirty years.

Social democracy has had little impact on the imposition of austerity/ immiseration capitalism. Indeed, it has colluded with it. Since the beginnings of the current crisis in 2007, social democrats have lost elections in Italy, Sweden, the Netherlands and Hungary. Crucially, as Stockton (2013) concludes, "There are no signs that François Hollande in France, Sigmar Gabriel in Germany or Ed Miliband in Britain will fundamentally reverse social democracy's subservience to capital or ideological decomposition that Lionel Jospin, Tony Blair, and Gerhard Schröder, carried on for so long."

In the U.S., the situation is spectacularly grim as the country is crawling back from what has been called the Great Recession. The unemployment rate rose from 5% in 2008 pre-crisis to 10% by late 2009, then steadily declined to 7.3% by March 2013. The ranks of the unemployed (Marx's reserve army of labor) rose from approximately 7 million in 2008 pre-crisis to 15 million by 2009, then declined to 12 million by early 2013. Even though we are coming out of the recession, most Americans are still experiencing downward mobility. It still remains a Gilded Age for the 1 percent who constitute the financial aristocracy. There is just one job available for every five individuals looking for work. Those finding jobs are finding pretty lousy jobs, often part-time and with fewer and fewer benefits. But it is appreciably different for those at the top. The richest 10 percent of Americans received an unconscionable 100 percent of the average income growth in the years 2000 to 2007. You would think that this would have driven most people in U.S. cities into the streets howling like a naked Allen Ginsberg with his angel-headed hipsters. But it did not (although it certainly contributed to the rise of the Occupy Wall Street movement). In 2009, the richest 5 percent claimed 63.5 percent of the nation's wealth. The bottom 80 percent, collectively, held just 12.8 percent.

According to Damon (2013), in the economic downturn that started in 2008, the U.S. economy lost 8.9 million jobs. Since the end of 2009, the economy has added only 5.7 million jobs. But these new jobs pay much less than those lost during the recession and an increasing number of them are part-time. The share of people working part-time has grown from 16.9 percent at the start of the recession to 19.2 percent. The percentage of the population that is employed fell from 63.3 percent in February 2007 to 58.5 percent at the present time. Long-term unemployment has likewise increased significantly. The slashing of government jobs will intensify as a result of the recent passage of $1.2 trillion in "sequester" job cuts. According to the Congressional Budget Office, the imposition of the sequester will result in 750,000 job losses, and increase by a wide margin the unemployment rate (Damon, 2013).

The unprecedented combination of mass unemployment, falling wages and an influx of free money from the Federal Reserve has led to a record-setting surge in corporate profits. Corporations are flush with capital but are just sitting on it, preferring at this time not to invest their vast windfalls in jobs. Instead of investing in production, major corporations, whose coffers are overflowing and whose stocks are hitting record levels, are paying out dividends and inflating their own stock values (Damon, 2013). CEOs are cashing in on stocks that are soaring in value with the rising market, with a growing number of CEOs reaping individual profits of $50 million or more.

Peter Hudis (2012b) and other Marxists have pointed out that the profits of speculative capital are largely invisible to the average person. But what is very visible to most U.S. citizens are the rising levels of state and federal debt and the accompanying cutbacks and fiscal restraint that come with it. This situation acts as an ideological cover, an alibi or smokescreen by making people believe that the reason for the declining conditions of everyday life is that the government is spending too much of their money. This is nothing short of an ideological scam.

The structural reasons for the current fiscal crisis in state and local governments, including massive layoffs in the private sector and reduced living standards, have been manipulated by the Right in their arguments that proclaim that our current fiscal crisis was caused by the government. By arguing that national debt levels threaten their economic well-being and by getting voters to agree to cutbacks in government spending and social programs, capital can redistribute value from labor to capital without revealing the very nature of the system—and, as Peter Hudis notes, the Right can then more easily blame the crumbling economic system on illegal immigration and other phony reasons. But here we need to understand that in order that capital accumulation proceeds apace and capital is able to sustain itself, the relative proportion of value going to capital as against labor must be increased. And we need to understand, as Hudis (2010, 2012a, 2012b) points out, that most of the value produced in capitalism is consumed not by capitalists or workers but by capital itself, through productive consumption, by capital consuming a greater share of the social wealth.

The economic stimulus package that U.S. President Obama installed shortly after he took office in 2009 was insufficient to stem the rise of unemployment. Still, an astronomical amount was pumped into the economy in the years immediately following the 2008 financial crisis—trillions of dollars by the U.S. Federal Reserve and over $1 trillion by the European Union. Hudis notes that this certainly saved global capitalism from going over the cliff, but it proved insufficient to reverse the deeper structural crisis plaguing capitalism itself (Hudis, 2012b).

Redistributing wealth to the poor by means of a Roosevelt-style "New Deal" would offer temporary help for those most immiserated by the current crisis of capital, but this would hardly be in the interests of the oligarchic bourgeoisie, who are currently profiting from the fusion of banking and monopoly capital and who are consolidating their power through an intersection of economic and political forms of domination. As capital moves freely, investing in production or in fictitious forms of capitalism, and as speculators, financier capitalists, stock and bond traders, investment bankers, hedge fund managers and others help to unleash the forces of capital accumulation globally, and as neoliberalism with its aggressive pro-market state policies allows this finance capital to restructure itself, to diversify its forms, to expand its accumulation opportunities through the growth of retail, financial and service industries, and enhance its global reach, then it is safe to assume that entire ecosystems of the planet have been harnessed exploitatively in a system of capitalist commodity production such that we cannot talk about capitalism at all without talking about capitalism as a world ecology.

The whole physiognomy of capitalism has changed, with finance capital requiring a parallel accumulation of political power, with financiers married to an unchecked political oligarchy spawning highly parasitic financialized forms of capitalism such as asset-stripping. The vampire of capitalism has grown a second set of fangs. The long shadow of Nosferatu falls across a systematic and ongoing attack on the living standards of the vast majority of the population.

Neoliberal policies are decimating social programs such as education, healthcare, police and public transit services, spending for the disabled and other areas of state services and employment. Conversely, subsidies to corporate elites in the form of the 2008 TARP bailout are given urgent priority, while officials speak of the need to cut back on educational spending.

Twenty-First-Century Socialism—An Alternative to Neoliberal Capitalism

All this begs the question: Is there a viable alternative to neoliberal capitalism? In 1998, President Hugo Chávez won the presidential elections in Venezuela by a landslide. At first, Chávez expressed an interest in Tony Blair's "Third Way," only to regret this soon after. As he put it in *Time* magazine in 2006: "I naively took as a reference point Tony Blair's proposal for a 'third way' between capitalism and socialism—capitalism with a human face" (Pabian, 2008). Following his first election victory, Chávez's views dramatically changed. Maria Paez Victor (2009) concisely summarizes Chávez's impact:

> Immediately the elites and middle classes opposed him as an upstart, an Indian who does not know his place, a Black who is a disgrace to the position. Hugo Chávez established a new Constitution that re-set the rules of a government that had been putty in the hands of the elites. Ratified in overwhelming numbers, the Constitution gave indigenous peoples, for the first time, the constitutional right to their language, religion, culture and lands. It established Human Rights, civil and social, like the right to food, a clean environment, education, jobs, and health care, binding the government to provide them. It declared the country a participatory democracy with direct input of people into political decision making through their communal councils and it asserted government control of oil revenues: Oil belongs to the people.

Chávez stressed the importance of "development from below" which could be achieved through the democratization of the workplace by way of workers' councils and a major shift of ownership of production, trade and credit in order to expand food production and basic necessities to the poor who inhabit the "internal market." Once President Chávez was able to control the oil industry, his government was able to reduce poverty by half and extreme poverty by 70 percent. Public pensions rose from 500,000 to over 2 million. Chávez helped turn Venezuela from one of the most unequal countries in Latin America to (after Cuba) the most equal in terms of income. Under the naked thrall of neoliberal capitalism, the U.S. has become one of the most unequal countries in the world.

While in Venezuela, I (McLaren) attended meetings of the *misiones*, social programs in health, education, work and housing, set up by Chávez when he came into office in 1999 to help the poor to become literate, to finish high school, to organize their communities and to get medical attention. *Misiones* involved citizen- and worker-managed governance and helped dramatically reduce poverty throughout Venezuela. These initiatives spanned education (Misión Robinson, Misión Ribas, Misión Sucre), the environment (Misión Energia), food and nutrition (Misión Mercal), science (Misión Ciencia), socio-economic transformation (Misión Vuelvan Caras), healthcare (Misión Barrio Adentro), housing (Misión Habitat), indigenous rights (Misión Guaicaipuro), land reform (Misión Zamora), rural development (Misión Vuelta al Campo, Misión Arbol), identity rights (Misión Identidad), civilian militia (Misión Miranda) and culture (Misión Corazon Adentro).

In 2006, when one of us (McLaren) was denounced by a right-wing organization as UCLA's "most dangerous professor" and the organization offered to pay students $100 to secretly audiotape my classes, or $50 to produce notes from my lectures, it was the Chavistas who first rallied to my support at the World Educational Forum in Caracas. I will never forget the solidarity. Other than close friends and colleagues, no educators on behalf of any U.S. educational organizations rallied to my support.

The other writer of this chapter (Cole) remembers the first visit to a local bar in Caracas. From the bustle and vibe emanating from inside, I expected to find a lot of noisy male football supporters shouting at a TV screen. Instead, the encounter entailed women and men from the local *barrio* engaged in serious and passionate discussions about the president and the direction of the revolution.

At the start of one of several seminars I (Cole) gave at the Bolivarian University of Venezuela in Caracas (UBV), a caretaker arrived to unlock the room. Instead of going on to other chores, he sat down, listened and actively contributed to the discussion. A lively interchange of views ensued about the meaning of socialism.

Since more than 70 percent of university students come from the wealthiest quintile of the population, Chávez instituted the Bolivarian University System, in which the students themselves were able to participate in the management of their institution. Education was designed to promote citizen participation and joint responsibility, and to include all citizens in the creation of a new model of production that stressed endogenous development, that is, an economic system that was self-sufficient and diversified. Misiones were created to create a social economy and a diversity of production and designed to meet the needs of Venezuela's poor and to counteract Venezuela's oil dependency. Higher education was de-concentrated from the urban centers in order to assist rural communities.

Education under Chávez was education for the creation of a "multi-polar" world. For Chávez, education either meant giving life support to capitalism's profit-orientation in order to bolster the remains of the welfare state, or education meant recreating a socialism for the twenty-first century. Chávez was not concerned with incorporating the oppressed within the liberal-democratic framework but rather with changing the framework through the reorganization of political space through education, that is, through making the state function in a non-statal mode by reorganizing the state from the bottom up through the education and initiatives of the popular majorities. Socialism, Chávez understood, could only be sustained by the subjective investment of those involved in the process.

Under Chávez, Venezuelan education was not only geared to help provide universal access to education (as Venezuela's poor had been shut out for generations), in particular, to those traditionally disadvantaged and/or excluded groups such as the urban and rural poor, those of African descent and indigenous communities, but also to help prepare the next generation of Venezuelans to enhance the conditions of possibility of a socialist alternative to capitalism. Venezuelan education aspired to be a combination of Freirean-influenced critical and popular education, where horizontal and dialogic (subject-subject) relationships were pursued using holistic, integral and transdisciplinary pedagogies and methodologies based on andragogical principles for a liberating and emancipatory education.

Under Chávez, little attempt was made to distance educational reform from a politicized approach. Education reform clearly directed itself towards an organic form of endogenous socialist development of the social-community context as part of a larger struggle for a participatory-protagonistic democracy. Against the privatization of education and approaches hegemonized by the neoliberal education industry, and its consumerist role grounded in egoism, competition, elitism and alienation, Venezuelan education aspired to be humanistic, democratic, participatory, multi-ethnic, pluri-cultural, pluri-lingual and intercultural. The development of a critical consciousness among the population was crucial, as was an integration of school, family and community in the decision-making process.

Venezuelan education favored a multidisciplinary approach linking practice and theory, curriculum and pedagogy, with the purpose of creating social, economic and political inclusion within a broader vision of endogenous and sustainable development, and with the larger goal of transforming a culture of economic dependency to a culture of community participation. This approach, for example, underwrote the courses at UBV where mentorship was provided to students who undertook projects in their local communities.

For instance, Community Health students worked with doctors within the *Barrio Adentro* health mission, and legal studies students established a community legal center to advise and support families with civil law issues, while education students worked in local schools with a teacher/mentor (Griffiths & Williams, 2009). And in the evening, during classes at the UBV, students discussed theory "linking back into and arising from their experiences in the project" and thus became part of a broader project of social reconstruction (Griffiths & Williams, 2009).

Of course, there were obstacles to be overcome with this approach. For instance, how do you prevent the social formation of schooling from being integrated into the educational system without reducing education to the functional needs and requirements of the national economy? And further, how do you create an approach that addresses the political formation of students in a way that is not simply a formalistic and uncritical response to official ideologies that support socialist objectives? Of course, this is not simply a challenge that faced Venezuelan education under Chávez, but is the challenge of critical pedagogy in whatever context it is taken up and engaged.

Despite these challenges, education under Chávez prospered. More than 93 percent of Venezuelans aged 15 and older can read and write. The Venezuelan government has more than 90 institutions of higher education and remains committed to the idea that every citizen should be able to have a free education. Education was conceived within an integrationist geopolitical conception of Latin American countries in a way that enabled Latin Americans to challenge economic dependency fostered on them by the imperialist powers, to resist colonialist globalization projects and to create spaces where students could analyze critically local problems from a global perspective (Muhr & Verger, 2006).

Under Chávez's leadership, the Venezuelan government invested significantly in *all* educational levels. In fact, between 1997 and 2002—under Chávez—*all* social classes benefited from an increase in access to higher education. Chávez refused to follow the neoliberal strategy of finance-driven reforms—i.e., transferring fiscal and administrative responsibilities to either lower levels of government or to individual schools for cost-saving and efficiency purposes—thereby challenging the dictates of the Washington Consensus policies (Muhr & Verger, 2006). He refused a shift of the cost of education to the "users" through privatization which would simultaneously instrumentalize "participation" as pecuniary and non-pecuniary household/community contributions (Muhr & Verger, 2006). Chávez's approach of *municipalización* refused to isolate universities from the rest of society and geographically de-concentrated the traditional university infrastructure and took the university to where the people are, to municipalities that had traditionally been underserved as well as factories and prisons, achieving what was known as "territorial equilibrium," i.e., harmonic development across the entire territory at the demographic, productive and environmental levels (Muhr & Verger, 2006).

Chávez was not about to let the business sector set the priorities for public education and thereby colonize the commons with the ideas of the transnationalist capitalist class in which the knowledge most valued is that which is the most exploitable in a capitalist economy, and where knowledge becomes fragmented, instrumentalized and narrowly specialized and is destined to produce self-alienating subjectivities. Consequently, Chávez created integral and permanent municipal education spaces called *aldeas universitarias* or "university villages," immersing higher education in concrete contextual geographies (geospatial, geohistorical, geosocial, geocultural, geoeconomic) in contrast to the model favored by neoliberal economics, that is, an economicist "efficiency" rationale or an approach that offers marketplace specialization (Muhr & Verger, 2006). The internationalization of Venezuelan education is not market-based but based on the logic of co-operativism, culture and exchange and forms an integral part of a broader counter-hegemonic proposal for regional integration— the *Alternativa Bolivariana de las Américas* (ALBA), replacing liberal "comparative advantage" with a "co-operative advantage" (Muhr & Verger, 2006).

Hugo Chávez's demonization and ridicule in the western press were lamentable but understandable. Television evangelist Pat Robertson called for the assassination of President Chávez on the August 22, 2005 television broadcast of *The 700 Club* on the Christian Broadcasting Network: "I don't know about this doctrine of assassination, but if he thinks we're trying to assassinate him, I think that we really ought to go ahead and do it. It's a whole lot cheaper than starting a war, and I don't think any oil shipments will stop."

The Christian Broadcasting Network reaches 360 million people in approximately 100 nations. Clearly, Robertson is a fumbling blowhard and dangerous demagogue, and his views and practices are far removed from the teachings of Jesus. Yet he wields tremendous influence as an opinion-maker. Bill Davis (2005) writes:

Hugo Chávez speaks at length to his people over the TV—and he reads to them. One of his favorite authors to read to his people is Walt Whitman. At the Youth

Conference in Caracas earlier this month he called the people of the U.S. "brothers" to Venezuela. He embraced the traditions of Walt Whitman and Dr. Martin Luther King Jr. and gave them as examples of the progressive history of the U.S. Walt Whitman understood spirit and America. Pat Robertson contradicts both.

Chávez took on President George Bush, Jr., whom he called "Mr. Danger," and showed the world that a more humane world could be had through a democratic socialist alternative. For weeks following Chávez's untimely death on March 5, 2013, newspaper stories throughout the U.S. condemned his alleged dictatorial brutality, thereby tarnishing the legacy of one of the world's most ardent visionaries of a world outside of capitalism, a man of courage and foresight whose resolute determination to fight the exploitation of the poor and the downtrodden will see history absolve him from condemnation by the western imperialist powers.

Nicolás Maduro, on being sworn in as acting president, declared: "We are here to guarantee peace, safety and political stability and the lifting up of the poor in Venezuela will continue: onward and upward with socialism!" ("Maduro Takes the Oath," 2013). Under Maduro's leadership, socialists will continue to press for the creation of a genuine, twenty-first-century socialism. In addition to the continuing expansion of the misiones, this must entail a major onslaught against capitalism, a massive re-distribution of wealth and the strengthening of participatory democracy.

La Lucha Continua (The Struggle Continues)

Writing about Europe, Peter Schwarz concludes:

> The only alternative to a relapse into mass poverty and barbarism is a socialist program. The banks and major corporations must be nationalized and placed under democratic control. Production must be reorganized so that it serves the needs of society and not the profit interests of financial speculators and parasites. Such a program can be achieved only through the united struggle of the European and international working class. It requires the formation of workers' governments and the establishment of the United Socialist States of Europe. (Schwarz, 2013)

The path to socialism entails participatory democracy. In representative democracies in place throughout most of the world, political participation is by and large limited to parliamentary politics which represent the imperatives of capitalism, rather than the real needs and interests of the people. Parliamentary politics and representative democracy are still major players in Venezuela, of course. There are, of course, numerous extra-parliamentary movements and processes throughout the world. Participatory democracy, conversely, involves direct decision making by the people. Twenty-first-century democracy must be participatory democracy and part of a program for the construction of twenty-first-century socialism.

Some socialist organisations such as the Socialist Equality Party, of which Schwarz is a member, reject the idea that Hugo Chávez was a socialist. We happen to believe that they are wrong.

By 2010, Chávez was asserting that, as well as being a Christian, he was also a Marxist (Chávez, 2010). He described Marxism as "the most advanced proposal towards the world that Christ came to announce more than 2,000 years ago" (Suggett, 2010). In arguing for the centrality of communal councils, Chávez made it clear that he was not arguing for the *reform* of the Venezuelan capitalist state, but rather its overthrow. As he put it, in perhaps his most clearly articulated intention to destroy the existing state:

> we have to go beyond the local. We have to begin creating … a kind of confederation, local, regional and national, of communal councils. We have to head towards the creation of a communal state. And the old bourgeois state, which is still alive and kicking—this we have to progressively dismantle, at the same time as we build up the communal state, the socialist state, the Bolivarian state, a state that is capable of carrying through a revolution. (cited in *Socialist Outlook* Editorial, 2007)

After his final re-election in October 2012, Chávez declared: "Venezuela will continue along the path of democratic and Bolivarian socialism of the 21st century."

It is our view that Chávez's death is a tragedy of immense proportions for socialism and for the Bolivarian Revolution. However, twenty-first-century socialism is and must be first and foremost a revolution of the people, as Chávez was well aware. The fact that masses of working people have taken socialism to heart ensures that the revolution he started will not die with him. While democratic socialism may sound utopian in the European context, and positively archaic in the U.S., there is in existence a viable alternative to the neoliberal model. It is incumbent on the Left to think seriously about what can be learned from the Bolivarian Revolution.

The Bolivarian Revolution can provoke us to imagine an alternative to capitalism and capitalist schooling, whether through forms of freely associated producers planning and allocating the social wealth, syndicalist and Marxist forms of socialism or self-governing popular assemblies or autonomous communities.

Revolutionary action today must be grounded in decisions pertaining to which past legacies, which historical determinants, should be used as a basis for action. We have a variety of experiences that provide us with multiple perspectives from among which we can choose. And we have offered the Bolivarian Revolution as an example that we, the authors, have experienced as a template for how to renew socialism in the twenty-first century. It should be stressed at this point that, while the innovations in Venezuela represent a major challenge to U.S. imperial hegemony, and its attendant ideological and repressive apparatuses (Althusser, 1971) and allow the export of socialist ideas and ideals, they are in themselves classic social democracy rather than socialism, somewhat akin to the policies and practices of the post-World War II Labor governments in the UK. What makes Venezuela unique, however, is that whereas these British Labor governments were posing social democracy as an alternative to socialism, and, indeed, attempting to fight off (sporadic) attempts by revolutionary workers to move towards participatory democracy and socialism, Chávez presented these reforms as a prelude to socialism.

Today, the most serious of the social movements for economic justice in the U.S., such as the Occupy Wall Street movement, will have no truck with promulgating a mendacious and sanitized history of capitalism, with giving away huge tax breaks for the rich, squandering taxpayer dollars on the pharmaceutical industry by making it illegal for Medicare to bargain for lower drug prices, rescinding financial regulations to enable Wall Street to operate like a Las Vegas casino and to enact legislation that has put nearly 6 percent of Americans out of work. As they stand, the best of the social movements are preparing us to be reborn with a transmuted consciousness, and taking us to the next step in the pursuit of socialism. But they have not yet created a new space of social emancipation, mainly because we do not know the spatial transformations necessary to prepare us for an alternative to the law of value. And while many of these movements have seen the old vanguard as a hindrance to further social change, they are still wrestling with the forms of organization needed to transform a world stage managed by a transnational capitalist class. These new social movements are the foreconscious of change, whereas what is needed is a change in the subconscious of the historical agent; that is, we need to raise the question of how we can gain an acceptance within the "deep mind" for the fact that a social universe outside of labor's value form is necessary for the very survival of humankind, not to mention extra-human life.

Some aspects of our goal must remain unspecified. Our path must remain trackless, our cry soundless and our destination uncertain, or else we will fall into the trap of imposing a blueprint, or re-coding old formulae. But at the very least we have to attune ourselves to history's migratory urge to sublate that which we negate as we struggle to create a world less populated by human suffering, exploitation and alienation. We can build upon the vestiges of past struggles and move into an entirely new terrain of resistance and transformation. We believe the best example at present to be the ongoing struggle of the Bolivarian Revolution.

The seething force force of the unmet shadow of capitalism has the potential to destroy the very form of our past struggles. New modes of organization are called for. The political imagination must be reconfigured to the challenges of the present. If we view the accumulation of capital and the production of nature as a dialectical unity, we need a new vision of the future that can break free from modernity's mega-strategies of revolution so that we can think of a socialist alternative to capitalism differently, not as some cataclysmic leap by which life advances but rather as steps—some precarious and some bold—by which life is prepared to evolve politically, economically and ethically. We must recover from our past what the past regarded as utopian and thus was rejected by our predecessors and offer new forms of rebellion that can better ensure that such knowledge will re-impact the present more effectively.

While we wrestle with what can replace immiseration capitalism—i.e., direct democracy, participatory democracy, grassroots democracy, autonomous communities—we maintain that such a struggle acquires a certain valence of authenticity in the example of the Bolivarian Revolution, despite some of its failings and shortcomings. As much as many want to believe that technology will rescue the planet from the destruction of its ecosystems and will help alter the disposition of capitalism to that of a benevolent uncle, it is likely that technology will have the reverse effect. Contrary to the wishes of science-fiction aficionados, there is no shortcut or "wormhole" to the future, even hidden in the bustling *barrios* of Caracas. There will be no steampunk dirigible of canvas, polished wood and sparkling brass fittings to float us away across the clouds to some distant horizon fashioned by the Inklings over fish and chips at Oxford's "Bird and Baby" pub. The future will be forged by rough-hewn hands and a fearless imagination directed in the here and now at rebuilding the planet on principles of socialist democracy.

The historical debates surrounding the legacy of Hugo Chávez have begun. Perhaps one day we will join these debates. But not now. Attacks on Chávez "the dictator" or Chávez the charismatic "opponent" of the U.S. will demand from the Left a spirited defense. Perhaps we will join such an effort in the months and years ahead. But not now. In this brief space we want to speak about Hugo Chávez as a leader who inspired a generation to believe that an alternative to capitalism could be fashioned from a reinvention of the state by the popular majorities.

The popularity of Chávez had a historic world reach, and it would not be a mistake to analyze his charismatic leadership in the context of a personality cult like that of Fidel, Che, or Subcommandante Marcos, for instance. To do this is not to diminish the importance of his role as a figure that could galvanize millions on the Left and animate their faith that a more humane alternative to capitalism was a possibility, once the battle against U.S. imperialism was won.

Chávez, whose father was of Indian descent and his mother, of African descent, was often the object of racial derision by Venezuela's white ruling elite, who did not hide their racial separateness from the rest of the Venezuelan population, four-fifths of whom could be described as indigenous-mestizo-mulatto-African. I (McLaren) remember one scorching hot day, after a particularly long march down the streets of Caracas supporting President Chávez, I went from store to store in an attempt to purchase a popular Chávez doll as a souvenir. But there was not a single doll to be found. I was told that I could find one in Altamira, an affluent east Caracas neighborhood. I was surprised. A fellow *camarada* laughed at my expression and told me that the white ruling elite—often referred to as *esqualidos* (a colloquialism for squalid people)—had plenty of Chávez dolls available in their upscale stores. Referring to Chávez as *ese mono* (that monkey), they would tie the dolls to the bumpers of their cars and drag them through the streets.

Insinuating itself into our daily life as an ideology as much as a set of accumulation practices and processes of production, neoliberal capitalism pretends to the throne of democracy-building but in reality it has hastened its demise. Capitalism wears a coquettish and self-effacing sheen of timelessness, inviolate consistency, and seamless immutability, but that sheen is not any more permanent than lipstick on a mirror, or the Barry Manilow hits played on vibraphone wafting through the shopping malls, or than an underwear stain from one of Charles Bukowski's famously wet beer farts.

What makes capitalism seem indelible yet imitable is the fact that it makes certain people very rich, and these paragons of the capitalist class are those that the state media apparatuses parade in their garish media outlets—the movie stars, the corporate moguls, the trendsetters, the celebrities and the culture brokers. News of celebrity cellulite shakes us awake with amphetamine alertness, in the columns provided by Hollywood gossip barons, equipped with the most profound and galvanizing lucidity available on which star has the best bikini body. At the same time, we remain emotionally drowsy to the pain and suffering of people who struggle and strain against falling household wealth, unemployment and lack of food and medical care. And we rarely cast our eyes south of the border.

Hugo Chávez raised the stakes for North Americans. He showed us that a president could be democratically elected many times and still direct the majority of his efforts at helping the poor and disenfranchised help themselves. He made us aware that the comfort we enjoyed in the U.S. was a direct result of the enforced dependency that the U.S. created with *las Americas*. He showed the world that the class struggle is no longer demarcated by men in boiler suits or railhead pants versus factory owners in top hats, continental cross ties and double-breasted vests. Or the sans-culottes versus the breeches-garbed ruling class. Or financiers with capes and silver-tipped canes exploiting the labor power of fruiters, cobblers and copper miners lugging lunchpails of lost dreams. The struggle, as he would tell us in his weekly television show, *Aló Presidente*, is against the transnational capitalist class. The struggle is to free those who depend upon wages for their labor from their enslavement to the capitalist class. He showed us that we need cultures of contestation that are transnational in scope to end the exploitation of capitalism and to bring about socialism for the twenty-first century.

Chávez's Bolivarian Circles (named after Simón Bolívar to serve as watchdog groups modeled after Cuba's Committee for the Defense of the Revolution and to function as liaisons between the neighborhoods and the government as well as fomenting support for Chávez) were important in combating business leaders and dissident army generals whom, with U.S. support, were trying to overthrow the Chávez government. Members of the Bolivarian Circles would bang on hollow electricity poles to warn against mobilizations by the opposition and to rally supporters across the city's working-class neighborhoods. They were an example of self-determination for sovereignty as evidenced by the Bolivarian declaration "Nuestra America: una Sola Patria" (Our America: One Country), which rejects an ideological loyalty to "America" as an America defined by a capitalist-laden value system that favors imperialism and exploitation for increased profit margins.

Chávez created an infrastructure for communal councils and for self-management in factories and cooperatives and for participation in social programs. This was an astonishing accomplishment because never before did the people living in the *barrios* have a real chance to participate in the government. For a leader to take the position of working from a preferential option of the poor and powerless and to be re-elected more times than any other leader in the Western Hemisphere (in the same amount of time)—and to survive a U.S.-supported coup in 2002 and oil strikes that crippled the economy—that is quite a feat. Even Jimmy Carter has praised the election process in Venezuela as among the fairest he has observed.

Capitalism works through a process of exchange-value, whereas Chávez was more interested in the process of communal exchange—that is, to cite but one example, exchanging oil for medical care in a program with Cuba in which Cuban doctors were brought into Venezuela and were set up in various barrios. I (McLaren) remember once I was very ill with a fever off the charts and had to call a doctor, but before the doctor arrived I struggled in vain to pull my Che T-shirt over my drenched body to express a sign of solidarity from this ailing gringo.

Chávez followed the principle of *buen vivir*, which can be translated as "to live well." But this term, which has indigenous roots, is very different from the North American term "the good life." *Buen vivir* requires that individuals in their various communities are in actual possession of their rights and are able to exercise their responsibilities in the context of a respect for diversity and in accordance with the rights of ecosystems. It's about social wealth—not material wealth.

I (McLaren) remember how much I enjoyed teaching at Universidad Bolivariana de Venezuela, located near the Universidad Central de Venezuela—part of Mission Sucre, which provides free higher education to the poor, regardless of academic qualification, prior education or nationality—housed in the ultra-deluxe offices of former PDVSA oil executives that Chávez had fired for their attempt to bring down the government. College enrollment doubled under Chávez. Student projects were insolubly linked to local community improvement. At a graduation ceremony in the early years of the university, Chávez famously said: "Capitalism is machista and to a large extent excludes women, that's why, with the new socialism, girls, you can fly free."

Chávez set up a structure to offer employment for the graduates of UBV through a Presidential Commission that enabled new graduates to be placed around the country in development projects. The graduates would receive a scholarship that was slightly above the minimum wage. Some of these projects involved Misión Árbol (Tree Mission), recovering the environment damaged by capitalism such as the Guaire River.

When I was first invited to Venezuela by the government to help support the Bolivarian Revolution, I (McLaren) remember speaking at Universidad Central de Venezuela. The students who attend this university are mainly the children of the ruling elite. Not many were Chavistas, well, at least not when I spoke there. After my talk where I announced to the students present that I was a Chavista (¿Tú qué eres, capitalista o chavista? Soy Chavista!), I was told that after my departure that some students in retaliation had ripped my portrait off a mural that a student had created of critical theorists. Yet I was able to have very good conversations with some of the students there in the years that followed.

I (McLaren) was privileged to be a guest several times on *Aló Presidente*, a popular weekly—and virtually unscripted—broadcast (popular among the poor and loathed by the rich) hosted by President Chávez, and run on Venezuelan state television and radio stations every Sunday at 11:00 a.m. and usually ending at 5:00 p.m. or occasionally even later. Once, when sitting directly behind the great poet, politician, and liberation theologian, Ernesto Cardenal, author of the magisterial *Evangelio de Solentiname* ("The Gospel of Solentiname"), I listened in awe to Ernesto wax eloquently about President Chávez, and Chávez's dream of bringing humanity together through a deep spiritual love. I silently reflected on the occasion that Pope John Paul II visited Nicaragua in 1983 and openly admonished Ernesto for refusing to resign from the Nicaraguan government: *Usted tiene que arreglar sus asuntos con la Iglesia* ("You must fix your affairs with the Church"). After a brief conversation with President Chávez in Palácio de Miraflores, he turned to the young female secretary who was working in the office where we had our meeting. In a friendly tone, he asked her questions about why she was working in the office and not attending university. He encouraged her to pursue her educational opportunities to the fullest and offered her his advice.

In 2005, when President Chávez offered residents of the Bronx, New York, a new type of program to heat homes, it was ridiculed in the U.S. media as a cheap publicity stunt. Chávez was using the profits from his nation's rich oil reserves to enact social spending programs and was offering residents of the Bronx the same deal, which meant he would provide home heating oil to economically disadvantaged residents at a major discount—through Citgo— provided the savings that were made were reinvested into programs that benefitted the poor. Veteran Representative José Serrano has since voiced his praise of Chávez for instituting this program in his district.

Although I (McLaren) met President Chávez half a dozen times, I had only one conversation with him. He thanked me for my work in critical pedagogy, and for my willingness to share some of my work with those in the Bolivarian Revolution. But he reminded me that I have as much to learn from the people of Venezuela, and that I needed to maintain that attitude in my work. Whatever critical pedagogy would emerge in Venezuela would, he said, be distinctly Venezolano. He turned out to be right.

La Salida

Unsurprisingly, all these progressive developments, both social democratic and socialist in character, have been met and continue to be met with fierce opposition from neoliberal capitalists and their supporters. Unrest in Venezuela at the time of writing (spring 2014) has gained a large amount of publicity worldwide, much of it hostile. The aim of the unrest, organized by *La Salida* (The Exit), is specifically to oust the democratically elected Maduro government and has taken the form of attacking and destroying the symbols of the Bolivarian Revolution such as community televisions, housing misiones, ambulances, the environment ministry, public transport and PDVSA (the state-owned oil and gas company) trucks. In addition, roads from farming areas to urban areas have been blocked to stop goods being transported, and food trucks have been burned (Pearson, 2014).

As the president himself points out, anti-government protestors have physically attacked and damaged healthcare clinics, burned down a university and thrown Molotov cocktails and rocks at buses. Other public institutions have also been targeted, such as the Supreme Court, CANTV (the public telephone company) and the attorney general's office (Maduro, 2014).

The headquarters of the Venezuelan government's housing mission in Caracas and an adjacent pre-school were also attacked. The housing mission is one of the government's largest social projects, aiming to construct three million homes by 2019 (Venezuelans living below minimum wage are eligible to receive free housing under the mission, while low-income families receive heavy government subsidies for the homes) (Mallett-Outtrim, 2014).

Tamara Pearson (2014) has pointed out that the aim of the opposition is:

> not just to intimidate, but to stop government institutions and social organisations on a practical level from getting on with other things. The violent opposition sectors

are not farmers, bus drivers, teachers, producers of anything, builders, etc., so they can't strike in order to bring things to a halt, they can only use violent barricades to stop others from working.

One group of barricaders strung up galvanized barbed wire 1.2 meters high so that motorcycle riders who tried to pass would be decapitated. This actually happened to two people (Dutka, 2014).

Luis Britto García (cited in Lovato, 2014) has quoted the Colombian novelist William Ospina who states that in the entire world, the rich celebrate and the poor protest. Only in Venezuela do the poor celebrate and the rich protest. Maduro sums up his view of the current situation in a similar fashion: "Today in Venezuela, the working class is in power: it's the country where the rich protest and the poor celebrate their social wellbeing" (cited in Milne & Watts, 2014).

While the violence was instigated by the opposition, and it is they who have perpetrated the vast majority of violent acts, it needs to be pointed out that Maduro and the attorney general have acknowledged the responsibility of the National Guard and the Bolivarian police in the death and mistreatment of some demonstrators (Ianni, 2014) and Maduro has pledged:

> A very small number of security forces personnel have also been accused of engaging in violence, as a result of which several people have died. These are highly regrettable events, and the Venezuelan government has responded by arresting those suspected. We have created a Human Rights Council to investigate all incidents related to these protests. Each victim deserves justice, and every perpetrator—whether a supporter or an opponent of the government—will be held accountable for his or her actions. (Maduro, 2014)

US Intervention in Venezuela

Maduro (cited in Milne & Watts, 2014) accuses the United States of using the ongoing street protests as an attempt at a "slow-motion" Ukraine-style coup against his government to "get their hands on Venezuelan oil." Maduro describes current events in Venezuela as a "revolt of the rich," adding that it will fail because the Bolivarian Revolution is more deeply rooted than in 2002 (cited in Milne & Watts, 2014). In that year, there was a coup that temporarily ousted Chávez, who was very soon reinstated by the will of the people.

Ed Vulliamy (2002), writing in the *Observer* newspaper, argues that his newspaper established shortly after the coup that it "was closely tied to senior officials in the US government … [who] have long histories in the 'dirty wars' of the 1980s, and links to death squads working in Central America at that time." According to officials at the Organization of American States "and other diplomatic sources," Vulliamy goes on, "the US administration was not only aware the coup was about to take place, but had sanctioned it, presuming it to be destined for success." Moreover, "the visits [to the White House] by Venezuelans plotting a coup ... began ... several months ago" and went on until weeks before the coup.

The "crucial figure around the coup," Vulliamy states, was Elliott Abrams, who was senior director of the National Security Council for "democracy, human rights and international operations," a leading theoretician of "Hemispherism," which "put a priority on combating Marxism in the Americas." It led to the coup in Chile in 1973, Vulliamy concludes, and sponsored regimes and death squads elsewhere in Latin America.

Venezuela, Maduro argues, is currently facing the "unconventional war that the US has perfected over the last decades," via U.S.-backed coups—from 1960s Brazil to Honduras in 2009. As he puts it, the aim of the opposition is to paralyze "the main cities of the country, copying badly what happened in Kiev, where the main roads in the cities were blocked off, until they made governability impossible, which led to the overthrow of the elected government of Ukraine" (cited in Milne & Watts, 2014). He goes on:

> [t]hey try to increase economic problems through an economic war to cut the supplies of basic goods and boost an artificial inflation ... To create social discontent and violence, to portray a country in flames, which could lead them to justify international isolation and even foreign intervention. (cited in Milne & Watts, 2014)

He then refers to 100 years of intervention in Latin America and the Caribbean: against Haiti, Nicaragua, Guatemala, Chile, Grenada and Brazil and the aforementioned 2002 coup attempt against Chávez by the Bush administration. He concludes, "[w]hy does the US have 2,000 military bases in the world? To dominate it. I have told President Obama: we are not your backyard anymore" (cited in Milne & Watts, 2014).

Maduro's points remind us how Wikileaks cables, Edward Snowden's exposés and U.S. state department documents reveal U.S. plans to "divide," "isolate" and "penetrate" the Chávez government, along with extensive U.S. government funding of Venezuelan opposition groups over the past decade (cited in Milne & Watts, 2014). Seumas Milne and Jonathan Watts (2014) point out that some were via agencies such as USAID and the Office for

Transitional Initiatives—including $5 million of overt support in the current fiscal year. They also note that Maduro's remarks follow admissions in April 2014 that USAID covertly funded a social media website to "foment political unrest and encourage 'flash mobs' in Cuba under the cover of 'development assistance'" which White House officials acknowledged was not "unique to Cuba" (Milne & Watts, 2014).

Maduro cannot forget that his primary goal is to assist the defenders of socialism in mobilizing against the opposition and to continue the deepening of socialism in Venezuela. The struggle against the counter-revolution in Venezuela will not only need to be won on the streets but also in the media where the social imagination of Venezuela is currently being fashioned by the opposition's manufactured lies: "hence the need for responding in an appropriate manner by creatively using not only all the traditional media (the press, the radio, television), but also the great opportunities given by the social networks" (Borón, 2014).

If Venezuela were to fall to the fascists in the opposition, then other Latin American democracies would be targeted with the same strategies soon after—Ecuador, Bolivia, Argentina, Brazil and Uruguay. Arlenys Espinal-Aporrea (2014) captures the essence of the struggle ahead when he argues that the goal is "to transform the extractionist model into a productive state without becoming a predator to nature, the struggle to transform our consumerist culture, to reclaim life on a human scale and promote self-sustainable community, or else what are the communes for?"

Maduro is in no doubt about the permanency of the Bolivarian Revolution: "The people will decide until when I can be here. Be certain that if it is not me it will be another revolutionary. What will be indefinite is the popular power of the people." As he puts it, "When Chávez said 'the 21st century is ours' in 1992 ... 'it was a romantic idea. Today it is a reality and no one is going to take it away from us'" (cited in Milne & Watts, 2014).

Cardinal Jorge Urosa and many of his followers in the Catholic Church in Venezuela are trying to take the revolution away from the people. The Catholic Church in Venezuela has long taken a strong stand against President Hugo Chávez and his successor. In warning the Venezuelan people of the dangers of socialism and denouncing Chávez, church officials sided, as they usually did, with the Venezuelan ruling class in its exploitation of the people of Venezuela.

The Catholic Church has a long history of conservatism in Venezuela although some clearly have heard the social gospel of Jesus Christ. The

Catholic faithful who are familiar with the struggle of liberation theology in America Latina can only hope that the spirit of Archbishop Óscar Romero will touch the hearts of their conservative brothers and sisters as they pray for the poor and the dispossessed of Venezuela, who are now able to read and write and engage in forging their own histories, thanks in part to the valiant and noble efforts of Hugo Chávez to create spaces of self-education for the people through the establishment of the misiones.

It is true that Chávez's successor, Nicolás Maduro, who sometimes sleeps in Chávez's mausoleum, claims that Chávez makes regular spiritual visitations to him (sometimes as a tweeting little bird) and often sees an image of Chávez on the Avila mountain overlooking Caracas (Strange, 2014). And yes, it is true that a version of "The Lord's Prayer" was recited at the end of a Socialist party workshop in Caracas that called on the spirit of Chávez to lead the country away from capitalism, oligarchy and contraband.

"Hallowed be your name, may your legacy come to us so we can spread it to people here and elsewhere. Give us your light to guide us every day," Maria Estrella Uribe recited in front of an image of Chávez (Strange, 2014) with President Maduro present. It is true that this has come to be known as the socialist prayer.

Since his death in March 2013, there continues to be great homage paid to the memory of Chávez.

And while there are many in Venezuela who say this move towards glorifying Chávez on religious grounds is merely a political strategy on the part of the ruling party, others will argue that this is clearly a matter of faith. Of course, the cynics who mock the religious fervor for Chávez among the poor, are quick to defend the poor who faithfully attend the Catholic masses in the churches overseen by the Catholic priests who are quick to denounce Chávez and who support the opposition party comprised of mainly the rich and middle class.

Equally, it could be said that the country's bishops who have lined up to condemn the insertion of Chávez into "The Lord's Prayer," such as Ulises Antonio Gutiérrez Reyes, Archbishop of Ciudad Bolívar, are doing so out of political considerations as much as religious ones.

Just as the figure of Che Guevara has been transfigured as "San Ernesto de La Higuera" by campesinos in Bolivia who offer prayers for favors in his name, so too has Hugo Chávez been canonized by the poor and the downtrodden in Venezuela. Just as Che's murdered body is now compared by campesinos to John the Baptist, similarly candles will be lit in the memory of Hugo Chávez, and his name will be whispered in cadences of love and respect and most of all, hope.

Hugo Chávez Frías rode the Angel of History like a wild stallion across the fiery firmament of revolution, drawing back the curtain on imperialism's "southern strategy," and advancing the cause of a twentieth-century socialism. He was a soilder, in essence, one with sufficient humanity to stare directly into the heart of capitalism and warn us that it pulsed with leakages of sequestered oil and that its "cap and trade" compassion was market regulated. Hugo Chávez was crowned by history with a red beret and made us proud to be warriors for social justice, marching towards a new future. His spirit remains with us. And that is something that even the U.S. cannot kill with the false precision of its drone strikes, even at the behest of Pat Robertson.

Bibliography

Althusser, L. (1971). Ideology and ideological state apparatuses. In L. Althusser, *Lenin and philosophy and other essays*. London, England: New Left Books. Retrieved from http://www.marx2mao.com/Other/LPOE70NB.html

Bercovitch, S. (2014, September 5). Maduro, Venezuelan Catholic church dispute 'Chavista' version of 'The Lord's Prayer' *Venezuelanalysis.com*. Retrieved from http://venezuelanaly-sis.com/news/10884

Borón, A. (2014, April 9). How to fight the fascist offensive in Venezuela. *Venezuelanalysis.com*. http://venezuelanalysis.com/analysis/10592

Chávez, H. (2010, April 11). *Coup and countercoup: Revolution!* Retrieved from http://venezue-la-us.org/2010/04/11/coup-and-countercoup-revolution/ (no longer accessible).

Ciccariello-Maher, G. (2013). *We created Chávez: A people's history of the Venezuelan revolution*. Durham, NC: Duke University Press.

Cole, M. (2011). *Racism and education in the U.K. and the U.S.: Towards a socialist alternative*. New York, NY: Palgrave Macmillan.

Cole, M. (2013). Neoliberal capitalism or twenty-first century socialism: What is the role of higher education? *Queries—Journal of the Foundation for European Progressive Studies (FEPS)*.

Cole, M. (2014). The Bolivarian Republic of Venezuela: Education and twenty-first century socialism. In S. C. Motta & M. Cole (Eds.), *Constructing twenty-first-century socialism in Latin America: The role of radical education*. New York, NY: Palgrave Macmillan.

Cole, M., & McLaren, P. (2013). Immiseration capitalism or twenty-first century socialism? In D. Hill (Ed.), *Immiseration capitalism and education: Austerity, resistance and revolt* (pp. 218–229). Brighton, England: The Institute for Education Policy Studies.

Damon, A. (2013). February employment report masks depth of U.S. job crisis. *World Socialist Web Site*. Retrieved from http://www.wsws.org/en/articles/2013/03/09/econ-m09.html

Davis, B. (2005, August 25). Is Pat Robertson out of his mind or in the loop? *Venezuelanalysis.com*. Retrieved from http://venezuelanalysis.com/analysis/1314

Dutka, Z. C. (2014, April 4). Mercal shooting highlights class polarization, psychologists fear 'fractured coexistence.' *Venezuelanalysis.com*. Retrieved from http://venezuelanalysis.com/analysis/10574

Espinal-Aporrea, A. (2014). Who dares evaluate the Bolivarian revolution? *Venezuelanalysis.com*. Retrieved from http://venezuelanalysis.com/analysis/10635

Griffiths, T., & Williams, J. (2009). Mass schooling for socialist transformation in Cuba and Venezuela. *Journal for Critical Education Policy Studies*, 7(2). Retrieved from http://www.jceps.com/?pageID=article&articleID=160

Hill, D. (2012). Immiseration capitalism, activism and education: Resistance, revolt and revenge. *Journal for Critical Education Policy Studies*, 10(2). Retrieved from http://www.jceps.com/PDFs/10-2-01.pdf

Hill, D. (2013). *Immiseration capitalism and education: Activist resistance to the neoliberal and neoconservative degradation*. Brighton, England: Institute for Education Policy Studies.

Hudis, P. (2010, December). *The critical pedagogy of Rosa Luxemburg*. Paper presented at the Encuentro Internacional del Pensamiento Critico: Marxismo y Educacion Popular, Morelia, Michoacan, Mexico.

Hudis, P. (2012a). From the economic crisis to the transcendence of capital. *The International Marxist Humanist*. Retrieved from http://www.internationalmarxisthumanist.org/articles/economic-crisis-transcendence-capital-peter-hudis

Hudis, P. (2012b). *Marx's concept of the alternative to capitalism*. Amsterdam, the Netherlands: Brill.

Ianni, V. (2014, March 31). The debate today is how to stop the violent offensive of the neoliberal right-wing. *Venezuelanalysis.com*. http://venezuelanalysis.com/analysis/10561

Leech, G. (2012). *Capitalism: A structural genocide*. London, England: Zed Books.

Lovato, R. (2014, April 2). Why the media are giving a free pass to Venezuela's neo-fascist creeps. *The Nation*. *Venezuelanalysis.com*. Retrieved from http://venezuelanalysis.com/analysis/10567.

Maduro, N. (2014, April 1). Venezuela: A call for peace. *The New York Times*. *Venezuelanalysis.com*. Retrieved from http://venezuelanalysis.com/analysis/10565

Maduro takes the oath as acting president and candidate for the coming elections. (2013, March 9). *MercoPress*. Retrieved from http://en.mercopress.com/2013/03/09/maduro-takes-the-oath-as-acting-president-and-candidate-for-the-coming-elections

Mallett-Outtrim, R. (2014, April 2). 'Terrorists' attack housing mission and preschool in Venezuela. *Venezuelanalysis.com*. Retrieved from http://venezuelanalysis.com/news/10568

McLaren, P. (2008). This fist called my heart: Public pedagogy in the belly of the beast. *Antipode*, 40(3), 472–481.

McLaren, P. (2013). The man in the red beret. *Speakout*. Retrieved from http://www.truth-out.org/speakout/item/14997-the-man-in-the-red-beret

Milne, S., & Watts, J. (2014, April 8). Venezuela protests are sign that US wants our oil, says Nicolás Maduro. *The Guardian*. Retrieved from http://www.theguardian.com/world/2014/apr/08/venezuela-protests-sign-us-wants-oil-says-nicolas-maduro

Minister David Cameron's speech to the World Economic Forum in Davos. (2013, January 24). *Gov.UK: The Official Site of the British Prime Minister's Office*. Retrieved from https://www.gov.uk/government/speeches/prime-minister-david-camerons-speech-to-the-world-economic-forum-in-davos

Muhr, T., & Verger, A. (2006). Venezuela: Higher education for all. *Journal for Critical Education Policy Studies*, 4(1). Retrieved from http://www.jceps.com/?pageID=article&articleID=63

Pabian, M. (2008, September 4). Venezuela: From 'third way' to socialist revolution. *Direct Action*. Retrieved from http://directaction.org.au/issue4/venezuela_from_third_way_to_socialist_revolution

Pearson, T. (2014, April 2). Demonising the 'Colectivos': Demonising the grassroots. *Venezuelanalysis.com*. http://venezuelanalysis.com/analysis/10569

Schwarz, P. (2013, January 10). Europe in 2013. *World Socialist Web Site*. Retrieved from http://www.wsws.org/en/articles/2013/01/10/pers-j10.html

Shaoul, J. (2012, March 12). Cuts push UK workers' living standards back 30 years. *World Socialist Web Site*. Retrieved from http://www.wsws.org/articles/2012/mar2012/wage-m12.shtml

Socialist Outlook editorial. (2007, Spring). Chávez: 'I also am a Trotskyist.' *Socialist Outlook*, 11. Retrieved from http://www.isg-fi.org.uk/spip.php?article430

Stockton, D. (2013, February). Is European social democracy in irreversible decline? *Workers Power*, 9(2). Retrieved from http://www.workerspower.co.uk/2011/12/is-european-social-democracy-in-irreversible-decline/

Strange, H. (2014, September 4). Saintly Hugo Chávez replaces God in socialist Lord's Prayer. *Vice News*. Retrieved from: https://news.vice.com/article/saintly-hugo-Chávez-replaces-god-in-socialist-lords-prayer

Suggett, J. (2010). Chávez's annual address includes minimum wage hike, maintenance of social spending in Venezuela. *Venezualanalysis.com*. Retrieved from http://venezuelanalysis.com/news/5077

Victor, M. P. (2009, December 4). *From conquistadores, dictators and multinationals to the Bolivarian Revolution*. Keynote speech given at the Conference on Land and Freedom, Caribbean Studies Program, University of Toronto, Ontario, Canada, October 31, 2009. *Venezuelanalyis.com*. Retrieved from http://www.venezuelanalysis.com/analysis/4979

Vulliamy, E. (2002, April 21). Venezuela coup linked to Bush team. *The Observer*. Retrieved from http://www.theguardian.com/world/2002/apr/21/usa.venezuela

Weisbrot, M. (2013, March 17). Chávez's death, like his life, shows the world's divisions. *Al Jazeera*. Retrieved from http://www.cepr.net/index.php/op-eds-&-columns/op-eds-&-columns/death-and-life-of-Chávez-demonstratedivisions

· 4 ·

COMRADE FIDEL,
THE FRENCH CANADIAN AND
A LITERACY CAMPAIGN

n the summer of 2000, I was invited, along with Ira Shor, to serve as an advisor for the doctoral degree program in critical pedagogy at the University of Saint Thomas (St. Paul and Minneapolis, Minnesota). I also had the good fortune to teach a summer course in that program that same year. In those days, many of us who had been engaged since the early 1980s in the difficult task of developing critical pedagogy into a legitimate program of study in graduate schools of education, dared to be optimistic about the future of the field. We were eagerly waiting to see our efforts reach fruition. Two of my former doctoral students (from Miami University of Ohio and the University of California, Los Angeles) became full-time faculty in the program at the University of St. Thomas. It was an exciting time.

I had hoped that critical pedagogy would catch fire at schools of education nationwide, and that this would lead to more doctoral programs with concentrations in critical pedagogy, and perhaps even doctoral degree programs. After all, UCLA had recruited me in 1992 to bring critical pedagogy to what is now called the Division of Urban Schooling. And colleagues of mine throughout the U.S. were being asked to develop courses in critical pedagogy at their institutions. Perhaps critical pedagogy was coming into its own. Of course, at that time (and to a certain extent today) critical pedagogy was used as an umbrella term that covered the domains of literacy, educational philosophy and theory, ethnographic studies of schooling, language acquisition and reading, the social foundations of education and multicultural education. So there was a lot from which to choose.

I had waited a long time for a doctoral degree in critical pedagogy to be established somewhere in the U.S., and when I heard about the program at the University of St. Thomas, a prestigious Catholic university, I was sure that more degree programs would be in the making. Those were heady days when public enthusiasm had been recalled from exile and was influencing the ranks of critical educators both in the public schools and the universities. Perhaps critical pedagogy could change the face of public schooling in the U.S. and perhaps even build a new social order where equality and justice prevailed.

Today, that enthusiasm has waned considerably, as both public universities and schools in general have been more completely taken over by corporate interests powered by neoliberal capital. The critical pedagogy program at St. Thomas exists no longer. And critical pedagogy barely seems to have survived the educational assaults of the Bush and Obama years.

The book *Rebel Literacy: Cuba's National Literacy Campaign and Critical Global Citizenship* is a stepchild of the Critical Pedagogy Program at St. Thomas, which ended after only four cohorts. Its author, Mark Abendroth (2009), was a member of Cohort Two. As a scholar-activist, Abendroth has produced a courageous and prescient volume that will impact the field of critical pedagogy for years to come. Each page of his book will repay the reader mightily in its creative retelling of the Cuban National Literacy Campaign— undeniably among the world's greatest educational accomplishments of the twentieth century. Of course, this book is much more than a retelling; it is also a rethinking of the very meaning of literacy and critical citizenship today. And for this reason it merits the attention of educators everywhere.

As a young man, Abendroth's interest in Cuba was partially fueled by the prohibition that exists for U.S. citizens to visit the island (one that Obama, to his credit, has begun to change). My own interest in Cuba came from a very different place. I grew up in Canada and I recall billboard and magazine advertisements inviting Canadians to enjoy their winter holidays in the sunny island of Cuba, and for Canadians, every potential tropical site was viewed as a paradisiacal haven for those of us who were confined to six long months of winter each year.

At the time of this writing, my years living in Canada outnumber the years I have lived in the U.S. by five. I immigrated to the U.S. in 1985 and became a dual Canadian-U.S. citizen in 2000. And while it is likely I will have lived longer in the U.S. than in my native Canada by the time my last

breath expires, I will always consider myself more Canadian than American.
My Canadian identity is in my red bones. After all, my political formation
began in the streets of Toronto in 1968. Maybe the biggest political lesson I
learned was walking down Yonge Street in the suburb of Willowdale in 1968
on whatever the hallucinogen of the day happened to be (an LSD blotter, as
I seem to recall), and flipping off a Metropolitan Toronto police officer. I was
thrown into a black and white and taken to jail, where the officers shone their
flashlights sadistically into the planet-sized pupils of my eyes, and whacked me
in the forehead with them when I tried to bat them away. My subsequent trip
to California that year was fraught with similar incidents, and I won't risk boring you with listing those. Nor will I attempt to compare Canada and the U.S.
But, thanks to the bohemian culture of downtown Yorkville (today a gentrified
area that resembles Rodeo Drive in Beverly Hills but was once a gritty section of the city where hippies lived and gathered), where I spent years in rapt
engagement with poets, writers, actors and musicians in the smoke-filled coffee
houses and hippie lofts, and in romantic moments with Pre-Raphaelite looking
lovers in velvet gowns and flower headbands whom I lovingly embraced in the
flickering shadows of Philosopher's Walk on the University of Toronto campus,
you could confidently say that I had imbibed the spirit of the Beat Poets, and
consumed as much of underground culture that I could hold in one brainpan
without flipping out—poetry, philosophy, Eastern religion, psychedelic drugs,
sex and the Kama Sutra, all kinds of new ideas and new artists—gestalt theory,
rational emotive therapy, Irving Layton, Leonard Cohen, Joni Mitchell, Buffy
Saint-Marie, Gregory Bateson, R.D. Laing, general semantics, psychoanalysis, anarchism, acid rock, John C. Lilly, the occult, pyramid energy, theoso-
phy, Darwin, Zen Buddhism, the Bloomsbury group, the Inklings, Dadaism,
McLuhan, Gordon Lightfoot, Luke and the Apostles (my guitar teacher was
Toronto's own David Wilcox), and Catholic saints. Well, where should I stop?
Stompin' Tom Connors? Anne Murray? Our pet, Juliet?

Even throughout the torment and joy of those troubling and troubled
years, I managed to find time to watch the occasional Hockey Night in Canada with my dad and enjoyed reminiscing with him about how we would go
curling together in matching sweaters during the four years our family spent
in Winnipeg. I really miss those days. That eclectic ecology of my mind at the
time no doubt influenced my (thankfully short lived) attraction to postmodernism in the mid-1980s. I still think of Toronto as one of the great cities of
the world, and I have visited many of them. But perhaps my perceptions of
the city are dipped in an all-too saccharine romanticism that from time-to-
time plagues me and my thinking. After all, right through the 70s, I dreamed

of leaving Toronto, riding a fire-apple red 1969 XLCH Harley Davidson 883
Sportster with an "Eye of God" pyramid on the gas tank, right across the
United States, sporting a Michael Parks "Then Came Bronson" wool watch
cap on my head. One thing that I learned from my countercultural days in
Toronto was that you make your path by walking and before you can travel the
path, you have to become the path. This is the essence of praxis. I had become
the path away from Willowdale, away from my home in "The Beaches", away
from everything I knew in order to step into the void of the United States.
But I had yet to find a path towards something, towards an understanding of
capitalist society and what would constitute a socialist alternative. My first
impression of the United States was of the vastness of the armies of the homeless, haunted by the slow death that stalked the dispossessed in the so-called
most progressive democracy in the world, or so the U.S. was described in those
days. It would take me years to understand that when the specter of progress
twists his hourglass watch upside down to mark the death-rattle countdown of
those millions who are dying on city streets of preventable diseases and who
lay unattended in hospital beds crammed into the corridors of decaying urban
medical centers; he is present around the world wherever the logic of capital
prevails. The pitted and pock-marked lungs of his victims are now unfillable,
their life force fading behind curtains of dust and dead memories. These casu-
alties of 'progress' are not restricted to one country. And they are not necessarily living in the streets. They occupy office buildings, schools, monasteries,
sanctuaries, offices, and shopping malls. They are often our own children, our
relatives, our friends, ourselves. They are not all victims of poverty, but victims of a logic that creates it.

    In January 1976, at the height of the Canadian winter (January 26, to
be exact), the charismatic Prime Minister of Canada, Pierre Elliot Trudeau,
stepped off an Armed Forces Boeing 707 at José Martí airport to meet Fidel
Castro in Cuba. I was teaching at a senior public school in a village outside of
Toronto at the time, and I remember well Trudeau's legendary visit. Trudeau
became the first leader of a NATO country to visit Cuba since the U.S. instituted its vicious 1960 embargo on the island, which the Cubans view (and
rightly so) as more of a blockade. During a speech in Cienfuegos, Trudeau
exuberantly exclaimed, "Viva Cuba" and "Viva el Primer Ministro Fidel Castro!"
And Margaret, his wife, declared Fidel to be "the sexiest man alive." And
while, as a burgeoning young leftist, I had my reservations about Trudeau's
liberal politics, I remember cheering Trudeau's remarks in a tavern when they
were televised throughout the country. At least for his three nights in Havana,

Trudeau had resisted the attempts of the U.S. to dictate Canada's foreign policy (although I am sure some of the U.S. military strategists saw an advantage to having a member of NATO that close to the devil himself).

Some analysts have made the case that Fidel's Jesuit education (grade five at the Colegio Dolores in Santiago de Cuba and finishing high school at the Colegio de Belén in Havana) and Trudeau's Jesuit schooling at the Collège Jean-de-Brébeuf in Montreal had something to do with their affinity for each other, but both their Jesuit educations occurred prior to an era marked by an openness to dialogue with others that was ushered in by the Second Ecumenical Council of the Vatican, or Vatican II, opened under Pope John XXIII on October, 11, 1962, and closed under Pope Paul VI on December, 8, 1965, and the 32nd General Congregation that followed it (although it is likely that Trudeau was at least at one time a student of liberation theology).[1]

I remember traveling to Ottawa in 1980 to appear on Margaret Trudeau's television show, and being warned by the production assistant not to refer to Ms. Trudeau as "Maggie." During all this time I was thinking fondly about the Trudeaus' visit to Cuba, as I fielded questions about a best-selling book I had just published about my teaching experiences in a school located in Canada's largest public housing project in the city of North York. (After the show, I was invited out to lunch by Ms. Trudeau and we were joined by Jan Rubeš, a Czech-Canadian opera singer and actor but as far as I recall, politics wasn't discussed.)

It was unthinkable that Fidel and Trudeau would become, in the words of former Canadian ambassador Mark Entwistle, "intellectual soulmates" at a time when all the political calculations of the era worked to prohibit such a relationship. Trudeau would not visit Fidel again until 1991, when the two men went snorkeling together, and he enjoyed three more visits with Fidel until the late 1990s. In fact, Jimmy Carter and Fidel both served as pallbearers at Trudeau's funeral in 2000. Later, it was learned that American mobster Meyer Lansky, who resented Fidel for confiscating his gambling enterprises in Havana, and who tried to have Fidel killed during Fidel's one and only formal visit to the U.S., also considered assassinating Trudeau.

Of course, the U.S. has repeatedly tried to assassinate Fidel, not only by recruiting mobsters John Roselli and Sam Giancana, but also through the pet project of Attorney General Robert Kennedy, Operation Mongoose, which saw the recruitment of Cuban-American militants who helped to carry out counter-revolutionary operations against Cuba, which included the bombing of hospitals, the sabotage of industrial and agricultural sites (including the poisoning of Cuba's sugar crops), as well as assassinations (when President Gerald Ford issued Executive Order 11905 in February 1976, prohibiting assassination as an instrument of U.S. foreign policy, the Cuban-American militants continued to terrorize the island and were still active years later, and the subsequent revelations about the Bush Jr. and Obama administrations have made a mockery of Executive Order 11905).

Today, as in the 1970s, there is a widespread habit of mind in the U.S. that is founded on the most pernicious of false generalizations and accordingly associates Cuba, socialism, Fidel and Venezuela's President Hugo Chávez with the greatest of evils. It is an era of "negative nationalism," to use the words of George Orwell. And this impacts not only foreign policy, but domestic policy as well. Consider the case of Obama's presidency. Fueled by a vehement racism, right-wing pundits and politicians and large sectors of the electorate are cheering for President Obama's policies to fail, even if it means the needs of the American people will not be served. Bolstered by a bottomless pit of corporate money, media support and right-wing officials giddy with partisan hatred, a reactionary street-protest movement is afoot, drawing at times tens of thousands of people to decry the bank bailout, the auto bailout, healthcare reform, the growing deficit and America's descent into socialism and communism blamed on the skullduggery of the forty-fourth U.S. president. Contrast this with the spirit and vitality of the Cuban people captured in *Rebel Literacy: Cuba's National Literacy Campaign and Critical Global Citizenship.*

In La Ciudad Libertad (City of Liberty), an educational complex situated in the western suburbs of Havana, known as the Playa district, in the sprawling former headquarters of brutal dictator Fulgencio Batista, there stands a small museum that commemorates Cuba's National Literacy Campaign (henceforth called the Campaign). This modest-looking white stucco structure is anything but a testament to negative nationalism; rather, it personifies what Abendroth calls "critical global citizenship"—a liberation movement designed to ensure the health and vitality of the revolution and independence from Cuba's colonial past. Few books have touched on this aspect of the Campaign, and it is to Abendroth's great credit that he makes this theme central to his work.

Driven by a need for equality, Fidel and Che moved to renew Cuba's infrastructure as quickly as possible, including instituting agrarian reform, healthcare reform, and educational reform, as the quality of life among the lowest sectors of Cuban society needed to be redressed in a serious fashion. Efforts at restructuring the country were put into effect, as many skilled workers had fled the country, creating a Cuban "brain drain." Workers had to be taught new skills to compensate for the loss of those highly skilled workers who had left the country. In addition, urban citizens and *guajiros* needed to learn how to cooperate and work together. Che encouraged Fidel to make 1961 the "year of education," a move desperately needed to counter the inequality of Cuban education that saw wealthy Cubans thrive in private institutions while working-class students received a sub-standard education, if they received an education at all. As a result "literacy brigades" were sent out into the countryside to teach illiterate *guajiros* (peasants) to read and write, and to build schools. Many of the Literacy Campaign's volunteers later became full-fledged teachers, and the annual graduation rate of teachers is now 11 times higher than it was prior to 1959.

Before the successful completion of the Campaign, almost a million Cubans lacked basic schooling owing to race, class, gender and geographic isolation (Elvy, 2007). But that was not to last long. Like the rapid brushstrokes of British narrative painter Ian Francis, voluntary literacy workers took to the streets and the fields, assembling in what was to become a massive enactment of the ethical imperatives of the revolution. A total force of 308,000 volunteers worked with 707,212 illiterate Cubans and helped them achieve a first-grade level of reading and writing (to be followed in later years by the Battle for the Sixth Grade and Battle for the Ninth Grade). Cuba's overall illiteracy rate was reduced from over 20 percent, according to the last census taken before the revolution, to 3.9 percent (Supko, 1998).

Volunteers included adult popular educators (178,000 *alfabetizadores* who taught in urban areas), workers from factories (30,000 *brigadistas obreros* who received their regular salaries while doing their literacy training), and 100,000 students, between the ages of 10 and 19 who came to be known as the *Conrado Benitez Brigadistas* and who carried in their knapsacks a pair of boots, two pairs of socks, an olive-green beret, a Conrado Benitez shoulder patch, a blanket, a hammock, a lantern and copies of *Alfabeticemos* (the Campaign's official teacher's manual) and *Venceremos* (a student primer).

City schools were closed down in order that students between the ages of 10 and 19, with a minimum grade six education, could leave their homes in urban centers and live with *campesino* families in the countryside. As Joanne C. Elvy (2007) puts it: "Integrated into peasant households, they worked alongside their new families by day, and then taught them how to read and write by lantern at night." This profound revolutionary condition marked an important exchange between Cubans from urban centers and those who worked in the fields. Of particular significance was the social and cultural shift of the role of women in Cuba's civic society. Over 50 percent of the volunteer teachers in the Campaign were young women, marking the first time that many of them left home and were given the opportunity to take on the same tasks as their male counterparts (Elvy, 2007).

Each act of shared labor and struggle with their *campesino* compatriots, each stroke of the pen made under the sturdy lanterns carried by the *brigadistas*, became gestures of solidarity, metonymical acts that reflected in their particular victories over illiteracy, the root metaphor of revolutionary praxis: making the revolution through revolutionary acts. Eventually, red flags were hung over doorways signaling *Territorios Libres de Analfabetismo* (Territories Free of Illiteracy).

The Campaign was able to develop appropriate strategies and tactics that were part of both methodological and doctrinal fronts. Paulo Freire (1985, p. 17) makes a distinction between strategy and tactics that are apposite in this context:

> Strategy is, as I understand it, the space in which I have my dream, my political dream, the objective of my life. It does not mean that my dream stays eternally, permanently, like it was at the beginning. Tactics, on the other hand are different. They concretize the dream. We have to be very consistent between tactics and strategy. It means that I cannot have tactics of a rightist man in order to concretize the dreams of a leftist … I remember Guevara said 'no contradictions between the means and the objectives.'

Not only did the Campaign have a strategy—building socialism—it also created pedagogical tactics that were consistent with that strategy.

The Campaign also benefited from Anibal Ponce's stress on creating both a methodological front—emphasizing collective work instead of the usual bourgeois call for increasing individual freedoms—and a doctrinal front— creating a curriculum that serves the interests of workers and *campesinos*. The methodological front was also evident in the emphasis placed on collaboration among all Cuban citizens—white, black, male, female. And the doctrinal front was further revealed in the creation of a curriculum that explored colonial oppression and promoted understanding of the transformative projects of the revolution. Of course, the Campaign also benefited from the insights of José Carlos Mariátegui, José Martí, Julio Antonio Mella, Augusto César Sandino, Mao and others.

At this present historical conjuncture, when we are living in the bowels of a crisis of capitalism, the likes of which we have not seen since the Great Depression, when increasing numbers of people are being thrown out of their homes and denied medical assistance because of a lack of health insurance, it is not as surprising as it is disconcerting that some educationalists, such as the illustrious William F. Pinar (2009), are attacking proponents of critical pedagogy for not acknowledging the lineaments of subjectivity or for paying insufficient attention to theorizing the "I" in their work, or for focusing too much on social structure and the role that education plays in the reproduction of inequality and injustice.

I beg to differ with the good professor. I do not believe that discussions of the importance of Che or Freire are attempts by critical educators to sell commodified "metasubjects" in a "symbiotic rhetoric" to students, creating a "doomed defiance" and an "impossible praxis." Having apparently ignored the search for a self-critical subjectivity in its eternal repetition of the same, Pinar argues that critical scholarship (that is, critical scholarship sans Pinar) has produced "no new insight, no accumulated knowledge or intellectual advancement" since 1968, despite the determination of the offspring of the *soixante-huitards* in Paris, Berlin, Grosvenor Square or Prague to carry on the struggle.

Pinar's aqueous clarion call to move 'beyond' the antediluvian categories of reproduction and resistance and to embrace Pinar's sanctified "I," just at a time when the work of critical educators, especially Marxist educators, is increasing in relevance because of the explanatory potential of historical materialist critique to unmask the current crisis of capitalism, to reveal the limitations of poststructuralism in its criticisms of Marxism as "deterministic" and to put class analysis back on the educational agenda,[2] can only be viewed by educators serious about educational transformation in capitalist societies as *jejeune*. Capital, it appears, has its way of making strange bedfellows.

Inspired by the examples of Fidel, Che and others, the hundreds of thousands of volunteers in the Cuban National Literacy Campaign were able to create a praxis, a possible praxis, without the benefit of Delphic utterances on the importance of self-critical subjectivity made by those who like to take refuge inside Foucault's metaphysical brainpan.[3] Nor does Venezuela's ongoing Bolivarian Revolution seem hindered by a lack of poststructuralist insight.[4]

Rebel Literacy: Cuba's National Literacy Campaign and Critical Global Citizenship is a shining example of the type of work that needs to be undertaken today. Abendroth links the revolutionary trajectory of this work to the foundations of critical global citizenship that today is reflected and deepened in critical race theory, in exploring the historical connections between indigenous struggles for sovereignty and the emancipation of the African Diaspora, in international feminist activity and scholarship and in Marxist critiques of transnational capitalism. It can also be seen in transnational struggles for socialism, in efforts of those developing a de-colonizing pedagogy as well as in anti-imperialist struggles worldwide.

Major accomplishments, such as the new "Organic Education Law" (see Suggett, 2009) which Venezuela's National Assembly passed unanimously shortly after midnight on August 14 following an extended legislative session, could not have been possible without the triumph of Cuba's National Literacy Campaign. Those fierce opponents of Chávez who claim the education law is unconstitutional, anti-democratic, politicizes the classroom, threatens the family and religion and will allow the state to take children away from their parents for the purposes of political indoctrination are reminiscent of the Cuban counter-revolutionaries who were against the Campaign. Of course, these condemnations by the Venezolano right wing are part of a well-orchestrated campaign, which, as in the case of Cuba's Campaign, is funded by Washington.

But the Organic Education Act is important in that the state has the responsibility to ensure that all citizens have a high-quality education, free of charge, from childhood through the undergraduate university level (Suggett, 2009). The concept of the "Educator State" (Estado Docente) is introduced in Article 5, which asserts that the state must guarantee education "as a universal human right and a fundamental, inalienable, non-renounce-able social duty, and a public service ... governed by the principles of integrality, cooperation, solidarity, attentiveness, and co-responsibility" (Suggett, 2009). The law also requires "progressive annual growth" in education spending as a percentage of GDP.

Article 6 lists nearly fifty aspects of the education system of which the state is in charge, including educational infrastructure, curriculum and other administrative tasks as well as specific duties that exemplify the principles of the education system established in Article 3. One of the key principles, in my view, advocates "equality among all citizens without discrimination of any kind." In fact, this new law mandates "equality of conditions and opportunities" as well as "gender equity," "access to the educational system for people with disabilities or educational needs" and the extension of educational facilities to rural and poor areas.

Spanish is listed as the official language of the education system, "except in the instances of intercultural bilingual indigenous education, in which the official and equal use of their [native] language and Spanish shall be guaranteed." In addition to promoting "the exchange of social and artistic knowledge, theories, practices, and experiences," the law sanctions "popular and ancestral knowledge, which strengthen the identity of our Latin American, Caribbean, indigenous, and afro-descendent peoples." Finally, Article 10 specifically pro-hibits speech and propaganda that promote hate and violence in classrooms or in the context of educational settings, including the news media.

Article 3 also stresses a recurrent theme: that of "participatory democracy." This is clearly important, and you can hear this echo throughout the new education act. Article 15 is perhaps the most controversial in the eyes of Chávez's opponents because it stipulates that one of the basic purposes of education is "to develop a new political culture based on protagonist participation and the strengthening of popular power, the democratization of knowledge, and the promotion of the school as a space for the formation of citizenship and community participation, for the reconstruction of the public spirit." Yet there are plenty of references to the importance of "learning to peacefully coexist," learning to learn and teach simultaneously, "valuing the common good," the necessity for education to be "integral" as opposed to highly specialized. The act emphasizes a "respect for diversity," and the importance of lifelong learning.

The legal definition of the educational community has been significantly broadened to include families, community organizations and wage laborers in addition to the formal educational workers. Article 20 states, "The educational community will be composed of all the fathers, mothers, representatives, students, teachers, administrative workers, and laborers of the educational institution. ... Spokespersons of the different community organizations linked to the educational centers and institutions will also be able to form part of the educational community." This new educational community is described in the article as "a democratic space of social-communitarian, organized, participatory, cooperative, protagonist, and solidarity-oriented character."

The Organic Education Act also deals with questions of labor rights, job security and benefits and training in "liberatory work." Article 15 asserts that the educational system must "develop the creative potential of each human being for the full realization of his or her personality and citizenship, based on the ethical value of liberatory work and active participation" (Suggett, 2009). There is also a stress on human rights and free speech. Additionally, the law maintains that education should encourage an end to nuclear weapons in the world, that it should fight racism and develop with students an ecological consciousness to preserve biodiversity and social diversity.

The Organic Education Act is a profound historical achievement, and continued struggles over these principles and practices are sure to animate Venezuelan politics for years to come. The historical struggles that continue to take place in Cuba, and now Venezuela, are indeed heartening, and give us reason for optimism.

While discussing Marxism and the struggle for socialism with educators in the U.S., a look of sullied astonishment sometimes comes over their faces, as if I am using an old and derelict language that looks like it has been scavenged from the linguistic equivalent of the cold war infrastructure of the Baikonur Cosmodrome, the space launch facility in the desert steppe of Kazakhstan where, in an abandoned hangar, the remains of the Buran Soviet space program (discontinued in 1993) lie in ruins, covered in dirt and bird droppings, the formerly glorious program that blasted the first human being, Yuri Gagarin, into space in his Vostok 3KA-3 spacecraft in 1961.

While the language of socialism may seem a once glorious but now anti-quated language to North American audiences, even progressive audiences, something that belongs today in a steampunk movie setting, where the high-tech North American hero is tracking an ex-KGB agent through the back alleys of Vladivostok, in search of a secret weapon hidden in the storage vault of a boat belonging to the Russian Pacific Fleet that is speeding down the Muravyov-Amursky Peninsula, the conditions that call for a socialist alterna-tive to capitalism are very much contemporary and real. Whether we choose to re-name our theoretical constructs or not is not the challenge here. The challenge is to find an alternative to the social universe of value production, using the best theoretical frameworks that are available.

I look back at the time of Prime Minister Trudeau's visit to Cuba and am not surprised that it took imperialist America so long to open up diplomatic relations between the two countries. And here I have to congratulate Pres-ident Obama for setting the conditions in motion for this to happen. I can only hope that the U.S. will similarly call off its hyenas and launch renewed diplomatic relations with Venezuela, but regrettably, that does not look like it is in the cards for Nicolás Maduro's administration, at least not at the time of this writing. Venezuela is a leading oil producer, after all, while Cuba produces sugar cane. Interestingly, Cuban President Raúl Castro has remarked recently that, after conversations with Pope Francis, he is willing to consider return-ing to his Catholic faith. Where Fidel stands on this, is still a mystery. Who knows, this could be a sign of the changing times, where the teachings of Jesus and his conquest of death can be discussed in the same breath as the struggle for justice for the poor. Discussions are one thing, of course, and actions are another. Global inequality looms large and we need a massive global cam-paign to overcome it, not to exacerbate it. And here we can learn from the accomplishments in Cuba and Venezuela. With Christ, all things are possible.

All things are possible because through Christ the people are inspired and emboldened by the light of the Holy Spirit to work towards justice, to eliminate differentiating wealth, and to help found a society, not on violently appropriated surplus value, but on love and understanding.

Poyekhali!—Let's go!

And let's pray.

The times I have spent in Cuba and Venezuela have given me hope that the conditions of possibility for the emergence of new human beings—a new humanity—can come into being and take root. Throughout his administrations, President Chávez had to fight against military generals who tried to get rich through Chavismo policies by skimming money designated for the poor; he tried to rid the country (with some success) of generation after generation of entrenched corruption, even among those who identified as Chavistas. He had, by his own admission, less success with fighting crime. But no revolution ever runs smoothly, nor is it ever finished. It is always in the making. President Chávez once told me during a visit to Palácio de Miraflores that education is essential to the success of revolutions. If that is the case, then there is no time to waste. There are only these times, the time for a revolutionary break with history.

Notes

1. Although today it appears as though the Vatican is softening its stance against Marx, Gregorian University professor Georg Sans, in a recent edition of *L'Osservatore Romano*, the Vatican newspaper, praised Marx, but not without qualification, distinguishing between Marx and Marxism, calling the latter a misappropriation of Marx's theories. The publication of Sans's piece in *L'Osservatore Romano* gives it the de facto imprimatur of Pope Benedict XVI, *The Times of London* reported. See Trudy Ring. Vatican: Marx, Wilde not so bad. *Advocate*, 2009. Retrieved from http://www.advocate.com/news/daily-news/2009/10/22/vatican-marx-wilde-not-so-bad. Of course, there is much more reason to be optimistic with Pope Francis at the helm of the Catholic Church, since he has received an extensive education in liberation theology, and he is instituting a welcoming revolution within the Catholic Church, making his top priority the living conditions among the poor and economically disenfranchised who struggle in peripheral countries.

2. Those educationalists (including poststructuralists) who accuse Marx of being a "determinist" confuse determination with determinism. Marx's *Capital* does not present a fatalistic theory that all peoples must or will endure. It presents an image of the trajectory of the logic of capital (Peter Hudis, personal communication).

3. Thanks to Joel Spring for alerting me to the Pinar critique.

4. This is not to say that the struggle for self-critical subjectivity is unimportant. What is problematic is the attempt by educationalists such as Pinar to denigrate the accomplishments

of Marxist critique (due in large part to their superficial characterization of Marxism) in their attempt to reinsert culture and subjectivity at the center of critical educational work. See Dave Hill, Peter McLaren, Mike Cole and Glenn Rikowski, eds., *Marxism Against Postmodernism in Educational Theory*, Lanham, MD: Lexington Books, 2003.

Bibliography

Abendroth, M. (2009). *Rebel literacy: Cuba's National Literacy Campaign and critical global citizenship*. Duluth, MN: Litwin Books.

Elvy, J. C. (2007, Fall). Women in the Cuban Literacy Campaign. *Literacies, 7*. Retrieved from http://www.literacyjournal.ca/literacies/7-2007/htm/elvy.htm

Freire, P. (1985). *Dialogue is not a chaste event. Comments by Paulo Freire on issues in participatory research*. Compiled by Paul Jurmo. Amherst, MA: The Center for International Education, School of Education, Hills House South, University of Massachusetts, Amherst.

Hill, D., McLaren, P., Cole, M., & Rikowski, G. (Eds.). (2003). *Marxism against postmodernism in educational theory*. Lanham, MD: Lexington Books.

Pinar, W. F. (2009). The unaddressed 'I' of ideology critique. *Power and Education, 1*(2). Retrieved from http://dx.doi.org/10.2304/power.2009.1.2.189 and http://pae.sagepub.com/content/1/2/189

Retamar, R. F. (1989). *Caliban and other essays*. Minneapolis, MN: University of Minnesota Press.

Ring, T. (2009). Vatican: Marx, Wilde not so bad. *Advocate*. Retrieved from http://www.advocate.com/news/daily-news/2009/10/22/vatican-marx-wilde-not-so-bad

Suggett, J. (2009, August 21). Venezuelan education law: Socialist indoctrination or liberatory education? *Venezuelanalysis.com*. Retrieved from http://www.venezuelanalysis.com/analysis/4734

Supko, R. (1998, September). *Perspectives of the Cuban National Literacy Campaign*. Paper presented at the meeting of the Latin American Studies Association, Chicago, IL.

· 5 ·

COMRADE CHE

oday socialist icons such as Che Guevara stare us from the crumbling walls of city slums reminding us of past struggles. Unlike the fate bequeathed to Frantz Fanon, whose memory is now partially eclipsed by the forces of history that have since enveloped his beloved Algeria (Macey, 2000), Che Guevara's popularity today is widespread not only in his adopted country of Cuba but throughout Latin America and beyond.[1] Despite Che's iconic stature as a matinee idol image that adorns T-shirts and posters, it remains a truism that regardless of the amative imaginings that his image provokes, he stands as a powerful thinker whose understanding of Marx and other radical theorists cannot be easily separated from his life as a revolutionary actor on the stage of world history.

In an article written to commemorate that intrepid revolutionary and daring thinker, Ernesto "Che" Guevara, thirty years after his death, Michael Löwy (1997) proclaimed:

> Years go by, fads change, modernisms are succeeded by postmodernisms, dictatorships are replaced by 'hard democracies,' Keynesianism by neoliberal politics, and the Berlin Wall is replaced by a wall of money. Yet Che's message still shines like a beacon in this dark and cold end of the century.

Nearly two decades after those words were written, we can safely say that the beacon of Che's message is as bright as ever, but at the same time the world has only grown darker and colder.

In a world torn between the oppressed on the one side, and those who esuriently exploit them on the other, there seems little hope today of a grand alternative for the wretched of the earth. They seem forever caught between the jaws of those scrupulously respectable people who offer them the slavery of wage labor and a lifetime of alienation in exchange for their labor power, and those who loathsomely criminalize their very existence, or feel justified in leaving them to suffer whatever cruel fate the market has in store for them.

The stages of liberation that were to follow lockstep from the contradiction between the forces and the relations of production—the accumulation of evolution powered by a law of dialectical development that would inevitably lead from the economic contradictions of capitalism to the establishment of a classless society under "the dictatorship of the proletariat"—did not follow in the wake of the quixotic predictions of the dogmatists (a condition into which a great many fundamentalist Marxisms fall), predictions that proclaimed the final victory of socialism over the cutthroat capitalists, the end of alienated labor and the flourishing of human culture.

What young radicals such as Che Guevara had discovered in the interim was that it was not history that should drive the revolution but the other way around—the peasants and the workers should direct their own fate, making economic decisions and deciding which share of production is to be assigned to accumulation and which share to consumption (Löwy, 2001; Tablada, 1998). But today, nearly fifty years after Che's death, when the contradictions at the heart of the market economy are more exacerbated than they were in Che's day (even in the industrialized capitalism of Marx's day!), there are no completed socialist revolutions to serve as a living model for the world, only those that have been ceaselessly and violently interrupted, or those that, following in the intrepid footsteps of Simón Bolívar, are being tested in the barrios and los altoplanos of Venezuela.

In the developed countries of the North, where we notoriously find a fawning acceptance of the benignity of American power and a postured accommodation to the idea of economic dignity, we also discover no real moral commitment to social and economic justice—especially if it means accepting a change in one's present standard of living. The capitalist world system binds us together as a democratic polity in a structure of relations made valid by little more than our own predilections of convenience.

Transnational civil society, bolstered by the foundation-non-governmental organizational world, continues to serve as a staging ground for the ambitions of the transnational capitalist class (Roelofs, 2006). Like the Christian missionaries of the American West who helped Rockefeller Sr.'s infamous company, Standard Oil, gather intelligence on the Native American communities that inhabited oil-rich land, the U.S. National Endowment for Democracy serves dutifully today as one of the many instruments of U.S. Manifest Destiny, offering to bring civil rights and elections to countries not yet democratized but on condition that those countries leave their door wide open to foreign capital, labor contracts, resource extraction and military spending (Roelofs, 2006).

Public-private philanthropies still work in conjunction with Christian missionaries and imperialist states in the long-abiding tradition of overthrowing any (organized or spontaneous) resistance to the exploitation of human labor, of disrupting revolutionary and reformist movements, of keeping marketized societies on a steady course and of destabilizing governments unfriendly to neoliberal capitalism. In fact, capitalism seemingly has become the secular equivalent of the Great Commission of evangelicals who are charged with making Jesus known to every person on earth. Just as the Christian evangelization process weakened the communal social structures of indigenous populations, leaving them defenseless against exploitation by the forces of industrial capital wielded by the ruthless sword arm of settler colonial conquest, so today the "symbiotic neo-conflation" (Adelman, 2006) of Christian values and capitalist "for-profit" ventures secures the hegemony of the U.S. (whose very national identity has been forged in the furnace of serial aggression, free-market triumphalism and white supremacy). So long as the banquet table of free-market democracy has been reserved exclusively for the capitalist class, and the mostly white capitalist class, there is little hope that the U.S. will break any time soon with the barbarism at the root of U.S. society. Hence, there will always be the need for a Che Guevara to rise up among us.

Democracy and economic (and military) imperialism are forged in the same baptismal fire of self-regard that fuels the slaughterhouse vision of an impending Armageddon—the U.S. has been chosen by providence to save the world by whatever means necessary (40 percent of Americans believe that the final countdown to the "end times" has already begun). Historically, those means have included accumulation by dispossession, by war, by "humanitarian" intervention, by bringing freedom to those nations still uncivilized enough to reject the profit motive as the sine qua non of democratic society.

Capital's cultural imaginary works by transcoding the violence wreaked by capital accumulation and dispossession into acts designed to protect the wealth of the homeland, both in terms of family values and private property, and channel the anger into larger Christian ideals directed at annihilating evil and protecting family, property and nation (Ebert, 2006)—all wrapped up in a brummagem patriotism of plastic flags and bumper stickers. While violence is condemned, it is sexualized and made more alluring by the stupe-fying impact of the media, and justified as a necessary action in a world where freedom is, as right-wing pundits are wont to say, "not free."

Disguised as free electoral choices, voters are invited to feed at the trough of a politics of "moral satisfaction" (attacking evil empires abroad and moral perversion at home) as a studied diversion from fighting for economic rights. The disenfranchised poor can continue to suffer economically but feel some national pride in being part of a country that is "liberating" dictatorships in oil-rich sovereign nations and ushering in "democracy." Illegal wars, secret wiretaps, government monitoring of library records and financial transactions, government attacks on an independent press, blatant war crimes and the fir-ing of university professors and high school teachers are all tolerated as long as it is understood as being in the service of the "greater good" of weeding out "terrorists" in our midst (or whatever country in which they happen to be hiding around the world). In a blatant display of legalized racial profil-ing, foreign nationals with visa violations can now be arrested in secret and detained indefinitely, and treated as guilty until proved innocent. Torture is now viewed as a necessary evil.

The fact that all Washington administrations are populated by a particu-larly venal cabal of career opportunists, theocratic sociopaths, anti-Enlighten-ment activists, pathological liars and vulpine opponents of democracy should in no way confound us into thinking that the problem of capitalism is rooted in acts of political malfeasance by clever but corrupted politicians. Such acts may be torturously accommodating to capital, and lead to impoverishment, bloodshed, repression, misery and eventually to genocide and even to the obliteration of entire nations, but they are not the source of the problem. The problem itself can be traced to Marx's world-historical discovery: the alien-ated character of the very act of laboring and the exploitation that is a funda-mental part of selling one's labor-power for a wage.

The collapse of statist communism and welfare state democracy and the creation of the U.S. as the world's sole superpower have made it easier to rewrite history and to control the future of the past. When young people are denied access to accurate scientific knowledge about the origins and evolution of life on earth through the promotion of creationism and intelligent design, when the Florida Education Omnibus Bill bars the teaching of "revisionist" history in Florida public schools (a law that astonishingly states: "American history shall be viewed as factual, not constructed, shall be viewed as knowable, teachable, and testable, and shall be defined as the creation of a new nation based largely on the universal principles stated in the Declaration of Independence" [Craig, 2006]), and when teachers are charged with teaching "the nature and importance of free enterprise to the United States economy" (Craig, 2006), then we have reason to be gravely worried about the future precisely because there is less and less opportunity to debate the past.

When seen in conjunction with President George W. Bush's 2003 vituperative and fustian attack on "revisionist historians" who challenged his justifications for using force against Saddam Hussein, and his 2005 warning on Veteran's Day in which he proclaimed that it is "deeply irresponsible to rewrite the history of how the war began" (Zimmerman, 2006), we know that such interpretive authoritarianism is both an index of the creeping fascism within the U.S. and a dire warning that disagreement with the official version of history (with its propensity for dehumanizing the poor and people of color) can be equated with misinterpretation, misrepresentation or even deliberate falsification. These days all of the above could be considered acts of treason during a time of "permanent" war.

When seen in conjunction with President Obama's withering push for educational standards linked to test scores and for private "charter" schools to replace public schools, the situation looks grim. Texas textbook standards now call for ruthless authoritarians such as the reviled anti-communist Senator Joseph McCarthy to be exonerated and for universally admired figures such as Martin Luther King to be downplayed.

For those who feel more comfortable donning veils of ignorance, placing history beyond the pale of interpretation and castigating those who lay claim to a different reading of tradition, the government may appear a valiant defender of U.S. democracy's unsullied origins, but such a view can only unfailingly undermine the capacity of society to change.

As much as the world appears to have forsaken socialism, socialism refuses to forsake the world. The message contained in one of the most famous writings in the history of socialism, Rosa Luxemburg's (1916) *Junius Pamphlet*, rings as true today as it did when Luxemburg wrote these words:

Today, we face the choice exactly as Friedrich Engels foresaw it a generation ago: either the triumph of imperialism and the collapse of all civilization as in ancient Rome, depopulation, desolation, degeneration—a great cemetery. Or the victory of socialism, that means the conscious active struggle of the international proletariat against imperialism and its method of war.

Few revolutionaries have put Luxemburg's choice to the test the way Che did. What was remarkable about Che was the way he went against the traditional Left of his day in the pursuit of new, more egalitarian and humane roads to this worthy goal, roads that he felt were more consistent with what he understood were the ethical principles of communism. Che rejected the Eastern European models of socialism that claimed to "conquer capitalism with its own fetishes." In his March 1965 essay, "Socialism and Man in Cuba," Che wrote:

The pipe dream that socialism can be achieved with the help of the dull instruments left to us by capitalism (the commodity as the economic cell, profitability, individual material interest as a lever, etc.) can lead into a blind alley. When you wind up there after having traveled a long distance with many crossroads, it is hard to figure out just where you took the wrong turn. Meanwhile, the economic foundation that has been laid has done its work of undermining the development of consciousness. To build communism it is necessary, simultaneous with the new material foundations, to build the new man and woman.

By conjugating contingency with necessity, Che was not only rejecting the layers of technocracy and bureaucracy that such a model would bring to Cuba, but also challenging the economistic view of socialism (which viewed the economic sphere as an autonomous system governed by its own laws of value or the market) with a more political view of socialism in which issues concerning prices and production are determined on the basis of social, ethical and political criteria (Löwy, 2007). It is important to underscore that Che's Marxism has an essentially undogmatic character. As Löwy puts it,

For Che, Marx was not a pope endowed by the Holy Ghost with the gift of infallibility; nor were his writings Tables of the Law graciously handed down on Mount Sinai. ... Che stresses that Marx, although an intellectual giant, had committed mistakes which could and should be criticized. (2007, p. 13)

Che's anti-dogmatism in the realm of theory (Che viewed Marxism as a guide to action, a philosophy of praxis, a theory of revolutionary action) was not unrelated to his pedagogical practice, as he rejected outright the Stalinist cult of authority (which he often referred to as scholasticism) and claimed it was impossible to educate the people from above. Echoing the question raised by Marx in his "Theses on Feuerbach" ("Who will educate the educators?"), Che wrote in a speech in 1960:

> The first recipe for educating the people is to bring them into the revolution. Never pretend that you can help them conquer their rights by education alone, while they must endure a despotic government. First and foremost, teach them to conquer their rights and, as they gain representation in the government, they will learn whatever is taught and much more. (cited in Löwy, 1997)

According to Che, students should not automatically defer to those who use their donnish authority to reaffirm society's unequal social division of labor. By contrast, they should challenge the ideological and material premises upon which such dismal measures of wealth dispersal are allowed to persist— including the "free-markets credo," the "pull-yourself-up-by-the-bootstraps" moralizing, the reflexive condescension on the part of the imperialist punditry towards the so-called Third World and the laws which strengthen guarantees of profit expatriation for multinational corporations. Critique was not auxiliary to the revolutionary struggle for liberation, but a fundamental part of it (McLaren, 2000).

Che began with the challenge of human capacity in the creation of the "new man," with the imperative of transforming the many-sidedness of aggrieved and suffering humanity under the yoke of imperialist aggression. What Che advocated was, in essence, a politics of self-transformation through revolutionary struggle, the struggle for humanity, dignity, freedom and justice from the standpoint of the proletariat fighting the class war.

Critics of Che's role as a guerrilla fighter have tried to point out the contradictions that the figure of Che is supposed to embody, particularly his advocacy of humanism and the importance he places on the sanctity of human life. How did Che reconcile his respect for humanity with the emphasis he places on guerrilla warfare and the taking of human life?

Löwy is correct in stressing that Che was highly critical of the tradition of Latin American national reformism (reformism via the electoral process), and he rejected the creation of a national-democratic revolution (a Menshevik-type conception) that would either collaborate with or offer a revolutionary role to the bourgeoisie. The Cuban experience convinced Che that the national bourgeoisie would never accept agrarian reform and the expropriation of imperialist monopolies and would eventually attempt a counter-revolution through alliances with the latifundia-owners, the dominant oligarchy and with perhaps the military assistance of North American imperialists or mercenaries.

Rejecting the then prevalent view of the traditional Latin American Left that the semifeudal and semicolonial character of the Latin American economies mitigated against a socialist revolution in favor of a national-democratic revolution, Che was absolutely convinced that only a socialist revolution based on an alliance of the workers and peasants could accomplish the permanent liberation of the Americas. The military-bureaucratic apparatus of the bourgeois state had to be destroyed because the politico-military machinery of the state would inevitably betray the people in support of the capitalists.

According to Löwy, "the principle of the inevitability of armed struggle" was, for Che, "derived precisely from the sociology of the revolution: because the revolution is socialist it can be victorious only through revolutionary war" (2007, p. 79). Löwy writes:

> Indeed Che, the theoretician of revolutionary war, of the liberating violence of armed struggle; Che, who insisted that "the oppressor must be killed mercilessly," and who believed that the revolutionary has to become an "efficient and selective" killing machine, this same Major Guevara always showed profound and genuine respect for human life. It is because he regarded life as a value that he criticized the blind terrorism which strikes down innocent victims; that he called on the guerrilla fighter to treat kindly the defenseless vanquished; that he urged clemency toward captured enemy soldiers, and categorically declared that a "wounded enemy should be treated with care and respect." (2007, p. 23)

Löwy makes clear the profound importance Che granted the concept of dignity, with its roots firmly planted within the Latin American humanist tradition. For Che, the "standard of dignity" to which all revolutionaries should adhere is reflected in the words of José Martí: "A real man should feel on his own cheek the blow inflicted on any other man's" (cited in Löwy, 2007, p. 24). Löwy writes:

> To hold life in profound respect and to be ready to take up arms and, if need be, to kill, is contradictory only in the eyes of Christian or pacifist humanism. For revolutionary humanism, for Che, the people's war is the necessary answer, the only possible answer, of the exploited and oppressed to the crimes and the institutionalized violence of the oppressors. (2007, p. 24)

Slavoj Žižek (2008) contends that the ultimate cause of violence is the fear of the neighbor. But he also describes what he calls "divine violence." He sees divine violence as an infusion of justice beyond the law. It is extra-moral but not immoral. It is not a divine license to kill. It is divine only in a subjective sense, in the eye of the beholder, or in the mind of the person enacting such violence. It is Walter Benjamin's Angel of History striking back, restoring equanimity to the history of the world. It is a violence that refuses a deeper meaning; it is the logic of rage, a refusal to normalize crimes against humanity, either by reconciliation or revenge. It is, in other words, a refusal to compromise. Žižek describes divine violence as pure power over all of life for the sake of the living; it is a type of sign that the world is unjust. It is not the return of the repressed, or the underside of the authoritarian legal order. Nor is it the intervention of some omnipotent God. Rather, it is the sign of the impotency of God. There are no objective criteria with which to judge divine violence.

Žižek uses the example of Che Guevara's two seemingly contradictory statements as a pristine example:

> At the risk of seeming ridiculous, let me say that the true revolutionary is guided by a great feeling of love. It is impossible to think of a genuine revolutionary lacking this quality.

> Hatred is an element of struggle; relentless hatred of the enemy that impels us over and beyond the natural limitations of man and transforms us into effective, violent, selective, and cold killing machines. Our soldiers must be thus; a people without hatred cannot vanquish a brutal enemy. (2008, p. 172)

Žižek claims that Che's comments are united in Che's motto: *Hay que endurecerse sin perder jamas la ternura* (One must endure [become hard, toughen oneself] without losing tenderness).

Paraphrasing Kant and Robespierre, Žižek notes that love without cruelty is powerless, and cruelty without love is blind. This paradox is what elevates love over mere sentimentality. So it seems here that divine love is inextricably linked with violence, which does not mean that all violent acts are acts of love. What it does indicate is that there is always a split in the beloved and the true object-cause of our love for him or her. Hatred can be the only proof that we love someone. The domain of violence that does not found laws of the state nor sustain them is the domain of love. So there is, then, the paradox of revolutionary love in that, according to Žižek, it continually overlaps with violence.

Che's two seemingly contradictory statements about hardening oneself without losing tenderness, of loving people yet hating the enemy, can be elucidated through some ideas put forward by James Cone. In his landmark theological work, *A Black Theology of Liberation*, Cone addresses the concept of the Creator God of the Old Testament who stresses obedience to the law of righteousness and the Redeemer God of the New Testament who emphasizes love, tenderness and forgiveness. The former God is one of retribution, wrath, reward and punishment while the latter God is most often seen as of a higher order since this God in the person of Christ stresses mercy and compassion. According to Cone, too often discussion of the God of Love in Jesus Christ "fails to take seriously the concept of God's righteousness and tends to make God's love mere sentimentality" (1990, p. 67). It is not true, Cone argues, that the idea of love in Christ is a negation of the Old Testament view of righteousness. And while Cone admits that love is the essential element of the Christian interpretation of God, he equally maintains that we can only understand such love if we view it in the context of "the biblical view of God's righteousness" (1990, p. 69).

Cone asks:

> Is it possible to understand what God's love means for the oppressed without making wrath an essential ingredient of that love? What could love possibly mean in a racist society except the righteous condemnation of everything racist? Most theological treatments of God's love are completely self-giving without any demand for obedience. (1990, p. 69)

Cone writes that a "God without wrath does not plan to do too much liberating," and he maintains that the two concepts should always be understood dialectically, in terms of each other, since they belong together. Cone writes: "A God minus wrath seems to be a God who is basically not against anything. All we have to do is behave nicely, and everything will work out all right" (1990, pp. 69–70). Che's statements, viewed within this seemingly contradictory context of wrath and forgiveness, make more sense.

Löwy (2007) also notes that the problematic of dignity also implied, for Che, the concept of freedom, and this does not refer in any way to bourgeois individualism but rather the liberation of humanity from alienation brought about by the capitalist production process. For Che, the transformation of human beings and the transformation of material conditions coincide, just as there is a dialectical relationship between means and ends. More specifically, Che was mediating the two apparently contradictory forces of violence and love and adapting them to the specific historical conditions of the armed revolutionary struggle in Cuba. He mediated these forces dialectically as two aspects of a process necessary for revolutionary consciousness. Similarly, he developed a reciprocal and indissoluble unity between the guerrilla revolutionary force of which he was a part and the people. According to Löwy (2005), it was the product of the *revolutionary praxis* during which the guerrilla force became popular and the people became revolutionary. The revolutionizing (umwälzende) praxis of the guerrilla force led to the destruction not only of the power of the ruling classes (the police, the army, the state machine) but of the foundations of that power in the people's consciousness (fear, passivity, apathetic fatalism, servile obedience). (p. 198)

It is important to remember, especially with comparisons being made between Jesus of Nazareth and Ernesto "Che" Guevara de la Serna, that the engine and axis of Jesus's ministry was to create the conditions of possibility for liberation from violence through the creation of what Jon Sobrino (1993) calls a "utopia of peace." Clearly, Jesus condemned what we refer to today as "structural injustice," "institutionalized violence," the "repressive violence of the state," or even "state terrorism" (i.e., institutionalized structures within the state apparatus that reflect formally sanctioned violence).

According to Sobrino (1993, p. 213), revolutionary violence may in some way be historically inevitable in the face of the unremitting atrocities of a militarized state. And while armed struggle may be justified in certain circumstances—i.e., when material life is at stake or when acts of violence seem assured to prevent even greater evils or in the context of 'just war theory'—all acts of violence generate forms of evil.

The fact that Jesus did not explicitly condemn insurrectionary violence does not mean that he approved of it. True, it is more likely than not that Jesus had followers—and perhaps even disciples—who were Zealots and involved in the political movement that was created to expel the Roman empire from the Holy Land through armed rebellion. And yes, it is telling that Jesus did not directly address the issue of revolutionary struggle against the Roman Empire (likely because he was expecting the imminent arrival of the Kingdom of God). And some may be surprised that Jesus even instructed his disciples to sell their cloaks and to buy swords in Luke (22:36), although he condemned the use of swords in Matthew (26:52). He also exhorted his followers to "carry your cross," a term which may have derived from the Zealot movement that demanded unconditional obedience to the point of death on the cross (Sobrino, 1993, p. 214). Yet, not once did Jesus call for armed revolution but rather preached forgiveness, an unlikely posture for a messianic insurgent.

While Jesus may have held some Zealot/Sicarii attitudes, evident in his attacks on the scribes, Pharisees, priests and the rich, and in his cleansing of the temple, he went so far as to ask God to forgive his executioners in Luke (23:34). Jesus was not motivated by religious nationalisms or theories of political theocracy which were shared by many Zealots; rather, Jesus believed the

Kingdom of God could be established by the power of truth, justice and love and the grace of God (Sobrino, 1993, p. 215).

The surplus value of capitalism is what we call profit (which is extorted from the laborer by the capitalist). The surplus value of state violence is fear (Sobrino, 1993, p. 216). It is political and religious authorities who help sanction the ideological and material conditions for the reproduction of state violence, for they often serve as "terrorists in white gloves, who hide the steel under the glove" while appropriating the surplus value of violence (Sobrino, 1993, p. 216). Yet even counter-violence against the state which could be rendered legitimate under certain circumstances will necessarily generate evil outcomes.

For Sobrino, Jesus offers "the utopia of peace" which is founded in loving one's persecutors, bearing injustice and taking the side of the victims of injustice. Here Marx and the Bible share a common thesis: "Sin and evil are not inherent to humanity and history; they began one day through human work and they can, therefore, be eliminated" (Miranda, 1974, p. 277). For Miranda, even though the "Marxist hope is that the world be transformed when the relationships among men become true bonds of love and justice," nevertheless "it is more utopian to believe in the resurrection of the flesh than in the abolition of all the injustices, enmities, and cruelties in the world"—which was for Miranda "something which Marx did not have the dialectics sufficient to reach" (Miranda, 1974, p. 277).

Clearly, there were certain circumstances in which Jesus felt violence could be justified, but this has to be understood in the context of the entire gospel of peace. All too frequently, Jesus's teachings have been turned into what Miranda (2004) calls a honey-sweet "candy theology" and "flabby theology" which has been used to defend the status quo. Miranda argues that Jesus's admonition to love your enemy "is not at variance with repulsion of the oppressor, even by violence" (2004, p. 76). Did not Jesus use a scourge of cords to drive the traders from the temple? Miranda goes so far as to argue the following:

> It is criminal to defend repression by the procedure of quoting to the oppressed the verse about "turning the other cheek" (Matt. 5:39). The supporters of official theology will have to be punished for discouraging the struggle against injustice with this verse. By the grace of God I will practice the heroism of presenting the other cheek when I myself have been struck on the first. But this is a personal and individual matter. *What Jesus never said is: If they strike your neighbor on one cheek, turn your neighbor's other cheek.* And the proletariat are defending the bread of their wives and children, and the lives of all their comrades. Furthermore, according to John 18: 22–23 Jesus did not present the other cheek when they struck him on the first. He protested with all his might. And who knows what he might have done if his hands had not been

bound (cf. John 18:12) ... Where is it written that the words of Jesus have a more normative character than his deeds? (Miranda, 2004, p. 77)

Those who ruthlessly and selfishly condemn the homeless and the working poor, who mock those standing outside of restaurants with pleading eyes and upturned hats, those who regard the poor as undeserving and weak-minded parasites who have not worked hard enough or lack sufficient faith in the market, help shape the ideological structures of violence that intergenerationally reproduce poverty by shielding the capitalist class from criticism. Those who believe they have been chosen to enjoy the comforts of economic prosperity by divine fiat, who bolster their claims of superiority by memberships in the Ayn Rand Institute or by bragging about having friends or relatives with Yale law degrees, those who cheer when their governor or congressional representative refuses to expand Medicaid health coverage or to increase taxes on the rich, and those who high-five their friends at the golf club when cuts in food stamps, school lunches and subsidized housing are announced on Fox News in the club lounge—all of those are perilously at risk of not being able to enter the Kingdom of God because they worship at the altar of the market.

Che fought to expel the forces of structural violence from Latin America. For him, as a military man, violence was a necessary weapon in this struggle. For Jesus, who chose the path of non-violence, revolutionary violence will always summon reactionary violence and the cycle of violence will forever repeat itself, and the Kingdom of God will never be established. It is not my intention to evaluate Che definitively in the terms laid out by liberation theologians, but only to emphasize that Che's actions can best be understood when viewed in the context of centuries of state violence inflicted upon the poor and the oppressed of Latin America.

As we examine contemporary socialist struggles for practices of direct and representative democracy, we recognize Che's signal insight that class struggle is more than an economic struggle, it is a struggle to become more fully human through the creation of ever-widening sociabilities, of a boundless horizon for human enrichment. In this context, a pedagogy of liberation becomes the self-education of the people through their own revolutionary practice as part of class struggle. And class struggle in this sense refers to the struggle for a class in itself to become a class for itself through direct participation and protagonistic action on the part of the masses themselves.

Che sought the abolition of the economic vestiges of capitalism not as the automatic result of the development of the productive forces (he rejected unconditionally the evolutionist strain of capitalist-industrial progress), but through the intervention of social planning (in contrast to the centralized planning practiced under Stalin). Furthermore, Che recognized the specific autonomy of social, political and ideological transformation that composed the social whole, and he valued the importance of political-moral motivation and the need for multiform action to change the consciousness of the masses in order to bring about the ideological hegemony of communist values.

Such a struggle and change of consciousness are necessary for the revolutionary struggle worldwide. As Che notes: "Socialism cannot exist without a change in consciousness that will bring about a more brotherly disposition toward humanity, both at the individual level in those nations where socialism was being, or had been, built and at the world level, with all the nations that are victims of imperialistic oppression" (1970, p. 574, cited in Löwy, 1997).

Today it is the informal sector that is keeping Latin America from sinking into a deeper abyss of poverty created by the politics of neoliberalism. Lands are being despoiled by international mining operations; lakes and forests have been destroyed by logging and toxic waste; air is clogged with lead and particulate matter; and healthcare, education, housing and sanitation are in shambles. The conditions which spurred Che Guevara to take up arms are still there; they have, in fact, worsened.

Civil society has increasingly become the stage upon which revolutions are now fought, with the state having been abandoned by many groups who feel that those who focus on seizing control of the state find themselves upholding the very relations of capital they originally fought to abolish. But it seems clear that we need more than just efforts to catalyze the self-organizing action of civil society against the state; we need to transform the very foundations of the state. Che can give us hope that smashing the old state and creating a new one is still a possibility, even today, while at the same time helping us to recognize that there is no certainty to our struggle for socialism because in many ways certainty is the enemy of revolutionary struggle. As Löwy (2002) notes, "We all are searching our way, no one can say he has found the true and only strategy."

While social movements today seem wedded to nationalized property and the statification of natural resources, it is obvious that these measures, while important, do not go far enough. In the 1980s, the great Marxist-humanist Raya Dunayevskaya asked: "Have we faced the harsh reality that, unless the inseparability between dialectics of thought and of revolution does exist, any country that does succeed in its revolution may retrogress, since the world

revolution cannot occur at one strike everywhere and world capitalism continues to exist?" (cited in Hudis, 2006). Che expressed a similar sentiment when
he wrote in his book *Guerrilla Warfare*, "A revolution which does not constantly expand is a revolution which regresses" (cited in Löwy, 2007, p. 74).

But are Che's sentiments and ideas those of a man who is hopelessly wedded to a bygone era that has all too quickly vanished, an era in which most
socialist regimes have disappeared under what seems to be the unstoppable
juggernaut of capital? In *The Marxism of Che Guevara* (2007), Löwy warns
readers that it would be grievously misguided to assume that Che is an anach-
ronism, who struggled in an ephemeral stretch of history. He writes:

> It would nevertheless be a mistake to suppose that Che was a man from the past, a
> survival from another epoch, an anachronism in the computer age. On the contrary, he
> was the avenging prophet of future revolutions, the revolutions of the "wretched of the
> earth," the starved, oppressed, exploited, and humiliated peoples of the three continents
> dominated by imperialism. He was the prophet who wrote in letters of fire on the walls
> of the new Babylon: Mene Mene Tekel Upharsin—your days are numbered. And it is
> as a prophet of the future, of the new man, the communist society of the twenty-first
> century, built upon the ruins of decadent and "one-dimensional" capitalism, that he
> has become the hero of the rebellious and revolutionary youth who are rising up in the
> industrial metropolitan centers of Europe and North America. (2007, p. 107)

Taking inspiration from this proletarian internationalist warrior, this horseman
of the impending apocalypse, we can find hope today in the enhancement of
the regional integration of many Latin American countries within a new "sol-
idarity-based" Latin America. Yet while there are calls for a new production
model, such models do not as yet refer to escaping from the current system
of open and deregulated markets and replacing the internationalized market
economy with an alternative system of allocation of productive resources. And
while we hope, at least, that these new rumblings from the South signal the
beginning of a new anti-capitalist initiative, we must admit that the struggles in
Venezuela and Bolivia have a long way to go before they begin to approximate
the socialist model of a Latin America free from the jackboots of imperialism
that Che dreamt of and for which he gave his life. Che sought to create the
conditions necessary for building a society that was qualitatively different from
that of capitalist society, a truly liberating alternative to capital in all its forms,
a total revolution that would transcend the value form of labor. A world free of
value production through the instruments of capital.

Che did not live to see his mission completed. Yet in another sense, Che
can be considered to be very much alive, his valiant and gallant spirit reflected

in every *camarada* ready to fight once again for the independence of *Nuestra America*. In fact, a case could be made that today Che's influence is felt more than during his lifetime. Löwy (1997) describes Che as a "seed of a different future planted in the Latin American soil; a star in the firmament of hopes of the people, a coal smoldering under the ashes of despair." He remarks (1997) that this seed "in the last 30 years has taken root in the political culture of the Latin American left, growing branches and leaves, bearing fruit. Or as one of the red-dyed threads that, from Patagonia to the Rio Grande, is woven into the fabric of dreams, utopianism and revolutionary actions."

But was Che's vision of the struggle for the liberation of Latin America a symptom of revolutionary romanticism? Some have criticized Che's struggle as a Blanquist or Bakuninist form of adventurism. As Löwy reports, "To the bourgeois philistine, Che was a utopian-romantic anarchist whose ideal of the future was nothing but 'The childish vision of Elysian fields without bureaucrats or soldiers, that eternal nostalgia for a 'saved world'" (2007, p. 110).

While Che's life illustrates overcoming the contradiction between freedom and necessity, he resisted falling prey to the most regressive manifestations of romanticism. And while he did admire elements of pre-capitalist societies, he did not remain trapped in the thrall of a Sturm und Drang superficial nostalgia. He did share, intuitively at least, a romantic sensibility in his rejection of the bourgeois-philistine tenets of social democracy that were so complacently restricted to reformism. To his credit, he did not retreat into a dilettante utopian idealism, a glorification of nature, a belief in socialism as a historical inevitability or Marxism as a kind of divine afflatus. He was able to bridge the gap between the radical demands of his revolutionary principles and his concrete actions on behalf of the dispossessed.

If we decide to call Che a romantic, we must at least acknowledge that he was no "mere" romantic; he was a revolutionary, forward-looking romantic who remained both appreciative of the achievements of modernity and at the same time critical of its shortcomings. In recognizing the potentials and contradictions of modernity, Che called the very logic of modernity into question. Clearly, he perceived the dangers in adhering blindly to the myth of progress. He was not interested in economic progress if that was not accompanied by a communist morality: "Economic socialism without communist morality does not interest me. We are fighting against poverty, yes, but also against alienation" (cited in Löwy, 2007, p. 59).

Löwy and Sayre (2001) have recovered aspects of romanticism that can play a useful and important role in the revolutionary process of social transformation, which they call a utopian-revolutionary romanticism. They warn that this form of romanticism

> would not be the abstract negation of modernity but its 'sublation' or 'absorption' (Aufhebung), its insistent negation, the conservation of its best gains, and its transcendence toward a higher form of culture—a form that would restore to society certain human qualities destroyed by bourgeois industrial civilization. That does not mean a return to the past but a detour via the past, toward a new future, a detour that allows the human spirit to become aware of all the cultural richness and all the social vitality that have been sacrificed by the historical process launched by the Industrial Revolution, and to seek ways of bringing them back to life. (2001, pp. 253–254)

Perhaps seen in the light of a utopian-revolutionary romanticism, Che's revolutionary praxis can be reevaluated today and can serve as a catalyst in the building of a new world, a world outside of capitalism's value form. It is a world to which Che's revolutionary praxis pointed, but a praxis that was cut short by Che's murder in 1967 by the Bolivian Rangers and the CIA.

Che's revolutionary praxis echos in many respects what Michael Steinberg refers to as a "negative politics":

> A negative politics … is grounded in the fact that our mutual self-constitution continues regardless of the ways in which we construe our experience. It opposes certainties and assurances of knowledge, but not in the name of either a different certainty or of a human characteristic that is presumed to lie beneath the social. It has hopes, not of a world that it already knows how to think about, but one that will not claim to be the culmination of time and that will not hold to ideas, ideals, or even values that seek to arrest the endless transformation of our lives together. It looks not to the perfection of detached knowledge but to an expanding attentiveness to embodied understanding. It is a path not to the future but to a deeper experience of the present. (2005, p. 180)

We can only speculate how the negative politics of Che Guevara might have developed. It is one of the great tragedies of history that his legacy was fatefully terminated before the full measure of his revolutionary project could be tested.

Clearly, the life and thought of Che Guevara mark an important distinction between those who have accepted the inevitability of capital and those who wish to pose a radical challenge to it, replacing it with a new world community that is qualitatively different. For this reason, it is important that this generation of scholars and activists revisit the intellectual as well as the historical legacy of Che Guevara. Che was no Blanquist, Bakuninist or adventurist since for Che the well-being of the popular masses resides in the heart of guerrilla struggle, which in turn serves as a catalyst for a much larger struggle for liberation (Löwy, 2003).

World historical events only add to the urgency of the legacy of Ernesto "Che" Guevara. The example of his life and thought works directly against concerted attempts by über-revisionists in Washington (and in other imperialist capitals throughout the developed world) to bury the history of genocide, epistemicide, slavery, the perdurable violence of colonialism and the wrath of Western imperialism—the structural unconscious of the U.S. nation-state—in the rag-and-bone shop of unwanted truths. Revisiting Che's legacy will open up new pathways for recognizing the life and thought of one of the world's great heroic warriors of the people who tried to create a place of freedom amidst the tyranny of capital.

Che's approach to education was dialectical, and he saw in the act of knowing and becoming fully human the struggle for economic development. Che wrote:

> I don't think education shapes up a country. This we even proved when with our uneducated Army we tore down an enormous amount of barriers and prejudices. But neither is it true that the economic process alone can bring about an economic transformation at that level. Education and economic development are constantly interacting and fully shaping themselves. (cited in Martí, 2008, p. 23)

Fernández Retamar (1989, pp. 44–45) has a wonderful quotation from Che Guevara, who, in accepting the position of professor, *honoris causa*, at the School of Pedagogy, University of Las Villas, in December 1959, proposed to the university professors and students the kind of transformation that all of them would have to undergo in order to be considered truly useful to the construction of a socialist society. And in Martí's terms, this meant moving from the European University to the University of the Americas:

> I would never think of demanding that the distinguished professors or the students presently associated with the University of Las Villas perform the miracle of admitting to the university the masses of workers and peasants. The road here is long; it is a process all of you have lived through, one entailing many years of preparatory study. What I do ask, based on my own limited experience as a revolutionary and rebel commandante, is that the present students of the University of Las Villas understand that study is the patrimony of no one and that the place of study where you carry out your work is the patrimony of no one—it belongs to all the people of Cuba, and it must be extended to the people or the people will seize it. And I hope—because I began the whole series of ups and downs in my career as a university student, as a member of the middle class, as a doctor with middle-class

perspectives and the same youthful aspirations that you must have, and because I am convinced of the overwhelming necessity of the revolution and the infinite justice of the people's cause—I would hope for those reasons that you, today proprietors of the university, will extend it to the people. I do not say this as a threat, so as to avoid its being taken over by them tomorrow. I say it simply because it would be one more among so many beautiful examples in Cuba today: that the proprietors of the Central University of Las Villas, the students, offer it to the people through their revolutionary government. And to the distinguished professors, my colleagues, I have to say something similar: become black, mulatto, a worker, a peasant; go down among the people, respond to the people, that is, to all the necessities of all of Cuba. When this is accomplished, no one will be the loser, we all will have gained, and Cuba can then continue its march toward the future with a more vigorous step, and you will need to include in your cloister this doctor, commandante, bank president, and today professor of pedagogy who now takes leave of you.

Shortly after his speech at the University of Las Villas, Che spoke to the problem of illiteracy in Cuba:

> There are more illiterates in Cuba today than there were twenty-five years ago, because the whole government educational policy has consisted of embezzling and of building a few insignificant schools at the more central crossroads of the country. Our task is another, *compañeros*; we can rely on the people as a whole. We do not have to go beg for votes by building an insignificant school next to a highway. We are going to put that school where it is needed, where it fulfills its educational function for the people's benefit. (cited in Supko, 1998)

Today, Che's example is needed more than ever as we witness the destruction of public education throughout the world and the role that schools and universities now play as handmaidens of the corporations in which consumer identity has replaced the quest for global citizenship. Will Che continue to serve as an indexical sign, an exemplum, or an allegorical trope for the politics of anti-imperialist aggression? Very likely he will. However, whether or not he deserves the status of a popular saint will always be a topic for debate. What remains certain is that now, more than ever, we need to forge a new sense of global citizenship that animated Che's life and the accomplishments he bequeathed not only to his own generation but also to future generations.

Mene, Mene, Tekel, Uparsin.

Che, as did the prophet Daniel, understood what this writing on the wall meant. But do we who inhabit modern Babylon?

Che Guevara, Presente!

Note

1. Che made Fanon's book, *The Wretched of the Earth*, available in Cuba.

Bibliography

Adelman, D. (2006, June 22–July 5). Neo-conservative's roots were planted first by Rocke-feller. *Republic News, 141*. Retrieved from http://www.republic-news.org/archive/141-repub/141_dan_adleman.htm (no longer accessible).

Cone, J. (1990). *A black theology of liberation*. Maryknoll, NY: Orbis Books.

Craig, B. (2006, June 1). New Florida law tightens control over history in schools. George Mason University's History News Network. Retrieved from http://hnn.us/roundup/entries/26016.html

Ebert, T. (2006, March–April). Romance novels, class and Abu Ghraib. *Against the Current, 121*, 20–23.

Elvy, J. C. (2007, Fall). Women in the Cuban Literacy Campaign. *Literacies, 7*. Retrieved from http://www.literacyjournal.ca/literacies/7-2007/htm/elvy.htm

Guevara, E. C. (1965). Socialism and man in Cuba. Retrieved from https://www.marxists.org/archive/guevara/1965/03/man-socialism.htm

Guevara, E. C. (1970). *Obras 1957–1967* (Vol. 2). Havana, Cuba: Casa de los Americas.

Hudis, P. (2006, May 13). *Retreat to statism? The debate over alternatives to neo-liberalism in the movements against global capital*. Paper presented at the 5th Annual Conference of Alternative Globalizations, the Global Studies Association, De Paul University, Chicago.

Löwy, M. (1979). *Georg Lukacs—From romanticism to Bolshevism*. (P. Camiller, Trans.). London, England: NLB.

Löwy, M. (1997). Che's revolutionary humanism—ideals of Ernesto 'Che' Guevara. *Monthly Review, 49*(5), 1–7. Retrieved from http://www.findarticles.com/p/articles/mi_m1132/is_n5_v49/ai_20039201 (no longer accessible).

Löwy, M. (1999). Under the star of romanticism: Walter Benjamin and Herbert Marcuse. In M. Blechman (Ed.), *Revolutionary romanticism* (pp. 197–213). San Francisco, CA: City Lights.

Löwy, M. (2001, June). 'Neither imitation nor copy': Che Guevara in search of a new socialism. *International Viewpoint*. Retrieved from http://www.europe-solidaire.org/spip.php?page=article_impr&id_article=5489

Löwy, M. (2002). Review of *Changing the world without taking power* by John Holloway. *Europe Solidaire Sans Frontieres*. Retrieved from http://www.europesolidaire.org/article.php3?id_article=2306

Löwy, M. (2003). *The theory of revolution in the young Marx*. Leiden, the Netherlands: Brill.

Löwy, M. (2005). *The theory of revolution in the young Marx*. Chicago, IL: Haymarket Books.

Löwy, M. (2007). *The Marxism of Che Guevara*. Lanham, MD: Rowman and Littlefield.

Löwy, M. (2009). Che Guevara—In search of a new socialism. *Against the Current, 142*. Retrieved from http://www.solidarity-us.org/node/2384

Löwy, M., & Sayre, R. (2001). *Romanticism against the tide of modernity*. (C. Porter, Trans.). Durham, NC: Duke University Press.

Luxemburg, R. (1916). The war and the workers. *The Junius Pamphlet*. Retrieved from http://www.marxists.org/archive/luxemburg/1915/junius/ch01.htm

Macey, D. (2000). *Frantz Fanon: A biography*. New York, NY: Picador USA.

Marti, L. T. (2008). *Notes on Ernesto Che Guevara's ideas on pedagogy*. La Habana, Cuba: Editorial Capitan San Luis.

McLaren, P. (2000). *Che Guevara, Paulo Freire and the pedagogy of revolution*. Lanham, MD: Rowman & Littlefield.

Miranda, J. (1974). *Marx and the Bible: A critique of the philosophy of oppression*. (J. Eagleson, Trans.). Maryknoll, NY: Orbis Books.

Miranda, J. (2004). *Communism in the Bible*. (R. R. Barr, Trans.) Eugene, OR: Wipf & Stock.

Retamar, R. F. (1989). *Caliban and other essays*. Minneapolis, MN: University of Minnesota Press.

Roelofs, J. (2006, May 14). The NED, NGOs and imperial uses of philanthropy. *Axis of Logic*. Retrieved from http://www.axisoflogic.com/artman/publish/Article_21977.shtml

Sobrino, J. (1993). *Jesus the liberator: A historical-theological view*. (P. Burns & F. McDonagh, Trans.). Maryknoll, NY: Orbis Books.

Steinberg, M. (2005). *The fiction of a thinkable world: Body, meaning and the culture of capitalism*. New York, NY: Monthly Review Press.

Supko, R. (1998, September). *Perspectives of the Cuban National Literacy Campaign*. Paper presented at the meeting of the Latin American Studies Association, Chicago, IL.

Tablada, C. (1998). *Che Guevara: Economics and politics in the transition to socialism*. New York, NY: Pathfinder Press.

Zimmerman, J. (2006, June 7). All history is revisionist. *The Los Angeles Times*. Retrieved from http://www.latimes.com/news/opinion/commentary/la-oezimmerman7jun07,0,5940045.story?coll=la-news-comment-opinions and http://articles.latimes.com/2006/jun/07/opinion/oe-zimmerman7

Žižek, S. (2008). *Violence*. London, England: Profile Books.

· 6 ·

REVOLUTIONARY CRITICAL PEDAGOGY

A Conversation With Peter McLaren

Peter McLaren and Sebastjan Leban

Sebastjan Leban: On your webpage you state that critical pedagogy, which you support and practice, advocates non-violent dissent, the development of a philosophy of praxis guided by a Marxist humanism, the study of revolutionary social movements and thought and the struggle for socialist democracy, which is diametrically opposite to the current neoliberal democracy. Can we say that you as a critical educator are basically leading a fight against a neoliberal global capitalist valorization of education?

Peter McLaren: Yes, that would be a very fair description. I am not alone, clearly, in this struggle. There are others within universities who work internationally towards the same goal. But it is also fair to say that in the U.S. there are very few of us in the field of education and the future in this regard looks irrepressibly bleak.

Well, let me put it this way. To their ongoing credit, there are those who are quite capable of engaging in a rigorous analysis of mounting sophisticated and nuanced attacks on the scoundrels and hypocrites of the White House, the gangster capitalists and political opportunists, the feckless cabal of Christian-Right "pro-family activists" who exercise their racism by warning about the coming "demographic winter" facing the U.S. unless the white population produces enough babies to achieve "replacement-level fertility," and on the evangelical economic zealots who call out for a renewed assault on the poor through neoliberal economic, political and social directives and principles. But these critics of the wretched havoc wrought by neoliberalism do not at the same time identify an alternative—at least one that is couched beyond very safe and I would say largely empty liberal pluralist principles.

Until about the mid-1990s, I found myself in the same dilemma. For me, the struggle was focused on democratizing the public sphere. But since that time I have been a staunch advocate of education as a means to further socialism, that is, to bring about a world outside capital's valorization process or, put another way, outside labor's value form. I have described capitalism and democracy as two thieves planning a joint robbery and simultaneously attempting to steal the spoils from each other.

I have been part of a movement to build a radical humanistic socialism—in part by de-writing socialism as a thing of the past and rewriting critical pedagogy as a struggle for a postcapitalist alternative—and in doing so I have taken the position that socialism and socialist principles are not dead letters, but open pages in the book of social and economic justice yet to be written or rewritten by people struggling to transform our capitalist prehistory and to build a truly egalitarian social order where, as Marx put it, the real history of humanity can begin.

We can do this in a number of ways, but I have been concentrating mainly but not exclusively on ideology critique, de-naturalizing what is assumed to be unchangeable, de-reifying human agency, and de-objectifying the commodity culture of contemporary capitalism. I have been trying to discourage progressive educators from a sole reliance on a politics of human rights antiseptically cleaved from the issue of economic rights and to unburden cultural studies emphases in education (identity politics, navigating subjective awareness, etc.) of its textuality of the negative, what Marxist professors Teresa Ebert and Mas'ud Zavarzadeh (2010, p. 40) refer to as a site of meaningfulness without meaning or "thoughtful unthoughtfulness" that presumably arrived on the wings of the Angel of History to save us from the old bearded devil: Karl Marx.

With the advent of the linguistic turn in the arts and social sciences—a time regrettably, where class struggle was rewritten in the aerosol terminology of the politics of difference, and difference was treated as difference within itself (how difference is different from itself)—Marxism was a popular target among progressive academics. But replacing class struggle with the politics of "difference" and "diversity" flattens out and empties the whole structure of antagonism or ensemble of relations of opposition within the structured hierarchy of capitalist social relations. Social relations of oppression are, in this case, dissolved into difference within or between two differences—into relations of supplementarity—rather than highlighting labor relations or struggles between workers and the capitalist class. Teresa Ebert, Mas'ud Zavazadeh, Deb Kelsh and others have written in great detail on this in a white heat but also with pristine clarity.

And yes, of course, I have at the same time been trying to challenge, along with my students and leftist colleagues, what Quijano calls "the colo-niality of power" (I very much admire the work of Quijano, Mignolo and Grosfoguel, although I have some difficulty with some aspects of their critique of Marxism). Educators, especially, need to get beyond the manufactured fear and the hysterical rhetoric, peddled by what we call the corporate-state-military-media complex (or simply, the "power complex"), and instead seek a deeper means of challenging repressive and violent social structures. In some instance we might slow down and reverse the current trend among legislative and policy-making bodies and political leaders who contribute mightily to the dreck and the moral refuse that has come to define the current war against the poor within the U.S. and the struggle against the working class by the trans-nationalist capitalist class.

Since 1987, I have been visiting radical educators, student groups, phi-losophers, counterculturalists, contrarians, culture brokers and pedagogical tastemakers internationally (most recently in Finland, Portugal, Greece, Venezuela, Brazil and Cuba), attempting to conscript their messages into a larger, transnational drumbeat that will help to entrain an activist movement towards a post capitalist alternative. Which, of course, I describe as socialism.

What has been different about my work over the last decade is that I am trying to delve deeper into the terrain of Marxist theory and with more exi-gency and urgency, in an attempt to create spaces/places in different scales and registers where students can apprise themselves of the opportunity to resist more fully the geopolitics of imperialism and comprehend how new social relationships can be wrought that can supersede those given birth by the U.S. underbelly of violence—a poisonous underbelly festering inside a hypocritical miasma of couth that floats everywhere and penetrates the very structure of our consciousness through electronic orifices that make up the neoliberal sen-soria of propaganda—propaganda that is imbibed by a duped citizenry under the aroma of "democracy." All of this is part and parcel of the geopolitics of imperialism that largely defines U.S. foreign and domestic policy—all of which, of course, impacts how we both view and develop our role as educated citizens (in my case, a citizen of the world, as I am against most forms of nationalism) and critical cosmopolites.

The gangrene-ridden wound in the soul of the country won't be healed by Obama or McCain (certainly not McCain who is a total nutcase). The issue goes beyond the U.S. itself. It has to do with the transnational capitalist class. But the U.S. certainly plays a major role.

In light of the Bush administration's "humanitarian" invasion of Iraq, and other U.S. war crimes too numerous to mention, its current war on the poor, its savage repression of 12 million immigrant workers, and its involvement in overthrowing democratically elected regimes worldwide, we must detach from the term "democracy" the connotations of equality before the law, free speech, right of association, universal suffrage and self-rule with which it has been saddled over the decades and recognize it as a vile condition that ensures the involuntary servitude of wage labor, the racial and gendered division of labor and the plundering of natural resources by the imperial powers.

The once grand refusal of critical pedagogy to reproduce dominant ideologies and practices inherent in capitalist schooling and the wider context of globalized capitalism and instead to embrace the possibility of decolonizing the conceptual, philosophical, epistemological and cultural dimensions of learning has been expurgated by the flatlined anti-politics of postmodernism. My work has set itself up in opposition to this fashionable apostasy undertaken by what I once termed the avant-garde "hellions of the seminar room."

Gore Vidal once presciently noted that the U.S. government prefers that "public money go not to the people but to big business. The result is a unique society in which we have free enterprise for the poor and socialism for the rich" (2002, p. 129), and the truth of this statement has never been more evident than in the recent nationalization of Fannie and Freddie where it is glaringly clear that the U.S. is a country where there exists socialism for the rich and privatization for the poor, all basking in what Nouriel Roubini (2008) calls the afterglow of "these Bush hypocrites who spewed for years the glory of unfettered Wild West laissez-faire jungle capitalism [and who have] allowed the biggest debt bubble ever to fester without any control, and have caused the biggest financial crisis since the Great Depression."

Indeed, socialism is only condemned when it profits the poor and the powerless and threatens the rich. But capitalists are quick to embrace a socialism for the rich—which really is what neoliberal capitalism is all about. But of course, it's called free-market capitalism and is seen as synonymous with the struggle for democracy. Which is why today we have democracy for the rich while the poor are cast into quasi-feudal steampunk landscapes of dog-eat-dog despair. Those whose labor is exploited in the production of social wealth—that is, the wage and salaried class—are now bearing most of the burden of the current economic crisis in the U.S and are being impaled by the pike of neoliberal capitalism.

SL: In the interview "Pedagogy and Praxis in the Age of Empire" (also the title of one of your books), published in the fall of 2007, you argue that revolutionary critical pedagogy operates from an understanding that the basis of education is political and that we have to create a space where students can be given resources to imagine a different world outside capitalism's law of value. Could you describe what space in particular you have in mind? Can you define the moment of the revolutionary in critical pedagogy?

PM: "The moment of the revolutionary." I like that term. I suppose that there are as many revolutionary moments as there are critical educators. Let me wind up to your answer by providing some theoretical context. As I expressed this dilemma and challenge in an article recently, while it is certainly true, as many poststructuralists unguardedly claim, that we are semiotically situated in hermeneutic horizons, in gendered and racialized positionalities riven by power-sensitive and power-expansive relations of asymmetrical privilege, and in social space aligned and vectored geopolitically and cross-hatched socio-culturally, it is also true that the totalizing power of capital has created an overarching matrix of exploitation in which all of these antagonisms have been accorded value in relation to the sale of human labor power in the global marketplace where, like force-fed swine who are made blind and crippled in preparation for mass consumption, men and women are led to the slaughter-house of capital hoisted on hooks of poverty and debt.

By this I meant that we certainly should not refrain from exploring and celebrating our ethnic heterogeneity and heterodox temporalities that power our subjectivity. I am not against this, or related issues such as building border identities that escape the lineaments of Eurocentric epistemes. This is all fine and good. But let's not forget that the totalizing power of capital creates constitutive limitations in which subjectivities are formed. This, I have argued, can be seen as a form of controlled consent made possible by the production of social amnesia both produced and enforced by the corporate media, and the deep psychology that turns the engines of mass propaganda disguised as a free marketplace of ideas (where the only free cheese available is in the mousetrap).

Democracy has become synonymous with profit making, requiring a roll-back of trade union power and a generalized hollowing out of social democracy, not by military dictatorship but by an endless stream of maledictions and execrations against leftist movements and Marxist analyses that deal with the totality of capitalist social relations and address questions of universality. We are immersed in a popular culture unswervingly saturated by endless spectacles meant to divert attention from substantive political issues and debates, and geared towards proselytizing in order to create silent accomplices in the ravages of corporate expansionism and imperialism. In the name of the most holy acts of consumption, the state media apparatuses, powered by turbines of moral turpitude, not only fail to resist the complete takeover of the public sphere by the logic of capital, but actively promote capitalist logic. In other words, under the guise of defanging the alienation produced by the social labor of capital, and making us more critically informed citizens, the media actively promote such alienation.

In order to address these issues and other related issues, critical pedagogy needs to be renewed—yes, it needs to bring itself face-to-face with the moment of the revolutionary. This time it has to be concerned with the problem of reasserting human action, and of finding forms of organization that facilitate human development. The depredations of progressive (i.e., left liberal) pedagogues have often subordinated praxis to the realm of ideas, theory and the regime of the episteme. But critical socialist pedagogy recognizes the pivotal role of public political action, what has been developed by radical educator, Henry Giroux, as "public pedagogy." It's a pedagogy of revolutionary praxis.

And here I would argue for a decolonizing, anti-capitalist pedagogy. I have talked already about an anti-capitalist pedagogy, so let me explain what I mean by a decolonizing pedagogy. A decolonizing pedagogical approach supports progressive initiatives such as smaller class sizes; improved low-environmental-impact school buildings; an end to school tracking; schools created on a human scale within or as local to communities as possible; cooperation between schools and local authorities rather than competition within the marketplace; vastly increased funding for education; increased powers for local governments to redistribute resources and participate in the development of anti-racist, anti-sexist and anti-homophobic policies and practices; and egalitarian policies designed to assist in more equal educational outcomes, irrespective of social class, gender, race, sexuality or disability, and a curriculum geared towards socialist cooperation and ecological justice.

But it also goes well beyond these initiatives. Decolonizing pedagogy in this instance does not only mean developing classroom strategies designed to contest neoliberal policies and practices, imperialism and militarism; it refers as well to developing a language of critique in which the concentration of corporate and state power is fundamentally challenged transnationally as well as locally. It is designed to understand society as a totality. Decolonizing educators realize that the concept of globalization alone is inadequate for understanding political and economic imperialism, wars of conquest and the pursuit of empire.

The decolonizing pedagogy that is being advocated here recognizes that as we exercise our neocolonial means of exploiting other countries (as the U.S. and other foreign capitalists have exploited the labor power of local populations, drawing them into the worldwide labor market), the mass media and culture in general constitute the central means by which the consent of the popular majorities are secured by the transnational capitalist class in pursuit of the consolidation of their profit-making practices. An important condition of possibility for economic exploitation is the subjective subordination of the popular majorities through education, entertainment, literature and art. Such strategies of subordination are made more transparent within a decolonizing pedagogy that employs critical media literacy in the manner suggested by philosophers such as Douglas Kellner.

Decolonizing pedagogical practices are fundamentally activities rather than a contemplation of abstract concepts; they are designed to undermine empire by creating connections between the subjective feelings of alienation experienced by students and an understanding of their objective location within the social division of labor. In other words, the project of decolonization involves a concrete historical struggle and not a struggle for an abstract utopia. It involves providing students with opportunities for learning some of the basic quantitative and qualitative tools of urban sociologists and activists, for undertaking analyses and projects in their neighborhoods and communities, and within the schools themselves.

More fundamentally, decolonizing pedagogy is the creation of an historical identity through understanding the origins of the system that produces the alienation and estrangement experienced by students. In helping students analyze how the symptoms of their alienation are connected to the objective conditions of class society, teachers contribute to opening up a relationship between students and the historical present. The overall purpose is to undermine the established social relationship among classes, individuals and groups as well as the state's overdetermined systems of meaning such that it is possible to redefine what it means to be human outside of the repressive restrictions of the state.

What is at stake here is more than following a methodology but developing the historical character of our social being. For instance, some radical educators such as Jeff Duncan-Andrade and Ernest Morrell are teaching high school students to become radical sociologists who can analyze their own schools as institutions of domination, colonization and social control. They call their approach, "thug life pedagogy" after the late hip-hop artist Tupac Shakur. Here critical pedagogy constitutes the building blocks for a relation with other people. In doing so, critical teaching helps hope resume its odyssey of struggle against the obstacles of fear, ignorance and self-doubt.

Tupac Shakur died at age 25. His theory of humanization was called THUG LIFE (The Hate U Gave Little Infants Fucks Everyone). Tupac used to call youth fighting against oppression as the "roses that grow from concrete." According to Duncan-Andrade, "They are the ones who prove society's rule wrong by keeping the dream of a better society alive, growing despite the cold, uncaring, un-nurturing environment of the concrete." (Duncan-Andrade & Morrell, 2008, p. 190).

Andrade's students create block-umentaries where groups of students organized by neighborhood document how the historical, sociological, psychological and educational tools of oppression are being used on their blocks to keep them and their families down. I think that's one way to utilize critical pedagogy. Of course, in doing all of this, it is also important to try to imagine what a post capitalist project might look like on the ground, in the streets—how would it look at the level of the system and structure, the state apparatuses and the lifeworld. These are challenges that as educators we need to face.

SL: Contemporary reality is contaminated with the neoliberal capitalist ideology of values that from the perspective of the current world's system has no intention to change. How can we make on the one side this process more visible and understandable to others, and how can we decontaminate it on the other?

PM: Well, first of all, we have to recognize what you just reiterated in your question—that the current world system has no intention of changing. So what's the point of doing nuanced and rigorous analytic work, and sophisticated and hard-knuckled research on capitalist neoliberalism if it won't make a dent in the system? We need to stop being academics and start becoming activists.

In 2006, I was placed on a list by a right-wing group, right at the top of the list known as the "dirty thirty" and denounced as UCLA's most dangerous professor—and the group that was responsible for this, a pro-Bush group, offered $100 to students who would secretly audiotape me, and $50 for lecture notes they made in my classes (or classes of other leftist professors). This story became international because of its resemblance to McCarthyism and was characterized as a resurgent McCarthyism brought on by the assault on civil rights by the Bush cabal. This would have been much more unlikely prior to September 11, 2001.

I think that the erosion of civil rights and the movement towards fascism here in the U.S. has really laid bare the serious threat we have to academic freedom in the U.S. We need to recognize that the social sciences themselves have helped to paralyze academics. There is only so much you can do when you are ensepulchered within a system of liberal modernity, liberal individualism and the doctrine of neoliberal economics.

As Takis Fotopoulos points out, the negative conception of freedom that is embedded in liberal democracy—that is, as the absence of constraints—has been abstracted from its economic base, leading to an erosion of "formal freedoms." They are now being taken away in the semi-totalitarian regimes of the West, as the heteronomous society in which we live is being usurped by the elites who serve the transnational capitalist class. Education helps the elites in their attempts to control the popular majorities, let's face it. Not just education in classrooms, but a larger educational practice that takes place in the realm of communication. I am talking about the perpetual pedagogy of the corporate media. Clearly, this is what representative democracy thrives upon. So in terms laid out by Fotopoulos, we need to struggle for an autonomous society in which the public space encompasses the entire citizen body, and where we can exercise a direct democracy (what he calls an inclusive democracy) where decisions at the macro-level (i.e., economic and political decisions) are part of an institutional framework of equal distribution of political and economic power among citizens.

Here we have a different conception of freedom—not freedom from constraints, but freedom to achieve self-determination and participate in society's reflective and deliberative activities and bring a substantive content to the public sphere. The view of freedom as an absence of constraints (i.e., on the market, on how much one can own, on how much power a single corporation can accumulate or on how much one can suffer need) has set the conditions of possibility for the capitalist class (or what we can now refer to as the transnational capitalist class) to defend its historical advantage, its existing hierarchies of power and privilege by out-maneuvering and manipulating the system so that it continually serves its own interests at the expense of the poor and the powerless.

So how do we create this society of autonomous individuals? We need to move beyond the modern hierarchical society. As educators we can't take the existing social system for granted. And this means fighting in our work not only against the marketization of scientific research but also against both the objective rationalism of science (that enforces the neutrality of knowledge) as well as its postmodern relativism, as argued by Fotopoulos.

Teresa Ebert and others have warned us against pedagogical practices developed by the poststructuralist avant-garde who theorize experience in relation to trauma, desire and affective relations in general as if these relations were antiseptically cleaved from relations of class, thereby replacing a conceptual analysis of the social totality with liberating pedagogical narratives grounded in local affective strategies—strategies that serve unwittingly as epistemological covers for economic conditions that help the subject cope with the objective material conditions of capitalist exploitation. So that most progressive pedagogical practices become little more than coping strategies that help students survive capital rather than transform it. This leads ultimately to a de-historicization of social life and draws attention away from the way in which all human beings who populate capitalist societies are implicated in some manner in international class struggles and the social division of labor.

As the bloody mailed fist of U.S. imperialism continues to hide itself inside a rose-petal glove, it is important to see its support of the self-determination of Georgia and Ukraine as part of a neo-imperialist practice of creating a neo-imperialist client state. Or what about Venezuela and Bolivia? Here the U.S. is trying to destabilize the government of Hugo Chávez and foster violence in the areas of Santa Cruz in Bolivia. Chávez was trying to free the poor from involuntary servitude to the forces of capital by, at the very least, fostering a vision of *un otro mundo*. In Bolivia we are witnessing opposition to Evo Morales by means of the violent tactics of the National Democratic Council (CONALDE), composed of five provincial governors, business associations, conservative civic groups and legislators of the right-wing Podemos party led by former president Jorge Quiroga, who are working now with the UJC (Unión Juventud Cruceña, or Union of Santa Cruz Youth) and the Santa Cruz Civic Committee. Not to see these struggles as class struggles is to miss the main point.

SL: The production of passiveness is a strategy led by the neoliberal system that enables the system to produce social and political apathy. In this perspective, how can we fight against the production of passiveness and how can we be (re)active to an already passive society so that it will be able to change the current neoliberal system?

PM: Well, first of all, we need to free ourselves from the *bête noir* of the progressives—positivism—which actually undergirds much of progressive educators' own work. One of the cardinal principles of positivism (that can be traced as far back as Hume and that involves a synthesis of idealism and empiricism) that was grandly pronounced as an antidote to the metaphysical belief in innate reason is that because all knowledge is derived through the senses, and because it is mediated by our subjectively conceived experiences through a conceptual system or various systems of intelligibility, the objects of our contemplation can never really be known. In other words, our subjectively conceived experience mediates reality such that we can never know it objectively but only approach it through systems of mediation that form an insuperable barrier—a necessary wall of mystification.

This has led to a passive theory of knowledge via a doctrine of experience that rejects understanding the world as a whole and resembles an empty solipsism where reality is reduced to a set of formal or logical statements (which leads to the existence of concepts because they are believed). This is a position that John Hoffman (1975) has called "positivism with a 'left' face." We can see this position reflected in the views of vulgar cultural relativists who believe that there is no real truth when it comes to values, and that one culture's values are no better than another culture's values and there is no basis for judging the values of one culture over another. Values in this view are subjectively held commitments of certain groups of people and not objective truths—they are, in other words, merely what different cultures hold to be true (I will discuss the issues of cultural values a bit later on in my answer and how such vulgar relativism leads to the imposition of Western subjectivism that can lead to what Grosfoguel (2005) calls epistemic genocide, or epistemicide).

My position is Hegelian/Marxist in the sense that I believe that we can't understand isolated bits of experience adequately without the whole—the absolute. We need to ask what makes experience possible, why do certain experiences count more than others, and what are the conditions of possibility for certain types of experiences. We read these dialectically against the absolute.

But here I must make a caveat. Quijano warns us that when thinking about totality, or sociohistorical totality, we need to avoid the Eurocentric paradigm of totality. We can do this by thinking of totality as a field of social relations structured by the heterogeneous and discontinuous integration of diverse spheres of social existence, every one of which is in turn structured by its own historically heterogeneous, temporally discontinuous and conflictive elements. Each element, however, has some relative autonomy and can be considered a particularity and singularity. But they move within the general tendency of the whole. We can't think of totality as a closed structure. Change affects components in a historical field of social relations in a heterogeneous and discontinuous manner, and history does not move from one homogeneous and continuous whole to another. We need to avoid the perception of total-ity as seen from Europe, for instance, and yes, we can see that in terms such as "precapitalist" or "preindustrial" or "premodern." As Ramón Grosfoguel pointed out at a recent workshop we participated in, so-called primitive accu-mulation has always existed in Latin America but it took David Harvey to bring this term into the spotlight recently in his excellent work on accumula-tion by dispossession.

I think it is important that we find a way to illuminate what is taken to be the natural (yet illusory) relation of human beings under capitalism and in doing so create a more "active" theory of knowledge. We can't have an active politics built on a passive theory of knowledge. That's one of the major issues. The current pedagogical concern with "experience" conceals from human beings that men and women are themselves the creators of these social facts, and there are no supportable reasons why we should accept the naïve but perhaps historically inevitable illusion of the inviolability and necessary per-sistence of capitalism as the truth.

This is why, for instance, I reject the position of Laclau and Mouffe, which denies that the material world has any significance outside of discursive artic-ulation since I presuppose that there are real material interests that can and should be articulated. Of course, at the same time I reject the concept of totality as some aprioristic abstract schema imposed as a prefabricated mold upon reality.

And, of course, I agree that Marxism may be misapplied in a militant or dogmatic manner, but it cannot be dismissed solely in non-sequitur fashion on the basis that it constitutes a universal theory. If it is driven by the spirit of self-assertion and totality such that it marginalizes, demonizes and excludes cultural others, then this is deeply objectionable. If that is the Hegelian abso-lute that confronts us, then we need to get beyond it. And many trajectories of Marxism, such as the Marxist-humanist tendency, have done so.

I don't believe that human agents are reduced in historical material-ist analysis to a one-sided determinism in which history repeats itself with crystalline inevitability. That is, I don't believe that human beings are relegated to a passive role in which they are swept away in a swift current consisting of historical laws of motion, or of nature-imposed necessity. I flatly reject this kind of mechanical materialism just as I reject, in contrast, a post-Marxist radical contingency and indeterminacy of the social.

We need to develop an active materialism that does not end up in a series of false dualisms such as human beings/nature or individuals/society. We need a pedagogy of what I have called "history-making," which is a revolutionizing practice that challenges capitalism's ability to invert our capacity for self-reflection so that we cannot understand capitalism's origins. As Teresa Ebert and others have argued, passive contemplation is not enough to alter those conditions in which human beings enter independently of their will. Rather, human beings must work to humanize those conditions and circumstances that shape them.

We need more than abstract principles by which to strive for social justice, such as those that guide anti-racist and anti-sexist curricula or eco-sensitive procedures for living in harmony with the planet. We must also challenge and transform those material circumstances seemingly beyond our control and this means developing a pedagogy of class struggle.

To reach for freedom is not an act of transcending reality but of actively reshaping it, as Michael Lebowitz has argued. Similarly, truth is not an account of what is but what needs to happen. Here I am indebted to classical Marxists such as Teresa Ebert and Mas'ud Zavarzadeh for helping us to escape the debilitating world of subjectivism and voluntarism.

Now what do I mean by class struggle? Well, I believe that it is more than an economic struggle between the propertied and propertyless but is a political struggle directed at the state (and here the hegemonic class is created through a system of alliances of class fractions that can best unify the power bloc). And winning the battle for democracy means much more than cultivating an ethical distaste for exploitation; it means actively working to end it.

The state is not a neutral site; it is not an autonomous region that miraculously floats above the messy world of class antagonisms. Many progressive educators fail to realize this and in their refusal to move beyond a reclamation of the public sphere and an embracing of an anemic and abstract conception of democracy and freedom, they unwittingly reflect the leftist face of the capitalist class in which appearances are created and preserved while reality is eroded. Here the state is viewed as a site where mechanisms to win consent are pivotal, and where the process of legitimization constitutes a struggle by competing groups with various social, economic and political interests. But semi-autonomous zones of engagement can be struggled for, where alternatives to capital can be seized and pushed forward, and this is the role of the educator in the decolonizing classroom.

It is important to note that my concept of materialism here and my belief in a world outside of our thoughts and experiences in no way denies the "objectivity in parentheses" mentioned by Walter Mignolo, since I reject a mutually exclusive transcendental ontology that is inhospitable to other ontologies or to observing our own acts of observation. My defense of a universality of social justice (and socialism) for all—creating the conditions of possibility for freedom from necessity for all—in no way rejects the pluriversity of knowledges. In fact, it affirms the legitimacy of knowledge disqualified by the imperiality of Eurocentered epistemology.

But at the same time I am not prepared to give up on a Marxist humanism, on knowing the world through experiences that cohere with other experiences and actions that cohere with other actions—with protagonistic actions in and on the world, a world in which the social is both the condition and outcome of human agency. And that also means I am not prepared to give up the fight for socialism.

We struggle here for the simultaneity of universal and particular rights. And in doing so we don't privilege the idea of culture as a signifying system, but as a form of embeddedness in the materiality of social life. In doing so, we can't abrogate the normative sense of what constitutes oppression; we consider it as a regulative idea.

That's why I agree that we can advocate an epistemic cultural relativism (in the serious rather than the vulgar sense) in arguing that there is no privileged access to the truth, and that there is no direct correspondence between an object and its representation, but at the same time I am opposed to a judgmental relativism—that there are no grounds, rational grounds, for advocating some beliefs over others (we do this through dialoguing, in the spirit of respect, with other cultures, that is, respecting the non-subjective character of their values). We can't fall into the trap of assuming all beliefs or arguments are equally valid. We need some explanatory adequacy or judgmental rationality in making decisions about various values, and we do this in relation to the material world, to things that exist independently of our attempts to explain them or account for them. And we don't impose this matrix of evaluation from our own Western geopolitical and epistemic location.

And at the same time, following Aijaz Ahmad, we need new forms of politics that constitute human subjects both in their heterogeneity and in their universality. We can't abandon the challenge of universality, of universal rights, as a basis of solidarity and struggle. We need to struggle to make sure such universality is not representative of the bourgeois male, heterosexist, imperial, Christian colonizing subject, of course, but we can do this without abrogating the concept of universality. We can achieve this without making this an ontological philosophy of power that eclipses the trans-ontological and abrogates our radical responsibility to each other in the most debilitating forms of social amnesia (such as what we saw during the Bush administration in the U.S.).

The principle of difference cannot provide us with the standards that oblige us to respect the difference of others, as Kenan Malik has pointed out. He notes that while difference can arise from equality, equality can never arise from difference. All universalisms are dirty, claims Bruce Robbins, and by this he means that universal standards are arrived at in conditions of unequal power. But he also notes that it is only dirty universalisms that will help us against the powers and agents of still dirtier ones. Similarly, we can't aban-don every and all notion of essence, of something that is beyond appearance, because if we do that—if we privilege the concept of difference—then the notion of appearance alone becomes evidence that there are different cate-gories of humanity that have little or nothing in common—or that they are incommensurable. If we do that, we fall into the same logic as positivist racial theory—which deduces categories of races from mere appearances of skin, hair and bone. Apprehension of formal difference then moves to an explana-tion for the existence of different ontological categories.

This is a dangerous move, just as I think a rejection of all humanism is dangerous, a rejection that follows the notion that modernity itself leads to an annihilation of the other. The barbarism of the twentieth century is, Kenan Malik argues, not so much a consequence of modernity as it was a product of specific capitalist social relations.

I object to the dismissal of universalism on the grounds of its hostil-ity to otherness and for its Eurocentric attempts to impose Eurocentric or Euro-American ideas of rationality on other peoples. I do believe it is import-ant to critique the false claim of universality inherent in the European par-ticular, of course. However, I agree with Eagleton when he argues that the Western, "First World," postmodern intelligentsia has mistaken "its own very local difficulties for a universal human condition in exactly the manner of the universalist ideologies it denounces." Those who are preoccupied with the "crisis of humanism" need to remember that it is not everyone's crisis (not even in the West). We need to remember, as well, that many Third World struggles of the postwar era drew upon the "logic of universalism" and that it remains crucial in many struggles for liberation.

Some might just dismiss this as Eurocentric Third Worldism, but such struggles could indeed set the conditions of possibility for decolonial struggles. Let's face it; humanist principles can be coercive or liberating, depending on who is employing them and for what purpose.

Here I am calling for a "non-abstract and non-homogeneous" form of universalism as a *political* referent. We need to distinguish between an abstract universalism that dissolves important differences among diverse phenomena and a concrete universalism that carefully draws such distinctions while upholding conditions that are binding for all. I have written elsewhere that the restricted and often dangerously destructive Western bourgeois character of Enlightenment universalism is a worthy and necessary object of critique, but to attack the idea of universalism itself is problematic. We need to be wary of conflating universalism with uniformity, because universals can be both various and locally diverse.

There is no question that, for instance, colonialism has been intrinsic to the kind of universality that we have had in much of world history and that the only universal civilization that exists today is global capitalism. The solution isn't getting rid of the concept of universalism but working towards a better universality—and some of this can be achieved in struggling for what has been called by Walter Mignolo and Grosfoguel and others as pluriversality.

A more useful alternative to "dismissing universalisms as masked particularisms" is to side with Terry Eagleton (1996) who writes that to be a socialist is, among other things, to recognize that

> universality *doesn't* exist at present in any positive, as opposed to merely descriptive or ideological, sense. Not everyone, as yet, enjoys freedom, happiness, and justice. Part of what prevents this from coming about is precisely the false universalism that holds that it can be achieved by extending the values and liberties of a particular sector of humankind, roughly speaking Western man, to the entire globe. Socialism is a critique of this false universalism, not in the name of cultural particularism but in the name of the right of everyone to negotiate their own differences in terms of everyone else's. (p. 118, emphasis in the original)

But I need to flesh out further what I mean. Where do other cultures come into play? I am committed to the objective truth of the values of other cultures;

I do not reject the non-subjective character of their values at all. I am a cultural relativist not in the vulgar sense of believing at the philosophical meta-cultural level that cultural values are simply subjectively held commitments. Rather, I give serious weight to the objective truth of other cultures in the sense of maintaining that all cultures have their own access to truth even though the values of other cultures might not be compatible with the values and conceptual schemes of my own culture. One has to guard against the imposition of a Western subjectivism calcified into an imperial universal.

As Nelson Maldonado-Torres so brilliantly argues, capitalism and coloniality have betrayed the oppressed at the expense of the trans-ontological, that is, at the expense of validating the knowledges and forms of being and the very humanity of the colonized, creating conditions of life founded on receptive generosity, or at the expense of "altericity" (a term that Maldonado-Torres uses to capture the priority of the relationship of responsibility between self and Others. The task then becomes, in Maldonado-Torres's view, eliminating what he calls "the coloniality of being" (the normalization of everyday warfare against colonial subjects that can be found in national ontologies and identitarian ontologies, etc.). He calls for the elimination of sub-ontological difference (ontological colonial difference or the naturalization of sub-Others as legitimate recipients of excessive violence) and restoring the meaning and relevance of trans-ontological difference (difference produced as a formative event in the production of being that makes possible communication between a self and an Other and the foundation of justice through the vertical relation between subjectivity and alterity).

As a Marxist humanist who finds a great deal of value in the writings of Hegel, let me take Hegel as an example of a philosopher of whom many multiculturalists are critical because of his undeniable racism and ethnocentrism. Of course, we must reject Hegel's ethnocentrism and racism. But Hegel's own philosophical position provides us with the tools to subvert Hegel's own ethnocentrism and cultural racism.

Philip Kain's (2005) book, *Hegel and the Other*, makes a good case that Hegel takes the position that every culture stands before the absolute such that the absolute is the expression of that culture and that culture is the expression of the absolute. Paraphrasing Kain, Hegel believes that it is philosophy's task to construct the absolute for consciousness, and because we construct it doesn't mean the absolute isn't real. Knowing, for Hegel, is part of the absolute—so it is impossible to know anything, really, before we know—so that we need, in other words, to start without any epistemological criterion because (as Kain, Norman and others remind us) to attempt to demonstrate an epistemological criterion that would claim to tell us what we can and cannot know already is a form of knowing, and this would presuppose the criterion it was supposed to demonstrate. So, we begin with the absolute, that is, we begin with something unproven and by abstracting from the absolute we eventually realize that this is impossible, so Hegel takes us full circle back to the absolute again by showing us how everything is internally related, how things are mutually constituted, that is, they are constituted by other things and fused by the whole, and this is what Marx's theory of internal relations was all about—and more.

Each culture constructs the absolute for consciousness in a different way; in doing so, each culture has access to its own truth. So that this absolute needs to be seen as open. The human spirit can be realized only through the spirit of particular cultures, and therefore we should not view the absolute as closed and we should welcome engaging cultural difference. In fact, the absolute demands its own subversion. We can't let the absolute be a totalizing juggernaut linked to Western imperial adventures, so we need to incite difference within the absolute. The absolute that is true for itself for a particular culture needs to be true in and for itself. It is impossible for something not to be absolute in itself and be absolute for a particular culture.

Thus, I am a cultural relativist in the manner that Kain describes, rather than a vulgar relativist. I am a cultural relativist who denies that cultural relativism is a self-refuting term insofar as I maintain that consciousness develops within a specific cultural context and a specific historical era or juncture.

That being said, it is also the case that culture can embody or embed truth. I reject the existence of a space station platform above culture—some kind of Death Star standpoint where the emperor, shrouded in a blood red cowl of Western epistemology, stands above culture and exercises a supercultural God's eye view, some kind of sky hook or observation platform nested in the metaphysical heights of Mount Olympus or neutral common coordinate system outside of the Matrix from which to transvalue all the meanings generated by the universe and pronounce indubitable judgment on all convention.

It's unlikely, at any rate that different cultures are completely incommensurable since different systems of intelligibility or different conceptual systems can provide some translation from one culture to another. I doubt very much that all truth can be captured within one system of intelligibility—at least consistently captured. We need to respect other conceptual systems—other perspectives—because no single system can capture all truths.

I have not given up on translatability. Paulo Freire once told me during a conversation we had about translating high theory into classroom practice that it was important to translate his work within the contextual specificity of where I was standing—where I was located—as a teacher and where my students were located as students. He told me that my job was one of translation—of translating his philosophical language into a language that impacted teachers in various pedagogical settings so that they could provide spaces of opportunity where critical learning could take place—that I should not simply impose his conception of knowing on my students—which would be a form of conceptual/cultural imperialism.

Our misunderstandings with individuals from other cultures does not mean that these cultures are incommensurable. After all, our conceptual systems can be different—and we can find such systems to be incompatible or inconsistent or both—but there is always the possibility of translation, no matter how limited. I am not advancing a moral obligation for tolerating other cultures; I want to be clear on that. We need other grounds for taking a position against intolerance.

We need to engage other cultures in order to better understand ourselves and others, our interdependence and mutual obligations towards each other and the world as a totality. We engage in the values and belief systems of other cultures, not in a vulgar way by according them only subjective merit and by denying them any non-subjective validity. We engage them by embracing a concept of truth. As Kain points out, if we believe that all values are subjectively held commitments and do not constitute objective truths—then we are going to fall into the trap of vulgar relativism—and this leads to epistemic violence inevitably. We need a commitment to the objective truth of other cultural values. All cultures have access—their own access—to the truth. The rejection of the non-subjective character of the values of other cultural beings (i.e., considering their views as just another position among many positions without any real truth value) is tantamount to the imposition of Western subjectivism.

Hegel, of course, is ethnocentric, but Kain argues persuasively that his system gives us a chance to subvert his ethnocentrism. Hegel was also a racist, and while Kain argues that he was not a theoretical or scientific racist, he certainly must be condemned for his ranking different ethnic groups according to their participation in the absolute and for his view of European superiority. It is simply indefensible. Hegel's ignorance of Africa is staggering, and his view of indigenous Americans must be criticized and denounced (see his ranking of cultures in *Philosophy of Mind*), as he not only describes Western ethnocentrism, imperialism and racism, but also actually endorses them.

Kain writes that in his rankings of races as higher and lower Hegel rejects a scientific justification of his ranking. Racial essences, which reside for Hegel in mind or spirit, are educable and are not unchanging. This, and the fact that Hegel includes different races for being part of the construction of the absolute, does not mean we should forgive him for his racism and ethnocentrism, but it does mean that we can look to Hegel's system for a way of subverting Hegel.

Kain suggests that we need to view Hegel's exclusion of other cultures from a dialectical perspective—they all contain the truth—in other words, world spirit does not belong to any one nation. There remains an outside to Western epistemology in Hegel's overall philosophical system. In this way Hegel invites a subversion of his own narrative of cultural ranking since, according to Kain, Hegel is committed to heterogeneity and does not focus on racial purity. It is important to keep in mind that Hegel does not want a single world culture—he is a pluralist at heart. He does not seek to absorb other cultures into an abstract universal. But undeniably, Hegel is ethnocentric at the philosophical, metacultural level. But his system carries within itself a mechanism for subverting itself.

SL: Anibal Quijano in his pathbreaking article, "Coloniality of Power, Eurocentrism and Latin America" (Quijano & Ennis, 2000) wrote that historically only through the colonization of the Americas could capital consolidate and obtain global predominance, establishing the new world order known as capitalism. Isn't it interesting and amazing that after five hundred years of the modern world system the new socialist revolution is actually happening precisely in Latin America, probably one of the most exploited geographical areas where colonialism through centuries allowed the expansion of capitalism (globally) up to now? Let me follow this with another question. It is quite obvious that if we want to build another perspective (and not only the capitalist one), we will have to engage in a fight against the current structure of power on all social levels. The fight against this hegemony is already going on but it seems that it is still a little bit dispersed (structured in different theoretical fields). Does radical critical pedagogy work together with other important de-linking projects, such as decoloniality (W. Mignolo), and do you think that it is time for a historical revolution on a global scale to take place?

PM: I very much admire Quijano's work and that of Walter Mignolo. They need to be read in my field of education and of course in other fields as well.

And of course there is the very important, and I would say urgently needed, work of Enrique Dussel, Ramón Grosfoguel and Nelson Maldonado-Torres.

But you mentioned Quijano. Well, for instance, Quijano draws attention to the production of a world system of classification, non-existent before the sixteenth century, and deftly argues that previous forms of domination (e.g., gender) were then reconfigured around the new system of racial classification. Knowledge and society were organized around the category of race (a precursor to Eurocentrism) to the extent that the division of labor itself was naturalized. With the help of capitalism, the idea of race helped to yoke the world's population into a hierarchical order of superior and inferior people and it became a central construct in creating and reproducing the international division of labor, including the global system of patriarchy.

Quijano is correct when he writes (2008, p. 220) that "domination is the requisite for exploitation, and race is the most effective instrument for domination that, associated with exploitation, serves as the universal classifier in the current global model of power." He also makes an important intervention when he argues that dualism and evolutionism situated the European subject as the most spiritually evolved while women and slaves were viewed as the most primitive, locked into their corporeality. Slavery, serfdom, wage labor and reciprocity all functioned to produce commodities for the world market. What Quijano calls a "colonial power matrix" (*patrón de poder colonial*) affecting all dimensions of social existence such as sexuality, authority, subjectivity and labor, Berkeley professor Ramón Grosfoguel conceptualizes as a historical-structural heterogeneous totality that by the late nineteenth century came to cover the whole planet.

Expanding on Quijano's work, Grosfoguel describes the coloniality of power as an entanglement of multiple and heterogeneous global hierarchies ("heterarchies") of sexual, political, epistemic, economic, spiritual, linguistic and racial forms of domination and exploitation where the racial/ethnic hierarchy of the European/non-European divide transversally reconfigures all of the other global power structures. As race and racism became the organizing principle that structured all of the multiple hierarchies of the world-system, Grosfoguel argues that the different forms of labor that were articulated to capitalist accumulation on a world-scale were assigned according to this racial hierarchy.

Cheap, coercive labor was carried out by non-European people in the periphery and "free wage labor" was exercised in the core. Such has been the case up to the present day. Grosfoguel (2005) points out that, contrary to the Eurocentric perspective, race, gender, sexuality, spirituality and epistemology are not additive elements to the economic and political structures of the capitalist world-system, but a constitutive part of the broad entangled "package" called the European modern/colonial capitalist/patriarchal world-system. This work is very important for educators to engage. We need to enter into dialogue with this line of work—I agree. But in some of the work based on moving beyond Eurocentrism there is a critique of Marxism that, I think, while it does a brilliant job of critiquing the Marxism of the Internationals, what could be called militant manifesto Marxism, it grievously ignores the Marxist-humanist standpoint and some work in classical Marxism by scholars such as Teresa Ebert and Mas'ud Zavarzadeh, and educationalists such as Valerie Scatamburlo-D'Annibale, Glenn Rikowski, Mike Cole, Deb Kelsh, Dave Hill, Paula Allman and others.

The last several decades have witnessed a concerted attack on "totality" by progressive educators of various stripes who purport to challenge the totalizing grand narratives informing Western domination and Eurocentrism. Decentering and recentering representational narratives have become the order of the day. Critiques of political economy and capitalist relations of exploitation have given way to a decentering of systems of signification that function within apparatuses of power-knowledge. The dualism of oppressor/oppressed has been replaced with the ambivalence of cultural difference and the notion that every subject is "always already oppressor and oppressed." The cultural differences of "in-between-spaces" are prioritized over the totalizing discourses of universal liberation. And while I recognize, with Gramsci, that consciousness can be "contradictory," I do not see the struggle for social justice as exploiting the ambivalence inherent in power relations or as a rupture of a signifying chain, but as the revolutionary praxis of the oppressed forged in class struggle.

Some works on coloniality and identity, in their theorizations of "difference" (usually in their discussions of race), circumvent and undermine any systematic knowledge of the material dimensions of difference and tend to segregate questions of difference from class formation and capitalist social relations. This is not the case with Quijano and Grosfoguel and Mignolo, which is why their work is so important for educators to engage. But some of the postcolonial scholars (those who work to consolidate "identitarian" understandings of difference based exclusively on questions of cultural or racial hegemony) tend to downplay or basically ignore the totality of capitalist social relations.

Therefore, I think it is important, as I have argued with Valerie Scatamburlo-D'Annibale, to (re)conceptualize difference by drawing upon Marx's materialist and historical formulations. Difference needs to be understood as the product of social contradictions and in relation to political and economic organization. We need to acknowledge that "otherness" and/or difference is not something that passively happens, but, rather, is actively produced.

Drawing upon the Marxist concept of *mediation* can help us to unsettle our categorical approaches to both class and difference, for it was Marx himself who warned against creating false dichotomies in the situation of our politics. He argued that it was absurd to choose between subjective consciousness and the material world, subjectivity and the way the world is socially organized, personal or agency and structural determination or determination by historical forces (see Bannerji, 1995). In a similar vein, it is equally absurd to see difference as a historical form of consciousness unconnected to class struggle. So we need very much to examine the institutional and structural aspects of difference, the meanings that get attached to categories of difference, and to understand how differences are produced out of, and lived within specific historical formations.

While it is important to create greater cultural space for the formerly excluded to have their voices heard (represented), at the same time we have to make sure that this does not simply reinscribe a neoliberal pluralist stance rooted in the ideology of free-market capitalism. In short, cultural politics becomes, in this case, modeled on the marketplace, and freedom amounts to the liberty of all vendors to display their "different" cultural goods.

What many postcolonial theorists fail to address is that the forces of diversity and difference are allowed to flourish provided that they remain within the prevailing forms of capitalist social arrangements. The neopluralism of difference politics (including those based on "race") cannot adequately pose a substantive challenge to the productive system of capitalism that is able to accommodate a vast pluralism of ideas and cultural practices and cannot capture the ways in which various manifestations of oppression are intimately connected to the central dynamics of capitalist exploitation. This is where Marxist-humanist analysis can help.

Why am I saying all this? Because the struggle for diversity through anti-discrimination has actually seen U.S. society adapt to its production of inequality and make the politics of difference work to bolster neoliberal capitalism. As you know, I have been creating anti-racist, anti-sexist and anti-homophobic curricula and pedagogical practices for decades, and have been challenging educational policies and practices from these same perspectives, but I have also been stressing the strategic centrality of class struggle.

It is not that I am trying to privilege class over race and gender or reduce race to an artifact of class, as some of my critics claim. Rather, I am trying to make the case that unless anti-racist and anti-patriarchal struggles are multi-pronged endeavors and conjugated with class struggle, their efforts could lead to a strengthening of inequality rather than bringing about its defeat. Why? Because while capitalist society is becoming less discriminatory, it is increasingly becoming unequal, not more equal.

In a recent article in the *New Left Review* (2008, p. 33; not a journal I read very much these days), Walter Benn Michaels has put the case succinctly and powerfully in the following terms:

> In 1947—seven years before the Supreme Court decision in *Brown v. Board of Education*, sixteen years before the publication of Betty Friedan's *The Feminine Mystique*—the top fifth of American wage-earners made 43 per cent of the money earned in the US. Today that same quintile gets 50.5 per cent. In 1947, the bottom fifth of wage-earners got 5 per cent of total income; today it gets 3.4 per cent. After half a century of anti-racism and feminism, the U.S. today is a less equal society than was the racist, sexist society of Jim Crow. Furthermore, virtually all the growth in inequality has taken place since the passage of the Civil Rights Act of 1965—which means not only that the successes of the struggle against discrimination have failed to alleviate inequality, but that they have been compatible with a radical expansion of it. Indeed, they have helped to enable the increasing gulf between rich and poor. Why? Because it is exploitation, not discrimination, that is the primary producer of inequality today. It is neoliberalism, not racism or sexism (or homophobia or ageism) that creates the inequalities that matter most in American society; racism and sexism are just sorting devices. In fact, one of the great discoveries of neoliberalism is that they are not very efficient sorting devices, economically speaking.

Michaels claims that the debates about race and gender are essentially empty unless the focus remains on capitalist exploitation. He goes on to say the following:

> Whether debates about race and gender in American politics involve self-congratulation, for all the progress the US has made, or self-flagellation over the journey still to go, or for that matter arguing over whether racism or sexism is worse, the main point is that the debate itself is essentially empty. Of course discrimination is wrong: no one in mainstream American politics today will defend it, and no neoliberal who understands the entailments of neoliberalism will do so either. But it is not discrimination that has produced the almost unprecedented levels of inequality Americans face today; it is capitalism.

In my mind, Michaels clearly identifies the central flaw of much Left politics today, whether in education or any other field. Given the current liberal pluralist framework that separates out economic rights from human rights, the most that can come of multiculturalism—or critical pedagogy for that matter—is one that is guided by a neoliberalism of the right or a neoliberalism of the left. Here is a section of his warning:

> [I]t is clear that the characterization of the race–gender debate as "empty" needs to be qualified. For the answer to the question, "Why do American liberals carry on about racism and sexism when they should be carrying on about capitalism?," is pretty obvious: they carry on about racism and sexism in order to avoid doing so about capitalism. Either because they genuinely do think that inequality is fine as long as it is not a function of discrimination (in which case, they are neoliberals of the right). Or because they think that fighting against racial and sexual inequality is at least a step in the direction of real equality (in which case, they are neoliberals of the left). Given these options, perhaps the neoliberals of the right are in a stronger position—the economic history of the last thirty years suggests that diversified elites do even better than undiversified ones. But of course, these are not the only possible choices.

So why am I so hard on the poststructuralists and many of the postcolonial theorists? For precisely this reason. By not conjugating anti-racism and anti-sexism with class struggle, efforts at ending discrimination could help to foster inequality. Consequently, critical pedagogy needs to remove itself from a left-liberal politics in which its antipathy for challenging neoliberal capitalism only strengthens the unholy grip of capital on the poor and the powerless. This is essentially the message of what I have been calling revolutionary critical pedagogy.

Now it is quite possible for Michaels to make a mistake here, and that would be to concentrate only on capitalism, and forget about colonial epistemology and pluriversality and the fact that multiple antagonisms are co-constitutive. If we want to challenge capitalism, we need to take on racism directly as well as delink from the Western rational episteme in the sense that such a delinking helps us recognize that it is the desire for wealth and capital accumulation that helps to provide the epistemic oxygen that nourishes capital. In other words, we need to negate capital but we need to negate what we have negated, and in doing so we can learn a lot from Hegel if we take seriously his concept of self-referential negation and what Raya Dunyevskaya referred to as absolute negativity.

Arrayed with the coxcomb of the court jester, the monk's cowl, or the pointed hat of some gnostic sectary, the faux-insurrectionary educator is dialectically subsumed back into the arena of not-knowing through the act of simple negation. Not-knowing is not the same as ignorance, however, it is merely the dialectical counterpart of all knowledge. Unless the educator herself is willing to be educated through the negation of the negation, no truly new world-creation is possible. With absolute negativity, the truly authentic insurrectionary educator joins the artificer's circle, creating new forms of knowing, forms in which justice is both externally struggled for and inwardly impressed, where knowledge is more enacted than spoken, where it becomes perpetually transfigured along with the agency of the learner, and made increasingly more protagonistic. Here, the coxcomb can be replaced with a red beret.

And we can learn a lot from epistemologies outside of Western ones, the epistemologies of *Les Damnés de la Terre* (*The Wretched of the Earth*) or who Frantz Fanon referred to as the racialized and colonized peoples of what some call the Third World—those who inhabit locations in the colonial matrix of power that are much different than our own, for instance. I am thinking here of the importance of the ethico-political project of the Zapatistas, whose geopolitics and body-politics provide the substance for what Mignolo calls "border thinking."

But at the same time I don't want to downplay the importance of some Western philosophical traditions—such as critical theory and Marxist theory—that can only be strengthened by our efforts to decolonize them; we need also to recognize their power and promise for creating a praxis of liberation that can challenge the power complex that Grosfoguel calls the "European/Euro-North American capitalist/patriarchal modern/colonial world-system." The Marxist-humanist tradition, for instance, cannot be simply dismissed as one totalizing episteme seeking to appropriate all of subjectivity into its voracious vortex of Western epistemology.

SL: You are working a lot with countries in Latin America (Bolivia, Venezuela) that are leading the socialist project (socialist revolution) of the twenty-first century. Slovenia, as one of the states of the former Federal Republic of Yugoslavia, had already been part of a similar socialist project with socialist self-government and collective (i.e., public) property. Soon after the fall of the Berlin Wall we entered the neoliberal order. Neoliberal ideology took place when the newborn Slovenian capitalists allowed for a reorganization of socialism into neoliberal capitalism. All socialist values have been replaced by the neoliberal ones. The same story happened in all the countries of the former Eastern European socialist bloc. Therefore, how can we imagine a socialist alternative to neoliberalism and what are the real possibilities for establishing a socialist democracy in countries such as Bolivia and Venezuela or elsewhere in the world?

PM: Yes, it has been a tragic history. The whole dismantling of the social-ist project by the West. I hope you will permit me to answer this question philosophically. But philosophy here means changing the world, not just interpreting it. But how to envision a new beginning? That is the challenge of our times. I believe we need to focus on human development through a renewed understanding of what the negation of the negation means. Because it will take us to a place of absolute negativity, and that is where we can forge spaces of hope and possibility.

Here I return to my Marxist-humanist roots and to the work of Raya Dunayevskaya and Peter Hudis. Hudis notes that the genius of Hegel was that he was fully aware that negation is dependent on the object of its critique. In other words, ideas of liberation are impacted, in one way or another, by the oppressive forms that one tries to reject, and that negation per se does not totally free one from the negated object.

But unlike the postmodernists that centuries later followed him, Hegel believed that there was a way for negation to transcend the object of its cri-tique. He therefore introduced the notion of "the negation of the negation." Hudis makes clear that the negation of the negation, or second negativity, does not refer simply to a continuous series of negations—that can potentially go on forever and still never free negation from the object of its critique. Hegel instead argues for a self-referential negation. By negating itself, nega-tion establishes a relation with itself—and therefore frees itself from depen-dence on the external object. According to Hudis, this kind of negativity, second negativity, is "absolute," insofar as it exists without relation to another outside itself. In other words, negation is no longer dependent on an external object; it negates such dependency through a self-referential act of negation.

According to Hudis, Marx did not dismiss the concept of the "negation of the negation" as an idealist illusion but instead appropriated the concept of the self-referential negation "to explain the path to a new society." Marx understood that simply to negate something still leaves us dependent upon the object of critique; in other words, it merely affirms the alienated object of our critique on a different level.

As Hudis and Dunayevskaya and other Marxist humanists have pointed out, that has been the problem with revolutions of the past—they remained dependent upon the object of their negation. The negation of the negation, however, creates the conditions for something truly positive to emerge in that absolute negativity is no longer dependent on the other. Here is how Hudis (2005) puts it in his own words, using the example of communism:

> Communism, the abolition of private property, is the negation of capitalism. But this negation, Marx tells us, is dependent on the object of its critique insofar as it replaces private property with collective property. Communism is not free from the alienated notion that ownership or *having* is the most important part of being human; it simply affirms it on a different level. Of course, Marx thinks that it is necessary to negate private property. But this negation, he insists, must itself be negated. Only then can the *truly positive*—a totally new society—emerge. (Emphasis in the original)

Marx believed that labor or human praxis can actually achieve the transcendence of alienation. But it is essential that one develops a subjective praxis, one that is connected in a vital way to a philosophy of liberation. Such a philosophy can't simply be all about critique. It must be dialectical and be able to illuminate the content of a post-capitalist society while projecting a path to a totally new society. After all, before any revolution can firmly take hold, humanity must be convinced that it is possible to resolve the contradiction between alienation and freedom.

We can't resolve such a contradiction within the social universe of capital and capital's value form of labor. In Hudis's (2005) terms, we need to concretize "Absolute Negativity *as New Beginning*, rather than repeating the truths of an earlier era that no longer have the power to seize humanity's imagination." And talking about seizing the imagination, well, that is certainly happening in Latin America with Bolivia, Venezuela and other places.

So what am I saying here? In conjunction with the centrality of class struggle, we need today a new form of philosophical comprehension and working out of what absolute negativity as a new beginning means today. We need to start to define the characteristics of a world outside of capital's value form— and we need the concepts of pluriversality and transmodernism to help us in doing so. We need, in other words, not only to acknowledge the priority of material necessity in historical development but to start constructing a post capitalist society, what we refer to as a socialist society in dialogue with other cultures, other values.

This understanding of absolute negativity as a seedbed for new beginnings is the motor of a renewed critical/revolutionary pedagogy guided by the imperative of class struggle, and the development of a decolonial philosophy of praxis. Now to a certain extent this is happening in Venezuela, where I have been invited to develop radical pedagogical alternatives. It is not a socialist society but the Chávez government is trying to create the conditions of possibility for socialism to emerge. And great experiments are taking place in attempting to create spaces for human development.

The teachings of Che Guevara have taught me a lot about the importance of human development. So many revolutionary leaders of his day thought that when the iron laws of capital were smashed by nationalizing the industries and centralizing the economy that socialist society would automatically spring forth. Che knew otherwise. He knew that socialist society needed socialist development—a socialist human development and the creation of new men and women.

Bibliography

Bannerji, H. (1995). *Thinking through: Essays on feminism, Marxism and anti-racism.* Toronto, Canada: Women's Press.

Duncan-Andrade, J., & Morrell, E. (2008). *The art of critical pedagogy: Possibilities for moving from theory to practice in urban schools.* New York, NY: Peter Lang.

Dussel, E. (1985). *Philosophy of liberation.* New York, NY: Orbis Books.

Eagleton, T. (1996). *The illusions of postmodernism.* New York, NY: Wiley-Blackwell.

Ebert, T. (2009). *The task of cultural critique.* Champaign, IL: University of Illinois Press.

Ebert, T., & Zavarzadeh, M. (2008). *Class in culture.* Boulder, CO: Paradigm.

Ebert, T., & Zavarzadeh, M. (2010). Hypohumanities. In D. Kelsh, D. Hill, & S. Macrine (Eds.), *Class in education: Knowledge, pedagogy, subjectivity* (pp. 39–65). London, England: Routledge.

Grosfoguel, R. (2005). The implications of subaltern epistemologies for global capitalism: Transmodernity, border thinking, and global coloniality. In R. P. Applebaum & W. I. Robinson (Eds.), *Critical globalization studies* (pp. 283–292). London, England: Routledge.

Gržinić, M. (2008, Summer). De-linking epistemology from capital and pluriversality—A conversation with Walter Mignolo, Part 1. *Reartikulacija*, 4. Retrieved from http://www.reartikulacija.org/dekolonizacija/dekolonialnost4_ENG.html (no longer accessible).

Hegel, G. W. F., & Wallace, W. (1971). *Hegel: Philosophy of mind.* New York, NY: Oxford University Press.

Hoffman, J. (1975). *Marxism and the theory of praxis.* London, England: Lawrence & Wishart.

Hudis, P. (2000, April 1). Can capital be controlled? *News & Letters Online.* Retrieved from http://www.internationalmarxisthumanist.org/wp-content/uploads/pdf/hudis-article-can-capital-be-controlled.pdf

Hudis, P. (2005, March). *Marx's critical appropriation and transcendence of Hegel's theory of alienation.* Paper presented at a session on 'Alternatives to Capitalism,' in the Left Forum, New York, NY.

Hudis, P. (2007–2008, December–January). Hegel's phenomenology today: A Marxist-humanist view. *News & Letters.* Retrieved from http://www.internationalmarxisthumanist.org/articles/hegels-phenomenology-today-a-marxist-humanist-view-by-peter-hudis.

Kain, P. J. (2005). *Hegel and the other: A study of the phenomenology of spirit.* Albany, NY: State University of New York Press.

Maldonado-Torres, N. (2008). *Against war: Views from the underside of modernity.* Durham, NC: Duke University Press.

Malik, K. (1997). The mirror of race: Postmodernism and the celebration of difference. In E. M. Wood & J. B. Foster (Eds.), *In defense of history: Marxism and the postmodern agenda* (pp. 112–133). New York, NY: Monthly Review Press.

Michaels, W. B. (2008, July–August). Against diversity. *New Left Review, 52.* Retrieved from http://newleftreview.org/?page=article &view=2731

Mignolo, W. (1987). *The darker side of the Renaissance: Literacy, territoriality and colonization.* Ann Arbor, MI: University of Michigan Press.

Mignolo, W. (1999). *Local histories/global designs: Coloniality, subaltern knowledges and border thinking.* Princeton, NJ: Princeton University Press.

Mignolo, W. (2005). *The idea of Latin America.* London, England: Blackwell.

Quijano, A. (1993). 'Raza,' 'Etnia' y 'Nación' en Mariátegui: Cuestiones Abiertas [Race, ethnicity and nation in Mariátegui: Open questions]. In R. Forgues (Ed.), *José Carlos Mariátgui y Europa: El Otro Aspecto del Descubrimiento* (pp. 167–187). Lima, Perú: Empresa Editora Amauta S.A.

Quijano, A. (1998). La colonialidad del poder y la experiencia cultural latino-americana [The coloniality of power and the Latin American cultural experience]. In R. Briceño-León & H. R. Sonntag (Eds.), *Pueblo, época y desarrollo: La sociología de América Latina* (pp. 139–155). Caracas, Venezuela: Nueva Sociedad.

Quijano, A. (2008). Coloniality of power, Eurocentrism and social classification. In M. Morana, E. Dussel, & C. A. Jauregui (Eds.), *Coloniality at large: Latin America and the postcolonial debate* (pp. 181–224). Durham, NC: Duke University Press.

Quijano, A., & Ennis, M. (2000). Coloniality of power, Eurocentrism, and Latin America. *Nepantla, 1,* 533–580.

Quijano, A., & Wallerstein, I. (1992). Americanity as a concept, or the Americas in the modern world-system. *International Journal of Social Sciences, 134,* 583–591.

Retamar, R. F. (1989). *Caliban and other essays.* Minneapolis, MN: University of Minnesota Press.

Roubini, N. (2008, September 18). Public losses for private gain. *The Guardian.* Retrieved from http://www.theguardian.com/commentisfree/2008/sep/18/marketturmoil.creditcrunch

Vidal, G. (2002). *Dreaming of war: Blood for oil and the Cheney-Bush junta.* New York, NY: Thunder's Mouth Press/Nation Books.

REVOLUTIONARY CRITICAL PEDAGOGY
IS MADE BY WALKING

In a world where many worlds coexist

Peter McLaren and Petar Jandrić

To anyone interested in contemporary critical education, Peter McLaren hardly needs an introduction. Dubbed "one of the leading architects of critical pedagogy" ("Peter McLaren," 2014), and "a teacher of all teachers" (Steinberg, 2005, p. xiii), he is widely recognized as "poet laureate of the educational left" (Kincheloe, 2000, p. ix).

Henry Giroux writes that "as a writer, he [McLaren] combines the rare gifts of the astute theoretician with that of the storyteller in the manner celebrated by Walter Benjamin" (1999, p. xxiii). On the back cover of *Critical Pedagogy and Predatory Culture*, William F. Pinar wrote: "McLaren's unerring sense of what is important as well as the remarkable range of his scholarship establish him as perhaps the central political theorist in the field today" (1995). Paula Allman (2000) describes McLaren's writing as follows:

> McLaren's writing is a brilliant blend of passion, commitment, and critical analysis and insight. It is poetry and prose in an intimate dance that touches, at once, readers' hearts and minds. McLaren's [*Che Guevara, Paulo Freire and the Pedagogy of Revolution*] is ... one of the most important books on critical education, and thus also education and social justice, to have been written in the twentieth century.

Last but not least, Peter's friend Paulo Freire wrote:

> Peter McLaren is one among the many outstanding "intellectual relatives" I "discovered" and by whom I in turn was "discovered." I read Peter McLaren long before

I ever came to know him personally ... Once I finished reading the first texts by McLaren that were made available to me, I was almost certain that we belonged to an identical "intellectual family." (Freire, 1995, p. x)

Among numerous awards, five books written by Peter have been winners of American Education Studies Association Critics Choice Awards, and his work has been the foundation for several dedicated institutions, including La Fundación McLaren de Pedagogía Crítica and Instituto McLaren de Pedagogía Crítica y Educación Popular in Mexico and La Cátedra Peter McLaren at La Universidad Bolivariana de Venezuela. In 2014, a sixth expanded edition of Peter's award-winning book *Life in Schools: An Introduction to Critical Pedagogy in the Foundations of Education* was published by Paradigm (2014).

Peter is Distinguished Professor in Critical Studies at the College of Educational Studies, Chapman University; Emeritus Professor of Urban Education at the University of California, Los Angeles; Emeritus Professor of Educational Leadership at Miami University of Ohio and Honorary Director of The Center for Critical Pedagogy Research at Northeast Normal University in China, where he also holds the position of Honorary Chair Professor. He has published forty-five books and hundreds of scholarly articles and chapters that have been translated into more than twenty languages, and his name has slowly but surely become almost synonymous with the contemporary project of critical education. Peter's academic work is blended with political activism. As he lectures all around the world and actively participates in various political struggles, Peter passionately lives theory and practice of revolutionary critical pedagogy.

In this chapter, Petar Mclaren discusses his ideas about the relationships between critical education and information and communication technologies with Petar Jandrić. Petar is an educator, researcher and activist. He has authored four books and various scholarly articles, book chapters and popular articles. Petar's work has been published in Croatian, English, Serbian, Spanish and Ukrainian. His current research interests are situated at the postdisciplinary intersections between technologies, pedagogies and society, and his ongoing projects are oriented towards collaborative research and editing. Petar worked at the Croatian Academic and Research Network, the University of Edinburgh, Glasgow School of Art and the University of East London. Currently, we works as Professor in e-Learning and Director of BSc (Informatics) programme at the University of Applied Sciences in Zagreb (Croatia), visiting Associate Professor at the University of Zagreb (Croatia), Professor and Director of Institute for Research and Knowledge Advancement at the Global Center for Advanced Studies (Michigan, US).

Petar Jandrić: Peter, thank you a lot for agreeing to this conversation. Please allow me to start with a brief overview of theoretical foundations. Your early work has been strongly influenced by postmodernism. For more than a decade, however, it has slowly but surely entered "the Marxist-humanist trajectory" spanning from authors with various Marxist tendencies and the neo-Marxism of the Frankfurt School to the original works of Marx (McLaren, McMurry, & McGuirk, 2008). The shift from postmodern Peter to Marxist Peter has been elaborated fairly extensively—for instance, in conversations with Marcia Moraes and Glenn Rikowski published in *Rage and Hope* (McLaren, 2006). Could you please summarize it in a few sentences?

Peter McLaren: As early as the 1980s, I was asking myself: How do we react to the cries of help from the youth of today, whose full-throated screams meet the immemorial silence of the pedagogical tradition? An answer to this question mandated a move away from the ironic distantiation and self-indulgent detachment of the vulgar divas of the academy who clearly chose identity politics over class politics (and in so doing became complicitous in the very relations of inequality they officially rejected) by a close reading of Marx and Marxist theorists, culminating with engaging the work of Marxist educators.

PJ: Departing from the Frankfurt School of Social Science, contemporary critical theories of technologies have developed in various directions (including, but not limited to, the elusive fields of postmodernism), and ended up quite far from their Marxist roots: nowadays, they seem stuck at the place which you left more than a decade ago. Could you please elaborate your return to Marxism as a theoretical base for reinvention of critical education in the context of information and communication technologies?

PM: Well, I began with an autonomous Marxist focus—the self-activity of the working class—and I was initially drawn to the work of important thinkers such as Antonio Negri, Michael Hardt, Raniero Panzieri, Mario Tronti, Sergio Bologna, Mariarosa Dalla Costa, Francois Berardi and others, although I didn't explicitly deal with their work in my writings on education. I moved towards an appreciation of more classical Marxist critiques, the work of Mas'ud Zavarzadeh and Teresa Ebert, for instance, then I became interested in the Marxist humanism of Peter Hudis, Kevin Anderson and Raya Dunayevskaya, and of course the work of British educators Paula All-man, Mike Cole, Dave Hill and Glenn Rikowski. So I began with an interest in what has been described as a new era of capitalist development that was variously described under the terms "post-industrialism," "post-Fordism" or "postmodern capitalism."

Here the emphasis was on information age capitalism via information technologies—computers and telecommunications—used by capital to cre-ate capital mobility across national boundaries and eventually the national security state of widespread societal surveillance. Even though my many vis-its to Latin America convinced me that we have not in any way left the smokestack era of factory production, I became interested in the various ways that capital has penetrated the entire society by means of technological and political instruments in order to generate a higher level of productivity and in order to monitor and reconstitute its response to the self-organization of the working class through these new technologies. Of course, innovations in the context of knowledge production and communication in the new information society do not merely serve as instruments of capitalist domi-nation but can be employed in creating alternative and oppositional move-ments in the larger project of transforming capitalist society into a socialist alternative.

PJ: There has been a lot of water under the bridge since Marx developed his theories. Could you briefly address some contemporary challenges to his dia-lectical thought?

PM: I am critical of autonomous Marxists such as Hardt and Negri who, in books such as *Empire* (2001), argue that the multitude, who have amassed the necessary "general intellect," are now in place as a web of resistance to capitalism—and they have done so simply by refusing to reproduce capitalism, without any unifying philosophy of praxis.

Here we see, as with Habermas, a rejection of all forms of radical tran-scendence and a refusal to conceptualize dialectically an alternative to capi-talism. As Anderson (2010) notes, doing so inspires a fear of utopianism, or worse, authoritarianism and colonial hubris. For Habermas, Hardt, Negri and Holloway, there appears to be a fear of the Promethean side of Marx's human-ism that, Anderson notes, points towards transcendence of the given. Thus, in the case of Habermas, we return to a reformist liberalism, and Hardt and Negri are moving towards a poststructuralist radicalism.

The solution, as Anderson proposes, is to "stare negativity in the face" (to cite Hegel), and work within a variegated dialectic that takes into consideration race and ethnicity, gender, sexuality and youth. We cannot just refuse to take state power, as John Holloway and others recommend, since the state with its pernicious logic of domination will continue to exist until we have created a new social order, one that consists of freely associated labor on a world scale.

The Neighborhood Has Just Become More Interesting

PJ: Nowadays, concepts such as "post-industrialism," "post-Fordism," "postmodern capitalism" and "information society" are often merged into an over-arching concept described in works such as Manuel Castells's (2001) *The Internet Galaxy*, and Jan van Dijk's (1999) *The Network Society*. One of the main differences between the industrial society and the network society lies in the structure of production: the first is predominantly based on production of physical artifacts, while the latter is predominantly based on production of knowledge. This brings us to the notion of knowledge economy, where hordes of information workers produce added value from juggling invisible and intangible bits and bytes. Certainly, it is hard to deny that you and I, teachers at universities from two different continents, have chased tiny immaterial lights on our screens in order to produce tangible value in the form of this printed interview. And we are not exceptions—as contemporary industry mercilessly reduces its workforce, virtuality is faced with a flood of "immigrants" who exchange production of physical artifacts for production of concepts and ideas.

Certainly, those trends are closely linked with historically embedded and economically entrenched social relationships. Theoretically, virtual immigrants have more chance of obtaining decent online jobs than clandestine immigrants from North Africa on the isle of Lampedusa—at least they are legal. However, making money online is still a rare privilege of a small bunch of your neighbours in Silicon Valley, or a socially and economically conceived exception that merely confirms the stereotypical image of a poor immigrant (Guy Standing explores this in depth in his excellent books, *The Precariat* [2011] and *A Precariat Charter: From Denizens to Citizens* [2014]).

On the one hand, Peter, we are obviously faced with dematerialization of economic activities. On the other hand, however, production of artifacts has no other choice but to closely follow the rise of worldwide population and its numerous lifestyles—as you previously said, "We have not in any way left the smokestack era of factory production." Obviously, those trends are closely related to issues of education and class. On that basis, Peter, could you please analyse the main contemporary changes in the structure of production?

PM: The knowledge society is premised on communication, on dialogue, on creating knowledge for the well-being of humanity. The knowledge economy, on the other hand, is interested in appropriating communication technology for the purpose of producing information that can be centralized, monitored and controlled partially through the systematic deskilling of workers. In fact, the knowledge-based economy is really an illusion. When we can eliminate underemployment, then perhaps that term will have some real salience. We already have a highly educated workforce with plenty of skills. What we need is a massive redistribution of wealth in the form of more jobs. So let's not be misled by all this talk about immaterial labor. Social exchanges are not equal, immaterial labor is not free of capital. Computers have not made us free and independent producers. Why are we even cooperating with generating high-caliber human capital to corporations?

Glenn Rikowski recently put it thus: "To become capital or to humanize our souls" (McLaren & Rikowski, 2000). I'd like to summarize some important points here made by Rikowski (McLaren & Rikowski, 2000). Human capital, as Marx pointed out, has become a condition of life in capitalist societies. The human is a form of capital and capital is a form of human life. While it is believed that competitive advantage comes from knowledge and innovation, knowledge workers are being exported all over the globe just like manual workers. The knowledge economy geared to employers' needs has narrowed the aims of education by marginalizing critical inquiry and skills. In fact, Rikowski goes so far as to note that education and training are actually a part of the knowledge economy, as higher education students from overseas bring in huge export earnings.

Capital, as Rikowski describes it, is a form of social energy, and is not self-generating. It depends upon our labor power which creates surplus value and then various forms of capital develop from this surplus value. Labor power produces immaterial as well as material commodities. Labor power is the most explosive commodity on the world market today, Rikowski points out, and education and training set limits upon the social production of labor powers, preventing the development of those powers that can break the chains imposed by the value form of labor. In order to change ourselves, to reinvent ourselves, to decolonize our subjectivities forged in the crucible of capitalism, we need to transform the social relations that sustain our capitalized life form.

PJ: Jan van Dijk juxtaposes *The Network Society* with its predecessor *The Mass Society* and links them with characteristics of the supporting media. Pre-digital media of the mass society, such as radio and television, support one-way communication between centers of power and peripheries: the chosen few perform and talk, while the rest of the population watches and listens. In contrast, the network society is associated with multi-directional digital social and media networks and "individuals, households, groups and organizations linked by these networks" (van Dijk, 1999, p. 24). Using the lingo of information sciences, technologies of mass society enable one-to-many communication while technologies of the network society provide many-to-many communication.

Another important difference between the two generations of technologies lies in their scope. Back in the 1980s, my parents' home was packed with many different one-purpose devices: radio, television, cassette player, vinyl record player, Walkman, telephone, photo camera, video camera ... and many of the devices could be found in multiples. Technologies of the mass society maintain firm borders between various media—cassettes cannot be reproduced on a TV set, and a Walkman cannot play vinyl records. They were made to last—as can easily be seen from the example of the audiophile scene, once you entered the world of vinyl records, you were stuck there for years and decades.

Technologies of the network society, on the contrary, are conceptually universal. The computer is "a medium of the most general nature" (Carr, 2011). Any form of analog information can be digitalized, processed and delivered in essentially the same way and using the same chip-set. In spite of the apparent diversity of things that can be done by computers, information and communication technologies have brought the great unification of human activities—contemporary work, communication and entertainment are all done using exactly the same hardware powered by different software. The mass society had been based on many technologies designed for specific and limited purposes, while the network society is based on adaptations of one technology for many different purposes. This is a mere outline of this complex topic—more about differences between various generations of media can be found in the very important book, *The Shallows: What the Internet Is Doing to Our Brains*, written by Nicholas Carr (2011).

There is something general about all technologies—despite obvious novelties contained in each generation of media, their dialectical relationships with the society are deeply historical and embedded in human nature. Therefore, I find van Dijk's juxtaposition between technologies of the mass society and technologies of the network society very important and suggest that we should kick off the discussion about digital media of today by analyzing their most influential analog predecessor—television.

PM: I have always appreciated the work of Joyce Nelson, especially her book, *The Perfect Machine* (1991), which reveals the ideological collusion between the television industry and the nuclear state in their quest for the perfect technological imperative: efficiency. Nelson undresses the relationship between the advance of television and defense contractors and the arms industries such as General Electric, DuPont and Westinghouse. I grew up in the 1950s, and we were one of the first families to own a TV because my dad started selling TVs when he returned from fighting the Nazis after World War II. Little did my father know that he was peddling the technological unconscious of our culture—a technological unconscious rooted in the nuclear unconscious.

Television is the eye of our unconscious, like the Eye of Sauron in *The Lord of the Rings* (Tolkien, 2012)—it colonizes our subjectivity, works through our organs of irrationality. It replaces the messy flesh of our bodies (which we secretly wish to discard) with the flesh of our dreams—it remakes us by re-valorizing the masculine self of conquest and control and allows us to live what is unmanageable and uncontrollable outside our heads inside our heads where we can stage-manage reality. We look to technology as we would to religion, for our salvation. It is the mirror in which we hope to find our perfection reflected back at us through our acquisition of universal knowledge, knowledge lost when we were supposedly thrown out of the Garden of Eden by God. David Noble has written on this theme with considerable insight and aplomb (see, for instance, his book *Digital Diploma Mills* [2001]).

PM: We can see the advent of television as giving birth to an ideological instrument connected intimately to human brain function, more specifically to the depression of the function of the frontal lobe. The frontal lobe organizes, plans and sequences our behavior. It is fundamental for making moral judgments, for making discriminating assessments about what we see. We know, for instance, that computer games can cause a decrease in activity in the frontal lobes by overstimulating parts of the brain associated with movement and vision. The work of Marie Winn (2002) has been helpful in addressing the effect on the brain of viewers engaged in the new media landscape. There is the whole question of TV ownership and viewing times of children correlating with a decline in students' SAT tests.

Winn has drawn our attention to extensive television viewing and the effects on young children's verbal development (as distinct from the development of their visual or spatial abilities) and reading scores. Research into the negative effects of TV watching on academic achievement is quite compelling. There is some evidence to suggest that visual and auditory output actually damages the child's developing brain. According to some brain researchers, when we watch TV, our brain actually shuts off and we are neurologically less able to make judgments about what we see and hear on the screen. I am thinking of Dr. Aric Sigman's work (2007) here on how television creates more separation between thought and emotion, and actually serves to enhance behavioral conformity—TV then becomes a great medium of social control and social engineering. It's a perfect instrument for advertisers, it's capitalism's wet-dream machine. As long as you can prevent the fibers connecting the neurons in the frontal lobe from thickening through TV watching, you can create an entire generation of hive dwellers, with little self-control, ready to be manipulated by television gurus and the propaganda machines of which they are a part.

One of my professors at the Ontario Institute for Studies in Education, Dr. Fred Rainsberry, who had a special interest in communication theory and curriculum development and was part of the Royal Commission on Violence in the Communications Industry, said that I should be working with Marshall McLuhan as part of my doctoral research, but the year I entered the program, in 1979, McLuhan suffered a stroke. I developed a children's television pilot, called *Kidding Around*, for the fledgling multilingual television station in Toronto at that time. The idea was to visit a different ethnic part of the city each week and interview regular folks and get a sense of their life. We couldn't find any sponsors and the show never got past the pilot.

PJ: Could you link these pre-digital insights to contemporary information and communication technologies?

PM: As David Harvey (1990) and others have pointed out, computerization creates a compression of time/space through an acceleration of capital accumulation, where accelerated turnover time in the process of capital accumulation and speedups in exchange and consumption help to produce superficial consumer needs though mass media (i.e., television advertising and the production of spectacles). We see ourselves as agents of change through these superficial commodities, which fester in our neoliberal bowels and are rapidly expelled in an uninterrupted peristaltic flow to make room for more superficial commodities.

Rather than producing durable goods and infrastructure for the public good, we are prone to the production of desire which replaces those very critical systems of intelligibility that could help us gain some critical purchase on what is happening to us. We become activists for types of cultural change that are dependent upon the very corporations that we rail against instead of agents for economic transformation that will produce the products and infrastructure necessary to help populations meet their needs rather than their digitally and electronically produced subjectivities—bodies without organs—that are nothing but what Alan Watts used to describe in the 1960s as "bags of skin" (1966). We retreat into a politics of immanence while thirsting for a politics of transcendence. But a politics of transcendence would mean we would have to give up the security of our embeddedness in the very corporate commodity culture we supposedly are fighting against.

According to this logic of commodification, revolutionaries are really just conformists, conforming to the desires of other revolutionaries, and it's better to become a conservative who seeks and finds pleasure in life than a humorless activist who suffers but makes some progress in creating a more just and equitable world. You are conditioned to think that a new cosmetic is as important as the crisis in Ukraine. They are featured in the media as commensurate. The greatest transcendent revolutionary was Jesus Christ. With Jesus, all commodities are relativized and re-contextualized and viewed in relation to the anti-Kingdom. The logic of commodification is not part of the word made flesh although in the anti-Kingdom Jesus functions as just another commodity.

Technological advances are functionally integrating us to the ideological circuits and global imperatives of the transnational capitalist class, prompting us to perform our identities according to the hidden transcript of the neoliberal agenda: to create consumer citizens through a comprador class cyber-citizenry who serve as sentinels that ensure the promulgation of a colonial mentality.

In this way, information technology serves to fire up the cauldron of domestic and political repression, to support the structural violence of capitalism, and to habituate us into the service of empire. No longer do we need to fear being press-ganged into the service of the empire; we have become ideological products of our own manufactured internal restraint, thanks to the technological advances that we all have come to "enjoy." We are all Julian Assange, lecturing through encryption devices from the balcony of the Ecuadorian embassy in London. We are all Edward Snowden, sitting in a Russian hotel room with his cell phone tucked away in a refrigerator freezer.

PJ: In the network society, many occupations have undergone significant transformations—and the mass media have obviously been hit harder than the rest of us (Bird, 2009). Could you please look back and analyze the main developments in mass media during the past few decades? What happens to traditional press in the age of the network?

PM: Journalism used to be a way of citizens holding people in power accountable for their actions—and the storied Upton Sinclair is often cited as the prototypical muckraker. But those journalists are few and far between and their careers in the corporate media rarely last very long. As Sonali Kolhatkar (2014) has noted recently in a conversation with Glenn Greenwald, the mainstream media engage in attack pieces on people like Greenwald and Snowden in ways they would never treat members of Congress. Greenwald and Snowden have become prominent examples of Orwell's "thought criminals" (1949) and the public has been conditioned to view them as traitors to the U.S.

I have long been of the opinion that Orwell's *1984* has been upon us for some time. At least since 2001, when the press became the echo chamber for the Bush administration in its heinous call for war in Iraq. When the U.S. started to believe its own mythology as the world's eternally invincible superpower, incapable of decline, then *1984* was constructed out of the debris of the dead and fallen corpses of American jihad. When the U.S. came to believe and act upon the notion that it could reshape the world, however it chose, through the wrath of the greatest military force in history, then we were all doomed in this country as the green light was given to the NSA and to corporations to act with the same rights as "religious people," and the government was cleared to hasten our extinction through policies that greatly enhance climate change, war, debt peonage that turns workers into wage slaves of the transnational capitalist class, and ecocide.

It is a marker of the sophistication of the U.S. media apparatus that many Americans still believe that they live in a country that exercises the freedom of the press. The press is free, of course. It is free to pursue the objectives and interests of the corporations that own the media outlets.

Even when there is a chance for reporters to investigate a story, other corporations jump into the act using bribery or whatever means available to purchase the silence of potential informants. Recently, for instance, a small town in Ottawa, Canada, will reportedly be receiving $28,200 from energy company Trans-Canada Corporation in exchange for keeping silent about the company's proposed Energy East tar sands pipeline project for five years. TransCanada has agreed to give Mattawa $28,200, so that town can purchase a rescue truck. You now can rescue a body in danger but you have put your humanity in mortal danger. The Energy East pipeline proposal has the potential to generate three greenhouse gas emissions each year; that is the equivalent of adding more than 7 million cars to the roads (Atkin, 2014).

Digital Cultures

PJ: I would like to point to the work done by Ivan Illich. From *Deschooling Society* (1971) through *Tools for Conviviality* (1973) to *Medical Nemesis* (1982), Illich offered many innovative insights and strategies for decolonialization of the complex web of relationships between technologies, cultures, education and ecology. Therefore, Peter, what are the most important lessons we can take from Illich?

PM: While Illich's idea of deschooling is obviously based on a utopian image of human beings (an in-depth critique of Illich's educational ideas in the context of the contemporary Internet can be found in the book called *Wikiworld* [2010], co-authored by Juha Suoranta and Tere Vaden), his lasting legacy lies in his profound analyses of the relationships between the human race and its environment. Barry Sanders, co-author with Illich of *ABC: The Alphabetization of the Popular Mind* (Sanders & Illich, 1989), shared the following story about Illich which has been described as follows by Richard Wall:

> At one point during a talk in Maine, in the midst of Ivan describing his mistrust of electronic technology and in particular his terror of email, a young man leapt to his feet and shouted out, "But, Mr. Illich, don't you want to communicate with us?" Ivan immediately shouted back, "No. I have absolutely no desire to communicate with you. You may not interact with me, nor do I wish to be downloaded by you. I should

like very much to talk to you, to stare at the tip of your nose, to embrace you. But to communicate—for that I have no desire." (Sanders & Illich, 1989)

Illich taught one to be fearless—on stage or in the audience. I would hate any kind of technophobia or dystopian imagination to destroy the fearlessness we need to move forward towards the future.

PJ: For now, we succinctly introduced your critical turn from postmodernism to Marxism and explored the changing modes of production in the network society. In order to systematize our thoughts, we approached those issues in neat sequence, one by one—but their real nature is anything but neat and sequential. Scientific discourses do not separate social phenomena because of their nature, but because isolated problems represent small(er) chunks of our reality that are much easier to comprehend for average human beings. However, the dialectic nature of our reality always finds its way to the surface. In the field of research methodologies, it is reflected in the need to explore the relationships between technologies and society using various interdisciplinary, transdisciplinary and even anti-disciplinary approaches (Jandrić & Boras, 2012). In everyday life, it is probably most notable in overarching, elusive yet unavoidable and inevitable concepts such as *digital cultures* (I am deliberately using plural in order to stress multiplicity of backgrounds, narratives and perspectives). What are the main features of the emerging digital cultures? What are their underlying values and ideologies? Paraphrasing Freire (2000), how do they relate to our reading of the word and our reading of the world?

PM: C. A. Bowers and I have had some spirited if not downright acrimonious debates over the decades, especially in relation to the work of Paulo Freire. At the same time I want to acknowledge the importance of some of his lucid observations about digital cultures (Bowers, 2014). First, it is absolutely essential that we understand the metaphorical nature of language, and that intelligence is not limited to what can be explained by scientific study of the neuro-networks of the human brain. Consciousness, as Gregory Bateson acknowledges, along with Bowers, includes the pathways of all unconscious mentation which includes those pathways that are automatic and repressed, neural and hormonal. Print-based cultural storage and thinking, which is relied upon by developers of technology, is not rationally based and objective but in fact impedes awareness of what is being communicated through the multiple pathways that differ from culture to culture.

Bowers is right about this, and he worries that computer technology and the digitalized mismeasure of man will offer us a truncated notion of ecological intelligence. Computer technicians and scientists working on artificial intelligence sanctify data and information grounded in print-based cultural storage and thinking, and this reinforces surface knowledge, ignores tacit knowledge, presents a false sense of objectivity and ultimately misrepresents the relational and emergent information-intense pathways of both cultural and natural ecologies. Bowers is very convincing here. Digital communication reproduces the misconceptions encoded in the metaphorically layered language that is often taken for granted by digital technicians.

Computer scientists are using a languaging process based on print literacy that reproduces the myths and deep cultural assumptions that influence thinking and awareness—what is being championed are the myths of individualism and progress and what is being silenced is the need to conserve the cultural commons of non-Western cultures that are able to provide largely non-monetized systems of mutual support that rely less on exploiting the planet's natural resources. I agree with Bowers's prescient understanding that you can't reduce culture, cultural knowledge systems and cultural ways of knowing to data and information—especially given the reliance of computer scientists on print, and given the fact that there exist 6,000 languages in the world. Words are metaphors whose meanings are framed, as Bowers explains, by the analogs settled upon in previous eras. What craft knowledge and indigenous wisdom traditions have been lost and replaced by Western corporate vocabularies of profits, efficiency and competition?

There are linguistic and cultural differences that cannot be captured by artificial intelligence. We can't capture what lies beyond the surface of the interplay of individual/cultural/linguistic ecologies. Here we should listen carefully to Bowers's criticism of the root metaphors of Western knowledge systems and the effects they have on the colonization of the life worlds of other cultural groups.

The digital revolution has encoded dangerous assumptions about endless growth, individualism and the deepening of the ecological crisis. Ecologically sustainable traditions need to be intergenerationally renewed. The traditions of civil liberties of the complex and non-monetized traditions of the cultural commons that are still viable within Western cultures must be preserved and the cultural commons of non-Western cultures that do not rely on the exploitation of natural resources need to be intergenerationally renewed. Computer technology is contributing to the ecological crisis as super-intelligent computers still rely on print-based cultural storage whose cultural assumptions have been shaped by root metaphors of Western ideas of progress and individualism. We need an earth-centered ecological intelligence. Critical pedagogy can join in such an effort.

PJ: Obviously, technologies have positive and negative impacts on our everyday lives and the society at large. Before moving on to its positive aspects, could you please briefly examine the dark side of technology?

PM: Erica Etelson has recently published a wonderful short piece on the perils of technology that I like very much, perils that include economic crisis, war, pandemic disease, and ecological collapse. While clearly technology has helped to sustain seven billion people on our planet, it is unlikely to be able to do so for much longer, even with anticipated innovations. Her point, of course, is that "modern communication technologies may have reached a tipping point where what is authentically created and shared is overshadowed by market-driven, corporate-generated content that is sold or imposed" (2014). I think by her definition I might be considered a neo-Luddite—a tradesman or artisan engaged in class protest against "all Machinery hurtful to Commonality"—or what Etelson (2014) describes as "forms of mechanization that damaged people and uprooted communities by forcing skilled workers to become wage slaves in factories."

Firstly, she argues forcefully that technology makes us less resilient, as we are "utterly dependent on the seamless functioning of a fabulously complex global superstructure with millions of impersonal moving parts, none of which most of us have even passing acquaintance with." To illustrate that point, she cites the history of the Arctic Ihalmiut who lost the ability to hunt with bow and arrow after they acquired rifles.

Secondly, she also notes that as techno-literacy expands, eco-literacy contracts. The more tech-savvy we become, the more eco-ignorant we become, as we now know more and more about less and less. Etelson also argues that environmental degradation created by technology spawns hubris, as we prefer our techno-nannies to care for us over human community and solidarity. She argues that technology fuels hyper-consumption, as products become cheaper and it diverts our focus "from natural to human-made wonders."

Thirdly, Etelson argues that "the wicked knot of inertia, corruption and hubris" in which we are inextricably trapped, which is part and parcel of our "techno-topian delusion" accelerates environmental ruin, resource depletion, and resource wars. We are on the cusp of the sixth mass extinction. Our non-renewable resources are being depleted, atmospheric carbon is at the tipping point, and renewable resources like forests, aquifers, and fisheries are being stripped faster than they are being regenerated. World conflicts now center around natural gas, water, oil, minerals, metals, and food.

Fourthly, she argues that technology carries very frightening risks. We can't presume products are safe until proven harmful. Etelson uses the example of cell phones and Wi-Fi, widely adopted despite 75% of non-industry sponsored studies that claim that cell phones damage our DNA. Brain cancer in children has increased 1% a year for the past 20 years.

If the cleaning up of Fukushima goes amiss (this kind of cleanup has never occurred before), the entire West Coast of the USA might have to be evacuated, not to mention what will happen in Japan itself. And then there is hydrofracking and the endless contamination of our water sources.

Fifthly, Etelson argues that technology often diminishes rather than enriches our quality of life. We turn to machines rather than to people. Etelson's sixth point is that technology erodes our privacy—do we need to go further here than the revelations of Julian Assange and Edward Snowden? Seventh, technology deepens inequality.

Within the U.S., manufacturing worker productivity has increased more than eightfold since 1947, thanks to robotics, etc. But we haven't seen higher wages for workers. Or shorter working hours. Corporations own 46% of global wealth. Even if we had a democratic socialist utopia, Etelson argues that too much productivity—even if the profits were shared more equitably—would lead to more pollution. Technology-induced unemployment is a serious problem. It would take five planet earths to enable everyone to have the same standard of living that we have in North America. We already have most of the technologies we need to live comfortably and we don't need more unnecessary technologies. Etelson offers some strategies such as stripping corporations of constitutional personhood, replacing the Gross Domestic Product indicator with the Genuine Progress Indicator (which takes stock of the risk factors of technology) and she has some other suggestions, of course. But Petar, the situation is dire, our world is shattering, imploding, and crying out to us to stop!

PJ: Digital cultures (I am deliberately using plural in order to stress multiplicity of backgrounds, narratives and perspectives) have recently acquired a lot of attention from various researchers, such as Sian Bayne, Jeremy Knox, Hamish A. Macleod, Jen Ross, Christine Sinclair and others. During the past several years, they have become an intrinsic part of curricula at various schools and universities—since 2009, there is even a scientific journal called *Digital Culture and Education* (2013). In this mash-up of postmodernist talk about grand narratives, glorifications of technologies, various scepticisms and/or primitivisms, practical inquiry into the ways people use the Internet for this or that purpose, analyses of the relationships between the local and the global, changes in various human activities including but not limited to arts, commerce, government and education, it is easy to forget that digital cultures are strongly linked to their non-digital background—particularly regarding power relationships. Based on your extensive international experience, particularly in the Americas, can you link digital cultures with the distinctions between the global South and the global North, with globalization of capitalism and the archetypes of identity?

PM: It's very easy to be distracted by the digital world and culture while you are building a personal identity created in a digital context. It is clear how individuals want to be represented in that world, and some prefer to live in that world than engage in the real world. Recently I returned from teaching a course in popular education and critical pedagogy in Mexico, where we discussed the negative impact of *narcocorridos*—songs that romanticize the Mexican drug cartels such as the Sinaloa Cartel, the Gulf Cartel, the Juárez Cartel, the Knights Templar Cartel (formerly La Familia Michoacana, who attacked the city of Morelia in 2011 while I was giving a speech there), the Tijuana Cartel, Los Zetas, Los Viagras, Jalisco New Generation, Independent Cartel of Acapulco and La Barredora—on youth. It is part of a movement around music that developed in Culiacán but is now a major commercial business venture in Los Angeles called *El Movimiento Alterado*.

Here are the words to an outlaw ballad in the Norteno musical style, sung by Alfredo Rios, or "El Komander," a song about a notorious drug kingpin.

> We take care of El Mayo
> Here no one betrays him ...
> We stay tough with AK-47s and bazookas at the neck
> Chopping heads off as they come
> We're blood-thirsty crazy men
> Who like to kill.

The songs glamorize torture, murder and decapitations. This particular song glorifies the Sinaloa cartel and its bosses, Ismael "El Mayo" Zambada and Joaquin "El Chapo" Guzman, and praises Manuel Torres, allegedly a top hit man for Zambada. At the end of 2011, the song had been downloaded 5 million times, and the accompanying video had been downloaded 13 million times (*USA Today*, 2011).

Banned on radio stations in parts of Mexico, *narcocorridos* are everywhere on the Internet. Twin brothers based in Burbank, California, developed the *El Alterado* culture, which admires the Sinaloa Cartel for their violent, murderous lifestyle. They won a Grammy award in 2008 for creating a singer who goes by the name of "El Chapo de Sinaloa." Drug trafficking and torture are being made socially acceptable. There have been roughly 40,000 drug war deaths since ex-Mexican President Felipe de Jesús Calderón Hinojosa of Partido Acción Nacional launched a major offensive on cartels when he took office in 2006 (followed in 2012 by the new president, Enrique Peña Nieto of Partido Revolucionario Institucional).

One of my doctoral students from Mexicali (home to the infamous maquiladora factories run by such corporations as as Honeywell, Kellogg's, Gulfstream Coca-Cola, Autoline, and Nestlé) presented on *El Movimiento Alterado*. He interviewed a number of his 12-year-old students in Mexicali about why they loved to listen to the narcocorridos. Their answers were chillingly very similar:

> Because we love violence.
> We want to be able to torture people.
> We want to grow up so we can kill people.

There is an entire Internet culture created by techno-experts from countries all over the world that celebrate violence. There are video games where you can rape women, you can kill effortlessly, where you can turn yourself into a super hero. So what is the appeal? Are you retreating into your unconscious and connecting with all the frustrations you feel about being just an ordinary bloke in real life? Will you be more prone to act violently to solve problems you might have in real life? To counter this music, we played political protest music, some very contemporary, such as that from Calle 13, a Puerto Rican band formed by two brothers, René Pérez Joglar, who goes by the name "Residente," and Eduardo José Cabra Martínez, who calls himself "Visitante," and their half-sister Ileana Cabra Joglar, aka "PG-13."

Anyway, I returned from Mexico and was walking around the train station and suddenly I was surrounded by superheros—Batman, Robin, Superman, the Flash, Wonder Woman, Wolverine, Zombies—as the city was hosting a comic book convention and what is called a "nerd prom." So I was thinking, where are the energies of these teens and young adults going? Do they think that by clicking on "Like" in their Facebook exchanges they are participating in a revolution?

The contrast between the discussions and work being done in Mexico and the invasion of the nerds in San Diego was striking. In Mexico, Internet culture based in Los Angeles was normalizing drug trafficking and brutal violence, while across the border in Gringolandia everybody was focused on the world of their superheroes. Capitalist consumer culture hijacks the archetypes of identity—and none of them is fighting capitalism. They might be fighting corrupt capitalists, but not capitalism as a system, as a structure of feeling, as social sin.

Critical Technological Consciousness for a New Humanity

PJ: Speaking of youth, Peter, we definitely should not take their ideas lightly—historically, youth movements have always been important agents of social change. Certain aspects of their struggle can be attributed to the universal clash of generations, while others might have some real potential to bring radical social transformations. In order to make a clear distinction between the eternal and the contemporary, between the basic human need to struggle against authority and the really important argument regarding the future of our society, between the battle to overtake positions of power and the principled struggle against positions of power, between the desperate fight against worldwide tyrants such as Saddam Hussein and the struggle for a better/more just/more democratic society, between genuine political change and mere replacement of one political mannequin with another, between real social development and digital Potemkin's villages, could you pinpoint some distinct features of contemporary youth movements which emerge from the context of the network society?

PM: Youth today are taking forms of insurgency from the past and grafting onto these forms new types of revolutionary praxis. In the plant-grafting process, when the vascular cambium tissues of the rootstock and scion plants have been successfully inosculated, the stem of the stock is pruned just above the newly grafted bud. But the joints formed as a result of the grafting process are not as strong as naturally formed joints. Social movements that have recognized their weak links with the past are not attempting to begin again from the beginning (as this is a constitutive impossibility), but are utilizing technological innovations never before imagined in the history of social movements to re-figure the ways in which student protest can be organized to resist the co-optation of the world capitalist aristocracy and to provide new networking potentialities for increasing the pressure on the sentinels of the transnational capitalist class.

Will you permit me another biological analogy? I have a pretty standard understanding of capitalism from a Marxist perspective. But I also like to think of capitalism as teletropic—and by that I am referring to psychotropic mechanisms that affect the body states—such as mood changes—of other people. Among other things, capitalism alienates and exploits workers dependent upon their labor power to make a wage and survive, but then also produces the mechanisms necessary to make those exploited populations feel better (or at least numb them emotionally) about being exploited—for instance, by making them feel good about being white people, or at least having a job, or supporting a winning sports team, or having the opportunity to win big with the lottery. And this lets the capitalist system reproduce itself relatively unimpeded by the very people that it is exploiting. Let me explain further what I mean.

Daniel Smail (2008) writes about teletropy in the world of biology. The Ichneumon wasp feeds within the living body of a host. It targets caterpillars and pupas, and the wasp eggs are injected through the ovipositor of the wasp which paralyzes the caterpillar. So we are a bit like the hosts, paralyzed into hatching the eggs of parasitic capitalism and reproducing the cycle.

But there is even a better example. Smail talks about certain parasites that exist in sheep pastures called the lancer liver fluke. This parasite spends part of its life cycle in the stomach of ants. Approximately fifty to a hundred free swimming larvae of this parasite, called cercariae, pass from the ant to a vertebrate host such as sheep or cattle. More specifically, the adult trematode or lancet fluke, lives in the gall bladder and bile ducts of their hosts. Their eggs (miracidia) are passed in the feces of the final host which are then swallowed by terrestrial snails.

The snails serve as the primary intermediate hosts, where the miracidia develop into cercariae within 3–4 months. The cercariae are excreted by the infected snails in the form of "mucus balls." These mucus balls are a source of moisture for the ants who ingest them. Then the cercariae bore holes into the esophagus of the ant and then miraculously close the holes with a special material so the ant doesn't die (if the ant dies the liver fluke is no more). The cercariae end up in the posterior part of the body of the ant, where they transform into metacercariae. One of the metacercariae encysts in the brain of the ant, which alters the behavior of the ant, producing a zombie-like state. The ant behaves normally during the day but instead of returning to its mound between dusk and dawn when the daytime temperature falls, the "brainwashed" ant does something unusual as a result of the chemical change in its brain—as if sleepwalking or under the influence of a zombie master, it climbs a blade of grass and clings there by its mandibular muscles, so that it is in an ideal position to be consumed by a grazing herbivorous animal—a sheep or a cow, in this instance.

Once the ant is ingested, the metacercariae excyst in the duodenum before entering blood vessels and traveling up the common bile duct to the capillaries of the liver. Boring through the walls of the capillaries they migrate to the bile duct in the liver and soak up nutrients from the sheep or the cow, which is the main host of the parasite. In the intestinal tract of their mammalian host, metacercariae develop into young flukes, where, in the liver of the sheep, the flukes produce eggs and complete their complex life cycle. That is the entire purpose of the lancer liver fluke, to make it from the ground, into a mucus ball of a snail to the stomach of a sheep or cow!

PJ: What an impressive journey… What does it tell us about the relationships between digital media and human beings?

PM: I see the mass media as a similar type of parasite that has both intermediate and final hosts. When we use technology we are the snails forming the mucus balls, watching television or spending time on the Internet using our smart phones or computers, we are the mucus balls being consumed by the ants, and by occupying ourselves in mundane activities instead of developing critical consciousness and actively resisting our exploitation we are becoming injected with the ideology of the dominant class through sound bytes, symbols, signs, images, and the like and are scrambling up the blades of grass and hanging by our mandibles; and once we are eaten by the sheep, we become just like the sheep—serving as hosts to reproduce the life cycle of capitalist exploitation.

Yet we fail to interrupt this cycle because the parasitic nature of capitalism is to make our exploitation pleasurable; it alters our mood much like a drug injected into our brains, or a parasite encysting in our ganglia. We take courses in university to become media literate, so that we do not become paralyzed by the thrall of the images that captivate us through carnal stimulation, yet this only makes us more vulnerable because we think our criticality immunizes us against ideological indoctrination, but it doesn't.

We teach about the dangers from the mass media to our students and then in the privacy of our homes or offices, out of sight of the students, we give ourselves a fix. After researching Walter Benjamin, we take a break and watch a Rambo film, or snicker at the bad plastic surgery jobs of the Orange County Housewives that we find in some random link on the Internet.

So I'm interested in how capitalism creates consent through mechanisms such as spectacles, television viewing, computer technology, etc., and altering our moods in various and sundry ways. I also wonder if we humans are planetary parasites that infect the earth, depleting the earth's natural resources and causing all kinds of diseases in our mother earth through our desire to find ways to enable us to cope in an ecologically devastated world that we have created.

PJ: Can you apply this fascinating analogy to the context of youth movements?

PM: Well, of course, I tend to think by analogy, and perhaps this analogy isn't perfect, but it gets some points across. We know, for instance, that ants and wasps serve useful purposes, as ants affect the level of nutrients in the soil by collecting food and building their nests; and we know that wasps help in pollination, etc. So I want you to know that I'm not against ants, snails, or wasps—or sheep for that matter! My interest is how youth movements can benefit from technology, but I fear the cure might be as bad as the disease.

The new youth movements have revealed that a decline in political activism among youth is not an inevitable fact of capitalist life nor is youth political apathy evidence of a deep normality. However, youth are pulled in sometimes crazed and mostly inconclusive directions. The spectacle of neoliberal capitalism would have us believe that youth protest should be enlivened by constant stimulation of the senses and thus opposed to the course of daily routine of regulation and self-restraint. But protest does not always require youth to shift registers between the everyday and the culture of contestation because contestation can, in fact, be part of everyday praxis, such as in the world of hip-hop culture. Protests can erode our subsequent capacity to endure the strenuous demands of our daily life, which is, of course, a good thing, because they create a space of liminality where youth can cultivate contestation as an art form. Historical necessity does not grant these movements success in advance, nor does divine fiat. This question can only be answered inside the struggles themselves, and in terms of the commitment that youth have to the poor, the powerless, the disfavored and the aggrieved.

Ruling elites who wish to turn greed into an inalienable right are now more fearful than ever that democratic social movements driven by youth who were previously politically unaware might now spawn a revolutionary upsurge among the popular majorities. So they make demands for more democracy for our youth undemocratically by enforcing brutal austerity measures and ratcheting up a permanent war on terrorism.

PJ: What is the role of social media in these processes?

PM: Imagine a grandmother has lost her grandson to lung disease. Her tears are rolling down the precipice of her sunken eyes like a bucketful of pearls. But when she passes the chemical factory responsible for her grandson's death, her tears shoot out of her eyes in great red molten sparks as if spewed from an ancient volcano buried deep in the sea of her grief. She can do little more at the moment than scream in a high-pitched rage that arcs around the smoke-stacks that killed her grandson. But can she do more than cry tears of grief and rage?

She can mount a social media campaign against the factory. She can peti-tion the government. She can become an environmental activist. She can enter the digital world of protest. I am not saying that social media are them-selves ineffectual. But so many protests these days are by digital petition. It takes less than a minute to sign. They give us the feeling that we are doing something, that we are making a difference, that the world is not hopeless, that we can intervene.

My concern is to form a coalition that organizes on the basis of class initia-tive, that cuts across race and ethnicity and sexuality, that directly confronts the rule of capital. Is this even possible in the digital age? Are we predestined for political fragmentation, for single-issue campaigns that bury struggles that are necessarily universal under a micro-politics of single issues antiseptically cleaved from relations of production?

PJ: Talking about social order, we must revisit contemporary transformations of the concept of the state. Sociologists such as Jan van Dijk and Manuel Castells repeatedly assert that global neoliberal capitalism constantly diminishes its role in everyday affairs. At a phenomenological level, it seems commonly accepted that most traditional functions of the state have been transferred to transnational institutions such as the WTO [World Trade Organization] and the IMF [International Monetary Fund], corpo-rations richer than many countries, and with increased individual respon-sibility for issues such as education and health. However, the left side of the political spectrum (McLaren, 2006; Standing, 2011, 2014) constantly emphasizes that the role of the state is as important as ever, and seeks to improve its functioning towards increasing social justice. Which con-cepts of the state are emerging from new social movements? How feasible are they?

PM: Before I answer your question, Petar, I want to make some brief comments on ways in which youth have been challenging the state using organizational approaches influenced by communication technologies. I am drawing here on the work of Todd Wolfson, who has written a great deal on the development of the Cyber Left. There has been much techno-evangelization surrounding the new media technologies and how they have been helpful in organizing social movements against the state, such as during Arab Spring, with the Indignados in Spain, the Zapatistas in Chiapas, and during Occupy Wall Street protests throughout cities in the U.S. I'm thinking specifically here of the famous "May of Facebook" uprisings in Greece in 2011.

I met anarchists and revolutionaries in Thessaloniki some years before the major Greek demonstrations. And later when the demonstrations broke out, I spent some time at Syntagma Square in Athens. I also met with intellectuals and activists in the storied Exarcheia district in downtown Athens, home to the anarchists. As well, I went on several marches in Ankara, Turkey as well as visited Occupy Wall Street in Los Angeles. So with that history, I am very interested in Wolfson's analysis and fundamentally agree with him on the problems with horizontalism, in which power is shared equally and no one is the leader. During the brief time that I observed meetings in Syntagma Square, and interviewed activists who had considerable experience working with Greek protesters, there seemed to be a consensus with whose whom I spoke with that meetings went on ad infinitum, with protestors feeling that too little was accomplished in terms of solidifying the structure and strength of the movement.

In an interview with Peter Handel (2015), Wolfson notes that horizontalism often leads to less formal organizational structures embedded in what Jo Freeman has called a "tyranny of structurelessness." He also reports that a lack of clear structures of accountability and leadership often found in horizontalist movements tend to favor white college-educated men, or people with more social and cultural capital. He writes that "without strong, transparent and accountable organizational structures, institutions have trouble building power over the long haul" (Handel, 2015). Wolfson reports that more successful movements no longer view the media as being a vestige of the movement itself, such as the sword arm of a movement, but view the media more in terms of a nervous system that can connect different features of a movement into a coherent whole. In this way the social media are able to play a more central, constitutive role in leadership development that includes as a priority building community relationships and trust. But Wolfson warns that the new social media cannot be a substitute for a strong movement infrastructure. In other words, an overreliance on technology is not a good thing—community rela-tionships come first. We need a media ecosystem, as Wolfson puts it, placing technology into organic relationship with communities of struggle, communi-ties trying to make important, long term changes.

Now back to your question. Youth resisters who assume the opinion that we live in the information age where we have a knowledge economy of "immaterial labor," where productive capital and the working classes are becoming increasingly irrelevant to social transformation, and that the nation-state is relatively powerless, are likely to adopt a "civil societarian" position (Holst, 2002) and put their faith in new social movements—in the "cognitariat" rather than the "proletariat." Many participants in the youth movements of today view the state as the "social state"—here I shall borrow some terms from Tony Smith (2009)—where symbolic and moral philosophy is the systematic expression of the normative principles of the Keynesian wel-fare state. In other words, it is a version of the state that offers wage labor as the normative principle of modern society.

Some of the more conservative and even liberal-centrist participants in new social movements take a neoliberal state as the norm, which we could call the entrepreneurial state—in which generalized commodity production requires a world market, and they follow Hayek's principle that capital's law of value (1948) in the abstract must be followed. Some of the new social movements look to create a new model of the state which could be called an "activist state" that is based, in large part, on the work of Polanyi (2001), and includes methods of aggressive state intervention into its industrial policy. International capital still predominates in this model, and there will be an inevitable government and global trade dependence on international capital. Of course, those who govern the activist state desire to place government restrictions on its rules and regulations for attracting global investment capi-tal. So there is a concerted attempt to lessen the worst and most exploitative aspects of the state. Then again, you have some left-liberal social movements who prefer the concept of the "cosmopolitan state." This model is largely derived from the work of Habermas (1970), where forms of global market gov-ernance can prevail that are intra-national rather than national; here there is a focus on the development of a global civil society.

Marxist and anarchist movements don't ascribe to any of these models, as it is clear to them that it is impossible to manage democratically wage labor on a global scale by placing severe restrictions on global financial and derivative markets. After all, wage labor only appears to include an equal exchange.

PJ: Being fairly close to anarchist ideas myself, Peter, I am extremely interested in your last claim. Does that mean that Marxism and anarchism have finally overcome the Bakunin–Marx split from the First International? Can we expect reconciliation of the two political philosophies as the theoretical and practical base for creating a massive anti-capitalist front?

PM: As is well known, there are wide variants of anarchism that have been described in the literature under various names, such as individualist anarchism, which rejects all forms of organization; "Black bloc"-style anarchism, which often engages in violent acts; anarcho-syndicalism and libertarian communism, which defend the interests of the working class and become involved in the class struggle; and "primitivist" and green anarchism, which challenge capitalist society or seek to create alternatives to it. Marxists and anarchists both agree on the goal of a stateless society. Some Marxists stridently maintain that a Leninist-style revolutionary party is necessary to rebuild society from its capitalist ashes, a strong collective, organizing force that goes beyond Bakunin's call during the First International for spontaneous organization of the masses.

I was a member of the Industrial Workers of the World, or "Wobblies" but felt that there needed to be a stronger emphasis on creating a philosophically driven praxis of liberation, and I have been drawn to the International Marxist-Humanist Organization (2013), which seeks to conceptualize forms of organization that escape an elitist vanguardism but which offers an organizing force towards developing a socialist alternative to capitalism. The challenge before us is to build such an alternative that can gain hegemonic ascendancy in the minds of the popular majorities worldwide so that we can fight to bring such an alternative into being.

Dreaming Inside the Technological Dream

PJ: In a way, Peter, this whole conversation talks about a very important matter: the relationship between information and power …

PM: Of course I believe that information is power. We need to know how institutions operate, how people inside of them behave. This is crucial. We can learn, for instance, about war from all the valiant work of Julian Assange and his WikiLeaks staff, and the efforts of Edward Snowden and Chelsea Manning. We've learned about the deaths of thousands who otherwise would be relegated to the annals of ignominy, to abstractions that we can ignore because we can't picture them in ghastly and gory detail in our minds.

There is a lot of information out there—all communication relies on information, but I am concerned here about the providers. Who provides the information, how is it framed or "punctuated" and what are the ideological effects? And how do human beings handle information? How do Americans cope, for instance, with the knowledge that their military has killed millions in its wars of aggression (which are disguised as preconditions for delivering "democracy" by "shock and awe" to those who won't play by our rules) and has viciously beaten recalcitrant countries into submission through their "humanitarian imperialism" until they become pliable client states? The U.S. appreciates those quisling nation-states that willingly bend over for whoever is in power in the White House.

How do young people react to the notion that their country is involved in a "forever war" against terrorism? Or with the knowledge that we could be saving millions of people by bringing them medical aid for what are known and treatable diseases—we have the technology to do that—but we don't. Capitalism creates such vast inequalities between groups within states and between states. Pollution of air, water and lack of sanitation and hygiene are responsible for more deaths than disease in the developing world. The rich countries can afford to export their pollution to the peripheral countries. We know that our fellow human beings, our fellow planetary citizens, are being poisoned by lead, toxic smoke from burning refuse in industrial dumps, from smoking cigarettes, from mercury, hexavalent chromium and pesticides which have become obsolete.

After a while the death toll is just too much to bear but we can fast-forward all the messy details out of our consciousness through digital distractions. Our coping mechanisms involve surfing the television channels or the Internet; we don't have to stay in any one place for too long. Our anti-war efforts are really activated in the arena of cultural protest—through music, dress, plays, Internet sites—that are connected to rebelling against bourgeois society—as if war were just another feature of bourgeois society.

What I am concerned with is how war is connected to class structure, to capitalism itself, and I agree here with Garry Leech (2012) that capitalism itself is a type of war, a "structural genocide" and it will take more than transgressions in the arena of culture to combat this genocide. All of us participate in this structural genocide as much by what we choose not to do, as by what actions we deliberately choose to take in our everyday lives. It is the concentration of capital within global corporations, their hegemonic control of the structures of ideological production through media, which largely make this genocide possible, and, of course, the policies of international regulatory agencies. Even when we choose to resist, we find ourselves regulated in the way in which we are permitted to violate the rules—we are given a certain part of the public square where we can picket, chant slogans and the like.

Postmodern anti-rationalism and anti-universalism from our avant-garde professoriate will not help us here. The struggle is up to us, to make sure we have a historical record that is truthful, and that we have safeguards in place so that corporations and government agencies cannot delete our national history. Because without memory, without collective history, education is impossible. Every educator should be involved in making history by struggling to make the world a better place, by connecting their local concerns to larger global concerns—war, industrial pollution, human rights, freedom from constant surveillance. Now there is another issue here about historical records. Who owns our personal historical record? This generation's personal history is recorded in some form—who owns it? Whoever owns it can control us.

PJ: Your analysis hits the nail on the head, Peter, and your last few sentences simply call for expansion. Nowadays, various gadgets and services collect enormous amounts of our personal data in exchange for "personalized" services. For instance, my new phone is structurally unable to browse the Internet without knowing my age, occupation, gender and marital status; in return, I get restaurant recommendations based on my favourite foods and flight discounts based on my usual destinations. However convenient, these developments bring along built-in ideological baggage which is painfully absent from our customer contracts. Whenever we subscribe to this or that digital service, a small part of our existence gets a digital life of its own. In the process, it moves out of our control—and returns as a control mechanism for our behavior. What is the real price of our "free" restaurant recommendations, flight discounts and heart monitors? Are we, like ancient American natives, giving away our best skins and gold in exchange for worthless glass pearls? What is the social role of metadata, and how does it relate to relations of consumption and production?

PM: As Evgeny Morozov wrote recently in *The Observer* (2014), our "techno-Kafkaesque" world is being subject to algorithmic regulation through technological innovation, and this will get exponentially worse in the coming years. Our daily activities will be monitored by sensors as part of the "smartification" of everyday life. Google will soon mediate, monitor and report on everything we do. Procter & Gamble has created a Safeguard Germ Alarm that uses sensors to monitor the doors of toilet stalls in public washrooms. The alarm blares once you leave the stall and can only be stopped by the push of the soap-dispensing button. Morozov mentions that Google plans to expand the use of its Android operation system to include smart watches, smart cars, smart thermostats and more.

Smart mattresses that track your respiration and heart rates and how much you move at night and smartphones that measure how many steps you take each day, or tools that measure how much you spend as opposed to how much you earn (to fight tax fraud) and "advances" such as remotely controlled cars that can be shut down from a distance if you are being pursued by the police— all of these will increasingly regulate your behavior. When Apple patented technology that deploys sensors in your smartphone that can block your texting feature if it is determined that you are driving and talking on your phone, and when face recognition systems are made public to prevent your car from starting should it fail to recognize the face of the driver (and send the picture to the car's owner), we can rejoice or be wary. I am inclined to feel wary.

The age of algorithmic regulation stipulates that we will be hived within a cybernetic feedback society in which the systems regulating our behavior maintain their stability by constantly learning and adapting themselves to changing circumstances. Morozov makes the important point that technologies that will detect credit card fraud or tax fraud will do nothing to hinder super-rich families who write tax exemptions into law or who operate offshore schemes that funnel millions into their bank accounts. These technologies will always be evaded by the rich and powerful.

Morozov cites the Italian philosopher Giorgio Agamben who writes about the transformation of the idea of government. We have traditional hierarchical relations between causes and effects. We used to be governed by causes. Now this relationship has been inverted and we are governed by effects. This is emblematic of modernity, according to Agamben. If the government no longer wants to govern the causes but only manage the effects, then we are in for some difficult times. Don't try to find out the causes of diseases; try to keep yourself out of the healthcare system by being healthy. It's the insurance company model of algorithmic regulation, according to Morozov. If our heart rate and our blood pressure can be tracked as a means of proactive protection, will we be considered "deviant" if we choose to refuse these devices? Will we be punished, in other words, with higher insurance premiums? In a cybernetically regulated world powered by the pro-privatization agenda of Silicon Valley, if we fail to take adequate responsibility for our health, will we be punished? Will we be seen as failures if we fail to keep healthy?

Well, Morozov makes a good point when he says that this lets the fast-food companies off the hook, and it doesn't address class-based differences and questions of inequality. We all should be monitoring the condition of our feces and if we don't self-track sufficiently, then it is our fault if we get sick. Forget the exploitation of the food and pharmaceutical companies! This is what Morozov calls politics without politics—a politics identified with the "nudging state" that relies on metadata. As correlating aggregate data on individuals becomes more sophisticated, data on individuals go to the highest bidder, as our personal data become state assets. The algorithmic state is reputation-obsessed and entrepreneurial. One day, everybody will be their own brand, and nearly every key social interaction will be ranked. This leads to the culture of resilience in which it is agreed that we cannot prevent threats to our existence, so we must equip ourselves with the necessary savvy to face these threats individually.

So this world that Morozov describes blithely glances over or studiously avoids serious issues facing humanity such as economic equality and emancipation—all that is important in the cybernetic world of feedback mechanisms in real time is the creation of social homeostasis in a world of polished surfaces, aerosol politics and epidermal social relations of consumption. What is blurred and discounted are the social relations of production and how these relations are connected to the ongoing centralization of the control of the provenance of information. We are faced with an uncritical rehearsal of *Brave New World* (Huxley, 1932), and while the soma might taste good, all life is etherized inside the Internet Box.

PJ: Following recent technological developments in collection, storage and manipulation of digital information, we have landed into the age of "big data"—and Huxley's *Brave New World* has indeed graduated from science fiction into real life. Therefore, it is hardly a surprise that various issues pertaining to big data provoke growing attention in diverse research communities from information science to education. (For instance, at the moment of writing this text, *Policy Futures in Education* has an open call for papers entitled "Big Data in Education and Learning Analytics," edited by Michael A. Peters, Robert Lingard, Tina Besley and Jillian Blackmore.) Could you please link big data to manipulation? What is the role of science in the struggle against the digital Brave New World?

PM: I am sure you are aware, Petar, that social scientists at Cornell University, the University of California, San Francisco (UCSF) and Facebook have revealed the result of a controversial experiment (controversial because it was covert and relied on proprietary data) in an article entitled "Experimental Evidence of Massive-Scale Emotional Contagion through Social Networks" published online in *Proceedings of the National Academy of Sciences of the United States of America* (Kramer, Guillory, & Hancock, 2014). In their attempt to alter the emotions of 600,000 people, these scientists egregiously breached accepted ethical research standards in discovering, apparently, that emotions can spread among users of online social networks, which can be taken to mean that emotions expressed throughout online social networks (in this case, in mood-laden texts) can influence or alter the moods of others (they did this via a Facebook-controlled ranking algorithm that regularly filters posts, stories and activities shared by friends).

It is still unclear whether this experiment was funded by the U.S. Army Research Office or some other branch of the U.S. military. Even if it wasn't, learning how to manipulate how we act and feel in social networks such as Facebook obviously has powerful potential for military attempts to control large populations via the Internet, populations worldwide that are fed up with immiseration capitalism and being forced to comply with government austerity programs that hurt the poor and benefit the transnational capitalist class. Of course, an experiment determining whether 1.28 billion Facebook users could potentially be manipulated through "massive-scale emotional contagion through social networks" (Kramer et al., 2014) is not simply a means of understanding what advertisements people are likely to respond to but is geared to shed scientific light on how to alter people's emotions so that they can be manipulated collectively.

When you sign up for Facebook you give a blanket consent to the company's research group to use you as a potential lab rat, as a condition of using the service, so the university researchers in this case obviously took advantage of the fine print to avoid requiring informed consent from the subjects involved. Apparently, however, in the case of the involvement of Cornell University, approval for the research was only given after the data collection had been completed. Because the responsibility for data collection and analysis was given over by the university researchers to Facebook, the academics involved were said to have "not directly engaged in human research and that no review by the Cornell Human Research Protection Program was required" (Cornell University Media Relations Office, 2014). Does this mean academic researchers can also team up with any organization, including the U.S. military, and escape ethical restrictions?

Everywhere you go today you are forced to consume information that has been tested in order to prompt you to contact certain companies, or purchase certain goods or remember certain information. At airports, in some supermarkets, at some movie theaters, and on billboards. It's very hard to escape this saturation society. But being the target of deliberate emotional manipulation puts us more squarely into the suffocating world of *1984* (Orwell, 1949). We are already there.

Have you ever had a dream, Petar, in which you are dreaming inside the dream? And then you awake from the dream in your dream, but when you are awake you are still in the dream. Advances in technology help us awake from the dream in the dream, but they do not help us to live outside of the dream, in the domain of wakefulness. Are the advances in technology worth it, when we no longer have the agency to create ourselves, but are merely flesh-like putty in the hands of the government and corporations?

This is why critical pedagogy is so urgent today. Another world is possible and critical pedagogy can play a part in its creation. Yes, I believe in transcendence, and unlike Vattimo or Agamben, I don't believe that transcendence cuts off questions prematurely. We need a philosophy of praxis, a Marxist-humanist pedagogy driven by the desire to live in a world of freely associated labor where value production is no longer the motor of human existence.

PJ: What does it mean to reinvent ourselves in the age of the network? Could you please analyze the role of critical pedagogy in that process?

PM: I'm answering your questions now, Petar, from Ensenada, Mexico. Yesterday at Instituto McLaren de Pedagogía Crítica y Educación Popular, I was speaking to my students about the importance of being attentive to the deep cultural assumptions that provide the deep moral and conceptual frameworks for our pedagogies. I was sharing with them some of the important work of C. A. Bowers (2014), who argues that digital technologies cannot represent the tacit knowledge and cultural norms that represent the daily exchanges in people's everyday lives, knowledges that sustain the natural ecologies of diverse groups of people who inhabit our planet.

How, for instance, are face-to-face mentoring relationships that have helped to create the educational commons being superseded by computer programs such as Blackboard and print-based storage systems and thinking that are so prominent in digital technologies? How does corporate-controlled media/digital culture promote a particular form of Western individualism dependent upon consumerism and, for instance, the notion that economic development and growth are automatically a good thing—all of which can lead, of course, to further poverty and the loss of natural resources?

Naturally, it can lead to much more—to structural genocide, ecocide and epistemicide. Information and data do not amount to wisdom. Bowers cites the neo-social Darwinian and neoliberal perspectives of Hans Moravec and Ray Kurzweil who argue that digital technologies are at the point of displacing human beings in the process of evolution by way of self-correcting machine intelligence. Here, in Ensenada, I am thinking of the history of the Cochimies, the Pai-Pai, the Kumiai, the Kiliwa, the Cucapa, the Guayaira, the Pericues— what were the so-called great movements of progress that destroyed their cultural commons generations ago? And how many other *pueblos originales* will be destroyed in the future by the evolution of machine intelligence?

Life Is Jerky

PJ: About half past three in the morning, during the peak period of our email exchange, I suddenly received the following email from Peter:

> When people started to use the Internet, I told my friends, the Neighborhood has just become more interesting.
> Sent from my iPhone

This sentence has served as inspiration for the first section of this chapter. More important, however, it provides a vivid example of Peter's modus operandi.

We started this conversation in the most traditional way: I asked questions, and Peter provided answers. To my great surprise, after not more than a few emails, things have turned upside down. At times, Peter would indeed reply to my questions with full-text answers—just like any other interviewee. More often than not, however, he would merely send a link or two or attach an article to an empty email. Out of the blue, he would send a phrase or sentence seemingly unrelated to the last thing we had been discussing—at all times of day, and often from his phone. Sometimes I could almost feel sources of his inspiration—queuing in the supermarket, sipping coffee in his favourite café in Los Angeles or talking to various people during his numerous travels.

Our relationship went much deeper than business. Emails have started to become fairly personal—yet they never completely lost focus. We talked about the general concept of humanity and about our love for our partners, about the changes in the contemporary structure of employment and about our personal work experiences, about immigration laws and their consequences to our families. In this way, my inbox slowly acquired an interesting collection of stories that do not really belong to the standard academic discourse. Yet, I felt that it would be a shame to keep those stories private, so I decided to make this small collection of thoughts which do not represent Peter the scientist, or Peter the critical theorist, but primarily expose Peter's personal feelings about technologies. In the context of revolutionary critical praxis, after all, context is equally important as content—and one's theoretical views about information and communication technologies cannot be separated from one's needs and feelings.

PJ: If you've got the time, Peter, I'd like to engage you in a wee thought experiment. Imagine two drawers. The first drawer contains all works of art, music and literature—Shakespeare, Hemingway, London, Kerouac … Picasso, da Vinci, Michelangelo … Zappa, Mozart, the Rolling Stones … you name it, it's there. The second drawer contains all scientific achievements—physics, chemistry, sociology, anthropology, history. Which drawer, in your opinion, contains more knowledge about the world around us?

PM: I would choose the first drawer but would try to steal as much from the second drawer when nobody was looking. Actually, I have an interest in quantum theory.

PJ: You are obviously well acquainted with the Internet. Ages ago, I found your website with the "Hasta Siempre" intro—very fashionable for its time. Now you've got the new design, though. … You also have profiles on various social networks such as Facebook and Academia.edu. What motivates you for such a strong online presence?

PM: I have two webpages, both started by other folks who volunteered to set me up. They are both interesting sites, one is in Spain developed by the brilliant Carlos Escaño and the other by Richard Kahn and Greg Martin. Greg is a professor in Australia, while Richard is a professor in Los Angeles. For a while it was run by Greg Misiaszek, who is also an academic. But he works in China and can only post items when he is out of the country. Now I have a new webmaster, Tim Bolin, from Chapman University. Occasionally I will post some talks I am giving or something I think readers who appreciate my work might be interested in. Now Facebook is another matter. I can't recall who set me up on Facebook, but I do post mostly visuals—posters, photos and the occasional essay or political notice. I don't like corresponding on Facebook at all. I get a lot of messages and I just don't have the time to answer questions.

PJ: So, you don't really like social networking?

PM: Facebook promotes people's narcissism. I prefer email. I have a certain visual aesthetic, I enjoy posting photos. It's mostly a vehicle to promote political causes, that's the best part of it—I am sitting at a coffee shop in LA. People are ignoring their companions. They are obsessed with their phones and iPads. People are redundant.

PJ: You are an avid user of digital gadgets—as far as I am aware, more than half of this interview has been written on your smartphone. How do you feel about the tremendous assimilation of information and communication technologies into our daily lives?

(During our online conversation, Peter provided three different short stories about these developments. They share the same general message but explore different angles and evoke different feelings. I do not feel that it would be right to publish only one of these stories and withhold from readers the pleasure of engaging with others. Therefore, I will merely list the three responses in reverse chronological order.)

PM: Story 1 (30 June 2014)
Today it was raining heavily in Jinhua, China. Black streaks were running down the cheeks of the buildings like mascara on mothers weeping for their lost children. I stopped by a water-logged restaurant that served countryside-style food, with a yearning for some Jiuqu Hongmei tea. After dinner, while I was admiring posters of Chairman Mao and Chairman Hua Guofeng, I noticed about ten young waitresses in orange uniforms in the upstairs dining area. They were all sitting together in the dark, their faces eerily illuminated by their large Samsung cell phones. They were playing games and watching videos. All of them were silent. There was no dialogue. Occasionally, a waitress would leave her chair to attend to a customer, and then it was back to the darkened room to the comfort of her cell phone. Outside the restaurant were unpainted concrete buildings and hydroelectric towers. They also stood silent.

PM: Story 2 (27 June 2014)

Recently I visited a thousand-year-old Buddhist Temple in Hangzhou. Sacred figures from Buddhist history were carved out of stone. Gold-painted statues of Buddha loomed over the visitors who were both pious and curious. In one temple at least a hundred monks were chanting in unison, as great clouds of incense wafted through the open doors. Winding my way down from the highest temple on the hill, I noticed one of the monks on his cell phone. Perhaps he was checking the World Cup results? Or calling his condo in Shanghai?

PM: Story 3 (25 May 2013)

I loathe technology, and yet, like many others, I am addicted to it. I hate cell phones, except for use in emergencies, yet I have an iPhone which I check regularly. I hate the Internet, yet I spend time on the Web each day checking what I have found to be reliable sources and authors. I am irritated when people around me are talking loudly on their cell phones. I greatly dislike the consumer hype around cell phone cases, and the like. There is just too much information available. It is overwhelming. Everybody creates their own Internet worlds, publishes their own journals and blogs, and sometimes you find something of interest.

PJ: Could you please link these developments to the world of academia?

PM: I remember professors in academic institutions who, when they published their first few books, suddenly became celebrities among their students. They started to cultivate their image as social critics, shopped carefully for their in-class sunglasses and black attire, and the men grew shadow beards. Their students have little knowledge about whether their professors' work is good or not but they have published some books, so their students treat them as academic celebrities. I feel it's a little bit like the film *American Psycho* (Harron, 2000), when so much fuss is made about business cards, the texture of the paper, the print, the color—it's all just image management. Academics get into their Internet worlds, advertise their work and all of that.

PJ: A recent issue of the *International Journal of Critical Pedagogy* entitled "Paulo and Nita: Sharing Life, Love, and Intellect" (2013) is dedicated to "revolutionary love" and its power to challenge oppressive social relationships. Your paper in that issue, "Reflections on Love and Revolution" (McLaren,

2013), shows that the concept of revolutionary love extends from the private sphere into important questions such as re-evaluation of the contemporary role of academics. However, Paulo and Nita Freire lived in the world of one-directional mass media such as television and newspapers. Could you please relate the concept of revolutionary love to information and communication technologies?

PM: I believe that love is a social relationship as opposed to an entirely private matter. I believe that love can be productive for the collective emancipation of people. One might think that technological innovations—the social media, for example—have enhanced the possibility of love expanding into the collective arena of social development. But the class interests embedded in the social media—i.e., the ideology of individual consumption, the commodification of subjectivities (especially the commodified individualism of neoliberal capital with its exclusive and singular morality), the exploitation of the social labor of others (the bourgeois treatment of people as commodities to be "owned" or possessed which is increased by economic dependency and the social division of labor dominated by property relations)—have disabled the emancipatory potential of love and collective solidarity.

Meeting the material needs of people—rather than treating people as "stranded assets" useful only when they can be maximized for their purchasing power by an embrace of market fundamentalism—creates the necessary conditions of possibility for radical love and the solidarity needed to create a world unburdened by value creation, a world committed to freely associated individuals.

PJ: As far as I am aware, Joe Kincheloe dubbed you "poet laureate of the educational left" (2000, p. ix). Your first book, *Cries from the Corridor* (reprinted and expanded in *Life in Schools* [McLaren, 2014]), is widely considered a masterpiece of literature. In recent years, you started writing poetry (a few of your poems can be found in *MRZine* [2013]). Overall, your unique expression has had a strong influence on the success of your academic work (more about your relationship to writing can be found in the 2008 interview for the University of Waterloo [McLaren et al., 2008]). In this question, I am interested in the "mechanics" of your writing. How do you write your poems? Do you use pen and paper, or type them on one of your gadgets? How do you write your articles? Do you do everything on screen, or print your articles and work on them in cafés? Why?

PM: Now as for writing—well, that's an interesting process. People approach me now about my idiosyncratic style, and that's something that they didn't do years ago, so maybe that's a sign that I am getting better. But I think people are starting to appreciate it more and more. My present style has to do with the writing I did in the 1960s, my affinity for the Beat Poets, encouragement I got from meeting Allen Ginsberg, Timothy Leary and a lot of very creative people. When I write a paper, there are sections that are meant to be read. Then there are just sections that are meant to convey ideas. I am trying to bring a lot more young people into critical pedagogy, and they like the spoken-word sense of some of my paragraphs.

Sometimes I will rip pages out of magazines, shuffle them and then just look for metaphors and strange combinations of words that have little to do with each other. I'm not sure who did the same, I think perhaps William Burroughs. Some people don't like my work because they find it too self-conscious, as if I am trying too hard to be hip, that kind of thing. But that's how I look at the world, I try to bring a little of a lot of different historical selves into my work—artist, poet, activist, essayist, teacher, student, interlocutor—and writing really does depend on how you feel when you put pen to paper. Sometimes I feel more didactic than at other times. Sometimes more like somebody provoking an idea.

I write mostly on scraps of paper with a pen. Then I put them on the computer. Then back to the pen. And back to the computer, and so on. I just hate reading on the computer. I can't do it, even with a big screen. I have to print out drafts and read them on paper. They only make sense to me on paper. The screen is just part of the work process. And then, I need to read my work in page proofs, in the final typeface. Only then can I judge my work. And I am notorious for making last-minute changes in the page proofs. Always, always there are errors in the book or published essays. I always spot them and they always annoy me. There are few good copy editors anymore—they have all been phased out by journals and publishers that want to pare down the publishing process.

PJ: I'm sure that our publishers will be delighted with your last-minute changes. … And what about your public talks? How are they related to your writing?

PM: I always hear my own voice when I read my work. I speak the words to myself. I think a lot of work comes to life when the right person is reading it. Richard Burton can read Dylan Thomas. But Dylan Thomas can read Dylan Thomas better than anyone else. (I'm not trying to compare myself with Dylan here, please!) I enjoy reading my work at conferences because I wouldn't dream of giving a talk unless I felt I had something to say, and the things I have to say I feel passionate about. I am not a conventional academic. I try not to be defined by the word 'scholar' and feel more comfortable with the term 'politically engaged intellectual' who is committed, in part, to blighting the calumniatory attacks on the Left by the corporate machine. I don't care much for academic conventions or academic life. In fact, it's a brutal world. I put a lot of energy into my talks, and few people complain that I "read my paper" instead of being spontaneous because they can see that I am very much emotionally invested in the causes that I write about. On occasion, I like to break off from reading my paper and be extemporaneous. Now you might be asking: Who cares? You are a revolutionary and you shouldn't really care about all the aesthetic details. Just get the message across. Write like a journalist in the most accessible style possible. I respect that type of journalism but I've never been able to sustain that kind of writing. I have given myself permission to be a stylist with the provision that style can never trump substance, and when it does, put away your pen!

PJ: With Carlos Escaño, you made a few videos about possibilities for social change such as *Sí se puede* (Yes it is possible) and a funny yet inspiring blend of technological reality and iconic images of Che Guevara called *Life Is Jerky*. What is that all about? Another vehicle to promote political causes, a new way of expressing your ideas, or a mere creative streak?

PM: I was impressed with Carlos's videos where the image jerks around. I thought to myself: That's what everyday life is like a lot of the time. There has been very little smooth sailing in my life. Life is jerky. It shifts around in fits and starts. It's like driving an old car that shakes and then falls apart. All that is left is you sitting on the seat. The rest of the car is in pieces lying all around you.

I feel that the journey we call life is a lot like that. I can deal with the jerks, and being jerked around by people, by circumstances, by the technological changes that speed me up or slow me down, but sometimes I wish the road had less bumps. Of course, my life has been filled with much personal trauma so the jerks usually don't seem so bad. But when you are jerking around, your imagination is more difficult to focus. So you need a reprieve. I get that in my writing or my creative work.

PJ: Now that we know what Peter the critical theorist thinks of the Internet, we have arrived at the obvious last question: How do you feel about the Internet?

PM: How do I personally feel about the Internet? I feel it is a tremendous source for cranial addiction. My invitations to contribute essays in journals and books used to arrive in the snail mail; you had around nine months to a year to produce a work. Invitations now come fast and furious and editors expect you to put something together in less than three months. So it does affect the quality of the work in a negative way, but you are able to get your ideas out there in vaster quantities, which is a good thing if you believe that what you have to say is worthwhile in making the world a better place.

But you pay a price. It is more difficult to read books carefully, without being interrupted by the Internet, or rather, allowing the Internet to interrupt you. It is a ferocious distraction from things that need to be done. Cell phones take priority over conversations with family and friends. Once you unplug yourself, you enter a world where everyone else is plugged in. It's become a tool of psychological and image management. It's an alternate reality that entraps you and enables you to feel you are bonding with people in a special way when, in fact, you probably don't mean much to those with whom you are corresponding. For many students that I know, it has become a source for bullying, for deception. Just going through hundreds of email messages a day, to see which ones are relevant to your life, takes hours. I have often fantasized about just getting away from technology, and keeping a ham radio available in case I'm on a boat crossing the Atlantic and a storm is approaching and, say, my companions in the boat are a tiger, an orangutan, a zebra and a hyena ...

Acknowledgements

This article is a modified and expanded version of an article McLaren, P. & Jandrić, P. (2014). Critical revolutionary pedagogy is made by walking – in a world where many worlds coexist. *Policy Futures in Education*, 12(6), 805–831. Translations of the original article, with various modifications, have been published in Croatian, Ukrainian and Spanish. Because of the large amount of gathered material, the conversation was published in two complementary parts. The other part of the conversation is: P. McLaren & P. Jandrić (2015), "The Critical Challenge of Networked Learning: Using Information Technologies in the Service of Humanity," in Petar Jandrić & Damir Boras (Eds.), *Critical Learning in Digital Networks*. New York, NY: Springer.

PJ: Some questions in this conversation borrow sections from my books: Jandrić, P., & Boras, D. (2012). *Critical e-learning: Struggle for power and meaning* *in the network society.* Zagreb, Croatia: FF Press & Polytechnic of Zagreb., and Jandrić, P. & Boras, D. (Eds.). (2015). *Critical Learning in Digital Networks.* New York: Springer.

PM: Elements of my critique of postmodernism and the shift to Marxism have been taken from another conversation with Glen Rikowski published under the title "Pedagogy for Revolution against Education for Capital: An e-Dialogue on Education in Capitalism Today," *Cultural Logic*, 4(1) (McLaren & Rikowski, 2000). Analysis of "the nuclear unconscious" is expanded and revised from my conversation with Glen Rikowski published in *Rage and Hope: Interviews with Peter McLaren on War, Imperialism, and Critical Pedagogy* (McLaren, 2006). The overview of the relationships between contemporary youth social movements and information and communication technologies is expanded from an earlier interview with Sam Fassbinder published in *CounterPunch* magazine (McLaren & Fassbinder, 2013).

PM, PJ: We give our special thanks to Christine Sinclair for her invaluable insights into and criticisms of this conversation.

References

Allman, P. (2000). Back cover. In P. McLaren, *Che Guevara, Paulo Freire, and the pedagogy of revolution.* Lanham, MD: Rowman & Littlefield.

Anderson, K. (2010, August 18). Overcoming some current challenges to dialectical thought. *International Marxist-Humanist.* Retrieved from http://www.internationalmarxisthumanist.org/wp-content/uploads/pdf/anderson-overcoming-some-current-challenges-to-dialectical-thought-20100818.pdf

Atkin, E. (2014, July 7). TransCanada buys town's silence on tar sands pipeline proposal for $28K. *Nation of Change.* Retrieved from http://www.nationofchange.org/transcanada-buys-town-s-silence-tar-sands-pipeline-proposal-28k-1404658137

Bird, S. E. (2009). The future of journalism in the digital environment. *Journalism, 10*(3), 293–295.

Bowers, C. A. (2014, March 15). Writings on education, eco-justice, and revitalizing the commons. Retrieved from http://www.cabowers.net/

Carr, N. (2011). *The shallows: What the Internet is doing to our brains.* New York, NY: Norton.

Castells, M. (2001). *The Internet galaxy: Reflections on the Internet, business, and society.* Oxford, England: Oxford University Press. Retrieved from http://dx.doi.org/10.1007/978-3-322-89613-1 and http://www.oxfordscholarship.com/view/10.1093/acprof:oso/9780199255771.001.0001/acprof-9780199255771

Cornell University Media Relations Office. (2014, June 30). Media statement on Cornell University's role in Facebook 'emotional contagion' research. Retrieved from http://

mediarelations.cornell.edu/2014/06/30/media-statement-on-cornell-universitys-role-in-facebook-emotional-contagion-research/

Etelson, E. (2014). Is modern technology killing us? *Truthout*. Retrieved from http://www.truth-out.org/opinion/item/26295-is-modern-technology-killing-us

Evans, T. L. (2012). *Occupy education: Learning and living sustainability*. New York, NY: Peter Lang.

Fassbinder, S. (2008). Capitalist discipline and ecological discipline. *Green Theory and Praxis*, 4(2), 87–101.

Freire, P. (1995). Preface. In P. McLaren, *Critical pedagogy and predatory culture* (pp. ix–xi). London, England: Routledge.

Freire, P. (2000). *Pedagogy of the oppressed*. New York, NY: Continuum.

Giroux, H. (1999). Preface. In P. McLaren, *Schooling as a ritual performance: Towards a political economy of educational symbols and gestures* (3rd ed.). Lanham, MD: Rowman & Littlefield.

Grosfoguel, R. (2008). Transmodernity, border thinking, and global coloniality. *Eurozine*. Retrieved from http://www.eurozine.com/pdf/2008-07-04-grosfoguel-en.pdf

Habermas, J. (1970). *Towards a rational society*. Boston, MA: Beacon Press.

Handel, P. (2015). Medium and movement: Todd Wolfson on the digital rebellion. February 2015. As retrieved from: http://www.truth-out.org/news/item/28954-medium-and-movement-todd-wolfson-on-the-digital-rebellion

Hardt, M., & Negri, A. (2001). *Empire*. Cambridge, MA: Harvard University Press.

Harron, M. (Director). (2000). *American psycho* [Motion picture]. United States: Lions Gate Films.

Harvey, D. (1990). *The condition of postmodernity: An enquiry into the origins of cultural change*. Cambridge, MA: Blackwell.

Hayek, F. (1948). *Individualism and economic order*. London, England: Routledge.

Holst, J. D. (2002). *Social movements, civil society, and radical adult education*. Westport, CT: Praeger.

Huxley, A. (1932). *Brave new world*. London, England: Penguin.

Illich, I. (1971). *Deschooling society*. London, England: Marion Boyars.

Illich, I. (1973). *Tools for conviviality*. London, England: Marion Boyars.

Illich, I. (1982). *Medical nemesis: The expropriation of health*. New York, NY: Pantheon.

International Marxist-Humanist Organization. (2013). Main page. Retrieved from http://www.internationalmarxisthumanist.org/

Jandrić, P., & Boras, D. (2012). *Critical e-learning: Struggle for power and meaning in the network society*. Zagreb, Croatia: FF Press & Polytechnic of Zagreb.

Jandrić, P. & Boras, D. (Eds.). (2015). *Critical Learning in Digital Networks*. New York: Springer.

Johnston, J. (2003). Who cares about the commons? *Capitalism Nature Socialism*, 14(4), 1–42. Retrieved from http://dx.doi.org/10.1080/10455750308565544

Kahn, R. (2010). *Critical pedagogy, ecoliteracy, and planetary crisis*. New York, NY: Peter Lang.

Kincheloe, J. (2000). Peter McLaren: The poet of the educational left. In P. McLaren, *Che Guevara, Paulo Freire, and the pedagogy of revolution* (pp. ix–xii). Lanham, MD: Rowman & Littlefield.

Kolhatkar, S. (2014, July 3). Orwell's dystopian future is almost here: A conversation with Glenn Greenwald. *Truthdig*. Retrieved from http://www.truthdig.com/report/print/orwells_dystopian_future_is_almost_here_a_conversation_20140703

Kramer, A. D. I., Guillory, J. E., & Hancock, J. T. (2014). Experimental evidence of massive-scale emotional contagion through social networks. *Proceedings of the National Academy of Sciences of the United States of America*, *111*(24), 8788–8790.

Leech, G. (2012). *Capitalism: A structural genocide*. London, England: Zed Books.

McLaren, P. (Ed.). (2006). *Rage and hope: Interviews with Peter McLaren on war, imperialism, and critical pedagogy*. New York, NY: Peter Lang.

McLaren, P. (2012). Objection sustained: Revolutionary pedagogical praxis as an occupying force. *Policy Futures in Education*, *10*(4), 487–495. Retrieved from http://dx.doi.org/10.2304/pfie.2012.10.4.487

McLaren, P. (2013). Reflections on love and revolution. *International Journal of Critical Pedagogy*, *5*(1), 60–68.

McLaren, P. (2014). *Life in schools: An introduction to critical pedagogy in the foundations of education* (6th ed.). Boulder, CO: Paradigm.

McLaren, P., & Fassbinder, S. (2013). His work, his visit to Turkey and ongoing popular struggles: Interview with Peter McLaren. *CounterPunch*. Retrieved from http://truth-out.org/news/item/16903-his-work-his-visit-to-turkey-and-ongoing-popular-struggles-interview-with-peter-mclaren

McLaren, P. & Jandrić, P. (2014). Critical revolutionary pedagogy is made by walking – in a world where many worlds coexist. *Policy Futures in Education*, *12*(6), 805–831.

McLaren, P., & Jandrić, P. (2015). The critical challenge of networked learning: Using information technologies in the service of humanity. In P. Jandrić & D. Boras (Eds.), *Critical learning in digital networks* (pp. 199–226). New York, NY: Springer.

McLaren, P., McMurry, A., & McGuirk, K. (2008). *An interview with Peter McLaren*. Waterloo, Ontario, Canada: University of Waterloo. Retrieved from http://english.uwaterloo.ca/PeterMcLareninterview.pdf

McLaren, P., & Rikowski, G. (2000). Pedagogy for revolution against education for capital: An e-dialogue on education in capitalism today. *Cultural Logic*, *4*(1). Retrieved from http://clogic.eserver.org/4-1/mclaren%26rikowski.html

Morozov, E. (2014, July 20). The rise of data and the death of politics. *The Observer*. Retrieved from http://www.theguardian.com/technology/2014/jul/20/rise-of-data-death-of-politics--evgeny-morozov-algorithmic-regulation

MRZine. (2013). Main page. Retrieved from http://mrzine.monthlyreview.org/

Nelson, J. (1991). *The perfect machine: Television and the bomb*. Toronto, Canada: New Society.

Noble, D. (2001). *Digital diploma mills: The automation of higher education*. New York, NY: Monthly Review Press.

Orwell, G. (1949). *Nineteen eighty-four. A novel*. London, England: Secker & Warburg.

Peter McLaren. (2014). *Wikipedia*. Retrieved from http://en.wikipedia.org/wiki/Peter_McLaren

Pinar, W. F. (1995). Back cover. In P. McLaren, *Critical pedagogy and predatory culture*. London, England: Routledge.

Polanyi, K. (2001). *The great transformation: The political and economic origins of our time.* Boston, MA: Beacon Press.

Sanders, B., & Illich, I. (1989). *ABC: The alphabetization of the popular mind.* London, England: Vintage.

Sandlin, J. A., & McLaren, P. (2009). *Critical pedagogies of consumption: Living and learning in the shadow of the 'shopocalypse.'* London, England: Routledge.

Sigman, A. (2007). *Remotely controlled: How television is damaging our lives.* London, England: Ebury Press.

Smail, D. (2008). *On deep history and the brain.* Berkeley, CA: University of California Press.

Smith, L. T. (1999). *Decolonizing methodologies.* London, England/Dunedin, New Zealand: Zed Books and University of Otago Press.

Smith, T. (2009). *Globalization: A systematic Marxian account.* Chicago, IL: Haymarket.

Standing, G. (2011). *The precariat: The new dangerous class.* London, England: Bloomsbury. Retrieved from http://dx.doi.org/10.5040/9781849664554

Standing, G. (2014). *A precariat charter: From denizens to citizens.* London, England: Bloomsbury.

Steinberg, S. R. (2005). Foreword. In M. Pruyn & L. M. Huerta-Charles (Eds.), *Teaching Peter McLaren: Paths of dissent* (pp. xiii–xiv). New York, NY: Peter Lang.

Suoranta, J., & Vaden, T. (2010). *Wikiworld.* London, England: Pluto Press.

Tolkien, J. R. R. (2012). *The lord of the rings.* Boston, MA: Mariner Books.

USA Today. (2011, December 21). Sinaloa cartel gives blessing to newest Mexican drug ballads. Retrieved from http://usatoday30.usatoday.com/news/world/story/2011-12-21/Alfredo-Rios-narcocorrido-Sinaloa-drug-ballad/52146296/1

van Dijk, J. (1999). *The network society.* London, England: Sage.

Watts, A. (1966). *The book: On the taboo against knowing who you are.* New York, NY: Pantheon.

Winn, M. (2002). *The plug-in drug: Television, computers, and family life.* London, England: Penguin.

· 8 ·

SEEDS OF RESISTANCE

Towards a Revolutionary Critical Ecopedagogy

Attention, young people of the future: September 6 of the year 2120, anniversary
of the first centennial of the world socialist revolution, which unified all the peoples of the planet around one ideal and one thought of socialist unity, and which
put an end to all enemies of the new society. Here remains only the remembrance
of a sad past of pain, suffering, and death. Forgive me. I was only dreaming when
I described those events, which I won't be able to see. But I had the pleasure of
having a dream.

—Chico Mendes (Quoted in Michael Löwy, *Ecosocialism:*
A Radical Alternative to Capitalist Catastrophe.

The earth, entire peoples and individual persons are being brutally punished. And
behind all this pain, death and destruction there is the stench of what Basil of
Caesarea called "the dung of the devil." An unfettered pursuit of money rules.
The service of the common good is left behind. Once capital becomes an idol
and guides people's decisions, once greed for money presides over the entire socio-
economic system, it ruins society, it condemns and enslaves men and women, it
destroys human fraternity, it sets people against one another and, as we clearly see,
it even puts at risk our common home.

—From Pope Francis's address for the World Meeting of Popular Movements
Expo Fair, Santa Cruz de la Sierra, Bolivia, Thursday, 9 July 2015.

ur Mother Earth is convulsing, choking on the filth, the dye, the pesticides,
the toxins, the effulgent splendor of chemicals and the dread unleashed

by the furnaces of human greed. Her death throes are imminent unless we decelerate the planetary ecological crisis. Unless we create a global commons purpose-built for the reclamation of our planetary home. That is, unless we create self-contained communities worldwide that are also phalansteries of hope and possibility.

The fast-approaching planetary dislocations brought about by the consolidation of the transnational capitalist state will also force the advance of fascism, whose specter already haunts the streets and communities across the U.S., in the form of resource wars for oil, gas and water, imperialist wars for strategic geopolitical advantage, the creation of a national security state, the militarism of the police and the war against economically imperiled U.S. citizens of color. In such a climate (no pun intended), should it surprise us that here in drought-ravaged California, at a time of shifting climate conditions, the state is still permitting companies to inject toxic chemical-laden oil industry wastewater and other fluids into protected sources of drinking water, and that over 2,500 oil and gas injection wells are still allowed in aquifers that could potentially be used as sources of drinking and irrigation water?

Let's consider some statistics. Theologian Elizabeth A. Johnson (2007) warns against the catastrophe that englobes us and threatens the survival of our species, not to mention countless other species: "Overconsumption, unbridled reproduction, exploitative use of resources and efflorescing pollution are rapidly depleting life-supporting systems on land, in the sea, and in the air." Underlying this catastrophe is an economy predicated on growth and the bottom line and relatively unconcerned about the ecological devastation that follows in its wake. Life-supporting systems on land, sea and air are being extinguished.

Johnson warns that 20 percent of the population of the planet uses 75 percent of the world's resources and produces 80 percent of the world's waste. She offers the example of Chicago, with 3 million people, consuming as much raw produce in a year as Bangladesh that has a population of 97 million. She reports alarmingly that in the year 1950, if somebody lived to be 80 years of age, the earth's human population will have multiplied five times during his or her lifetime. In the year 2030 it is predicted that there will be 10 billion persons on the planet. And she notes, too, that in the last quarter century 10 percent of all living species went extinct.

This information comes from Sr. Johnson's extraordinarily important book, *The Quest for the Living God: Mapping Frontiers in the Theology of God*, which, regrettably, provoked the United States Conference of Catholic Bishops (USCCB) to issue a statement of censure on March 24, 2011, in which the USCCB found the book inadequate in expressing the faith of the Catholic Church. Whether this statement is a result of Catholic theologians being pressured to express their faith through predetermined formulae taken from neo-scholasticism or for some other reason, it is heartening to see theological treatises dealing with important ecological issues and placing them within the context of our spiritual commitment and responsibility to the planet. Contemporary theologians often must create spaces of hegemonic rupture to enable their messages to be received or 'enfleshed' by the 'feeling body' of their listeners (McLaren, 1999).

Critical educators, who have addressed for decades and with firm commitment topics of race, class, gender, sexuality, disability and other social justice issues are now casting their eyes to the antagonism between capitalism and nature to ask themselves how we can rationally regulate the human metabolic relation with nature. In our struggle for a "transformed economy founded on the nonmonetary values of social justice and ecological balance" we don't follow a productivist socialism or capitalist market ecology. We emphasize use value, not exchange value and "a liberation from the alienating economic 'laws' of the growth-oriented capitalist system" (Löwy, 2015, p. 89). We fight for the collectivization of the means of production and for the requirement that our goals of investment and production be defined collectively by the people, and that means including the popular majorities. I have a message for the plutocrats who own the planet: Your dark money and undisclosed gifts to the corporatocracy silence the voices of the popular majorities, but we will drag you out of the shadows and expose your forked arbitration tongues and fine print smiles to the people! As the global power complex reduces human life and Mother Earth to mere production and consumption, revolutionary critical ecopedagogy is developing new, unalienated forms of self-presence. Ecopedagogy is inspired by and inspires a new social arc, rooted in practices of ecological struggles by the working classes and the poor—an unabashedly utopian dreaming of a post capitalist future not unlike the dream of Chico Mendes cited at the opening of this chapter.

The crises of global capitalism, including grotesque inequalities and ecocide, are not self-standing—they form an organic unity. In capitalist societies such as ours, self-alienating subjectivity is always already social alienation linked to the social relations of production, to racialized and gendered antagonisms and to the normative constraints of what Best, Kahn, McLaren and Nocella (2011) refer to as "the global power complex" that reduces everything to production and consumption. It is this alienation that generates the self which remains isolated from its Other, including the natural world. Living within the state of planetary ecocrisis so aptly characterized by Richard Kahn (2010) as constituting "geographies of genocide, ecocide, and zoöcide," we cannot experience our self-presence except through the anamorphically distorting mirror of capital.

Now that Keynesian stimulus measures no longer suffice to resolve the structural crisis of capitalism, and now that the frontiers of cheap resources are closing down, we are witnessing the dynamic increase in asset-stripping capitalism. Financial channels are used to plunder and pillage, as profit making is linked to the fastest and largest rates of return inextricably tied to the world of fictitious commodities that dilapidate the sources of past revolutions of productivity. For instance, the agro-food transnationals seek to capture profits through price inflation rather than through advances in productivity. Petty commodity producers saw their profits drop as finance capital subordinated all commodity logic to the competitive logic of global financial markets. In other words, finance capital makes all parts of the world ecology commensurable in productivity.

Asset Capitalism and Imperialism

Asset capitalism and the juggernaut of imperialism that follows in its wake have the potential to wreak further havoc upon the world in terms of imperialist wars as well as the ecological destruction of the entire planet. Sociologist William I. Robinson (2008) has discussed the development of a new transnational model of accumulation in which transnational fractions of capital have become dominant. New mechanisms of accumulation, leading to the dramatic expansion of capital, as Robinson notes, include a cheapening of labor and the growth of flexible, deregulated and de-unionized labor, where women experience super-exploitation in relation to men; the creation of a global and regulatory structure to facilitate the emerging global circuits of accumulation; and neoliberal structural adjustment programs which seek to create the conditions for unfettered operations of emerging transnational capital across borders and between countries. To this list we might add epistemicide, the wholesale 'disappearance' of indigenous knowledges and practices and ecosystems of the mind carried out by the guardians of Eurocentric knowledge production and their soldiers of conquest and destruction, and the wholesale destruction of life which Richard Kahn subsumes under the term zoöcide.

Financial oligarchies like the corporate elite, and their allies in the corridors of U.S. political power, benefit from the consolidation of numerous matrices of power, whose generation of surplus value potential is transnational in reach, and whose multifarious and decentralized institutional arrangements are organized around the industrial, bureaucratic and commodity models associated with the military-industrial complex. All of these "power complexes" have intersecting social, cultural and political spheres that can be managed ideologically by means of powerful, all-encompassing corporate media apparatuses and the culture industry in general, including both popular and more traditional forms of religious dogma and practice. Assuming a position of major importance today is the religious-industrial complex that provides the moral alibi for U.S. acts of war and military incursions throughout the world, so necessary for imperialist expansion.

We are witnessing the profound dismantling of national economies and the reorganization and reconstitution of national economies as component elements or segments of a larger global production and financial system. As Robinson (2008) observes, there is a decentralization and fragmentation of the actual national production process all over the globe while the control of these processes, these endless chains of accumulation, is concentrated and centralized at a global level by a transnationalist capitalist class. All of these power complexes overlap and interpenetrate each other at the level of capital accumulation and value production. At the same time, the sovereign ideologies of the capitalist state are reinforced through both new and old media technologies, resulting in an imperfect but nonetheless over-determined ideological climate that enables major "class" conflicts to be avoided.

Grosfoguel (2007a, 2007b, 2008a, 2008b) reminds us that this power complex has an ignominious history. The rise to power of Reagan and Thatcher is often traduced for being the midwife to neoliberal capitalism, but the horror of accumulation by dispossession was well established long before their violent attacks on miners and air traffic controllers.

In 1492, it was not just economic colonization that visited *las Americas*, but multiple antagonisms. This included a global class formation where a diversity of forms of labor coexisted, including slavery, semi-serfdom, wage labor and petty-commodity production. These diverse forms of labor, organized by capital, became a source of production of surplus value through the selling of commodities for a profit in the world market. Simultaneously, an international division of labor between core and periphery countries emerged, where capital organized labor in the periphery around coerced and authoritarian forms.

As Grosfoguel reports, an interstate system of politico-military organizations controlled by European males and institutionalized in colonial administrations supported a global racial/ethnic hierarchy that privileged European people over non-European people. This was organically intertwined with a global gender hierarchy that privileged males over females and the system of European patriarchy over other forms of gender relations, alongside a sexual hierarchy that privileged heterosexuals over gays and lesbians. A spiritual hierarchy privileged Christians over non-Christian/non-Western spiritualities, institutionalized in the globalization of Christianity, while an epistemic hierarchy upheld Western cosmology and systems of intelligibility over non-Western knowledge and cosmologies, institutionalized in the global university system. This was complemented by a linguistic hierarchy consisting of European languages and non-European languages that privileged Eurocentric knowledge as true communication and rational knowledge/theoretical production yet denigrated indigenous knowledges as "merely" folkloric or cultural and not worthy of being called theoretical.

The consequences of the simultaneous emergence of a transnational form of capitalism based on the exploitation of human labor and the endemic crisis of capitalism—based on the political, class conflicts taking place given the exploitative relations of production—are also the origin of the current ecological crisis. In the same ways that the exploitation of human labor sustains the conditions of possibility of all other antagonisms, including profound, globalized racial hatreds—which is not to reduce them all to class—transnational forms of capitalism today and their historical precedents are preconditions for ecocide.

In a recent lecture, Christian Parenti (2014) lucidly remarked that the modern capitalist state—what he calls "the environment making state"—does not *have* a relationship with nature, it *is* a relationship with nature. Capitalist institutions control the entire surface of the earth—the biosphere—and here the state exercises considerable power and influence over enforcing their property rights. Citing Jason Moore, Parenti notes that human economic activity is grounded in biophysical reality and that capitalism doesn't so much act upon nature as it does, in a very strong sense, develop through nature-society relations. While capitalism can be configured as a social system, Parenti reminds us that it is also a process that has an outside upon which it is dependent, and this "outside" can be understood in terms of places and social relations.

Parenti points out that human history begins to emerge as ecological history, and production begins to emerge as the production of social nature, in Marx's discussion of labor power. Marx's concept of labor power, as I have summarized it in many books, is the capacity to labor. Parenti likens labor power to the motive force of a waterfall, or the calories in a potato, or the infinite energy of the sun. He does this to stress the fact that labor power is "a *pre-existing force external to capital*" (2014, p. 6). He writes:

> The capitalist uses money to buy labor time, a quantity of money for a quantity of time, and in that labor process the capitalist attempts to capture as much labor power as possible. The key point: labor power is eternal to capital and pre-existing; it is the capacity to labor. In that regard it is like the waterfall. Labor power, like the other natural forces, becomes a force of production in that it is captured in the labor process by capital in a process of micro-level energetic enclosure; an enclosure not of territory, but of energies; human, biophysical, kinetic and solar. (2014, p. 6)

The argument mobilized here by Parenti is important: capital uses the biosphere, exploits it, but before capital can harness the energy of the biosphere, the state must control it. Labor power here is conceived of as the transferred value of non-human nature or pre-existing 'rents' that make up portions of the surface of the earth where these utilities exist as commodities controlled by the state. This transferred value must be controlled militarily and legally and completely 'encased' within the techno-managerial apparatus of administration, science and governance.

This is what is known as 'geopower.' Here, geopower refers to "the ensemble of state practices that *make environments*," and geopower technologies include "exploring, describing, cadastral surveys; building roads, canals, dams, railroads, telegraphs; establishing property rights, borders, policing and identification systems; scientific surveys, and all the applied natural sciences, like botany, agronomy, and geology" (2014, p. 7). This is what Parenti refers to as the "geopower matrix of state-centric, earth-focused techno-rational practices that help produce capitalist social nature" (2014, p. 7).

We are all up against this state. Those of us who are critical educators must be called to challenge the territorially defined modern state which is linked inextricably to capital's value form. This is no small task, for it means combating the state's "immutably fundamental nature." Parenti warns: "The state appropriates nature for capital directly by force; during conquest, enclosure and the creation of functional property rights; and indirectly by its development of landscape and its infrastructure" (2014, p. 10).

Capitalist Ideology and Capitalist Discipline

The preconditions for exploitation, alienation and ecocide are not only material, although of course it is also that, but ideological as well. The global power complexes tacitly and manifestly teach values, and produce ideational schemata that serve as interpretive templates or systems of intelligibility through which the popular majorities make sense of everyday life via the language of technification, corporatization, bureaucratic administration and commodification. These are knitted together (in the U.S.) by ideological imperatives of religious ideology, American exceptionalism and the coloniality of power. The ecological devastation of the planet must be understood as partly a product of the ideologies and discipline of capitalist imperialism.

We are inured to the catastrophic suffering of Mother Earth. Capitalism has a Bhasmasuriac touch. Like the devotee to the god Shiva Bhasmasura, who was granted the gift of causing anyone whose head he touched with his hand to burn up and turn to ashes (bhasma), capitalism turns to ashes all that it touches. Even surpassing its Medusean stare, which turns living labor into stone-dead labor through the logic of commodification, capitalism's touch utterly turns all living objects to cinder, creating a living hell on a dying planet.

In the meantime, capitalist discipline, "that which people do to prepare themselves for exchange on the money economy" (Fassbinder, 2008), binds the self to a lifetime of alienated, capitalist labor. The social relations of production then divide people into a class of owners who control the money-economy by manipulating exchange for the sake of capital accumulation, and a class of people-commodities whose lives are dedicated to preparing themselves to sell their labor power to capital. Everyone outside of the owning class is at least a potential member of this second class—see, for example Marx (1967) on the "industrial reserve army," which, as Marx said, "belongs to capital just as absolutely as if the latter had bred it at its own cost" (Marx, 1967, p. 784). Under capitalism we of the working class must continually (re)commodify ourselves in order to survive, regardless of the odds of actual survival. Needless to say, this commodification of the self is simultaneously an alienation from the Other and from the natural world.

From Pedagogy to Ecopedagogy

Larry Summers, president emeritus of Harvard University and former director of the White House U.S. Economic Council, made a telling comment when he was chief economist of the World Bank: "The economic logic behind dumping a load of toxic waste in the lowest wage country is impeccable and we should face up to that" (Porter, 2014, p. B1). The late Brazilian environmental minister, José Lutzenberger, one of the principal architects and most outspoken advocates of Brazil's environmental movement, responded that Mr. Summers's reasoning was "perfectly logical but totally insane" (Porter, 2014, p. B1).

Making poor countries a dumping ground for the refuse of the rich wasn't something that spoke with an inevitable and inescapable moral exigency to Mr. Summers, pricking his conscience, as one would have hoped in the case of one of the country's most esteemed economic luminaries. But should we be surprised? Summers made millions as a managing partner at the hedge fund D. E. Shaw & Co. by giving speeches attached to hefty honoraria to major financial institutions, including Goldman Sachs, JPMorgan Chase, Citigroup, Merrill Lynch and Lehman Brothers. That sheds some light on what presidents of Harvard stand for these days and the condition of the knowledge factory itself. This pristine logic of Summers simply obnubilates the Other, situating the Other in non-being by imputing to the world neocolonial and imperial patterns of understanding as part of an invisible (to many in the U.S.) Western ontology of Totality.

Summers's mental ecology seems preoccupied with axiomatic or classical de-contextualized logic. That is the logic generally used by U.S. academics when attempting to deal with social problems. He obviously doesn't work from a dialectical analysis. Dialectics is not a logic, per se, but a philosophical conceptual framework that deals with interactive reality; in other words, it deals with reality in motion, including contradictions, oppositions (which motivate change) and contextual knowledge. Marxists use a dialectical explanation of social problems that captures the social totality in transition—an explanation that does not separate economics from politics or ethics—so that we can intervene in the conflicts created by the capitalist system.

We understand, of course, that there is a single material reality that is not independent of our thoughts; in other words, how we think about issues affects the workings of our society. In abstracting from reality, our thoughts can never completely correspond with that reality. The world is neither independent of nor determined by our thoughts—because history is made by an interaction between thinking and doing, an interaction of our collective thinking and doing for the purpose of changing the world through our obligation to the suffering Other and our commitment to take action on behalf of the oppressed.

This is what critical ecopedagogy does: it uses a Marxist dialectic framework to invade prevailing notions of neoliberal education; it undermines certainties about what can or cannot be done about bringing justice to the world through education; it casts doubt upon the harsh inevitabilities of school life for urban populations; it proves the immutability of capitalism to be false; it subverts the tyranny of educating for political docility; and it converts a broad obligation to serve the poor into a fervent aspiration to use education to subvert the apparently unchangeable suffering of the working classes and to deploy teachers and students alike as agents for the public good. And it does so by imagining a better future determinatively and creatively.

Whether other Harvard professors and the new mandarins of academic life have followed in the wake of this aseptic preceptor of Western academic nobility is of course a case for debate, but if Summers is representative of what is happening at Harvard and other world-class universities, then we can better understand the dogmatic slumber that has affected "higher" education in this neoliberal era, especially when it comes to questions about the deterioration of the biosphere. Hence, the urgent need for a critical ecopedagogy. But perhaps a broader question relates to whether or not the very functionality of capitalism can satisfy the ethical criteria by which that system ought to be judged (Barber, 1998).

Despite the long-standing threat of capitalism to planetary survival and the more recent intensification of that threat through transnational forms of asset capitalism, environmental questions have been largely undiscussed in recent decades. In the 1980s and 1990s, as a result of the unrelenting onslaught of consumer culture and progressive education's overweening emphasis on identity politics as a solution to creating a more vibrant and critical public sphere, issues of environmental sustainability maintained but a lifeless presence, including within critical pedagogy. Now, at the outset of the twenty-first century, motivated by the sustainability crisis and emboldened by the courageous activities of various planetary social movements, critical ecopedagogues have arrived on the scene and not only developed a powerful argument about how to respond to the crises of sustainability but also offer a very timely and important contribution to critical pedagogy and community action at a time of resource shortages, climate change, economic instability and ecological breakdown.

Richard Kahn (2010) emphasizes that critical pedagogy has evolved consciously to become ecopedagogy as a planetary universal state of community-based emancipatory education.

Youth today are beginning to refuse the cult of individualism as an anti-dote to their loss of a sense of self, to their being situated as impersonal agents in a rationalized society that is highly competitive and achievement oriented and psychotherapeutically oriented. Contemporary youth do not feel them-selves embedded in a living reality that will endure within years to come because youth are taught to concentrate on their immediate personal status and well-being. They and their loved ones are not assured of protection from misery and oblivion.

The 2011 student mobilization in Chile; the activism of Nigerian youth at the Niger Delta crude oil flow station; the clenched-fist protests against the ruling establishments of Tunisia, Egypt and Libya; the resistance to the austerity measures by the youth in Portugal, Spain and especially Greece; the South African public school students who struggle to secure basic teaching amenities, such as libraries, in their schools; the Occupy Wall Street move-ment in the U.S.—all of these are part of a growing culture of contestation with its roots buried in the past, and its arabesque of tendrils arcing towards the future, the result of grafting what is desirable from the past onto new prac-tices of revolt.

Many of these movements self-consciously resist capitalism's transna-tional reach, while insisting that concerns with capitalism and ecology are all of one entangled piece. For instance, youth in these movements examine how their food is produced in terms of sustainable water and land use, critique the harsh treatment of small-scale farmers, raise the alarm around climate change while outlining the negative implications of global warming for food produc-tion and sound the charge against the exploitation of women and immigrant workers in food production and agricultural distribution. Capitalism, as Jason Moore (2011) has articulated, is understood increasingly as a "world-ecology" that connects the accumulation of capital to the exploitation of nature and working-class peoples in a toxic and unholy alliance. New social movements, led by the world's youth, are increasingly insisting upon this connection.

Towards Revolutionary Critical Ecopedagogy

I am using the term "revolutionary critical ecopedagogy" in a special sense as a reconfiguring force of socialism. I specify this because the term "revolution" has become domesticated in consumer culture, and I don't want to replicate the hegemonic, if ludicrous, conception of this insurgent process in such a way that confuses it with some new "revolutionary" version of a laundry detergent. Some would argue that ecopedagogy is already revolutionary and critical and should simply be denoted as "ecopedagogy." But the term "revolutionary critical pedagogy" draws attention to my conception of ecopedagogy as denoting a transformation of capitalism into a democratic socialist alternative, that is, a transformation of institutions of power on behalf of social justice.

In this view, any state that fails to provide food, home, education, shelter and medical assistance to its populace is considered "unnatural" and should not be left to die out but should be overturned and a new regime replanted in the soil of the old. At the same time, this socialist challenge is an ecological challenge. In the words of John Bellamy Foster (2009, p. 34):

> The socialist goal of transcending the alienation of humanity is impossible to achieve to any considerable extent unless it coexists with the goal of transcending the alienation of nature. Likewise, the ecological goal of transcending natural alienation is impossible to attain without addressing social alienation. Socialism is ecological, ecologism is socialist or neither can truly exist.

With contributions from authors and activists such as Richard Kahn, Tina Evans, David Greenwood, Samuel Fassbinder, Sandy Grande and Donna Houston (to name just a few), the field of ecopedagogy is now on a potent trajectory. Bringing their contributions into conversation with the efforts of Vandana Shiva, Joan Martinez-Alier, Joel Kovel, Jason W. Moore and John Bellamy Foster, ecopedagogues have cultivated a landscape of important transnational activism.

We are now witnessing a profound demonstration of an efficacious integration of the social, educational and ecological justice movements. In opposition to capitalist discipline, as it contributes to the ongoing crisis, ecopedagogic practices can be organized into a sort of "ecological discipline" (Fassbinder, 2008) which would bind people to the defense of diversities both ecosystemic and social as against capital's manipulation of them as people-commodities.

In this sense, *Occupy Education* (2012), a book by Tina Lynn Evans, is very much a critical pedagogy of convergence and integration bound together by ecological discipline, as the work of European sustainability scholars and activists is brought into dialogue with powerful emergent voices from las Americas, both to interrogate the rust-splotched and steampunk metropolises and tumbleweed hinterlands of neoliberal capitalism and to work towards a vision of what a world outside of the menacing disciplines of neoliberal capitalism might look like.

Evans's work is built upon in-depth theories about the nature and purposes of sustainability itself, and Evans is acutely aware that the politics of
sustainability is not a pitch-perfect love story and can easily be co-opted by
the guardians of the state, who make empty promises to manage the crisis
in the interests of the public good (really in the interests of private greed).
The discourses of sustainability can be hijacked by the very interests that
Evans is out to unmask (see, for example, Josee Johnston's "Who Cares about
the Commons?" which argues that "sustainability has come to imply sustainable profits as much as 'saving the earth'" [2003, p. 1]). Indeed, as Kahn
argues in his introduction to *Greening the Academy* (Fassbinder, Nocella, &
Kahn, 2012), the academy itself is managing sustainability for private greed
in exactly this way—and this despite the fact that its own knowledge workers
document the catastrophic ecological conditions that we have created and
that we now face.

Evans's answer is to anchor "sustainability" in place-based theory and
action, rooted in multiple contexts of practical lived experience—experience
that has been inestimably impacted by neoliberal capitalist globalization and
sustained opposition to it. In this context, the starting point for a meaningful
understanding of sustainablity is the suffering of the planetary oppressed.

Understanding how such hijacking takes place and how the imperial
instinct remains alive and well among progressive educators and comes with
a fixed-rate and non-negotiable commitment to reform over revolution can
be brilliantly assisted by engaging with the works of the decolonial school.

Exponents of this school have charted out the conflictual terrain known
as the "coloniality of power" (patrón de poder colonial), and "the Eurocentric pattern of colonial/capitalist power" (el eurocentramiento del patrón
colonial/capitalista de poder). Scholars and activists working in the areas of
decolonizing epistemologies and praxis include Ramón Grosfoguel, Anibal
Quijano, Linda Smith, Enrique Dussel, Sandy Grande and others.

In addition to addressing the coloniality of power, a revolutionary critical pedagogy of sustainability is as much about creating what Kahn calls a
"revitalized ecology of body/mind/spirit" and the struggle for "planetarity" as
it is a praxiological undertaking to achieve specific, cumulative goals (2010).
Thus, for instance, Grosfoguel (2008), as well as Quijano, Dussel and other
"decolonial" thinkers, suggest new approaches to ecology through viewing the
dependent hierarchies of capitalism, spirituality, epistemology, jurisprudence
and governance, patriarchy and imperialism as an entangled and co-constitutive power complex akin to a global ecology.

Ecopedagogy in Dialogue With Marx

My own approach to revolutionary critical pedagogy and revolutionary critical ecopedagogy is not so much theoretically multiperspectival as it is dialectical, emerging from the Marxist-humanist tradition and beginning with the works of Marx himself. Marxist educators need to include an ecological dimension in their work: In the discourse of "asset" or predatory capitalism, is not the exploitation of human labor and endless consumption a logical corollary of the extermination of indigenous peoples? More importantly, "labor" is itself a category within "nature" which, as Marx recognizes, exists, from capital's perspective, as a "free gift."

Jason W. Moore (2011) fingers capital as the owner of this perspective. Moore argues not only that "capital externalizes nature through the appropriation of extra-human nature as "free gift" (Marx, 1967, p. 745), but also asserts that nature's free gifts are not "limited to minerals, soil, and so forth: they also include human labor power (re)produced outside the circuit of capital" (Marx, 1967, p. 377). Thus capital exploits both society and nature in the way ascribed to its exploitation of nature as such. Moore (2011, p. 109) is worth quoting in full on this point:

> In privileging labor productivity over land productivity, capital reconfigures the relations between humans and the rest of nature (Marx 1967). Value, Marx argues, *internalizes* nature through the alienated elevation of human labor power to primacy. Labor power, as abstract social labor (which might be thought of as the average labor time inscribed in the average commodity), becomes the decisive metric of wealth in capitalism. At the same time, capital *externalizes* nature through the appropriation of extra-human nature as "free gift" (Marx 1967III: 745). Nor are nature's free gifts limited to minerals, soil, and so forth: they also include human labor power (re)produced outside the circuit of capital. (Marx 1976: 377–378)

At the same time, environmental activists need to follow Moore's lead (and that of Joel Kovel and John Bellamy Foster) and engage directly with the writings of Marx. No longer can environmentalists continue to rely upon capitalism for solutions to the problems which were caused by the capitalist system: thus Marx's critique of political economy, which helped guide his devastating critique of capitalism, is appropriate for mounting proactive responses to today's environmental crisis. But not only can Marx's work reveal to the educational Left how attempts to harmonize revolution and reform serve to diminish both, but his work can also be used to find some helpful markers for charting out what a post capitalist future might look like.

Curry Malott (2013) offers a succinct summary of Marx's work that I believe must be foregrounded in the ecopedagogy debate insofar as that debate is limited, too often, to altering existing capitalist social relations in order to make way for ecological progress:

> In other words, altering exchange-relations, that is, redistributing wealth to workers directly through wage increases, or indirectly through taxation and social programs ... (which of course would be a huge victory for labor), leaves production relations intact, and thus the substance of value, abstract labor, unacknowledged and thus unchallenged. In other words ... it is not issues of distribution (i.e., poverty and inequality) that so offends Marx regarding capitalism, partly because they are but mere consequences of the alienating nature of the social relations of production within capitalism. In other words, Marx objects to the alienation or self-estrangement of capitalism (i.e., abstract labor, the substance of value) because it excludes the possibility of the full, healthy, normal, cultural-social development of the human being. Because abstract value represents the substance of capitalism, the only way to transcend the alienation of capitalism is to transcend capitalism itself. Even if markets and private property were abolished and wages were equalized, as suggested above, alienation and dehumanization would continue if the social relations of capitalist production represented by the existence of socially necessary labor time, or the generalized standard separating thinking from doing, persisted. Working toward a post-capitalist society that is humanized might include a critical education against capitalism focused on imagining a world without abstract labor. This is the foundation needed for a world of inclusion, or a world inclusive of humanization and against dehumanization.

As Peter Hudis (2012) formulates it in his path-breaking book, *Marx's Concept of the Alternative to Capitalism*, when labor is determined by necessity and external expediency ends—that is, when we exist outside the social universe of value production and are no longer defined by material production, and our tribulations as human beings seeking to survive the world of vampire capitalism are no longer measured by labor time—then, and only then, are we able to take the first real steps towards freedom. This is because production and consumption will be based, according to Hudis, "on the totality of the individual's needs and capacities." Drawing our attention to Marx's storied phrase, "From each according to their abilities, to each according to their needs," Hudis corrects those who might interpret this phrase as some kind of a quid pro quo.

Here, we need to understand that Marx is not saying that needs are met only to the extent that they correspond to the expression of a given set of abilities. If this were the case it would mean that human relations are still governed by material production. But the true realm of freedom lies beyond material production. Even when we move from socially necessary labor time to actual labor time, we still are outside of the realm of freedom—entering the realm of freedom only occurs when actual labor time also ceases to serve as a standard measure, and labor serves as an end in itself, as part of an individual's self-activity and self-development.

As Hudis makes clear, free development for Marx could not be possible when human activity and products acquire an autonomous power and limits are externally imposed on the range by which individuals can express their natural and acquired talents and abilities. Marx went so far as to stress the elimination of the basis of both modern capitalism and statist "socialist" alternatives to value production.

From the point of view of ecopedagogy, the re-centering on needs suggests an important reining in of unsustainable extractive practices. In the shift from consumption to the expression of natural and acquired talents lies the promise of better ecological stewardship. More specifically, a world society whose members subscribed to some form of ecological discipline, as taught by ecopedagogy, would shift from value production to sustainable participation in ecosystems. Joel Kovel (2007) calls this activity "ecocentric production" (pp. 234–241).

And Hudis gives us something else to consider. He writes that the subjective development of the individual is, for Marx, a crucial precondition of a truly new society; in fact, for Marx it was as significant as such objective factors as the development of the forces of production. Here, he took the position that human subjective activity should never be constrained by the forces of its own making. He went so far as to argue that it is not the means of production that create the new type of man, but rather it is the new human being that will create the means of production. Marx understood that there was no way that progressive political forces could just "will" a new society into being by force of the imagination or by interlocking fingers with the capitalists in a Faustian toast to avoid the eco-sins of the father. Any new society would have to come into existence imminently from the womb of the old society, with its specific conditions of capitalist production and reproduction and the forces in play that challenge such conditions.

One of the promises of indigenous struggles within the current context, without romanticizing them, is the possibility that indigenous ways of being and knowing can be reimagined for a post capitalist world. That is, from the existing struggles will come a new society, one that is ecologically viable partly because human needs are the focus and not endless consumption for an insatiable market.

Why, one might ask, did Marx not specify more about the time frame that societies could use as a reference for the point at which they could expect to achieve certain steps in the progress towards freedom? According to Hudis (2012, p. 201), Marx is "cautious about getting ahead of what individuals could or could not achieve in the course of their practical history, precisely because he is wary of imposing any conceptions upon individuals that are independent of their own self-activity." Marx understood that changes would arise from the nature of new forms of production in a post capitalist society and, as such, he did not feel the need to advocate new forms of distribution.

Marx clearly supported the idea of a non-statist and freely associated form of self-governance that emerged from the Paris Commune. But this was a mediatory stage in which capitalist social relations had not become fully overcome. He advocated the rule of the proletariat—democratic, inclusive and participatory communities of association—as such rule could work progressively to eliminate the social dominance of capital.

While I do not claim the proletariat as the sole subject-agent of revolutionary truth, the revolutionary dictatorship of the proletariat, as articulated by Marx, has much value for us today. In addition, decolonial thinkers such as Grande, Martinez-Alier, Shiva and others suggest to us the possibilities for radical self-organization and democratic governance that gets away both from the domination of the state and of capitalist world markets, a direction that Kahn (2010, p. 114) calls "the new science of the multitude."

Marx stressed the development of the forces of production (in part, because he did not live to witness the most destructive power in the forces of production), whereas, as Hudis notes, we are witnessing today the need to limit the destructive power of many of these forces before they overtake us completely. Time is running out in the effort to save the planet from capital's vicious self-expansionary nature, and this is where the works of new ecopedagogy activists can provide us with a crucial intervention. Their work suggests links to existing work by Southern/indigenous thinkers, insofar as it emphasizes a new worldview grounded in a recognition of human beings as part of the land and natural world.

Linking Ecopedagogy to Praxis

Today's ecopedagogues are able to accomplish the charting out of a comprehensive critical pedagogy of sustainability with considerable skill and by displaying tremendous courage. The characteristic virtues and underlying tenets of such a pedagogy include trenchancy, a commitment to social and economic justice, a challenge to those who are engrossing disproportionate amounts of surplus value that are immiserating the world's peasants and a rage against those liberals who in their blinkered thinking remain at best evasively critical of capital. To this list I would only add the thought that in order to have a critical pedagogy of any kind, we first need to develop a philosophy of praxis, which requires that we recognize that all philosophy is determined by its dialectical relationship to praxis. And I would emphasize that this relationship between philosophy and praxis is imminently ethical in that it is manifested in a preferential option—no, preferential obligation!—whereby thematic priority is to be given to the oppressed to present their counter-stories and testimonies of resistance. It is also imminently pedagogical in that it recognizes that the languages and discourses of the oppressed have been domesticated, if not destroyed, by the pedagogical practices of the state (in its role as a client to the owning class) and that new languages of resistance are often coded in the interstices of popular struggles. It is imminently transformative in that it adopts a class position in solidarity with the oppressed and remains united in popular, ideological, racial, gender and cultural struggles.

In other words, ecopedagogy must join up with existing decolonial struggles, of all kinds, as natural allies in the battles against an unsustainable world capitalism. In this regard we might consider Vandana Shiva's advocacy of the Chipko movement (Mies & Shiva, 1993) as an ecosocialist struggle for the rights of forest use, as well as her advocacy of farmers' rights to seed and land through the organization "Navdanya" (Navdanya Trust, 2013). Shiva's general principle of "earth democracy" (2005) is congruent with the idea that the foundations of the means of production in land, seed, water and so on need to be kept in perpetuity by an arranged social commons (Shiva, 2005, pp. 2–4).

In general, we can regard struggles for a post capitalist world of ecological discipline as being guided by what Joan Martinez-Alier (2002) called the "environmentalism of the poor," the defense of ecosystems by those who live in and among them. He identifies three distinct types of environmentalism, which I have summarized from Fassbinder (2008, p. 97):

1. The "cult of wilderness," preservationism which "arises from the love of beautiful landscapes and from deeply held values, not from material interests" (p. 2). In this thread Martinez-Alier includes the "deep ecology" movement and the organization, "Friends of the Earth."

2. The "gospel of eco-efficiency," connected both to the "sustainable development" and "ecological modernization" movements and to the notion of the "wise use" of resources. Martinez-Alier tells us that "ecological modernization walks on two legs: one, economic, eco-taxes and markets in emission permits; two, technological, support for materials and energy-saving changes" (p. 6). This, then, is a reformist movement attaching itself to industrialism, and for it, ecology "becomes a managerial science mopping up the ecological degradation after industrialization" (p. 6). It promotes "eco-efficiency," which "describes a research programme of worldwide relevance on the energy and material throughput in the economy, and on the possibilities of 'delinking' economic growth from its material base" (p. 6). And most important—

3. The "environmentalism of the poor," which has as its main interest "not a sacred reverence for Nature but a material interest in the environment as a source and a requirement for livelihood; not so much a concern with the rights of other species and of future generations of humans as a concern for today's poor humans." This is the "environmental justice" movement, and it is centered on what Martinez-Alier calls "ecological distribution conflicts" (p. 12). Its protagonists are locals whose livelihoods are threatened by environmental impacts.

One problem with the Martinez-Alier position is that it makes it seem as though green ecology and animal liberation are bourgeois movements solely. Of course, they can be and have been and quite clearly are dialectically related to that history.

But total liberation pedagogy and politics are not about bourgeois formulations but about the utopian struggle to overcome the domination of nature in every form of its matrix. That is why, for instance, Kahn and others cannot approve of a speciesist environmental justice struggle as ecopedagogy, nor can they approve of environmental justice being turned into a secular struggle about distribution of resources.

There are decidedly spiritual implications, since, for example, many fundamentalist Christians believe that the earth was given to humankind to plunder as it sees fit all the resources it deems necessary. As I remarked in an earlier interview with Samuel Day Fassbinder:

> To all those good Christians out there who believe the Bible has given humankind the authority to use nature as it pleased, I would argue that Jesus did not mean for his followers to be baptized in the toxic waste of drilling retention ponds. The coal ash in surface impoundment ponds was not meant to be worn on the foreheads of believers on Ash Wednesday. As an educator, I believe it is my duty to promote a socialist agenda, and I make no apologies for that. (McLaren, cited in Fassbinder, 2013)

The Arc of Social Dreaming

As a philosophy of praxis, revolutionary critical pedagogy in the service of eco-sustainability will need to remain critical, self-reflexive, ethical and practical. Such a praxis is self-relating, it is immanent, it is an inscription into the order of being, a pulsion towards alterity, and it is also connected to the larger language of multiplicity and the historical traditions that can help guide it. It is an arc of social dreaming, a curvature of the space of the self as it is inscribed in our quotidian being. I emphasize this feature of revolutionary critical pedagogy as a process of becoming, not as a set of instructions for effective practice.

We generate truth by searching for it and the search itself becomes part of this truth. We don't select the circumstances in which we live; the conditions that impact our choices have arisen from the past and make up the objective conditions in which we live and act. But as Žižek notes, we also make our history through our actions that actively create the propositions of our activity—we posit, in other words, the very necessity that determines us (2012, p. 466). This means we are obligated to political mobilization. And it is here that the work of ecopedagogy and indigenous struggles, the most radical of which consistently emphasize protection of the earth and oceans, serves as an important guide.

On a recent trip to the small mountain town of Cherán, one of the eleven *Municipios* that are officially devoted to the Purépecha nation, I accompanied some educational activists from Morelia to observe attempts by the townspeople to break away from the Mexican state and function as an autonomous community. One aim of the autonomous movement was to form its own citizen militia to protect the surrounding forests from illegal loggers armed with automatic weapons and who are protected by the feared drug cartels. Here one could see the causality of capital's awkward brutality and unprecedented repression as not simply a relationship for export but rather a home ground violence that permeates the unequal societies of the earth, sprouting in the soil of value production. At the same time, the struggle of the townspeople speaks to ongoing efforts to defend ecological rights (see Martinez-Alier, 2002) from capitalist exploitation linked with the worst forms of terror and violence. This is a lesson for ecopedagogues, in the form of praxis, of everyday struggle. This is the arc of social dreaming, whether or not it is informed by explicitly revolutionary rhetoric.

In Cherán, Michoacán, where *el pueblo Purépecha en rebeldía* is in a life-and-death struggle, I could see the spirit of Paulo Freire at work in the attempts of the people to become a self-governing community. Here, Freire's entire pedagogical *crasis* stands for the God of the Poor against both the egregious-ness and good intentions of the God of the Rich (the God of Violence or the God of Unlimited Progress). The fragrance wafting from Freire's axiological thurible is not cassia or sandalwood or frankincense and myrrh; rather, it is the sacred sage of the indigenous peoples of *las Americas*, signifying unwith-holding love and salvific grace. Here Freire's face is hidden behind a signa-ture Zapatista handkerchief, his pedagogy of liberation bent on creating the necessary albeit insufficient conditions for a world where the boulevards of the lonely and the despised will no longer be drenched with tears from poor mothers carrying pictures of their murdered daughters, sons and husbands.

In such moments of struggle, we act not from some divine fiat, but from our own compassion, from our love for our brothers and sisters and non-human animals, from our thirst for justice and from our desire to end such needless suffering in the world. Yet the struggle will not be easy. On this path we are threatened by our own human frailty, by those who would betray us and the principles of revolutionary *comunalidad*, by those who would use us for their own ends, and by the faux revolutionaries who wish to be part of the struggle without sacrificing their own positions of power and privilege. It is these indi-viduals who will take us down the path of working in "collaborative partner-ships" with statist institutions all too eager to co-opt limited environmental resources, using what Kahn calls "public relations alchemy." (2012, p. 304)

But at the same time, there is another kind of imagining that is crucial to critical pedagogy. Ecopedagogy carries with it the implicit but powerful lesson that we need to talk about the future and to ignore those who tell us that normative considerations and utopian thinking are inappropriate for rev-olutionary critical pedagogues. This would be, in Marx's view, a self-refuting statement as "what will be" is always inscribed within the "what is." Marx tells us that all transformation must begin in the crumbling edifices of the old society, cobbled together by the smoldering debris left by the laws of motion of capitalist social relations—or, if you prefer something more messianic, piled up by Benjamin's Angel of History. To talk about different futures is desirable as long as such reflection is grounded in reality. Normative statements about the future are inescapable for any revolutionary. The elements of the future are contained within the very structure of the present. But we need to have more than a vision of the future—we need to be committed to a vision that arcs towards the justice that eludes us under the ironclad thrall of capitalism.

Our return to our humanity requires that we posit a new world outside of the well-worn path of American custodianship, and this is a retroactive process in which our presuppositions occur after the event. There is no metaphysical springboard from which to propel ourselves into the future; rather, we propel ourselves from where we are, from being energized by the truth effect of our own commitment to a praxis of liberation—what we may consider a concrete universal—and our full fidelity to such a praxis (Žižek & Milbank, 2009).

While we have no original source from which to act (we act from a position of exteriority beyond the totality of social relations) and from which to accept the entreaty of the oppressed, that should not stop us from participating in the struggle to build the world anew. This struggle, at once practical and imaginative, must be one for a world beyond class but also a world in harmony with social justice. It must be a social universe that refuses to reduce the natural world and everything in it to generic income streams, as surplus value that can be extracted in the absence of a revolution in productivity.

David Harvey instructs us that converting the current social system into one where worker ownership prevails can be gradually accomplished by means of the Rehn-Meidner plan, which was developed in Sweden. According to the plan, there would be a "20 per cent tax on corporate profits [which] would flow into wage earner funds controlled by the unions to be reinvested in the corporations," and this would "steadily reduce the significance of private ownership and ... build towards collective ownership managed by the representatives of the workers" (2005, p. 112, cited in Maeshiri, 2014a), thus eroding the power of the capitalist class. In a similar vein, Roberto Unger (2009, p. 43) suggests a tax on inheritance would be an effective means to democratize the market because "hereditary transmittal of economic and educational advantage through the family continues drastically to restrict mobility among generations" and notes that "the simple abolition of the right of inheritance ... for everything except a modest family minimum would everywhere amount to a revolution" (quoted in Maeshiri, 2014b).

We have other alternatives available right now that move beyond protesting in the form of shop floor revolts of rank-and-file labor. We now are witnessing mass protests against the neoliberal capitalist globalization of the entire planet. Whether we are referring to the Indignados, the Zapatistas, the Landless Peasants Movement in Brazil, Occupy Wall Street or Idle No More!, we can look to some experiments in transitioning towards worker-owned and -run cooperatives.

A co-operative was launched 60 years ago by a Roman Catholic priest, José Maria Arizmendi, in the Basque region of Spain. It grew to become Mondragon and is now the largest exporter of durable goods and one of the largest firms in Spain. Maeshiri (2014b) writes that Mondragon "prefigures socialism and economic democracy *within* the very framework of a capitalist order, within which it thrives, even in the throes of financial crisis." Mondragon has maintained a zero unemployment rate in a region that suffers from 12 percent unemployment. The default rate of Mondragon's central bank is less than half of other Spanish banks. Now, thanks to the cooperatives that have been developed, the Basque region, once one of the poorest in Spain, is one of the wealthiest; at the time of this writing it has the highest standard of living and the lowest rate of unemployment in all of Spain.

There is also an example of the recuperated IMPA factory in Buenos Aires which I visited in 2009. I am using the term "recuperation" from my experiences with what have been called the "occupied factories" of Argentina, factories that have undergone on the part of the workers a collective refusal to leave the premises when the owners decided to close the factories down, following the economic collapse of the country (see Jaramillo, McLaren, & Lázaro, 2011). What initially became occupied spaces were transformed into recuperated spaces of work, and in the case of IMPA (Industrias Metalúrgicas y Plásticas Argentina, located in Buenos Aires), sites of pedagogical, cultural and artistic production as well.

I met with factory workers on the recovered company IMPA's grounds in 2009, at the invitation of Fernando Lázaro, one of the founding members of the secondary school housed in the factory. As a fellow researcher and I approached the IMPA factory on a damp and chilly night in September, we met several of the workers and students who had come together to discuss the history of the recuperation and their ongoing struggle with the state to maintain ownership of the factory (this group included a middle-aged woman who had just ended a 30-day hunger strike in defense of IMPA). We walked through the production line and examined the small aluminum tubes these workers produce to package (among other things) toothpaste, epoxy glue and hair dye. We were led up the stairs to the classrooms, a haphazard arrangement of student desks with sporadic displays of student work hanging on the factory walls. And as we wound our way back down to the factory floor, we entered the large open space dedicated to artistic and theatrical production, part of *La Fabrica Centro Cultural*, the cultural center that had given IMPA widespread recognition throughout broad swaths of Buenos Aires's European-inspired urban enclaves.

The IMPA experience, and the work of recuperated factories across Argentina in general, offers us a unique look into those unconventional spaces where, in this life-and-death agon for workers worldwide, visions of alternative arrangements among workers, intellectuals and artists become reality, where individuals gather as a collective voice, indivisible from their struggle for self-determination, speaking the ineffable and enacting horizontal forms of organization that fulfill the social, economic and cultural necessities of everyday life. Here, a cross section of the city's working and middle classes has not only grasped the paradigmatic sociality constituting individuals, they have also revitalized the arts as a way of sustaining a critical community.

The first "recuperated" secondary school for young people and adults in Argentina was set up in 2004 at the premises of IMPA. This was preceded by the cultural center that opened in 1999, following the recuperation of the factory in 1998. The workers not only produced commercial "products," they produced art as well. The sheer novelty of society's popular classes engaging in the production of art gave them widespread visibility among the country's media elite, thus allowing them to communicate an aesthetic dimension to their historical and political struggle as disenfranchised workers (Benito, 2010).

In the case of IMPA, bringing together the spaces of work, culture and education generated a synergistic and multipronged effort as part of a broader social movement during the economic collapse of the country, to support the workers' struggle and to advance the needs of the community. In the simplest terms, the secondary school and the cultural center became part of a general working-class movement. From one day to the next, artists, educators, students and workers began to occupy the same space, diminishing the social distinctions among them. Together, these individuals began to see themselves as cultural workers, as public pedagogues, as subjects of social transformation who shared in a vision and struggle to occupy and recuperate social, cultural and pedagogic spaces of factory life. In this sense, IMPA became a resource for discovering the nexus between personal experience and history.

What is particularly inspiring are the women-initiated projects such as the Chipko movement in India in which women risk their lives preventing lumber interests from cutting down the trees, ensuring clean water, fruits and fuel, and the Green Belt movement which was initiated by Wangari Maathai in Kenya, winner of the Nobel Peace Prize in 2004, who inspired women to plant millions of trees and receive a small income for nurturing them (Johnson, 2007).

Ecopedagogy at a Time of Capitalist Cholera

The biosphere is disappearing into itself, and it is no coincidence that those of us living in regions of the geopolitical center, in the very locations where the forces of exploitation are most acutely developed, will be able to resist (with the help of the arms race and the war economy) this collapse for a longer duration than those laboring in the peripheral countries.

In this ominous moment of capitalist cholera, I do not know whether critical pedagogy will be the outcome and expression of historical necessity, or whether it will be a contingent force that will be erased by the sands of empty, unproductive time—that is, it is unclear whether critical pedagogy will be the result of the constitution of a deeper historical praxis needed at a future historical moment or whether it is merely the contingent construction of such a praxis. And we must live with the realization, as difficult as it might be, that we cannot know the outcomes of our actions and teaching, whether they will be futile or whether they will be part of the struggles that bring into being a new world out of the current world of suffering, exploitation and greed. We have no choice but to live with this uncertainty. Moreover, given the stakes of a dying earth, we have no choice but to engage in revolutionary struggle. We are all part of the politics of incompleteness!

Standing polemically against and serving as a crucial antipode to the narcissistic individualism of the consumer citizen—to a society founded on the commodity form—is revolutionary critical pedagogy. Critical pedagogy seeks those spaces where production is not wholly capitalist, and where new subjectivities can be given birth, subjects unsparingly reflective enough to remain at odds with the consumer subject. The consumer subject, skulking behind the facade of representative democracy, remains bereft of how self-knowledge is tied to the fetishism of the commodity, of how life becomes burdened with subjectivities that are monomaniacal, ungrateful, intellectually insecure, which are given to Trump-style fantasist ravings, which are at sea in judging the competitive worth of others, which never stint at distributing faults, and which are most comfortable in accepting the patronage of overly corrupt corporate leaders.

In Cherán, there is a thirst for revolutionary subjectivity. There is no dismal hunger for orthodoxy, nor lofty gestures for revolution. While there is an atmosphere fraught with foreboding, there are increasing occasions for multiple points of dialogue in which the inhabitants huddle together in discussions of new vistas of revolutionary consciousness and organization.

We cannot have market freedom, hierarchical harmony or authentic democracy within the social universe of capital—this monstrosity of monopolistic imperialist capitalism—that is unable to distribute overproduction and unable to function even minimally without the extraction of surplus value. We must not be deceived. We must reject liberal pluralism and methodological individualism, as they only serve to bolster neoliberalism and the capitalist state. Our job on the left is to cobble together strategies and tactics from the debris of human suffering that surrounds us and that can unite us in a common cause. An ecopedagogical approach that understands the ways that human suffering is tied to a larger toxic politics of ecocide is a necessary part of this Left strategy.

Critically, however, this will not be a socialist strategy that denies the different ontological and epistemological realities of the world's peoples, particularly subordinated classes. We must recognize that we live in *un mundo donde muchos mundos coexistan* (a world where many worlds coexist), and this means that we have an opportunity to resignify the notion of critical agency from the position of subaltern exteriority—that is, from the subaltern side of colonial difference in the spirit of the Zapatista *dicho* (saying) of *mandar obedeciendo* (to rule by following) and *andar preguntando* or *preguntando caminamos* (walking we ask questions), which means we make our road of liberation by walking (i.e., as we go along). This horizontal approach to organization (emphasizing interclass unity) contrasts with *andar predicando* or *predicando caminamos* (walking I tell you), which is a vertical form of organization in which one group tells another which way to go (often described as a form of Leninist vanguardism and supraclass harmony). Of course, this is organizing from a base of affection, or what has been called *política afectiva* (affective politics) or *horizontalidad* (horizontalism), where one organizes at one's own pace: *caminamos, no corremos, porque vamos muy lejos* (we walk, not run, because we are going very far).

My own preference is the term *¡Que se vayan todos!* (Out with them all!), as I think that life against and beyond capital requires more than local struggles for self-sustainability, direct democracy and participatory democracy, as important as these struggles are. We need to figure out how to organize the totality of everyday life and, for that to occur, we must first articulate the revolutionary subject. And our struggle must not only be local, to cease creating capitalism as much as resisting capitalism; rather, it must be massively universal—stronger, in fact, than the corporations that have hijacked the state. Resistance must be as global as the worldwide threats that capitalism poses to the complexity of global ecosystems but also as global as the transnational suffering caused by capitalist exploitation.

As more and more people now exist outside the control of the state, in vast slums and favelas throughout the world, the struggle to bring down capitalism and replace it with a more democratic and sustainable alternative must have a viable vision of what a social universe outside of capitalist value production will look like.

Tellingly, guerrilla fighters in Latin America, like indigenous groups worldwide, have often identified their struggle with the permanence and sanctity of nature. In Nicaragua, the vicious Reagan-backed counter-revolutionaries known as the Contras deliberately terrorized the rural communities in the 1980s, especially teachers, as a tactic for destroying the morale of the Sandinistas. David Craven reports that "the U.S.-backed Contras executed, for example, as many as 189 Nicaraguan school teachers in an effort to terrorize psychologically the populace of rural areas" (2002, p. 154). Craven writes of the Nicaraguan guerrillas' "belief during the insurrection that mountains had a 'mythical force' as 'our indestructibility, our guarantee of the future'" (2002, p. 148). He summarizes Carlos Fuentes's opinion that "Sandino and the Sandinistas were victorious against imperialism because their adversaries could not defeat nature, no matter how formidable the Western-backed technological edge was in military terms" (2002, p. 148).

Craven describes the significance of the volcano, Momotombo, which signified in revolutionary Nicaragua technological progress because it became the site of a geothermic electric plant which used volcanic steam to generate over 12 percent of Nicaragua's energy needs. Craven (2002, p. 149) notes: "Mountains thus came to signify national self-sufficiency in an entirely new sense. ...

A traditional respect for nature was combined with a modern mastery of energy sources that left the ecosystem unharmed" (a fact entirely at odds with the ecological devastation endemic to capitalist industrialization under Somoza).

Tragically, today's capitalist buccaneers do not share such a perspective. It has brought us a bloated Behemoth with a rictus of poisoned fangs, breath reeking of the stench of GMOs, agrotoxics, water-polluting mines and frack-ing fluid coursing through its veins. We live in the Golgotha of the planet, in which global colonial relations between Europeans/Euro-Americans and non-Europeans is increasingly organized in a hierarchical division of labor that is nothing less than a massive form of global apartheid.

Not only do we need a pedagogy that does not avert attention from con-templating problems of social, political and cultural domination and does not obfuscate its own complicity with the coloniality of power, we also need a mass struggle determined by our collective engagement with the world econ-omy as it participates in the natural world. This will surely require new forms of radical subjectivity and agency. It is to the task of building those new forms of political and pedagogical agency that revolutionary critical ecopedagogy must dedicate itself.

Noam Chomsky (2013) pitches the challenge as follows:

In future, historians (if there are any) will look back on this curious spectacle tak-ing shape in the early 21st century. For the first time in human history, humans are facing the significant prospect of severe calamity as a result of their actions— actions that are battering our prospects of decent survival. Those historians will observe that the richest and most powerful country in history, which enjoys incom-parable advantages, is leading the effort to intensify the likely disaster. Leading the effort to preserve conditions in which our immediate descendants might have a decent life are the so-called "primitive" societies: First Nations, tribal, indigenous, aboriginal. The countries with large and influential indigenous populations are well in the lead in seeking to preserve the planet. The countries that have driven indigenous populations to extinction or extreme marginalization are racing toward destruction. Thus Ecuador, with its large indigenous population, is seeking aid from the rich countries to allow it to keep its substantial oil reserves underground, where they should be. Meanwhile the U.S. and Canada are seeking to burn fossil fuels, including the extremely dangerous Canadian tar sands, and to do so as quickly and fully as possible, while they hail the wonders of a century of (largely meaningless) energy independence without a side glance at what the world might look like after this extravagant commitment to self-destruction. This observation generalizes: Throughout the world, indigenous societies are struggling to protect what they sometimes call "the rights of nature," while the civilized and sophisticated scoff at this silliness.

Moving from an abstract universalism to a pluriversalism (see the work of Ramón Grosfoguel), from modernity to transmodernity (completing the unfinished project of decolonialism), from a *vanguardismo* to a *retroguardismo*, from an abstract utopia to a concrete utopia, from *andar predicando* to *andar preguntando*, from a postcolonial critique to decolonial pedagogy and an appreciation for the *comunalidad* of First Nations peoples and *pueblos originarios*, and from environmental education to ecopedagogy and the politics of sustainability, revolutionary critical pedagogy is positioning itself for a transnational struggle for a socialist alternative to capitalist value production.

In this age where we work within an asset economy that makes profits from fictional investment markets imbued with the stench of greed while much of the world's population suffers, revolutionary critical pedagogy is poised to form transnational alliances with social movements that are working towards a vision of a social universe where labor processes are organized autonomously by the direct producers, where direct and participatory democratic administrative arrangements flourish, and where there exists a strong emphasis on social relations and human development that focus on service to others and the common good.

This vision must include recognition of plural worlds, of indigenous worldviews and ways of being, as well as a shared commitment to the stewardship of the natural environment. As I have written elsewhere (McLaren, 2008, p. 475) we live in a suspended present in the future anterior, and this requires an immediate choice:

> One thing is clear: the trajectory of history is non-linear. It is not mechanical. In the stretching and tearing, folding and collapsing of time there is only the now of our struggle, of the embattled toilers of the world. Daniel Bensaid (2002) writes that the key political task is to anticipate the present in the dialectical conception of historical time. The present is strategic, it is a suspended present, not a transition. It is a place where the past, present and future are non-temporal. It is a fork in the road. It is the crossroads. It is the time to struggle for a different life. A life outside of labor's value form. It is a time for teaching, a time for pedagogy, for the development of critical pedagogy—revolutionary critical pedagogy.

The questions that remain point to an urgent challenge for the Left: How extensive should be the uprooting of existing society and what should be the new social relations and new forms of social consciousness that replace current relations of exploitation and alienation?

Towards a Planetary *Comunalidad*

My experiences at IMPA and other workers' cooperatives have taught me that not only must we struggle for solidarity with the oppressed, we must also struggle for the conditions of *comunalidad*. Jaramillo, McLaren and Lázaro (2011, pp. 754–755) describe the conditions that must obtain for *comunalidad* to be realized, and these observations are worth quoting at length:

> Comunalidad is a Oaxacan concept that serves as a type of cosmovision, and it deals with 'the complex intertwining of history, morality, spirituality, kinship and communal practices' (Meyer et al., 2010, p. 387). Out of this concept is cultivated the concept of reciprocity. We believe that reciprocity is a more appropriate term than solidarity, as it is inflected by the Aymara's concept of ayllu (we are reminded here of the way in which Mariátegui articulated the Inca ayllu as a prototype of society) and by the Oaxacan term comunalidad. Solidarity is a selective and individuated term and does not speak to relations of equality, as it is essentially a one-way, unidirectional relation, which is by and large temporary. The concept of reciprocity, by contrast, is a set of practices that requires the other or others to make an equivalent response, and it is meant to be a permanent relation and inclusive of all members of the community (Meyer et al., 2010, p. 389). The left clearly needs to concern itself with ways of establishing a global comunalidad—one that is constantly renovated in the context of human development and revolutionary praxis, what Marx referred to as 'the coincidence of the changing of circumstances and of human activity or self-change' (as cited in Lebowitz, 2003, pp. 178–181). Here, it is important to link the reciprocity of global comunalidad with interculturalidad, which is a 'model constructed from below based on territorial and educational control, self-sustainable development, care of the environment, reciprocity and solidarity, and the strengthening of communal organizations, languages, and cultures' (Meyer et al., 2010, p. 393). Here, we are reminded that 'our activism must be embedded within, and never separate itself from, the multivoiced hemispheric conversation on resistance, hope, and renewal' (Meyer et al., 2010, p. 397). The concept of comunalidad resonates with ideas generated by the decolonial school of ethnic studies represented by such figures as Ramon Grosfoguel, Enrique Dussel, Walter Mignolo, Catherine Walsh, and Anibal Quijano. The decolonial school seeks to dismantle the epistemic hierarchies embedded in an institutionally globalized Eurocentric fundamentalism with its false objectivity and epistemic neutrality. In contrast to the 'ego-politics of knowledge' produced within Eurocentric epistemologies, the exponents of the decolonial school seek to promote a 'geo-politics of knowledge' and a 'body politics of knowledge' in their production of systems of intelligibility. In addition to a decolonization of colonial and neo-colonial epistemologies produced by European settler societies, the decolonial school supports the production of knowledges from below, that is, knowledges produced by subalternized and inferiorized subjects. Not only does this approach open up pathways of resistance to the epistemicide resulting from the 'coloniality of power' (Quijano &

Ennis, 2000), but encourages an epistemic diversality in opposition to 'white male hegemonic identity politics, which are hidden as the norm within knowledge production' (Grosfoguel, 2011, p. 84). In contrast to essentialistic and reductionistic approaches to identity politics, the decolonial approach reflects what Angela Davis (1997) refers to as 'identities in politics.' Addressing the challenges facing the organizing practices of women of color, Davis explains that 'this political commitment is not based on the specific histories of racialized communities or its constituent members but rather constructs an agenda agreed upon by all who are a part of it.' 'In my opinion,' she writes, 'the most exciting potential of women of color formations resides in the possibility of politicizing this identity—basing the identity on politics rather than the politics on identity' (1998, p. 320). According to Grosfoguel, 'identities in politics' is a concept based on 'ethico-political-epistemic projects which are open to all regardless of ethno/racial origin' (2011, p. 85). Grosfoguel offers as examples the Zapatista movement in Chiapas, Mexico and the movement in Bolivia led by Evo Morales that are 'open to all people and groups who support and sympathize with their political proposals as well as those who criticize them in constructive ways' (Grosfoguel, 2011, p. 85). In these movements, there is 'no correspondence between the ethical-epistemic identity of the project ... and the ethnic/racial identity of the individuals who participate in the movements' (2011, pp. 84–85). Such a position is not meant to disparage or deflect from the importance of race, ethnicity, culture, and history in fashioning a local, regional, or global political project, but to emphasize the importance of diverse and multi-voiced forms of alliance-building in a world ravaged by the globalization of capital and its divide-and-rule strategies and tactics.

Given the dire ecological situation but also the reality that the very wealthy are insulated by their wealth and physical protection from the immediate effects of such devastation, how can a new transformative understanding of the human place in the natural world be forged and practiced? While there is no effective indemnity against failure, we have no choice today but to move forward as concrete utopian workers who refuse to conceal our partisanship for a radically different future. We may not choose to call this future socialist. We might instead call for a form of planetary *comunalidad*. But whatever we choose to call the future, it will require a simultaneous revolution in our relations with nature and in our social relations of production.

Mad troubadour poet and cloth-maker Francesco di Bernardone, more commonly known as St. Francis and considered the patron saint of ecology, is often held in high regard by environmentalists. Yet, you don't have to be seen weeping, howling, screeching and writing canticles to Brother Sun, dancing in your undergarments and exhorting sinners to give up their possessions to engage in ecological praxis. Nevertheless, you are required to make a pedagogical commitment to unpacking the strong metabolic relationship between human beings and society and in so doing recognize that ecological degradation and the destruction of biodiversity that are currently engulfing the planet is not only tied to economic crises but are built into the very way human beings relate to ecosystems in their wish to dominate or master them.

If St. Francis, who loved the poor and the downtrodden and who was anything but anthropocentric, could be considered the Angel of the sixth seal in Revelation (7:2–3) "ascending from the east … saying, Hurt not the earth, neither the sea, nor the trees," as some Catholics claim, then Hugo Chávez is a John the Baptist figure, warning imperialist nations to recant their ways and to take up the indigenous principle of buen vivir "to live well." This term has become popular among ecopedagogues in Latin America because it affirms a respect for biodiversity and the rights of ecosystems.

In 2001, Chávez's congress, overseeing one of the world's most biodiverse countries, required millions of acres of untilled land where plantation owners squatted to be sold to the landless. Misiónes Zamora, Árbol and Agro Venezuela were set up to protect the environment, native peoples and campesinos (agricultural workers). Environmental benefits have accrued from de-urbanizing the population and reducing food miles (distance food is transported from the place of its production to the consumer). Chávez also ushered in improved land-ownership structures that resulted in improved environmental stewardship and associated gains in biodiversity and efficiency.

But we do not need to be saints to enter the struggle, to develop a communal metabolism to fight the class-based accumulation of capitalism. We can start now by engaging in acts of prefiguration, that is, by living and thinking as if we were in the future right now, by promoting the idea of living well. Perhaps it is Evo Morales (2008) who says it best:

> As long as we do not change the capitalist system for a system based in complementarity, solidarity and harmony between the people and nature, the measures that we adopt will be palliatives that will be limited and precarious in character. For us, what has failed is the model of "living better," of unlimited development, industrialisation without frontiers, of modernity that deprecates history, of increasing accumulation of goods at the expense of others and nature. For that reason we promote the idea of Living Well, in harmony with other human beings and with our Mother Earth.

We don't have to wait until we have a perfect society, we can begin to create the alternative worlds we wish to create right at this very moment, as what we have at hand contains the lineaments of what could be. A movement towards the future exists in every breath that we take. All the acts that we take in the here and now have a prefigurative potential. What we call for is a prefigurative praxis. There are always cracks in historical time, where the light shines through. The battle for that future will be illuminated by this light. And it will be fought with fierceness. So if we must be burdened by nostalgia, let it be nostalgia for the future. And that requires permanent revolution:

> History's osteoporetic spine can be crushed under the weight of the burden we place on it to find its own way. We can help it lurch in the direction of freedom only by apprising ourselves of the pedagogical dimension of the political and re-membering the political by living it pedagogically. And creating pedagogical spaces for self and social transformation, and for coming to understand that both are co-constitutive of building socialism for the twenty-first century—a revolutionary praxis for the present in the process of creating a permanent revolution for our times. (McLaren, 2008, p. 480)

As urgent as the struggle for our future has become, we need always to be measured in our steps. Not because there is time to waste, but because time has now been turned into waste. And the hounds of both heaven and hell are sniffing our tracks:

> The omnicidal regimes of our Anthropocene Era have brutalized our planet to the point of bringing ecosystems and the energies of evolution and speciation to the point of devastation and Homo sapiens to the brink of extinction. Even as we shrug off visions of hollowed-out buildings, cyclopean skeletons of smoldering steel gesticulating to an unforgiving sky, cars abandoned on highways or hanging precariously on collapsed bridges as the death wish of writers of dystopian fiction, the pace of the escalation of ecological destruction might appear to less stimulated minds as unhurried and even unperturbed. But let's not fool ourselves: Time is running out quickly. We are being chased by the hounds of both heaven and hell "with all deliberate speed" and we are being continually outflanked. The struggle that this impending tragedy mandates from all of us will not be easy. It will require all of our energy and strength as well as our courage. And it will be brutal. But the energies of love and solidarity will, I am confident, give us the fortitude necessary to bring about a new world. And critical pedagogy can serve as a red lantern, perhaps even a beacon projected skyward, signaling the beginning of a new history. This is not a guarantee of victory, by any means. For in a world besotted with tyranny, poisoned with unslakable greed, and stung by hubris, there are no guarantees. (McLaren, 2015, p. 261)

Bibliography

Barber, M. (1998). *Ethical hermeneutics: Rationality in Enrique Dussel's philosophy of liberation.* New York, NY: Fordham University Press.

Benito, K. (2010). Free stone for all the buddies: Analyzing the experience of IMPA La Fabrica ciudad cultural. *Nómadas, 32*, 45–57.

Best, S., Kahn, R., McLaren, P., & Nocella, A. J. (Eds.). (2011). *The global industrial complex: Systems of domination.* Lanham, MD: Lexington Books.

Brookfield, D. S., & Holst, J. D. (2010). *Radicalized learning: Adult education for a just world.* San Francisco, CA: Jossey-Bass.

Chomsky, N. (2013). Can civilization survive capitalism? *RSN: Reader Supported News.* Retrieved from http://readersupportednews.org/opinion2/279-82/16453-focus-can-civilization-survive-capitalism

Craven, D. (2002). *Art and revolution in Latin America: 1910–1990.* New Haven, CT: Yale University Press.

Darder, A. (2011). *A dissident voice: Essays on culture, pedagogy and power.* New York, NY: Peter Lang.

Davis, A. Y. (1997). Interview. In L. Lowe & D. Lloyd (Eds.), *The politics of culture in the shadows of capital.* Durham, NC: Duke University Press.

Davis, A. Y. (1998). Reflections on race, class, and gender in the USA. In J. James (Ed.), *The Angela Davis reader* (pp. 307–325). Malden, MA: Blackwell.

Evans, T. L. (2012). *Occupy education: Learning and living sustainability.* New York, NY: Peter Lang.

Fassbinder, S. (2008). Capitalist discipline and ecological discipline. *Green Theory and Praxis, 4*(2), 87–101.

Fassbinder, S. (2013, June 7–9). His work, his visit to Turkey and ongoing popular struggles: Interview with Peter McLaren. *CounterPunch.* Retrieved from http://www.counterpunch. org/2013/06/07/interview-with-peter-mclaren/

Fassbinder, S., Nocella, A., & Kahn, R. (2012). *Greening the academy: Ecopedagogy through the liberal arts.* Rotterdam, the Netherlands: Sense.

Foster, J. B. (2009). *The ecological revolution: Making peace with the planet.* New York, NY: Monthly Review Press.

Freire, P. (1985). *Dialogue is not a chaste event. Comments by Paulo Freire on issues in participatory research.* Compiled by Paul Jurmo. Amherst, MA: The Center for International Education, School of Education. Hills House South. University of Massachusetts, Amherst.

Freire, P. (1997). *A la sombra de este árbol* [In the shadow of this tree]. Barcelona, Spain: El Roure Editorial S.A.

Freire, P. (2000). *Pedagogy of the oppressed.* New York, NY: Continuum.

Grande, S. (2004). *Red pedagogy.* Lanham, MD: Rowman & Littlefield.

Grosfoguel, R. (2007a). Descolonizando los universalismos occidentales: El pluriversalismo transmoderno decolonial desde Aimé Césaire hasta los Zapatistas. In S. Castro-Gomez & R. Grosfoguel (Eds.), *El giro decolonial: Reflexiones para una diversidad epistémica más allá del capitalismo global* (pp. 63–77). Bogota, Colombia: Siglo del Hombre Editores.

Grosfoguel, R. (2007b). The epistemic decolonial turn: Beyond political economy paradigms. *Cultural Studies, 21*(2–3), 211–223.

Grosfoguel, R. (2008a). Para descolonizar os estudos de economia política e os estudos póscoloniais: transmodernidade, pensamento de fronteira e colonialidade global. *Revista Crítica de Ciências Sociais, 80*, 115–147.

Grosfoguel, R. (2008b). World-system analysis and postcolonial studies: A call for dialogue from the coloniality of power approach. In R. Krishnaswamy & J. C. Hawley (Eds.), *The postcolonial and the global* (pp. 94–104). Minneapolis, MN: University of Minnesota Press.

Grosfoguel, R. (2011). The dilemmas of ethnic studies in the United States between liberal multiculturalism, identity politics, disciplinary colonization, and decolonial epistemologies [Special issue]. *Human Architecture: Journal of the Sociology of Self-Knowledge, 9*, 81–90.

Harvey, D. (2000). *Spaces of hope.* Berkeley, CA: University of California Press.

Harvey, D. (2005). *A brief history of neoliberalism.* Oxford, England: Oxford University Press.

Hudis, P. (2005, November). *Marx's critical appropriation and transcendence of Hegel's theory of alienation.* Paper presented to the Brecht Forum, New York, NY.

Hudis, P. (2009, June 1). Today's global financial/economic crisis and the legacy of Rosa Luxemburg. Retrieved from http://www.internationalmarxisthumanist.org/uploads/hudis-article-20090601-Todays-Global-Financial-Economic-Crisis.pdf

Hudis, P. (2010, December). *The critical pedagogy of Rosa Luxemburg.* Paper presented at the Encuentro Internacional del Pensamiento Critico: Marxismo y Educacion Popular, Morelia, Michoacan, Mexico.

Hudis, P. (2012). *Marx's concept of the alternative to capitalism.* Amsterdam, the Netherlands: Brill.

Jameson, F. (2009). *Valences of the dialectic.* London, England: Verso.

Jaramillo, N., McLaren, P., & Lázaro, M. (2011). A critical pedagogy of recuperation. *Policy Futures in Education, 9*(6), 747–758.

Johnson, E. A. (2007). *The quest for the living God: Mapping frontiers in the theology of God.* New York, NY: Continuum.

Johnston, J. (2003). Who cares about the commons? *Capitalism Nature Socialism, 14*(4), 1–42. Retrieved from http://individual.utoronto.ca/joseejohnston/CNS2003.pdf

Kahn, R. (2010). *Critical pedagogy, ecoliteracy, and planetary crisis: The ecopedagogy movement.* New York, NY: Peter Lang.

Kahn, R. (2012). Afterword. In T. L. Evans, *Occupy education: Learning and living sustainability* (pp. 301–310). New York, NY: Peter Lang.

Kovel, J. (2007). *The enemy of nature: The end of capitalism or the end of the world?* London, England: Zed Books.

Lebowitz, M. A. (2003). *Beyond capital: Marx's political economy of the working class* (Rev. ed.). London, England: Palgrave Macmillan.

Löwy, M. (2015). *Ecosocialism: A radical alternative to capitalist catastrophe.* Chicago, IL: Haymarket Books.

Maeshiri, K. (2014a, March 11). For socialism. *The Harvard Ichthus.* Retrieved from http://www.harvardichthus.org/fishtank/2014/03/for-socialism/

Maeshiri, K. (2014b, April 19). The kingdom of God, or what shall Christians do? *The Harvard Ichthus.* Retrieved from http://www.harvardichthus.org/fishtank/2014/04/the-kingdom-of-god-or-what-shall-christians-do/

Malott, C. (2013). Questioning the American Dream: An essay review of Marsh's *Class dismissed. Education Review, 16*(3). Retrieved from http://www.edrev.info/essays/v16n3.pdf

Martinez-Alier, J. (2002). *The environmentalism of the poor: A study of ecological conflicts and valuation.* Cheltenham, England: Edward Elgar.

Marx, K. (1967). *Capital* (Vol. 1;. F. Engels (Ed.); (S. Moore & E. Aveling, Trans.)). New York, NY: International.

Marx, K. (1976). *Capital vol. I.* New York: Vintage.

Marx, K. (1977a). *Capital* (Vol. 1;. (B. Fowkes, Trans.)). New York, NY: Knopf Doubleday.

Marx, K. (1977b). *Capital* (Vol. 3;. (F. Engels (Ed.); (S. Moore & E. Aveling, (Trans.)). New York, NY: International.

McLaren, P. (1999). *Schooling as a ritual performance: Toward a political economy of educational symbols and gestures.* Lanham, MD: Rowman & Littlefield.

McLaren, P. (2008). This fist called my heart: Public pedagogy in the belly of the beast. *Antipode, 40*(3), 472–481.

McLaren, P. (2012). Objection sustained: Revolutionary pedagogical praxis as an occupying force. *Policy Futures in Education, 10*(4), 487–495. Retrieved from http://dx.doiorg/10.2304/pfie.2012.10.4.487

McLaren, P. (2015). *Life in schools: An introduction to critical pedagogy in the foundations of education.* Boulder, CO: Paradigm.

McLaren, P., & Houston, D. (2004). Revolutionary ecologies: Ecosocialism and critical pedagogy. *Educational Studies, 36*(1), 27–44.

Meyer, L., Kirwin, J., & Toober, E. (2010). An open-ended closing. In L. Meyer & B. M. Alvarado, *New world of Indigenous resistance: Noam Chomsky and voices from North, South and Central America.* San Francisco, CA: City Lights Books.

Mies, M., & Shiva, V. (1993). *Ecofeminism.* London, England: Zed Books.

Moore, J. (2011). Ecology, capital, and the nature of our times: Accumulation and crisis in the capitalist world-ecology. *Journal of World-Systems Research, 17*(1), 108–147.

Morales, E. (2008). 'Save the planet from capitalism,' *Links.* Retrieved from http://links.org.au/node/769

Navdanya Trust. (2013). *Navdanya.* Online. Retrieved from http://www.navdanya.org/

Ollman, B. (2003). *Dance of the dialectics: Steps in Marx's method.* Urbana, IL: University of Illinois Press.

Parenti, C. (2014, December 11). The 2013 Antipode AAG Lecture. The environment making state: Territory, nature, and value. Antipode Foundation Ltd. As retrieved from *http://onlinelibrary.wiley.com/doi/10.1111/anti.12134/epdf*

Porter, E. (2014, December 10). In Latin America, growth trumps climate. *The New York Times,* pp. B1, B5.

Quijano, A., & Ennis, M. (2000). Coloniality of power, Eurocentrism, and Latin America. *Nepantla: Views From South, 1*(3), 533–580.

Robinson, W. I. (2008). *Latin America and global capitalism: A critical globalization perspective.* Baltimore, MD: Johns Hopkins University Press.

Shiva, V. (2005). *Earth democracy: Justice, sustainability, and peace.* Cambridge, MA: South End Press.

Smith, L. T. (1999). *Decolonizing methodologies.* London, England/Dunedin, New Zealand: Zed Books and University of Otago Press.

Unger, R. (2009). *The Left alternative.* London, England: Verso.

Žižek, S. (2012). *Less than nothing: Hegel and the shadow of dialectical materialism.* London, England: Verso.

Žižek, S., & Milbank, J. (2009). *The monstrosity of Christ: Paradox or dialectic?* Cambridge, MA: MIT Press.

· 9 ·

RADICAL NEGATIVITY

Music Education for Social Justice

Edgar Bauer, hurt by some chance remark, turned the tables and ridiculed the English snobs. Marx launched an enthusiastic eulogy on German science and music—no other country, he said, would have been capable of producing such masters of music as Beethoven, Mozart, Handel and Haydn, and the Englishmen who had no music were in reality far below the Germans who had been prevented hitherto only by their miserable political and economic conditions from accomplishing any great practical work, but who would yet outclass all other nations. So fluently I have never heard him speak English.[1]

Music can turn people on to politics, draw crowds to rallies, feed the soul with revolutionary fervor, expose the ruling class, etc. Pete Seeger, however, was correct in saying, "If music alone could change the world, then I'd only be a musician." Most musicians are members of the working class and need to get down and dirty with their fellow workers if they are serious about changing the world. Just recently for example, we organized a benefit concert to promote California's Proposition 47, and Delia and I also went knocking door-to-door to tell people to vote for it. This was a community effort that resulted in victory. We like to think that our part as musicians and activists played a small but important role. Now imagine if every band did the same.[2]

I've sometimes been described, mostly throughout Latin America, as having red bones, referring to my socialist politics. My imagination, it has been said, is surrealist and situationist, my spirit is ecumenical and my soul has been humbled by the martyrdom of saints such as Archbishop Óscar Romero.

But I can say firsthand that my heart perpetually sings the blues. I've been a bluesman as long as I can remember. As a teenager, I was shown some licks by John Hammond Jr. on his Gibson acoustic guitar at Yorkville's Riverboat Coffeehouse in my native Toronto. Muddy Waters graciously permitted me and some other white boys to jam with him during a break at The Colonial Tavern, and Charlie Musselwhite would always be kind enough to answer my dumb questions about playing the blues harp—not by actually talking to me but by playing slowly enough on some of his songs that I could tell what he was doing. But I didn't play well enough, it seems, since the Grateful Dead threw me and my harmonica off the stage during a concert at the Carousel Ballroom, San Francisco, in 1968. But that was probably because I had spent the evening with Timothy Leary with whom I had ingested some purple tabs courtesy of Stanley Owsley.

Around that time Allen Ginsberg gave me some sage advice about my poetry, and I thought I could accompany my poetry on guitar with my Hohner Marine Band harmonica safely tucked into a Lee Oskar Harmonica Holder, Dylan-style. I was never very good, but found that the blues helped my soul in times of great distress, and there were many occasions of great distress, and there still are. Congenital deafness in one ear and too much time spent in front of blaring Marshall "Plexi" amplifiers didn't help, and the ravages of old age have made things even worse. However, I'm spry enough to notice that interest in critical pedagogy in music education has come at a very precipitous time not only for music educators but educators in all fields of endeavor.

Revolutionary critical educators are mindful of the tragic humanism [of acknowledging our own incompleteness and unfinishedness] that undergirds our work, and in this way we reject the liberal humanism that distinguishes much of mainstream critical pedagogy. In addition, what distinguishes us from many other Marxist groups is that we employ dialectical reasoning. This type of reasoning stipulates that we must attempt to become conscious of and transcend the limits that prevent us from developing protagonistic agency. To develop such agency demands externalizing, historicizing and objectifying our vision of liberation. So, for instance, we don't treat theory and practice as distinctions but see them as a part of a larger dialectical process. In other words, we don't see them as isolated from each other. We treat theory as a form of practice and practice as a form of theory. In this way the production of knowledge can never be separated from praxis, just as reading the world can never be separated from reading the word. The ultimate ground for advancing and verifying theories as well as for providing warrants for our knowledge claims is practice (Stetsenko, 2002). But of course we must always understand that there are both good and bad ethical practices. The knowledge claims we make are thus understood by examining both the ideological and ethical potentialities of a given theory as a form of practice (Stetsenko, 2002, 2008, 2009).

In addition, it's been my observation for some time that critical educators have largely failed to read the word and the world both dialectically and historically. By "historically" I don't mean the history of discourses taken in isolation but rather the history of the relationship among discourses, capitalist social formations and production relations. This stipulates paying close attention to the temporal and spatial dimensions of knowledge production but with an eye to the production of silences, of lacunae, of interstices where, like an octopus that can fold itself into small cracks and crevices and camouflage itself, great power can hide and then emerge unexpectedly to wreak havoc on the most vulnerable groups. At the same time, we need to be careful not to fall prey to philosophico-anthropological generalizations that educators use to deflect our attention from class struggle and to identify the concrete sociopolitical analysis that needs to be done to move the Left forward towards socialism.

Critical educators need to identify that which may be forbidden to say since it is not always clear what is considered extreme or ridiculous from a dominant perspective and what is actually forbidden to think or to utter. Conversely, it is important to identify which educators are likely to be heard in the dominant culture, how their ideas affirm the ruling ideas (which are, as Marx noted, most often the ideas generated by the ruling class) by serving as an ideological alibi for the production of commonsense knowledge, and why such educators allow their messages to be conscripted by the dominant media apparatuses. Second, it is important to identify educators whose ideas are discontinuous and disruptive to the pro-capitalist imperatives of the ruling regime, to affirm the aberrant, the incongruous and offensive, and to advance their work.

Radical Negation

The revolutionary critical pedagogy that I support is directed at understanding the world dialectically, as an effect of multiple antagonisms whose conditions of possibility are intensified by the contradiction between labor and capital. Revolutionary critical pedagogy questions the official, hegemonic view of ahistorical educational change, isolated from the capitalist social and production relationships. As revolutionary critical educators, I believe that we need to understand how the dynamics of the capitalist system—its movement from global capitalism to transnational capital, for instance—have guided the meaning and purpose of educational reform and have impacted institutions and approaches with respect to what counts as educational change.

There has been little transformation wrought in the attitude of critical educators to Marxism. Like an artifact packed in a tea chest and left sitting in the rust-splotched storage room of an abandoned freighter, Marxism has been all but forgotten in the field of critical pedagogy. This has been, in part, because Marxism has been criticized for its hermetic vocabulary that apparently reduces class to a categorical stasis and allegedly participates in a dehistoricizing economic reductionism commonly associated with the orthodoxies of what has been termed "mechanistic or manifesto Marxism." This lack of understanding of Marx and the Marxist tradition has ensured a fixed place in the future for a very specific and circumscribed concept of Marxism, along with the company of other "isms" such as totalitarianism and authoritarianism.

The Marxist-humanist approach with which I strongly identify has a very different take on Marx's writings, viewing Marx's work as indispensable for the development of a philosophy of praxis, and human development in general. I don't have the space to discuss this work, but I would argue that Marxist educationalists have, in the main, been able to develop an important dialectical conception of knowledge production, which is formed internally through analyzing the continuous contractions of external influences on the lives of human beings. One founding assumption of this approach is that by means of negativity, human beings are able to surmount those contradictions that block the development of their humanity, and they are able to come to recognize the positive content of their original acts of negation or what philosophers have called "the negation of the negation." I call this process "radical negation."

I discussed the negation of the negation in terms set out by Hegel and Marx, as summarized by Peter Hudis, in Chapter 1, and now I would like to further expand on the concept of radical negation, this time borrowing from the work of Anne Fairchild Pomeroy (2004). All movement is the negation of what is. As Pomeroy notes, what is, might not be, and what is not yet, might be. But acts of negation that move beyond mere acts of negation are those that negate the negation itself, and this occurs when we recognize the positivity of acts of negation as negativity. We are all beings of negativity. We are dialectical beings and our self-determination is our absolute right. Pomeroy's (2004) premise is that if the human being is in her very being the source of negation and that negation is the continual transformation of the real, then the lived being of humanity is the appropriation of this very being. It is, therefore, a revolution in permanence.

Paraphrasing Pomeroy (2004), the first negation (she is referring here to Hegel's negation of the negation) occurs when we negate our status as objects of history, when we refuse to be commodities in the service of neoliberal capital, when we shout a resounding "no" to serving as wage labor for capital. This is when we take the position: I am NOT wage labor. Here, the emphasis is on the NOT. We do not want to fit into this destructive society of commodified, monetized relations of capitalism. We refuse to live within relations of subordination wrought by capital with its ever-increasing rate of exploitation. We will not let capital define and redefine us according to its need to maintain its rate of profit. We are misfits and we choose to be so rather than allow ourselves to be re-patterned according to the requirements of value production. We refuse to be buried by abstract labor. We shake our fists at the sky in defiance. We assert our determination against all pre-existing capitalist social relations.

The second negation occurs when "the human being as self-determination hears herself speak that she truly understands what freedom is" (Pomeroy, 2004). Freedom here has become self-conscious; it knows itself. When we, as human beings, recognize ourselves as the source of negativity that produces the contradiction that is the source of movement and life, then we are in the self-possession of our creativity, of our freedom, of our potentiality, of the "not yet." Here, self-recognition is the second negation, when freedom becomes conscious of itself, when it knows itself. In this instance, we escape from the prison house of being determined to the precincts of self-determination. The second negation is this self-determination hearing itself speak in the subject's own voice, that is, when our knowing becomes merged with our doing, and our reaching out becomes part of a collective doing (Pomeroy, 2004).

Paraphrasing Pomeroy further, when we become self-conscious of our act of negating our role as wage labor for capital, that is, when we become more critical and self-reflective about it, then we are participating in a second negation, and this is greatly facilitated by the kind of self-reflexivity engaged in by critical educators who work in the field of critical pedagogy. When teachers can create spaces of learning where students are able to HEAR their denial of their status as capitalist labor, they can help them see the positive content of their original act of negation, and thus assist them in recognizing their own act of self-determination: I AM not wage labor. I AM not capital.

Here the emphasis is on the AM. Individuals in this second negation become more self-conscious about their power to become subjects of history. In Pomeroy's terms, individuals recognize themselves as the one with the power to say no, as the very source of the negation, and thus through this recognition they become the subject of the movement of history itself. Here, we are able to plant the seeds of the new, and begin our escape from the deadening fixity of capitalist social relations, creating a counter-public sphere, a counter-world with a different logic of being, "a time-space in which we try to live as subjects rather than objects" (Holloway, 2010, p. 54).

A critical education, in my view, should provide the space for students to recognize themselves as the very source of the valorization of capital that oppresses them but also as the primary source of capital's undoing. Teachers can make a strong case that individuals have the capacity to alter what it is about their world that they no longer want to be—slaves to capital and to capital's co-constitutive antagonisms of racism, sexism, homophobia, patriarchy, colonialism and imperialism. They can begin to take charge of their own creative capacities and realize that it is possible to build a future outside of capital's value form, outside of the social universe of capital and value production itself. When individuals realize the power of their acts of negation and simultaneously understand this negativity as positivity, then they can come to the conclusion that it is through their great refusal of capitalism that ideas are produced anew.

Students also begin to realize that "mere" acts of negation are inadequate for changing the world, without the second negation. The negation of the negation is the return of human beings to themselves, as we recognize that capitalism is that which enslaves the negative, that requires the subservience of this critical self-consciousness, of the I AM not wage labor. Here we find the freedom to create organizational forms that will enable us to live outside of capital's value form, to discover the freedom in our particular acts of struggle that we also recognize as absolute freedom, because negation is the source of all movement. Here we find, in Marx's words, "the true resolution of the strife between existence and essence, between objectification and self-confirmation, between freedom and necessity" (1964, p. 135).

We recognize that there is no freedom that does not simultaneously will the freedom of the other, and that, as Pomeroy notes, our form of being becomes the Absolute Idea (in Hegel's terms), that is, our simultaneous individual and universal realization that I am the movement of the real, that my own self-consciousness takes on the burden of freedom, of responsibility, of sociality. At this point, critical pedagogy as radical negation becomes a brimming reservoir from which to draw numerous practices of criticism and possibility. For instance, to recognize that you are NOT capital (the first negation), followed by the understanding that you ARE not capital (the second negation or the negation of the negation), is also both to acknowledge and confront the series of antagonisms unleashed by capital—racism, sexism, homophobia, and other social relations of power and privilege supported by capitalist social relations of exploitation.

One of Karl Marx's germinal contentions is that it is insufficient for philosophers to interpret the world; rather, they must seek to transform the world. This idea is what sets in motion Marx's revolutionary praxis. Hegel's notion of the Absolute Idea is the lifeblood of the dialectic, and far from representing a closed totality, it represents the culmination of Hegel's dialectic of self-movement—absolute negativity! In the language of dialectical materialism, a knowledge that enables the social negation of the social negation of creative labor constitutes the foundation of all critical knowledge (Reitz, 2000) which is the process of absolute negativity. Marx's focus on Hegel's concept of self-movement through second negativity is what led Marx to posit a vision of a new society that involved the transcendence of commodity production for exchange value. In fact, it involved the very self-transcendence of the totality of human powers. There has never been a more urgent time to embrace such a philosophy of praxis, of absolute negativity, of self-transcendence, of the transformation of our social universe outside of value's social form.

Radicalizing Education in and Through Music

One of the most prominent Latin American Marxist theorists was José Carlos Mariátegui. Rejecting dogmatic objectivism, Mariátegui believed that revolutionary consciousness could be achieved in the very process of revolutionary struggle. Mariátegui was an iconoclastic Marxist in that he did not believe the proletariat was a passive spectator bobbing and eddying in the wake of the laws of motion of capitalist development. Rather, from within Mariátegui's open, non-deterministic, subjective Marxism, he sought to salvage Marxism from the economic determinists. Mariátegui's statement—that "for poor people the revolution will be the conquest not only of bread, but also beauty, of art, of thought, and of all the pleasures of the spirit" (Becker, 1993, p. 137)—has influenced many on the Left. Following Mariátegui's lead, it is easy to see how music can serve as a vehicle for challenging oppression through a form of radical aesthetics.

In their path-breaking book, *Radicalizing Learning*, Stephen Brookfield and John Holst (2011) describe what they call "the educational functions of radical aesthetics," summarizing T.V. Reed's ten functions of art in social movements that can be equally applied to music: to "encourage, empower, harmonize, inform internally, inform externally, enact movement goals, historicize, transform affect or tactics, critique movement ideology, and make room for pleasure" (p. 152). They go on to identify six functions of art in radical adult education: sounding warnings, building solidarity, claiming empowerment, presenting alternative epistemologies and ontologies, affirming pride and teaching history. Here, they maintain that songs play a vital role:

> Art that sounds warnings is art that works on two social levels. First, it solidifies and encapsulates an emerging movement in a way that feels accurate and real to members of the movement. Song is particularly suited to this owing to its short gestation time. A song can theoretically be written and learned in a couple of hours, recorded and mixed in a few more, and then be available for download on the web almost immediately and on the streets a little later. It is more compact than a blog posting and works in visceral and emotional ways that an op-ed piece or blog cannot. From the Trouveres to the broadside ballads, from "Joe Hill" to "Strange Fruit," song has a directness and immediacy that appeals to memories and instincts deeper than mere prose can. (Brookfield & Holst, 2011, p. 153)

Woody Guthrie wrote a song based on the novel *Grapes of Wrath* by John Steinbeck that exposed the suffering of migrant farm workers in California during the Great Depression. Steinbeck once confessed: "he [Guthrie] got the entire story of a thing that took me two years to write" (McLoughlin, 2009, p. 73). I've often felt that music can reach inside your chest and place a string of lights around your heart, enabling you to feel your way through some very dark times. There is a scene in the movie, *Quartet*, where Reginald, a retired opera singer, is teaching music to a group of high-schoolers, comparing opera to hip-hop. Reginald exclaims, "Opera is, when a guy is stabbed in the back, instead of bleeding, he sings. In rap, when he's stabbed in the back, instead of bleeding, he speaks."

Of course, there's no real class analysis regarding rap and opera in the film, but I thought that the line was telling. What song and "musicing" can do—along with theater and other 'unorthodox' approaches to teaching and learning—is to provide alternative and oppositional ontologies and epistemologies that can then serve as mediating languages for reading the word and the world dialectically. This is certainly true in the music of Rage Against the Machine, a group that actually makes reference to Frantz Fanon ("grip tha canon like

Fanon and pass tha shells to my classmate") in a track entitled "Year of tha Boomerang" on their 1996 album, *Evil Empire*. Other references to Frantz Fanon can be found in a track that Zack de la Rocha (the lead singer of Rage Against the Machine) did with artists Last Emperor and KRS-One called "C.I.A. (Criminals in Action)," and in other songs by The Coup, Digable Planets and Earthling.

Inspired by the life and work of Tupac Shakur, Jeff Duncan-Andrade and Ernest Morrell (2008), in their book, *The Art of Critical Pedagogy*, developed what they refer to as "THUG LIFE" pedagogy that does an exceptionally fine job of drawing upon the "hatred/rage/hostility/indignation that result from any group of people systematically being denied their right to food, clothing, shelter, education, and justice" and channels these feelings "into the courage to act and fundamentally change the direction of a society, even in the face of the broader society's cowardice" (p. 143). Music in this instance helps to bridge the gap between our inner and outer worlds, as difficult and agonistic as those worlds might be.

In her book, *A Pedagogy of the Blues*, Shirley Wade McLoughlin (2009) successfully challenges dehumanizing techno-rational approaches to education that devalue what she sees as the spiritual and physical aspects essential to humanity. She does so by establishing a pedagogy that utilizes the blues metaphor and that conceives of pedagogy as an art form that can break the established hegemonic order of society. She believes that "[b]y looking at teaching as an art, the process of educating is seen more clearly in terms of its potential for creating change" (2009, p. 88).

McLoughlin's pedagogy of the blues centers on what she calls "critical testimony." She writes:

> A pedagogy of the blues looks and feels different than the type of education so prevalent today. One of the distinguishing characteristics is in the incorporation of testimony in the daily work in the classroom. Teachers and students relate their personal experiences to the educational setting, interpreting them and relating them to the content with which they are working with intent for deeper learning and understanding to occur as these stories are shared. In essence, they are sharing their selves and elements of their private interpretation of experience and knowledge of the way of the world. ... The use of critical testimonies is an essential component of working within educational environments that are essentially controlled by members of the dominant society. To teach and learn within such spaces, especially as marginalized members of society, requires deep reflection and consideration of appropriate manners in which to best approach issues, especially those of social justice. (2009, pp. 88–89)

The idea behind these critical testimonies is to acknowledge the oppressive circumstances surrounding the lives of marginalized peoples, to "embody" theory production by revealing the author's voice through personal narratives that accompany theory production, and to create a community that can support the struggle for social justice. In this respect, these critical testimonies are similar to the counter storytelling so vital to the practice of teaching informed by critical race theory.

Tracing the blues metaphor in country music, folk, jazz and hip-hop, McLoughlin identifies six themes that have come out of the thematic universe of her classroom experiences and are engaged through the testimonies of her students: truthfulness, pain, criticality, hopefulness, joyful/playfulness and autobiography.

My own previous work on the topic of gangsta rap and hip-hop touched on some of these themes, as well as attacks on music that can be traced to the creative production of artists working within different historical junctures and musical genres. As I wrote in 1996:

> Gangsta rappers follow a long line of musicians denounced by the moral custodians of US culture as prime instigators of juvenile delinquency—a list that includes, among others, Frank Sinatra, Elvis, the Beatles, the Sex Pistols, Metallica, and Prince. Members of my generation … reflecting on the earlier public debates surrounding the subliminal messages purportedly inserted into songs by Judas Priest and Ozzy Osborne, are perhaps reminded of earlier controversies that accompanied the Rolling Stones' hit "Satisfaction," or the two-and-a-half-year analysis by J. Edgar Hoover's G-men of the Kingsmen's 1963 hit, "Louie Louie." The investigation by FBI sound technicians and cryptographers of this pop chant (which merely recounts a lovesick sailor's return to his Jamaican sweetheart) seems ironic now, given the fact that the teen anthem has since appeared as the backdrop of numerous films, charity telethons, and wine cooler ads. The debate over gangsta rap has captured the public imagination at a time when the nation is vigorously reevaluating public policies surrounding affirmative action and urban reform. This has given gangsta rap an urgency and public visibility far greater than earlier debates over rock 'n' roll and morality. (McLaren, 1996, pp. 10–11)

Gangsta rap and hip-hop clearly have a visceral sensibility of embodying life in the streets. Again, as I wrote in the same article:

> With its numbing psychorealism; with its fixing of "in-your-face" rhymes to social meltdown and bass rhythms to urban disaster; with its commodification of black rage through high-volume and low-frequency sound; with its production of sexualizing fugues for an imploding Generation X; with its ability to provoke a white hellification

of black youth with "attitude"; with its seventh sons in blue or red bandanas and ten-dollar gold tooth caps "droppin science" and warning their homeboys against "tell-lie-vision," the "lie-bury," and public school "head-decay-tion"; with its dance culture of the Hanglide, Flow, Headspin, King Tut, Windmill, Tick, Float, Wave, and freestyle; with its production of affective economies of white panic around a generalized fear of a black planet; with its sneering tongue-flicking contempt of public space; with its visceral intensity and corporal immediacy; with its snarling, subterranean resistance; with its eschatological showdown of "us" against "them"; with its "edutainers" down with the brothas in the street; with its misogynist braggadocio; with its pimp-inspired subjectivity; with its urban war zone counternarratives; with its home-brewed polymerized anarchism; with its virulent autobiographical hype; with its irreverent first-person narratives powered by malt-liquor; with its rhythmic macho boastfests by brothas in Carhartt jackets; and with its dissentious themes and high-pitched contempt for the white petit-bourgeoisie and the yuppie heirs of the overclass who can afford to sidestep the frenetic dizziness of reality. ... (McLaren, 1996, pp. 13–14)

And while hip-hop clearly has become commodified and commercialized, it has pullulated, and continues to branch out, into new forms. Hip-hop can provoke classroom debates as students examine not only the sexism and use of language in some of the lyrics but also the ways in which the four pillars of hip-hop (MCing, DJing, b-boying and graffiti writing) embody a way of life, have been embraced by youth globally and have produced politically and socially conscious messages that speak within a larger framework of social justice.

And while many are drawn to hip-hop, it would be a mistake to rule out the appeal and the power of the protest songs that grew up around the Great Depression created by the Industrial Workers of the World, also known as the Wobblies (my old union). These can be found in the *Little Red Songbook* that was created by a committee of locals in Spokane, Washington in 1909. I'm thinking of songs such as "Workers of the World, Awaken!" or "One Day as I Lay Dreaming" and songs written by T-Bone Slim and Joe Hill. The ravages that capitalism has wrought, especially for workers in the factories and the mines, have turned so many workers into what the late singer, Alistair Hulett, described as "a wheezing bag of bones with lungs half clogged and filled with clay."

Musician and activist Billy Bragg has produced rousing songs about the importance of unions, the struggle for socialism and warnings about not breaking a picket line. And of course, what could be more inspirational than "The Internationale!" And what about the protest music of the 60s, which

I was raised on, such as songs by Pete Seeger, Bob Dylan, Buffy Sainte-Marie, Sam Cooke, Phil Ochs, John Lennon, Ramblin' Jack Elliot, and of course Joan Baez? This music needs to be shared with and cultivated by generations to follow.

Urban Life, Capitalism and Music Teaching

The focus on urban music is an important advance in music education, not just in terms of how such music is consumed but how it is produced, how it is taught and the assumptions that underlie such approaches. Critical approaches to music teaching in urban areas have focused a great deal on so-called at-risk students and the importance of teaching music that embodies the kind of "difference" that would be relevant to their lives. But, of course, this begs the question of what constitutes the operative multicultural imaginary in use and the kind of music that would embody the idealized normative conception of music against which such "difference" defines itself.

When Gaztambide-Fernández (2011, p. 11) raises the question, "differing from what?" he notes that "the reference to the 'ideal student' that these urban students differ from" also makes clear "that the 'reality of urban schools' is constructed in opposition to the normalized ideal implied in most pre-service teacher education"—which he recognizes as embodied in a concept of a white and middle-class student surrounded by nurturing (i.e., non-pathological) environmental conditions.

When one deterritorializes this discourse of normativity in music education, it often reveals an invisible backdrop of Eurocentric values and the hierarchy of worth buried therein. When we call for diversity, we are usually referring to instances when a non-Western culture enters Western culture while maintaining its identity as one of difference (Gonzalez, 2008, p. 31). This notion remains trapped in the discourse of cultural hybridity and counter-hegemonic mixing and cross-cultural forms of semiotic blending that too often ignores the history of the often genocidal (and epistemicidal) encounters between non-Western cultures and Western cultures. Often this hidden backdrop of the Anglosphere, this curtain that European epistemologies have unnervingly drawn across the front of the world, affords the white music educator the opportunity to problematize students of color as pure negativity (often engaging in a prurient sensationalism under the cloak of "being down with people of color who live in the hood") while assuming the role of the solitary protagonist of "reason" and accountability. It also clears the ground for a well-intentioned pathologizing of the situated cultures of non-white students, as well as naturalizing the hierarchy that grants the Western musical canon sacerdotal status over other, "different" musical formations.

What often goes unrecognized, however—even in the discourse of critical music educators—is that the preemptory quest for the equal worth of cultures, is underwritten by a homogenizing notion of cultural worth mediated by the capitalist marketplace. Here, multiculturalism—even within the critical tradition—becomes a means of imposing a new form of mystification based on exchange value where different cultures can be made "equivalent" when, in fact, within neoliberal capitalist societies these different cultures are all parasitic on the notion of the nation-state that assumes the parity of colonized and dominated peoples.

What is left out here is a reading of difference against the totality of capitalism's division of labor and the history of colonization. In addition, addressing the postmodern cultural configuration of difference allows some white music educators to indulge in conversations about pluralism, heterogeneity, local knowledges and non-essentialized identity politics without acknowledging how the social division of labor impacts communities of color differentially. This form of multiculturalism fetishizes the local and heterogeneous and refuses to see difference as part of a differentiated and dynamic totality (a concrete unity of contradictions) that is historically determined—such as neoliberal capitalism and the history of colonialism. In the absence of socio-economic conditions for political equality, the notion of cultural pluralism is simply reduced to an empty plaudit of the ruling class, hiding what is in essence a form of cultural imperialism.

I agree that approaching music as a form of cultural production—be it ska punk, reggae, indulgent rock, Icelandic post-metal, bluegrass, jazz, blues, lo-fi garage, folk or psychedelic rock—is a crucial step forward in the field of music education. But of equal and vital importance is to recognize that a cultural entity is not a totality in and of itself and must be read in the context of the larger social totality of capitalist social relations and the history of the rank colonization and imperialism that has followed in its wake.

To see cultural production as essentially a discursive affair, as in many poststructuralist accounts, can draw our attention away from the way that power relations are historicized in concrete material conditions of production and reproduction. As E. San Juan (1998) notes, recognition of the equal worth of cultures cannot be possible in a social system founded on relations of commodity exchange and on the reification associated with bourgeois culture:

> In this system of discrete and separate individuals, aggregated together in various collectivities, the hegemony (ideological plus political supremacy) of one group over the rest implies the ascendancy of a particular philosophical, ethical or cultural world view and form of life that subordinates others in a hierarchy that resembles the pre-capitalist formation—except now it is disguised in the language of democracy and equality. While lip service is paid to the value of diverse interest-groups, lifestyles, and so forth, in a society based on the logic of accumulation, the form differentiation and abstract universality of the whole operates to reproduce segregation, discrimination, and exclusion. (1998, p. 147)

Approaching music education from the perspective of revolutionary critical pedagogy will require music educators to take the ethical-political role of those most hated not only by the right-wing establishment but by the liberal establishment as well. Revolutionary critical pedagogy demands our engagement with the notion of the proletarian subject, given that what we stand to lose today is the entire human race (and non-human life as well) and the planet through capital accumulation, war and environmental catastrophe. We do this through our protagonistic identification with the oppressed and by enacting a praxis of interculturality. The revolutionary struggle here is resolutely transnational, self-emancipatory, and lies beyond petty-bourgeois democracy. The revolutionary subjects (be they knowledge workers, cultural workers or manual workers), far from being scorned as "louts besotted with barricades," are to lead the struggle through their own enlightened and creative initiatives. This stipulates further that music educators not only enter into a radical negation of all that exists but begin to envisage a world outside of commodity production, the violence of exchange value (both of symbolic and material values) and the abstract measure of equivalence inherent in capitalist social relations.

This is a task that both liberals and conservatives are bent against, and they are counting on the fact that the educational establishment, including the progressives in their ranks, will resist any move to put capitalism itself under siege. It is my hope that you will profoundly disappoint them. Anarchist preacher, Emma Goldman, allegedly didn't want to be a part of anyone's revolution if she couldn't dance. If I can't bring my telecaster, then count me out.

Capitalism cannot survive without remaining eagerly functional for a parasitic, panoptic and profit-making control over its workers. And that means control over people's sensuous selves, their eyes, ears, noses, throats, and loins.

It must, as Adorno (1968) warned, cast a spell over how everyday life is organized and transformed into things. It must insinuate its shamanic power within today's capitalist relations of production that instrumentalize life and commodify and fetishize our subjectivity and the technocratic contexts in which such subjectivity is produced. It must be met by the institution of popular self-government where the people act for themselves, by themselves—without relying on consciousness introduced from without—having freed themselves autonomously by their own efforts. The popular self-government must be a consistent and transparent interpreter of the dreams and aspirations of the popular masses, and the educator a liminal midwife that can help learners—young and old—relate their inner lives to the outer hard-knuckled realities of capitalist life. Music is one such liminal midwife. And vastly important in any revolutionary process. Music reaches into the past and echoes back to us from the future. It is a fibrillating aperture through which the spirit beckons us and makes demands upon us. We must welcome such demands and beware of them at the same time.

Notes

1. *Karl Marx: Biographical Memoirs*, by Wilhelm Liebknecht. First German edition, Nuremberg, 1896; first English translation (by E. Untermann), 1901. Reprinted by Journeyman Press, London, 1975. Retrieved from Eyewitness: A London Pub Crawl with Karl Marx, 1850s. http://www.mytimemachine.co.uk/pubcrawl.htm
2. The Last Internationale. In Mimi Soltysik (2014). Interview with the Last Internationale. *The Socialist*, November 6. Retrieved from: http://w.w.w.thesocialist.us/the-socialist-interview-with- the-last-internationale/

Bibliography

Adorno, T. (1968). Late capitalism or industrial society? (D. Redmond, trans.) Opening Address to the 16th German Sociological Congress. Retrieved from http://members.efn.org/~dredmond/AdornoSozAddr.PDF

Becker, M. (1993). *Mariátegui and Latin American Marxist theory*. Ohio University Monographs in International Studies, Latin America Series, No. 20. Athens, OH: Ohio University Center for International Studies.

Brookfield, S., & Holst, J. (2011). *Radicalizing learning: Adult education for a just world*. San Francisco, CA: Jossey-Bass.

Duncan-Andrade, J., & Morrell, E. (2008). *The art of critical pedagogy: Possibilities for moving from theory to practice in urban schools*. New York, NY: Peter Lang.

Gaztambide-Fernández, R. (2011). Musicking in the city: Reconceptualizing urban music education as cultural practice. *Action, Criticism, and Theory for Music Education, 10*(1), 15–46. Retrieved from http://act.maydaygroup.org/articles/Gaztambide-Fernandez10_1.pdf

Gonzalez, J. (2008). *Subject to display: Reframing race in contemporary art installation.* Cambridge, MA: The MIT Press.

Holloway, J. (2010). *Crack capitalism.* London, England: Pluto Press.

Marx, K. (1964). *Economic and philosophic manuscripts of 1844.* New York, NY: Parker Press.

McLaren, P. (1996). Gansta pedagogy and ghettoethnicity: The Hip Hop Nation as counter-public sphere. *Socialist Review, 25*(2), 9–55.

McLaren, P. (2011). Radical negativity: Music education for social justice. *Action, Criticism, and Theory for Music Education, 10*(1), 131–147. Retrieved from http://act.maydaygroup.org/articles/McLaren10_1.pdf

McLoughlin, S. (2009). *A pedagogy of the blues.* Rotterdam, the Netherlands: Sense.

Pomeroy, A. F. (2004). Why Marx, why now? A recollection of Dunayevskaya's *Power of negativity. Cultural Logic, 7.* Retrieved from http://clogic.eserver.org/2004/pomeroy.html

Reitz, C. (2000). *Art, alienation and the humanities: A critical engagement with Herbert Marcuse.* Albany: State University of New York Press.

San Juan, E., Jr. (1998). *Beyond postcolonial theory.* New York, NY: St. Martin's Press.

Stetsenko, A. (2002). Vygotsky's cultural-historical activity theory: Collaborative practice and knowledge construction process. In D. Robbins & A. Stetsenko (Eds.), *Vygotsky's psychology: Voices from the past and present* (pp. 122–135). New York, NY: Nova Science Press.

Stetsenko, A. (2008). Collaboration and cogenerativity: On bridging the gaps separating theory-practice and cognition-emotion. *Cultural Studies of Science Education, 3*(2), 521–533.

Stetsenko, A. (2009). Vygotsky and the conceptual revolution in developmental sciences: Towards a unified (non-additive) account of human development. In M. Fleer, M. Hedegaard, J. Tudge, & A. Prout (Eds.), *Constructing childhood: Global-local policies and practices* (pp. 125–142; World Year Book of Education series). London, England: Routledge.

· 1 0 ·

DEPLOYING GUNS TO EXPENDABLE COMMUNITIES

Bloodshed in Mexico, U.S. Imperialism and Transnational Capital—A Call for Revolutionary Critical Pedagogy

Peter McLaren, Lilia D. Monzó and Arturo Rodriguez

The violent unanimity that pervades daily life in the U.S. with such disarming spontaneity does not affect merely those born into communities plagued by the forlorn circumstances of poverty but threatens the very fabric of our existence as a nation. Of course, we can expect to see violence escalate in this, the first generation of Americans in modern history expected to endure lower living standards than their forebears (Haque, 2013), at a time when prosperity is diminishing at an alarming rate, when economic growth is rising while living standards simultaneously fall, when master limited partnerships (or MLPs) create "pass through" companies that do not retain their savings and thus avoid corporate tax, and that have the management of big private-equity companies circumventing rules that apply to conventional public companies, and when the rich are becoming inexorably richer without creating goods of real value for the public.

Discourses of violence also appear in the academy and are sometimes carried forward by theories associated with the linguistic turn that dismiss class antagonisms (which are dependent upon the appropriation through wage labor of the surplus value over and above the cost of the production and reproduction of the laborer) and which all but dismiss class-based critique. Here scholarship is ensepulchered in a self-enclosed and aggressively insular understanding of culture that mystifies how the social relations of production produce a culture of alienated labor and how socially produced surplus labor produces classes. Class relations are rewritten by these fashionable apostates of post-structuralism as a drama of unrepresentable self-difference in which the material is translated in terms of the cultural (i.e., what is outside culture is really the inside of culture), occluding the totality of the social relations of production (Ebert & Zavarzadeh, 2007).

Few Americans cotton to the idea that they must give up their right to bear arms, but that does not mean that they believe gun laws should be treated capriciously or with puckish abandon. Especially after the Newtown and Aurora shootings, national polls reveal that most Americans support stricter gun laws (Stableford, 2013). And this poll took place before the June 17, 2015 mass shooting at Emanuel African Methodist Episcopal Church in downtown Charleston, South Carolina, where nine people were slaughtered, including the senior pastor. Yet the right to bear arms remains the fabric of American identity.

The right to bear arms is part of the Second Amendment to the U.S. Constitution and is based partially on English common law and the English 1689 Bill of Rights. It has been described as an auxiliary right, supporting the natural right of self-defense against attack and in keeping with one's patriotic obligation to defend the nation state under assault by foreign powers. While the right to bear arms was meant to be used in a defensive stance or posture, it has become cathected ideologically to America's structural unconscious where white men envisage themselves as embodying Superman-like strength and courage and a God-given right to demonize and conquer darker-skinned nations, or those otherwise deemed inferior, while simultaneously charming women into a faint-like docility under the watchful eye of patriarchal convention.

The Rag and Bone man who trolls the dank recesses of historical memory for its refuse has taken the rotten rifle stock clutched in Charlton Heston's "cold dead hands" and transformed it into a symbol of right-wing defiance against all enemies of the state—be they women, gays, immigrants or people of color. This hyper-masculine fantasy of killing by means of guns and other weapons of destruction—lodged in the structural unconscious of the nation-state—is defended by an aging clientele of white men who view the right to keep and bear arms as their last hold on their own racial privilege while bemoaning the days of the Wild West when their power and privilege went unquestioned and was rarely contested (Karlin, 2013b).

Debates over gun control are often fraught with romantic images of an untamed frontier patrolled by John Wayne and Clint Eastwood, occluding the fact that gun manufacturing today is a billion-dollar industry that wields enormous power domestically and internationally and which, under the auspices of the NRA (National Rifle Association), lobbies aggressively to maintain the loose standards of control that murderously permit guns to be deployed to communities deemed expendable and undesirable for the purpose of maximizing surplus accumulation of capital (Graves, 2013).

Gun control activists have become increasingly bellicose as they witness our most vulnerable populations ravaged by the gun industry with its devastating capacity to kill, cripple and maim children and teachers in schools, with the offenders sometimes being children themselves. But these isolated incidents only dramatize the everyday reality of communities constantly under siege and presumed to be easily disposable, here and across the world.

The idea that guns preserve democracy constitutes an unconscionable and egregious swindle of benevolence that is unfathomable in the face of continuous bloodshed. The capitalist class and the U.S. government—in guileful cahoots—create an illusion of necessity by initiating a culture of devastation and depravity where they can conspire to create internal massacres to which they then heed a clarion call to intervene benevolently with yet more guns. The winners, of course, are the gun industry and the broader military-industrial complex, U.S. imperialism, and the transnational capitalist class—what Best, Kahn, Nocella and McLaren (2011) call the "power complex."

The border patrol is a case in point. Guns, illegally taken to Mexico from the U.S. through what has been called the "iron river," supply a murderous narcotrafficking project that terrorizes the people and destroys communities (Karlin, 2012). The U.S. media sensationalize this drug war, depressing travel to Mexico and further impacting an already crippled economy and increasing the vulnerability of those who find no rescue from their impoverished existence but to join these glorified *narcotraficantes* who promise a respite from want and dehumanization. U.S. citizens, whose own communities of color sometimes resemble these war zones, are led to believe that our "benevolent" role is to wage a war on drugs and to build systems of protection against invaders that are perceived as inhuman—sustaining and intensifying the brutal racism that has been developed in the service of capital accumulation since colonial times (Monzó & McLaren, 2014). Donald Trump, iconic personification of the Great White Capitalist Id and perennial presidential hopeful, is a representative example of the crass, narcissistic and bloviating guardian of the Anglosphere constitutively given over to hate-mongering. A recent case in point: Employing language designed to inflame even further white supremacists and Tea Party constituents against Mexican immigrants, the New York business magnate and television personality with the feisty Ewok or related Star Wars biped living on top of his head labeled undocumented Mexicans trying to enter the country criminials and rapists. Not surprisingly, he was able to boost his poll ratings among New Hampshire primary voters. But there are limits to what the transnational capitalist class will tolerate when one of their foreign members insults their homeland. Mexico's Carlos Slim Helú, worth $63.3 billion, and the world's richest man, severed a project with Ora TV, a television production and on-demand digital network, and Trump Enterprises, after Trump made his racist comments. Another Mexican billionaire, Emilio Azcárraga Jean, broke ties between Trump and NBCUniversal and Televisa, the largest television network in Latin America, for the same reason. Felix Sanchez (2015) has labeled the groundswell of response against Trump by Latino communities throughout the Americas, "Latino Spring." As of this writing, none of the presidential candidates has spoken out against Trump's remarks in anything more than tepid phrases. Presidental candidate Marco Rubio has (so far) remained silent while Ted Cruz shockingly endorsed Trump's comments. Both Rubio and Cruz are Cuban American and as such have a different sociopolitical history than other Latinos in the U.S., with a large conservative and Republican base that was established by the Cuban capitalists who fled at the onset of the Cuban Revolution. Sanchez is scathing in his rebuttal:

> Had Trump called a woman the B-word, one would imagine that every single presidential candidate would have immediately responded and condemned the remark, but call a Mexican a rapist and what is the response? It seems to be: Just ignore the clown.

In this chapter, we argue that the gun industry, as part of the broader military-industrial complex, serves a specific function of both producing and securing the interests of capital, extending the reach of U.S. imperialism and legitimizing racism and that these work conjointly to augment value for the benefit of the transnational capitalist class. A revolutionary critical pedagogy is advanced to support the mass mobilization of a people worldwide who are fed up with having their labor and dignity extorted and who are ready to imagine and create a socialist alternative, free of class inequality, a social universe that honors their humanity and that of every human being and where guns and the destruction that they wage are no longer seen as necessary nor desirable.

Guns in the Service of Capital

We live in a world that is plagued by inhumanity—the effects of the treachery of a capitalist system that promises the virtues of democracy, including freedom and equal opportunity but instead delivers war, hatred and greed (McLaren, 2012). Karl Marx prophesized that capitalism would extend its looming darkness over not only our economy but also our cultural ways of being and doing, that it would encroach on our psyche to such an extent that we would come to revere its logic of consumption, competition and greed (Fischer, 1996). A world structured by class relations in which an elite capitalist class owns the means of production—the labor power of a mass of workers—and continually seeks to extract the greatest surplus value from their labor for the purposes of their own capital accumulation can only be sustained through multiple ideologies that create hate, distrust and destruction among workers themselves (Ebert & Zavarzadeh, 2007).

Regardless of rhetoric, guns are mass-produced to kill and maim and they are man-made (sexist language intentional), not a divine invention. While some guns are created for recreational purposes such as hunting, sports competition, and personal self-defense purposes, in the main they are designed to assist the military and police forces in responding to local, regional and national security threats, to repel aggressors in the theater of war or advance a nation's interests through military means. In the U.S., guns are manufactured for two main markets: the military/law enforcement market and the civilian consumer market. As such, guns form part of the broader military-industrial complex that encompasses our military, the prison system, the law enforcement industry, the border patrol industry, weapons manufacturing corporations, marketing strategists, training schools and gun safety and crime prevention programs. The U.S. produces more guns than any other nation, and we have virtually the only legal market for personal use (Marra, 2012). This is no surprise, since a market economy and the insatiable demand for capital accumulation necessitate the constant search for new markets within which to sell products (Hill, 2012).

As in other sectors of the U.S. economy, the profit margin or the bottom line is what's at stake. Shareholders who watch the New York Stock Exchange, or NASDAQ, fluctuate seldom see the living expression of gun violence, except to cry out in horror when another shooting occurs in a middle-class neighborhood, crowded shopping mall, movie theatre or elementary school. They seem not to care that gun violence exists on a daily basis and with greater rapidity than the fluctuation of their share prices. It exists across the liminal horizon and in abandoned neighborhoods and housing projects as well as middle-class neighborhoods in Detroit, Los Angeles, Chicago, New York, New Orleans and Miami and on the streets of Torreón, Monterrey, Morelia and, lest we forget, Medellín.

We see the interests of the elite capitalist class too clearly in the failure to restrict guns even after such atrocious events as the recent massacre at Sandy Hook Elementary in Newtown, Connecticut, that took the lives of 20 first-grade children and six school employees. The attacker was in possession of several guns, including the semi-automatic rifle used in the attack, which allowed this bloodbath to occur in less than five minutes. With little remorse, however, the National Rifle Association (NRA) once again waged a multimillion-dollar campaign that stopped a bill from passing the Senate that would have required background checks prior to purchasing guns. While some restrictions have been put in place in certain states, a greater number of state legislative actions in the past year have expanded gun rights. It is believed unlikely that the gun-control movement will be an effective match against the power and money of the NRA (McVeigh, 2013).

The credo of the NRA is that "the right to keep and bear arms shall not be infringed upon." Read another way, the right to remain in power will be forever a privilege of wealthy and white property owners. Although the NRA is a non-profit organization, its membership consists of corporations whose combined contributions of millions of dollars have ensured that the NRA watches over their vital interests by making sure that dark money finds its way into political campaigns (Stone, 2013).

The NRA also lobbies aggressively for support from its primarily white, middle-class, male clientele who defend gun rights primarily on ideological grounds that cite the Second Amendment and their God-given right (as property owners) to protect themselves (Karlin, 2013b). Indeed, white Americans often turn a blind eye to violations of constitutional rights when these are sold to us as strategies of protection against the terrorist Other or the Minority Other. Whether from outside or within our own borders, the Other is often viewed as a threat from whom we must protect our "democracy," our English language and the Anglosphere that nurtures, educates and civilizes all who bask in the warm modernist afterglow of its civilized delights.

The proliferation of closed circuit television, cell tower dumps, state-sanctioned wiretaps, access to your cell phone by providers like Verizon and AT&T are part of what Michel Foucault (1978) refers to as disciplinary devices designed to exercise state power over the will and the interests of the people. The mass media create horrific spectacles of isolated acts such as the 9/11 bombings and the Sandy Hook massacre through continuous live feed of events and images of pain and suffering that are strategically deployed to keep us in a state of fear and to sell us more guns. Yet, every year the death toll from gun violence exceeds by far the number of deaths that resulted from 9/11 (Cohen, 2013).

Astonishingly, after such tragedies, Americans flock by the tens of thousands to gun shops and sporting goods stores to protect themselves and feel in control; meanwhile, the feral, vampire-like gun capitalists laugh all the way to the bank (and we are not talking about the blood bank). In the wake of the Sandy Hook tragedy, gun-manufacturing companies have found a new market for protective gear for children. Suburban males mount their new super-sized SUVs, defiantly slap the brims of their baseball caps to the rear of their heads, and rush off to martial arts classes to learn how to disarm potential terrorists Chuck Norris-style in venues where they are unable to reach for their guns and order would-be assailants to "Reach for the sky hombre"!

Racism and Expendable Communities

A heated debate exists among the Left with respect to the relationship between class and race (Cole, 2009). Some scholars argue that racism is independent of class and a more salient oppression in the lives of people of color (Taylor, Gillborn, & Ladson-Billings, 2009), whereas others argue that racism and other antagonisms are conceived within capitalism in order to keep workers ideologically and materially divided and unable to band together against capital interests (Darder & Torres, 2004).

We take this latter Marxist perspective that class and race are dialectically related. That is, they are mutually constituted but class relations—ownership of the labor power of a mass of workers by an elite few—create relations among workers that sustain a divided workforce in the service of capital accumulation. Ebert and Zavarzadeh (2007) argue that capitalism did not just begin with the industrial revolution but rather evolved out of previous historical economic formations that also constituted relations between owners and workers.

Racism is created through a complex system of ideologies and material conditions that remain historically entangled. The idea that racism is independent of class stems from a view of class as an identity parallel to racism and patriarchy rather than as a system of interlocked relations and forces of production that creates dependent hierarchies that keep workers divided (McLaren & Jaramillo, 2006).

From a Marxist perspective, racism is so ideologically entrenched in capitalist society that it cannot be undone overnight even if a different political economy replaces capitalism and is unlikely to diminish under the current system of transnational capitalism. Racism is highly implicated in the sustenance of the gun industry, the prison-industrial complex and the broader military-industrial complex.

In the U.S., guns take the lives of predominantly black and Latino youth in urban "killing grounds" (Karlin, 2013a)—impoverished communities forgotten by a society too intent on a superficial consumerism that is designed to mask the injustices outside the precincts of secluded gated communities populated by whites. The daily destruction of urban communities that previously produced white flight has intensified, as schools cannot ameliorate the underclass conditions of their students and jobs for youths of color become increasingly non-existent. As Mark Karlin (2013a) plainly states in Truthout:

> There's always violence in destitute areas that provide only two job opportunities of any significance: selling drugs and being a police officer patrolling the economic wastelands like an occupying military force. (para. 6)

Guns are then made readily available to these youths of color who fall prey to their promise of power as they evidence the lack thereof in their own racialized existence and develop a silent cry for justice in the desolate shrillness of their lost worlds. While poverty and racism may lead youth of color to succumb to gang activity and other types of violence, it is also evident that black and Latino men are heavily and mercilessly targeted for criminalization to support the (increasingly privatized) prison-industrial complex through a racially discriminatory justice system, with harsher penalization, greater incarceration and police brutality.

The guns that kill these youths are often purchased through a thriving black market that further sets them up for criminalization. While their white counterparts are easily able to purchase guns "for their own protection," youths of color are rarely granted gun permits even though they live in communities where protection is said to be more necessary. Under the horrendous and painful history of slavery and other inhumanities directed towards black, indigenous and Chicano communities, guns were legally restricted from the poor and people of color to prevent armed dissent (Tahmassebi, 1991). While the protection of gun rights may have ideological roots for some people, the reality is that they destroy black and Latino communities through death, criminalization and imprisonment in what is increasingly recognized as twenty-first-century slavery and the new Jim Crow (Alexander, 2010).

Outrage over gun violence occurs mainly when white children are involved. Where are the heartstrings of America when yet another black or Latino youth is gunned down because of a perceived threat against the white dominant group? Ideologies of fear, spawned by the unquestionable browning of America, are constructed to secure a growing and unfettered market for guns and other weapons of destruction. Racism incites hate, anger, fear and distrust, and these emotions, coupled with guns, are lethal, as is evident from the recent killings of 17-year-old Trayvon Martin and 13-year-old Andy Lopez, teens of color misperceived as violent threats because of the color of their skin.

Mexican immigrants and other Latinos are marked through anti-immigrant and nativist spectacles that define them as a deficit and criminal Other that belies their proud historical roots in once Mexican and indigenous lands. Under the auspices of saving jobs for 'real' Americans, undocumented immigrants are hunted down and humiliated, imprisoned, deported and torn from their families. They are described as the "dangerous and dirty Mexicans" who come to the U.S. to have welfare babies and steal our resources. In some cases, they may be perceived as the progenitors of "anchor babies" who will be programmed to insinuate themselves into U.S. culture only to inflict terror against white people years later under instructions from terrorists outside the country. This character assault is often exercised by those who would never consider taking or perhaps even withstanding the backbreaking work that undocumented immigrants do for miserly wages and substandard working conditions—slave labor that increases the profit margins for businesses and corporations.

The racism and exploitative conditions that Mexican immigrants experience in the U.S. have a deep impact on Latino immigrant communities that in the past few decades have seen anti-immigrant legislation introduced and sometimes passed across the country that attempts to curtail their use of Spanish and their access to resources, including schools, and that criminalizes undocumented status. For example, laws banning or limiting the use of bilingual instruction have been introduced in numerous states and have passed into law in California, Arizona and Massachusetts. More recently, legislation in Arizona (SB 1070) has passed requiring police to determine legal status when there is suspicion that someone is not in the U.S. legally, which is likely to lead to police profiling, as those who will be investigated are likely to look Latino. An action that previously fell under border patrol jurisdiction now serves to effectively criminalize undocumented status. To date, copycat legislation has passed in Alabama, Georgia, Indiana, South Carolina and Utah.

In Alabama (H.B. 56), this copycat legislation extends beyond putting bounty hunter Duane Lee "Dog" Chapman or Reserve Deputy Sheriff Steven Seagal (of both Hollywood and Maricopa County fame), on the hunt for undocumented workers but attempts to drive out entire families by requiring schools to document the legal status of their students and prohibiting landlords from renting apartments to undocumented workers. This racialized hatred directed against a hardworking people and their children is an attempt to retain a mythic monolithic white America (Rodriguez & McLaren, 2014). But myths have considerable power since America's structural unconscious is fashioned out of the language of myth and these myths have their roots buried in the brutal European conquest of Las Americas, myths which even today are watered by the blood, sweat and tears of poor people of color. We need to remember that it was not that long ago, at the beginning of the 18th century, that over 40% of white New York families owned enslaved Africans and the city taxed all slave sales at the site so that the municipal government could financially benefit from African enslavement. Thousands of African American slaves helped to build colonial New York, and over seventy streets in Brooklyn alone are named after slave-holders (Singer, 2015). As Alan Singer (2015) notes, "For too long, the African American role in the building of colonial New York and the New York economic and political elite's complicity with slavery, including financing of the 19th century trans-Atlantic slave trade, have been erased from history."

Many Americans have little understanding of how the U.S., NAFTA and global capitalism are implicated in Mexican immigration to the U.S. NAFTA, with its provisions of security measures for corporations, lax implementation of workers' rights and expropriations of *ejidos* (lands that were constitutionally granted collective ownership to the Mexican people for agricultural production in rural Mexico upon which many indigenous communities relied) to be opened up for sale to corporations, has resulted in extremely exploitative wages and working conditions for Mexican people. Many Mexican families from rural towns have been pushed out of their communities and, desperate for work, they have left for the cities, driving Mexican wages further down in the U.S. and Canadian *maquiladoras*. Add to this the terror and devastation that the war on drugs has created and it is easy to understand why Mexicans will move north in search of the "American dream" that the U.S. incessantly dangles before the world's poor and destitute only to snatch it away when they enter our borders.

Mexican Bloodshed

The border between the U.S. and Mexico is a heavily guarded panopticon of surveillance devices designed to control illegal Mexican immigration. Yet it is evident in the failure to stop undocumented Mexicans from entering the U.S., that even after billions of dollars have been poured into militarizing the border, people will stop at almost nothing to feed themselves and their families. Without an ounce of compassion, federal and state agents torture and sometimes gun down undocumented Mexicans as they attempt to enter the U.S., and in some cases they shoot first and investigate later. Murder is made acceptable under the guise of the federally funded war on drugs and war on terror.

It is also evident, however, that the attempt to curb Mexican immigration, even with all the funding that has gone into the narco-terror border patrol industry, is merely a symbolic gesture. Only a third of the 2000-mile border dividing Mexico and the U.S. has an actual fence that obstructs passage. Mexicans endure a host of possible deadly scenarios while crossing the border into the U.S. in the hope of a better life, including being shot, physically abused, tortured and even raped at the hands of coyotes who promise safe passage for exorbitant fees. Many also must endure dehydration in the desert heat or dash perilously across the freeway between speeding cars, their families in tow. However, since the border patrol became part of the Department of Homeland Security, not one terrorist up to this point in time has been apprehended, nor has any terrorist activity been evidenced, at the U.S.–Mexico border.

What is clear, however, is that the militarization of the border patrol is a billion-dollar charade from which numerous national and transnational corporations hugely profit. Karlin (2013c) recounts how both government agencies and private corporations are introducing new surveillance equipment, weapons and other products to enhance the effectiveness of the U.S. border agents at keeping terrorists out of the U.S. and winning a war on drugs that U.S. involvement has only intensified, particularly as suppliers of the guns used in this murderous rampage against predominantly Mexican people.

Where squatters' rights as well as the right to own property were once protected in Mexico, entire communities might be razed in a day as narco-soldiers identify areas needing tighter control and then fiercely descend upon them. Those who don't want to die either leave or pay for protection.

According to McDougal and his colleagues (McDougal, Shirk, Muggah, & Patterson, 2013), the illegal trafficking of guns to Mexico suggests a conservative count of 253,000 guns on average that are taken across the border to Mexico each year, and increasingly these include military-style semi-automatic weapons. We quote Parakilas (2013) in full:

> Of primary interest to drug traffickers are the so-called assault weapons. These rifles are effectively identical to the standard arms of infantry soldiers the world over, lacking only the provision for automatic or burst fire. Most modern assault weapons fire intermediate cartridges with effective ranges of 300 yards or more, and can be equipped with magazines holding between 30 and 100 rounds, allowing extended fire without reloading—a massive tactical advantage.
>
> Other favoured weapons for Mexican drug trafficking organizations include large-calibre sniper rifles and anti-materiel rifles, particularly the .50 caliber Barrett models, which are reputed [to be] capable of destroying a car's engine block with a single shot from a mile away. Semi-automatic personal defense weapons (the civilian versions of submachine guns such as the Heckler and Koch UMP and FN P90) are also frequently recovered by Mexican security forces, along with a wide range of shotguns and semi-automatic pistols. The cost of acquiring such weapons are negligible for trafficking groups whose profits are estimated in the billions of dollars: variants of the AR-15 rifle (the civilian version of the U.S. military's M-16) can be bought brand new for a little over $1000, pistols and shotguns for a few hundred dollars, and the hugely powerful Barrett M82 for about $10,000. Even factoring in the labor cost of the straw purchaser (an individual with a clean criminal record who legally purchases the weapons at an American firearms dealer), the cost of procuring ammunition and the cost of moving the weapons across the border, the advantages to traffickers are considerable.
>
> Combined with the benefits of being able to bulk-purchase weapons in brand-new condition, it is easy to see why buying American is so popular amongst Mexican drug trafficking groups. An exact estimate is difficult to come by, but the U.S. Bureau of Alcohol, Tobacco and Firearms (ATF) found in 2011 that 20,504 of 29,984 firearms (68%) recovered in Mexico from 2009–2010 were either manufactured in or imported into the United States before being moved into Mexico. (paras. 9–13)

McDougal and colleagues (2013) suggest that revenues of legitimate gun sales in the U.S. would be significantly reduced without this Mexican market. Further corroborating this evidence is the fact that on average there are more than three licensed gun dealers for every mile along the U.S.–Mexico border. Indeed, the most popular guns used among the drug cartels in Mexico are both manufactured and bought in the U.S.

It is virtually impossible for Mexican citizenry to purchase guns in Mexico, and they have only one store that sells guns and that is operated by the Defense Secretariat in Mexico City and serves the military. It bears emphasizing that Mexican citizens are strictly monitored in terms of gun ownership. Mexican laws prohibit the possession of weapons that can fire military-caliber ammunition. Legally, Mexican citizens are restricted to small-caliber handguns, hunting rifles and shotguns.

While attempts to keep Mexican migrants out of the U.S. intensify, little seems to be done to squelch the straw sales that create this iron river gun trade to Mexico. In a system in which capital accumulation takes priority, the Mexican people become merely collateral damage and expendable. We cite Parakilas (2013) again:

> The results of this trade are nothing less than horrific. While these arms may be marginally less effective than purpose-built military equipment on account of their lack of selective-fire capability, they are infinitely more dangerous than the small-calibre revolvers and bolt-action rifles available on Mexico's civilian market. Semi-automatic weapons with high magazine capacity allow for much more indiscriminate fire, and the military-calibre ammunition fired by such weapons is more than capable of penetrating cover and causing casualties unseen or unintended by the shooter. These capabilities increase violence at both the high and low ends of the market: professional *sicarios* (hit men) become emboldened by their ability to take on police and military forces, while the many who are not are far more dangerous for both their targets and anyone else nearby.
>
> This is important because violence in Mexico is not simply an internecine war between drug traffickers. Targeted victims of the conflict have included police officers, journalists, peace activists, and migrant workers. The dead have also included civilians who were either misidentified or were simply in the wrong place at the wrong time. In all of these cases, the scope and lethality of these attacks are vastly enhanced by easy access to military-grade small arms. (paras. 14 & 15)

Sting operations described as "gunwalking" or "letting guns walk" were part of the tactics of the Arizona Field Office of the U.S. Bureau of Alcohol, Tobacco, Firearms and Explosives (ATF), which ran some of these operations out of the Tucson and Phoenix areas, where the ATF purposely allowed licensed firearms dealers to sell weapons to illegal straw buyers whom they hoped to track inside Mexico to cartel leaders. However, during Operation Fast and Furious, the largest of the "gunwalking" probes, the ATF monitored the sale of about 2,000 weapons and recovered only 710 of them. And many of the guns tracked by the ATF have been found at crime scenes on both sides of the U.S.–Mexico border and at scenes of mass murder inside Mexico.

More recently, CBS news correspondent, Sharyl Attkisson (2011), uncovered another twisted U.S. program that may prove more deadly to Mexican citizens than Fast and Furious. Direct Commercial Sales is a U.S.-approved program that allows sales to foreign countries with less stringent control and disclosure measures than having to go through the Pentagon. The program has seen a "massive" increase in sales to Mexico, Attkisson (2011) reports:

> Here's how it works: A foreign government fills out an application to buy weapons from private gun manufacturers in the U.S. Then the State Department decides whether to approve. And it did approve 2,476 guns to be sold to Mexico in 2006. In 2009, that number was up nearly 10 times, to 18,709. The State Department has since stopped disclosing numbers of guns it approves, and wouldn't give CBS News figures for 2010 or 2011.

Not surprisingly, the CBS disclosure noted that the Mexican military recently reported 9,000 police weapons missing. These will likely end up in the hands of the cartels, just as they did in 2009 when over a quarter of all gun sales to Mexico were "'diverted' into the wrong hands, or had other 'unfavorable' results" (Attkisson, 2011). The commentary by a gun industry spokesperson suggests a naïve belief that the State Department always acts in the interest of our national security. What many may be duped into believing is that "national security" refers to our safety and well-being, when history has shown that it often refers to securing the interests of capital.

The war on drugs, spawned at the urging and financial backing of the U.S., has resulted in more than 50,000 mostly civilian deaths, more than 10,000 persons missing and more than 180,000 people displaced from their homes. An important understanding is that the drug industry has now become the second largest export industry in Mexico (Livesey, 2013a). This is a direct result of NAFTA and has virtually devastated Mexico's agricultural industry through the cheaper sales of American produce, the displacement of farmers to make lands available to transnational corporations and a highly exploitative maquila industry that pays wages that are too low to sustain Mexican families. Thus, many Mexican citizens have had to find employment that is directly or indirectly related to the drug cartels, a harsh and unyielding reality that may create a culture of complacency.

Indeed, Livesey (2013b) reports that Juárez has now become the most dangerous city in the world, with seven to ten murders occurring daily as a result of a war between essentially two major cartels, the Juárez and the Sinaloan. The military that was brought in to subdue the growing violence in 2008 has actually taken sides and seems to be taking part in the drug war between the cartels. Thus, the gun sales to Mexico may not even need to be "diverted" to play a part in the destruction of Mexican lives. Livesey points out that while it is difficult to know how far up the military ranks the corruption reaches, there are U.S. DEA (Drug Enforcement Administration) agents on the ground who have to be aware of this corruption but who are unlikely to make public that the U.S. is essentially backing a military that is aligned and implicated in the bloodshed of the very cartels with whom they are allegedly at war.

This tsunami of pain and destruction can be considered a lucrative business for the U.S. since it provides the means for expanding military presence, training and other measures to enable the U.S. to keep a vigilant watch over an often-volatile political arena in Latin America and in this way ensure the "national interests" of U.S. transnational corporations. That is, securing political stability and putting power in the hands of U.S.-friendly governments ensures open markets and flexible regulations for U.S. corporations.

Furthermore, the war on drugs also aids in keeping a citizenry in fear and more willing to acquiesce to authority. Indeed, in some cases U.S. government officials have allied themselves to and even assisted the drug cartels when it has served the interests of the U.S.—defined in truth as the interests of the transnational capitalist class. During recent visits to communities in Michoacan, Mexico, one of us (McLaren) has witnessed teachers and community members involved in the creation of *autodefensas*, or armed civilian militias designed to protect their communities and schools from violence inflicted by the cartels.

The Border Patrol, the War on Drugs and Hemispheric Hegemony

The backing of particular regimes by the Central Intelligence Agency (CIA), military training, surveillance operations and other CIA activities throughout the world guarantee new U.S. markets and work prophylactically against socialist alternatives (Robinson, 2008). The military-industrial complex aids in this imperialist project by developing the mightiest military in the world with the most destructive arsenal. The need to condition soldiers psychologically to indiscriminately kill other human beings requires a host of ideologies and practical strategies to mark the Other as deficient, immoral and expendable; to desensitize the military and its adoring public to pain, torture and death; and to create increasingly efficient guns that can destroy in seconds a mass of people. Racism, an appeal to patriarchy and other related antagonisms are employed strategically to negate the humanity of the Other and enable soldiers to see them as expendable in the context of war.

When the word "terrorism" reverberates through the mass media, white Americans cringe at the perceived threat to their way of life. Shout the word "terrorism" and the dominant group acquiesces to the Patriot Act, Foreign Intelligence Surveillance Act (FISA), violations of the amendments to the Constitution and the Bill of Rights, not to mention the suspension of Posse Comitatus during the Boston bombings or any time local police forces claim exigent circumstances to apprehend a known suspect or fugitive.

Under the cloak of building "democracy" across the world, the U.S. squashes dissent, defeats its international opposition and maintains its position as the world's superpower. This agenda is waged primarily in the so-called developing world where poverty and unfreedoms are too evident to be ignored and uprisings are increasingly common. The racist attack on Mexican immigrants and Chicano communities within the U.S. extends beyond our borders through the exploitation of Mexican workers in the *maquila* industry. Within this framing of the Mexican people, our society is duped into seeing the U.S. government and U.S. transnational corporations as benevolently providing jobs to those poor souls from the developing world who cannot sustain themselves within a global economy.

The border patrol and the narco-terrorist industry provide an increasingly militarized gateway that secures a mass population of desperate workers in Mexico whose only recourse is the *maquila* industry and also serves as an excuse and opportunity for the surveillance of Latin America against any insurgent forces that may threaten capitalist interests. Through torture and surveillance training, the CIA and other U.S. government agencies support the coercion of the Mexican people and oftentimes financially and sometimes militarily back regimes likely to legislate favorably for U.S. capitalist interests.

Our guns supply both sides of the war on drugs and serve to terrorize Mexican communities in Mexico, push them out of Mexico and across la frontera into the U.S. and then terrorize them again once they are in the U.S. This "service" of extracting the greatest surplus value from the Mexican worker and controlling the political arena of the entire hemisphere to secure open markets for exploitation of people and natural resources by U.S. corporations stems not from an incessant and inhuman greed but instead is a result of the monstrous logic of capitalism. Under such logic, capitalism must continue to plunge into every possible venue of profitability and power in order to survive.

The debate over mass shootings, gun ownership and gun control within the U.S., and their relationship to the thousands of people killed in the Mexican drug wars (largely carried out with small arms) will continue unabated. Although the first major congressional action on gun control in nearly two decades occurred in the wake of 2012's spate of mass shootings, a small group of senators supported by the National Rifle Association blocked the legislation from passage and ensured a plump U.S. civilian market for the Mexican drug cartels and condemned thousands more Mexicans to an early death (Parakilas, 2013). According to Parakilas (2013):

> The NRA's five million-strong membership roll and its strong financial links with major firearms manufacturers give it a deep war chest and unmatched political clout in American domestic gun politics, and in recent decades its opposition to gun control has evolved from nuanced opposition to outright hostility. In recent years, having successfully lobbied for the expansion of concealed-carry laws and against any new federal gun control measures, the NRA has also moved into the international sphere by opposing the UN Arms Trade treaty and attempting to globalise a civilian right to bear arms. The federal judiciary has also recently proven hostile to gun control measures, overturning some of the more restrictive statutes, such as Washington, DC's handgun ban. With gun control stalled at the federal level, the border states could in theory pass their own measures with some effect. But in practice, Texas, Arizona and New Mexico all have extremely lenient gun laws and have not evinced any willingness to strengthen them. (paras. 18 & 19)

Revolutionary Critical Pedagogy: After the Future Is the Past

Revolutionary critical pedagogy is an educational agenda for creating a mobilized mass of critically educated people in schools and university classrooms, in labor union meetings, among church groups and factory workers and in any formation where people can come together to explore their particular social conditions and human potential, where clarity can be developed and action that leads to greater clarity can be taken for the sake of confronting critically our existing capitalist reality (Freire, 1970). With an increased understanding of our combined knowledges and resources and our stolen humanity, we can learn to imagine our true potential, to labor creatively beyond necessity and to seek changes, small and large, towards a socialist transformation.

To expel the culture of gun violence to the outer darkness and exile racism past the stark hinterlands of the Anglosphere means defying outright customary duties and affiliations associated with this domain, and this means more than desacralizing the role that violence plays in our everyday lives or radically condemning the violence at the heart of the founding of modernity, or proscribing the sale of guns or forcing official culture into a rigid Victorian corset of prohibitions against violence. To require the public to abandon guns is not perforce the augury of a peaceful world, since the founding slaughter over our modern civilization needs to be understood critically in order that the violent culture of guns does not recalibrate or refurbish itself through aerosol homilies about American exceptionalism or the role of the U.S. as the sword arm of divine justice or through deodorized and dehistoricized theories of culture that obscure the class struggle at the heart of capitalist social relations and the liberating potential that is located in a materially oppressed subject foreclosed from narrating her own oppression and therefore serving as a critique of it. To mortally deform, definitively compromise or leech from within the divine violence associated with the founding genocide of the U.S. requires an understanding of the unprecedented role that violence has played in the construction of American identity. It requires collective action in building a democratic socialist alternative to labor's value form and regime of private property.

We denounce guns and all destruction of humanity. Yet we are not naïve enough to imagine that the capitalist class will simply put down their ideological weapons of death on the basis of sound reasoning or moral imperative and allow the precariats, the cognitariats, and the proletariats of our techno-capitalist present to march towards a socialist alternative without a fight. It is not our task to determine the course of this transformation. We understand the ideological contradiction that we espouse. As critical educators, we work to reach those who will engage with us and to encourage those who are initially reluctant to engage in anti-capitalist struggle and in the forging of a socialist democracy that will free us to be fully human and teach us to love truly and radically.

Bibliography

Alexander, M. (2010). *The new Jim Crow: Mass incarceration in the age of colorblindness*. New York, NY: The New Press.

Attkisson, S. (2011, December 6). Legal U.S. gun sales to Mexico arming cartels. CBS *News*. Retrieved from http://www.cbsnews.com/news/legal-us-gun-sales-to-mexico-arming-cartels/

Best, S., Kahn, R., Nocella, A., & McLaren, P. (2011). *The global industrial complex: Systems of domination*. Lanham, MD: Lexington Books.

Cohen, M. (2013, April 20). Why does America lose its head over 'terror' but ignore its daily gun deaths? *The Observer/The Guardian*. Retrieved from http://www.theguardian.com/commentisfree/2013/apr/21/boston-marathon-bombs-us-gun-law

Cole, M. (2009). *Critical race theory and education: A Marxist response*. New York, NY: Palgrave Macmillan.

Darder, A., & Torres, R. (2004). *After race: Racism after multiculturalism*. New York, NY: NYU Press.

Ebert, T., & Zavarzadeh, M. (2007). *Class in culture*. Boulder, CO: Paradigm.

Fischer, E. (1996). *How to read Karl Marx*. New York, NY: Monthly Review Press.

Foucault, M. (1978). *Discipline and punish: The birth of the prison*. (A. Sheridan, Trans.). New York, NY: Pantheon.

Freire, P. (1970). *Pedagogy of the oppressed*. New York, NY: Continuum.

Graves, L. (2013, November 1). ALEC is a corporate lobby masquerading as a charity. *Truthout*. Retrieved from http://www.truth-out.org/news/item/19749-alec-is-a-corporate-lobby-masquerading-as-a-charity

Grosfoguel, R. (2013). The structure of knowledge in westernized universities: Epistemic racism/sexism and the four genocides/epistemicides of the long 16th century. *Human Architecture: Journal of the Sociology of Self-Knowledge, 11*(1), 73–90.

Haque, U. (2013, December 9). America's economy is officially inside-out. *Harvard Business Review Blog Network*. Retrieved from https://hbr.org/2013/12/americas-economy-is-officially-inside-out/

Hill, D. (2012). Immiseration capitalism, activism and education: Resistance, revolt and revenge. *Journal of Critical Educational Policy Studies, 10*(2), 1–53. Retrieved from http://www.jceps.com/archives/709

Karlin, M. (2012, March 20). Murder incorporated: Guns, the NRA and the politics of violence on the Mexican border. *Truthout*. Retrieved from http://truth-out.org/news/item/8004-murder-incorporated-guns-the-nra-and-the-politics-of-violence-on-the-mexican-border

Karlin, M. (2013a, February 6). Why does the cry for gun control become impassioned only when white kids are shot? *Buzzflash at Truthout*. Retrieved from http://truth-out.org/buzzflash/commentary/item/17791-why-does-the-cry-for-gun-control-become-impassioned-only-when-white-kids-are-shot

Karlin, M. (2013b, February 26). Gun zealots are more interested in being seen as dangerous than in using guns for self-defense. *Buzzflash at Truthout*. Retrieved from http://truth-out.org/buzzflash/commentary/item/17827-gun-zealots-are-more-interested-in-being-seen-as-dangerous-than-in-using-guns-for-self-defense

Karlin, M. (2013c, March 10). Fear, corporate profiteering, and government expansion of the security surveillance state on the US borderland. *Truthout*. Retrieved from http://truth-out.org/news/item/14993-fear-corporate-profiteering-and-government-expansion-of-the-security-surveillance-state-on-the-us-borderland

Kovel, J. (2002). *The enemy of nature: The end of capitalism or the end of the world?* Nova Scotia, Canada Fernwood and Zed Books.

Lichtman, R. (1982). *The production of desire: The integration of psychoanalysis into Marxist theory*. New York, NY: The Free Press.

Livesey, B. (2013a, May 3). Behind Mexico's bloodshed, part 1. *The Real News*. Retrieved from http://therealnews.com/t2/index.php?option=com_content&task=view&id=31&Itemid=74&jumival=5572

Livesey, B. (2013b, May 3). Behind Mexico's bloodshed, part 2. *The Real News*. Retrieved from http://therealnews.com/t2/index.php?option=com_content&task=view&id=31&Itemid=74&jumival=5577

Marra, J. R. (2012, December 12). Guns in America: Marketing military lethality. *The Socialist: The Official Publication of the Socialist Party USA*. Retrieved from http://www.thesocialist. us/guns-in-america-marketing-military-lethality/

McDougal, T., Shirk, D. A., Muggah, R., & Patterson, J. H. (2013). *The way of the gun: Estimating firearms traffic across the U.S.-Mexico border*. Igarapé Institutes and University of San Diego Transborder Institute. Retrieved from http://catcher.sandiego.edu/items/peace-studies/way_of_the_gun.pdf

McLaren, P. (2006). *Rage and hope: Interviews with Peter McLaren on war, imperialism, and critical pedagogy*. New York, NY: Peter Lang.

McLaren, P. (2012). Objection sustained: Revolutionary pedagogical praxis as an occupying force. *Policy Futures in Education, 10*(4), 487–495.

McLaren, P., & Jaramillo, N. (2006). Critical pedagogy, Latino/a education, and the politics of class struggle. *Cultural Studies: Critical Methodologies, 6*(1), 73–93.

McVeigh, K. (2013, December 14). Sandy Hook: One year on, campaigners prepare for new push on gun control. *Readers Support News*. Retrieved from http://readersupportednews. org/news-section2/433-2nd-amendment-rights/20951-sandy-hook-one-year-on-campaigners-prepare-for-new-push-on-gun-control

Monzó, L. D., & McLaren, P. (2014). Critical pedagogy and the decolonial option: Challenges to the inevitability of capitalism. *Policy Futures in Education, 12*(4), 513–525.

Parakilas, J. (2013, July 30). A trade in iron and blood: The impact of American guns on armed violence in Mexico. Retrieved from http://aoav.org.uk/2013/impact-of-american-guns-on-armed-violence-in-mexico/

Robinson, W. I. (2008). *Latin America and global capitalism*. Baltimore, MD: Johns Hopkins University Press.

Rodriguez, A., & McLaren, P. (2014). Human rights, states' rights, and linguistic apartheid. In P. W. Orelus (Ed.), *Affirming language diversity in schools and society: Beyond linguistic apartheid*, (pp. 77–93). London, England: Routledge.

Sanchez, F. (2015). CNN News. How Trump's comments unleashed 'Latino spring'. July 2. Retrieved from: http://edition.cnn.com/2015/07/01/opinions/sanchez-latino-spring/index.html

Singer, A. (2015) Recovering New York City's black history. Huffington Post. July 2. Retrieved at: http://www.huffingtonpost.com/alan-singer/recovering-new-york-citys_b_7713048.html

Stableford, D. (2013, April 3). Poll: Most Americans want stricter gun laws. *Yahoo News*. Retrieved from http://news.yahoo.com/blogs/lookout/poll-stricter-gun-laws-155122502. html

Stone, P. (2013, April 2). Inside the NRA's Koch-funded dark-money campaign. *Mother Jones*. Retrieved from http://www.motherjones.com/politics/2013/04/nra-koch-brothers-karl-rove

Tahmassebi, S. B. (1991). Gun control and racism. *George Mason University Civil Rights Law Journal, 2*, 67. Retrieved from http://saf.org/LawReviews/Tahmassebi1.html

Taylor, E., Gillborn, D., & Ladson-Billings, G. (2009). *Foundations of critical race theory in education*. New York, NY: Routledge.

· 1 1 ·

EDUCATION AS CLASS WARFARE

The Socialist: How is your work, broadly speaking, informed by Marxist theory?

Peter McLaren: As a Marxist, I look to Marx's writings and to contemporary Marxist scholars to help analyze the current crisis of capitalism. And within this context I try to understand the history of education, particularly in the U.S. and in my native Canada, but also educational trends worldwide, as part of the formation of the transnational capitalist class and the transnational capitalist state. Since 1987, I have had the opportunity to speak in approximately 30 countries (many of which I continue to visit, and some of which I visit on a regular basis, such as Mexico and Venezuela), to academics, teachers and social activists and in numerous cases to form active alliances.

One of my projects has been to enlarge the scope of critical pedagogy into that of a social movement, a movement that I call "revolutionary critical pedagogy" (after British Marxist Paula Allman) in order to underline its central aim—to work towards a social universe outside of capitalist value production. I work in the area of anti-capitalist struggle and in the arena of epistemology, educating against the coloniality of power, and trying to create a pluriversal approach to indigenous knowledges through a critique of Eurocentric

knowledge production and through working with subaltern groups who have
been victims of European and U.S. imperialism. So I begin with a critique
of neoliberal globalization, financialization, the autonomous functioning of
the monetary economy, working-class standards of living being sacrificed at
the altar of the enrichment of finance capital, the declining rate of profit (a
number of my students at UCLA took classes with Robert Brenner), over-
accumulation of capital and accumulation by dispossession as developed by
David Harvey.

But I also work within the analysis of the transnational capitalist class
and the development of a global capitalist historical bloc composed of the
transnational corporations and financial institutions, the elites that manage
the supranational economic planning agencies, major forces in the dominant
political parties, media conglomerates and technocratic elites, as developed by
William I. Robinson at UC–Santa Barbara. Here I am specifically interested in
how the class practices of a new global ruling class are becoming condensed in
an emergent transnational state in which members of the transnational capitalist class have an objective existence above any local territories and polities.

I am very interested in work being done in epistemology within the decolonial pedagogy school, and here I am starting to work within a framework
developed by the decolonial school, whose exponents include Enrique Dussel, Ramón Grosfoguel, Walter Mignolo, Catherine Walsh, Nelson Maldon-
aldo-Torres and others. Here, I expand the idea of what happened when *las
Americas* were transformed by capital. I try to think of capital as more than the
limited sense of an economic logic but as an integrated network of cultural,
political and economic processes that are all internally related. We need to
account for the complex entanglement of gender, racial, sexual and class hierarchies within global geopolitical, geocultural and geo-economic processes of
the modern/colonial world system.

We need to keep in mind the global racial/gender/sexual hierarchy that
emerged with European colonial expansion and that continues to be reproduced in the modern/colonial/capitalist world system. We are trying to bring
this perspective to the Marxist left in Venezuela, and this summer (2014)
we hope we will begin training cadres in the countryside in this decolonial
perspective as part of a project that we organized with the Ministry of Education. These multiple hierarchies, or "heterarchies," are not epiphenomenal to
capitalism but are constitutive of capitalism, when we look at the historical
formations that capitalism has taken, especially from the beginning of the
conquest of *las Americas* right up to the present working of the coloniality of

power, or the persistence of thinking within Eurocentric perspectives absent actual colonial administrations.

Now it is important when doing this work to keep the eyes on the prize—the abolition of capitalism. And here I try to remain faithful to Marx's own writings, his criticism of the presuppositions and premises of classical political economy, and this causes me to be very critical of some of the formations of revolutionary organizations of the past and present. As Peter Hudis, Kevin Anderson and other Marxist-humanist scholars and activists have pointed out—and which has been supported by my own reading of Marx—Marx did not support control of society by a single state party, he did not endorse authoritarian regimes, nor did he support state control of the economy. Of course he criticized private property, but he also opposed the notion that economic life should be controlled by the state as in a centrally planned, state-run economy that supposedly counters the anarchy of the deregulated market. Both of these positions were roundly rejected by Marx as expressions of alienated social relations. Marx identified the central problem of capitalism as the production of value.

What is value production? Well, it is different than the production of wealth. As Peter Hudis notes, value is wealth computed in monetary terms. It is the reduction of concrete, living labor—or "doing" directed towards satisfying real human needs—to abstract, alienated labor (the commodification of labor power) that operates to increase value as an end in itself, as in the drive to augment value through the creation of exchange value (i.e., the exchange of commodities as the universal medium of social interaction as in surplus value production). Capitalist social relations take on a certain form of value in which human relations take on the form of relations between things. It is this form that needs to be abolished, and this can only be done through the abolition of value production.

Labor in Marx has a twofold nature—useful labor or concrete labor (purposeful doing or conscious life activity) and abstract or alienated labor (which Marx argued was the substance of both value and surplus value). These forms of labor are in a dynamic and living antagonistic relationship due to the fact that capitalism requires the worker to sell her labor power to the capitalist for a wage. John Holloway identifies two forms of struggle here—the struggle of purposeful doing (concrete labor) against abstract labor (the struggle of doing against labor, or the struggle of workers against their own existence as a working class) and the struggle of labor against capital (as in the struggle of the labor movement against capitalist exploitation, i.e., wage labor and capital). We need to see these two struggles as being related.

For instance, I am critical of labor movements and teachers' unions for many reasons. But mostly because they define the struggle as that of labor against capital, when, in fact, they actually support abstract labor, or value production. They believe that value production can be made less exploitative or that abstract labor can be reconfigured in less alienated ways. While this might be true in the short run, with redistribution from capital to labor, it will actually exacerbate the crisis of capitalism in the long run.

I am against value production and believe the only way to create a new society is through the abolition of value production. We can't tinker with relations of distribution and circulation by bringing them under the control of the state and believe we can create a socialist society. We need to abolish the production relationship itself, or we will create an even greater despotism than the one that exists under free-market capitalism. We can't abolish value production by altering the mechanisms by which surplus value is extracted from the worker.

Real freedom cannot be won in a society governed by exchange value and value production. Even cooperative, non-statist forms of production will not lead to freedom if they remain tethered to exchange value, money and value production. Here, workers only become their own exploiters. As Peter Hudis notes, such cooperatives have eliminated the need for the capitalist but have not eliminated themselves from the capitalist relation itself, a message that I tried to deliver convincingly to factory workers in Argentina who were part of the occupied factories movement, and who invited me to speak at a recuperated factory in Buenos Aires because they are setting up schools in these "recuperated factories."

TS: As a Marxist, how would you explain the current state of public education and how would you characterize the latest attempts at school reform?

PM: Education is now a subsector of the economy. Public education is now on a fast track towards privatization; it is part of the overall trend of neoliberal globalization, the two central axes being privatization and deregulation, which, by the way, has been forced upon nation-states, especially after Reagan's crushing defeat of the air traffic controllers and Thatcher's defeat of the miners who went on strike in the UK in the 1980s. This has led to the current crisis of world capitalism, and yet its policies and practices are precisely those endorsed to an even greater extent by Republicans (and in a softer version by Democrats) today. This is all part of the overall pattern of neoliberal globalization in which the World Bank (controlled by the U.S.) and International Monetary Fund have forced national governments to develop economic policies that emphasize economic growth and property rights over social welfare and personal rights.

Market-driven education (the voucherizing of education) has led to today's corporatization of education and the for-profit and corporate-style charter school movement. Education is one of the largest market industries around, and it is now controlled by hedge fund managers and bankers and speculators with the support of the Walton Family Foundation (Walmart gives $50 million a year to the charter school movement). The Bill & Melinda Gates Foundation wants to close thousands of broken inner-city schools and replace them with charters. And in some cases, for-profit corporations have created non-profit foundations to obtain charters and then hire themselves to run the schools.

Hedge fund managers and CEOs become rabid advocates for market reforms which are driven by the desire to create a less expensive teaching force, one that is shackled by narrow-minded test-based accountability measures, and one that has less union power to fight back. Federal education mandates have moved away from supporting equality of access and outcome and have focused instead on cutting back on school funding, on promoting shame-and-blame policies, on merit pay or on firing school staff, on supporting standardized tests based on Common Core standards which have little to do with the production of critical, meaningful knowledge and problem solving, on giving grants to the school "winners" instead of those high-needs students who are most in need of financial assistance, and on corporate control of the curriculum. As Stan Karp has pointed out, the most complete study of charter school performance, by Stanford University, found that only 17 percent of charter schools had better test scores than comparable public schools and more than twice as many did worse. Traditional public schools accept all children, including much larger numbers of high-needs students, whereas charter schools are very selective in who they admit.

Charters—endorsed with enthusiasm by Arne Duncan—have become the new commonsense option for the poor and the dwindling middle class who want to escape the crumbling, under-funded inner-city schools with failing track records on standardized tests and who can't afford full-blown private schools (at least for those that can get through the admissions requirements and who can afford it, as the stipends for charters won't pay for everything). For those desperately trying to escape the ravages of public schools, especially in decaying urban centers, the world of charters has been presented by Duncan and his ilk as the only feasible option. But the very people who push for charters are those who have spent years driving down public schooling. If you examine public schooling as part of the logic of neoliberal globalization, you can see that the assault on public education is really just part of the final frontier in a move by corporate America and the transnational capitalist class to privatize all public resources, at least as many as the public permits.

The whole privatization movement in education wants to smash the power of the teachers' unions and to destroy decent public wages for workers, be they teachers or other public employees. You have to see this in the context of the larger logic of neoliberal capitalism.

It's not only the Republicans but the Democrats as well that support the candidacy of pro-charter candidates for public office, even when they know full well that their selective advocacy avoids the fact that there are twice as many failing charters as there are successful ones and that a number of their principals have been indicted for embezzlement.

We are told by the state that there is a shortage of professionals in the U.S. in technology, mathematics, engineering and the sciences. But in reality there is no shortage of professionals in the U.S. in these areas. According to the World Economic Forum, the U.S. ranks first in the world in global competitiveness and about 6th out of 134 countries in all categories related to these professions and availability of expertise. So if this is the case, why does Obama's Race to the Top justify its program by claiming the U.S. needs to keep up with the rest of the world? We already keep up with the rest of the world. We know that students in schools that are well funded score as well as or higher than students from other countries in international tests. But all of this masks the fact that the U.S. has the highest percentage of children in poverty of all the industrialized countries, and we know that children from poor families who attend under-funded schools score below the international average.

So it is clear that poverty is a problem. And it's a problem that's not being addressed because we ignore the fact that we live in a class-based society. We use the term "economically disadvantaged" or "low socioeconomic status" when we should be saying "working class"! When we use the term "low socioeconomic status," we naturalize and legitimize inequality and try to rationalize it.

In our sociology of education studies, we don't look to Marx to provide an explanatory framework for poverty; we look instead to Max Weber, who frames class more in terms of consumption habits and lifestyle than objective conditions of exploitation. While Weber wrote about the irrational logic of capital, the paradoxes of capitalist rationality and the illusions of progress, he did not exhibit much concern about workers and even defended aspects of capitalism as part of the Protestant work ethic. So is it any wonder that when vouchers are proposed, or charter schools, teachers can easily find a way to rationalize them, too, when the only language they know about class from their teacher education programs is from Weber?

When the commissioner of the New York State Department of Education, David M. Steiner, told critical educator Henry Giroux at the Nexus Conference in Amsterdam in 2007 that "social justice promotes hatred. Hatred for the established order," it became clear that the object of attack of many establishment leaders in education is critical thought itself. These thinkers, including Arne Duncan, support what Giroux calls instrumental and practical classroom methodologies that, especially in the case of African Americans, function as part of a circuit of power that produces the school-to-prison pipeline. Reactionary political values are smuggled under the guise of technical reasoning and remain immune to the criticism that education has succumbed to the idiom of the corporation, to the business ethic of self-interest, to knowledge as a prepackaged commodity, to the unlimited pursuit of the accumulation of capital, to the notion that progress is measured by the quantitative growth of consumption.

Somewhere around the late 1980s, the output of the affiliates of transnational corporations outside their home countries overtook the volume of world exports of manufacturers—and there was a dramatic shift in the ability to shift capital outside of government control. This is reflective of the shift in the nature of the power relationship between the nation-state and transnational corporations.

The role of public schools has shifted accordingly. Schools are no longer preoccupied with cultivating democratic citizens for the nation-state (creating the codes for citizenship and transmitting the deep character of the national state by legitimizing the superiority of elite bourgeois culture), but instead with helping the nation-state serve the transnational corporations. Schools themselves are becoming corporate enterprises. We are training students to become consumer citizens, not democratic citizens. The future of education is now in the hands of corporate rule as the hedge funds, finance capital and betting on the stock market overdetermine the fate of public schooling.

TS: With all the discussion around school reform, it seems that the conversation has been rather limited in its scope. What would you like to see added to the conversation and what effect do you think this would have?

PM: Well, I would like to see a renewed emphasis on fighting poverty as a means of creating more equality of educational opportunity. The logic of conservative educational critics for years has been that public schools already overspend; that they have failed poor, urban students; that the teachers' unions won't allow bad teachers to be fired; and that until we fire the bottom 10 percent of the lowest performing teachers (some school boards are demanding that value-added measures on tests should account for 30 percent of teachers' evaluations, and in some cases, 50 percent), our nation will never break out of its sluggish economy and we will not be able to compete economically with other nations.

But it is not a lack of education that creates poverty and economic inequality; it's a lack of jobs. It's the very nature of the capitalist system. Successful educational reform can close the achievement gap by increasing the number of working-class and minority students who do well in school, but a good education cannot rescue the majority of children from poverty because there are too many jobs that pay poverty-level wages.

The ruling classes want to blame poverty on the failure of our education system because it is the community that assumes the burden of paying for schools, whereas it would cost the capitalists more to pay decent wages to workers. I agree with John Marsh, who in a forthcoming book, *Class Dismissed*, makes the case that education should be treated as a political—not a market—phenomenon. We need social programs and non-educational interventions into the market, whether through redistributive tax rates, massive public works projects, a living wage law or a renaissance of labor unions. More workers with college degrees will not stem the rise of low-wage jobs nor will they reduce inequality. We need to decrease the total number of people living in poverty. We can't use educational programs to reduce inequality, because this just won't work in a capitalist economy, and then when education doesn't do the trick, when unemployment is rampant and jobs are scarce, then the public educational system can be blamed.

Part of the reason that the U.S. is one of the most unequal countries in the world is that we have limited economic rights. Our main vehicle for economic success is linked to our right to a decent education. We can't simply use education as our main economic right. As Marsh argues, we need more economic rights and it is important that they not be tied to education.

Every right we have must have an independent status, such as the right to a useful and remunerative job, the right to adequate food and clothing, the right to a decent education, etc. Education is seen as a requirement for all the other rights, and it is assumed that once you are given the right to a good education all the other rights will take care of themselves. But you can't make these rights dependent upon one another or an outgrowth of one another. They must remain separate. The only economic right we can exercise in the U.S. is the right to a good education, and this right has been transformed into the right to a good corporate education.

Even in 2000, when the unemployment rate in the U.S. fell to 3.9 percent, and the poverty rate fell to 11.3 percent, we had 30 million people living in poverty in this country—and that is approximately the population of Canada. But, as Marsh reports, the U.S. does not generate many more poor people than other countries. European countries achieve lower poverty rates because they provide more social programs aimed at the poor and unemployed. Without government programs, Sweden would have 26.7 percent of its population living in poverty, but with their social programs, the poverty rate is 5.3 percent.

Sure, education helps some people enter the labor market, and indirectly might create a few more jobs, but what we need are jobs, higher wages and better redistribution programs. Marsh cites Douglas Willms, a Canadian professor, who found that among children whose parents have identical levels of education, those children who lived in unequal countries performed worse on tests of adult literacy. Children of parents with college degrees in general perform the same, whether they live in Finland, one of the most equal countries, or the U.S., one of the most unequal. But children in the U.S. whose parents only attained a high school diploma will perform worse on literacy tests than will children in Finland whose parents only attained a high school diploma. This is because economic inequality affects the quality of family life, in areas of health, security, rates of substance abuse, etc. So yes, we need educational reforms, but we need to reduce inequality and poverty just as much if we want to increase the quality of educational opportunity.

Now of course we don't stop here—we do what we can to reduce poverty and inequality, but we need to struggle internationally to create a social universe outside of the value form of labor—that is, outside of value production altogether. At least, that should be our long-term goal.

TS: What role, if any, do you see the Left playing in the future of school reform?

PM: Well, I believe that the Left cannot isolate the current crisis of education from the global crisis of capitalism and larger struggle against capitalism and the structural necessity of an equitable transition to a zero-growth economy. We need to take up the task of defining how another socialism or communism is possible and how to take up the transition to these possible alternatives. What will a social universe outside of capital's value form, outside of value production altogether, look like? And how do we get there? David Harvey calls this "organizing for the anti-capitalist transition." We know that capitalism can survive this present crisis and that the costs to the popular majorities will be catastrophic as we will witness increased political repression, militarization and state violence.

How can the Left create a new revolutionary politics that can take us down the path of organizing social life in such a way that augmenting value—through acquiring money—is no longer considered the highest good? In fact, it is abolished outright. Harvey argues that we need a co-evolutionary theory derived from an analysis of Marx's account of how capitalism arose out of feudalism. He notes that social change arises through the dialectical unfolding of relations between what are essentially seven moments—considered as ensembles or assemblages of activities and practices—that occur within the body politic of capitalism, and these include: technological and organizational forms of production, exchange and consumption; relations to nature; social relations between people; mental conceptions of the world, embracing knowledges and cultural understandings and beliefs; labor processes and production of specific goods, geographies, services or affects; institutional, legal and governmental arrangements; and the conduct of daily life that underpins social reproduction. Harvey argues that each of these moments, while marked by tensions and contradictions, is co-dependent and co-evolves in relation to the others.

The Left has a tendency to look at these moments in isolation and focus on just one of them, viewing it as the magic path to social transformation. But when capitalism renews itself, it does so by co-evolving all these moments (admittedly, there are many more than seven). This is how capitalism arose out of feudalism. So the transition from capitalism to socialism or communism must co-evolve in the same way. Our strategic political interventions must move within and across these different moments. So educators need to look beyond epistemological critique in the classroom.

This is why I have been trying to treat revolutionary critical pedagogy as a social movement. Most educational reform never questions capital as a social relation. When this happens, you might be able to make some progress through reform efforts within capitalism, but likely these will be short-lived. This doesn't mean we shouldn't try—we must. Yes, we should not abandon a redistributive socialism but we should keep in mind the larger struggle of developing the path to a social universe without value production.

Reform and revolution are not mutually exclusive. Dialectics is about mediation, not juxtaposition, so the challenge ahead cannot be framed simplistically as that between reform versus revolution but working to reform the system within the larger political optic of anti-capitalist struggle. It is true that reform and revolution are certainly not complementary terms. However these two terms may not be conflictually disjunctive or mutually exclusive if viewed dialectically.

It is not a question of either reform, i.e., incremental change within the system, or revolution, i.e., an overturning of the system from the bottom up by the people. It is a question of *both* reform *and* revolution. In other words, we can work within the system to make the necessary changes which we are able to effect, without losing sight of the revolution that must occur in our social universe if we are going to create a world that is not ruled by the anti-Kingdom of value production (i.e., profits via wage labor). In theological terms, it is Jesus who mediates between the anti-Kingdom and the Kingdom of God, and it is clear today that the anti-Kingdom plays an enormous role in structuring reality for suffering humanity. Why, we must ask, have we rejected the Kingdom of God and the divine mediator, Jesus? In my work, I see the anti-Kingdom as largely constituted by capitalist social relations of exploitation, by structural violence, by social sin.

And I see the Kingdom of God as a world where love and justice as proclaimed by the Suffering Servant of God are made manifest through the gospel of the cross and the resurrection.

But we can't just see capitalism in isolation from other dependent hierarchies that are co-constitutive historically with capitalism. Another way of looking at this is from what I call the decolonial Marxist perspective, utilizing some insights from Latin American social theorists, including the work of Anibal Quijano, Enrique Dussel, Gloria Anzaldúa, Catherine Walsh, Walter Mignolo and Ramón Grosfoguel. When we on the Left are trying to challenge capitalism, we need to imagine what capitalism was like for an indigenous woman in the Americas, when capitalism arrived in the fifteenth century. We must, in other words, shift our geopolitics of knowledge. What arrived was not just an economic system of capital and labor for the production of commodities to be sold for a profit on the world market. What arrived was a set of global entangled hierarchies that Grosfoguel calls a European/capitalist/military/Christian/patriarchal/white/heterosexual/male power matrix. So in adopting an anti-capitalist perspective, teachers need to pay attention to this entangled global power matrix. These formations of domination are internally related or co-constitutive "heterarchies." So as the Left participates in educational reform, it needs to pay attention to all of these internally related heterarchies—but in terms of the transition to an anti-capitalist future and in terms of creating a decolonial approach to knowledge production.

The Left also needs to realize that global problems cannot have national solutions. If we are to participate in school reform, it needs to be linked to anti-capitalist struggles, to decolonial struggles, to critical border thinking that can help us rethink our socialism by thinking with, and not about, indigenous knowledges and epistemologies of subaltern groups. We need a feasible alternative to existing forms of societal organization that reproduce labor's value form. And this will require educators who can work with economists, philosophers, rural and urban planners, critical geographers, anthropologists, sociologists, technology specialists, communication experts, social theorists and community activists coming to work together with this aim in mind.

TS: As we go through a school of education, many of us are taught critical pedagogy and method, but it seems that this does not get put into practice once people enter the classroom. What advice do you have for teachers who are working under the restraints of Obama's Race to the Top program who want to implement critical pedagogy in their classroom?

PM: What Obama's Race to the Top program is doing is essentially increasing the privatization and corporatization of education in such a way that results in the re-socialization of the perceptions of the popular majorities into the dominant legitimizing myths of U.S. capitalism. The NEA and the AFT overwhelmingly accept neoliberal capitalism and so are not interested in long-term structural transformation or a re-scaling of power from the bourgeoisie and private managerial elite to those toiling in the barrios. The school system is not obligated to prepare students for anything more than the lowest-level jobs.

Our regressive tax structure is never challenged. U.S. representative democracy is never questioned or ever compared to or contrasted with participatory democracy, which emphasizes the social, political, economic and cultural aspects of human agency based on human rights, or direct democracy, which focuses on popular control of the means of production and organization by workers' councils. The focus is on teaching to the test, which occupies itself with technocratic problem solving and technocratic knowledge but does not produce meaningful knowledge, knowledge grounded in contexts that require critical analysis and a philosophy of praxis and an ethics of social justice.

What is taught in today's schools is technocratic knowledge or technical problem solving—means-ends thinking. What is missing is meaningful knowledge, that is, the ability to make moral and ethical choices and to interpret and critique. What is missing is intellectual engagement. Schools train students to become consumers. In a world facing ecosystemic breakdown, we clearly need to approach teaching through the optic of an ecosocialist pedagogy grounded in the notion of sustainability, and as socialists we need to recognize that socialist developmentalism has often co-opted indigenous movements. Clearly, we need to bring to our teaching practices a pedagogy of looking beyond Western/Euro/U.S.-centric ways of knowing the world that are based on capitalist wastefulness and a lack of regard for the planet, in order to consider alternative and oppositional ways of thinking about and acting towards/against the imperialism of free-market neoliberal capital.

I am talking about seeking solidarity with non-dominant groups—in particular, silenced groups, marginalized groups, indigenous groups—in bringing together the collective imaginaries of all peoples who seek freedom from necessity and dignity for themselves and their communities by denying epistemologies of empire and the destructive and genocidal practices of Western imperial regimes and their fraudulent narratives of historical innocence. We need different perspectives of justice, rights and social change, and we must take up indigenous perspectives but in ways that do not exploit indigenous peoples in the process.

In other words, I am talking about challenging our conceptions about modernity, and our European-based epistemologies in order to affirm the epistemic rights of the racially devalued. This means challenging the colonial matrix of power grounded in phylogenetic and ontogenetic Western theories. Critical pedagogy gives us critical distance in examining our own epistemological and ontological formation, but not so much distance that we cannot slay the hydra-headed beast of capital and its razor-toothed companions—racism, sexism, imperialism, colonialism.

But how do you fight against oppression from the classroom when teachers and students are both evaluated in standardized tests that are making a lot of money for the companies that are producing and developing the tests? Standardized tests are a form of social control that keep students from exploring their own experiences through epistemological approaches grounded in critical reflectivity.

Education should be grounded in a non-capitalist, decolonial, intercultural dialogue. The engine for this change is a commitment to the oppressed, to marginalized and subaltern groups. So, I often ask my students to join a community group, a social movement, and in their act of struggling alongside and with their group, they will develop critical consciousness which can be augmented by reading and examining texts.

But how can teachers use this approach in public school arenas? Teachers will need to educate their communities about the crisis of education to try to get the parents on their side. Teachers will need the parents as allies against repressive administrations. They need to educate their communities about the dangers of charter schools, how charter promoters pump money into charters to prove they are better than public schools, how charter schools are undermining teachers' unions and the quality of teaching, and how underfunded public schools often result in poor-quality education and how this then is used as another excuse to further gut public school funding.

Sarah Knopp, a Los Angeles teacher, talks about the practice of whipsawing, which has to do with the process of destroying unions by subcontracting to create lots of small workplaces—in place of large, highly unionized ones—so that when workers in smaller, spun-off shops get inferior contracts, those contracts are used to pressure workers in bigger plants to accept similar concessions. We need to show the community that charter schools are a stepping-stone to privatization and that corporate funding depletes state funds and that publicly funded schools are a basic right. Teachers need to create organizations dedicated to fighting standardized testing. They can't do this alone, working in their respective schools. They need to form larger communities of struggle. And they need to educate their communities about socialism as an alternative to capitalist society and capitalist schools.

TS: Teachers' agency comes up against limitations of structural inequality. What are the limits on what a teacher can do? What can a teacher do to break through those limits?

PM: Here I draw on my work in Venezuela in support of the Bolivarian Revolution. I am currently working with the Ministry of Education to train cadres of decolonial Marxists. The idea is that we need a revolution in our structures of knowledge, and in our political roles as educators. For instance, we could learn a great deal from the term *buen vivir* (sumac kawsay), a term that comes from the indigenous peoples of the Andean region, and the Aymara people in particular, that refers to harmony and equilibrium among men and women, among different communities, and among human beings and the natural environment. We also need new technological and scientific knowledges to develop alternatives to neoliberal capitalism, and to resist the academic repression we are experiencing in our schools and universities when we bring the language of Marx to bear on helping us to solve the current crisis of capitalism.

While educational transformation is a necessary but not sufficient struggle for creating a new social universe outside of the value form of labor, we need a new geopolitics of knowledge guided by an anti-capitalist imperative in order to play our part as teachers and cultural workers. The challenge for us is how to recreate the state from the bottom up, while working towards the long-term goal of socialist transformation.

The debates we encounter are usually between those who believe in taking state power, such as the Chavistas, and the anti-statist autonomists and anarchists, and often the Zapatistas are cited here as the alternative to follow. Again, I don't think it is an either-or choice. I appreciate the *andar preguntando* (asking we walk) of the Zapatistas to the *andar predicando* (walking we tell) of the standard recitation and repeat approach of conventional pedagogy. But I also believe that we need to struggle to rebuild the state from the bottom up as a step towards eventually doing away with the state altogether.

We certainly need state control over the distribution of the surplus in order to diminish inequalities, but the old Keynesian model is no longer sufficient in this time of neoliberal capitalism and we need new forms of left statism, created from the bottom up using participatory democracy and direct democracy as potential models. I agree with John Holloway that revolution is not about destroying capitalism but instead refusing to create it. There are ways we can stop producing capitalism now, such as creating public gardens, fighting against corporate control of the schools, protesting the G8, etc. Crying out "Ya Basta!" or "Que se vayan todos!" in the face of education cutbacks is another option. But I also believe we need a coherent philosophy of praxis linked to an epistemological revolution that can incorporate and negotiate both indigenous and Westernized knowledges—ecologies of the mind that are able to contest the paradogmas of Western colonial rationality (what Anibal Quijano calls the "coloniality of power," or *patrón de poder colonial*) and open up strategic spaces for engaging with new conceptualizations of living in Pachamama.

My position is that we need a subjective praxis connected with a philosophy of liberation that is able to illuminate the content of a post capitalist society and project a path to a totally new society. This can be done by making convincing arguments that it is possible to resolve the contradiction between alienation and freedom. The key here is that our forms of organizing society must be consistent with our philosophy of liberation. We need obviously to prioritize human development and search for new epistemological frameworks and refuse to continue to participate in epistemicide, or the silencing and destruction of indigenous ways of understanding and negotiating the world.

Not all of us can use the political language of socialism. Speaking at a high school outside of Medellín, Colombia, a few years ago, I learned that the military had earlier attacked the community with helicopters, a tank, artillery and troops, and the paramilitary, and while the teachers had asked me to speak at their school, they rejected my language of socialist struggle because it put them and their students at risk for their lives. They created their own language of critical pedagogy. We need a pluriversal approach to critical pedagogy—there is no one universal approach. Teachers will develop these approaches in their communities according to the contextual specificity of their struggles, their commitment to the oppressed and their commitment to creating a post capitalist future.

TS: Many parents, particularly working-class parents, seem to have bought into the rhetoric of "choice and competition," "academic rigor" and "achievement" and the idea that school should be more academic earlier. What ideas would you offer parents when thinking about the quality of their children's education that might counter the ideas they are being offered by the mainstream debate?

PM: Yes, working-class parents often want for their children the kind of education that the children in Beverly Hills are getting. You can't blame them for that. They believe that education is the only vehicle available to them, and it's really a question of the kind of teachers they are able to hire at their neighborhood public school. They have bought into the notion of meritocracy and the capitalist propaganda that charters are the best option for their children. They often don't realize that for-profit charters have less public accountability and transparency requirements than do public schools. That charter proponents are those behind the shame-and-blame policies of the Obama administration, behind the weakening of teachers' bargaining rights, behind the giving of grants to the "winners" instead of those high-needs students who are most in need of financial assistance. I do know some very successful neighborhood charters, but the charter school movement in general is destructive of what remains of public schooling.

Public schools accept all children, including much larger numbers of high-needs students. The move to privatize education can be traced as far as the World Bank and transnational efforts to weaken teachers' unions and create international standards to put students globally into a lockstep with the needs of transnational capitalism, and the directives of the transnational capitalist class. But at the same time, we need to face the ugly reality that as cities are becoming more segregated, schools are resegregating and racially tracking students, with students of color denied equal access to educational resources, healthy school environments and higher learning.

Parents can be allies in fighting the current assaults on education that can be traced to the deregulatory policies of free marketization, the neoliberal religiosity of corporate intermarriage and the corporatist managerialist assault on the welfare state that took place during the 1980s and 1990s and that brought about low public expenditures and the hoovering up of state subsidies and support back to capital.

I was part of the New Left in the 1960s, and part of the problem is that we dropped the ball as far as labor issues were concerned, as we focused more on issues of civil rights. We need to pick up that ball again and run with it, while maintaining our defense of civil rights, many of which are in the process of being rolled back to a frightening degree. Parents must be invited into our meetings, into our community struggles, into our broad alliances in which single-issue politics gives way to understanding how the major struggles of our day are struggles that are all "entangled" and have a transnational reach.

Academic rigor is of course an issue, but rigor can lead to rigor mortis. The issue for me is critical thinking with revolutionary intent. My approach is to encourage students to engage various languages of critique and possibility through which they can help gain some critical purchase on their experiences and the objective social world in which they are variously positioned in terms of race, class, gender, sexuality, disability. In too many cases, the languages students are given in school settings to interpret their experiences are restrictive and truncating. For instance, teaching classical economics and rational choice theory, and leaving out a Marxist critique of political economy, won't get us out of the current crisis of capitalism.

Ideas have effects, and so do pedagogies. A truly transformative pedagogy takes students' experiences seriously, challenges those experiences without taking away the voice or agency of the students and is undertaken with the overall purpose of transforming the world in the interests of making it less oppressive, less exploitative. Academic approaches to knowledge are often based on a passive approach to learning. What we need is an active theory of knowledge production and pedagogies that can produce the knowledge/action needed to create alternative futures for ourselves and the world in which we live and labor.

Bibliography

Grosfoguel, R. (2013). The structure of knowledge in westernized universities: Epistemic racism/sexism and the four genocides/epistemicides of the long 16th century. *Human Architecture: Journal of the Sociology of Self-Knowledge, 11*(1), Article 8. Retrieved from http://scholarworks.umb.edu/humanarchitecture/vol11/iss1/8

Harvey, D. (2010). *Organizing for the anti-capitalist transition.* Talk given at the World Social Forum, Porto Alegre, Brazil. Retrieved from: http://davidharvey.org/2009/12/organizing-for-the-anti-capitalist-transition/

Karp, S. (2013). Charter schools and the future of public education. *Rethinking Schools, 28*(1). F. Retrieved from http://www.rethinkingschools.org/archive/28_01/28_01_karp.shtml

Mignolo, W. D. (2002). The geopolitics of knowledge and the colonial difference. *The South Atlantic Quarterly, 101*(1), 57–96.

Quijano, A. (2000). The coloniality of power, Eurocentrism, and Latin America. (M. Ennis, Trans.). *Nepantla: Views From the South, 1*(3), 533–580.

· 1 2 ·

CRITICAL RAGE PEDAGOGY

From Critical Catharsis to Self and
Social Transformation

For Allen (I hear your howl from heaven)

Twelve figures draped in black and between 20–80 years of age assemble on a dimly lit stage and face the audience. Placed about ten feet in front of them are fifteen to twenty standard-issue school desks and chairs. Behind them is a white screen upon which various images can be projected. These images are chosen from various descriptions offered throughout the chapter and will be flashed on the screen once the performance begins. The figures draped in black represent the ghosts of former teachers who, reluctant to speak out during their lifetimes, have now been given the opportunity to return to the land of the living in order to deliver their final lecture. Each desk facing them features a propped up photograph of the person whom is supposed to be sitting at that desk. These photographs are turned backwards so that the audience watching the performance can identify them. They include photographs of various Presidents of the United States including Jimmy Carter, Ronald Reagan, and George W. Bush, well-known capitalists, representatives of the CIA, the NSA, the Pentagon, the U.S. Department of Education, political operatives and well-known right-wing media figures who are being forced to listen to what the teachers have to say. The ghosts begin a reading of this chapter, each taking turns, with spirit-breath aflame, naming themselves to their calling.

allegro asai

And so, to the final question, yes, the final question: where should critical pedagogy take us and where should we take critical pedagogy? We can only answer this with a response from our guts. To the plaintive and indignant voices of our establishment critics, we say this: We are inadaptable! We are maladaptable! We answer your charges of sedition with a burst of laughter. We will not be treated as overactive children with behavioral disorders. We will not swallow your pills.

We do not live in treehouses but underground, in the sewers of Bogotá, in the slums of Calcutta, in the Lacandon jungle of Chiapas, in *las calles de* downtown Los Angeles, in *casas de carton* in Culiacán, in the *favela bairro* of Rocinha in Rio's South Zone, in classrooms without books, in restrooms without toilets, in boardrooms without CEOs, in prisons without guards! We speak Chontal, Ch'ol, Tzeltal, Tzotzil, Tojolabal, Chicomuceltec, Mocho' and Akatek.

Are these not the new sites of Galilee, of which the Gospel of Mark (16:7) commands: "But go your way ... into Galilee: there shall ye see him, as he said unto you"? Are these not places where the wretched of the earth have chosen to live as a risen people? Is this not where the poor and the despised have taken on the burden of history and where the hope that springs from the resurrected Christ can be found, even among the rivers of despair and inquietude, hope that the risen Christ will triumph over injustice? Is this not where Christ's definitive irruption into the continuum of history impregnates the present with remembrances of all things past, as the storm from paradise abates, the blind forces of history regain their sight, the bonds of repression are unyoked and the task of redemption is made possible?

We are the children of 1968 and of hip-hop; we will not accept bribes; we will not accept financial compensation; we refuse to let our subjectivities be cooked in the ovens of the state; we refuse to ask permission for anything; we refuse to be colonized or to colonize; we refuse to be exiled from our own flesh; we refuse to let our languages, our songs, our histories and our dreams be expropriated by the mass media. We will not let capital disfigure us. We understand the hidden transcript of capitalist normality and we are making it manifest for the world to see.

In his most famous work, *The Wretched of the Earth*, Frantz Fanon (2008, p. 201) opines: "It's not because the Indo-Chinese discovered a culture of their own that they revolted. Quite simply this was because it became impossible to breathe, in more than one sense of the word." Do you now understand why Fanon's name went viral on the Internet shortly after the New York City grand jury decided not to indict the police after an unarmed black man named Eric Garner was choked to death by an arresting officer?

We are the WikiLeaks of the seminar rooms and classrooms and we will expose the lies and corruption of all Ministries of Education. We will not burn our copies of Marx and genuflect at the altar of neoliberal capitalism. It's been a capricious ruse of corporate media to confuse capitalism with democracy. We know that we exist as inter-subjective beings and will not let wage labor tear us from our friends, our families, our communities. We refuse to be decomposed by the social machinery of the state apparatuses. We will not be the subjects of your social experiments. We understand fully that there is no separation between the definition of justice and our obligation to do justice.

We aren't proud to announce that The Forever Café has been closed forever; it just goes with the economic territory. We aren't embarrassed to wear vintage shirts from Pendleton Woolen Mills, turquoise jewelry and 50s glass frames; so go ahead, be our guest, criticize us as petty bourgeois, we don't care. If we want to stuff gloves in our hip pocket and go barefoot like Billy Jack or choose to dress like a NASA scientist, then so be it. You follow YouTube instructions on how to look like a hipster, so by definition you can't call yourself one. We're freeskiers and do backflips off fluffies and shart on impact.

We read Hegel and Marx in an abandoned Porta-Potty near our favorite road house, so don't expect us to be impressed when you read your Wittgenstein under a table in Ralph Lauren's new Polo Bar. Give our best to Ralph, will you? Tell him that he looks most elegant in fitted Scottish wool suits.

We lost our front teeth playing hockey in the minor Canadian leagues, and we aren't interested that you drove your Holland & Holland Range Rover with a custom gun box to your field-level seat for game 6 of the World Series at Fenway Park. We say, good for you! We were just as content to drive to the nearest bar on our Harleys and watch the game on the big screen.

If we appear overburdened by a rash of obloquies and excoriating invectives directed against the transnationalist capitalist class, please know that it is not because we are especially prone to rage but because we are morally exhausted in our refusal to accept their constant barrage of lies and deceptions. If this sounds like I miss the 60s, you're right, but you're wrong if you think my critique is fueled by nostalgia alone.

We read the following quotation by Noam Chomsky and not only do we agree with it, we see it as an understatement:

> Europe has a very bloody history, an extremely savage and bloody history, with con-stant massive wars that were all part of an effort to establish the nation-state system. It has virtually no relation to the way people live, or to their associations, or anything else particularly, so it had to be established by force—centuries of bloody warfare. That warfare (in Europe) ended in 1945—and the only reason it ended is because the next war was going to destroy *everything*. So it ended in 1945—we hope; if it didn't, it *will* destroy everything. The nation-state system was exported to the rest of the world through European colonization. Europeans were barbarians basically, savages: very advanced technologically, and advanced in methods of warfare, but not culturally or anything else particularly. And when they spread over the rest of the world, it was like a plague—they just destroyed everything in front of them. ... They fought differently, they fought much more brutally, they had better technology—and they essentially wiped everything else out. The American continent is a good exam-ple. How come everyone around here has a white face and not a red face? Well, it's because the people with the white faces were savages, and they killed the people with red faces. (2002, p. 314)

And hasn't the U.S. exceeded Europe in its brutality? And isn't this brutality largely a result of attempts to augment capitalist value production? Do we need to go through all of the U.S. invasions since 1945? And the horror it has produced in Southeast Asia and Latin America? You find all of this untrou-bling to your souls, don't you? It's part of the spiritually stultifying continuity of your minds.

And do you think the history of Christianity will protect you? Did not religious leaders in Spain justify the war against indigenous peoples in *las Americas* on the grounds that they be converted to Christianity? Did anybody utter a peep about this in your holy Council of Trent? Didn't Bishop Moscoso of Cuzco condemn the rebellion by Tupac Amaru against indigenous slave labor and didn't he describe Tupac Amaru as a "rebel against God, religion, and the law"? Didn't the Vatican's Holy Office officially deny on June 20, 1886, that slavery was contrary to natural law? Before the Spanish executed him by decapitation, did not Tupac Amaru cry out, "Ccollanan Pachacamac ricuy auccacunac yahuarniy hichascancuta" (Mother Earth, witness how my enemies shed my blood)?

We don't care if you live in a converted granary with handmade clay tiles. Take your make-believe ruralism and shove it up the copper pipes of your neo-vernacular estate! We proudly sing "Rejoice, O Virgin" from Rachmaninoff's *Vespers*, wearing denim overalls from the Dust Bowl and if Putin wants to put us into prison, we say, let him try! We don't appear every 200 years like Brigadoon. We are on the streets every day!

Capitalism has made us feel alone together and homesick at home and we won't allow you into our community unless you can enrich the debate about the future of humanity! We want to engage in acts of self-creation, you have forced us to act in self-preservation because you compel us into acts of self-alienation for our survival. We want to be self-motivated; you want to coerce us! You want ownership in severalty, we want collective ownership! You want to create our needs, we want to create our future! You want to manufacture our consent when we are unable to consent to having a life!

We will not be cast into your world; we will not let your despotic capitalist mind lead us to suffocate in the urban sprawl of an extractive economy.

You can fly the fish you catch on the U.S. coast to Japan for processing and then send it back here to fancy seafood restaurants at Pier 39 in Fisherman's Wharf, but we are not impressed. We don't care how many frequent-flyer miles your fish have accumulated. We would rather eat corn grown in an urban garden than be part of this insanity!

You are interested in science for preserving your hair and teeth until you die. We are interested in fathoming the mysteries of the universe. Don't try to send us into a brick cell with a whiteboard and then have us read a book about nature. We prefer to live *in* nature than read *about* nature in a classroom that supports the expropriation of the means of production.

Every time one of you Republicans talks about abolishing Social Security because it's socialist you are sentencing Americans to death. Every time one of you Democrats runs away from the word "socialism," you are sentencing the entire world to death! Your corporations pretend to be one-worlders, but they always turn to their national government when they are in crisis and need to be bailed out.

We are not interested in *The Expendables* or *Independence Day*, or Adam Sandler films, so decry us as elitist post-universal cosmopolitanists or post-national liberals, we don't care. We prefer to stay at home and watch Pier Paolo Pasolini's *The Gospel According to St. Matthew*. We stand against all racists, including steroid-powered white men with buzzcuts, blue uniforms and skull tattoos who make up the military-and-police state machine. We also stand against orthorexic hipsters and computer geeks in chic-nerd glasses and shadow beards who have infiltrated the academy on behalf of the Rand Corporation, the NSA, the FBI and the CIA in order to assist vice-provosts in monitoring politically subversive professors. You donnish fake progressives in your fashionable spectacles who sit in judgment of those of us who have tried to live our politics in our everyday lives, you remind me not of the guardians of academic freedom but of self-styled ruffians who dedicate themselves to cleaning up the streets of academe and whisking away the barbarians who have entered the gates. In fact, you remind me of academic equivalents of the muscadin, dandyish henchmen from the 1790s street gangs of Paris who wielded their "constitutions" or wooden clubs with savage aplomb as they beat to death any Jacobins or sans-culottes who got in their way. You would have fit right in with the aristocratic subcultures of the Incroyables and the Merveilleuses, the jeunesse dorée of the day.

By the way, while your nerd couture doesn't impress us, we'd still appreciate it if you gifted us your Nintendo bow-tie and muted red jacket.

You want an integral capitalist state; we want a counter-hegemonic state that is transnational, transversal, and transformative! You want to produce corporate knowledge; we want to produce counter-knowledge! You see time as unified and stationary and controlled by the logic of the capitalist state. We operate from a plural temporality and work for a unitary time under freely associated labor and the end of the pre-history of humanity! You want to re-legitimize the capitalist state and the class relations that it maintains through your western-based NGOs in order to further integrate civil and political society. We see right through your plans!

We are interested in cosmic intelligence, not central intelligence. Go tell that to the head of The Company or Homeland Security! Should we be alarmed that Erik Prince, who owns the infamous U.S. mercenary army, Blackwater, is the brother-in-law of Domino Pizza entrepreneur Dick De Vos? In De Vos's failed bid for governor in Michigan in 2006, he put forth a program to weaken unions, institute vouchers in Detroit public schools and deny benefits for public sector workers with same-sex partners. This is what Laurie Wimmer calls "the Blackwatering of public education." Why doesn't this surprise us? We will not live compliantly in a society so sickened by such hatred!

You want to create international ideological consent for your binge capitalist interests. We want to multiply the struggles to replace the current capitalist hegemony! You extort consensus with your lies! We fight consensus with absolute negativity as a revolution in permanence! You want spaces of capitalist discipline. We want new geometries of struggle and converging networks of tactical subversion! And if we have to decamp from the lecture halls and seminar rooms to the streets, so be it!

You seek an enterprise business culture; we want to breach your entrepreneurial backside and managerial models and fill the classrooms with living labor, with militant co-research that creates a consummate synthesis among and crossbreeds with autonomous knowledge production, class struggle, and a philosophy of praxis that radicalizes the global commons through self-education!

You want to invite foreign providers unleashed by the World Bank and the General Agreement on Tariffs and Trade (GATT) to colonize our educational system. We will fight your efforts to spawn a culture of outlawry in our campuses where you chain students to the masthead of eternal debt!

Please try to understand us: We don't want to break with the history of the last century, we want to break with the history of the past two thousand years! Now do you get it?

You can gawk at Miley Cyrus's twerking buttocks all you want and whip up sentiment about her "freeing the nipple," but we are more interested in freeing workers from necessity. But if Miley's butterfly pasties, tinsel wig and psychedelic thong draw attention to her worthy causes of helping homeless and GLBTQ youth, then we say: All the more power to happy hippie Miley! Anyone who can write a beautiful song for her dead blowfish, Pablow, has a childlike sweetness of spirit and love for the living that is missing among too many of us. (We are aware that not everyone agrees with us. Celebrity Christian evangelist and curator of Kentucky's Creation Museum, Ken Ham, has recently condemned Miley Cyrus's "wicked" and "debased" lifestyle and warns her that God may rain terror down upon her; yet still he believes that God might be in her heart because she draws the line against having sex with animals and anyone under 18. That's an awful strange and creepy criteria for being a closet believer, Ken! Especially for somebody who is building a life-size Noah's Ark for his theme park, hopefully not to save all those animals from Miley, should she suddenly lose her faith!)

We know that you know that you have created a mass society of dopamine-deprived, stressed-out citizens and that you need to modulate our brain/body chemistry—deliver to our brains enough dopamine, serotonin, epinephrine and all the neurotransmitters and hormones and all the other systems of comfort needed to prevent us from storming the barricades blocking our emancipation that you have constructed and seizing our freedom and our rights. You can addict us to reality television shows, expand the sports channels, disorient us in your shopping malls so that we can only relieve our anxiety with a purchase. Yes, you can do all of these things. Go ahead and hijack our neurotransmitters, make us feel our submission, pump up our stress hormones and then, like missionary heroes, offer us a means of relieving our stress by patting us on the back and calling us good consumers who are helping to strengthen the economy. We won't buy your lies and we won't purchase your consumer goods, either!

And then literally take over our working-class youths by offering them a free education in the military so that they can go and beat up little countries every so often—intermittent reinforcement, catch them unawares—and let the world know that we mean business. And of course, we are talking about business. You have decided to give your corporations free rein. We say to you: We're going to rein your corporate asses in!

You have predisposed us to acting like your serfs, but we know that we are predisposed to violating our own predispositions and that the hardwiring that has gone into our brains, courtesy of your schoolmasters and clergy, can be overruled (see Smail, 2008). We hereby overrule you!

You underestimate us by thinking that we are fools who haven't the intellectual insight or ethical fortitude or courage to challenge your everyday threats, to peel away your lies, to undress your outlawry, to denature the tissues of deceit and fear-mongering that constitute your empire? Or perhaps you believe that we will sit by idly as you create the anti-Kingdom? Or do you think that the media propaganda churned out by the engines of your ideological state apparatuses as a perpetual pedagogy of hate and demonization of the Other has paralyzed us politically?

Do you think it will prevent us from challenging you, from creating the Kingdom of God here and now? Do you think we fear martyrdom? Do you really believe that we lack faith in Jesus of the cross, in Jesus of the resurrection, in Jesus the Christ? Do you think our faith in Jesus makes us less prone to embrace Eugene Debs's "Speech of Acceptance" that appeared in the *International Socialist Review* (Debs, 1912)? Well, you are wrong!

Do you think we exercise our Internet skills only to gaze at Kim Kardashian's backside? We read our history! We put Noam Chomsky and Howard Zinn and Margaret Randall on our course reading lists since the corporate press refuses to publish the facts that these intellectuals have so courageously unpacked. Eugene Debs's outrage against capitalist misrule under which working-class people "suffer slavery and the most galling injustice" is our own outrage today as profit maximization and market share is the dominant logic of the current historical moment.

We hereby withdraw our support from capitalism in order that it might die, and we pledge our support in building a socialist alternative!

Do you think your corporate entertainment industry has dulled our emotions? That we listen only to the muzak piped through your shopping malls and hotel lobbies? Do you think you have desensitized us so much that we are no longer moved to tears when we hear "Gentle on My Mind" sung by Glenn Campbell and John Hartford, or "Strange Fruit" by Billie Holiday? Do we not feel a knife slice through our hearts when Odetta sings, "Sometimes I Feel Like a Motherless Child" with the choir from Church of the Master? Do you think we don't worship at the Church of John Coltrane? Do you think we are deaf to A Love Supreme? Think again!

We will not let the commons be privatized! We will fight your institutionalized logic and market calculations alongside our indigenous brethren to preserve the commons—our biosphere—for the common people!

Sure, go ahead, call us conspiracy theorists. That tactic has worked so far to preserve your state power. We know that you perceive the general population as your enemy. Encourage the public to laugh at us or to dismiss us as extremists. But how long do you feel the larger public will remain indifferent?

Let me give you one example. Do you really believe that the public will continue to willfully ignore GEO Group, one of the largest private prison companies in the country? Not if we can help it. Do you think we are too indifferent to care that GEO lobbyists send direct campaign contributions, mostly to Republican lawmakers, and expect—and receive—favors in return? Do you think we don't know that they lobby for harsher sentencing laws so they can fill up their prisons—and maximize their profits—with more inmates who will work for little or no wages?

What an obedient and compliant workforce inmates make, since they are prohibited from unionizing and punished if they protest. And it is not necessary to provide them with health insurance or sick days or vacation pay or raises. How convenient for Mr. Moneybags! And if they refuse to work, then throw them into solitary, or make them fight in your private gladiator arenas, you modern-day Neros!

The 2.3 million American prisoners locked behind bars make up 25 percent of the world's prisoners—and this occurring in a country with just 5 percent of the world's population (Khalek, 2011). Shame on you! Do you think we don't know that Indiana lawmakers guaranteed GEO a 90 percent prison capacity? And who doesn't know that there are disproportionately black and Latino prisoners in our prisons throughout the country? Even dumbed down Fox News listeners know that! What does this make our prisoners? Legally Sanctioned Slaves!

And what about the federal government? We are not fools, we can see your sleight-of-hand—that you subsidize the use of inmate labor by private companies through lucrative tax write-offs. We know that you reward these companies for hiring "risky target groups." Do you think we don't know that this is an immoral scam? Do you think we don't know that each time that you 'lawmakers' increase the mandatory sentencing laws and turn misdemeanors into felonies, that you increase corporate profits? Inmate workers generate 2.4 billion in revenue annually (Khalek, 2011). You sicken us with your scandalous degradation of human life!

Perhaps you yourself wear some of the prison-chic fashions. You don't? Well, then the license plates of your cars were more likely than not stamped by prison labor. And do you shop for your Revlon products or your Pierre Cardin sweaters at Macy's? Do you buy your jeans at Target Stores? And you continue to think you are superior to those governments in Mexico, Indonesia and China on whose soil sweatshop workers toil and suffer for the sake of your sartorial reputation. Hypocrites, all of you! Your anti-union laws are forcing inmates into work that was formerly done by unionized workers. Everybody's wages are pushed down because of your loathsome policies! You bloodsuckers!

And Christian evangelicals, you and your nativist brethren are being deceived, since the policies you have been manipulated to support are destroying the country for your children and your grandchildren.

We are at an historical tipping point. Heed our words: the decisions we make today will determine whether or not our planet will survive.

You have ripped Marx's ideas out of their revolutionary soil by decades of toxic bombardment by the corporate media and repotted them in greenhouse megastores where, under hydrofarm compact fluorescent fixtures, they can be deracinated, debarked, disarmed and made trendy for university seminars on economic stratification and for au courant condominium living alike and where highly committed twentysomethings who like to whistle to ballpark tunes in their faux-Victorian bathtubs can impress their fellow junior managers during drunken vacations at Club Med Cancún with terms like "the cash nexus". You think you are so subversive because you decorate your den with an unread copy of Das Kapital. You care more about whether Foucault is out this year or whether Rancière is in than about the objective conditions of the exploited and the immiserated. Shame on you!

Your meticulous disparagement of life and your well-nurtured cyncism has cultivated a neurosis that has left our minds in ruins. Do you think we will forgive you because you read Rimbaud in college?

And shame on you for disturbing my slumber. Now, when I dream, I discover myself squatting atop a Gothic cathedral, whose gargoyles perched below my feet are spouting the blood of history's time-enduring saints to quell the maelstrom of angry crowds below—crowds made up of the powerless, the forgotten, the excluded, victims caught in the crossfire of capitalism (the result of watching too many of your Zombie or vampire films, no doubt). I peer down at the collarless, blood-covered, and spindle-shanked figures below, shafts of brilliant light slicing through the clouds that hover hesitatingly over the entangled gloom, and then the noxious exhalation of putrid effluvia wafting upwards from the dank and pungent sewer mist rises to meet the light, and suddenly everyone is playing and celebrating in the city streets, like neighborhood kids who have yanked open a fire hydrant during a heat wave. But what are they celebrating? Their new credit card advance?

Suddenly I am sitting at a long mahogany table inside the Crystal Cathedral, before it was purchased by the Catholic Church. Around the table are a group of graduates from Patrick Henry College, now evangelical Bible salesmen chomping on huge wads of Purple Grape Dubble Bubble Gumballs. Some of them are Grace Movement Dispensationalists, some are Hyper-Dispensationalists, some are Post-Tribulational Pre-Millennialists, some are Pre-Tribulational Pre-Millennialists, some are just plain Post-Millennialists and some are even Anti-Millennialists—all of whom embrace historical grammatical interpretations of the Bible.

In walks Pat Robertson calling again for the assassination of Hugo Chávez (apparently not realizing that Chávez was already dead) followed by Oral Roberts, who was followed by a 900-foot Jesus holding hands with a farting Robert Tilton.

The last person to enter the room is Karl Marx, who, after listening to the conversation, quickly excuses himself. Unblinking, he grabs a taxi and leaves for John Wayne Airport and then catches a flight to San Salvador. He finally makes his way along Avenida Monseñor Óscar Romero to the Cathedral of San Salvador. On the marble slab behind Romero's crypt, he lays a wreath in memory of the thousands slain by U.S.-trained death squads. The faces of the dead appear in clouds slowly floating southward, as Marx exits the Cathedral.

When you start interfering with my dreams like this, I know it's time to decamp for an uninhabited island out of the reach of your bandwidth! But do any exist?

You are the heirs of the Magna Carta, that 800-year-old document signed at Runnymede on the banks of the Thames between Windsor and Staines. Congratulations on that! I'm glad that King John was finally subjected to some oversight by a panel of wealthy barons! I'm glad that world historical document resulted in some limitation on taxation without representation; that certainly helped out a lot of important aristocrats. That's just great! And I'm gratified that my ancestral homeland, Scotland, was able to survive as an independent state, and the king was prevented from turning it into his own feudal stomping ground. No king (or queen) is above the law these days, so thank you for that, heirs of the Magna Carta.

Excuse our bad breath, but are not the poor and the powerless also heirs to the Magna Carta, and what about them? Now taxes are no longer extracted in an arbitrary way by an acquisitive king, but systematically by the state, advantaging the rich white property owners, as always. Free men are no longer arbitrarily imprisoned, except for African American men caught "being black" and warehoused in our penitentiaries as part of the school-to-prison pipeline. I suppose they are the modern-day equivalents of feudal serfs. Well, we have the U.S. Constitution, you tell us. But that mainly protects the rich white property owners, courtesy of the extermination of most of the indigenous population. Damn any concentration of power—be it church or state—that dares to mess with white male property owners! And so the rich have always presented themselves as the oppressed each time the law prevents them from buying up everything, including us!

White Christian smugglers and drug traffickers who sold opium to the Chinese in the early 19th century are responsible not only for creating over 11 million Chinese opium addicts but for contributing mightily to the massive fortunes of some members of the U.S. ruling elite, such as F.D.R.'s grandfather, Warren Delano, the Cabot family of Boston who endowed Harvard with opium money, and the Russell family who endowed Yale's famous Skull and Bones society through the opium trade (Braswell, 2015). And we can't forget the opium trade in consolidating the fortunes of John and Robert Forbes—of the Boston Forbeses—whose relatives include current U.S. Secretary of State, John Forbes Kerry.

And what about your hero, Samuel Adams, one of the so-called Founding Fathers of the U.S., whose namesake beer you quaff down in buckets and whose praises you used to sing during your internship at the Cato Institute?

And whose name (along with James Madison's) you sometimes mixed into your witty retorts and bon mots at Vaucluse on Sunset Boulevard in West Hollywood or the Algonquin Hotel in New York City, both of which were happy to serve you a $10,000 diamond martini (thanks to your calling in advance to pre-order the diamond). Did you know Samuel Adams drafted the Riot Act that suspended habeas corpus so that debtors and protesters could be kept in jail without trial? That didn't sit well with a group called the Regulators, who wanted to shut down the courts and turn debtors out of jail. Adams believed that while all men were equal under the law and in the eyes of God, they would always be unequal in beauty, talents and fortunes. James Madison argued that the abolition of debt and the institution of an equal division of labor was absolutely wicked. Sorry, but I'm with Shays' Rebellion, led by Revolutionary War veteran Daniel Shays, the spirit of which I hope is reflected in this book.

We also take our inspiration from the communism of the early Christian Church, the Gospel message of the Kingdom of God and the rich homiletic material made available in the parables of Jesus. You take the parable of the "talents" (Matthew 25:14–30; Luke 19:12–27) to argue that Jesus preached the glories of capitalism and usury, but we see it as a warning to the rich not to exploit their workers! You bring your own desire to the interpretation; we try to understand it from the worldview of a first-century Palestinian.

The human logos will not suffice to explain the mystery which is inexpressible, impenetrable and wholly other, unable to be represented by our eyes that lust for the visible or any of our other senses. We can only reply to your theologians that we know God through our admission that God is unknowable. And for that matter, ours is a suffering God—the scourged Christ—who suffers along with the poor and the oppressed and yours is the triumphant Christ ruling all from His heavenly throne!

We struggle with the texts of scripture in community while you sit in your suburban church pews. You see the Bible as some kind of aperture through which you can know how God worked in the days of old; we see the Bible as a reflection of our lives as we suffer the daily indignities of life under capitalism.

We are not heresiologists and are not here to condemn your orthodoxy but to challenge your orthopraxis. We are not here to give you some cosmogenic revelation and propel you to the thirteenth aeon where you can discuss metaphysics with the lion-faced Yaldabaoth. You will not find us scouring the rubbish heaps of Oxyrhynchus. We are more interested in the here and now.

But all this talk is about ancient history, you tell me. Okay, let me talk about something closer to home. Okay, squint hard, will you?

How about Los Angeles? Can't you see in the distance the Sheriff of Skid-berry, patrolling San Pedro and San Julian streets, tipping his bald pate to The Hurricane, Bow Leg, Slow Bucket and Thick 'n' Juicy? Can't you see him handing out a donated hygiene kit to a woman shooting heroin between her toes, while nearby a beer baron sells $2 bottles outside of AA meetings (O'Neill, 2015)? You can't? Well, have you ever been to downtown Los Angeles, not far from City Hall? Have you ever gone "sliding down The Nickel," you know, made the trek to Skid Row, where the city warehouses its homeless population from Third Street on the north, Seventh Street on the south, Alameda Street to the east and Main Street to the west (O'Neill, 2015)? Do you know that the 2,000 down-on-their-luck men, women and children who live under tarps strewn across shopping carts in this one square mile are now at risk of losing their squalid surroundings to gentrification, since urban development—residential lofts, trendy bistros, influx of yuppies, etc.—has brought 50,000 people next door and developers are lining up, salivating to grab more territory for their urban hipster clients (O'Neill, 2015)? Have you ever wondered what happened to low-income housing?

Have you ever been on the mean streets of LA, this city of angels, and watched thousands of hardscrabble members of Marx's always unpopular reserve army of unemployed and their blank-faced children line up uncomfortably outside of the Los Angeles Sports Arena to get their yellow wristbands, their one-in-a-million ticket to see in the flesh a doctor, a dentist, a healthcare volunteer? When thousands line up all night, in the desert-climate chill, to see a dentist, what does that portend for their future, aching molars aside?

Even the healthcare aides of the Orange County sick wait patiently beside their own brittle-boned patients, who wait beside undocumented day laborers, who wait beside formerly affluent housewives abandoned by their gambling husbands, who wait beside teachers seeking mammograms and treatment for their diabetes.

What will it take for you to be outraged? Do you have to be pushed into the ranks of the living dead to fight back?

Will this population perhaps be the first to be shipped off to a labor camp somewhere should fascism consolidate its legal, economic, criminal justice and affective regime (i.e., the manufacturing of public opinion through the news, popular culture, commercial media) in the U.S.? Will we muster a fight or be compelled to join them? Will we all end up singing "Tomorrow Belongs to Me" from the film *Cabaret*? And does a "volkisch" community have to be fascist?

Can't an effect precede its cause? Can't our American tradition be led not to be some jerry-rigged assemblage of backward-looking times, some broken remnants of the past, but by a dream of the future—by a feeling of contemporaneity, of sharing the present time collectively, whose arc is wide enough to harness our collective, generalized affect for the liberation of humanity from capital, even in this prevailing apotheosis of despair? The present, after all, is no longer mostly the past. Well, at least for those who are wired to the World Wide Web. Our struggle is eschatological, the possibility of making a dialectical leap into a new aeon where the Gospels and education can create synergistically a transitional functionality for building a world free from necessity and needless suffering.

[Excuse me, I've got to stop raging for the moment, a man in a nightgown, dragging a suitcase and sporting a smile like shattered glass has just entered the coffee shop here in Orange, where I am writing this book, and has beckoned to me to give him some spare change. Okay, I'm back, $2 poorer but feeling less guilty.]

The notion of free clinics for the poor has stoked the ire of those who think this is "socialism," helping all those "freeloaders," and especially the scraggly immigrants south of the border, while those responsible for the over-exploitation of *las Americas* sit in their mahogany offices, wet their kerosene lips on shipwrecked 1907 Heidsieck champagne (which, at $275,000 a bottle, could subsidize all those diagnosed for root canals and then some) and watch the fascism of the nation unfold, as Hannity, Beck and O'Reilly call for liberal heads to roll.

Francisco Franco, beloved fascist dictator of Spain, allegedly slept beside the incorruptible arm of Saint Teresa de Avila. Can't you see him waving it, white knuckled, in a death bed frenzy to fend off Old Scratch? Perhaps George Bush Jr. has hidden some religious relic under his bed, perhaps even the skull of Geronimo (allegedly stolen from Yale by his grandfather, Prescott Bush, and some other Yale Bonesmen), while Barack Obama, needing no protective relic, sleeps soundly, unperturbed by terrorists or undisturbed by columns of the homeless and the unemployed (Marx's reserve army of labor) snaking around the block in the City of Angels, as his own angels of steel hover overhead, their tactical control systems operated from a remote hangar in Arizona by a cowboy clutching a joy stick humming "Yankee Doodle Dandy." Instead of calling upon Michael, Gabriel, Uriel or Raphael, our beloved leader feels safe enough under the watchful eyes of Predator, Global Hawk, Fire Scout and Hunter as he calls for the birth of new nations under god, liberated by the mighty F-16s and his Luftwaffe of drones. May God bless America. And nobody else.

Do you think we are unaware that the Pasco police force in Washington State has shot and killed four people in the past six months? We are used to police killing people here in the U.S. so much that we don't think much about this statistic. But the Pasco police force has killed more people than the police in the entire United Kingdom in the past three years combined! Pasco has 59,000 residents and the U.K. has a population of 60,000,000. And do you not brag with your friends as you gulp down your Blue Moons in your favorite police bars that we live in the greatest country in the world?

You sicken us with your senseless slaughter of unarmed black men, immigrants who do not understand your commands, the homeless, and people suffering from psychological problems. We may walk the streets in fear, but we will still walk the streets! And we will not let our fear freeze our obligation to stand up to your brutality!

Long after your bones and excrement have been fossilized and studied in a spaceship circling a space station where earth's survivors were first sequestered after experiments in engineered algae and synthetic biology failed, your ancestors will look back at you in disgrace, and it won't be with heroic recrimination but just plain, measured disgust. Time will forever be out of joint and Yorick's lips that hung in frozen merriment will not be rejuvenated.

George W. Bush, do you think your career as a painter has humanized you, has redeemed you in the eyes of the world? Your cute paintings of French poodles and dignitaries and your toes sticking out of your bathtub don't impress us, although your use of color does seem to be improving (keep working at it, bro!).

Do you think it has distracted us from your 2003 "war of aggression" against Iraq, the type of war which the Nuremburg Tribunal judges in 1946 termed a "the supreme international crime, differing only from other war crimes in that it contains within itself the accumulated evil of the whole" (cited in Pilger, 2015)? Do you think we don't see the connection between your war and the rise of ISIS? And don't you think the famous photo of your televised arrival in your groin-enhancing S&M flightsuit aboard the USS *Abraham Lincoln* is now made all the more absurd in light of the absolute chaos you created in Iraq!

Do you think the public execution of Libyan president Muammar Gaddafi by a mob of "rebels" (many of Libya's rebels were secretly trained by Britain's SAS and went on to join ISIS, but you want us to keep that secret, I'm sure) who sodomized him with a bayonet during his fatal beating was funny? Hillary Clinton, then U.S. Secretary of State, apparently did, when, chuckling at first hearing the news of Gaddafi's death, she exclaimed: "We came, we saw, he died." That is a pretty clear echo of the famous Latin phrase, "veni; vidi; vici" which translates as "I came; I saw; I conquered." The phrase reportedly originates from a letter written to the Roman Senate around 46 BC by Julius Caesar, after achieving an easy victory in a war against Pharnaces II of Pontus. Yes, Hillary, you are the new Caesar, or at least you represent the Roman legions of the 21st century. Although they at least did not disguise their conquering of other countries as 'humanitarian' interventions.

You hypocrites! Do you think that the 'maquilas' extending beyond la linea that separates us geographically from Mexico are not our future? Do you think that Baotou, the largest industrial city in Inner Mongolia—is not our own future? Do you think the factories and container ships that bring you your flatscreens and smartphones from China—and even your green technologies like wind turbines—are not also bringing the wrath of God? Do you think you will not be drinking your hubris from history's tailings ponds, from Baotou's toxic lake? Think again!

Aristotle freed us from the bondage of the gods. However, we cannot transcend reality through rationality alone, through our waking consciousness. So I cannot convince you by any known system of intelligibility to halt the coming planetary catastrophe. Therefore I beseech you in the name of the Kingdom of God that has already arrived: Abandon your altars of capital and the path of imperial war! And I can only repeat again and again these words of Che Guevara: "Si fuéramos capaces de unirnos … qué hermoso y qué cercano sería el futuro" (If only we were able to become united … how beautiful and near at hand the future would be).

Okay, we can appreciate that the U.S. military provides its officers courses on the ethics of launching nuclear strikes. And, yes, we know the Air Force cites St. Augustine's "Qualifications for Just War." That has some possibilities. But his *City of God* stipulates that we honor the legal imperatives imposed by emperors, kings and princes. We are sorry, but we reject that.

I have visited the City of God, but it's not the same city to which St. Augustine was referring. It's the neighborhood of Cidade de Deus in the West Zone of the city of Rio de Janeiro, Brazil and resembles far too many cities I have visited.

So I reject the stipulations of St. Augustine and the similar advocacy of Luther, Calvin, and all the other great defenders of the church. Their God only allows the privileged to disobey! The immiserated must remain immobilized in their chains. Your notion of freedom allows the rich man to sleep under a bridge with a poor man, but it does not allow the poor man to enjoy the security of being able to feed his family or ensure that they always have a room over their heads and receive the medical attention that they need.

We no longer believe that the most unspeakable offense is rebellion against the laws of earthly empires with their legalized hierarchies of oppression. Didn't you read the title of this book? It's called *Pedagogy of Insurrection*. Do you think I chose the title because it has a nice cadence? It is the cadence of memory that occupies my work, the cadence of the memories of those silenced by the history of the victors!

But I'm afraid that, when all is said and done, we have to denounce roundly and vociferously all of your tongue-wagging Christian-themed teachings in your nuclear weapons ethics training sessions. And especially when you trot out Werner Von Braun as a moral authority. Do you remember the V-1 and V-2 rockets smashing into London? Do you remember the sound of those buzz bombs? Of course you don't, you're too young. So what makes you think you can quote Von Braun? Citing Von Braun on the ethics of warfare is the medical equivalent of using Blackbeard the pirate's urethral syringe to inject mercury into your bladder for the treatment of syphilis. This is not 1718. Or haven't you noticed?

The struggle for civil rights marches valiantly onwards but has been rolled back considerably since the days of our prominent predecessors, Martin and Malcolm, has it not? Our society is about as tolerant today of racial differences as a busload of Sigma Alpha Epsilon fraternity brothers on their way to a white tie soirée. Nobody is fooling us anymore!

And what, dare say, about the struggle for economic rights? It took Hurricane Katrina to get us even a few meager news clips from the corporate media about persistent class divisions in the U.S.

If you are concerned about class inequality and come out in the academy as a socialist or a communist, it's not going to fast-track you to a coveted research scholarship, that's for sure. True, you won't be tethered naked to a mast and flayed alive. But being exiled to the academic equivalent of Palookaville isn't exactly fun and games, either. From your perch in your cage, you can watch your liberal colleagues chuckle and cluck their tongues at the mere mention of my name, while squatting on their academic bed-pans until they overflow with research that dares not jolt the system except by the stench of its anti-politics.

William Morris, among the world's most illustrious and politically pre-scient environmentalists, poets and artisans, was roundly denounced by those who had eagerly gathered to hear him speak at University College, Oxford, in 1883, because he announced to the starched shirts in attendance that he was a Socialist. Do you think the sentinels of today's global plutocracy are that much different? True, they pretend to share some sympathy with our ideas, but it's clear that they listen to us with extreme sufferance.

Don't try to pull the wool over our eyes! We know how the game is played. When push comes to shove, you Democrats join yourselves at the hip with your Republican partners in order to re-sanctify and consolidate your unholy pact: Block any real threat to the capitalist system at all costs!

Please don't let me be misunderstood. I'm not interested in blaming the wealthy. Everybody knows some wealthy philanthropist who donates socks and golf clubs to the local town assistance league. I'm interested in uncovering the process that enables people to become wealthy through the exploitation of the labor power of others. The occult curtain that shrouds the mysteries of capitalism must be rent, its Wizard of Oz machinations revealed. Then, and only then, will we be able to move forward in our efforts to abolish the capi-talist class.

Haven't you heard the latest news? We're no longer content with democ-ratizing already existing socialist societies. We are looking to build a new type of socialism, one that was supported by Marx, a society beyond value production. Yes, you heard correctly, we are struggling to build socialism out-side of value production.

We know enough to ascertain that value is not a property of things. It's not labor that exists as a commodity. Marx regarded labor as an activity (Hudis, 2015). His genius was in revealing that a worker does not sell his or her labor but rather sells his or her labor power, or capacity to labor.

Marx instructed us on how we can take a significant step towards cre-ating a social universe outside of capital's value form by explaining how to divide the aggregate product by freely associated producers. Social consump-tion should be shared by individuals, and this should be determined by actual labor time. Actual labor time, not by socially necessary labor time. Actual labor time does not produce value (monetized labor).

The social average of necessary labor time creates value (i.e., which is established behind the backs of the direct producers) by means of an average that operates out of their control (Hudis, 2015). *Necessary labor time* is the time (per day or per week) which workers *must* work in order to create the equivalent of their own livelihood or what they need in order to survive and reproduce generations of workers for the capitalists (at the socially and historically determined standard of living of their day).

When Marx explained that the share of each individual producer in the means of subsistence is determined by his or her labor time, Marx was not positing an identity between commodity production and social relations of production that will prevail after capitalism has been dethroned; rather he was simply suggesting a parallel (Hudis, 2015). He understood that we have to transcend value production altogether, and that is just what we aim to do!

But that means crossing the river of fire. We can cross the river of fire and not be scorched because we are José Clemente Orozco's "El Hombre en Llamas" and have been reborn in the flames of revolutionary struggle. We are holding counsel with the universe, and the oceans, lakes, rivers, rocks and trees are shouting in unison with us: Vivos se los llevaron! Vivos los queremos!

Some of us like to read. And some of our friends and comrades learned how to read as a result of literacy campaigns in Cuba and Venezuela. And some of us learned to read the word and the world from Paulo Freire, who was my mentor, my teacher. We do not read simply out of pleasure but because we want to learn what you don't want us to know.

We know, for instance, from recent cables released by Wikileaks the degree of hostility with which the Vatican of Pope Benedict viewed the doctrine of liberation theology and the continued obsession of the U.S. State Department with liberation theology (Kovalik, 2013). The attack on liberation theology dates back to before the days of John Paul II and President Jimmy Carter and Ronald Reagan. But try as it might, the U.S. government has so far been unable to destroy advocates of liberation theology and its teachings within the Catholic Church.

Witness the recent comments by Pope Francis on capitalism and climate change in *Laudato Si!* You probably know by now that we revere the life and legacy of Archbishop Óscar Arnulfo Romero of El Salvador. You probably have this information in your reports. Be that as it may, you can't take Romero away from us. We can only applaud the valiant effort of Pope Francis in officially declaring the late archbishop a martyr, for it has cleared the way for eventually proclaiming him a saint. Romero was killed celebrating the mass in 1980, not long after pleading to President Jimmy Carter to halt U.S. military aid to the murderous Salvadoran government regime. Carter unsurprisingly remained silent. And then Ronald Reagan helped to ratchet up the attack on liberation theology.

Of course, we are aware that it's been over 20 years since the signing of the Chapultepec peace accords, which effectively put an end to the 12 years of fighting between the military-led government of El Salvador (whose death squads were trained in the United States at the School of the Americas in Fort Benning, Georgia and who also received training from the U.S. Army John F. Kennedy Special Warfare Center and School at Fort Bragg, North Carolina) and the Farabundo Marti National Liberation Front (FMLN). And it is incontrovertibly the case that the government forces of El Salvador were, with U.S. assistance, overwhelmingly the worst perpetrators of war crimes during this decade-long conflict.

The U.S. could not—and cannot to this day—tolerate organized movements for social justice in Latin America which it views as a threat to its economic domination of the region. Hence, in the late 1970s, it had to step up its insurgency against the influence of liberation theology within the Catholic Church (Kovalik, 2013). After 1962, and Vatican II, the U.S. government tried to neutralize the efforts of Pope John XXIII to return the Church to its roots in the Social Gospel of Jesus Christ. Priests were removed, censured, and defrocked, and religious and base communities were attacked throughout Las Americas (Kovalik, 2013). With the help of Cardinal Ratzinger (later Pope Benedict XVI), who at the time was head of the Congregation for the Doctrine of the Faith (known in earlier times as the Inquisition), John Paul II officially condemned in 1984 and 1986 important aspects of liberation theology. Neither one of these powerful figures within the Catholic Church appreciated liberation theology's Marxist analysis of class struggle. That's very clear to us!

Archbishop Romero was unable to acquire a Vatican condemnation of El Salvador's regime, for violations of human rights and its support of death squads that eviscerated women and children.

And then there was Nicaragua. I remember so fondly my meeting with Ernesto Cardenal, a Nicaraguan priest, poet, and former Minister of Culture, during a television appearance we made for the program, *Alo Presidente*, hosted by the late President Hugo Chávez of Venezuela. During a trip to Managua, Nicaragua, in 1983, Pope John Paul II condemned the popular church and ecclesial base communities. Cardenal was there to greet John Paul II and when he knelt to kiss the papal ring, the pope withdrew his hand and rebuked him for his position on liberation theology.

How could this be? How could this collusion between state terror and the Catholic Church have happened? We Catholics want to know!

In 1989, a Salvadoran army patrol—including members of the infamous and feared Atlacatl Battalion—executed six Jesuit priests (as well as their housekeeper and her 16-year-old daughter) as they lay face down on the ground at Central America University. We are aware that the United Nations's Truth Commission Report on El Salvador in 1993 identified most of the officers who took part in the executions as being proud graduates of the School of the Americas. We know that U.S. Special Forces doctrine directly advocates training paramilitaries, participates in surveillance of private individuals and groups sympathetic to liberation theology, practices censorship and press control and creates restrictions on labor unions and political parties. As far as the conflict in El Salvador was concerned, President Reagan was not much interested in achieving a negotiated settlement between the warring sides, hoping instead to obliterate the FMLN and the liberation theology that was informing the religious education of many priests in El Salvador, Nicaragua, Brazil, and elsewhere throughout Latin America. We know this!

The slaughtering of thousands of *campesino* and human rights and labor activists by the Atlacatl Battalion was vehemently opposed by priests sympathetic to liberation theology. And, of course, the U.S. labeled these priests as communist sympathizers with great propaganda skill. We know this U.S.-trained battalion was given a carte blanche license to kill anyone that they pleased, and so they tortured and slaughtered men, women and children with impunity.

Let's take one example, the villagers of El Mozote. The villagers of El Mozote, including women and children, were raped and beheaded with machetes. We know that infants were thrown into the air and skewered on bayonets; we know that pregnant women had large rocks dropped on their bellies, and we know that during the attack on El Mozote, 900 peasants were slaughtered. We know that President Reagan disputed this massacre and argued that the government of El Salvador was making a concerted and significant effort to comply with internationally recognized human rights. Assistant Secretary of State for Human Rights and Humanitarian Affairs, Elliott Abrams (a future Iran-Contra criminal and subsequent George W. Bush National Security Council director), praised the "professionalism" of the Atlacatl Battalion. He even described this death squad as having a commendable combat record. We would laugh at this report if we were not so sickened by it. Such reports do not surprise us in the least! We stand in solidarity with Archbishop Óscar Romero who once said, "¡No se mata la justicia!"—"Justice cannot be killed!"

Do the recent Wikileaks cables that reveal an ongoing concern by the U.S. Embassy to the Vatican about the impact of liberation theology surprise us? About as much as learning that the Catholic hierarchy in Nicaragua was being financed by the CIA and was coordinating with the Reagan administration's destabilization strategies in that country.

The archbishop of Managua, Cardinal Miguel Obando y Bravo, was one of the most vocal domestic opponents of the Sandinistas. Yes, we know about him. He also opposed the "people's church" and banned the Nicaraguan peasants' mass known as the *Misa Campesina Nicaragüense*. On May 25, 1985, the pope named him cardinal for Central America. And in 1986 Obando y Bravo traveled to the United States where he stated his support for the murderous U.S.-trained Contras and approved military aid from the U.S. Does anybody doubt reports of CIA funding for Nicaragua's Catholic Church during the 1980s? Haven't reports from congressional intelligence oversight committees revealed that to be the case?

I hope you get our point. We are sympathetic to liberation theology and to the struggle of the peasants—to all of the oppressed! And history tells us that you will oppose us. We expect your subterfuge. Yet there is for the moment a light that is shining in the darkness, the light of Pope Francis. And we hope this light will continue to shine, that it is not temporary, and that it will intensify.

We are among the generations whose families were peasants and farmers and who knew Hugo Chávez and visited Venezuela and Colombia during Chávez's presidency of Venezuela. We witnessed how vile the opinion of Chávez was among the rich and learned of the shameful cooperation between the Venezuelan ruling class and the CIA in their failed attempts to topple Chávez and the Bolivarian revolution. We witnessed a similar hostility to Chávez in neighboring Colombia where to be a member in a leftist teacher union was often to risk assassination by the paramilitary, the pit bulls of its ruling class. We learned from conversations in Bogotá and Medellín that there were concerted efforts to keep "Chavismo" on the other side of the border, even if it meant crossing into Venezuela and murdering Chávez sympathizers. Interesting, isn't it, how contempt for the poor is not restricted to individual countries but is pervasive in all countries where achieving wealth and power is praised as the highest good? Do you think we are surprised that over 800 members of the Colombian army have been jailed so far in the "false positive" scandal in which civilians were murdered and their bodies passed off as those of FARC (Fuerzas Armadas Revolucionarias de Colombia— Ejército del Pueblo) rebels in order to boost the army's combat kill rates?

Do you think we believe that the former head of the Joint Caribbean Command, retired General Gonzalez-Peña and the former army commander, retired Gen Mario Montoya Uribe, are simply oblivious as to what went on in their battalions? Do you think it surprises us that the victims of the "false positives"—victims of extra-judicial killings—were often poor farmers who were lured with the promise of work to remote places where they would be killed? One group of poor young men had been recruited from the slums of Bogotá, promised lucrative jobs in the province of Norte de Santander, then mercilessly killed and dressed up in FARC uniforms as having been slain during official combat operations.

Do you think we don't know that soldiers were being sent to round up homeless people to be murdered in cold blood so that members of the army, police and navy could be promoted to a higher-paying and more prestigious rank and be given "perks" such as days off? Do you think we don't know that those who dedicate themselves to helping the poor in their struggle for the basic necessities of life are as loathed as the poor themselves? Do you think that we don't know that the poor are taught to loathe themselves?

I am from a lineage of farmers and petty merchants with a special affinity to the land and kinship, the silent folk whom today are derided as hicks and lumbering, fumbling know-nothings. Did not Jung (1973, p. 149) say:

> He who is rooted in the soil endures. Alienation from the unconscious and from its historical condition spells rootlessness. That is the danger that lies in wait for the conquerors of foreign lands, and for every individual who, through one-sided allegiance to any kind of –ism, loses touch with the dark, maternal, earthy ground of his being. Our barren souls yearn for a harvest of the will, where we do more than sanctify our possessive investment in our superiority, our purity.

andante con moto

You modern-day shallow rationalists, you bloodless phantoms of the intellect, you have addled our brains with such dogma and stripped knowledge of the numinous! You re-echo the sterile sounds of the eugenics laboratory, and your unseemly ebullience for technology has withered the vine of spirituality. Yet your abysmal ignorance does not exempt you from the task of redeeming yourselves.

My father fought the Nazis in Europe from 1939 to 1945. My uncle, who flew his Royal Navy Fairey Swordfish off the Arc Royal, helped to disable the German battleship *Bismarck* with a torpedo. I am proud there is a Canadian postage stamp to honor my uncle's heroism. I am proud that King George VI (whom Hollywood made famous for his stuttering) personally pinned onto my uncle's courageous chest the Distinguished Service Medal. I honor the service of those who fight for their country. But today in the U.S. we fight continuous wars of aggression, not because our country is under threat of invasion, but because it bolsters business and protects our already established economic and geo-political hegemony. Wars against "terror" are often fought because they good for business.

And while we are on the topic of war, stop putting Biblical quotations on your sniper rifles, and stop making Jesus into a pro-nuke Christian warrior! And stop defending *American Sniper!*

We remember you, Private Danny Chen, when you were part of 2nd Platoon, C Company, 3rd Battalion, 21st Infantry Regiment, that belongs to the 25th Infantry Division's 1st Stryker Brigade Combat Team at Fort Wainwright, Alaska. You "committed suicide" on October 3, 2011, after you were deployed to Kandahar province, Afghanistan, and then hazed about your Chinese ancestry, forced to crawl on your belly on gravel for over a hundred yards while carrying your equipment, at the same time that your fellow soldiers were throwing rocks at you and calling you "gook," "chink" and "dragon lady." But before this you received 6 weeks of similar hazing by your fellow soldiers back in the U.S. And now the unit leader of 2nd Platoon is under investigation for allegedly encouraging soldiers to use racial slurs against each other every Thursday as a way to build morale and camaraderie—a practice the soldiers call "racial Thursdays."

U.S. military veterans are not cowards, but neither are all of them heroes to us and we do not buy into the slogan, "my country, right or wrong." We are critical patriots and believe that we must not be led into war by the lies and machinations of politicians. Which is why we challenge you to let us offer courses in critical pedagogy at West Point!

The U.S. invaded Iraq before Al-Qaeda or ISIS were established entities in that country. The U.S. destroyed a nation that was trying to defend itself from a U.S. invasion and occupation. We mourn the American and Iraqi lives that were lost. These lives were destroyed by a war that was premised on the lies of our politicians and could have been avoided. Should have been avoided! We stand for peace. We are revolutionaries for peace. Peace through socialism! We believe in a social revolution through critical education!

Should we forget the decimation of Fallujah (where white phosphorus was used) and other cities where resistance occurred? Do you want to erase the memory of the barbarity in Abu Ghraib? Do you want to pretend the massacre in Haditha didn't happen? Do you want simply to whitewash the gang rape of a 14-year-old Iraqi girl and the murder of her family in Al-Mahmudiyah? Do you even know about the war crimes committed by the group of U.S. military personnel in Baghdad known as the "Leavenworth 10," the murders carried out by Marines in Hamdania, the Baghdad airstrike known as "Collateral Murder," and countless other atrocities? Well, do you?

Do you know what depleted uranium does to the body, and do you know the birth defects from that unholy substance that appear generations later? Have you heard the screams from the victims of U.S.-trained death squads throughout Las Americas? I have seen the tears of their sons and daughters and wept alongside them.

We will not be living fragments of your mythology! We will not be consoled by the promise of your dream! Especially your dreams of world domination, or world destruction, which really amount to the same thing.

Don't you think we know that the Tokyo stock market soared after Japan's army butchered the people of Nanking, torturing and executing 300,000 civilians? What, do you think we live in shells? Do you think we don't notice the relationship of the economy to war? Do you think we don't notice that the ruling classes everywhere behave like the ruling classes anywhere? Ah, yes, the glorious victors, that's us! What happened to the native Americans, and black soldiers, and Mexican immigrants who fought for the U.S., when they returned from the "good war"?

Don't you think we know that Atticus Finch's home was spared demolition when the police came to evict the remaining residents from Chávez Ravine in Los Angeles and sold by the developers of Dodger Stadium to Universal Studios for a dollar, later to be seen in the 1962 film, *To Kill a Mockingbird?* We cried at the end of that movie, but who cried for the Mexican residents who were evicted from Chávez Ravine?

Don't you think we know our history? Do you think you are going to escape your karmuppance for that? And, trust me, it will be more than a shoe thrown at your pompous head. Or do you think the topic of exploitation is too picayune for you? We reside in the unmanifest universe! There is no total expression, no words of wisdom that can embrace the totality of our universe. We know a little bit about hubris. If you want to escape your destiny, I say, come and join us on the right side of history. But bring your own towel!

Do you think your Manichean narratives of "us against them" can get past our gut check? Do you think our guts are separated from our brains? Do you think your repeated fallacies have any currency with us? Well, think again!

We were listening as Dr. Yu Wei of Northeast Normal University remarked recently that all children are philosophers. They ask basic philosophical questions such as: What is politics? Why do people grow old? What happens when you die? Too often we are taught to stop asking these questions as we get older in order to become more "realistic" and "practical" citizens whose primary goals are to produce commodities for exchange value and surplus value for capital. At the risk of being criticized for being irretrievably stuck at some stage of arrested development, we have some news for the grand masters of empire: We refuse to stop asking these questions!

We are nobody's pre-history. We live outside the pale of bourgeois democracy. Tell your lawyers that their degrees are not valid here. In the court of the people, their doctrinaire fanaticism and spurious morality will be annihilated by their own questions. You are only reaping the value judgments of your dogmatic self-assertion about those whom you have already cast into the pit of poverty and robbed of any cognitive validity.

A pox on your house!

Your conventionally established rules are no better than our ancient tradition. Your cosmopolitan consensus is fake. We do not bid the dialectic goodbye!

Doesn't Daniel 9:7 say something about the whips of the Lord? You are forced to kiss the whip of those whom you elect (and you hypocritically condemn Cuba for not allowing its elections to be purchased by rich Cubans in Miami!). We do not believe that God has imprinted and engraved inviolable eminence and grandeur on the hearts and souls of our overlords. Therefore, we rip the whip from our rulers' hands! I have choked on the tear gas of riot police in Ankara, and felt the force of their boots on my legs. I have heard machine gun bursts from La Familia Michoacana fighting government troops on the outskirts of Morelia.

My tears have marked the floor of the Museum of Japanese Aggression at the Imperial Palace of "Manchukuo" in Changchun, and the Memorial for Compatriots killed in the Nanjing Massacre by Japanese Forces of Aggression in Nanjing. I have trembled in horror before the starvation cells of Auschwitz and the gas chambers of Birkenau. I fear what fascism could bring to the streets of our cities and towns. Let us not sink into a retrospective posture of lament—a melancholy mourning—but rather connect this remembering to the horrors of the present and those already fomenting in the terrible womb of our discontent.

The militarization of the police, the quickening pace of the jackboots of riot police, the denial of climate change, the shooting of unarmed black men in the streets of our cities, the expansion of the school-to-prison pipeline and the Charleston massacre in the Emanuel African Methodist Episcopal Church are not the result of some psychopathic deviation from the grandiose triumph of modernity but the apocalyptic tumult of its murderous hubris latent in all your talk of economic progress and profits and your unwillingness to see racism eating away the very foundations of the American Dream like termites gorging a block of damp Oregon timber. Do you think you can distract us with photos of a champagne glass perched upon Kim Kardashian's butt? Do you think creating a hundred sports channels will siphon away our resolve and disintegrate our revolutionary spirit into digital sparkle dust? If you do, you're crazier than I thought.

You empiricists make me sick. You worshippers of the false idol of data! You are gloriously oblivious to inequality. You say that we live in a meritocracy and that this can be provably shown. Well, I'll tell you what can be shown to be true! Let me show you inequality. Let me show you how the rich live in their gated communities and how the poor suffer. Come with me on my visits to teachers and activists in Colombia, in Venezuela, in Mexico, in Brazil, in India. You don't have time for this, you tell me. Well, let me tell you that you cannot empirically verify equality. Equality is the logical consequence that all of us should be treated with equal dignity. Historically, this is derived from Jesus dying for all of humanity. As Porfirio tells us—and do I need to scream this into your brain?—affirming equality is our moral duty! Love and justice, they mutually inform each other.

When in La Paz, Bolivia, on July 8, 2015, President Evo Morales presented Pope Francis with a crucifix carved into a wooden hammer and sickle, we understood immediately the significance of this, and the common struggle that can be waged on behalf of struggling humanity by Christians, communists and socialists alike. The crucifix was a replica, originally designed by Jesuit activist Luis Espinal, who was assassinated in 1980 by suspected paramilitaries during the months that preceded a military coup. Following the publication of the photo of this event, we happened upon an article entitled "Here's a Picture of the Pope Being Given a Really Weird Crucifix" in *Time Magazine*, written by Joanna Plucinska (2015). *Time Magazine* might consider the crucifix weird, but consider the figures gracing the covers of their magazine as Persons of the Year throughout the decades: Adolf Hitler, Joseph Stalin, George H. W. Bush, Newt Gingrich, Ken Starr, Rudolph Giuliani, George W. Bush and Ben Bernanke, to name only a few "weird" choices.

We do not ramble quaintly about the dignity of humankind. We don't rely on empirical showable facts but on moral principles! We are not memorably rousing the "we happy few" but rather calling our brothers and sisters into full humanity. Do you think you can dismiss our ravings because our thoughts are disorganized? Well think again!

You support an economic system that kills millions of children annually from preventable hunger-related causes; you support capital punishment; you supported sanctions against Iraq that killed 500,000 children according to the U.N. Food and Agriculture Department and UNICEF; you supported the invasion of Iraq that killed hundreds of thousands of innocent victims; you support Obama's drone warfare policy of extrajudicial killings, and you call those who are pro-choice killers? You oppose regulating firearms; you oppose universal health-care, claiming it is socialism, putting millions of children at risk; you think climate change is a fraud and you oppose sex education classes.

When will you express concern for unwanted children that emerge from the womb in the same way you express concern for the unborn? You want to legally end abortion (by making little personal sacrifice in calling for a change in the law) but not reduce abortion, is that it? The lowest abortion rates in the world are in countries such as the Netherlands and Belgium where abortion is legal. But they have state programs for mothers and children. Yes, socialized programs. You can't stop abortion by making it illegal but you can manifestly reduce abortion not by criminalizing it—but by providing social programs for children that you so vociferously demand to see born! And by fighting a capitalist system that creates such disparities in wealth, access to health, and access to financial security.

When the Zapatista Army of National Liberation (*Ejército Zapatista de Liberación Nacional*) publicly declared war against the Mexican government on January 1, 1994, the day the North American Free Trade Agreement (NAFTA) went into effect, the Zapatistas knew how this trade agreement would affect indigenous populations throughout Mexico. They predicted with uncanny accuracy the cataclysmic impact of NAFTA on the Mayan communities in Chiapas. What, did you think they were simply ignorant peasants? We have stood behind them since they issued their First Declaration from the Lacandon jungle and their Revolutionary Laws and we will continue to stand behind them.

There is another NAFTA looming, being hatched behind closed doors among the panoply of power in Washington. We reject this attack on the poor, this new Trans-Pacific Partnership deal among thugs, and a thousand Zapatista armies must be launched throughout the world to stop it.

We do not call for violence, but civil disobedience. We do not try to sharpen the contradictions between the workers and ruling class but educate all through revolutionary critical pedagogy!

We reject ISIS and Al-Qaeda, but we also reject decades of colonialism, violent aggression, exclusion, and vilification of Muslims around the world and in the U.S. We reject these racist policies that have been abetted by an organized Islamophobic, anti-immigrant ideology. While we reject the ideologies of hate and violence undergirding oppressive regimes and non-state actors in Muslim-majority societies, we also reject Western anti-Muslim propaganda that fuels their rise. Most Muslims are not interested in terrorism. So stop telling us otherwise. You are only feeding into the strategies of the terrorists and their Faustian hunger for power! The more Al-Qaeda can foster Islamophobia, the more it can ripen the minds of Muslim youth for its strategy of ideological colonization. The closer the KKK or the National Front comes to initiating pogroms against Muslims, the more they are playing right into the hands of the terrorists.

You cannot master the powers that you have summed up. We see cracks in your armor. You have vilified the past of those who have struggled and sacrificed the most for social justice.

The upper echelons of your bureaucracy in charge of the apparatuses which function to inculcate ideology cannot instill fear in me despite the virtual unanimity of your persistent political persecution, because I am prepared to fight you with a fearlessness that is stronger than your fear-mongering! I am prepared to de-Stalinize your entire system.

The sun does not travel across the sky and set in the evening. Joshua's scientific mistake does not cast the word of God into the rag-and-bone shop of discarded trust. It tells us that we should reengage the scriptures in the context of the unfolding present, including scientific knowledge. But we will not let your scientific consensus drown our souls.

And now I shall turn to you, you faux Fisher King with pinewood crown and empty loins waiting for your Percival to rescue you from your frozen emptiness. I haven't forgotten about you. Yes, you work outside of the sterile laboratories of the state, immersing yourself in your incense, your chanting, your incantations, your Giordano Bruno, your H. P. Blavatsky, your Israel Regardie, your Aleister Crowley, your knowledge of the Hermetic Order of the Golden Dawn. That's fine, impress us when we come to visit you in Sedona. But this does not stop you from altering the narrative of history for the sake of protecting yourself. As hard as you might try, you can't escape the eye in the triangle on the back of our dollar bill. We say, let the money rot!

We do not believe the gold is worth saving in the fire. The only thing worth saving in a fire is the act of saving life itself; for in such an act we can save ourselves.

We will not be pulled into the future by a carriage with chestnut-colored warmbloods with ribbon-braided tails. Likely we will be pushed into the unknown by our own ignorance and by meekly following the coattails of those who purchase our labor power. Paulo Freire urges us to be a subject of history and not a casualty. So let's get on with the revolution! The stakes are high. They always are.

Was it not Jung (1973, p. 147) who said:

> No one can make history who is not willing to risk everything for it, to carry the experiment with his own life through to the bitter end, and to declare that his life is not a continuation of the past, but a new beginning.

I have stood on the banks of the Yangtze River, which flows 3,200 miles across central China to the sea, waters in which Mao liked to swim. Like Mao, we will swim against the current and arrive on the opposite bank and show the goddess of the mountain a new world!

Your breezy tone and cheery smile suggest you are feeling quite chipper today. We're glad you enjoy being white, and all the power privilege that goes with that identity, but stop breathing the sea air and then telling people of color to 'man up.' And why don't you stop acting like you white folks are the real victims. That's easy enough for you to say, speaking from your yacht and wearing your silly jacket with a patch pocket crest of some phony coat of arms you made up so you could wear it on your intellectually quaint Christian Broadcasting Corporation television show. You are only victimizing people of color by pontificating like that, perched on top of your throne of lies like some carnival huckster. You would like to force us to digest any opposition by the independent media to your lies as an attack on decent white folks. We know how you play that game, you corporate dreamer, because some of us are white, like me, and trust me, it doesn't fool anybody. You spew hate, you walk back your comments, you wait a bit and then spew hate again. You think we don't know how you do it?

And you gossip mongers, please take heed. We won't quail in our efforts to confront your fortified residential enclaves, your corporate luxury zones, your self-enclosing maze-like bureaucracies populated by state functionaries bent on creating an imperial administrative apparatus. Because we're bent on creating transnational spaces of liberated humanity who are willing to move beyond critical cosmopolitanism to create a counterpublic sphere consisting of autonomous communities of ecosocial struggle.

We know that the Marxist taboo is functionally necessary for capitalist rule. We're not foolish enough to think that this is orchestrated by a cabal of conspirators hidden away in a luxury hotel in the Bahamas. But to let the suggestion settle in the minds of Americans that socialism has worked successfully in other countries would be self-subverting and therefore the idea must be discredited through undirected messages we receive every day in your corporate media outlets about failed alternatives to capitalism. We know that the state serves as a gold card filter removing by taboo contrary knowledge from the system. If you advocate for socialism you are shunned, ridiculed and condemned in the media and we know that this brings about self-censorship. Don't think we are fools. We will take this risk!

We don't care to know when Kim Kardashian changes her hair color. We're too busy discussing Manuel Zapata Olivella's work. Are you okay with that, or would you rather we retreat instead to your teak-paneled living room den and play Twister after the Super Bowl game is over?

Dear National Security Agency courtiers and quislings of the ruling regime, you shame all of humanity. We know what goes on at the intersection of the Baltimore Parkway and Maryland Route 32. Don't for a moment think we aren't watching what's going on inside the Special Sources Operations unit of the NSA or that we don't know all about your Corporate Partner Access portfolio, thanks to the heroic actions of Chelsea Manning, Julian Assange, Edward Snowden and Pulitzer Prize-winning journalist Glenn Greenwald. We thank you Daniel Ellsberg for inspiring all of them. We know about the secret agreements between the NSA and Facebook, Yahoo, Apple, Google and Microsoft.

We know about Five Eyes and we are millions of eyes watching you! Contrary to President Obama's aerosol assurances to the contrary, the NSA intercepts the communications of US citizens continuously and thuggishly disregards "probable cause" warrants as laughable while unsparingly prosecuting whistleblowers and the few authentic journalists that still exist in the US (Greenwald, 2014). Speaking of what is considered to be laughable, we know that the Foreign Intelligence Surveillance Act court is a joke that would be hilariously funny were it not for the unassailable fact that it is a puppet entity that rubber stamps all requests from this ubiquitous spying machine, including requests to monitor all electronic communications by US citizens.

We know that the US government has been implanting surveillance mechanisms in their network devices that possess the lurid capacity of remotely activating all cell phones and converting them to listening devices—to "roving bugs"—so we put our phones in the kitchen freezer with our restaurant leftovers when we want privacy. We know all about your "false flag" operations, your "honey traps," your "deception strategies" and your "information ops" designed to annihilate a person's reputation. We know that the NSA outlawry threatens the very foundations of democracy under the pretense of keeping us safe from terrorism. The reality is that such an egregious abuse of power is driven by the need for the US government to spy on its capitalist rivals, to manipulate its corporate and military advantage and to control the world through the exercise of limitless power with no accountability. We are the sources for your metadata as you monitor our emails, our web browsing and our search histories and our chats. We know you do "real-time" monitoring of all our online activities and likely are reading what I am writing at this very moment, keystroke by keystroke. All of you neuroscientists, sociologists, anthropologists and behavioral scientists on the payroll of GCHQ in Britain, or the NSA, do you really think you are doing humanity a favor?

We ask why we need fetid right wing media hacks to bolster the infrastructure of the national security state when liberal critics distort the facts just as effectively and perhaps more so? You liberals masquerading as radicals, we see how you dutifully abide by the established fear-driven and unscrupulous discourses that foster a passive and compliant citizenry produced on the conveyor belts of false neutrality. What, you thought we were sleeping through our critical theory classes? You censor yourselves unblinkingly then wrap yourselves in the heroic posture of a rebel. You make a quiet ruckus, resisting only halfway, thereby amplifying the very forces of domination that you claim to want to subvert. You mastermind a swindle of rebellion without so much as the courtesy of introspection.

Do you think we the people (not we the citizens!) don't know how to learn? Do you think we need teachers? Do you think we are not ourselves teachers? Do you think we can't teach what we don't know? Give us a space, that is all, and we will figure it out.

Do you think we don't see the American government as hypocritical? You condemn terrorism but you have waged terrorist attacks in Vietnam, in Guatemala, in El Salvador, and Cuba. All over the world! Our teachers won't admit this so we find this out ourselves.

Do you think your Camelot president John F. Kennedy was a good man? We know he ordered the U.S. Air Force to authorize napalm and chemical warfare to destroy crops and livestock in Vietnam. But let's get to Latin America and the Caribbean. Okay, the Bay of Pigs. John Kennedy and his brother Bobby Kennedy, what a team! On their orders, the CIA worked with Cuban exiles based in the U.S. to destroy the Castro regime.

On the advice of Arthur Schlesinger, the U.S. tried to lure Castro to attack other countries so that the U.S. would have a pretext for invading Cuba. Operation Northwoods, as it was called, was a plan signed by all the Joint Chiefs of Staff which recommended blowing up a U.S. ship in Guantanamo Bay and saying it was sabotaged by Castro, developing a communist terror campaign in Florida and Washington and blaming it on Castro, shooting down a drone aircraft and making it appear as though an airliner full of vacationing U.S. college students had been shot down by Cuban jets. And while these plans were not implemented, we know the kind of mentality that goes around in Washington.

We know that in 1962, under the directive of National Security Memorandum No. 181, covert action teams from the U.S. strafed Cuban hotels, blew up a Cuban industrial facility killing 400 workers, contaminated sugar shipments. We know Nixon directed terrorist attacks on Cuba, blowing up fishing boats, embassies and overseas offices of Cuban officials. We know that Cubana airliner 455 was blown up, killing 73 passengers. We know attacks continued well into the late 1990s.

Don't think we don't know about Luis Posada Carriles and the Cuban exile terrorists living in Florida and their CIA history? Don't you think we know that Posada also helped U.S. Colonel Oliver North direct terrorist attacks in Nicaragua? Don't you think we know that Posada and Orlando Bosch were responsible for the Cuban airliner being blown to smithereens? And they also planned the attack on a freighter bound for Cuba?

You threaten to ridicule us as conspiracy theorists but we are not a meek cadre of gelotophobes. We know you are experts on destroying reputations. We know you offered money to students to secretly audiotape my lectures when I was at UCLA. We know you offered to pay students for lecture notes made in my classes. We know you put me on top of the dirty thirty list as the most dangerous professor at UCLA. And we know you continue to monitor left-wing professors. And so what else is new?

We know about Operation 40, a CIA assassination squad. And Operation Condor. We agree with George W. Bush that those who harbor terrorists are themselves terrorists, and by Bush's very definition of terrorist he is admitting that he, himself, is a terrorist.

We therefore proclaim that we will treat our fellow human beings as ends in themselves and not as a means for something else. As far as entering your normal universe is concerned, we are on permanent strike. And this is but a short prelude to a path for social change. We stand firm for a multi-tendency revolutionary democracy that advocates direct forms of mass self-rule.

Just because I have disturbing dreams of the Roberts Supreme Court bedazzled in ruffle frill lace shirts tucked under rhinestone-studded sharkskin suits playing cowpunk songs with lyrics by the ghost of Ayn Rand doesn't mean that I am crazy. The nightmares began after viewing a video clip of Karl Rove as "MC Rove" rapping at the Radio and Television Correspondents' Association Annual Dinner on March 28, 2007. David Gregory, host of NBC's Meet the Press and tepid courtier of ruling class ideology, appears in the background of the video, dancing along with MC Rove, symbolizing that this show does little more than shamefully showcase the views of political power-brokers, left or right, no matter how loathsome their opinions or beliefs. (Gregory was reportedly given $4 millon to leave NBC as a result of falling ratings.) In the words of Glenn Greenwald, Meet the Press is "a place where political power goes to be amplified and flattered, where only the most staid conventional wisdom is heard, where only the narrowest range of political views is permitted" (2014, p. 217). Perhaps it is not me but the country that has gone mad.

Save the Children Fund honored George W. Bush as Father of the Year, 2015. Do you find this difficult to fathom? After all, there is ample reason to believe that this honor might be disputed, at the very least, by Iraqi fathers who lost their children during the US invasion and occupation of their country. I am sure the US commanders of the notorious prison, Abu Graib, balanced their family duties and their professional duties as torturers quite effectively. Do you think they will be nominated next year? Didn't Hannah Arendt warn us about the banality of evil?

Perhaps it is time that I put this angry pen to rest and recast my tone. It is not you, dear readers, to whom this rage is directed. It is the capitalist machine. So permit me to take a more measured tone in the final pages of this book.

allegro ma non troppo

Today, during the worst economic crisis since the Great Depression, we know that corporations are reaping huge profits but they are not spending their profits to hire workers or build factories but to enhance their own share prices. In contrast to this reality, we all live with a certain image that is constantly being embellished: that we live in a meritocracy where we are rewarded fairly for our hard work and perseverance. Hagiographers of American life surely will describe the first decade of the twenty-first century as a decade of disaster piled upon disaster. The misery of everyday life in capitalist society comes for many in the form of a pink slip or a home-foreclosure notice.

As critical educators, we search for a reprieve. We know from the alienation and suffering that have afflicted humanity for centuries that history can never be trusted to bend one particular way or another. Our purpose as revolutionary educators has never been to trust history, or whatever prophetic insights we believe we have pertaining to the fate of humankind, but to understand history's movement and give it direction and momentum in the interests of social justice. Viewed from any point within the socio-historical panorama of despair that now confronts us, such a task seems more daunting than ever. Besotted by ideological belligerence, capitalism relies to a greater extent today than ever before on ideological rationalizations and obfuscations to defuse and deflect criticism of its recent developments.

When we look around us at the age in which we live, we see a ruling class with an unimaginably dense accumulation of wealth undertaking innumerable efforts to establish new organizations to reproduce the same social practices. Those who control capital control the government, forcing governments to become part of a corporate superstructure, overseeing capital's base. And there has been an accompanying corporate colonization of civil society as well, effectively stifling any ameliorative function that might be offered by new educational movements, those very pragmatic organizations that have become a more capital-friendly substitute for revolutionary manifestos and for groups bent on overthrowing the regime of capital.

Those of us who have to sell our labor power for a wage remain ensepulchered by the realities of the global meltdown and the militarization of the country. The poor are left to face the organized burden of being American in the gold-paved paradise created by the rich and for the rich.

Dr. King noted that the United States is the greatest purveyor of violence in the world today. Well, has anything changed? Haven't you rich folks done anything since Dr. King left us for a better world? Sorry, we don't need your flatulent words or your philippics, or your 'scholarshit,' or the voice from the spinning dust cloud of your mind, for that matter. You've rigged the statistics to preserve your hides. Excuse us if we are intruding into your carefully planned universe and stepping on the surety of your conscious gaze. Like Dr. King, we have a dream. And you are not our dreamer.

We need the prophetic voices of Dr. King, of Abraham Joshua Heschel, of Dietrich Bonhoeffer, of Óscar Romero, and of Tsunesaburo Makiguchi (who, while in prison, asked loudly enough for people in other cells to hear: "Isn't not doing good the same as doing evil?") more than ever today. You want Aristotelian reason with a beginning and a middle and an end. We prefer dialectical reasoning from a prefigurative standpoint as well as figurative standpoint. That's why we nod in agreement with Hegel's statement, "the fact is, before it exists," and C.L.R. James's comment, "the future that is in the present." We are, after all, interested not only in resistance, but emancipation.

You applaud the politics of the Obama administration and yet know nothing of his attacks on Venezuela, declaring that country a threat to U.S. national security. Don't you know that in Latin America many regard, with good reason, U.S. governments over the past 30 years as no better than Chile's former military junta led by Augusto Pinochet, or the Alianza Republicana Nacionalista (or ARENA) led by Salvadoran Roberto D'Aubuisson. You probably won't like me saying this, but I am happy to have met the late President Hugo Chávez of Venezuela and participated, however modestly, in the Bolivarian Revolution. It was a time of great accomplishments for the working class. It is an experiment that is still worth defending. In fact it is crucial that we defend it, although the U.S. is ratcheting up its clandestine operations to destroy the revolution and we can only pray that the revolution will succeed.

We have dreams, and they are not your dreams. We have interests, and they are not your interests. We know the steps you take to destroy nations whose philosophies and practices of social justice are deemed a threat to the corporate interests of the United States. We know that those suffering the most under today's buccaneer capitalism of prosperity through pillage will not self-organize unbidden, as if following lockstep the echoes of their genetic unconscious. They need spaces of hope and possibility and that's what we are now transforming into schools—spaces of resistance and transformation. We are not going to lead the oppressed; we are creating spaces where the oppressed can lead themselves.

You political leaders with your grandiose prerogatives, your regal pretentions, your monarchial authority and desire for Hollywood celebrity; you who dispatch your enemies through secret drone strikes and then target the funeral participants; you who disgrace your office when you lie to the American people, I condemn you!

Dear reader, are you starting to get the point? "Hypocrite lecteur,—mon semblable,—mon frère!" ("Hypocrite reader!—You!—My twin!—My brother!") Can we not learn from Baudelaire about our own hypocrisy? Can we not admit, for instance, that our standard of living in the United States today rests on the backs of the exploited countries of Las Americas? Can we not see the blood on our hands? This is not a problem that can be solved by your Christian campfire experience where you pray for your God-ordained prosperity and ask Jesus for a Corvette Stingray. Nor can it be solved by your mega stadium Billy Graham experience where you sang, "All to Jesus I Surrender," as you slowly made your way through a flood of tears to the stage to receive Jesus as your "personal Lord and savior." We respect that you have given over your life to the saving grace of Jesus the Christ, as have many of us, but please don't expect every word that springs from U.S. church pulpits to be pleasing to the Lord.

The attempt by the Right to exorcise the insinuation of too much diversity into the U.S. Anglosphere, and the mass media's long-imposed separation between dialectical thought and everyday life have united to bring about a terrifying calcification of the public mind that has turned politics into a circus of pantomime, and has helped to secure both political parties as organs of interest for the corporations, which have become the servo-mechanisms of the corporate state. Are you being entertained to death? We are!

It is the daily taunt of many on the Right that socialism leads to mindless conformity. But what could be gloomier than the politics that has arisen out of the ashes of bourgeois capitalist democracy? The word "socialism" is disparaged in the U.S., and rather than socialism being an unsettled question, it is used as an unsettling noun, intended to frighten and to create panic among the popular majorities. The Left has yet to overcome this obstacle. But we are working on it!

The cataclysmic social and political changes of this present historical moment have unleashed the most unholy aspirations among the modern Manicheans of the Christian Right. The Tea Party, the prehensile tail of libertarianism, has made a vertiginous descent into the bowels of the American Armageddon psyche, resurrecting itself in the gratuitous sepulchral cant of Christian dominionism and reconstructionism. Armed with a message that is an eerie amalgam of generalized resentment, a nympholepsy of self-hatred, and nativism sutured together by theocratic aspirations, these activists are clawing their way towards the New Jerusalem with their rabble-rousing war cry of dismantling the federal government. Are we seeing the Confederacy rise again, absent the white sheets?

Television personality and Republican necromancer, Glenn Beck, makes a messianic overture to masses of Tea Party supporters gathered at the Lincoln Memorial in Washington, DC, while at the same time immolating the historical memory of the civil rights movement, by claiming Martin Luther King Jr. as his forebear. In an atmosphere of big-tent religious revivalism dripping with a fascist miasma of national rebirth, a furor of white backlash zealotry, political demagoguery, fear-engendering and resentment-mongering, he grandly asserts that the civil rights movement was not really about black people, but rather about white conservatives under assault from evil liberals. Dear Glenn, Ringling Bros. currently has two circus train-based shows with full three-ring production. Have you thought of signing up for the Blue or Red Tours? You could certainly draw bigger crowds than the mistreated elephants. And you would look dashing in a top hat!

As advocates of revolutionary critical pedagogy, we stand at the turning point in this process. Critical pedagogy is an approach that we have chosen as a necessary (albeit insufficient) vehicle for transforming the world. The work that we do has been adapted from the path-finding contributions of the late Brazilian educator, Paulo Freire, whose development of pedagogies of the oppressed helped to lay the foundations for approaches (feminist, poststructuralist, Marxist) to teaching and learning that utilize the life experience of students inside and outside of traditional classrooms to build spaces of dialogue and dialectical thinking.

We have renamed our pedagogy "revolutionary critical pedagogy." We have done so because we believe that dialogical approaches to teaching can help to create a critical citizenry capable of analyzing and transforming capitalist societies worldwide. In doing so, we denounce the domesticated versions of critical pedagogy that are insufficiently critical of capitalism and even hostile to a socialist alternative.

Critical pedagogy has been discredited by the Right's circling drain of a brain as administering propaganda for a communist insurrection, and it has been domesticated by those on the Left who do not want to challenge capital and state power directly. But critical pedagogy as a revolutionary praxis must never be extinguished. The jackboots of fascism can try to stamp it out, as is happening today, but we're rekindling it on a daily basis to serve as a funeral pyre for the imperialist regimes we are bound to serve as long as we remain citizens of transnational capital.

We are so reverentially preoccupied with what others have to say about the struggle for socialism that we fear to trust our own understanding and consequently we have no eyesight left to look upon these historical events themselves. Marx's writings that tell us untraditional truths about the social and economic order tap a world-weary longing that stretches back through the centuries. Here the term "world-weary longing" is not meant to refer to the existential despair often experienced by intellectuals as fathomless as the abysses of the earth. We are talking about the anguish that accompanies what have been for the majority of humanity the failures of attempting to overcome necessity. Current struggles to overcome oppression, anchored to liberal appeals for fairness and equality and built upon the crusted-over sediments of past choice, are no longer options for the present day. Please excuse our decision but we have decided to look elsewhere before our lungs explode from toxic gas!

Critical pedagogy teaches us that we have the collective power to overcome the inimical forces of capital. The Promised Land can promise only to be a place of struggle, springing up where hope is conjugated with the movements of the people toward an anti-capitalist future. We are all merely seeds in the moist soil of the counter-world. It is up to us to decide what that world is to look like and how to get there.

We need to extend the ambit of critical pedagogy from persons with "authority," to whom, by convention and precept, education has hitherto been confined, to those who are "least" among us, not in numbers, surely, but in social legitimacy—the poor and the dispossessed. We are not talking about the dispossessed as passively dispossessed, but as a revolutionary force for socialism. They are carrying a much larger freight than their single selves. It is in their name that we begin to fathom that which we have been formed to be, and begin the arduous and painful process of remaking ourselves in a deliberately new way that often takes us on a collision course with the systems of intelligibility, ways of knowing and received terms that we have inherited to create habitual and resigned agents of the status quo.

The fact is, surely, that we are faced with two choices about how to live our humanity—the liberal model of pleading with corporations to temper their cruelty and greed, and the reactionary model that has declared war on social and economic equality. And on the evidence that each of these models is fiercely and hopelessly entangled in the other's conflictual embrace, we can accept neither. So don't take it personally you wise guys, it's just business, in our case, revolutionary business.

Critical pedagogy is more than throaty bursts of teacherly impropriety, more than enumerating in ironic detail the problems faced by the youths of today, more than hurling invective at government policies—it is a sustained march towards a revolutionary consciousness and practice.

We must become more like the unknown sailor who tried to smash the head of Napoleon's statue with a brick during the days of the Paris Commune, or like the Iraqi journalist who threw his shoe at the head of President George W. Bush while Bush was standing tall before cameras of the transnational corporate media like a Texas version of the Vendome Column wrapped in a jock strap.

Revolutionary critical pedagogy questions the official, hegemonic view of ahistorical educational change, isolated from the capitalist social and productive relationships. As revolutionary critical educators, we need to understand how the dynamics of the capitalist system—its movement from global capitalism to transnational capital, for instance—have guided the meaning and purpose of educational reform and have impacted institutions and approaches with respect to what counts as educational change.

We follow Che's dialectical conception of education which is formed internally through analyzing the continuous contradictions of external influences on the life of individuals. We agree with Paulo Freire that dialogical pedagogy can achieve the kind of class consciousness necessary for a powerful social transformation. It also suggests that as we participate in an analysis of the objective social totality that we simultaneously struggle for a social universe outside the commodity form of labor. If we are to educate at all, we must educate for this!

Statist socialism has collapsed and weighs heavier on the minds of the living with its inevitable decay into the oblivion of historical time. Libertarian socialism as well lies rotting on its deathbed, as capitalism continues to wreak its revenge, despite its present state of unprecedented crisis. Anti-systemic movements of all shapes and stripes are still around but have, for the most part, become domesticated into reformist shadows of their previous revolutionary selves, forming enfeebled and enfeebling popular fronts that collapse on the heels of any real challenge to capitalism. Are you with us?

Critical educators must take a stand, working for political or direct democracy, for the direct control of the political system by citizens, for economic democracy, for the ownership and direct control of economic resources by the citizen body, for democracy in the social realm by means of self-management of educational institutions and workplaces, and for the ecological justice that will enable us to reintegrate society into nature. The struggle for a new historic bloc built up by the working class will not be easy. If critical educational studies are to avoid being corralled into accepting the dominant ideology, or annexed to pro-capitalist forces among some on the Left, or transformed into a recruiting ground for liberal reform efforts, or even worse, turned into an outpost for reactionary populism, it will largely be due to our efforts as revolutionary critical educators.

We advise you to democratize access in your institutions so that working families from urban and rural sectors can attend, and give the poor the same chance to prepare for higher education as the rich, since the goal of education is to create an egalitarian society. Don't just create another educational elite but use critical non-positivist problem solving to bring about an endogenous development and the reparation of communities through holistic, integral and critical educational practices.

Give the schools autonomy! And while you are at it, don't shift the cost of education to the users and don't make social mobility the goal. Social mobility is for the neoliberals who just want to maintain the two-tiered system we have for the rich and for the poor and for the imaginary community we call the middle class. The goal should be empowerment of the communities and the sustainable development of the society where a participatory culture can become permanently robust and vibrant and co-operativism rather than competition can prevail. Take critical pedagogy into the factories and the prisons! Rub shoulders with all sectors of society and level out the advantage between them.

Eliminate high-stakes testing, period. There is no room for that. Don't employ tests that can't help you become a better teacher and students better learners. Look beyond helping your students get to university; help them get to universities, yes, but give them the foundations for building future pluriversities, or even better, commoniversities for the global commons. Don't teach them about how to make it rich with copyright laws, teach them copyleft— to create new networks of critique, solidarity, transformation based on free access!

Help them to build revolutionary theory so that rebellions against fascist repression can become true revolutions. Think outside the box. Think Zapatismo and Bolivarianismo! Siga el Humanismo Marxista! Imbibe the creative spirit of Faro de Oriente! Follow the heart of the workers and students at Industrias Metalúrgicas y Plásticas Argentina (IMPA) in Buenos Aires.

We need to awaken from our dream into another dream, but one dreamt with open eyes, a collective dream that will take us out of the homogeneous, monumental and chronological time of capital and beyond the consolatory pretensions of the bourgeoisie to create the "time of now" discussed so poignantly by Walter Benjamin—the time of the revolutionary. We need to capture the revolutionary fervor of the communards, whose battle-tested hearts managed, if only for a brief time, to dump the muck of ages into the sewers of history. It is precisely the socialist partisanship of critical pedagogy—not to the point of dogmatism or inflexibility—that reveals its power of critique. We need to reclaim the power of critique as the sword arm of social justice and not relinquish it. For in doing so we reclaim our humanity and the world.

We cannot be evasive in our search for justice, tranquilized by self-deception, led to political hibernation by our own torpor, or unwarrantably adventitious in our actions. We must reach out to those whom Jesus reproved with "fierce censure" for not bearing fruit (i.e., for not loving one's neighbor) and for not recognizing that the end of history has already arrived in history (Miranda, 1977) with the coming of Jesus as the Messiah. For those of us who call ourselves Christians, we must challenge those in our communities of faith who prevent the Messiah from being truly recognized (i.e., prevent love and justice from being seen as one and the same), those who relegate Jesus to an indefinitely postponable future, keeping him "eternally pre-existent" or "eternally future" but never existing in the "now," that is, in the "supra-individual reality" that is the Kingdom of God (Miranda, 1977). The Kingdom of God is where faith and justice determine our being as we confront history in its totality and as we bring forth through faith and class struggle those fruits of love, *comunalidad* and peaceful intercultural existence that have been annulled by the forces of capital.

We ground our teaching in compassion, but not the paternalistic compassion that is close to pity. Our compassion is biblical, it refers to compassion and goodness and is "closely linked to a sense of justice: its is compassion-on-the-poor-and-the-oppressed, identical to indignation over the violation of the rights of the weak" (Miranda, 1977, p. 152). This is the word made flesh. As Miranda (1977) warns, in keeping with the biblical indignation towards oppressors, Jesus of Nazareth denounces the scribes and the Pharisees seven times as "hypocrites!" He denounces them five times as "blind!" and once as "stupid!" while at the same time teaching with compassion and goodness.

You who fear all prodigalities and parsimonies of the world, all diverse centralities of human emancipation, you are a scream with no echo! You who are born in the latrine of "white stream" culture, who are engulfed in some supple and intoxicating middle ground, clutching in your cold dead hands a seamless and incandescent veil used to drape over the messy contradictions of your existence, you are a wager with no consequence, a vine with no roots! You who slumber wide-awake in a sanctified equilibrium consoling yourself with seraphic melodies from the Parisian avant-garde, you are a photograph with no image, a mirror with no tain, a heart without blood! Listen to your Erik Satie, let Gymnopédie No.1 nurture your soul, since those notes turn the keys to the door of heaven and the streets of the sublime.

But also listen to Rage Against the Machine because those notes will lighten your fist as you raise it to the sky and storm the offices of Wall Street and the musty corridors of the Supreme Court. Above all, remember the words of Che: "Hay que endurecerse sin perder jamas la ternura" (One has to grow hard but without ever losing tenderness). How callous are your dreams, you men and women of little faith! Any mystical ardor that can be found in the pedagogy of rage is sure to founder if it is not tempered by a revolutionary militancy that seeks to dismantle the social relations of capitalist exploitation. Be a sojourner in the metaphysical hinterlands of divine mystery by all means, but once you abandon yourself to agape use both your hardships and your epiphanies dialectically, in the service of building the global commons.

Tell your teachers to become attentive to their self-transforming potential, to stop loitering around the trashcans of tradition and to stop resisting the prospect of a possible future. Please tell them to leave the shepherd's crook and the winnowing whip in a stone reliquary for old school hand-me-downs; they don't need them anymore. Instruct your teachers that they have become endowed with the capacity to become more aware of their mission. Ask them to remove the cover from the straw basket at their feet. In it, they will find a serpent coiled in three and a half turns. Tell them to place the serpent in an empty baptismal font or a crystal aspersorium and anoint themselves.

Insist that the teachers take up the ladle of public service and drink from the elixir of immortality. Invite them to partake of its grace. For if you are committed to serve the people, you are serving all of eternity. For time was brought into existence out of nothing to give us an opportunity to share an infinite compassion and active receptivity to the anguished cries of our people and a graced realization that we are one with all those who suffer and are heavily burdened. The sound of Einstein's equation $E = mc^2$ is "OM."

And may I tell some of you mainstream scientists something you might think sounds a bit strange? Some things that you might consider to be dead—such as, for instance, inanimate objects like stones and fossilized Yak dung—may in fact be very much alive! So walk with reverence across the earth, and be in harmony with the universe.

Your teacher education reforms, with their compensating subtleties of incremental measures to make oppression more tolerable, roil me. But what bothers me more are the twisted reaches of groupthink emerging from the Department of Education, where in the subterranean depths of disunion between the intellect and the spirit, and its covert implication for the creation of legions of homo economicus, we create not critical citizens but consumer citizens, thereby breaching the inviolable will of the people.

We make no accommodating gestures towards your threat, "America, love it or leave it!" Do you think your patriotic injunction holds any power over us?

Coda

presto

Advise your teachers to abandon their notions of America the Invincible Force for Good. Advise your teachers to abandon their altars of capital and the slaughter bench of imperial war. It's time to put aside such childish myths about America's providential mission to civilize the world; our rulers cling to this myth, even if it means bombing that world back into the Stone Age. It is time to put aside such dangerous and vile ideas.

The abyss-like presence of alienation from nature (both inwardly and outwardly), and from our divine nature, can be defeated and the divine destination of our lives can be realized. Be one with the people—not only meditatively but through praxis—through acting on and in and even alongside the world with them. You are not them, but you are not Other to them.

Accustom yourself to wonder. Abide in the miracle of life. As Saint Francis de Sales put it, the only measure of love is to love without measure.

St. Gemma Galgani has beckoned you to go forth and teach, acting lovingly. For it is only by teaching that you can learn, and only by learning that you are fit to teach. And it is only through love that we can transform this world.

When we contemplate our state of spiritual infinitude, we are confronted with a myriad of choices. We can imagine the putrid stench of flesh decaying from regret; ambition lying fallow from an over-tilled darkness; voices rasping, hollowed out by unwelcomed perseverance; hope rattling like a dust-choked dream coughing in our brainpan. We can let death jeer at us, its chilling rictus pulled tight over our fears like a Canadian winter cap, or we can use the past, not as the deathbed of our last remorseful slumber, but transformed into a bow forged from our weary heartstrings, sending us spinning, a delirious flame shot into the temple of fate.

Let us always be fearless teachers, even unto our last breath, and hope that such fearlessness will lead to wisdom. And such wisdom will lead to a transformation of this world to another world where love and justice prevail.

Dear reader, the falcon is "turning in the widening gyre," beware! Do you not hear Yeats's anguished cry as "things fall apart," as the center collapses like a sunken lung? Beware the Spiritus Mundi, blackened with pitch and winter catarrh, carrying portents from lost scrolls hidden in the damp abode of billionaires' yachts. A new messiah is being spawned from the curdling afterbirth of history's raw defeat, its spine bent forward like a twisted compass pointing to Silicon Valley. This "rough beast," this "rising Sphinx" with a smile of infinite bandwidth and burning fiber optic eyes encoded with apocalypse wades slowly through deep deposits of NSA data, gleefully sinking in the muck of its own creation.

But Leonard Cohen taught us the secret chord that David played to please the Lord. And we are all singing Hallelujah!

I think it was the poet June Jordan who said, "we're the ones we've been waiting for," a line made famous in a song by Sweet Honey in the Rock. Well, what can I say except, "we're the ones we've been waiting for!" Let go of the shore and push off into the river of love, and ride into the whirlpool. Know that when you come out the other side, that the river has a destination. When you arrive there you will find that the river of love and the destination of justice are one and the same.

Perhaps one day, while decamping from your conference on the Common Core, or value-added instruction, you'll find time to ponder this choice. After your continental breakfast at Motel 6, you might consider glancing across the street at the empty lot of jimsonweed, concrete shards, gasoline-soaked soil and mercury vapors. There you will find a man in seamless twill-woven pants, clutching his rake handle with a long iron-ridged nail driven into the tip colorfully festooned with collapsed Styrofoam cups and Chuck E. Cheese's and Happy Meal coupons. He's the one spearing paper wrappers along the spongy gutters. Look to the right and you will notice a communion chalice and a bagel crust sitting on a collapsed lawn chair. Are you telling me that it's really a can of Coca-Cola? Then focus your imagination and open the eyes of your heart. The new world exists already in our hearts and our hearts are always learning. The heart is more than a physical muscle that pumps blood throughout our body; the heart is a space of possibility, the potential for living in a hoped-for world. The heart is the organ of all pedagogy, activated by relationships, by engagement with community and sustained by love, solidarity and hope. The heart is a battleground in the struggle for freedom. Listen to the language of your heart.

Perhaps in the distance you will hear John Coltrane's saxophone playing A Love Supreme. Can you hear the chau gong? Can you hear the cymbal washes? Can you hear the hard bop tenor sax meld with modal and free jazz styles in a homage to God? Listen softly. Can you hear the words, "Elation. Elegance. Exaltation. All from God. Thank you God. Amen"?

Can you hear the trumpet blast from Gabriel, signaling the Lord's return to earth? Perhaps then you will see Jesus in the groundskeeper, in your neighbor, in the man who sweeps the laundromat, in the woman who folds your linen, in the waiter who spills tomato soup on your shirtsleeve, in the bartender who comforts you when you despair of life, in your students who bring both frustration and joy. Perhaps then your spirit will arise from the ashes of your discontent. Perhaps then you will find the path to what Jon Sobrino (2001) calls "a journeying faith" where all of humanity is presented with an absolute demand to take down all victims from the cross. Perhaps then you will discover history in the making of it.

References

Braswell, S. (2015, May 1). The drug that bankrolled some of America's great dynasties. Today's OZY. Retrieved from http://www.ozy.com/flashback/the-drug-that-bankrolled-some-of-americas-great-dynasties/40555#ixzz3Z6BeYkRb

Chomsky, N. (2002). Understanding power: The indispensable Chomsky. P. R. Mitchell & J. Schoeffel (Eds.). New York, NY: The New Press.

Debs, E. (1912, October). Speech of acceptance. International Socialist Review.

Fanon, F. (2008). *The wretched of the earth.* (R. Philcox., Trans.) New York, NY: Grove Press.

Giroux, H. (2015, April 27). The perils of being a public intellectual. *CounterPunch.* Retrieved from http://www.counterpunch.org/2015/04/27/the-perils-of-being-a-public-intellectual/

Greenwald, G. (2014). *No place to hide: Edward Snowden, the NSA and the surveillance state.* London: Hamish Hamilton.

Hudis, P. (2015, February 20). Yes, there is an alternative—And it can be found in Marx. *The International Marxist-Humanist.* Retrieved from http://www.internationalmarxisthumanist. org/articles/yes-there-is-an-alternative-and-it-can-be-found-in-marx-by-peter-hudis

Jung, C. G. (1973). *Psychological reflections: A new anthology of his writings, 1905–1961.* J. Jacobi & R. F. C. Hull (Eds.). Princeton, NJ: Princeton/Bollingen Paperback.

Khalek, R. (2011, July 21). 21st-century slaves: How corporations exploit prison labor. *AlterNet.* Retrieved from http://www.alternet.org/story/151732/21st-century_slaves%3A_how_corporations_exploit_prison_labor

Khalek, R. (2011, November 29). The shocking ways the corporate prison industry games the system. AlterNet. Retrieved from http://www.alternet.org/story/153212/the_shocking_ways_the_corporate_prison_industry_games_the_system

Khalek, R. (2011, December 1). How private prisons game the system. *Salon.com.* Retrieved from http://www.salon.com/2011/12/01/how_private_prisons_game_the_system/

Kovaliek, D. (2013, March 5). The Wikileaks revelations: US still fighting 'threat' of liberation theology. *Counterpunch.* Retrieved from http://www.counterpunch.org/2013/03/05/us-still-fighting-threat-of-liberation-theology/

Miranda, J. P. (1977). *Being and the messiah: The message of St. John.* (J. Eagleson, Trans.). Maryknoll, NY: Orbis Books.

O'Neill, A. (2015, January 3). On patrol with skid row's 'angel cop.' *CNN.* Retrieved from http://www.cnn.com/2015/01/02/us/skid-row-cop/

Plucinska, Joanna. (2015). "Here's a Picture of the Pope Being Given a Really Weird Crucifix." July 10. *Time Magazine.* As retrieved from: http://time.com/3952444/pope-francis-crucifix-hammer-and-sickle/

Smail, D. (2008). *On deep history and the brain.* Berkeley, CA: University of California Press.

Sobrion, J. (2001). *Christ the liberator.* Maryknoll, NY: Orbis Books.

AFTERWORD

Lilia D. Monzó

Comrade Peter: Marx Meets Ginsberg

Peter McLaren is a giant in the field of education, especially among radicals on the Left. His extraordinary and groundbreaking body of work, spanning hundreds of articles and fifty books, read extensively in the United States and abroad, has had an enormous influence on the way we understand the current conditions of our world and develop a revolutionary praxis toward a socialist alternative. Peter McLaren evidences a brilliance and a broad wealth of knowledge that can rival any of history's major thinkers. He is unwavering in his commitment to social justice. With an unmistakable poetic flare and an intensely powerful and passionate voice, he is a scholar-activist-poet who, in his works and in person, has a magical allure that is a force to be reckoned with—unforgettable and impossible to dismiss.

Pedagogy of Insurrection is a prophetic and visionary exposé. McLaren sheds layers of politeness and rhetoric to pinpoint with uncanny precision and denounce the despots who protect corporate interests by casually and ironically deploying armies of working class women and men (mostly of color) to kill and maim in defense of democracy, while they sit around drinking diamond martinis on their million-dollar estates. He explodes with both rage and visceral longing in a way that ruptures the structural unconscious that has obfuscated reality in the service of capital for far too long and lights a fire of indignation and inspiration. With fierce passion and poetic fervor, he demands that we set aside the multitude of excuses we make for our apathy and inertia amidst the suffering inflicted upon humanity and take up the revolutionary call to rise up against capital, establish a socialist alternative, and save our souls. His words, majestic and ethereal, awaken us sharply from the catatonic state in which many of us simply sway to the whims of capital—the result of our alienated existence that robs us of our human potential to love and to develop a collective agency. *Pedagogy of Insurrection* forces us to strip naked and examine our own complicity in acceding to the lustful fetishes and greedy excesses of the market that numb us into passivity within a global war zone.

We have come to expect McLaren to both incite and inspire us to revolutionary action but *Pedagogy of Insurrection* surpasses our expectations. Karl Marx takes up permanent residence in its pages and is called upon by a series of extraordinary heroes whose praxis of liberation has left an irrefutable and indelible imprint on history and who, as men, illustrate the potential for love and courage within the human spirit. It is well known that Che, Fidel, and Paulo have long inspired McLaren to heed the call of praxis and engage in the struggle for freedom. We see snippets of McLaren's own philosophy of praxis—traveling far and wide across the globe, clutching *Das Kapital* to his chest as he decries the exploitation and dehumanization that capitalism and imperialism breed and brings the word of communism and revolutionary critical pedagogy to students, teachers, educational scholars, workers' unions, and other activists and revolutionaries across the world, even in risky contexts affected by violence and war. Long the master of poetic inspiration, he brings a beauty and compassion, intellectual rigor, and ethical reflexivity to his praxis that draws audiences of all types. His travels and experiences talking, planning, and marching with people across the world provide a repertoire of remarkable stories—stories of anguish, but also stories of hope—that re-energize, that inspire us to be stronger and more ethical and more loving, and that help us to create a radical dream for the future. His latest critical insurgency is in China, where he is working with various universities to establish a center for critical pedagogy.

McLaren makes a daring move by bringing to us in *Pedagogy of Insurrection* an unexpected and controversial but revered star guest—Jesus Christ, himself, is at the door, and he comes claiming his copyleft to communism and declares that the kingdom of God must be sought here on earth. Undoubtedly, the

Jesus McLaren refers to is the Jesus of the Left, depicted brilliantly in Pasolini's (1964) *The Gospel According to St. Matthew*. Without mincing words McLaren examines history from our current condition of greed, violence, and human suffering under capitalism and brings us the biblical texts that support his proclamation that communism is the only possible solution to reverse the apocalypse on the horizon—a Christian and a moral imperative.

Through *Pedagogy of Insurrection* we come to realize that we may be living through one of Walter Benjamin's (1940) messianic moments, one that will eventually and inevitably break with history and put us on the path toward socialism. Here McLaren is the prophetic Angel of History that enables the renewal of the past in a moment of spectacular significance that brings redemption—the realization that Jesus was sent to help us create heaven on earth by condemning the rich and the process of production that creates "differentiating wealth," including private property and profit. Going beyond the righteous call of liberation theology to make the plight of the poor "the preferential option," McLaren argues that for Jesus, the fight against poverty and exploitation is not merely an option but an obligation—a condition for entering the kingdom of God. The messianic moment signals a revolutionary break with past understandings and a clarity and hope that galvanize humanity to action and bring history into a new realm for the future. In contrast to a series of unending steps leading us toward a predetermined destiny, the messianic moment recognizes history as non-linear with particular junctures and shifts. We become the subjects of history rather than mere objects of time. Many Left radicals may, perhaps, remain skeptical of this alliance with the Bible, but they will undoubtedly admire McLaren's penchant for constantly challenging himself to develop new avenues to bring forth a socialist revolution. And what better way than to enlist millions of new disciples from the Christian faith? *Pedagogy of Insurrection* provides a trailblazing vision for the future and new spiritual paths to revolution.

McLaren will, inevitably, face stern critics for this courageous move. The conservative Christian Right will decry his stance as blasphemy—unwilling to give up their claim to divine providence as justification for the horrific ravaging across the world that ensures their comfortable "middle-class" existence. Here, I echo Canadian educator David Geoffrey Smith (2014), who points out that people often have intense responses to Peter McLaren and his work. He writes, "As a former theologian I judge Peter McLaren to be a prophet and prophets are seldom recognized in their own countries especially when they tear away veils of hypocrisy ..." (p. 145). Indeed I have seen firsthand how loving, ethical, and generous people often fear Marxism and those of us who seek a socialist alternative even though minimal probing reveals they have never engaged Marx or Marxist work seriously and do not understand even the foundational aspects of Marxism. Many of these folks follow the Christian faith, which has traditionally subjugated the commandment to love thy neighbor to maintain a social and political order that supports the ruling class and that asserts itself decidedly as anti-communist.

Jodi Dean (2012) provides a strong account of the U.S. campaign of fear and hate created to delegitimize the Soviet Union that had notable early successes in establishing measures of equality. This campaign against communism was so successful that it has rendered any association with socialism as evil and created a trembling fear of communism among the U.S. populace. Capitalism has been ironically coupled with democracy even though its emphasis on individualism and capital accumulation results in severe wealth disparities and unfreedoms that are antithetical to democracy. The campaigns against the Soviet Union and communism were one and the same, even though scholars recognize that the Soviet Union strayed from its original Marxist approach and became a form of state capitalism. Communism (and by extension any other socialist or communist nation or movement) continues to be associated with human rights violations and censorship, persecution, and indoctrination—all practices that have consistently been present within our own capitalist domestic and international relations (in recent times, consider the police brutality against communities of color that is legally condoned, the persecution of whistleblowers against the government, the killings of hundreds of thousands of Iraqi civilians, the secret and widespread surveillance of our own citizens and U.S. allies). Yet the mainstream media and education system that present normalized versions of history and limit criticality are rarely recognized as anesthetizing propaganda that serves capitalist interests.

In the final act, McLaren powerfully engages a mind-blowing pedagogy of rage by exploding into an angry and sarcastic tirade reminiscent of Allen Ginsberg's (1956/2001) Howl to denounce the transnational capitalist class and proclaim his (and our eventual) adamant and uncompromising refusal to accept the oppression and inhumanity that exist. Here, McLaren decries the tendency to humiliate workers, artists, and revolutionaries of all types as a means of invalidating resistance. He condemns those who in their greedy excesses and narcissistic need for exaltation enact a praxis of hypocrisy in order to justify their capitalist existence as deserved and God's will. He goes after every form of manipulation that attempts to befuddle the imagination so that we will see capital and the dehumanization it breeds as inevitable. He drives home the point that we must become savvy to the ideological formations that keep us under siege and courageously confront the capitalist assault on our humanity. McLaren points out with breathtaking beauty that all of us exist as possibility and therefore can remake ourselves in the image of God and create a world that is moral and just.

Pedagogy of Insurrection and Peter McLaren stand as testaments to the historical disfigurement of communism. A profound love for humanity seeps out of every page of this book. The words that stayed with me include love, hope, inspiration, solidarity, social justice, heroism, generosity, humanism, and compassion. McLaren inspires us to dream of a future devoid of what Henry Giroux (2012) calls the culture of cruelty—the unmitigated acceptance and glorification of violence and suffering. McLaren's vision for a better world is a classless society where every human being and all other life forms are worthy of respect and dignity simply because they exist in the world and where love, equality, freedom, and social responsibility are the basis of life.

I can reluctantly accept that some people may be skeptical of communism's viability since we have yet to see sustained examples of a truly Marxist communism, because they do not understand why Marx proclaimed the inability to create a blueprint or because they are not well versed in Marxist theory. However, the fear and disdain for all that is Marxist, socialist, or communist seem inconceivable upon the recognition that communism, following Marx, is the praxis of love.

I must clarify that even among self-proclaimed anti-communists, Peter McLaren is beloved. Few can resist his appeal. He emanates a love for humanity that is manifested in a kindness and generosity that goes beyond most of our expectations of human beings. He instinctively opens his heart to anyone he meets and readily shares his knowledge, his time, and his many resources. He treats everyone with a genuine respect and quickly finds their strengths and beauty. Those who know him well will attest to the fact that to the best of his ability (given that he is in and of this world) he lives out the ethical revolutionary praxis that he proclaims. With little hesitation he challenges oppression and injustice wherever he encounters it, but he does so always dialogically and with remarkable humility. He is always poised to learn with and from others, regardless of their academic degrees or their social positioning in the world. In many ways he has evolved beyond the disfigured human that capital spawns and that most of us exemplify to some extent even in our best moments. At his best, he epitomizes the "new man" that Che Guevara (1965) proclaimed would develop under socialism—a human being with the freedom and courage to love freely.

I know these things about Peter firsthand, for he took me under his mighty wings two years ago when I was questioning my future in academia and my purpose in life, and he has taught me to soar. With tremendous confidence in my potential and a very gentle approach he has mentored me to a Marxist revolutionary critical pedagogy that comes alive in his everyday actions. In my view, it is this synchronicity that provides a vision of possibility and which is absolutely necessary to move humanity to act collectively toward a future founded on love, solidarity, and justice.

References

Benjamin, W. (1940). *On the concept of history.* Retrieved from https://www.marxists.org/reference/archive/benjamin/1940/history.htm

Dean, J. (2012). *The communist horizon.* Brooklyn, NY: Verso.

Ginsberg, A. (2001). *Howl and other poems.* San Francisco, CA: City Lights.

Giroux, H. (2012). *Disposable youth, racialized memories, and the culture of cruelty.* New York, NY: Routledge.

Guevara, E. (1965). *Socialism and man in Cuba.* Retrieved from https://www.marxists.org/archive/guevara/1965/03/man-socialism.htm

Pasolini, P. P. (Director). (1964). *The Gospel according to St. Matthew* [Motion Picture]. Italy and France: Arco Film, Lux Compagnie Cinématographique de France.

Smith, D. G. (2014). Engaging Peter McLaren and the new Marxism in education: An essay review of McLaren's *Rage + Hope.* In D. G. Smith, *Teaching as the practice of wisdom* (pp. 145–176). New York, NY: Bloomsbury.

INDEX

ABOUT THE AUTHOR

Peter McLaren is Distinguished Professor in Critical Studies, International Ambassador of Global Ethics and Social Justice and Co-Director of the Paulo Freire Democratic Project, College of Educational Studies, Chapman University in Orange, California. He is also Chair Professor at Northeast Normal University in Changchun China where he serves as Honorary Director of the Center for Critical Pedagogy Research. Professor McLaren served as Professor of Education, Director of the Center for Education and Cultural Studies and Renowned Scholar-in-Residence for 8 years at Miami University of Ohio and 20 years as Professor of Education at The University of California, Los Angeles. Professor McLaren is the author and editor of 45 books and several hundred scholarly articles. His writings and political activism have received major national and international awards. His work has been translated into thirty languages. Professor McLaren is considered one of the architects and leading exponents of critical pedagogy worldwide.